STATE AND LOCAL GOVERNMENTS

McGraw-Hill Series in Political Science

STATE AND LOCAL GOVERNMENTS

CHARLES R. ADRIAN
PROFESSOR OF POLITICAL SCIENCE
UNIVERSITY OF CALIFORNIA, RIVERSIDE

SECOND EDITION

McGRAW-HILL BOOK COMPANY
NEW YORK   ST. LOUIS   SAN FRANCISCO   TORONTO   LONDON   SYDNEY

STATE AND LOCAL GOVERNMENTS

Acknowledgments

Page 72: quotation from "Letter from Birmingham Jail" by Martin Luther King, Jr. Copyright 1963, Christian Century Foundation. Reprinted by permission from the June 12, 1963 issue of *The Christian Century*.

Pages 424, 429, 430, and 433: tables from William Brink and Louis Harris, *The Negro Revolution in America*, Copyright © 1963, by Newsweek, Inc. Reprinted by permission of Simon and Schuster, Inc.

PREFACE

As in **Governing Urban America,** I have attempted in this book to relate the subject matter to the total political process, including the social and economic environment in which it exists. I have thus drawn materials from all of the social sciences, as well as from the humanities. My goal has not been to provide a factual reference book—I have been liberal with citations for that purpose—but to give the reader a tool for the analysis of politics at the state and local levels. A strong effort has been made to incorporate recent empirical findings from all of the social sciences, though I would describe my approach as eclectic rather than behavioral.

My own participant-observer roles have been useful, I believe, in providing insights and giving balance in the selection of materials to be included. I have served as a member of the planning commission in my suburb. At the state level, I was formerly administrative assistant to Governor G. Mennen Williams of Michigan and have been a member of the Governor's Advisory Committee on State Reorganization and chairman of the Michigan Study Commission on Metropolitan Area Problems, among other assignments.

This edition seeks to incorporate recent research pertinent to state and local politics and to reflect the direction in which research is taking the field. The particularly important advances in understanding state legislative behavior and the large amount of valuable data stemming from studies of legislatures have made it seem appropriate to add a separate chapter on the subject, and the central importance of state and local politics to civil rights and liberties is the basis for a separate chapter on that subject.

The strongly favorable response to the original edition of this work has convinced me that the style and spirit should be retained, but advances in the field have dictated a substantial updating and revision of all chapters.

Unfortunately, I cannot give proper credit to the many persons in the academic world and in government who have helped me as critics and in supplying information; I cannot even name them here. One person must be singled out for special appreciation, however. Richard H. McCleery of Antioch College reviewed the original manuscript in great detail. His notes were a model of effective criticism, and I owe much to him as a result.

I am also indebted to many persons who have used the original edition and offered their criticisms and suggestions. My thanks to them.

It is conventional, and quite proper, to add that all conclusions—and errors of fact—are my responsibility alone.

Charles R. Adrian

CONTENTS

STATE AND LOCAL GOVERNMENTS

1

THE NATION WE LIVE IN

The automobile; the telephone; the suburb; the owner-occupied, heavily mort-gaged, single-family home; the expectation of a right to a high standard of liv-ing; public education from kindergarten to the doctorate; a superb medical profession, jealous of the sphere of activity it has staked out for itself; a popu-lar feeling of inferiority despite enormous wealth and power; urbanism; social conflict; professional entertainment; mass culture; heroes made-to-order on Madison Avenue; ambivalence toward governmental services and administration, toward civil rights, toward subcultures other than one's own; confidence in an ability to meet crisis situations, even to the point of overconfidence; resent-ment toward an involuntary world leadership role and the insecurities it pro-duces; neuroticism over neuroses; faddism; social climbing; a scramble for prestige and security, and an opportunity to achieve both; public servants of greater ability than is their credit—this is all a part of America.

All this and much more—the demagogue; the traffic accident; inadequate protection for those who fail in the socioeconomic struggle; the apartment, the multifamily flat, and the flophouse, which collectively shelter nearly 20 percent of our population, some in luxury, some in grinding poverty; the jail cells, which hold 2 million men—and not a few women—each year; switch blades and comic books; huge metropolitan areas, decaying at the center; bright neon signs; impatient traffic; puritanical soul-searching and self-doubt; a political system designed to give us the kind of government and governors we deserve. This is all a part of America.[1]

Every aspect of American culture, every social need, every problem affects government and is in turn affected by government—national, state,

[1] See also Charles R. Adrian and Charles Press, **The American Political Process**, McGraw-Hill Book Company, New York, 1965, chap. 2.

and local. Because this is so, and because the state and local agencies of government are deserving of special attention in their important social activities, this book was written. Throughout its chapters, emphasis is placed upon the *political process* as a method by which individual wants, which become social wants, are met by government and sociopolitical policies emerge as imperfect compromises among the conflicting interests of society.

The Analytical Approach

Many possible approaches could be taken to the study of political institutions. In this book, the emphasis is placed upon a study of the *political process* with the objective of supplying to the reader a method that will provide him with *a tool for the analysis of political events* that affect him and his society. Encyclopedic detail concerning each of the thousands of local units of government in America is not supplied. It is available in the nearest library, and the footnotes and bibliography list ample citations. Neither is there an effort made to outline a set of ethical norms for the reader's guidance, since analysis requires an objective, or amoral, examination of relevant data if understanding of politics is the goal. A word of warning, however: Although the author has tried to avoid introducing his own preferences into the materials of the book, values—the beliefs one holds dear—are an essential ingredient in the decision-making process of politics. When one votes, or joins a group that seeks to influence governmental policy, or otherwise takes political action, he uses his sense of values of what is right or wrong, good or bad, in deciding what to do. At such times, personal values are of critical importance. However, to introduce one's personal preferences into an analysis of the political process is to blur the image: this the author has tried to avoid doing. But no reader should assume that "One choice is as good as another," or that "No matter what I do, things will turn out the same anyway." The analysis given in this book does not imply or justify such conclusions.

Government sets the boundaries of action for other social groups and for government itself. It is the final means of enforcing controls. The decision makers in government, therefore, decide which groups and ideas will be favored and which will not. They do this even when they generally permit groups in society to decide the relative places that each will occupy in society, for at any point government may intercede in the process and make rules that help or handicap a particular group or idea. They have done so, for example, in holding that relations among races will no longer be determined without formal governmental regulations being involved in the process. Similarly, governmental policy has imposed a rule against plural marriages of the type once practiced within the Mormon church.

In a democracy, government exercises controls or gives rewards that are favored by the effective social forces in the society, subject, however, to certain procedures and to certain rights of minorities. Even in a democracy, the actions of government remold social forces. But as society is modified, it in turn modifies government. For example, action by government outlawed slavery. This action, in turn, shifted the balance of social forces in America; it has gradually resulted in the reshaping of many other governmental policies in respect to descendants of freed slaves, and to other minority groups as well.

The Parts of the Governmental Process   Government, then, allocates the resources of society among its members. How does it do this? Does a democratic government always represent an accurate reflection of social forces? What, in fact, are the social forces that shape governmental policy?

These questions have frequently been discussed by political scientists in recent years. There is, as yet, no consensus concerning an answer. We cannot, therefore, present a neat theoretical model of how the American policy-making process operates. To the extent that there is agreement, it is reflected in a quite imprecise formula stemming from a phrase coined by Pendleton Herring. Political decisions, he concluded, stem from "a working union of interests, ideas, institutions, and individuals." These are the four I's of political science.

One group of political scientists has attempted to combine these variables under the one heading of the organized interest group. In the shared attitudes and interactions of individuals forming an organized group, they see the root of all ideas, individual action, and institutional arrangements. In one of the major modern theoretical contributions to political science, David Truman has presented an extensive statement of the group approach.[3] This approach, however, has not in itself provided an adequate explanation of all political phenomena. But it is useful and has provided insights that have permitted analysis of previously neglected aspects of politics.

Governmental structure and rules are now recognized as being not neutral, but a means of access or advantage to selected groups and ideas. For example, most state legislatures long were apportioned in ways that gave rural and small-town groups and ideas an advantage in policy making. Complicated registration procedures discourage political participation by the low-income, less educated groups.

Some political scientists have moved from an examination of legal institutions to a study of the roles * established by both the legal and informal processes, because every institution of government provides for certain roles that lead to expectations concerning the proper activities of role performers. The stimulation of the other sciences—notably sociology and psychology— has increased emphasis on the study of interpersonal relations among decision makers and the formal and informal communications networks among them. What, for example, is the effect on policy making if the governor's brother is named highway commissioner? What is the effect on legislation when a club or clique feeling arises among members of the legislature? What is the relevance of the personality characteristics of decision makers to actual policy decisions?

[2] Pendleton Herring, **The Politics of Democracy,** Holt, Rinehart and Winston, Inc., New York, 1940, p. 421.
[3] David Truman, **The Governmental Process,** Alfred A. Knopf, Inc., New York, 1951.

*ROLE. The manner in which a status position is supposed to be filled; it is the group's expectation of conduct in a status. An individual's STATUS is his position in relation to other positions held by other individuals in a social group or grouping. The essence of status is a defined superior-inferior relationship, that is, dominance and subordination—always within a set of rules.

Some political scientists have emphasized the importance of the social backgrounds of decision makers, including voters, on the decisions that are made. Others have assumed that the political ambitions of decision makers offer explanations of their behavior.

A number of studies have centered on what sociologists call "institutional values," that is, the ideology * developed by organized groups such as business firms or professional associations. Others have considered the ideologies of collectivities that are not formally organized groups, but are, in fact, subcultures within a larger society—a particular class, race, or ethnic group. Finally, there has been an examination of what Gabriel A. Almond has called the "political culture"—the grouping of political ideas associated with a particular nation-state.[4] The Swedish sociologist Gunnar Myrdal once concluded that America has possessed such a mystique from its beginning.[5] He called it "the American Dream" and saw it as a vague grouping of ideals that derived mainly from the British liberal tradition and from rationalist thinkers such as Thomas Jefferson, who embodied these ideals in the Declaration of Independence. The dream, he concluded, borrowed from concepts implicit in our English common-law heritage and from ideas about individual conscience that were held by the dissenting religious groups that formed our nation. These ideas will be examined in a later chapter.

*IDEOLOGY is "folk philosophy" concerning the good life. It is not so systematic nor so sophisticated as philosophy; it evolves gradually, not as the product of any single thinker. In this sense, it resembles folk songs more than works of serious composers. Ideology consists of a network of interrelated normative values that emerge from a particular life-style and environment. It serves a double task: It helps to direct action toward the satisfaction of existing wants and to establish new goals for an individual or group.

But how do these four I's—interests, ideas, institutions, and individuals —mix? Some political scientists seem to hope that one day we may be able to describe in detail how particular policies are made and applied. But this may be unduly optimistic, for a particular policy or decision may hinge on minute or fortuitous factors. What difference would it have made in the civil rights struggle if Lincoln had lived out his second term? Would a particular bill have taken precisely the same form if a key senator had not fallen asleep during a crucial period at the hearing? Such questions lead to the "What did he have for breakfast?" kind of analysis. Individual events probably can never be predicted in precise detail in the social sciences. What the social scientist

[4] Gabriel A. Almond, "Systematic Theory," in Heinz Eulau and others, **Political Behavior,** The Free Press of Glencoe, New York, 1956, p. 34.
[5] Gunnar Myrdal, **An American Dilemma,** Harper & Row, Publishers, Incorporated, New York, 1944.

can do, however, is to state probabilities. How likely and under what conditions is variable A influential in the making of policy? Political scientists appear today to be refining the four I's. The statement of probabilities in mathematical terms, while occasionally attempted, awaits further detailed data and refinements of theory.

Often individual events are at least partially irrelevant to broad ends. The 1963 murder of Medgar Evers, an NAACP official in Mississippi, led to increased demands for civil rights legislation. But if this event had not occurred, probably something else would have spurred action, though policies might not have been precisely the same or the timing of their adoption identical in all circumstances.

We are not left with total despair, however. Gross patterns of policy development can be discerned through existing tools of observation. In a democracy, there is some rough reflection in governmental policy of the effective social forces of the day. Policy making, while not a perfect reflection of social forces, does seem to mirror the ideas and wants of effective groups and individuals in the society. Somehow these institutional arrangements, with all their imperfections, do permit the peaceful coexistence of competing groups, institutions, and ideas. Peaceful change does occur.

Until a more accurate theory is proposed and tested, we can only detail what seem to many political scientists today to be the principal social forces influencing the legitimate allocation of benefits and rewards. This book will seek to describe what is known about how ideas, interests, individuals, and institutions interact in the political process to form policy.

Classifications of the American Political System

Political resources are unevenly distributed in society. However the elements that make up the effective social forces of a society are defined, an equal distribution of such resources among all members of society rarely occurs. Some individuals possess more than others.

The Theory of Ruling Elites   The unequal distribution of resources, combined in our culture with a general emphasis on the primacy of economic resources, has encouraged some to devise theories in which ruling elites are seen as controlling government, while the mass has no influence. Karl Marx developed such a theory, based on economic and class interest. An Italian, Gaetano Mosca, argued in the early twentieth century that there was a ruling class in every society and that it was based on the resources most valued by the society. Other Europeans, such as Pareto and Michels, have elaborated on this theory of a single elite that is united in opinion and action. In America, such a theory has been reflected in the findings of a school of sociology that has studied American communities. The Lynds in the 1920s and 1930s, C. Wright Mills in the 1940s, and Floyd Hunter in the early 1950s all saw American communities as dominated by single elite groups that made the important decisions. In Middletown (Muncie, Indiana), it was the X family.

In the upstate New York cities studied by Mills, it was the large corporation—
as was also the case in Atlanta as seen by Hunter. Both Mills and Hunter wrote
books describing the whole of American society in elite terms. In Mills's case,
it was an elite group of military, governmental, and corporation officials that
made all the major decisions. Hunter did not make such precise categoriza-
tions. He found corporate officials especially important, however.

Theories of cohesive elites have been widely criticized. For example, if
the X family actually controlled Middletown, why was it unable to get the
citizens to vote for an adequate sewage system despite several attempts? In
summer, the X family was unable to use the patios of the houses it had built
along the river into which Middletown's raw sewage was dumped. Critics have
argued that the notion of a few corporations or unions or Wall Street running
America is an oversimplification of decision making. Simplistic elite theory is
seen by many scholars as an example of the fallacious One Great Cause Theory,
which was once common in the social sciences.*

* The ONE GREAT CAUSE THEORY holds that all important social events can be
traced to a single event or phenomenon that is the exclusive or overwhelmingly dominant cause of other events or phenomena. Most social scientists are now convinced
that there are usually many causal factors in social events, no one of which is ordinarily predominant.

Probably no social scientist denies that a structure of economic power
may exist. Certainly large corporations in America do commonly work together
in seeking to influence policy, and they exercise influence and probably dominate decision making of some types. But this type of power is only a part of
the total system. For one thing, the resources of influence are more than simply
economic—though these resources, of course, can be used to purchase others,
such as skills and publicity. But the market of total resources is too great to
corner. The sit-in is a political resource, and for a group with the few economic
resources Negroes collectively possess, it has proved to be effective. Votes, of
course, are also resources. Family prestige is a resource, as is organization
into solidary groups (e.g., the Catholic Church, the United Steel Workers, or
the American Legion).

In a democracy, money, numbers, and group cohesiveness are perhaps
the most important resources. The combination of these and other resources
in efforts to influence a specific issue is often of great importance, and the
leaders who control such resources are often of dominant importance in policy
making *in a specific area of public policy.* If this is the normal pattern, as it
seems to be, the designation of certain individuals as being part of "the
power structure" is not meaningful. The only justifiable conclusion is that the
individuals who have the highest positions in economic, social, and governmental spheres probably, on the average, have considerable influence and
therefore can be designated as an elite. This does not, however, imply that
they are united, for they may actively oppose one another.

Time and effort are political resources. The individual who makes a
nuisance of himself long enough may eventually influence a particular policy

in the way he desires. The assassin of Huey Long decisively influenced policy. He was willing to make the effort—and pay the costs—involved in killing a political leader. In this sense, no one is without some political resource. One cannot know, of course, whether a political resource will be spent skillfully or whether it will be used at all. One wealthy American may prefer to spend his money on chorus girls, another to further the election of Senator Zilch. Most persons do not care to spend their time in politics—many do not even vote. Lack of political activity by the individual is, however, not necessarily irrational or irresponsible behavior. It was perhaps as well for the Western world that Mozart and Beethoven did not divert their energies toward becoming precinct captains.

The resources distributed among individuals and groups to some extent cancel one another out. Labor's strength in numbers is countered by the financial resources of business. Individuals seldom identify completely with a single influential group or community subsystem. No group can expect to mobilize all of its membership in support of any one issue. The Catholic businessman and the Catholic laborer do not oppose each other on every issue, nor do their Methodist counterparts.

The Classification of Political Systems   Aristotle, noting the unequal distribution of society's resources, concluded that it resulted in different kinds of political systems: the rule of one, the rule of a few (less than a majority), and the rule of the many. He called the resulting systems "monarchy," "aristocracy," and "polity" (democracy). He also identified corrupted versions of each form. Further observation led him to conclude that a mixed system was both possible and preferable. The social basis, or "social constitution," for a mixed system was, he said, a large middle class that encouraged a widespread distribution of political resources.

Modern political scientists have revised and refined Aristotle's typology. Max Weber classified governments according to the basis on which an elite held its political power—the basis of its legitimacy. Another classification might be made according to the number of political subsystems that possess some degree of autonomy. Combining these elements, one political scientist has devised a classification system providing for sixteen different types.[6]

An alternative classification system has been devised by students of comparative government. Gabriel A. Almond and James S. Coleman, building on the sociological theories of Talcott Parsons, have offered a "functional" model for political analysis.[7] It assumes that in every viable political system, certain functions must be performed. Some institutional means must exist, they conclude, for rule making, rule application, and rule adjudication, as well as for social methods of interest articulation, interest aggregation, and political recruitment. These functions may or may not be handled by separate institutions. In American government, both administrative boards and the courts

[6] Robert A. Dahl, **Modern Political Analysis,** Prentice-Hall, Inc., Englewood Cliffs, N.J., 1963, pp. 25–38.
[7] Gabriel A. Almond and James S. Coleman (eds.), **The Politics of Developing Areas,** Princeton University Press, Princeton, N.J., 1960, chap. 1.

are concerned with rule adjudication, for example. The courts, in turn, are concerned with both rule adjudication and rule making. Almond and Coleman see political institutions as typically performing more than one function. Their method of analysis is logical and has attracted much interest, but it is not widely accepted by political scientists—at least at the present time.

There is as yet no consensus on classifications in the field of political science. Classification is, of course, always determined in part by the purposes of the classifier. But rough consensus does exist about the American political system of today. The effective social forces in America result in a system that is pluralistic rather than one ruled by a small group from the top. Many social components are politically effective. The allocation of benefits and rewards is accomplished through a complex process in which the many exert influence, though most of the time minorities with resources to spend join in compromises among themselves that produce policies not too different from present ones. The result offers only partial fulfillment for the goals of any group. The legitimacy of ruling elites is achieved by regularized procedures and is accepted by most citizens. Political subsystems (states, counties, cities) are many and have a relatively high degree of autonomy. Most political scientists are content to classify such a system of allocation as one form of democracy. Even though the classification is gross and crude, it will serve as the basis for the definition used in this book.

Structure and Process in Politics

The process of public policy making is modified by the structure of government, just as the path of a turbulent river is modified by natural and artificial barriers. Structure helps shape the process, but the process influences the character of the structure. In other words, it is not accurate to say that only the beliefs of a people and the interests of groups determine what policies a government will follow. The institutional arrangements themselves modify the outcome of the policy-making process.

The structure of American government includes an independently elected governor. This allows the chief executive to behave differently from the way he would behave if he were chosen by the legislature. The seniority system in the legislature, which often determines who will head a committee, produces a different pattern of legislative leadership and a different set of leaders with different values and policy goals from what would be the case if these leaders were chosen by a political party committee, for example. The seniority system most frequently produces committee heads who are conservatives from "safe" or noncompetitive districts, that is, who face little competition in staying in office and who, therefore, have little incentive to be concerned about the most recent political demands. A party committee would probably represent primarily the larger cities in a state. Its concerns would be principally matters of current controversy, particularly those of an urban character. The differences in policy would be considerable if changes of the kind mentioned here were to be made.

The point is, then, that the structure of government is only one of the influences upon policy and hence only one of the things to be studied in an examination of the workings of American government. Structure, on the other hand, is not to be dismissed lightly. It too affects the pattern of decision making.

American Panorama

The American states and their subdivisions are individual communities with individual personalities. The nation is a collection of geographic areas and of subcultures. It is a land of almost infinite variety and is in many ways an enigmatic nation, one seemingly of uniform mass culture but also one of great variety by regions and by cities. The citizen speaks of an American way of life, but the sociologist sees a collection of cultural groupings based upon geographic location and ethnic associations, each with its own values and behavior patterns. America is a nation of uninspired place names and of romantic and beautiful place names, of Sixteenth Street and of Perdido Pass, of two political parties and of a thousand political parties masquerading under well-known labels or under no labels at all.

The States as Cultural Entities   Although sociologists have tended to ignore the states as units, seeing them as arbitrary political structures, such is not entirely the case. Time and differing laws, ethnic settlements, racial and rural-urban balances, and economic combinations have all contributed toward the creation of vast differences between adjoining states, not to mention between states of different regions of the nation (see Table 1).

Oregon was first settled by New Englanders; it is conservative and traditionally Republican. Washington, which was strongly influenced by the gold rush, Scandinavian settlement, and Populism, is Democratic and liberal. There are other differences, too.[8] North Dakota is wheat and potato country, the home of agrarian radicalism—and is overwhelmingly Republican. South Dakota is wheat country only in the northeast; the southeast is devoted to corn-hog farming of the type found in Iowa, and the west is range. The state contains some of the most conservative rural folk in the Midwest—and is overwhelmingly Republican.

Ohio and Michigan are both highly urban, industrial states with strong Republican histories. But Ohio has remained conservative, and it is difficult to predict whether the Republican or Democratic candidate for a major office will be the more conservative. In Michigan, the Democratic party follows a consistently liberal position which, in the postwar years, drew the Republican candidates for statewide office farther and farther away from their traditional conservatism.

Nevada is a remnant of the Old West, a wide-open gambling state known for quick divorces, even though there are many Catholic politicians. Politics

[8] See John Gunther, **Inside U.S.A.**, Harper & Row, Publishers, Incorporated, New York, 1947, p. 87.

is very personal, with conservative Democrats vying with conservative Republicans for office. Utah, in contrast, is an "extraordinary combination of theocracy, dogoodism, industriousness, and flint-hard belief in the virtue of a living God, the Church of Jesus Christ of Latter Day Saints." [9] About 60 percent of the people are Mormons, but the influence of the church is even greater than that percentage. The politics of the state is conservative and tends to be Republican.

Table 1   Varying Characteristics, Selected States

	DEL.	N.Y.	IOWA	N. MEX.	W. VA.	MISS.
Per capita income (1962)	$3,102	$2,930	$2,189	$1,824	$1,810	$1,285
Selective service rejection rate (1963)	44.7	49.5	36.6	58.9	62.6	67.3
Murder rate (1962)	3.8	3.6	1.1	6.1	3.7	7.3
Persons per auto (1960)	2.8	3.4	2.6	2.6	3.9	4.1
Percent urban (1960)	65.6	85.4	53.1	65.7	38.2	37.7
Percent Negro (1960)	13.6	8.4	0.9	1.8	4.8	42.0
Newspaper circulation per 1,000 population (1963)	271.0	424.4	341.4	186.6	270.0	130.1
Death rate (1962)	9.1	10.4	10.3	6.4	10.5	10.1
Average days school attendance (1964)	167	167	163	158	167	151
Per pupil expenditure (1964)	$498	$705	$456	$440	$300	$241
Per pupil expenditure as percent of per capita income by state (1963–1964)	3.98	4.69	5.05	6.57	4.37	5.04
Classroom shortage, percent (1963–1964)	3.04	13.34	2.40	8.23	N/A	6.66

SOURCE: U.S. Bureau of the Census and U.S. Office of Education.

There are anomalous arrangements within states, too, however. North Idaho is within the area of dominance of Spokane, Washington, and the politics of the state centers on a north-south split.[10] West central Wisconsin faces toward the Twin Cities of Minneapolis-St. Paul, while Michigan's Upper Peninsula has long felt isolated from the rest of the state and has tended to identify with Wisconsin. Oregon is divided down the middle by the Cascades, with one economy in the humid western and another in the dry eastern parts of the state.

[9] *Ibid.*, p. 190.
[10] *Ibid.*, pp. 113–114.

Vast differences exist between the states, of course (see Table 1). These extend to differences, among others, in size, population, urbanization, per capita income, and period of settlement. Texas is over 220 times the size of Rhode Island. New York has seventy-four times the population of Alaska. New Jersey is around 90 percent urban; North Dakota is 65 percent rural. Nevada had a per capita income of $3,278 in 1964, Mississippi had $1,285. The first permanent settlement was made in Virginia in 1607, in Oklahoma in 1889.

The Community Faces toward the Capital One study of high school students in three cities, each about twenty-five miles from one another, but each in a different state, shows the strong orientation of citizens toward their own state government and institutions. The cities of Angola, Indiana, Reading, Michigan, and Montpelier, Ohio, are all located within a few miles of where the three states meet. The cities share a common hinterland, overall economic situation, and transportation network. However, the school systems face inward toward their own states for various activities and concerns. They have their backs to one another, as it were. In terms of athletic and other nonacademic school activities, they are closer to cities in their own state than to one another. School officials are oriented toward the state departments of education in the state capitals, hundreds of miles away. High school students in the three towns show a much greater awareness of activities in their own state and of pub- licized persons and institutions in their state than they do of activities, per- sons, and institutions in neighboring states. In responding to a survey ques- tionnaire, the great bulk of citizens could name the governor of their own state, but relatively few could name the first-term governors of Indiana and Ohio if they were not residents of those states. Michigan's governor, George Romney, was better known nationally, and this was reflected in the fact that he was better known to more students in Indiana and Ohio. The parents of the high school students overwhelmingly lived in the state in which they were em- ployed. Of those living in Indiana, 92 percent were employed in the state; in Ohio, 95 percent; in Michigan, 90 percent. The students preferred radio sta- tions and newspapers from their own state. They overwhelmingly preferred to see a Big Ten school from their own state go to the Rose Bowl. Pride in one's own state and in the leaders and institutions of that state characterized the responses throughout the study.[11]

Capitals and Capitols The capitals of European states are characteristically the largest cities of the nation. There are, in fact, few exceptions to the rule. These nations, accustomed to a strong central government about which eco- nomic and social life tends to cluster, have found this natural. A different pattern developed in the United States, however. State capitals were sometimes located in the wilderness somewhere near the center of the state's population, following the precedent of the establishment of Washington as the nation's capital. Other factors also contributed to a general tendency to establish the

[11] Arthur R. Stevens, "Political Culture in the Tri-state Area of Michigan, Indiana, and Ohio," term paper, Michigan State University, East Lansing, Mich., 1965.

seat of government in a city other than the largest of the state. Americans have traditionally regarded urban life as corrupt and of a lower morality than the rural life which was for many decades regarded as the norm. A nation of farmers tended to prefer small towns for the capitals. In other cases, transportation problems helped determine the site: Bismarck, Denver, Des Moines, Indianapolis, Sacramento, and Springfield are all examples of centrally located capitals. Montpelier, Vermont, was started in a forest clearing in 1809, and so was Columbia, South Carolina, in 1786. Columbus, Ohio, was platted on the prairie in 1812. Cheyenne is perhaps the best example of a capital located on the basis of rail transportation considerations—although Wyoming is the ninth largest state in area, its capital barely manages to squeeze within its southeast boundary.

Even today, some capital cities are hardly more than small towns. The 1960 census showed Carson City, Nevada, with a population of 5,163; Pierre, South Dakota, with 10,088; and Montpelier, Vermont, with 8,782. Alaska, Kentucky, Maine, New Hampshire, North Dakota, and Washington also had capitals with populations under 30,000.

State names are noted for their variety and for their euphony. Some names are clearly historical. The Carolinas are named for King Charles I, who gave a land patent to Sir Robert Heath. Virginia was so named by the gallant Sir Walter Raleigh in honor of the Virgin Queen, Elizabeth I. Delaware was named for Lord De La Warr, the first governor of the Virginia Company. One-fourth of the states have names based on variants of Indian words, quite a few of them involving matters of controversy as to the original meaning. Four states have Spanish names; two, Maine and Vermont, are French in origin; and Montana is Latin. Counties, cities, villages, and townships have interesting and varied names, too, although many of them are simply named for now-obscure local persons or for Presidents or governors.

Domes and Other Decorations Architects find the state capitals interesting "for their often handsome domed government buildings, which, like the courthouses, bear testimony to the fact that all levels of American government have given a place to art in cities which would otherwise be so lacking in decoration, painting, and sculpture." [12]

But artistic quality varies a good deal. Some capitols were constructed of shoddy materials under conditions involving graft and corruption, the most notorious example, perhaps, being that of Pennsylvania in the early years of the present century when the taxpayers of the commonwealth [13] were swindled out of over $5.5 million. Some are poor imitations of the nation's Capitol, with the proportions seriously distorted; others, with adequate American Grecian or American Roman exteriors, have gloomy, cluttered Victorian interiors. The capitol at Salem, Oregon, seems to be an attempt at "early contemporary"; that at Columbus, Ohio, looks like a Greek temple with a submarine conning

[12] Christopher Tunnard and H. H. Reed, **American Skyline,** New American Library of World Literature, Inc., New York, 1956, p. 63.
[13] According to their constitutions, Kentucky, Massachusetts, Pennsylvania, and Virginia are "commonwealths." All others are "states." There is no legal distinction.

Fig. 1-1   **State Variation in Ability to Support the Expectations of the American Life Styles.**
The southeastern states have the lowest income and lowest tax capacity.
SOURCE: U.S. Advisory Commission on Intergovernmental Relations, **Measures of State and Local Fiscal Capacity and Tax Effort,** 1962.

tower atop; and Baton Rouge, Louisiana, and Lincoln, Nebraska, both cities of modest size, seem like strangely inappropriate places for capitols built in the style of the American skyscraper. But generally it is the Roman basilica dome which has come to symbolize American democracy and, despite the possible criticisms that may properly be levied, "government in America, more modest than business, less obvious than the churches, has done as much as both of these to shape the scene about us." [14] Certainly the capitols of Massachusetts, North Carolina, Virginia, and West Virginia, among others, are examples of good American architecture.

Regions and Regionalism   For all the talk about American uniformity and conformity, the diet, dialect, language, degree of urbanization, ethnic patterns, and political traditions of the various regions of America differ considerably from one another. Perhaps the similarities among the regions are greater than their differences, but there are important differences.[15]

It is easy to exaggerate these differences, of course. There is a dull monotony about a great many American cities when they are compared, and this is especially true of the middle-sized cities. Often, the city has failed to develop its own individuality, to exploit its traditions, to use its opportunities to make the community a place where life is richer because of its own partic-

[14] Tunnard and Reed, *op. cit.,* p. 27.
[15] Although the statistical evidence to support its sweeping generalizations is weak, see David Cort, "The Variety of American Cities," **Harper's Magazine,** November, 1957, pp. 46–49, for an argument that the nation "is filled with real and different cultures, people—and prices."

ular attributes. But the differences do exist, especially if distinctions are made by regions rather than by comparing cities or counties. And while these regions cannot be accurately defined, they are of political importance.

Population Patterns and Politics

The 50 states and 100,000-odd local units of government in the United States are social service agencies. Their size, shape, and reason for being are a result of historical accident and tradition. Often they are a heritage from more simple and primitive times. But their tasks, functions, and problems are posed by the populations they contain. Population does not, of course, mean mere numbers of people. It also means density, ethnic and racial patterns, rate of growth, percentage of very old and very young, of school age, of rural or urban, and of stability and mobility. Before any attempt is made to inquire into the services performed at the state and local levels of government or into the politics surrounding those services, the general pattern of demographic trends should be clearly before us.

Urbanism and the Western World

The city in Western civilization is primarily a product of the industrial revolution. To be sure, Europe had cities before 1770 (roughly the time of the beginning of the revolution, which lasted for over a century thereafter and has never really ended), but they were chiefly capitals or trading centers.

The American Pattern   With the rise of a machine technology, steam power, the factory system, and modern agricultural techniques, cities grew at phenomenal rates. Europe and America, predominately rural from prehistoric times, rapidly urbanized. In the United States, only small towns existed at the time of the Revolution, and 90 percent of the population was rural. The towns grew, however, and at an almost continuously accelerating pace. Between 1820 and 1840 the number of people engaged in manufacturing increased by 127 percent. Between 1840 and 1850 alone America's urban population increased by nearly 50 percent.

After the construction of railroads, the heavy influx of foreign investment capital, and the Civil War (1861 to 1865), urban growth, which earlier had occurred on the East Coast and especially in New England, spread into the Middle West. The rise of the great corporations and the never-ending developments in technological knowledge continued to raise the American standard of living even as it changed the American mode of living. Immigrants who before had hurried to the rich clay loams of the Middle Western farm belt now remained in New York, Cincinnati, or Chicago to become a commodity called "labor" in the factory, the steel mill, or the stockyard. The children of country bumpkins yearned to become city slickers and hurried off at the earliest opportunity to what was often their disillusionment. But they did find greater opportunity, and it was the most competent of the rural youth who were most likely to make the big change.[16] And this probably continues to be the case today.

A Growing Nation   On March 1, 1966, the United States had a population estimated at over 197 million. Fewer than 4 million persons lived in the United States at the time of the first census in 1790. This figure thereafter doubled approximately every twenty-five years for the next century. Rural America had a high birthrate, and immigrants arrived from abroad with little restriction. An all-time high of 1,285,349 foreigners reached our shores in 1907. This figure dropped sharply after a quota system of immigration was applied following World War I. For a while the rate of increase of population declined rapidly, especially during the Great Depression of the 1930s.

The history of America has been almost continuously a history of urbanization. In every decade since the Constitution went into effect, except for the period 1810 to 1820, the urban growth rate has been greater than that of rural areas. Between 1950 and 1960, the urban population increased by 29 percent and for the first time in our history rural population decreased both relatively and absolutely.

The City Today   The population of American cities doubled between the beginning of the Civil War and 1900. In the next quarter of a century, it doubled again. By 1920, over one-half (51.2 percent) of the American people were living in urban areas; * and in 1960, over two-thirds of them.

* URBAN AREAS. In the census of 1960, the Bureau defined urban, as distinguished from rural, areas as (1) places of 2,500 inhabitants or more incorporated as cities, boroughs, villages, and towns (except towns in New England, New York, and Wisconsin); (2) the densely settled urban fringe, whether incorporated or unincorporated, of urbanized areas; (3) towns in New England and townships in New Jersey and Pennsylvania which contain no incorporated municipalities and have either 3,500 inhabitants or more or a population of 2,500 to 25,000 and a density of 1,500 persons or more per square mile; (4) counties in states other than the New England states, New Jersey, and Pennsylvania that have no incorporated municipalities within their boundaries, but have a density of 1,500 persons or more per square mile; and (5) unincorporated places of 2,500 inhabitants or more.

The movement toward the cities is further indicated by the fact that nearly one-half of the counties in the nation showed a population decrease between 1950 and 1960. These were, of course, the rural counties. Some of the changes that have taken place in the last generation are truly revolutionary in character. Carroll County, Mississippi, for example, lost 25 percent of its population between 1940 and 1950. A large number of Negroes left the county to move into urban areas in either the South or North, but more startling is the fact that two-thirds of the white population emigrated from the county during that decade. In contrast, Harrison County, Mississippi (Biloxi-Gulfport),

[16] See Noel P. Gist and C. D. Clark, "Intelligence as a Selective Factor in Rural-Urban Migration," **American Journal of Sociology**, 44:36–58, July, 1938.

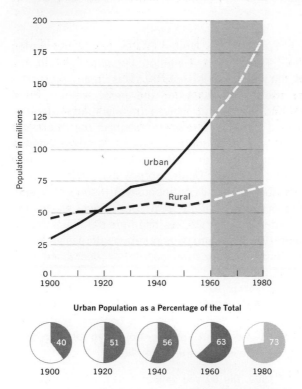

Urban Population as a Percentage of the Total

1900	1920	1940	1960	1980
40	51	56	63	73

Fig. 1-2　The United States Is an Urban Nation.
SOURCE: Municipal Manpower Commission, **Governmental Manpower for Tomorrow's Cities,** McGraw-Hill Book Company, New York, 1962.

increased by 66 percent and Hinds County (Jackson), by 33 percent. The rural-to-urban movement continued after World War II, and so did the pattern of movement in counties such as these. Carroll County, Mississippi, lost another 28 percent of its population between 1950 and 1960, with the white out-migration somewhat outnumbering the Negro. Harrison County continued to gain; during this decade its increase was 42 percent. Hinds County gained 32 percent, almost as high a percentage as in the previous decade.

Outside the cities, the population was often sparse. For example, the seventeen northernmost counties of Wisconsin cover one-third of the state's land area, but have only 7 percent of its population.

It was not cities but metropolitan areas * that were undergoing the most rapid change in the mid-twentieth century. By 1960, one American in five was living in the metropolitan areas (not necessarily within the core-city limits, of course) of New York, Chicago, Philadelphia, Los Angeles, and Detroit. And 64 percent of the population lived within the 216 metropolitan areas. Yet, these areas covered only about 7 percent of the land area of the continental United States.

* STANDARD METROPOLITAN STATISTICAL AREAS contain at least one city of 50,000 population, by Bureau of the Census definition. The nucleus of the area is the county or counties containing the core city or cities. Contiguous counties are included in the area if they are densely settled by nonagricultural workers and are socially and economically integrated with the core city.

The metropolitan areas account for about two-thirds of the total retail volume and about 90 percent of the total wholesale volume of the nation. It is in these areas that the great bulk of the nation's population increase has taken place since the end of World War II. In 1960, 87 percent of the California population lived in metropolitan areas; in Rhode Island, 86 percent; in New York, 85 percent, in Nevada, 74 percent.

The general pattern of urban population development is fairly consistent throughout the nation, however. Everywhere, even in the Rocky Mountain and other less populous states, the principal area of growth is around the major cities. For example, Wyoming, with only 332,000 people in 1960 and a tradition centering around "the wide open spaces," had 57 percent of its people living in urban areas.

The Urban Region   Only four of the fifty states contain no metropolitan areas. These are Alaska, Idaho, Vermont, and Wyoming. Of course, it is around the metropolises that the population continues to cluster. In fact, these areas are growing into one another, so that Charlton F. Chute has found it advantageous to define "urban regions." These consist of two or more contiguous standard metropolitan areas. The greatest of these is the Eastern Seaboard region, which stretches for 600 miles from the vicinity of Haverhill, north of Boston near the New Hampshire border, to the southernmost suburbs of Washington, in Virginia. This vast region contains around 20 percent of the total national population. The Chicago and Cleveland urban regions are also huge, and the Los Angeles region stretches from the northwest suburbs of Los Angeles to the southern suburbs of San Diego, a distance of over 200 miles, and became the second largest region in the nation in the 1960s. Eighteen urban regions existed in 1958 and included about 40 percent of the nation's population. The complexity as well as the cost of government increases disproportionately with density.

Between 1950 and 1960, the larger the metropolitan area, the greater was its population density, the larger its proportion of minority-group populations, and the higher its average family income.[17] For all of these reasons, it can be expected that these will be the areas where governmental problems will continue to make their greatest challenge.[18] About 84 percent of the total national population increase in the decade preceding 1960 was in the SMSAs. The metropolitan areas grew by 26 percent during the decade, the rest of the country by only 7 percent.

The suburban movement also continued in the pattern that has charac-

[17] Leo F. Schnore, "Some Correlates of Urban Size," **American Journal of Sociology,** 69:185–193, September, 1963.
[18] See Charlton F. Chute, "Today's Urban Regions," **National Municipal Review,** vol. 45, June and July, 1956.

terized America since World War II. While the core cities of standard metropolitan areas increased by 11 percent, their suburbs increased by 48 percent.
Suburbanization took place most rapidly in the largest metropolitan areas and,
in general, a direct relationship existed between size of metropolitan area and
rate of suburban increase, but this can be explained in part by the fact that
the larger the city, in general, the less vacant land there is available in the

Table 2   Metropolitan Proportion of the Population, by States, 1960

STATE	PERCENTAGE OF POPULATION IN SMSAs	STATE	PERCENTAGE OF POPULATION IN SMSAs
California	86.5	Louisiana	50.0
Rhode Island	86.2	Indiana	48.1
New York	85.5	Wisconsin	46.3
Massachusetts	85.2	Georgia	46.0
Hawaii	79.1	Tennessee	45.8
New Jersey	78.9	Oklahoma	43.9
Maryland	78.2	Nebraska	37.6
Pennsylvania	77.9	Kansas	37.4
Connecticut	77.6	Kentucky	34.1
Illinois	76.9	Iowa	33.2
Nevada	74.2	South Carolina	32.2
Michigan	73.1	West Virginia	30.9
Arizona	71.4	New Mexico	27.6
Ohio	69.5	North Carolina	24.6
Delaware	68.9	Montana	22.6
Colorado	68.0	Maine	19.7
Utah	67.5	Arkansas	19.1
Florida	65.6	New Hampshire	17.7
Texas	63.4	South Dakota	12.7
Washington	63.1	North Dakota	10.6
Alabama	63.0	Mississippi	8.6
Missouri	57.9	Alaska	0.0
Minnesota	51.3	Idaho	0.0
Virginia	50.9	Vermont	0.0
Oregon	50.4	Wyoming	0.0

SOURCE: U.S. Bureau of the Census, **Census of Population:** 1960, vol. I, parts 2–51, 1963.

core city. Furthermore, the larger the city, the less willing areas surrounding it
are to be annexed to it. In addition, the larger the city, the more likely it is to
be surrounded by already incorporated suburbs which serve to block off any
possibility of growth through annexation. Even so, between 1950 and 1960,
8.8 million people were taken into core cities by annexation; core cities in
more than 75 percent of the metropolitan areas annexed some territory. Some
of the core cities actually lost population and the larger the metropolitan area,
the more likely this was to be the case. Of the eighteen largest cities in the

country, fourteen lost population and two of the remaining—Houston and Milwaukee—grew only because of major annexations. Leo Schnore has calculated that if the 1950 city boundaries had been held constant, the core cities would have grown by only 1.5 percent, while their suburbs would have grown by 61.7 percent.[19]

Before 1920, core cities grew faster than did their suburbs. The two increased their populations at about the same rate in the 1920s, and since the census of 1930, the suburban growth has been faster, with the rate of increase constantly expanding.[20]

About one-third of the American population lives within core cities now, but the population of core cities in coming decades will decline. Another one-third, roughly, lives in metropolitan suburbs. This is the population class that is increasing most rapidly. The remaining one-third of the population is scattered around the rest of the country. It is increasing at only about 1 percent per year, or at one-fourth the rate of the metropolitan suburbs.[21]

This rapid rise in population has not taken place without significant changes in the American way of life, including the American way of earning a living. It was because we ceased to be a rural nation, as were our colonial Founding Fathers, and because we became the greatest of all industrial nations that we could support so rapidly increasing a population at a standard of living never before dreamed of. Yet there is no one America; while most states are gaining population, a few are losing population; while most cities grow, some shrink and others remain static.[22]

The Negro Leaves the Farm   Perhaps the most dramatic population shift has been made by American Negroes. These people are descended from persons who were brought to the New World as slaves. Their ancestors labored on plantations in the South, and nearly all of them were rural dwellers. After the Civil War, most Negroes remained in the Deep South, becoming sharecroppers on land subdivided when the great plantations were broken up. Their number increased with each census, but a lower economic standard, leading to a higher death rate, combined with an almost all-white immigration caused the percentage of the population, which had been nearly 20 percent Negro in 1790, to drop to 14 percent in 1860 and to about 10 percent in 1930. The percentage has increased only slightly since.

Even before slavery was abolished, some movement of Negroes out of the South took place. However, as late as 1900, only 10 percent of the Negro population lived in the North. The big change, the one that brought economic opportunity to the poverty-ridden Negro sharecropper, was the demand for his

[19] Leo F. Schnore, "A Planner's Guide to the 1960 Census of Population," **Journal of the American Institute of Planners,** 29:29–39, February, 1963; Leo F. Schnore, "Municipal Annexations and the Growth of Metropolitan Suburbs," **American Journal of Sociology,** 67:406–407, January, 1962.
[20] Data from the U.S. Bureau of the Census.
[21] York Willbern, **The Withering Away of the City,** University of Alabama Press, University, Ala., 1964, pp. 20–21.
[22] Population statistics used are from various publications of the U.S. Bureau of the Census. A good and convenient summary of statistics, including recent estimates, may be found in the annual edition of **The World Almanac,** published by the **New York World-Telegram and The Sun.**

Table 3 Population and Urbanization Data, by States

STATE	POPULATION (1960 CENSUS)	RANK	DENSITY (PER SQ MI)	PERCENT URBAN	NUMBER OF PLACES OVER 50,000	POPULATION CHANGES 1950–1960, PERCENT		
						TOTAL	URBAN	RURAL
Alabama	3,266,740	19	64.0	54.8	6	6.7	33.6	14.3
Alaska	226,167	51	0.4	37.9	0	75.8	150.3	48.8
Arizona	1,302,161	35	11.5	74.5	2	73.7	133.3	−0.6
Arkansas	1,786,272	31	34.0	42.8	3	−6.5	21.4	−20.2
California	15,717,204	2	100.4	86.4	43	48.5	58.9	4.8
Colorado	1,753,947	33	16.9	73.7	3	32.4	55.5	−6.6
Connecticut	2,535,234	25	517.5	78.3	10	26.3	27.4	22.5
Delaware	446,292	47	225.6	65.6	1	40.3	47.0	29.0
District of Columbia	763,956	40	12,523.9	100.0	1	−4.8	−4.8	—
Florida	4,951,560	10	91.3	73.9	10	78.7	101.9	34.8
Georgia	3,943,116	16	67.7	55.3	6	14.5	39.8	−6.5
Hawaii	632,772	44	98.6	76.5	1	26.6	40.3	−3.9
Idaho	667,191	43	8.1	47.5	0	13.3	25.6	4.2
Illinois	10,081,158	4	180.3	80.7	15	15.7	20.4	−0.6
Indiana	4,662,498	11	128.9	62.4	9	18.5	23.5	11.1
Iowa	2,757,537	24	49.2	53.0	7	5.2	16.9	−5.5
Kansas	2,178,611	28	26.6	61.0	3	14.3	33.8	−6.8
Kentucky	3,038,156	22	76.2	44.5	3	3.2	24.8	−9.4
Louisiana	3,257,022	20	72.2	63.3	5	21.4	40.0	−1.3
Maine	969,265	36	31.3	51.3	1	6.1	5.3	6.9
Maryland	3,100,689	21	314.0	72.7	5	32.3	39.5	16.5
Massachusetts	5,148,578	9	654.5	83.6	20	9.8	8.7	15.7
Michigan	7,823,194	7	137.2	73.4	17	22.8	27.4	11.5
Minnesota	3,413,864	18	42.7	62.2	4	14.5	30.6	−4.9
Mississippi	2,178,141	29	46.1	37.7	1	0.0	35.2	−13.6

Missouri	4,319,813	13	62.5	66.6	6	9.2	18.2	−5.2
Montana	674,767	42	4.6	50.2	2	14.2	31.2	1.0
Nebraska	1,411,330	34	18.4	54.3	2	6.5	23.2	−8.3
Nevada	285,278	50	2.6	70.4	2	78.2	119.0	23.5
New Hampshire	606,921	46	67.3	58.3	1	13.8	15.3	11.8
New Jersey	6,066,782	8	806.7	88.6	17	25.5	28.4	6.7
New Mexico	951,023	37	7.8	65.9	1	39.6	83.2	−4.3
New York	16,782,304	1	350.1	85.4	19	13.2	13.0	14.1
North Carolina	4,556,155	12	92.9	39.5	7	12.2	31.7	2.2
North Dakota	632,446	45	9.1	35.2	0	2.1	35.1	−9.9
Ohio	9,706,397	5	236.9	73.4	18	22.1	27.7	9.1
Oklahoma	2,328,284	27	33.8	62.9	3	4.3	28.5	−21.1
Oregon	1,768,687	32	18.4	62.2	2	16.3	34.3	−4.8
Pennsylvania	11,319,366	3	251.5	71.6	20	7.8	9.4	4.0
Rhode Island	859,488	39	812.4	86.4	4	8.5	11.3	−6.5
South Carolina	2,382,594	26	78.7	41.2	3	12.5	26.2	4.6
South Dakota	680,514	41	8.9	39.3	1	4.3	23.3	−5.2
Tennessee	3,567,089	17	85.4	52.3	4	8.4	28.4	−7.4
Texas	9,579,677	6	36.5	75.0	21	24.2	48.6	−16.7
Utah	890,627	38	10.8	74.9	2	29.3	48.3	−6.5
Vermont	389,881	48	42.0	38.5	0	3.2	8.9	−0.1
Virginia	3,966,949	14	99.6	55.6	9	19.5	41.3	0.2
Washington	2,853,214	23	42.8	68.1	3	19.9	29.3	3.9
West Virginia	1,860,421	30	77.3	38.2	3	−7.2	2.4	−12.3
Wisconsin	3,951,777	15	72.2	63.8	7	15.1	26.9	−1.2
Wyoming	330,066	49	3.4	56.8	0	13.6	29.7	−2.3
United States								
Total	179,323,175	—	50.5	69.9	333	18.5	29.3	−0.8

SOURCE: U.S. Bureau of the Census.

labor in the urban factory. The first great demand for this purpose came during World War I, when a shortage of factory hands caused an imbalance in supply and demand of labor. It was the younger, more adventuresome who first made the long trek to Chicago, Detroit, or New York. The word they sent back was that one could make far more money in less time under better conditions of labor in a factory than in the almost hopeless atmosphere of the tenant farm. As early as 1914, Henry Ford created a sensation when he offered a $5-a-day minimum wage. He also established a quota for Negro employees.

Recent Developments   After World War I, only the Great Depression served temporarily to stop the urbanization of the Negro. Every other important economic and political consideration—the closing of the gates to immigrants (1924), World War II (1941–1945), and the prosperous years after 1945— encouraged the movement to cities. In the decade following 1940, 3 million Negroes made the rural-to-urban change. By 1950, 28 percent of the Negro population lived in the North and nearly 60 percent of the total was urban, for Southern Negroes also moved into Southern cities.

In 1960, the percentage of the Negro population located in urban areas was very nearly as large as that of the white population. In the years following the beginning of war preparations about 1940, the nonwhite growth in urban population was far greater than that on the farm. In cities of over 50,000 the nonwhite population increased at a rate five times that of the white population (49.2 percent as against 10.4 percent) between 1940 and 1950. The Los Angeles and Detroit nonwhite populations doubled; that of San Francisco increased by 156 percent. New York's Harlem became the largest Negro community in the world.

The Negro has been moving from rural America into the cities. He has also been moving from the South to the North. Each of the fifty largest cities in the United States had increases in the percentage of nonwhites between 1950 and 1960. Using metropolitan areas as a basis for measurement, large increases in Negro population occurred in the North, but more than 60 percent of the metropolitan areas in the South showed a lower proportion of Negroes in 1960 than in 1950.[23]

The Negro is at a disadvantage in comparison with the urban white by almost any standard of measurement. He has a lower level of education, a lower average income, a smaller dwelling place, poorer sanitary facilities, poorer health and less medical care, and fewer avenues for social or economic advancement. Even so, the disadvantage of the Negro is becoming less with each generation. In the Philadelphia metropolitan area in 1960, for example, 74 percent of the white population lived in homes owned by their families. For Negroes, the percentage was only 45, but in the preceding decade it had increased at a faster rate than that for whites and the percentage was equal to that of whites twenty years earlier. The commonly heard criticism that no

[23] See Harry Sharp and Leo F. Schnore, "The Changing Color Composition of Metropolitan Areas," **Land Economics**, 38:169–185, May, 1962.

progress toward equality is being made is statistically inaccurate. The real normative question is whether the gap is being closed at a satisfactory rate of speed.[24]

Negroes continue to be concentrated in a relatively few sections of cities, although a tendency toward the spread of Negroes into the suburbs of Northern cities can be seen. In 1960, 88 percent of the Negroes in Syracuse, New York, lived in eight of the sixty census-tract areas. One study concluded that, "in view of the total Negro population increase in the years 1950–1960, the degree of segregation has probably increased." [25]

By 1960, one person in five within the city limits of Chicago was a Negro; in Detroit the proportion had reached one in four. In 1966, over 90 percent of the public school children in Washington, D.C., were Negro. Because Negroes tend to concentrate in the core cities and because their rate of urbanization is much faster than that of the white population, we may expect that they will become the dominant racial or ethnic group in the core cities of many metropolitan areas in the coming decades. This will likely mean dramatic changes in the political patterns of those cities, with Negro majorities on the council and a Negro mayor in city hall an eventual possibility in such cities as Chicago, Cleveland, Detroit, and St. Louis. It is a matter for speculation as to the effect that such developments will have upon metropolitan area government, intergovernmental relations, partisan conflicts in state legislatures, the suburban movement, interracial friction, and a host of other political and social matters.

Population: In Summary   In the 1960s, America was an industrial nation with two-thirds of its population living in urban areas and chiefly in metropolitan communities. The large core cities had almost stopped growing: nearly all of the population growth after 1950 was centered in the suburban areas.

Small-town population continued to hold its own, and farm population, which had reached an all-time high of 32.4 million in 1915 and had been declining almost without interruption since, continued to drop.

In the metropolitan areas, the flight to the suburbs by the bulk of the middle-class and many working-class families was still being counterbalanced by the continuing arrival of migrants from rural and small-town areas. Negroes, in particular, were moving into the core cities from the rural South.

In the mid-1960s, the American birthrate was slightly lower than it had been just after World War II, but evidence indicated that the American attitude toward family size, early marriage, and economic opportunities had undergone a pronounced change from the time of the Great Depression. With more medical-treatment discoveries each year and a larger proportion of the population receiving professional medical care, the death rate was expected to continue to decline. As a result, each year, nearly 3 million additional Americans were demanding food, clothing, and shelter.

[24] George W. Grier, **PENJERDEL, Region in Transition,** Penjerdel, Philadelphia, 1964, p. 41.
[25] Alan K. Campbell and others, **The Negro in Syracuse,** University College of Syracuse University, Syracuse, N.Y., 1964, p. 34.

The Effects of Physical Mobility

Ours is a nation of seminomadic people. Opportunity for advancement, the necessity for going to the job that will not come to the individual, the practice of business and industries that operate over the entire nation, or over even larger areas, to send men from assignment in one city to assignment in another while moving up the organizational ladder, all contribute to this mobility. As William H. Whyte, Jr., has said, "The man who leaves home is not the exception in American society, but the key to it." [26] In the postwar years, one-fifth of the population has changed place of residence each year. Some people move more often than the average, of course, and some Americans still are born, live, and die in the same house; but it is estimated that in the five years after 1950, one-half of the people in the United States changed their places of residence.[27] Most of these moves are within the same county, although about 5 percent of the total population annually moves to a different county within the same state and another 5 percent moves to a different state.

Why Do People Move?   To some extent people move to escape unemployment. Some people shuttle back and forth between their old home town or farm and the city several times during a lifetime as it suits their momentary needs or whims. But, for the most part, moves are made as the result of, or in search of, economic advancement.[28]

This mobility of the American people has been criticized as undesirable. "Observers who would like to see less change argue that change breeds anxieties, tensions, and frustrations. This is true, and certainly the suburban [or core city] transients pay a great price for the up-rooting that has put them there. But how ideal for them would be the alternative?" [29]

In the fifty years following 1902, the population of the nation doubled, the general price level tripled, per capita state and local expenditures increased fifteenfold (even if one corrects for the diminishing value of the dollar, they increased fivefold), and per capita state and local debt, holding constant the value of the dollar, increased by over 2½ times [30] (see Figure 3-1). America is and always has been an optimistic, changing nation with great emphasis upon meeting the needs of society as society sees those needs. This confidence is no doubt partly a result of a continuing conviction that "the routes to advancement are not closing down, our classes are not freezing; quite the opposite, there have never been so many people moving in so many different ways." [31] Whether it is the Southern sharecropper moving into the Northern

[26] William H. Whyte, Jr., **The Organization Man,** Doubleday Anchor Books, Garden City, N.Y., 1956, p. 297.
[27] U.S. Housing and Home Finance Agency, **Housing in the United States,** 1956, pp. 8–9.
[28] Noel P. Gist and L. A. Halbert, **Urban Society,** 4th ed., Thomas Y. Crowell Company, New York, 1956, pp. 354–365; and Whyte, *op. cit.,* chap. 21.
[29] Whyte, *op. cit.,* p. 309.
[30] U.S. Bureau of the Census, **Historical Statistics on State and Local Government Finances,** State and Local Government Special Studies No. 38, 1955, p. 1. Dollar values adjusted by use of the consumer price index of the Bureau of Labor Statistics.
[31] Whyte, *op. cit.,* p. 309.

city to become a factory worker or the son of a clerk becoming an "organization man" and a middle-class suburbanite, the result is viewed by the migrant as another step toward the fulfillment of the American dream.

Political Consequences A great many aspects of state and local government are affected by the changing population pattern in America. To name a few:

1. Urbanization has produced demands for more urban representation in legislatures; rural areas have been fighting a rearguard action against this, but the courts have been pressuring for reapportionment.

2. The suburban trend has produced conflict and service problems in metropolitan areas which contain dozens, sometimes hundreds, of governmental units.

3. The movement of Negroes off the Southern farm into Northern cities is accompanied by a development of an awareness of the potential use by Negroes of political power.

4. The throwing of people of many subcultures into close physical proximity in urban areas is contributing to increasing social conflict, which becomes political conflict.

5. The insecurities created because the urbanite is dependent upon someone else—the employer—for work have produced demands for governmental programs of many kinds.

6. The agricultural transformation is causing economic distress to many farmers. Marginal farmers are moving into cities. Both farmers and rural-to-urban migrants are looking to government at all levels for several types of assistance.

These phenomena, among others, will be explored in later chapters. In sum, they indicate an expanded role for state and local governments.

Culture and Society

The way in which people choose public officials, the manner in which public policy is made and carried out, the behavior patterns of the bureaucracy, the services expected of government, the concept of ethical behavior on the part of public officials and employees, the type of government personnel, the priorities placed upon those things to be done by government, the share of the national income to be spent by government—all of these are determined by the social environment which envelops a society of human beings. The relationship between the individual and the state is dependent upon a system of values—ideas or beliefs which people within a society cherish. These values are the cornerstone upon which the culture * of a group of people is built. American government cannot be understood unless we understand American culture.

* CULTURE is the pattern of all those arrangements, material or behavioral, which have been adopted by a society as the traditional ways of solving the problems of its members.

Dynamism in American Society

André Siegfried, a French economic geographer, writing about his impressions of the United States in the 1920s, offered the opinion that the nation had arrived at the early stages of maturity. He thought events in that decade indicated that European cultural domination of the United States had come to an end, and that America was now in the process of creating its own mass-oriented culture. This new culture he saw as unique, not merely an adaptation of various segments of the culture of European nations. Although America had borrowed extensively from the Old World, she had added so much of her own that the result was a truly new and different way of life.[32] Some characteristics of this unique culture are worth noting.

Rootlessness   The general pattern of population movements in the United States was discussed earlier in this chapter. High physical and social mobility have been characteristics of American society from colonial times. Physical mobility has been of advantage in developing new opportunities for people who feel that they have reached a stalemate in their present location. It permits manpower to be available wherever it may be needed, and gives variety to otherwise jaded life interest. But high physical mobility helps create serious social problems. The breakdown of primary controls * in the rooming-house and deteriorated apartment-house areas of the zone of transition † leads to higher crime rates, increased insecurity feelings, and other personal and social problems. Since migrants are usually marginal workers—last to be hired and first to be fired—their presence in large numbers in a city makes the public-welfare problem more complicated than in a stable society.

* **PRIMARY GROUP** behavior is controlled through shared values and goals of persons in small groups who deal with one another on a personal basis, rather than in terms of the functions they perform in society. **SECONDARY GROUPS** are usually larger, more dispersed in space, and share fewer values. The individual is seen not as a whole person, but as someone performing a particular role. Secondary group controls emphasize formal rules and procedures.

† **ZONE OF TRANSITION.** The area outside the central business district, where retreating higher-class residents have left an area now consisting of rooming houses, cheap hotels, and business places that do not require prestigeful locations.

From the point of view of participation in democratic government, high mobility is important in that large numbers of migrants fail to identify themselves with their adopted communities.[33] Their civic pride is likely to be

32 André Siegfried, **America Comes of Age**, Harcourt, Brace & World, Inc., New York, 1927. Nearly three decades and many visits later, Siegfried wrote another book, **America at Mid-century**, Harcourt, Brace & World, Inc., New York, 1955, which seems less insightful and reflects European stereotypic attitudes and prejudices about American culture.
33 See Robert C. Angell, "The Moral Integration of American Cities," **American Journal of Sociology**, vol. 57, part 2, July, 1951; Basil G. Zimmer, "Participation of Migrants in Urban Structures," **American Sociological Review**, 20:218–224, April, 1955; Basil G. Zimmer, "Farm Backgrounds and Urban Participation," **American Journal of Sociology**, 61:470–475, March, 1956. A classic statement, though no longer fully accepted by social scientists, of urban living as contrasted with rural may be found in Louis Wirth, "Urbanism as a Way of Life," **American Journal of Sociology**, 44:1–24, July, 1938.

almost nonexistent. There is no loyalty to the city as such. If the migrant happens to live in a suburb, he may not even know whether it is actually an independent unit of government. Politically, this means that appeals to community responsibility will fall on deaf ears. It means that elections will be ignored. Government will be left in the hands of others—and the others may be grossly unrepresentative of the interest of the newer arrivals.

The Transient as a Community Participant   Vast suburban growth has created special problems in the matter of rootlessness and a lack of belonging. The values of the middle class call for individual participation in political, social, and civic activities. Yet, members of this group often lack the deep roots that at once command and, at the same time, clear the way for the assumption of local social responsibilities. Still, if nearly everyone in communities such as Levittown or Park Forest (suburban Chicago) is a newcomer, some way must be found to get people to serve on city councils, on planning commissions, on united community fund boards. Thus, we come to the question: [34]

Are the transients a rootless people? If by roots we mean the complex of geographical and family ties that has historically knitted Americans to local society, these young transients are almost entirely rootless. They are very much aware of the fact; surprisingly often they will bring up the home town, and though they have no intention whatsoever of going back, they dwell on what they left behind. . . .

Whyte, in his examination of Park Forest, found that there was indeed a good deal of apathy toward community problems in a new town made up entirely of persons who are rootless in the traditional sense. But he also found that many residents took up the real issues of providing for schools and public services because of a feeling of a need for "ties more meaningful than those of bridge and canasta and bowling." [35]

Trade Unionism   The factory worker, like the middle-class organization man, is also faced with the problem of establishing some kind of roots in lieu of the traditional type. He, too, is accommodating himself to the new American way of life. A study of Detroit automobile workers, for example, found that the great bulk of them (82 percent) are American-born, in contrast to the factory worker in Andrew Carnegie's steel mills or to Jurgis Rudkus, the Lithuanian who slaved in the stockyards of Chicago at the beginning of the present century.[36] Over one-half of them (52 percent) had immigrant fathers, however. Most automobile workers are living in towns where they did not grow up, and they are to some degree culturally marginal. The home-ownership level of 59 percent is high, almost as high as that of Detroit in general (65 percent), but much lower than that of the middle-class and upper-working-class suburban dwellers. (In Chicago, a pre-automobile-age city of apartments, home ownership is only 30 percent and would be lower than that for factory workers. Detroit, like many other industrial cities is, however, a post-automobile-age city consisting prin-

34 Whyte, *op. cit.*, p. 318.
35 *Ibid.*, pp. 325–327.
36 In the novel by Upton Sinclair, **The Jungle,** The Viking Press, Inc., New York, 1906.

cipally of one- and two-family homes. Home ownership in most types of suburbs runs around 90 percent.)

One-fifth of Detroit automobile workers grew up on farms, another one-fourth in small towns. Only 44 percent were raised in large cities. Two-thirds of them are the only breadwinners in their families. One-half of them are church members, but factory workers seem to be quite inactive in church groups, fraternal organizations, veterans groups, neighborhood associations, and parent-teacher associations—a matter of considerable importance so far as social and political representation of interests is concerned.[37]

In suburbia, neighbors are the mainstays of social relationships, since organization-man families are often forced to live far from any of their relatives. Residents of the core city, including factory workers, find that relatives are more important than are next door neighbors. Unskilled workers probably migrate more to areas where relatives have already located than do middle-class persons. The latter have less of a choice of destination, being required to go where their skills are demanded. In Detroit, 89 percent of core-city working-class couples have relatives living in the community; more than one-half of them have relatives in the same neighborhood. Two-thirds of the couples see their relatives once or twice a week at least, and over one-fourth see some relative nearly every day. Family gatherings at weddings, funerals, birthdays, and holidays are important. Of the people who see relatives once or twice a week, more than one-half see neighbors less than once a month.[38]

Core-city residents are thus less neighborhood-oriented than are sub-urbanites, though they seek to maintain primary relationships of some kind. When relatives live within driving distances, they are likely to concentrate their social activities upon them (and upon the impersonal aspects of urban recreational activities), thus emphasizing traditional family ties in preference to amalgamation into the impersonal community and its activities. This difference between core-city and suburban dwellers may have important effects upon the pattern of politics in the community and upon political participation. It should be noted, however, that persons with family ties are probably more likely to develop an interest in the community than are isolated persons.

Trade Unions in Politics   In contrast to the frantic, reformist periods of the 1930s, trade unionism became an accepted part of the American way of life after World War II. By no means are all members of unions enthusiastic over the necessity of membership, and collective security by way of the union runs counter to American values of individualism; but only the wistful consider it even remotely possible that unions will not remain a dominant social and political force in America. The day when working-class people had no voice, or only the voice of the political machine, in state or local politics is gone.

In the mid-1960s, union members and their immediate families made up one-third of all the eligible voters in the United States. In urban industrial

[37] See Arthur Kornhauser, Harold L. Sheppard, and A. J. Mayer, **When Labor Votes,** University Books, Inc., New Hyde Park, N.Y., 1956, pp. 26–28.
[38] Survey Research Center, University of Michigan, 1955 report of the Detroit Area Study. See also Joel Smith and others, "Local Intimacy in a Middle-sized City," **American Journal of Sociology,** 60:276–284, November, 1954.

centers, over one-half the potential voters were in this category. In state and local elections, in the consideration of legislation pending before city councils, county boards, and state legislatures, the working class, represented by the highly professional bureaucracy of the trade union, will continue to make its position known and its votes felt.

Conformity

The Lonely Escape Erich Fromm has suggested that the contemporary urbanite seeks to avoid the isolation of modern life in "automation conformity." [39] Man fears freedom and individuality. In an interdependent world, he is afraid to go it alone. He does not desire to emphasize creativity or opportunity for individual action. The person who deviates from the norm, even very slightly, is subject to immediate criticism from a mediocre, unimaginative, fearful society. It is *safer*—it is more conducive to security—if he conforms. No one will attack him; no one will have a reason to exclude him from the children's play group, the country club, the Kiwanians, or a deaconship in the church if he loses his individuality in entire, uncritical conformity. He becomes *accepted,* and it is a deep-seated need for social acceptance that he feels.

David Riesman, building on the concepts presented by Fromm, has shown that until late decades Americans sought security in conformity to parental, and particularly paternal, authority.[40] The middle-class urban American of today, however, seeks social approval, not from his family and close personal friends, but from his associates and for the most part from associates in secondary relationships. And this process begins before he, as a child, enters school and does not end until his funeral.

The individual seems doomed to frustration in Riesman's analysis, however, for he desires to come closer to other people by conforming to whatever they tell him to do; yet because almost all of his contacts with others are superficial rather than warm and personal, "he remains a lonely member of the crowd."

Conformity in a Bureaucratic Society In the postwar years, orthodoxy and conformity became a matter of concern to social psychologists and others. It should be remembered that conformity to prevailing value patterns is a universal device for maintaining social control. Most persons are content to follow the leadership of those in whom they have established confidence. Yet, some critics feel there is a possibility that a society may place such great emphasis upon conformity as against creativity and originality as to create stagnation. The reasoning goes somewhat as follows: American society is becoming increasingly a collection of large, complicated, self-perpetuating bureaucracies.*

* **BUREAUCRACY.** Any large organization characterized by specialization of the work assignment of personnel, essentially impersonal relationships both among persons in

[39] Erich Fromm, **Escape From Freedom,** Holt, Rinehart and Winston, Inc., New York, 1941; see also Margaret Mary Wood, **Paths of Loneliness: The Individual Isolated in Modern Society,** Columbia University Press, New York, 1953.
[40] See two works by David Riesman, **The Lonely Crowd,** 1950, and **Faces in the Crowd,** 1952, both published by Yale University Press, New Haven, Conn.

the agency and with those in external clientele groups, and a formal hierarchical structure.

These large organizations—it does not matter whether they are public or private—are made up of people with a definite set of attitudes, all of them leading to a general atmosphere of conformity: "If the bureaucracy is to operate successfully, it must attain a high degree of reliability of behavior, an unusual degree of conformity with prescribed patterns of action. Hence, the fundamental importance of discipline, which may be as highly developed in a religious or economic bureaucracy as in the army." [41]

If these assumptions about bureaucrats are correct—and evidence that they are universally valid is lacking—it follows that there is a danger that one's abilities and training become blind spots, that the individual becomes so accustomed to reacting in a well-inculcated manner under a given set of stimuli that he becomes inflexible under conditions requiring flexibility. The individual is thus unable to adjust to changes in the environment, and this situation, if applied to a large portion of the population, could under certain conditions result in disaster. The process is thus along these lines: (1) Devotion to rules is required in order to achieve efficiency in a large, impersonal bureaucracy; (2) this devotion ultimately causes rules originally created for practical reasons to become absolutes not to be questioned by anyone and not to be tempered by the application of "commonsense" modifications; (3) the uncritical acceptance of absolutes leads to inflexibility of bureaucratic policy and bureaucratic personality; and (4) finally, then, the elements originally established to create efficiency lead to inefficiency through inadaptability to changing social and economic environments.

Such, at least, is the theory. That it is to some degree true is scarcely to be questioned. But whether or not human beings can really become complete automatons in spite of themselves and whether or not the theory applies more to America with its organization man than it does to such highly bureaucratic nations as France, England, Germany, or Denmark has not been demonstrated empirically. Some outstanding students of bureaucracy, including the German social scientist Max Weber, thought this general behavior pattern to be a universal characteristic, but the reader might, in the scientific spirit, reserve judgment.[42]

Town and Country

Rural Life in America   Urban life now dominates America, but rural life has been important in shaping traditions. This is especially true of politics, where rural America affects policy in considerable disproportion to its population strength.

---

[41] Robert K. Merton, "Bureaucratic Structure and Personality," **Social Forces**, 18:560–568, May, 1940. Merton was drawing upon the earlier ideas of Max Weber, Thorstein Veblen, and John Dewey. On the effect of widespread norm evasion in American culture, see Robin M. Williams, **American Society**, Alfred A. Knopf, Inc., New York, 1951, chap. 10.
[42] For more on bureaucracy, especially in government, see below, chap. 12.

In mid-twentieth-century America, ever fewer farmers are producing ever more in food and fiber. Rural and urban life are becoming steadily less distinguishable both as to working conditions and mode of life, including values. A declining need for manpower on the farm has produced a seemingly chronic economic and social problem as the harsh facts of economics put pressure on farm families to move to the city, when that is not their wish.

In 1966, only 7 percent of our population lived on farms. During the preceding decade, the farm population declined by about 5 percent a year. During this same period, the number of farms decreased by 1 million. Increasing mechanization and the amount of capital investment in machinery required larger acreage per farm for efficient operation and a profitable return on investment. While in 1915 the typical Iowa farm of 160 acres required the labor of the farmer, a hired man, and help from the children, two generations later a single farmer could handle considerably more acreage and still work fewer hours than did his grandfather.

This smaller farm population was feeding an enormously increased national population and was still faced with surpluses. It was not just a larger population, however, that was being fed; it was the best-fed nation in the world eating the best-balanced diet.

Further changes may be expected. In 1960, when only about 10 percent of all Americans were members of families securing their support fully from farming, Department of Agriculture statisticians estimated that 40 percent of all farm youths would have to find city employment after they left school. Department specialists also thought that one-third of existing farms were too small to be economically efficient. There was every indication that in the future the size of farms would increase and farm population would continue to decrease.

It can be expected that the continuing social and economic revolution in rural America will require government action of many kinds. Although the part that state and local government could play had not become clear by the mid-1960s, the problems relating to the relocation of ruralites will no doubt become increasingly matters for these levels of government and will be especially felt in connection with such items as employment counseling, social welfare, public health, vocational and adult education, and technical consulting services to farmers.

Although rural dwellers continue to become increasingly like urban dwellers, largely as the result of the automobile, television, and the consolidated school, significant differences in the cultural backgrounds of rural and urban dwellers still exist. Only 30 percent of the population is now classified as rural and small town, but 43 percent of all Protestants live in these areas. Nearly four out of five Roman Catholics live in urban areas, as do 96 percent of the members of the Jewish faith. Rural family size is still larger than that in cities and rural areas continue to be major population suppliers to urban areas. The core cities of metropolitan areas have a larger percentage of pre-school children and retirement-age people than is the case in rural areas. Education is both more needed and more common in urban areas. In 1960, the average urbanite (white) had had 11.5 years of schooling while the average person in a small town or on a farm had somewhat less than nine. Urbanites of all age groups beyond eighteen are more likely to be in school than are rural dwellers, but this may partly reflect the fact that rural dwellers who seek higher education may move off the farm and into cities. In other words, some of the urbanites are ex-small-town or farm dwellers. A large proportion of the nation's poor are concentrated in rural rather than urban areas. In 1960, only about 4 percent of urban families received incomes under $1,000, but more than 15 percent of farm families were in this category, most of them located in the Deep South on sharecropper farms and in the valleys of Appalachia.

The Anomaly of the Small Town   Village and small-town life has been a traditional part of America, honored in memory and song and satirized in novel and poem. The town has its origins as a service center for a small rural area. Throughout much of the nation, towns were originally spaced close enough together to allow any farmer to reach one by horseback or buggy within a reasonable length of time, perhaps an hour. County seats were generally situated so that they were not more than a day's buggy ride from the farthest farmer. They were larger than ordinary trading places, since they contained the incipient bureaucracy of government, the offices of lawyers who dealt with that bureaucracy on behalf of clients, livery stables, hotels, and other establishments catering to the citizenry that found it necessary or desirable to visit the seat of government.

The ordinary town contained a general store, repair shops, a physician, a veterinarian, a weekly newspaper, a bank, a school, and a few churches. If the community was large enough, it also served as a market. With the coming of the automobile and telephone, this pattern began to change. After World War II, the general store came more to resemble the corner grocery of the city or, in larger towns, became a supermarket (which is, in fact, a reconstitution of the old general store except that modern merchandising techniques have been added and the traditional function as a news and gossip center has declined). The physician found he could serve more people and make more money by moving into the nearby city. The weekly newspaper, in the face of high labor and newsprint costs, was beginning to disappear. The bank had become a branch of a city institution or had disappeared. The school now represented the consolidation of a great many formerly rural districts with an elaborate system of school bus routes. The churches continued to perform some, though not all, of their traditional functions. The population was made up of locally employed persons, a considerable number of retired farmers, and a new element—the commuters. Many persons, either because of a preference for the small-town life or because of shortages in low-cost housing in the cities, have taken up residence in the town but may drive twenty-five and more miles each day to their jobs in the city.

Small-town Politics   Politically, the villages and towns tend to be, throughout the nation, centers of conservatism. Most of them are one-party communities, either Democratic or Republican depending upon local traditions. Although their governments provide basic community services in the areas of water, sewage disposal and sewerage, police and fire protection, the small community remains a center of opposition to the social service state. Town dwellers are likely to view with skepticism—closely reflected by their representatives on the county board and in the state legislature—labor and social welfare legislation, fair employment practices commissions, laws on minimum wages or on conditions of labor, public housing, programs for the aged, and the like. Lacking experience in the social problems of large cities or in living together with cultural groups having different values from their own, they tend to be intolerant of proposed legislation dealing with problems that do not exist or exist in minor ways in their communities. To them, the fact that such problems exist in large cities is taken to be evidence of the degeneracy or moral inferiority of urban life.

Yet the town is itself a political, economic, and social problem. Its difficulties stem from several things: the declining farm population, which produces a declining market; the preference of many farmers for the more specialized and hence more expert services in the nearby city, now easily available by modern auto and good roads; the lack of opportunity in the town while our culture emphasizes the desirability of opportunity, with the resultant draining off of the most able young people; extreme conservatism in a day when many attitudes which this produces do not fit into the value systems learned in the consolidated schools and on television by young people; and, finally, current highway department practices of bypassing practically all towns, thus cutting off the transient business that had earlier helped to sustain them. The changes taking place in town life will have continuing effects upon state and local government throughout the nation.

A Study in Stagnation [43] Carsonville, a rural, Midwestern village of 487 persons, might be examined as an example of the generalizations made above. The village began its existence in 1853, continued its settlement period until about 1880, then enjoyed a period of expansion as the surrounding rural community came to depend upon it. The expansion phase ended around the beginning of the twentieth century, however, and the plateau that had been reached lasted until the coming of the automobile age after World War I. Since that time, Carsonville has been undergoing a very slow decline in population and in economic importance.

The young people have for years tended to leave the village after being graduated, or withdrawing, from high school. Thirty percent of the population is sixty years of age or older (as against a national average of about thirteen percent). There are many widows and retired couples who had come off nearby farms and from cities some distance away. Kinship considerations remain important as a basis for social intercourse.

Few economic opportunities exist in Carsonville and many people who

[43] This section is based upon Laurene A. Wallace, **Carsonville: An American Village Viewed Sociologically**, University Microfilms, Inc., Ann Arbor, Mich., 1957.

live there work in a nearby trading center. The village leaders would like to attract small industry to the village, but have found this to be extremely difficult. Social mobility is low in the community, with status positions of each individual relatively fixed and known to other residents. There are few recreational facilities, and the automobile is depended upon to transport people to surrounding towns and cities for this purpose.

In keeping with Midwestern patterns, most voters are staunchly Republican of a very conservative type. They are apathetic about politics and distrustful of all governmental leaders of both party labels beyond the village. Local politics is of a personal sort, and policy is determined for the most part by consensus.

Carsonville, then, has seen its best days. But it continues to serve a useful social function as a trading and educational center for the hinterland and as a place for retirement for both farmers and some city people. A sociologist has described its future as "uncertain."

Culture and Classes

Mass Culture　Pundits often write about American mass culture. By this rather vague term—with "culture" used in its popular sense—is meant that American entertainment, along with American material things, has been standardized so that Americans watch the same television shows coast to coast, watch the same movies, read Book-of-the-Month Club literature, sing the same popular tunes, follow the same comic strips, talk about seeing the same Broadway shows (at least members of the middle class do), get interested in the same fads, dress alike, and eat the same foods—though it is easy to exaggerate these generalizations.

Americans purchase more than 1 million paperback books each day. The United States has more than 1,150 symphony orchestras—more than one-half of all symphony orchestras in the world. Americans spend more money each year for tickets to serious music concerts than they do for tickets to baseball games, despite the contrary popular impression in both this country and Europe. More than 5,000 community theaters exist in the United States, and nearly 800 groups produce operas. (Unlike Europe, nearly all our fine arts groups consist of amateurs or semiprofessionals, but this is probably more an economic than a cultural factor.) [44]

Mass culture has been aided, without doubt, by the existence of mass communication through the telephone, radio, television, and motion pictures, by mass transportation and mass education. Mass communication has developed "hucksterism," or high-pressure advertising, into a mammoth industry so that its symbol, Madison Avenue, has become a household word. [45]

In every nation, mass culture is to be found, of course, since it is a generic term applying to "lowbrow" and "middlebrow" tastes as distinguished

[44] See Richard Schickel, "That Cultural Explosion," **The Progressive**, October, 1961, pp. 45–48.
[45] For a set of commentaries, see Bernard Rosenberg and David M. White (eds.), **Mass Culture**, The Free Press of Glencoe, New York, 1957.

from the *avant-garde* concerns of the "highbrow." [46] It is popular among intellectuals to criticize mass culture as if it were a demoralizing, degenerative influence upon society. Actually, the American of today has artistic tastes infinitely above those of the medieval common man or the common man in such nations as India or China, where mass communication has as yet had a very limited impact.

Members of the general public have tastes and interests higher than they are generally given credit for. We can expect that they will never become highbrow. They do not want radio and television to be an uplift medium but rather an entertainment medium. We can expect them to continue to improve their level of taste (using highbrow standards) and that sufficient opportunities will be afforded them to do so through the various mass media.

So far as politics is concerned, mass media of communication have had a vital effect upon the means of reaching the public, although the basic style of American politics has remained fairly constant since the 1830s.[47] Without radio and television, American politics tended to center upon emotional symbols and personalities. With these mass media, it has remained about the same. A rising level of education throughout American history has likewise not been accompanied by increasing rationality in politics or a trend toward an emphasis upon issues. Rather, the politician finds that the public prefers to have political controversies translated into terms of the prevailing political ideology.[48] This the politician does today as he did a century ago, though he must now cope with a more sophisticated audience and can less easily resort to the purchase of votes or the intimidation techniques of the old-fashioned machine.

Social Classes in America   Although it has always been popular among tellers of the great American myth to say that this nation is lacking in classes,* that all are equal, and that anyone can do anything that his ability and determination dictate, less romantic sociologists point out that while we have a good deal of mobility between classes, the classes do, indeed, exist. Some sociologists would go further and say that, because of the inferior social position of the Negro, America has both a class and a caste † system, although the rapid postwar changes in the status of Negroes have encouraged a trend away from a caste concept.

* CLASS (SOCIAL). In some social models, a self-conscious group whose members occupy similar social positions, and who share a similar life style, set of values, and behavior pattern. In practical terms, members of a class have little internal communication and the class is commonly identified by certain quantitative indicators— in particular, wealth, income, education, and occupation.

† CASTE SYSTEM. A stratified society in which social position is determined entirely by parentage, with no provision for achieved status.

[46] See Russell Lynes, "Highbrow, Lowbrow, Middlebrow," **Harper's Magazine**, February, 1949, pp. 19–28.
[47] See chap. 2.
[48] See chap. 2.

America has no national class structure for several reasons, the three most important being (1) because the nation has always had a great deal of vertical mobility, with much movement up and down the status ladder; (2) because the nation has until after World War I had a population made up largely of recent arrivals with widely varying national backgrounds; and (3) because of the egalitarian influence of the frontier which discouraged class-differentiated behavior for many decades.[49] Under these circumstances, "the emergence of fairly uniform classes over an extended geographic area, such as are clearly discernible in England," never took place.[50]

Class systems, within a particular locality, are based upon relative wealth, occupations, education, manners, mode of life, and such things as membership in an "old family" or a recent immigrant family. But migration and mobility and the distribution of material things throughout all except the lowest income tiers have tended to have a leveling effect upon American manners and way of life.[51]

Social Role and Social Status   The continuing trend in America—and this among many other things distinguishes the American from the European life style—is away from status determined by class position, even within the local community, to status determined by occupation. In other words, one's social function has become more important than one's class position.

The structure of the American economy itself discourages the development of a clear-cut class system, and many social critics regard this as desirable. American business management, as compared with that of Belgium, France, or Italy, allows far more room for advancement in ranks and access to managerial status.[52] Decision making in business is more decentralized in America, and businessmen are much more conscious of expanding industry as against merely retaining control over it. Management of business in Europe tends to be concerned with security, which encourages working classes to look in the same direction, thus making business enterprise static. The European system does not, by its nature, work toward raising the standard of living and improving the health of the economy, as the American system does.[53] It does, however, tend to perpetuate existing class patterns.

Social Striving and Political Conflict   Sociologists find that social mobility remains high in America but that the prestige of white-collar work is diminishing. This will perhaps have a tendency to accentuate the traditional political struggle between the lower middle classes and the working classes. The former have long been the most insecure group in society, clinging desperately to identification with higher status groups and seeking to differentiate themselves

[49] See Arnold W. Green, **Sociology,** 4th ed., McGraw-Hill Book Company, New York, 1964, pp. 185–186.
[50] *Ibid.,* p. 186.
[51] *Ibid.,* chap. 12.
[52] See C. H. Coates and R. J. Pellegrin, "Executives and Supervisors," **Social Forces,** 35:121–126, December, 1956.
[53] See F. H. Harbison and E. W. Burgess, "Modern Management in Western Europe," **American Journal of Sociology,** 60:15–23, July, 1954.

from workers. Yet, in their struggle they have been faced with a continuing improvement in the lot of the working man. This situation has made the lower-middle-class member a particularly sympathetic reactor to the nostrums of the demagogue. Current trends seem to indicate increasing friction along the rough edge between the middle classes and the working classes.

Politics and Classes Politically, a class or caste system is an important determinant of the strategy and tactics of campaigning. Politicians appeal to Negroes, the foreign-born, Jews, Puerto Ricans, homeowners, renters, and other socially or economically identifiable groups. These appeals may be basically harmless or they may arouse virulent intergroup prejudices.[54] Because of the prestige factor, which in turn has economic repercussions that affect, for example, property values, many political battles are fought over the issue of invasion.* Such controversies most commonly involve Negroes moving into white neighborhoods, but the opposite may be the case; and invasion may also center around other racially or ethnically identifiable groups, or it may involve the moving of business or industry into previously residential neighborhoods, proposing multifamily dwellings in areas exclusively of single-family homes, or the developing by subdividers of a previously rural area for urban land uses.

* **INVASION is a term for what happens when a new type of people, institution, or activity enters an area previously occupied by a different type.**

The problem of social prestige may appear in many different ways. In Park Forest, Illinois, for example, it arose in connection with the building of a swimming pool (in keeping with the expectations of suburban Americana, it was called an "Aquacenter," of course). A municipal pool was first discussed, but this might have required the admission of people from adjoining Chicago Heights, a community of less prestige and one, furthermore, that contains a large number of Negroes. The alternative, finally accepted, was a private pool. But this produced fears of a first step toward social stratification of the all-new suburb. Even though pool fees were set very low, many appeared to fear that their very existence was a move toward the creation of an unwanted country-club set.[55] In both Park Forest and Levittown, classlessness does not extend to the admission of Negroes, and in Levittown, Pennsylvania, there were open demonstrations during 1957 against a Negro family's moving in.

Closing Note Some of the characteristics of American life and the values that guide our decisions concerning governmental policies have been presented in this chapter. Others will be discussed in the following two chapters. The issues of policy raised in connection with various functions of government will be developed in more detail in the appropriate chapters throughout the book.

[54] For examples of the latter, see Carl O. Smith and Stephen B. Sarasohn, "Hate Propaganda in Detroit," **Public Opinion Quarterly,** 10:24–52, Spring, 1946; Forest Frank, "Cincinnati Loses P. R.," **National Municipal Review,** 46:534–535, November, 1957.
[55] Whyte, *op. cit.,* pp. 343–344.

SELECTED READINGS

Banfield, Edward C., and Morton Grodzins: **Government and Housing,** McGraw-Hill Book Company, New York, 1958.   (On the rising political importance of the Negro in urban areas.)

Bell, Daniel: "Crime as an American Way of Life," **Antioch Review,** 42:131–154, June, 1953.

Cantril, Hadley: **The Psychology of Social Movements,** John Wiley & Sons, Inc., New York, 1963, paperback. First published 1941.

Douglass, H. Paul: **The Little Town,** The Macmillan Company, New York, 1927.

Drake, St. Clair, and H. R. Cayton: **Black Metropolis,** Harcourt, Brace & World, Inc., New York, 1945.   (Chicago's Negro community.)

Dullard, John: **Caste and Class in a Southern Town,** 3d ed., Doubleday & Company, Inc., Garden City, N.Y., 1957.   (Study of social status.)

Dunham, H. Warren (ed.): **The City at Mid-century,** Wayne State University Press, Detroit, Mich., 1958.

Fitzgerald, F. Scott: **The Great Gatsby,** Charles Scribner's Sons, New York, 1925. (Account of complacency, conformity, and superficiality.)

Fromm, Erich: **Escape From Freedom,** Holt, Rinehart and Winston, Inc., New York, 1941.

Glazer, Nathan, and Daniel Patrick Moynihan: **Beyond the Melting Pot: the Negroes, Puerto Ricans, Jews, Italians, and Irish of New York City,** The M.I.T. Press and Harvard University Press, Cambridge, Mass., 1963.   (A refutation of the "melting pot" theory. The larger ethnic groups in New York, and in other large cities, do not become assimilated into a distinctive American culture, but often remain clustered in self-segregated neighborhoods.)

Kornhauser, Arthur, and others: **When Labor Votes,** University Books, Inc., New Hyde Park, N.Y., 1956.   (A study of members' political attitudes in the United Automobile Workers.)

Lampard, Eric E.: "The History of Cities in the Economically Advanced Areas," **Economic Development and Cultural Change,** 3:81–136, January, 1955.

Lerner, Max: **America as a Civilization,** Simon and Schuster, Inc., New York, 1957.

Lewis, Sinclair: **Main Street,** Harcourt, Brace & World, Inc., New York, 1920. (A satirical novel which attacks the romantic image of the small town.)

Linton, Ralph: **The Study of Man,** Appleton-Century-Crofts, Inc., New York, 1936.

Lipset, Seymour Martin: **The First New Nation,** Basic Books, Inc., Publishers, New York, 1963.   (Analyzes the American character as seen by Americans and foreigners who interpret our partially inconsistent values of equality and achievement.)

Lynd, Robert S., and Helen M. Lynd: **Middletown in Transition,** Harcourt, Brace & World, Inc., New York, 1937.   (Study of Muncie, Indiana. Atypical of present patterns. Conspiracy theory of economic elite.)

Merton, Robert K.: "Bureaucratic Structure and Personality," **Social Forces,** 18: 560–568, May, 1940. (Summarization of ideas of Weber, Veblen, and Dewey.)

Mumford, Lewis: **The City in History,** Harcourt, Brace & World, Inc., New York, 1961.   (A learned, opinionated study.)

————: **The Culture of Cities,** Harcourt, Brace & World, Inc., New York, 1938.

Munro, William B.: **Municipal Government and Administration,** The Macmillan Company, New York, 1923, and later revisions.   (Account of ancient and medieval cities.)

Park, R. E., and E. W. Burgess: **The City,** The University of Chicago Press, Chicago, 1925.

Pirenne, Henri: **Medieval Cities,** Princeton University Press, Princeton, N.J., 1925.

Riesman, David, and others: **Faces in the Crowd,** Yale University Press, New Haven, Conn., 1952.   (A sequel to **The Lonely Crowd.**)

——— and ———: **The Lonely Crowd,** Yale University Press, New Haven, Conn., 1950.   (An interpretation of metropolitan man.)

Roethlisberger, F. S., and W. J. Dickson: **Management and the Worker,** Harvard University Press, Cambridge, Mass., 1939.   (Individual desire for belonging.)

Rosenberg, Bernard, and David M. White (eds.): **Mass Culture,** The Free Press of Glencoe, New York, 1957.   (Influence of mass communication and mass media advertising.)

Rostow, W. W.: **The Stages of Economic Growth,** Cambridge University Press, New York, 1960.   (A theory of industrial development.)

Schlesinger, Arthur M., Jr.: **The Age of Jackson,** Little, Brown and Company, Boston, 1945.

Schroth, Thomas N., and others: **Congress and the Nation, 1945–1964,** Congressional Quarterly Service, Washington, 1965, chap. 12.

Shannon, Lyle W., and Elaine Krass: "The Urban Adjustment of Immigrants," **Pacific Sociological Review,** 6:37–42, Spring, 1963.   (Education and length of urban residence are important, but are not the only factors. Minority group members have rougher time advancing.)

Smith, Carl O., and Stephen B. Sarasohn: "Hate Propaganda in Detroit," **Public Opinion Quarterly,** 10:24–52, Spring, 1946.

Vidich, Arthur J., and J. Bensman: **Small Town in Mass Society,** Princeton University Press, Princeton, N.J., 1958.

Warner, W. Lloyd, and Paul S. Lunt: **The Social Life of a Modern Community,** Yale University Press, New Haven, Conn., 1942.

Weber, A. F.: **The Growth of Cities in the Nineteenth Century,** Columbia University Press, New York, 1899.   (Still the best study available.)

White, Morton, and Lucia White: **The Intellectual versus the City,** Joint Center For Urban Studies, Harvard University Press and The M.I.T. Press, Cambridge, Mass., 1962.   (Two philosophers review intellectual critics of cities from Benjamin Franklin to John Dewey.)

Whyte, William H., Jr.: **The Organization Man,** Doubleday Anchor Books, Garden City, N.Y., 1956.   (A study of the middle-class bureaucrat in private corporations.)

Williams, Robin M.: **American Society,** Alfred A. Knopf, Inc., New York, 1951. (Widespread norm evasion in America, chap. 10.)

Wirth, Louis: "Urbanism as a Way of Life," **American Journal of Sociology,** 44: 1–24, July, 1938.   (Classic article on social characteristics of the city; the theory is now somewhat modified by subsequent research.)

Zorbaugh, Harvey: **The Gold Coast and the Slum,** The University of Chicago Press, Chicago, 1929.   (Status and class differences near the lakeshore on Chicago's North Side.)

2

IDEOLOGY FOR THE GRASS ROOTS

Ideas affect politics. So do emotions. The effective politician knows how to mix the two in the proper proportion. He seeks to find the ideas that will make the most effective appeal in a given situation. He knows, too, that the typical citizen often responds more readily to an emotional appeal than he does to a closely reasoned argument. Since this is the case, the politician becomes interested in ideas as weapons. They become devices through which people can be manipulated. Ideas are stated in terms that reflect existing value patterns of society. They are repeated with variations and elaborations; they are tied together with clichés that are already well established in their ability to produce a desired response, and through skillful reiteration, ideas are boiled down until they become slogans or proverbs that produce a conditioned response in the individual who is exposed to them. But politicians, in seeking to influence people, are limited and restrained by the existing value structure and they cannot move effectively except within that structure.

An understanding of ideas, attitudes, ideals as goals, and cultural values is important not just to the politician seeking to sway the minds of citizens, however. To know something about these concepts is vital to anyone who wishes to understand the political process. The materials in this chapter and the next, then, are some of the most important analytical tools that are necessary for the citizen to make a meaningful analysis of the political events which take place about him and which affect him as a participant as well as an observer of politics.

The Nature of Political Ideology

Philosophers attempt to explain social phenomena, including of course political phenomena, in terms of ultimate causes, and they seek to develop logical relationships among the various phenomena which they observe. In their pursuit of an understanding of the meaning of life, philosophers frequently write about the function of government and of its politics, but the effect that these writings may have upon the general public or upon the structure and functioning of government has not been clearly determined. Certainly some philosophers affect the actions of future generations, as Jefferson did in setting the scene for a frontier democracy and as John Dewey did through his influence upon the public schools, but others probably simply reflect the values of their own day or of a past or future day, expressing them in more formal and systematic terms than would the politician or journalist. Whatever may be the ultimate effect upon government of the writings of the men whose views were so painstakingly set out by Sabine and Parrington,[1] we know that the typical citizen does not read such works and that his views on politics stem from far more visceral impressions than those created by the systematic and rational (though not always unemotional) writings of the philosophers, even though the "temptation to assign a controlling influence to the place of ideas in the operation of democracy is very great." [2] For the ordinary man in any society, far more important than systematic philosophy is the network of verbalized values that social scientists call ideology.

Symbolism is found below philosophy and ideology. A symbol is any term or concept that is intentionally used to stand for or represent something else. Symbols have meaning both because they appeal to the emotions and because they are the outward, shorthand expressions of the loosely clustered ideological values that hold society together and enable the political system to function. Symbols are important in the development of public policy, for whenever they are not effectively used in the justification of policy, widespread dissatisfaction results.[3]

Ideologies: The Web of Government Politics has its "rituals, sacred objects, saints, dogmas, devotions, feasts, fanaticisms, mummeries, and its Bible of sacred writings." [4] That is, it has an elaborate system of symbols, not as pervasive or enduring as those of religion, perhaps, but certainly an analogy can easily be drawn. Symbols have meaning because they are outward, shorthand expressions of the loosely clustered value systems that hold society together and enable its political system to function. These symbols can be manipulated so as to influence people, even people who scarcely understand the myths upon which they are based.

Ideologies or myths are "the value-impregnated beliefs and notions that men hold, that they live by or live for. Every society is held together by a

[1] George H. Sabine, **History of Political Theory,** rev. ed., Holt, Rinehart and Winston, Inc., New York, 1950; Vernon L. Parrington, **Main Currents in American Thought,** 3 vols. in one, Harcourt, Brace & World, Inc., New York, 1930.
[2] Herbert McClosky, "Consensus and Ideology in American Politics," **American Political Science Review,** 58:361–382, June, 1964.
[3] Murray Edelman, **The Symbolic Uses of Politics,** The University of Illinois Press, Urbana, Ill., 1964, p. 167.
[4] Ross Lockridge, Jr., **Raintree County,** Houghton Mifflin Company, Boston, 1948, p. 776. Available in paperback.

myth-system, a complex of dominating thought-forms that determines and sustains all its activities. All social relations, the very texture of human society, are myth-born and myth-sustained." [5]

Ideologies may exist independently of their truth or falsity, of their relationship to the eternal verities. They are too general, too broad, too unscientific to be proved or disproved as to their intrinsic worth. They are accepted on *faith,* and when faith in their rightness gradually fades away, the myth passes into the shadow, except for its vestiges which are no longer recognizable in their original form. Changing economic and social conditions may create new ideologies which are antagonistic to, and which directly challenge, the old ideologies. On the other hand, the old ideologies are frequently renovated in order to meet a changing environment and may be applied to situations far removed from those that originally created the ideology. [6]

Various ideologies, new and old, prevail at any one time in a nation, of course, and not all people even in given regions of the land accept the same ideology at the same time. [7] The important thing is that there normally exists an ideology that is accepted by a dominant group of citizens, and as a result politicians are able to condition their appeals to fit the beliefs that their constituents treasure. A further point about ideologies: Their relationship to the environment is something like that of the chicken to the egg. Existing ideologies condition emerging political, social, and economic circumstances, while these circumstances in turn tend to modify the existing ideologies. Ideologies and the environment in which they exist are hence interdependent, each affecting the other. [8]

Political Organization and Ideology   With the exception of America's early days under the Constitution, when our political system had not yet jelled and the upper-class Federalists controlled the national government, the nation's history has been dominated by three major domestic ideologies, one *gradually* shading into the next and the older ones living on in vestigial form. The political parties at any time in history are necessarily concerned with making appeals to the existing ideologies, and as a new value system begins to appear out of the old, or as a replacement for it, one political party or another may be expected to try to gain votes by espousing the new ideology. Since this is likely to be the party in power at the time, the ideology becomes accepted, *the general public tends to associate the dominant ideology with a particular political party,* as it will be seen below. Except in single-party areas of the nation, one party claims to own the ideology, and as long as the ideology is dominant, that party will be dominant and can expect to win most of the elections. The history of parties in most states is not of two closely balanced organizations frequently

[5] Robert M. MacIver, **The Web of Government,** The Macmillan Company, New York, 1947, p. 4.
[6] *Ibid.,* p. 6.
[7] Only *domestic* myths are discussed here. Foreign relations are controlled by similar value clusters. The best known of these involve the set of concepts that surround the ideologies of isolationism and of internationalism.
[8] For additional material on the ideology, see two works by Ernst Cassirer, **The Myth of the State,** Dover Publications, Inc., New York, 1946, and **Language and Myth,** Doubleday & Company, Inc., Garden City, N.Y., 1946.

exchanging control of public office, but of long control by a single party, often for decades on end, with rare shifts whereby a Republican-dominated state, for example, becomes a Democratic-dominated state.[9] A political ideology, once established, is highly persistent and seems to change only after it has become very seriously out of step with the existing social and economic environment.

The "out party," which in American politics plays the special role of serving as the vehicle of *protest,* is constantly faced with a dilemma of pursuing a policy of "me too" (that is, "We support the prevailing beliefs but think we can do a better job, especially since the other party has been in too long") or a policy of "not me." In the latter, the line is taken that an older ideology is better and is still "really" accepted by the people. Since history would seem to indicate that, once a substantial section of the public has lost faith in an ideology, it does not return to it again, it is possible to answer the question as to whether a me-too or a not-me policy can most profitably be followed by the out party: ordinarily the only hope is to take, no matter how unpalatable it might be, a me-too position. Since this is the case, the two parties are under strong pressure to take approximately the same general positions when they take positions on issues at all.

Individualism and Public Policy   Without going into details, the basic continuing importance of the credo of individual responsibility, free enterprise, thrift, and hard work upon public policy in America can be seen in connection with a great number of values which Americans hold, once held, or are told they should hold: the continuing emphasis upon the importance of a balanced budget for the sake of a balanced budget; the view that individual effort toward the solution of one's own problems is ultimately more satisfactory than group effort through the use of governmental facilities; the continuing resistance— not alone from the high-income recipients—to the income tax as an economic equalizing device; the underlying belief that welfare recipients are shiftless and should receive a bare minimum of assistance; and the widespread skepticism concerning retirement plans, especially government social security plans.[10] These views could no longer be described as dominant, but all of them have a restrictive influence upon governmental policy and continue to have an effect upon state legislatures, governors, the judiciary, and governmental officials at all levels, because these values are still held by a large number of citizens—although these same citizens may have ambivalent feelings about them and, in fact, may simultaneously hold to conflicting values.

The Revolutionary Era

It was an agricultural nation that declared its independence from the mother country in 1776. Only about 3 percent of the people lived in nonrural communities, and there were not more than twenty-four incorporated municipalities

[9] See V. O. Key, Jr., **American State Politics,** Alfred A. Knopf, Inc., New York, 1956, chap. 4. The points made here will be further developed later in this chapter and in the chapters on politics.
[10] Charles Press and Charles R. Adrian, "Why Our State Governments Are Sick," **Antioch Review,** 53:100–120, June, 1964.

in all thirteen of the new states. There was an important aristocracy: in the South, the slave-owning planters concentrated along the coast and in the river valleys; in the rest of the nation, the bankers, exporters-importers, shipowners, and manufacturers. Yet, at least outside the Deep South, most Americans were neither rich nor poor but rather were lower-middle-class yeomen farmers.* There were property requirements to vote, but these appear to have been quite easily met in rural areas—it is estimated that nearly 90 percent of the adult white males of Massachusetts could vote at the time of the Revolution.[11]

* YEOMAN FARMER. A farmer who owns, is buying, or hopes to buy his own land, which he works himself with or without hired help. His ideology differs sharply from that of the European peasant, who lacked both social and physical mobility and could never hope to own land.

The Nature of Government during the Green Years   The state legislatures, which had championed the colonists against the royal governors representing the British government, became the dominant agencies in government. The governors, on the other hand, had to bear the burden of the unfavorable image of the executive created when their prerevolutionary counterparts sided against the resident population. The legislature usually chose the state officials, including the governor, who was limited to a one-year term, had no veto except in Massachusetts, and could not succeed himself. It also selected the judiciary.[12]

In these early days of the Republic, the values of thrift and hard work were already firmly established. But neither these values nor the importance of property had as yet produced the doctrine of *laissez faire,* which called for the government to keep its hands off business. As a matter of fact: [13]

The colonists were accustomed to the mercantile system of intensive state regulation of economic affairs. Their argument with England had not been that the system was evil but that it was being used to colonial disadvantage.

. . . state governments followed the practices that they knew and in which they believed. They fixed prices for transportation services, licensed inn-keepers and peddlers, constructed and operated turnpikes, and began issuing special charters to businesses.

In the cities, the pattern of organization also reflected the beliefs and disillusionments of the times. The urban structure was modeled upon a system that had been familiar to the colonists in their native England. There was no separation of powers between the legislative and executive branches. The council possessed virtually all authority. It was headed by the mayor, who had no veto * power and practically no executive power. His task was to preside over meetings of the council as one of its members and to perform the ceremonial functions of the city.

[11] Robert E. Brown, **Middle-class Democracy and the Revolution in Massachusetts,** Cornell University Press, Ithaca, N.Y., 1955, chaps. 1–5 in particular.
[12] See Allan R. Richards, "The Traditions of Government in the States," **The Forty-eight States: Their Tasks as Policy Makers and Administrators,** The American Assembly, Graduate School of Business, Columbia University, New York, 1955; Herbert Kaufman, "Emerging Conflicts in the Doctrines of Public Administration," **American Political Science Review,** 50:1057–1073, December, 1956.
[13] Richards, *op. cit.,* p. 42.

* VETO. The act of disapproving a proposed ordinance or statute, done by the chief executive. Usually, he is required to veto within a given period of time and must return the proposal to the legislative house of origin, together with his objections. Normally, the legislative body may enact the ordinance or statute over the veto by repassing it with some specified extraordinary majority.

The Ideology of Frontier Individualism

The Federalist party never had a chance for long life. It was a class party in a nation that was increasingly subjected to the egalitarian influences of the frontier. While Federalists were looking to the advancement of commerce, industry, and the plantations, Thomas Jefferson, with the help of others, "had steadily gathered behind him the great mass of small farmers, mechanics [skilled tradesmen], shopkeepers, and other workers." [14] These were gradually molded into a party of the common people, the development of which was a bud that was to reach its complete flower three decades later, in the age of Andrew Jackson.

The Jeffersonian Period   Immediately after the beginning of the nineteenth century changes took place in state government. Almost all of the new states omitted property qualifications for suffrage from their constitutions. In the 1820s and 1830s, the older states dropped their property requirements for voting—requirements that might otherwise have had important connotations for the expanding urban proletariat. Because of behavior that caused a decline in public confidence, state legislators, who had been the heroes of the day during and immediately after the Revolution, fell into disfavor and constitutional restrictions began to be placed upon their powers.[15] The most common were those prohibiting the chartering of banks, except for a single state bank (the frontier yeoman farmer was already in conflict with those who controlled the credit, as he was to remain throughout American history). Legislatures were also prohibited from granting individual divorces by special acts—formerly a common practice available especially to those with political influence. Lastly, salaries of major state officials were written into the constitution, and the legislatures were prohibited from raising them.

Governors   The governorship, too, changed during the first two decades of the nineteenth century. In fact, the changes are a good example of the way in which the attitudes of a group in society will change according to whether or not its friends currently hold political power. The conservative Federalists favored a strong Chief Executive when the new United States Constitution was being framed. After this group lost power, however, it came to oppose such an institution, while its opponents, now generally triumphant and especially along the frontier, wanted to strengthen the executive.

The conservatives resorted to the "Whig theory" of the executive, so

[14] Allan Nevins and Henry Steele Commager, **The Pocket History of the United States**, rev. ed., Pocket Books, Inc., New York, 1951, p. 144.
[15] Richards, *op. cit.*, pp. 42–44.

called for the party of opposition to a strong monarch in England. This view held that the President or governor should not play a part in policy making, should have few administrative powers, and if he had a veto at all, should use it only against legislation he regarded as unconstitutional and not against that which did not agree with his personal ideology. The Jeffersonians did not offer an adequate theory to counter this one. Their view was largely empirical: the executive could rightly exercise power if he did so in the interests of his constituents. It was not until many decades later that the "stewardship theory" * (so called because Theodore Roosevelt said that the President was the "steward of the people") was advanced. It held that the Chief Executive should be both an administrative leader and a leader in the formulation of public policy, with the veto a proper means of seeking to achieve the policies he favored. This theory was defended on the ground that the Chief Executive was elected by the people of the whole city, state, or nation and hence had a mandate from them to take firm action.

* **STEWARDSHIP THEORY.** This theory holds that the executive has something akin to inherent powers of office, which permits or even requires him to do anything necessary to protect the nation—so long as his acts are not unconstitutional. The theory is also closely associated with the idea that the executive has an obligation to provide leadership in policy development. The Whig theory, in contrast, holds that the executive can do only those things clearly authorized by the Constitution or the legislature and should leave policy development to the legislature.

In the Jeffersonian period, governors began to acquire the power to veto legislation, and the beginnings of administrative power came to them through a right to require reports in writing from other state officers. (Both of these provisions had earlier been written into the Federal Constitution.) Judicial review * increased in importance in the states (Jefferson opposed it on the national level—the Federal judiciary had become the last refuge of the Federalists).

* **JUDICIAL REVIEW.** Action by a court to rule on the question of whether a statute, ordinance, or administrative order is constitutional.

Internal Improvements   The states, during this period, were intensively active in seeking to break down the obstacles that were preventing the westward movement of the frontier. They sought to connect the frontier with the established East and its ports, business firms, and institutions of credit. The Missouri constitution of 1820 stated the case: "Internal improvements shall forever be encouraged by the government of this State, and it shall be the duty of the general assembly, as soon as may be, to make provision by law for ascertaining the most proper objects of improvement. . . ." Pennsylvania invested heavily in banks and transportation companies. Massachusetts encouraged the development of business by issuing 300 franchises to manufacturing corporations in the first twenty years of the nineteenth century.[16] New York constructed a great 400-mile highway to the West in the Erie Canal, completed in 1825.

[16] *Ibid.*, p. 44.

Public Education   During the early years of a democratic America education became public. Jefferson insisted that the states must assume the responsibility for education, and, led by New England and New York, they did. Beginning with the admission of Ohio (1803), the democrats in Congress sought to prod the new states by requiring, as a condition of statehood, that the sixteenth section in each township be reserved for the common schools. In contrast to the usual pattern of establishing new democratic institutions first along the edge of civilization, however, the frontier states were somewhat slower in providing free public education than were the Eastern states. The practice, by the frontier states, of charging back part of the costs to parents was probably more an indication of their relative poverty than of lack of sympathy toward the principle.

The Frontier in Full Command: The Prototype Politician   The difference between the philosophy of Jefferson, the man of reflection, and the ideology of the Jacksonian frontiersman, the man of action, has been described as one in which the former sought the ideal of equality in order to develop *individuality*, while the latter sought the same ideal as a means toward providing opportunity for ambition and a chance to climb the ladder of wealth and power.[17] Jefferson was an intellectual who had an academic interest in mankind. He loved humanity, but he had less direct contact with individual common folk than did the Jacksonian politician of three decades or so later. The true frontier campaigner concentrated upon exploiting the commonly shared values of his constituents; he did not seek to make philosophers out of them or to teach them the alleged beauties of individuality. In this sense, he became the prototype of nearly all subsequent American politicians.

The Frontier in Full Command: The Ideology   The values of the frontiersman came out of his everyday experiences in the struggle for survival, for success, for wealth. His outlook on life was pragmatic rather than introspective, functional rather than universal; and it was applied to state, county, township, village, and city governments alike. An excellent statement of his beliefs may be found in the novel **Raintree County** by Ross Lockridge, Jr.: [18]

It was the code of the early Hoosier, the backwoodsman or river man, a type already [in 1859] becoming extinct in Indiana. The code of Flash Perkins was the code of a people who had become great fighters and talkers in a wilderness where there was not much else a man could do for diversion except fight and talk. It was the code of the tellers of tall tales who tried to live up to their tales. It was the code of a competitive people, who had fought the Indian and a still greater antagonist, the wilderness itself, the stubborn, root-filled pioneer earth, the beautiful and deadly river, the sheer space of the West. It was the code of breezy, cocky men, who had no fear in heaven or earth they would admit to. The code involved never hitting a man who was down, never turning down a drink, never refusing to take a dare, never

[17] J. C. Livingston, "Alexander Hamilton and the American Tradition," **Midwest Journal of Political Science**, 1:209–224, November, 1957.
[18] Lockridge, *op. cit.*, p. 174.

backing out of a fight—except with a woman. The code involved contempt for city folks, redskins, varmints of all kinds, atheists, scholars, aristocrats, and the enemies of the United States of America.

Actually, every Raintree County man had a little of the code in him. It was simply the Code of the West, and though the West had already passed over Raintree County and left it far behind, nevertheless the County had once been and would always be a part of the West. As Professor Jerusalem Webster Stiles was wont to say,

—To the true Easterner, everything on the other side of the Alleghenies is the West. And in a way that's right. . . .

Moral Superiority in the Soil   The rustic idyl that was the America of the dream of Thomas Jefferson began to disappear as an actual possibility well before that philosopher and statesman had completed his days on earth. Jefferson firmly believed that democracy, if it were to be successful, must find its strength in the individual farmer working in soil that he could call his own. Directly, he did not know very much about large cities (except for what he had seen in Paris), but he was an insatiable reader, and what he read about them did not please him. His opinion was stated trenchantly in **Notes on Virginia** (1782): "The mobs of great cities add just so much to the support of pure government, as sores do to the strength of the human body." So long as he lived, he urged that the United States remain an agricultural nation.

But the cities came anyway, and with them the urban proletariat that Jefferson thought spelled doom for democracy. The rise of the city was accompanied by ideas for its proper government. Ideas came via Jefferson and the frontier to the rising urban centers, where they were embraced by the working-man. The ideology involved an attitude toward government ·accepted by those who labored on the farm and in the city alike; it was an ideology of a rapidly growing nation, constantly pushing westward, founding new towns, building up old ones through the rise of a new industrialism; it was a viewpoint of a people constantly in debt, yet perennially optimistic as they realized, or at least hoped for, the unearned increment of increasing site value of land; and it was the thoughts of the common man about a nation that was now his own and that no longer belonged to an oligarchy of propertied aristocrats. Together it made up the political ideology of Jacksonian democracy, and it provided a rationalization for government that survived nearly intact the remainder of the nineteenth century and is still important in our thinking today.

Jacksonian Principles   Probably antecedent to all other Jacksonian principles in importance was the concept of government by the common man. Government existed, not for a privileged class, but for the general citizen. Any one man was equal to any other man. Jefferson had said so in 1776, when the country was controlled by an aristocracy; now the words were to be taken quite literally, even though only the visionary extended the concept beyond the white man in the 1820s. If this were the case, then it followed that any man was as good as any other man in public office—no special qualifications were needed, no special training, nothing other than willingness to serve the community.

Out of this concept came the principle of universal manhood suffrage. It followed logically from egalitarianism, it was necessary to the development of Jacksonian thought, and, furthermore, it was the natural result of the effect of inertia upon the already existing tendency to broaden the electorate—a tendency that had begun even before the Revolution. Change in this respect took place at a great rate during the 1830s especially, and by 1850 virtually all property restrictions had disappeared from voting requirements and universal manhood suffrage had been achieved. (The extension of the vote to women in later decades proved to be of very little immediate political importance.) The general public now possessed the potential for the control of government in its own interests. Universal manhood suffrage made it possible for any man to run for office, to get support from all kinds of people, and to be elected. Jacksonians were not greatly concerned with the education, background of experience, or private calling of a candidate. This viewpoint, incidentally, made a career as a professional politician or even as a political hack * legitimate.

* **POLITICAL HACK.** An individual who is a perennial office seeker and who depends for a livelihood upon scraps from the political table. His competence and public faith in him are questionable. A **PROFESSIONAL POLITICIAN** is a person who secures his livelihood from political jobs, but his competence in a public job is assumed or has been demonstrated.

Following from the above, Jacksonians believed that public officeholders, as servants of the people, should hold their mandates directly from the people. It was therefore desirable to elect public officials rather than to appoint them. Gradually this came to mean the election of many officers, thus imposing upon Americans the unique institution of the long, or "bedsheet," ballot. To further ensure proximity to the people, a short term of one or two years in office and rapid turnover of personnel were advocated. In rural and small urban communities, government could be *personal;* and the long ballot was therefore less of a handicap to the casual voter, for he probably knew all or most of the candidates either personally or by reputation. Similarly, while rapid turnover of personnel meant inexperienced officeholders, this was no great problem where government was on a neighborly basis and administration was simple and nontechnical. The public thought it more important that the bureaucracy be representative of the interests of the common man than that it be skilled and neutral.[19]

In the nineteenth century, even the conservatives were pragmatists rather than doctrinaire supporters of *laissez faire,* however, and Thomas Williams of Pennsylvania, a founder of both the Whig and Republican parties, defended the protective tariff on four grounds in an 1844 speech. He said free trade would: [20]

1. Place the United States in "a degree of dependence not exactly consistent with our dignity or security"

[19] This point is made by Kaufman, *op. cit.,* pp. 1058–1059.
[20] Burton A. Konkle, **The Life and Speeches of Thomas Williams,** Campion & Co., Philadelphia, 1905, vol. I, pp. 180–181.

2. Raise prices on untaxed goods because of high transportation costs

3. Condemn us to a single industry—agriculture—and not leave our energies "free as the wind to roam over the boundless and varied fields" of industry

4. "Thwart and counteract the obvious high destiny of the magnificent country which has been committed to our hands."

Administrative Trends   The trends begun during the early years of the nineteenth century continued on through the period preceding the Civil War. The chief executive officer continued to gain back some of the ground he had lost during and after the Revolution. Terms of office were lengthened in some instances, restrictions against succeeding oneself were eased, impeachment was made more difficult. But governors and mayors, though given some appointive powers previously vested in the legislative body, had little administrative authority because of the prevailing fashion of the long ballot. Oregon later went so far as to make the state printer elective [21]—state printing contracts were lucrative and subject to abuse. It was assumed that direct public control over the printer through election would help eliminate the threat of corruption.

Party organization developed during the Jacksonian period. Through organization, the party controlled patronage, and through the use of conventions and caucuses (the primary election appeared much later) it controlled nominations. Parties tended to be alliances of sectional interests, but the Democratic party, which had sponsored the expansion of the suffrage and with which the ideology of frontier individualism was associated in the popular mind, was much stronger than its opponents, who had gathered together in the Whig party.

State constitutions were lengthened as the public, distrustful of legislatures that were often corrupt, wrote a good deal of statute or ordinary law into them, a pattern that has generally prevailed to the present day. The constitution is the fundamental law, setting forth the structure of government and providing the basic rules of the political process. Lawyers and political reformers have argued that it should not include statutory law because of the inflexibility thus created.[22]

Bribery, blackmail, the shakedown, and outright theft on the part of legislators began before the Civil War and grew worse immediately afterwards. Nearly all states were affected. The Southern Pacific Railroad in its early history virtually bought control of the California legislature. The copper-mine owners did the same in Montana. A party boss in Georgia used state money to buy into a railroad car company, had the legislature appropriate funds to buy cars from him—and then did not deliver the cars. The reconstruction-period legislatures of the South reached the lowest ebb. Northern visitors organized slumming expeditions to watch the Louisiana legislature, which was manned by drunks offering obscene amendments, making vulgar speeches

[21] Richards, *op. cit.*, p. 45.
[22] *Ibid.*

from the floor, and refusing to be offended by charges that they accepted open bribes.[23]

In some states, a section was written into the constitution providing that the question of holding a constitutional convention be submitted to the voters periodically, commonly every twenty years (Jefferson thought a revolution each generation might be a good thing; his practical successors settled for this sublimated form). The provision is still a feature of eight state constitutions. There was also a pronounced trend toward the submission of constitutional amendments directly to the voters. Their approval was required before changes went into effect. This practice eventually became almost universal.

Constitutions continued to have added to them increasingly long lists of "don't's" directed toward limiting the legislatures' discretionary powers. The use of state credit for the encouragement of internal improvements had been greeted enthusiastically in the early years of the century, but road and canal building by state governments ran into a series of misfortunes. Some routes were poorly chosen or cost so much to develop that subsequent traffic did not liquidate the debt; the panic of 1837 had disastrous consequences for state finances; building was sometimes done inefficiently with political patronage a factor; and, as the final blow, while canals and turnpikes were still being built or before they were paid for, the railroad came along as a more efficient form of transportation. The result was a spate of constitutional provisions prohibiting the use of the state credit in such undertakings. (The pragmatic frontiersman, though he believed that the individual could best depend upon himself, did not oppose state activity in the transportation field on theoretical grounds, but the failures in this area were cited later, in the last half of the nineteenth century, as "proof" that government was too inefficient to engage in activities that might conceivably be performed by private enterprise.)

The Case of Ohio   Ohio offers an example of the trends of the day. The constitution of 1851 (with amendments, still in effect) hemmed in the previously almost unrestricted legislature by limiting the amount of debt that might be contracted by the state and by establishing biennial sessions to replace the annual sessions provided for in the constitution of 1802—the less often a legislature met, the less damage it might do. The state was prohibited from buying stock in, or loaning its credit to, private business, and no debt was permitted for the sake of making internal improvements.

The judiciary was made elective (the legislature had previously selected judges). Only the governorship did not fit the fashion of the day; no provision was made for a veto, and none was made until 1874. In other respects, however, Ohio (and other states) followed the prevailing style in writing a new constitution, and the style settled upon was pragmatically determined from the ideology and life styles of the day.

The Doctrine of States' Rights   A heterogeneous nation with widely varying cultural traditions and economic patterns could not be expected to become

23 C. G. Bowers, **The Tragic Era,** Houghton Mifflin Company, Boston, 1929; James Bryce, **Modern Democracies,** The Macmillan Company, New York, 1921, vol. II; Richards, *op. cit.,* pp. 40–64.

a single, closely knit nation overnight—or even over several decades. In opposition to the nationalism of the Federalists, a vigorous states' rights movement appeared early in the history of the Republic and has never since disappeared. This doctrine has regularly done service as a device for rationalizing a variety of protests against the establishment of a single policy for the nation as a whole.

As early as 1798, the Kentucky and Virginia Resolutions restated the anti-Federalist position that the nation was a compact among sovereign states, as had been the case under the Articles of Confederation, and not one established by the people directly. The resolutions (those from Kentucky drafted by Jefferson, from Virginia by James Madison) held that states might take steps to veto any legislation they held to be unconstitutional. In this particular case, the objection was to the Alien and Sedition Laws of the Federalists.[24]

In 1828, the South Carolina legislature passed a resolution of "Exposition and Protest" against the protective tariff adopted that year—the agricultural South opposed a high tariff which would encourage the development of industry in the North but would raise the cost of finished products to the consumer. The legislature attempted to nullify the tariff, ran into strong opposition from President Jackson, was forced to retreat when the rest of the South did not give it full support, and finally achieved some measure of success by winning a downward revision of the tariff. The principle expressed in the Constitution held, however, and neither South Carolina in this instance nor any state at a later time has succeeded in nullifying a Federal law.

Calhoun's View Perhaps the doctrine of states' rights found its most eloquent spokesman in John C. Calhoun of South Carolina. To Calhoun, states' rights became "an instrumentality primarily for the protection of property rights, with the protection of slavery foremost in his consideration." [25] Calhoun continued the classic struggle of the agrarian against the vested financial interests, but his agrarians were the Bourbon aristocracy * of the Deep South. Calhoun's arguments for the preservation of the Southern way of life as he knew it centered around the view that the Constitution was a compact among the states and that the Federal government, through its Supreme Court or oherwise, could not be the judge of its own powers. Rather, he argued, the states should properly resolve for themselves all conflicts.[26]

* BOURBON ARISTROCRACY. The plantation-owning elite of the South and its descendants.

The Tidelands Issue The Civil War did not settle the issue of states' rights, although it made clear the fact that the national government would not tolerate secession any more than it would tolerate nullification. The doctrine was used later by the great financial, business, and industrial combines of the last half of the nineteenth century to protect themselves from control by any government, national or state. It was used again by oil companies interested in

[24] See any introductory American history text.
[25] Robert J. Harris, "States' Rights and Vested Interests," **Journal of Politics**, 15:457–471, November, 1954.
[26] See John C. Calhoun, **Disquisition on Government** (1851), The Liberal Arts Press, Inc., New York, 1953. For a vigorous contemporary defense of states' rights, see J. J. Kilpatrick, **The Sovereign States: Notes of a Citizen of Virginia,** Henry Regnery Company, Chicago, 1957.

controlling the tidelands oil, that is, the offshore oil deposits under the oceans. However: [27]

> The solicitude of the oil companies for states' rights is hardly based on convictions derived from political theory but rather on fears that Federal ownership may result in the cancellation or modification of state leases favorable to their interests, their knowledge that they can successfully cope with state oil regulatory agencies, and uncertainty concerning their ability to control a Federal agency. The position of the oil companies [has] . . . depicted the actions of the Federal government as the "Tidelands grab" by an oppressive central government from sovereign states. . . .

The tidelands controversy ended differently from earlier contests: those wearing the states' rights mantle were this time successful. The Republicans, with one eye on votes in California, Texas, and Louisiana, promised in 1952 to vacate Federal title to the tidelands if elected. The party won the Presidency and Congress and delivered on the campaign commitment.

The Integration Issue   States' rights, once again, became a part of the arsenal of those who in the South opposed the integration of schools before and after the United States Supreme Court decided in favor of a single national policy on this delicate but basic question.[28] States' rights is an argument well suited for the protection of regional attitudes against a contrary national view.

Similarly governors, including liberal governors strongly committed to vigorous Federal action, have not hesitated to use the states' rights argument if it was in their interests to do so. Thus, Governor Franklin D. Roosevelt of New York once denounced a Federal court decision favorable to the utilities of that state as an invasion of a state's right to regulate such businesses within its border.[29] The decision had not been helpful to Roosevelt's personal political plans.

The states' rights type of argument, running as it does throughout American history, is thus a fine example of the fact that values held dear by a people are verbalized into an ideology, are told and retold until they become virtually folktales, and finally become instruments for the manipulation of attitudes and for the achievement of desired political goals by the manipulators.

Frontier Individualism Today   Ideologies probably never die entirely. "They depart farther and farther from reality with the passing of time, thus representing the original truth less and less perfectly. At the same time they tend to command ever greater strength and ever wider acceptance partly because, since they have little to do with reality, no interest can be injured by protestations of platitude." [30] Thus the values of the frontier continue to influence the symbolism of politics today. In particular, Americans still believe that "small" government is better than "big" government; that an officeholder is more responsible to the people and likely to be more honest if he is directly elected;

[27] Harris, *op. cit.*, p. 467.
[28] *Brown v. Board of Education of Topeka*, 347 U.S. 483 (1954). See below, chap. 18.
[29] Frank Freidel, **Franklin D. Roosevelt: The Triumph**, Little, Brown and Company, Boston, 1956, chap. 8.
[30] Roscoe C. Martin, **Grass Roots**, University of Alabama Press, University, Ala., 1957, p. 87, which discusses the fact that the Jacksonian value of small government close to the people has come "to be associated with everything good and virtuous in American life."

that rural government is more democratic and probably of a higher type than is urban government; that a local government of neighbors is more efficient and effective than a local government in the hands of a professional bureaucracy; and so on. At the same time, the individuals who accept these slogans also hold other views resulting from their modern day needs, so that *an individual's political attitudes are always of an ambivalent character.* Thus the citizen who believes that rural government is more democratic than city government because rural life is better than city life may also believe that all rural justices of the peace are incompetents who should be replaced by professional lawyer-judges at the county seat. A person who believes that small government is better than big government also wants services of various kinds from government, and each of these contributes toward making government bigger. The suburbanite who wants a government of neighbors may also think that the village public works department would operate much better if it were headed by a fully qualified engineer.

In the 1960s, the ideology of the frontier could be found in a special, frustrated version in the romantic, confused, angry protests of the far right. These reactionary movements came to be known popularly as "the radical right."

According to one study: [31]

The individuals attracted to such activities have been shown to suffer from "anomia," Durkheim's term for alienation from warm and meaningful social relationships, which is another way of characterizing the absence of symbolic reassurance. Such people, feeling intensely alone, are likely to assume that the threats they perceive are caused by a conspiracy of hostile elements. Their behavior takes on the characteristics that have come to be called "mass society": extreme susceptibility to suggestions for mob action, intolerance, easy excitability, ready arousal to violence. The vigilante action such groups initiate is irrational in the sense that there is no logical reason it should allay the threat they fear or produce the benefits they claim. It is often not clear whether a threat objectively exists. The succession of nativists movements in American history, the antiradical hysteria after World War I, and the McCarthyism of 1951 to 1954 exemplify this kind of departure from political quiescence.

The findings of one study of right-wing extremists indicated the following: [32]

1. Rightists are more likely than are other persons to have experienced social mobility, particularly in a downward direction;

2. Rightists experience more status anxieties than do others;

3. Rightists perceive significant differences between the traditional values in which they strongly believe and those of the rest of society;

4. Rightists accept simplistic explanations of social and political events and tend to be dogmatic;

5. Rightists tend to displace their hostilities upon persons whom they see as possessing undesirable qualities; and

6. Rightists manifest general feelings of personal alienation and powerlessness.

[31] Edelman, *loc. cit.*
[32] Ira S. Rohter, "Some Personal Needs Met by Becoming a Radical Rightist," a paper read at the meeting of the American Psychological Association, Chicago, 1965.

This same study concluded that extremists of the right attempt to increase their personal sense of self-esteem and of social status through identification with extremist movements. By measuring persons who possess what others consider to be higher social status and influence and those with different values in life styles in terms of their own values and life styles, they gain a greater degree of self-worth than society accords them.

To members of the far right, ideology is especially important: [33]

It appears that while any group of ideologists may be deeply committed to ideological precepts, [extremists] are people whose ideology seems to play a more central role in their lives than do the ideologies of other groups. These are "deviant" political ideologies—ideologies subscribed to by relatively few people and in which the preferred type of regime differs markedly from that in most other political ideologies.

Advocates of frontier individualism who are merely conservative in character tend to be much less alienated than are extremists. They are negative regarding proposed public policies or proposed expenditures to meet changes in public policies. Many of these persons are elderly people living on relatively fixed incomes, and some of them seem to be neighborhood, as distinguished from central business district, merchants. They usually have a spokesman or two on the city council—though these in most cities do not constitute a majority. They have a number of spokesmen in state legislatures.

The Program of the Right   Extremists of the right wing, in contrast to the conservatives, or caretaker ideologues, do have a positive program. Because they are looking back on a frontier America, one which was preindustrial and preurban in character, their ideology is necessarily reactionary, nostalgic, and sentimental. It also tends to emphasize simple, conventional wisdom in preference to explanations learned through the scientific method and modern research.

Extreme rightists, sometimes but by no means always supported by conservative caretakers, commonly urge public policy programs that characteristically include certain things. They advocate support for the local police, for example. Even though they favor minimizing governmental budgets, they may urge an expansion in the size of the police force. They also favor broader authority for the police, even though they may at the same time decry the decline in civil rights and liberties in America. They defend the law and urge upon all citizens the importance of obeying it, although, like all extremists groups, they will sometimes disobey the law themselves. When they do so, as in the case of members of the extreme left wing, they argue that the end justifies the means, although they may not be willing to admit that this is in fact the nature of their argument. They tend to take the old Puritan's view of welfare, urging that conditions under which an individual is eligible for public welfare should be extremely restricted and arguing that persons on welfare are probably essentially shiftless. Even in cases where they might concede that individuals are in real need through no fault of their own, they argue that

---

[33] Robert E. Agger, Daniel Goldrich, and Bert E. Swanson, **The Rulers and the Ruled,** John Wiley & Sons, Inc., New York, 1964, p. 31.

welfare allowances are too generous and that there are many professional welfare "chiselers." [34]

Right-wingers sometimes take the position that the taxpayer is subsidizing immorality if aid to dependent children is granted to illegitimate children. In terms of the general population, a disproportional percentage of illegitimacy is to be found among low-income groups, and particularly among those on welfare. Within this group, illegitimacy is particularly common among Negroes, which introduces a racial tone into the issues, even though right-wingers generally protest that they are not prejudiced against Negroes as such. Except in the South, this is probably generally the case. The principal objection of Negroes to the right-wing position centers around the fact that it adds to their problems of recognition, acceptance, and upward social mobility.

Those on the right generally favor a traditional school curriculum and an inexpensive one. They have sometimes opposed the fluoridation of water, arguing that it is against nature, or that it may cause cancer, or that it offers an opportunity for subversives to poison the water system. (In some cases, such efforts backfire. The city of Antigo in northern Wisconsin abandoned fluoridation in 1960 as the result of a conservative drive, but it was restored by an 11 to 1 vote of the council in April, 1965, when scientific evidence was called to the attention of the council—in this case, the results of a state health department survey which showed that tooth decay in Antigo kindergarten children had increased by 92 percent in the years since the abandonment of fluoridation. Even in this case, however, although the council voted 11 to 1, a referendum advisory vote on fluoridation passed by only 1,822 to 1,685.)

Crime, Punishment, and the Rightists   Right-wing ideologues sometimes object to controls over the shipment and sale of guns and ammunition, but, holding to the traditional Protestant ethic, urge that mandatory long sentences be meted out for the use of guns in crimes. An illustrative contrast between the ideology of the past and that of the present took place in the Illinois legislature in 1965. A committee on organized crime legislation, appointed by Mayor Richard J. Daley of Chicago, recommended that all guns possessed by private citizens be registered, just as are all automobiles. The conservative reaction to this was to propose that, instead, there be a mandatory prison sentence of two years for the first time an individual is convicted of using a gun in a crime, five years for a second offense, and seven years for a third. The former proposal emphasized prevention; the latter, punishment.

A similar attitude toward the law as a device for retribution is to be found in connection with a conservative point of view toward the death penalty for crimes.[35] The death penalty is essentially an instrument of primitive societies. The trend has been away from it for a long time and it has almost disappeared in Europe and in much of Asia. Statistical evidence that the death penalty is not a deterrent to crime is overwhelming. Persons dedicated to the nineteenth-

---

[34] Carl Selby and Anne Selby, "California's Jackpot for the Jobless," **Reader's Digest**, June, 1965, pp. 67–70, and many other articles on public welfare written for the **Digest**. This magazine also prints articles from other periodicals which use the same theme.
[35] See John W. Johnston, "The Death Penalty and Self-defense," **Chicago Daily News**, May 24, 1965.

century ideology, however, insist that punishment is effective, despite scientific evidence to the contrary. For example, one has argued that, "it is not coincidence that with growth of maudlin sentimentality in the treatment of all manner of offenses, the crime rate is rising and brutality flourishing." [36]

Labor Unions and the Rightists   Advocates of the frontier ideology also tend to be skeptical of labor unions and of their place in contemporary society. In general, they tend to oppose all legislation which they believe will be of advantage to labor unions and to support legislation weakening or controlling unions. In 1957, when the movement to provide right-to-work laws * was at a peak, twelve of the seventeen least urban states had such laws while only three of the seventeen most urban had them. In contrast, at that time none of the seventeen least urban states had fair employment practices laws, while nine of the seventeen most urban had them. The advocates of frontier individualism did not oppose fair employment; they did oppose making the matter one of public policy and permitting the government at any level to enforce rules relative to the matter upon employers.

* **RIGHT-TO-WORK LAW. A law forbidding "union shop" contracts by which all hourly rated employees must join a union within a specified period of time.**

Table 4   "Right-to-work" Legislation

STATE *	DATE OF "RIGHT-TO-WORK" LEGISLATION
Florida	Nov. 7, 1944
Arizona	Nov. 28, 1946
Virginia	Jan. 21, 1947
Arkansas	Feb. 19, 1947
Tennessee	Feb. 19, 1947
North Dakota	Mar. 13, 1947
North Carolina	Mar. 18, 1947
Georgia	Mar. 27, 1947
Texas	Apr. 8, 1947
Iowa	Apr. 28, 1947
Nebraska	June 10, 1947
South Dakota	July 1, 1947
Nevada	Feb. 1, 1953
Alabama	Aug. 28, 1953
Mississippi	Feb. 24, 1954
South Carolina	Mar. 19, 1954
Utah	Feb. 10, 1955
Louisiana †	Aug. 1, 1956
Kansas	Nov. 4, 1958
Wyoming	Feb. 8, 1963

* Indiana passed but later repealed a "right-to-work" law.
† Law covers agricultural employees only.
SOURCE: Richard C. Einbecker, " 'Right-to-work' Laws vs. Union Security," **Business and Economic Dimensions**, 1:5, July, 1965.

[36] Statement of William F. Buckley, Jr., published in the **National Review**, July 13, 1965, pp. 586–589.

Urbanism and the Rightists   When William F. Buckley, Jr., announced he would be a candidate for mayor of New York City in 1965, his opening statement indicated he felt that the mayor of the city had in the past failed to use his powers to "reverse the crime rate." He advocated a "much larger police force" than existed at the time. He opposed a civilian review board—a device that had been urged by liberals who were concerned about alleged police brutality and alleged discrimination by the police against minority groups and races. In referring to persons on public welfare, he reflected the traditional attitude of the frontier that work is good for the soul. He recommended that those who "are able-bodied, and who are not needed at home to care for the children, should report for duty in our parks, in our streets, in our development projects, pending their absorption into the labor market." [37] He urged that a full year of residence be required for eligibility for public welfare aid, "to discourage the thoughtless flow of men and women into New York." He also urged that the "obsession with urban renewal" be "tranquilized" lest the city lose "its hold on human sentiment."

At the local urban level, however, the frontier ideology is no longer appropriate and hence has little acceptance. When Buckley was asked whether he thought he had any chances of winning the office of mayor of New York, he replied, "No." He apparently was right.

State Government and Frontier Individualism   In legislatures, the nineteenth-century ideology has been far more obvious than it has been in city councils. In urban areas, pressures on the political system tend to produce public decision makers sympathetic to or at least willing to accept the urban situation. At the state level, such a situation does not necessarily exist. The pattern of apportionment of legislatures in the past has encouraged legislative leaders to emphasize the small-town ideology which has, for the most part, been a reflection of the values of the nineteenth-century frontier. (In the mid-1960s, the frontier attitude was sharply emphasized by the opposition to apportionment based on strict population and by support of the so-called Dirksen Amendment, which would allow one house of a state legislature to be based on other factors.)

As people have moved into the cities and become accustomed to the social problems of the urban way of life, this legislative viewpoint has become increasingly insufficient as a basis for explaining or proposing solutions to problems as the typical urban citizen sees them. Therefore: [38]

The small-town viewpoint, now on the defensive, sometimes achieves a shrill note with irrational overtones. Low taxes and simplicity in state government are the goal for a group of legislators who see most modern-day conditions as a mammoth conspiracy against their views of truth and beauty. Big-city schemers seem to surround them. Legislators of the small town paint pictures—in a day of widespread prosperity and the most conspicuous forms of consumption—of the beleaguered and almost bankrupt taxpayer who cannot afford to have rivers unpolluted, or mental

[37] *Ibid.*
[38] Press and Adrian, *op. cit.*, p. 159.

institutions with rehabilitation facilities for their patients, or highway systems designed to minimize the danger of head-on crashes.

One political analyst, describing the small-town legislative bloc in his own state said, "they have 'tantrums' for a platform." And this nicely sums up the decline of what once was the most dynamic political viewpoint in America. A querulousness about governmental "frills" is almost all that remains of the once proud doctrine of small-town individualism.

The frontier ideology is today, then, a minority ideology, but still an important one. It is centered in the American small town and increasingly is a reflection of frustration rather than a symbol of the good life.

The Ideology of Industrial Individualism

America industrialized rapidly in the decades following the Civil War. She became increasingly an urban nation, and the system of big business with large capital investments, a high degree of mechanization, and the impersonalization of labor became the order of the day. The dominant ideology of the times, that of industrial individualism, was a modified and modernized version of frontier individualism, moved into the city and made to fit a new pattern of life. In the place of the frontiersman, the new hero was the self-made man of industry in the Horatio Alger tradition. In the place of the long-dominant Democratic party, the new Republican party emerged from the war as, except in the South, the strongest political coalition and the one which successfully associated itself with the new ideology. In place of a dominant legislative branch of government, the judicial branch came to the top as stronger than the legislative or executive. It became the energetic protector of the new myth. Through the Fourteenth Amendment to the United States Constitution (ensuring due process of law in connection with property rights), economic individualism was written into the fundamental law of the land.

The period after the Civil War to the time of the Great Depression, which began in the fall of 1929, was one of many facets, the most important of which included (1) disillusionment with universal suffrage among intellectuals and business leaders, (2) changes in state and local government under the impact of rapid industrialization and urbanization, (3) the development of the "efficiency-and-economy" reform movement which sought to reestablish government dominated by middle-class values, and (4) agrarian radicalism as a protest against laissez-faire extremism.

Poor Boy Becomes Millionaire Horatio Alger wrote more than one hundred stories, uniformly low in literary merit, telling the nineteenth-century youngster that opportunity was his for the taking, that success can be measured in terms of material accomplishments, and that it results from virtue and hard work. Perhaps not every boy believed that he could, by this simple formula, become another Vanderbilt or Carnegie, but he was constantly bombarded with similar propaganda from all the media of communication, controlled as they were by persons whose interests coincided with those of the newly created titans of business and industry.[39] Undoubtedly these teachings profoundly affected Americans, urban and rural, rich and poor, and had much to do both with conditioning their own behavior and with the way in which they permitted the new giant corporations to create "clusters of private government which first neutralized state powers and then overcame them." [40]

The new ideology included the idea that business and industry was the nation's most important institution, that what was good for business was good for the nation, that other institutions, social or political, should play a second-ary role and must not interfere with the activities of the business community. Free enterprise and *laissez faire* became key symbols; government was regarded as inefficient, and its control over business was held to be not only a threat to the progress of the nation but in fact immoral.

States' rights were considered important, especially by the courts which used legal arguments in support of the doctrine in order to prevent Federal regulation of the economy, and at the same time, set aside state regulation as interference with the interstate-commerce powers of the Federal government. The Federal and state courts, frequently occupied by ex-corporation lawyers, became guardians of free enterprise. In order to legitimatize the frustration of the popular will to regulate as expressed by legislative bodies, heavy reliance was placed on the Constitution. It became an institution, a spirit that hovered over the land, over the courts, and over the elected officials. The idea was developed that the Constitution had a meaning all its own and that it was the duty of the judges, not to use their own values in interpreting the document, but to seek to "discover" its true intent.

The people accepted these ideas in general, but, as always, their atti-tudes were ambivalent. They believed in hard work; they believed that it would be rewarded. They believed in government's staying out of the way of their own efforts. But where this belief failed to help individuals in their time of troubles—as was the case with the farmers toward the end of the nineteenth century—they also continued to accept the frontiersman's faith in expediency. They would seek help wherever they could find it.

Immigration, Urbanization, and Disillusionment   At the 1885 commencement-day exercises on the campus of the State University of Iowa, graduating seniors in their orations deplored the "irreverence and restlessness generated in our over-crowded cities," the peasant immigrants who were "clogging the wheels of progress," the extreme tendencies toward utilitarianism and materialism which were destroying the "cultural unity of society" and dividing men into "discordant classes." [41]

Frank O. Lowden, son of an Iowa Granger radical, later to become Gov-ernor of Illinois (1917–1921) and a man who, in 1920, came within a razor's

---

[39] For the impact of the industrial age upon Americans, see Samuel P. Hays, **The Response to Industrialism,** The University of Chicago Press, Chicago, 1957.
[40] Harris, *op. cit.,* p. 461.
[41] William T. Hutchinson, **Lowden of Illinois,** The University of Chicago Press, Chicago, 1957, vol. 1, p. 27, quoting the campus newspaper.

edge of the Presidency of the United States, criticized the intellectual leaders of the French Revolution for spreading "that fallacious theory of man's absolute equality" and the demagogues who, using this belief, sought "the plaudits of the vulgar crowd." Along with many intellectuals and businessmen of the age, Lowden concluded that "all tendencies toward socialism are toward the rule of mediocrity." [42]

During the decades following the Civil War, **The Nation,** the **Atlantic,** and other periodicals carried the protest of intellectuals and businessmen. They commented unfavorably upon the rise of the ignorant and poor to political power. They saw the demagogue and city boss as results of the common man's demand for a controlling voice in social and economic questions which had once been settled rationally by intelligent, responsible persons. The people now wanted, not "great minds" in political office to lead them, but obedient agents to help them meet "their overpowering anxiety about their daily bread." [43]

Yet, while the intellectual defended free enterprise as a system of economics, he came to disapprove of its social results. Eventually multimillionaires were seen by the editors of **The Nation** as an even greater threat to America than was the common man. Both were regarded as self-seeking and self-centered, but the former were thought to be the more dangerous because of the power of their money. In this period of our history, then, there was a disenchantment with the common man—he was not to be romanticized again until the days of the New Deal—and the business leader was thought to be on the right track. But this viewpoint lasted only until the businessman's own selfishness caused him to lose his place on the pedestal where he had earlier been placed by the intellectual, the farmer, the workingman. He was eventually to lose the support of all except the growing middle class. However, the business leader of the days of industrialism had two advantages that the pre-1860 businessman did not have and that gave him an enormous advantage in the political arena: he and his kind were now incomparably wealthier, and the business community was far better organized with a better set of internal communications. Both of these advantages did much to give the businessman a strong voice in state and local government.

Government in an Unprincipled Age.   There was little room for moral principles unconnected with the immediate business at hand in an age when tycoons were piling up fortunes, exploiting the consumer, seeking to destroy one another, and doing whatever was necessary to make money. Never had Americans come closer to believing that the end justified the means. Corruption existed in state and local government and reached up into Congress itself, even to the Speaker's chair, and to the Cabinet. If bribery, spying, throat cutting (literal and figurative) existed in private business, why should the business-

[42] *Ibid.*
[43] Alan P. Grimes, **The Political Liberalism of the New York Nation,** The University of North Carolina Press, Chapel Hill, N.C., 1953, chap. 3; also Vernon L. Parrington, **Main Currents in American Thought,** Harcourt, Brace & World, Inc., New York, 1930, vol. 3, pp. 58–59.

man not apply the same methods in getting governmental obstacles out of the way? Small wonder that: [44]

Venality characterized the state legislatures and so profitable was it that many legislators sought their offices in order to turn a quick profit. Ready to protect his interests, Jay Gould is reported to have once come to Albany with $500,000 in his satchel. If the vested interests did not immediately approach the lawmakers, the latter introduced bills inimical to their interests, not with the intent of passing them, but with the intent of collecting for not passing them. . . .

Bosses and machines became powerful in cities and states. Legislatures took over the aspects of municipal government that were profitable or of political importance despite a tradition stemming from colonial times giving municipalities a good deal of leeway in handling their own affairs.[45] Franchises, contracts for public works, even seats in the legislatures were sold to the highest bidder. The public confidence in government, generated by the Jacksonian policy of government by neighbors, gave way to cynicism. Only the Constitution remained sacrosanct.

The Efficiency-and-economy Movement   Well-meaning but poorly organized amateurs began their efforts to reclaim state and local government from the boss and the political machine as early as the 1870s. They lacked experience and organizational skills and were often politically naive. The movement, like its Jacksonian predecessor, was pragmatic, unsystematic, and loosely coordinated. It had no single intellectual leader and was not part of a general philosophy, although it did have definite Hamiltonian overtones. Its strength was centered in the middle-class businessman with additional aid coming from a handful of academicians.[46]

The difficulties which confronted reformers were at first almost overpowering. Political machines, often headed by a well-known boss, resisted by using any technique that would destroy or discourage the neophytes. The machine was usually well organized, with an army of workers and large numbers of voters who were obligated to it, and hence was generally able to defeat any attempts at reform. The minority of businessmen who turned reformers were in a particularly vulnerable position. A strong political machine in control of the state and city had many weapons at hand to injure those who dared oppose it. It could, for example, increase the assessment of their properties, refuse them permits and licenses, or harass them through overenforcement of health, fire, building, and other codes.

Many industrialists and businessmen refused to cooperate with reformers. They were convinced that it was cheaper and more effective to buy off the machine. The general public was almost completely cynical regarding the

[44] Richards, *op. cit.*, p. 51.
[45] Charles R. Adrian, **Governing Urban America**, 2d ed., McGraw-Hill Book Company, New York, 1961, pp. 52–54, gives an account of this.
[46] *Ibid.*, pp. 56–63. For classic statements on the efficiency-and-economy movement positions, see Robert C. Brooks, "Bibliography of Municipal Problems and Conditions of City Life," **Municipal Affairs**, vol. 5, 1903.

efforts of the do-gooders and, in the slums of the burgeoning cities, a great many people found the machine a helpful crutch in time of need. To slum dwellers, the destruction of the machine would not be triumph; it would be sheer tragedy.

Reforms and Renovations   The principal slogans of the reformers centered around belief that "all politics is crooked" and that state and local government is essentially a matter of "efficient business administration." Disillusionment with the mechanics which had been proposed by Jacksonians in order to bring America truly democratic government resulted in a skepticism of unbridled majority rule, of legislative supremacy, of the spoils system, of the practice of electing in preference to appointing public officials. Reflecting the views of the times, **The Nation** took a series of editorial positions urging changes. To strengthen executive leadership and restrict the incompetent, irresponsible legislatures, it endorsed the executive budget (1882), the item veto (1886), administrative reorganization with the governor or mayor responsible for the actions of department heads (1885), and the establishment of legislative staff agencies to provide professional advice to legislators (1866). Eventually the lexicon of reform mechanics also came to include the Australian secret ballot, corrupt-practices legislation, publicity for campaign receipts and expenditures, proportional representation * to give the intelligent minority some voice in legislation, the direct-primary election to overcome machine control of caucuses and conventions and to permit the intelligent members of the community at least to put up candidates, and the appointment of judges so as to remove them as far as possible from politics.[47] But perhaps the basic reform issue became that of the merit system for the civil service. Most of the reformers believed that no other reforms could be effective until the spoils system had been eradicated.

* **PROPORTIONAL REPRESENTATION. A device for electing the members of a legislative body in such a way as to reflect all groups or factions in proportion to their strength. It is used in multimember districts rather than single-member districts and is an alternative to geographic representation. Proportional representation is less common in America than in Europe.**

The civil-service reformers saw their goal as being the achievement of neutral competence in public employment. What they sought was "ability to do the work of government expertly, and to do it according to explicit, objective standards rather than to personal or party or other obligations and loyalties." [48] The reformers believed that a clear line could be drawn between politics and administration. The former was the proper sphere of the elected representatives of the people, the latter of the experts, and neither could properly become involved in the arena of the other. Such was the model, though its application proved to involve many difficulties.[49]

[47] Grimes, *op. cit.*, pp. 44–51.
[48] Kaufman, *op. cit.*, p. 1060. See also L. D. White, **The Republican Era**, The Macmillan Company, New York, 1958.
[49] See below, chap. 14.

Organizations and Results   Dozens of organizations were created as the reformers became more skillful in the techniques of political activity. These included such groups as the National Short Ballot Organization, the National Popular Government League, the Proportional Representation League, the National Municipal League, the Bureau of Municipal Research of New York, and dozens of local reform clubs, taxpayers' leagues, local government committees of chambers of commerce, and various research agencies.

In 1891, the voters of Ohio refused by a 3 to 2 vote to call a state constitutional convention, but by 1910 there was so much pressure for reform that the legislature submitted the question of holding a convention a year earlier than was required by the constitution. The voters returned a verdict 10 to 1 in favor and subsequently adopted most of the amendments proposed by the convention. In the 1916 Illinois gubernatorial campaign, Frank O. Lowden, who had been criticized by his opponents for his big-business connections, based his campaign essentially on this straightforward, if somewhat unrhetorical, statement: "It is time for someone who has had some experience in even what is called big business to introduce some things into the form of our state government, if we are going to have efficient administration." [50] And the people elected him. His subsequent reorganization efforts were widely lauded by reformers.

Other changes were made, too: the recall of public officers, begun in Los Angeles in 1903; the initiative and referendum, dating from 1898 San Francisco charter provisions; the commission and council-manager plans of city government at, and shortly after, the beginning of the twentieth century. Nonpartisan elections, eight new state constitutions, the executive budget in one-half the states, corrupt-practices acts, secret-ballot laws, and other reforms were accomplished before the energy of the movement had spent itself in the uncongenial atmosphere of the 1920s. [51]

Reform: An Appraisal   The reform movement made a real contribution to local self-government by recovering a certain amount of responsibility, by replacing the checks and balances of Jacksonian democracy with a more modern system of centralized leadership, and by reestablishing at least a modicum of public respect and confidence in state and local government. However, it did some damage, too. It placed a misleading overemphasis upon forms and structures of government. It led people astray with its preachings to the effect that government was principally a matter of "efficient business management"—which it was not and never can be in a democracy which seeks to be responsive to the demands of voters.

The reform movement failed, for the most part, to make state and local government more representative of a cross section of the community. [52]

---

50 Hutchinson, *op. cit.*, p. 290. For an account of administrative reorganization under Lowden, see Hutchinson's chap. 13.
51 These various devices are discussed in chaps. 4 and 8.
52 The failure of the movement to include a "solid basis in mass support" was pointed out many years ago in John A. Vieg, "Advice for Municipal Reformers," **Public Opinion Quarterly**, 1:87–92, October, 1937.

The old-style politician was rather thoroughly repudiated, but the balance of power in government was not fundamentally altered. The business community continued to dominate. Formerly it had had to do this indirectly, through the state and city machines. Now a new type of control grew up. Businessmen began to participate directly in government. Influence over the voter was now achieved, not through the traditional devices, but through the media of mass communication.

Agrarian Radicalism   As America matured, changing from a frontier nation of farmers to an industrial nation of urbanites, the basic emphasis gradually shifted from opportunity to security, from individual to collective activity. It is perhaps ironic, though certainly understandable, that the first significant efforts at collective action came on the part of the farmers, the very men who were thought to represent, in Charles Beard's overworked phrase, "rugged individualism."

The farmer, through neglect of the political arena as a medium for protecting his interests, had gradually fallen into an impossible economic position and had lost his political dominance by the end of the nineteenth century. "His was the only considerable economic group that exerted no organized pressure to control the price he sold for or the price he paid." [53] He had voted away the public domain to the railroads in his desperate need for transportation facilities—and the railroads were now repaying him with excessive freight charges.[54]

He took pride in the county-seat towns that lived off his earnings; he sent city lawyers to represent him in legislatures and in Congress; he read middle-class newspapers and listened to bankers and politicians and cast his votes for the policy of Whiggery that could have no other outcome than his own despoiling.

Political Action   But in the decades after 1870, the farmer began to protest against "ten cent corn and ten percent interest." He was told to "raise less corn and more hell." But he had determined to become politically active at a time when "legislatures were bought and sold like corner lots; senatorships went to the highest bidder; judges were more responsive to the wishes of bankers than to those of farmers." [55] The road to political success was as rut-filled and as full of obstacles as the one that ran past his deteriorating farmhouse.

William Jennings Bryan told the farmer (and the city dweller) that social problems were essentially moral questions and that moral solutions to them required equal rights for all and special privileges for none. The urban worker, faced with job competition from immigrants and Southern sharecroppers leaving the farm, was slow to respond. The farmer, however, took action. He seized control of several state legislatures, in some cases elected a farmer to sit in the governor's chair, and demanded state action to replace the free enterprise

[53] Parrington, *op. cit.*, p. 262.
[54] *Ibid.*
[55] *Ibid.*, p. 287.

system which he had temporarily accepted. He returned to his old demand for cheaper currency; he sought, among other things, control over transportation, banking policies more helpful to the debtor, a standard system of grain grading, the construction of publicly owned grain elevators, and state crop insurance.[56]

Both the farmers and the business corporations, especially the railroads, established lobbying on a professional basis in the state capitals and in Washington. The conflict between the farmer and his historic business-world enemies came about in the years after the Civil War, when the railroads developed rapidly and came virtually to monopolize control over the transportation of the farmers' products. At the same time the great industrial trusts began to control the productive and consumptive goods the farmers needed. Grain elevators, too, were essential to the farmers' welfare, since they controlled the sale price of his grain and the conditions under which he could sell it—and these were owned by absentee landlords in cities miles from the farmers who used them. Bankers controlled credit, and their policies permitted a continuing deflation of the currency which forced upon the farmer unbearable long-term debts.

Granger Legislation   The Granger movement * (the National Grange carried much of the farmer's political burden) was not a success. It flourished for a few years in a few states. But it often failed to get enacted the legislation it wanted, or its laws were set aside by the courts. The farmers elected to legislatures were often unable to deliver on their promises. Yet the movement greatly affected subsequent legislation. Its proposals involved principally the setting of railroad-rate charges, controlling the maximum charge for the storage of grain, and setting rules concerning "dockage" (the allowance made for weeds, straw, and other waste before calculating the net weight of grain offered for sale at an elevator). Massachusetts established the first of the "railroad and warehouse" commissions in 1869, although it was only a fact-gathering agency. Greater control was vested in the Midwest commissions, where Illinois led the way (1871), followed closely by Minnesota, Iowa, and Wisconsin. The state Granger legislation, aimed as it was against the biggest of big business, was of course challenged in the conservative courts and ultimately in the United States Supreme Court itself, which at that time was regarded as the ultimate bastion of the doctrine of free enterprise.

* GRANGER MOVEMENT. The agrarian radical movement of the 1870s and 1880s designed to raise agricultural profits and protect the farmer from big business exploitation. So called because leadership was provided by The American Patrons of Husbandry, generally called the National Grange. The Grange is today the most conservative of major farm organizations.

The Supreme Court, however, sided against unbridled *laissez faire* and, in a historic decision,[57] held that the state of Illinois (and thus by implication

[56] See *ibid.*, pp. 262–287; Richard Hofstadter, **The American Political Tradition**, Alfred A. Knopf, Inc., New York, 1948, chap. 8.
[57] *Munn v. Illinois*, 94 U.S. 113 (1876).

other states) could establish maximum charges for the storage of grain without depriving the granary owners of their property without due process of law. Businesses, such as granaries or railroads, which were "clothed with the public interest" could be regulated.

The pattern had thus been set, and although the Court a few decades later had some doubts about its decision, especially when it was faced with early labor legislation, the principle of regulation "in the public interest" had been established, and the way opened for the social service state in the years following the Great Depression.[58]

Industrial Individualism and the Businessman   As the political ideology undergoes gradual modification, individuals do not all adjust to its changes in the same manner. Some are out leading the parade, demanding that the public recognize the need for a new point of view. Others accept new ideas passively but without much hesitation if they seem to fit the current environment; still others accept change very slowly or not at all. This is the case with individuals in every group in society. However, within the business community, and especially among small businessmen, the strongest continuing commitment probably continues to be the values of the ideology of industrial individualism.[59]

The Small Businessman   Most small businesses are service rather than productive operations. They are intensely competitive, struggling against one another, against the large corporations that supply them, and against the potentially more efficient corporate form of organization of their businesses, as in the case of the large chain supermarkets which have left little room for the traditional corner grocer. In these circumstances, it is understandable that the small businessman would continue to believe in the values of the American agrarian frontier. To him, success is still not to be found so much in luck or in environment, as in self-reliance, hard work, and thrift. He recognizes that big business, big labor, and subsidized farming pose serious threats to him by raising both his business costs and his taxes.

In an effort to cling to a fading part of the American way, "the thinking and temper of the small businessman indicates a profound ideological attachment to the values of a preindustrial order—indeed, he has become a contemporary advocate of the spirit and virtues of agrarianism." [60] Because he is suspicious of all the many things alien to the world in which he lives and to his idealized version of the same, he is especially distrustful of foreign ideologies, internationalism, the upsetting of established traditions, cosmopolitanism, urbanism, and collectivism. In state and local politics, he favors a

[58] For a brief summary of Court decisions which finally cleared away legal obstacles to the social service state, see Harris, *op. cit.*, pp. 461–471; and J. W. Hurst, **Law and the Conditions of Freedom in the Nineteenth Century United States,** The University of Wisconsin Press, Madison, Wis., 1956.
[59] See William H. Whyte, Jr., **The Organization Man,** Doubleday & Company, Inc., Garden City, N.Y., 1956, chap. 2.
[60] John H. Bunzel, "The General Ideology of American Small Business," **Political Science Quarterly,** 70:87–102, March, 1955; also A. J. Vidich and Joseph Bensman, **Small Town in Mass Society,** Princeton University Press, Princeton, N.J., 1958, pp. 116–117.

weakening of the power of organized labor, discouragement of corporate advantages over small businesses (hence such legislation as chain store taxes), and minimum government spending as a general policy. On the other hand, with the ambivalence typical of everyone's political value patterns, he favors legislation to improve his competitive position, such as fair-trade laws and publicly financed parking places. He opposes legislation that will potentially increase his costs, including fair-employment-practices legislation and the application of workmen's compensation or unemployment-compensation programs to his business. Since virtually all programs under the social service state are seen as costing him more than he gains from them, he becomes an advocate of minimal governmental "interference" in business, of free enterprise, and of states' rights constitutionalism.[61]

The small businessman suffers from a great many fears and anxieties. In one study, the most frequently mentioned "problem" was that of competition. Of the respondents in the survey, 37 percent mentioned this problem and their concern was more with competition from large national companies than from other small businessmen. Taxes were mentioned by 31 percent. Many were concerned that current state and national policies did not give the small businessman a "break." The third most common complaint was one of the problem of finding and keeping good employees. This was mentioned by 29 percent of the respondents. It reflected the difficulty of the small businessman in attracting high-quality employees, most of whom prefer to work for larger companies where the pay is usually better and the threat of corporate collapse is small.

About 23 percent of the respondents indicated that trade unions were a problem. Here the most common complaint was that unions expected small businesses to equal the wages, hours, and conditions of labor of the large corporations. Government "interference" with business was mentioned by only 19 percent. Other items frequently mentioned included cost-control problems, marketing problems, government red tape (mentioned by 9 percent), recruitment of capable managers, and their own personal shortcomings. The study concluded by noting that "in many lines of activity the future of the small businessman does not appear to be bright. This conclusion follows from his combined inability to attract managerial talent and supplement it with skilled staff personnel. Both are essential if any business is to remain competitive in today's market." [62]

The Business Bureaucrat   The organization man has views considerably different from these, however. Whyte has pointed out that the corporation executive lets the personnel and financial departments of the company handle his savings for him, that the advertising agency for the company is busy convincing people to spend, not to save. ("The same man who will quote from

[61] See John H. Bunzel, "Comparative Attitudes of Big Business and Small Business," **Western Political Quarterly**, 9:658–675, September, 1956.
[62] Winston Oberg, "Some Problems Faced by the Small Businessman in Michigan," **Michigan Economic Record**, 4:3ff., December, 1962.

Benjamin Franklin on thrift for the house organ would be horrified if consumers took these maxims to heart and started putting more money into
savings and less into installment purchases.") [63]

Of course, the big-business bureaucrat does not reject the rhetoric of
individualism. The language of individualism is still useful in a variety of
ways: in seeking to preserve the essentially unnatural alliance of friendship
between big and small business; in seeking to prevent the adoption of proposals for governmental policy where those policies would threaten the company welfare; in making goodwill appeals to the public through the use of
essentially meaningless, but favorably perceived, symbols to which all pay
lip service whether they still live by them or not.

Yet, the big-business bureaucrat, in contrast to the small-business pro-
prietor, has no strong motivation to fight the social service state. Organized
labor is not his problem unless he serves in the industrial relations department, and big business has by and large accepted the existence of big labor
and feels able to live with it. He is not directly concerned with costs, except
in his own department, and the taxes paid by the company are not his immediate worry. Top management will, of course, seek to minimize the direct tax
burden on the company, but the bureaucracy not directly affected will not
necessarily give more than perfunctory support to the cause. The same is true
when the corporate leaders lobby against proposals that could lead to a
strengthening of organized labor.

The organization man may, therefore, be one whose political views vary
considerably according to his background and interests. Because he must
conform to the expectations of his bureaucracy, he will likely speak in traditional individualist terms, but he has far less incentive to take political action
in support of these views than has the small businessman. And if his personal
avocational interests should lead him to become active in an interest group
seeking appropriations for some expensive program—mental-health rehabilitation, say, or a recreation program in the slums—his hobby will probably not
cost him his job.

The Social Service State

As the nation changed from an individualistic, rural society to one that was
economically interdependent and urban, much social dislocation took place.
When industrial individualism failed to meet felt needs, people turned to
collective effort through government. The pattern first followed by the farmer
was later taken up by the workingman and then even the businessman.

The New Ideology   The shaking experience of the Great Depression, which
began in the fall of 1929 and lasted until the nation began to prepare for
World War II a decade later, convinced many that job security, guaranteed
payments in the event of unemployment or industrial accident, government
assistance in preparing for retirement, help in finding a job, and other hedges

[63] This section is based upon Whyte, *op. cit.*, chap. 2. Quote is from p. 19.

against starvation were more important than opportunity or the abstract principle of freedom from government control.

As **The Nation** noted in 1868, "if the doors of the future are once thrown open to what are called 'the masses,' and they catch even one glimpse of the splendid possibilities which lie within it, it is in vain to close them again. The vision never leaves their minds." [64] And indeed, in a series of movements—the farmers' activities beginning in the 1870s, Theodore Roosevelt's "Square Deal," Robert LaFollette's progressive movement, Woodrow Wilson's "New Freedom," and others—the common folk had come to realize that government was potentially a powerful weapon in their hands and that each of them had a vote equal to that of any banker or corporation president. The doors had been opened.

It was not only the workingman who sought government support for himself and protection for his labor union. Farm organizations, if not all farmers, for the first time in the 1930s came to fully understand the techniques of political activity. The businessman turned to government for credit when he could not get it elsewhere; the home builder sought government aid for his business; the transportation industries sought government subsidies; even the banker, traditionally the most conservative of businessmen, accepted the idea of government insurance on bank deposits so as to stabilize *his* business.

Wherever the hopes of men had been frustrated under industrial individualism, people were now able to turn to government to bridge the gap between what the person could provide for himself and what he believed he needed in order to possess a reasonable degree of psychological security. Even those who sincerely believed in individual self-reliance came to recognize that the great bulk of the breadwinners worked for someone else who decided, almost arbitrarily from the point of view of the individual, whether he was to be hired, fired, promoted, transferred, or raised in pay. Under such circumstances, the ideal way of life might lie beyond one's grasp and governmental activity in some areas might be a necessary evil in order to give the individual protection that the corporate system did not provide.

Rural versus Urban Social Systems   There was another factor, too, that made for collective action in the modern era: the trend toward an urban nation. The farmer and small-town dweller could, throughout American history, provide most of his own household services. He built his house on top of a knoll—there were usually plenty of them to choose from. He dug his own well. He constructed his own outhouse—it was inexpensive sanitary engineering, and the inconvenience caused on a winter's night was, like dying, taken to be one of the inevitabilities of life. In the large frame farmhouse, there was room enough to care for retired parents (physical disability was the only consideration in retirement, and it generally came gradually, without the shock that sudden retirement on one's sixty-fifth birthday later came to be) and for widowed or orphaned relatives. If a farmer or small-town merchant became ill, his relatives and neighbors saw to it that his work was carried on for him until

[64] Quoted in Grimes, *op. cit.*, p. 40.

such time as he was restored to health. Involuntary unemployment was un-known. True, profitless years were common enough; but the garden and hog lot provided food even during the worst depression, and the woodlot or corn-crib could supply fuel.

An urban society was a totally different society, however. Not everyone could live on the hill, and on flat or low land only the government could pro-vide the type of drainage needed. Where great numbers of people lived in close proximity, water and sewage were both matters of prime public-health consideration. Ultimately, the only safe way was through providing carefully engineered—and expensive—physical plants to supply water and to dispose of sewage. Again, it was government that could best handle the situation; certainly it was unthinkable for the individual to do it alone. Houses became smaller—there was no longer room for retired parents, widowed sisters, or orphaned nephews. Relatively few people found that they could provide ade-quately for their own retirements independently of their children. Yet the chil-dren too often could afford neither to feed nor house their parents. And even the elderly person who was willing to work found that there were no jobs to be had—he was "too old."

Illness or injury now spelled economic disaster to the factory worker or the white-collar clerk whose pay offered little opportunity for saving. Certainly friends or relatives could not take over his job for him temporarily—and busi-ness and industrial leaders refused to consider such personal tragedies as a social cost chargeable to the firm. Unemployment of an involuntary nature became not merely a potential threat—it became commonplace. A man who worked for another man, or worse, for an impersonal corporation, might be laid off at any time for being ill too much of the time, for becoming superannuated, because the nature of the business was cyclic or seasonal, because of a de-pression or financial panic, or even because of a personality conflict with the foreman or personnel officer.

Urban society, therefore, produced economic interdependence where independence had once existed. It produced insecurities nearly unknown in an agrarian society. These circumstances caused people to look around for a social institution to help them regain the poise and security that had slipped away from them. The most likely candidate—perhaps the only one available, in fact—was government. And its politicians responded to the call when it came.

The new ideology brought another party—at least on the national level—into the position of dominance. The Democratic party came to be associated with the ideology of the social service state. The complicated and elaborate system of government that resulted, and the need for direction to be given the movement, resulted in a renewed emphasis upon the executive branch of government. Governors and the President became the individuals from whom policy leadership came to be expected. The new hero was the common man for the working class and the conformist for the middle class. How long the ideology would retain its vitality or how it might be modified with the passage of time, no one could anticipate. But it was significant that many Republicans, including some who were conservative by personal conviction, talked "modern Republicanism" and had come to see that, in most parts of the United States, elections could be won only by a basic acceptance of the social service state.

As this ideology has spread deeply into both major political parties, suburbia, and most of the major interest groups, liberal reformers—in order to remain in the vanguard—have had to move on to new positions. In the 1960s, their fundamental concern was with the civil rights movement. Economic and social issues were interpreted in terms of their meaning for minority-group, and especially Negro, advancement.

One observer has commented on contemporary American left-wing ideology in the following fashion: [65]

The liberal ideology of the 1930s which linked together students, trade unionists, Negroes, the poor, the unemployed, the teachers, anti-fascists, and political radicals, no longer exists. Teachers are non-political members of guilds and associations, the unions are conservative in social philosophy, some are anti-liberal. The tension between labor and capital that gave an ideological flavor and a moral content to political and social action has disappeared into a dialectic of bargaining strategies supported by economic and social ambitions on both sides.

Contemporary advocates of liberalism, particularly the leaders of the civil-rights movement, emphasize their belief in the essential unity of the United States, while right-wing leaders emphasize the desirability of local decision making. Thus, the well-known Negro leader, Martin Luther King, has commented: [66]

I am cognizant of the interrelatedness of all communities and states. I cannot sit idly by in Atlanta and not be concerned about what happens in Birmingham. Injustice anywhere is a threat to justice everywhere. We are caught in an inescapable network of mutuality, tied in a single garment of destiny. Whatever affects one directly affects all indirectly. Never again can we afford to live with the narrow, provincial "outside agitator" idea. Anyone who lives inside the United States can never be considered an outsider anywhere within its bounds.

The radical left of the 1960s, as well as the far right, has engulfed state and local governments in social movements. In the past, government played a relatively small part in most social movements and, where it was involved, it was usually the national government that was the active participant. In the 1950s, right-wing leaders came to recognize that many of the changes they advocated could be brought about only by bringing pressure to bear upon state and local governments. These were, of course, the governments they hoped could replace the national government in many areas if, indeed, nongovernmental institutions could not replace the national government.

Beginning around 1960, left-wing leaders also began to pressure state and local governments. In the past, local governments had been principally records keepers, providers of consumer amenities, and executors of state

[65] Harold Taylor, "American Idealism, 1965," **Saturday Review,** June 26, 1965, pp. 14–16.
[66] Martin Luther King, Jr., "Letter from Birmingham Jail," **Christian Century,** June 12, 1963, p. 767.

criminal laws. State government had established the basis for criminal law, commercial relationships, higher education, the custody of felons, and the care of the mentally ill. Its functions had not been much broader than this until the 1930s. At that time, it began to provide financial aid from its more substantial tax base to local governments for health, education, and welfare functions, in particular. In the 1960s, however, pressures began to be exerted upon both state and local governments by social reformers, for they were the agencies that determined, fundamentally, which laws were to be enforced and to what extent. In particular, state and local governments controlled the fundamental decisions on matters of greatest importance to the civil-rights movement. In demanding equality in the enforcement of the law, in employment opportunities, in housing, and in the general amenities of life, the reformers tended to be as intolerant as were their counterparts on the right. They were unwilling to compromise and refused to abide by the traditional approaches to state and local policy making through negotiation and compromise. They borrowed many techniques used by the leaders of organized labor in the 1930s, and by European reformers and student movements, such as picketing and sit-ins. The result was to make state and local governments more dramatic, more newsworthy, and the center of more significant decision making than had been the case at perhaps any other time in American history.

The Need for Executive Leadership The new social service state required political leadership, and candidates for the offices of President, governor, and mayor responded with a will. But the increasing complexity of government also brought about considerable concern over the problem of the place of a large public bureaucracy within a democracy and over the seemingly endless yards of red tape that were being produced in Washington, Albany, Austin, and every state or city.[67]

The professional level of public administration in the United States had undergone a decline in the years following the Civil War. Yet, at the same time, in the face of an urbanizing trend and an increase in the need for specialization and competence at all levels of government, the need for better administration increased. Advocates of the efficiency-and-economy movement had stressed the need for neutral competence in the bureaucracy, but this goal had proved inadequate to meet modern needs, principally because the advocates had assumed a sharp distinction between policy making and policy administration, a distinction which did not actually exist.

A new doctrine of administration arose at this time, one that might be called the doctrine of executive leadership.[68] In a day when the chief executive had emerged as a public hero, as the chief innovator of policy, and when the earlier doctrine had helped to encourage fragmentation of government rather than coordination among its parts,[69] it was natural to think of this officer as a potential chief administrator. The new attitude was reflected in the

[67] On the problems of bureaucracy, see chap. 12.
[68] See Kaufman, *op. cit.*, pp. 1062–1073.
[69] On administrative concepts and problems, see chap. 14.

trend toward executive budgets, and in control over the personnel system by a personnel officer responsible to the chief executive, a practice which originated in cities with the council-manager form of government. Administrative reorganization movements became popular. On the state level, they sought concentration of administrative power in the governor (a policy also supported by efficiency-and-economy-movement advocates who had, however, not supported giving the governor control over personnel). In cities, the movement centered in the drive for the strong-mayor and council-manager forms. Movement toward streamlined administration was delayed, however, especially in state governments, because of obstructionism by interests seeking preferred status for agencies of special concern to them and by conflicting rural-urban points of view, and by continued skepticism on the part of many persons concerning the legitimacy and adequacy of proposed administrative reorganizations.

States' Rights in Modern Times   The trend toward bigger government brought increased confidence to many citizens concerning the trustworthiness of government as an instrumentality for social action. The concept of cooperative federalism became widely accepted. But the older idea of states' rights retained much of its vitality, as did that of individualism.

It was noted earlier that states' rights was used as an argument for those who, like many small businessmen, remained unreconciled to the concept of the social service state. It was used as an argument by the oil companies seeking to deprive the Federal government of control over offshore oil reserves. It was also a principal weapon of many of the opponents of desegregation in the struggle for equal facilities.

Watching government grow, many a conservative has complained of a continuing march on Washington. State governments, which his cynical father had bribed or ignored, became objects of admiration for the person seeking to preserve the *status quo*. His point of view was nicely expressed for him by the best known of all the protagonists for the social service state. Said Franklin D. Roosevelt, the Governor of New York, in a 1929 complaint: [70]

If there is a failure on the part of a State to provide adequate educational facilities for its boys and girls, an immediate cry goes up that a department of education should be established in Washington. If a State fails to keep abreast with modern [health] provisions, immediately the enthusiasts turn to the creation of a department of health in Washington. If a State fails adequately to regulate its public service corporations, the easiest course is to ask the Interstate Commerce Commission or the Federal Trade Commission to take jurisdiction.

But the facts do not support the charge that state and local governments are vacating their policy-making responsibilities, and the doctrine of states' rights remains essentially a weapon of ideological warfare.

Closing Statement   This chapter has dealt with the way in which various ideas and values become intertwined and become the basis for attitudes and senti-

[70] Quoted in Freidel, *op. cit.*, pp. 71–72.

ments which in turn serve as landmarks for the individual to use in determining his personal position on any issue of public policy or toward the statements of any politician. The concepts set out here, together with this brief administrative history of American state and local government, will be referred to again from time to time in later chapters.

SELECTED READINGS

Abcarian, Gilbert, and Sherman M. Stange: "Alienation and the Radical Right," **Journal of Politics,** 27:776–796, November, 1965. (Contains a good bibliography. Right extremists are found to have a distinctive ideology and political style, a latent sense of alienation.)

Adams, Henry: **Democracy:** New American Library of World Literature, Inc., New York, 1961, paperback. (First published, 1880.) (A novel, published anonymously, by a member of one of America's most aristocratic families. Adams viewed with horror and disdain the vote buying and election rigging that was part of the status striving of the immigrant Americans of the 1870s.)

Bernstein, Marver H.: "The Political Ideas of Selected American Business Journals," **Public Opinion Quarterly,** 17:258–267, Summer, 1953.

Billington, R. A.: "How the Frontier Shaped the American Character," **American Heritage,** April, 1958.

Blau, J. L. (ed.): **Social Theories of Jacksonian Democracy,** Hafner Publishing Company, Inc., New York, 1947.

Brown, Robert E.: **Middle-class Democracy and the Revolution in Massachusetts,** Cornell University Press, Ithaca, N.Y., 1955, chaps. 1–5.

————, and B. Katherine Brown: **Virginia, 1705–1786: Aristocracy or Democracy?** The Michigan State University Press, East Lansing, Mich., 1964.

Bryce, James: **The American Commonwealth,** The Macmillan Company, New York, 1888.

Buck, S. J.: **The Granger Movement,** Harvard University Press, Cambridge, Mass., 1913.

Bunzel, John H.: "The General Ideology of American Small Business," **Political Science Quarterly,** 70:87–102, March, 1955.

————: "Comparative Attitudes of Big Business and Small Business," **Western Political Quarterly,** 9:658–675, September, 1956.

Calhoun, John C.: **Disquisition on Government,** The Liberal Arts Press, Inc., New York, 1953. (First published, 1851.)

Childs, Richard: **Civic Victories,** Harper & Row, Publishers, Incorporated, New York, 1952.

Cochran, T. C., and William Miller: **The Age of Enterprise,** The Macmillan Company, New York, 1942.

de Tocqueville, Alexis: **Democracy in America,** many editions, original publication, 1835.

DeVoto, Bernard: **The Literary Fallacy,** Little, Brown and Company, Boston, 1944. (Discusses the tendency of Americans to misrepresent their homeland.)

Grimes, Alan P.: **The Political Liberalism of the New York Nation,** The University of North Carolina Press, Chapel Hill, N.C., 1953.

Harris, Robert J.: "States' Rights and Vested Interests," **Journal of Politics,** 15: 461, November, 1954.

Hartz, Louis: **The Liberal Tradition in America,** Harcourt, Brace & World, Inc., New York, 1955.

Hays, Samuel P.: **The Response to Industrialism,** The University of Chicago Press, Chicago, 1957.

Hicks, John D.: **The Populist Revolt,** The University of Minnesota Press, Minneapolis, 1931.

Hurst, James W.: **Law and the Conditions of Freedom in the Nineteenth Century United States,** The University of Wisconsin Press, Madison, Wis., 1956. (Shows that frontiersmen were pragmatists and not doctrinaire advocates of *laissez faire*. By a law professor.)

Kaufman, Herbert: "Emerging Conflicts in the Doctrines of Public Administration," **American Political Science Review,** 50:1057–1073, December, 1956.

Kramer, Dale: **The Wild Jackasses: The American Farmer in Revolt,** Hastings House, Publishers, Inc., New York, 1956.

Lerner, Max: **America As a Civilization,** Simon and Schuster, Inc., New York, 1957.

Lockridge, Ross, Jr.: **Raintree County,** Houghton Mifflin Company, Boston, 1948, paperback. (Excellent statement of frontier individualism in a novel.)

MacIver, Robert M.: **The Web of Government,** The Macmillan Company, New York, 1947.

Martin, Roscoe C.: **Grass Roots,** University of Alabama Press, University, Alabama, 1957. (A study of rural ideology.)

Miner, David W.: "Ideology and Political Behavior," **Midwest Journal of Political Science,** 5:317–331, November, 1961. (Examines the usefulness of ideology in analyzing politics.)

Parrington, Vernon L.: **Main Currents in American Thought,** Harcourt, Brace & World, Inc., New York, 1930.

Parsons, Talcott: **The Structure of Social Action,** McGraw-Hill Book Company, New York, 1937. (Chap. 14 has a summary and development of the Weberian thesis.)

Perkins, Dexter: **The American Way,** Cornell University Press, Ithaca, N.Y., 1957.

Richards, Allan R.: "The Traditions of Government in the States," **The Forty-eight States: Their Tasks as Policy Makers and Administrators,** The American Assembly, Graduate School of Business, Columbia University, New York, 1955.

Rossiter, Clinton: **Conservatism in America,** Alfred A. Knopf, Inc., New York, 1955.

Schlesinger, Arthur M., Jr.: **The Age of Jackson,** Little, Brown and Company, Boston, 1945.

Shannon, Fred: **American Farmers' Movements,** D. Van Nostrand Company, Inc., Princeton, N.J., 1957.

Sutton, Francis X., and others: **The American Business Creed,** Harvard University Press, Cambridge, Mass., 1956.

Tawney, Roger H.: **Religion and the Rise of Capitalism,** Harcourt, Brace & World, Inc., New York, 1926. (Criticism of Max Weber.)

Taylor, C. C.: **The Farmers' Movement,** American Book Company, New York, 1953.

Vidich, Arthur J., and Joseph Bensman: **Small Town in Mass Society,** Princeton University Press, Princeton, N.J., 1958.

Walter, Rush: **Popular Education and Democratic Thought in America,** Columbia University Press, New York, 1962. (Chap. 4 deals with 1830s and 1840s and Jacksonian Democrats' views.)

Weber, Max: **The Protestant Ethic and the Spirit of Capitalism,** English trans. by Talcott Parsons, George Allen & Unwin, Ltd., London, 1930. (A classic theory of motivation and the generation of ideology. Challenges the ideas of Karl Marx.)

White, Leonard D.: **The Federalists: A Study in Administrative History,** The Macmillan Company, New York, 1948.

————: **The Jeffersonians,** The Macmillan Company, New York, 1951.

————: **The Jacksonians,** The Macmillan Company, New York, 1954.

Whyte, William H., Jr.: **The Organization Man,** Doubleday & Company, Inc., Garden City, N.Y., 1956.

Williams, Robin M.: **American Society,** Alfred A. Knopf, Inc., New York, 1951.

3

FEDERALISM AND INTERGOVERNMENTAL RELATIONS

Government as we know it in the United States is based on the principle of federalism. It is characterized by a decentralization of power that was strongly favored in the early days of the Republic when means of transportation and communication were slow, patterns of life and cultural values differed widely from one part of the country to another, and the frontier commitment to individualism included support of grass-roots government. The structure that was developed over time provided for many tiers of government with greatly varied organizational patterns.

Americans today remain attached to the early principles of the federal system * and of grass-roots government, but modern means of transportation and communication, the growth of a nationwide economic organization, the almost nomadic tendencies of contemporary Americans, and other factors have contributed to the breakdown of political barriers. The popular concept of each level of government serving a specialized purpose and operating largely independently of government at other levels has had to be extensively modified in the twentieth century, especially after the Great Depression, in order to fit the characteristics of society as we now know it.[1]

* FEDERAL SYSTEM. A system in which power is divided between a central government and regional governments, each legally supreme in its own area of jurisdiction. Relationships between central and regional governments may be either competitive, cooperative, or a mixture of both.

CONFEDERATION OF STATES. A political association of independent states brought together for certain purposes, usually foreign diplomacy and mutual defense. Power

[1] The theory of federalism and the principal kinds of intergovernmental relations are discussed in detail in Charles R. Adrian and Charles Press, **The American Political Process**, McGraw-Hill Book Company, New York, 1965, and bibliography below.

relationships between levels are determined by agreements among the states, and the central unit possesses only delegated powers.

Table 5   Degree of Centralization in the American Federal System

	FUNCTION	CA. 1790	CA. 1850	CA. 1910	CA. 1964
1	External affairs	4	1	1	1
2	Public safety	5	4	4	4
3	Property rights	5	5	4	4
4	Civic rights	5	5	5	3
5	Morality	5	5	5	5
6	Patriotism	3	3	3	3
7	Money and credit	3	4	3	1
8	Transport and communication	4	4	2	2
9	Utilities	5	5	5	4
10	Production and distribution	5	5	4	2
11	Economic development	3	4	3	2
12	Resources	—	—	2	2
13	Education	—	5	5	4
14	Indigency	5	5	5	2
15	Recreation	—	4	4	3
16	Health	—	—	4	3
17	Knowledge	1	1	1	2
	Average	4.1	4.0	3.5	2.8

One interpretation of the relative importance of various levels of government. The higher the number, the greater state government influence is as compared with national.
SOURCE: William Riker, **Federalism**, Little, Brown and Company, Boston, 1964, p. 83.

The States in the Federal System

Why a Federal System?   The reasons for the existence of federalism in the United States or in any other federal nation are not known with certainty. Two generations ago, Charles Beard suggested that the federal system was the result of a plan by the economic elite of the late eighteenth century to continue to dominate the nation and to protect their own wealth. He saw domestic issues as being the overwhelming cause of the writing of the Constitution in 1787.[2] More recently, William Riker has suggested that the more centralized type of government under federalism as provided for in the Constitution was preferred over the earlier decentralized pattern provided in the Articles of Confederation out of considerations of military security. He concludes that the Constitution was written by men who were determined to establish a government better able to hold off the threats being made by the British and the Spanish against the young and weak American nation.[3] We need not examine the arguments in detail here, but perhaps it is relevant to note that both Beard and Riker may have been ensnared by the One Great Cause fallacy. It is rea-

[2] Charles A. Beard, **An Economic Interpretation of the Constitution,** The Macmillan Company, New York, 1913.
[3] William H. Riker, **Federalism**, Little, Brown and Company, Boston, 1964.

sonable to assume that both domestic and defense considerations were involved in the motivations of those who sought a new constitution in 1787 and who preferred a federal system to a confederation.

Federalism as Limited Government   Democracy in the United States is limited in a variety of ways. Powers of government are divided among the executive, legislative, and judicial branches, and this serves to limit to some extent the latitude permitted officials in each branch. A doctrine of civil rights is designed to reserve for the individual certain liberties which in theory may not be interfered with by government. A federal system further limits government by assigning certain powers and functions to each of the component parts of the system. Although in a nation as large as the United States is in both population and area, regional and local governments would probably always be necessary for administrative purposes, the federal system tends to preserve the states and local governments and to protect their policy-making powers. The states are formally recognized as existing independently of the national government, and this recognition actually predates the United States Constitution itself.[4]

The Federal System   In a formal sense, in a federal system of government, power is divided between a central government and various regional governments, each of which is supreme in its own area of jurisdiction. This system stands in contrast to that of the unitary system, in which the central government is supreme and the regional governments, if any, have only the powers assigned to them. And, of course, powers assigned by the central government may also be taken away.

In discussions of the preferred relationships between the national government on the one hand and state and local governments on the other, most discussions today tend to assume either the states' rights model of federalism, which presumes that the relationship is a competitive one in which the gains of the one side represent losses to the other, or the model of cooperative federalism, which assumes that domestic policy in the United States is made through the interaction of a large number of persons and institutions. It sees public policy as the result of shared decision making—a sharing among the national, state, and local levels of government, each having a voice and, frequently, an effective veto over proposed changes in that policy.

The model of cooperative federalism recognizes that some competition takes place within the federal system, but that it does not dominate the pattern of behavior. The principal divisions within the decision-making system are not between and among levels of government, but rather are between and among different functions of government. This is so because the functional specialists at all levels share the same values, goals, and professional associations. Public-health workers at one level of government have more in common with

---

[4] The national government is, of course, popularly referred to as the "Federal government," and the practice is continued in this book, even though technically the latter term should apply to the combined state-national system of government.

public-health workers at another level of government than they do with, say, highway engineers or educational officials at their own level of government. They share a common set of values which they believe to represent desirable public policy. As a result, they do not regard themselves as being exploited by or dominated by bureaucrats at a higher level of government. Friction is seen as taking place primarily between professionals and nonprofessionals at the same level of government or within the same governmental function and between the bureaucracy and the legislative branch. Professionals, chosen for their competence based on training and experience, will clash with persons in a particular functional area who hold their jobs as a result of a patronage personnel policy. The conflict between bureaucracy and legislature stems from the fact that the former seeks to defend professional values and standards, while the latter sees its social function as that of defending and furthering grass-roots values and goals.[5] This pattern of intergovernmental cooperation is not new in the United States. It has been characteristic of American federalism from the beginning.

As one specialist on the subject has noted: [6]

Because of the present pervasiveness of government in the United States, this means that every level of government is involved in virtually every governmental activity. Intergovernmental relations may involve informal co-operation, contracts for simple sharing, interchange of personnel, interdependent activities, grants-in-aid, tax offsets, and shared revenues. The precise character of the co-operative relationship is tailored to fit each program through the political process in which representatives of the Federal, state, and local governments and concerned private interests all participate.

In emergency situations, the cooperative effort of all levels of government is best exemplified. The great Alaska earthquake of 1964 and the Mississippi River flood of 1965, which was the worst in the history of the great river, produced responses involving the cooperative efforts of many different agencies, such as Civil Defense, which is a national, state, and local activity. The National Guard has a part to play at such times. So do national, state, and local engineers and public-health officers. And if the President can be persuaded to establish a disaster area, a large number of Federal agencies are activated.

The cooperative pattern has become all-encompassing in domestic policy making: [7]

The American citizen of today is involved in intergovernmental relations, whether he knows it or not. The basic problems in this field are just about universal among governments, whether federally organized or unitary in structure. Intergovernmental relations are not a sporadic or a specialized type of activity, they are part and parcel

[5] Charles R. Adrian, "State and Local Government Participation in the Design and Administration of Intergovernmental Programs," **Annals,** 359:35–43, May, 1965.
[6] Daniel Elazar, "The Shaping of Intergovernmental Relations in the Twentieth Century," *ibid.,* pp. 10–22.
[7] W. Brooke Graves, **American Intergovernmental Relations,** Charles Scribner's Sons, New York, 1964, pp. 927–928.

of the everyday operation of government. American government is not a three-layer cake; involvement is widespread and interpenetrating. It is useless to attempt to "unwind" the federal system, as some recent attempts to solve intergovernmental problems have advocated.

The Influence of Lower Levels of Government   Shared decision making offers an opportunity for influence to flow upwards as well as downwards. Public officeholders and bureaucrats at one level of government influence decision making at higher levels of government in at least four different ways. The first of these is lobbying. Not only do individual states and populous cities and counties sometimes have their own lobbyists in Washington and local units in the state capital, but many special organizations permit various groups to lobby collectively. The Council of State Governments speaks for many state positions in Washington. In recent years, the Council has been controlled by relatively conservative groups and has tended to accept the states' rights model of federalism, but in earlier years it had placed greater emphasis upon cooperation. Perhaps it will do so again in the future. The Council has spawned many organizations which, in turn, also lobby. For example, the National Governors' Conference, the National Conference of Chief State School Officers, and the National Association of Attorneys General are important. For cities, the United States Conference of Mayors and the American League of Cities lobby. At the local level, similar agencies exist for collective lobbying of state government. There is, for example, the state educational association (which has its national counterpart in the National Educational Association), the state leagues of cities, and such specialized organizations as the state association of justices of the peace.

Second, and somewhat related to the first, is the continuous interaction through common interests, and often a common political party, of officeholders at all levels. Legislative districts have traditionally—although there are many exceptions—been based upon the county or groups of counties. This has led in many cases to close working relationships between county officers and state legislators. The county officer who wants or opposes a particular piece of legislation, therefore, frequently has direct access to the critical decision makers. Frequently they share a set of interests that provide the basis for understanding relationships. Governors are in frequent contact with congressmen and senators relative to legislation affecting their states. Mayors, particularly those of the largest cities in the state, also have such contacts.

Third, persons in offices at higher levels of government are frequently sympathetic to the policy demands of lower levels of government and frequently carry to the higher office a set of experiences and policy preferences which they had accumulated at the lower office. Many a United States senator and congressman is a former governor or mayor, or has held some other state or local office. Many legislators are former county or municipal officeholders. Few persons are elected to the governorship without previous experience in some other state or local office.

Finally, one level of government influences policy at higher levels through imitation. Much of the domestic policy enacted by Congress reflects in part, at least, experiences in particular states which serve to pioneer legislation on the subject. State legislation, too, is frequently a modification of practices developed at the local level. In particular, the larger cities and counties of the state seem to be important innovators of policies that are later applied on a statewide basis. In addition to these vertical patterns of influence, states often pattern their own legislation on that already adopted in other states, and local governments tend to imitate other local governments.

The Weaknesses of the States

A study of high school students in three small cities in 1965 showed that the great majority of them had a favorable image of government at all levels. But it was significant that all of the students collectively rated the national government ahead of either the state or local government in terms of its effectiveness. Local governments were viewed as the least effective of the three levels. All levels of government were believed to show considerable concern for the problems of people. Significantly, the Federal government was rated about equal to local government in this respect.[8]

Even though the states are active in a very large number of areas of public policy development and administration, the expansion in their activities since the 1930s is largely a result of shared activities, by working jointly with local and national governments. In referring to the states, former Governor Terry Sanford of North Carolina has noted that, "because of their timidity and lack of initiative, it has become the pattern to turn to the Federal government for the solutions of problems."[9] After the Alaska earthquake of 1964, the executive director of the American Municipal Association raised the question whether there was not a need for a national policy of disaster aid. He also called for a disaster insurance program. In both cases the appeal was to the national government rather than to the states. At about the same time, Congress began to consider laws controlling the mail-order shipment of guns and ammunition and other laws to control the purchase and possession of arms. Again, Congress was considering public policy in an area where most of the states had failed to adopt modern regulations reflecting a metropolitan as distinguished from a frontier nation. After professional heavyweight boxing reached a new low in public confidence in the middle 1960s, there were many demands from sportswriters and others for some kind of Federal control of boxing. Again, the states had failed to provide adequate legislation.

In 1964, Lansing, Michigan, urban renewal officials inspected renewal programs in three Ohio cities, Akron, Canton, and Cleveland. Akron and Cleveland had used Federal aid in their renewal program, while Canton used only municipal and private funds. A reporter noted:[10]

---

[8] Arthur R. Stevens, "Political Culture in the Tri State Area of Michigan, Indiana, and Ohio," term paper, Michigan State University, East Lansing, Mich., 1965.
[9] Terry Sanford, press conference, Washington, D.C., Apr. 6, 1965.
[10] State Journal (Lansing, Mich.), Oct. 20, 1964.

The trip left the visitors with a strong impression that the Canton program, while to be admired for its "bootstrap" and independent attitude, was lagging behind those in its two sister cities.

Governor Sanford has observed that while he was in office he was forced to conclude that state governments had not become "the instruments of aggressive, imaginative, innovational service to the people." With assistance and leadership from the better-qualified Federal bureaucracy and financially stronger Federal government, however, the states are playing an active cooperative role.

Pressures for innovation and change commonly come from outside the state-local complex of governments. In the mid-1960s, action on social reform was taking place in the South, but largely not as the result of actions initiated by governments in the region. Those Southern states that had, up to that time, made only token efforts toward integration, speeded up their activities. Integration became closer to a reality. The reason for this could be found in provisions in the Civil Rights Act of 1964 which required that each school district file a plan and timetable for integration. Districts failing to file a satisfactory plan were to be deprived of Federal aid. The Federal government was, at first, relatively generous and few districts were actually deprived of their funds in most of the states of the old Confederacy. But the pressure had been applied and was not likely to be relaxed.

Cooperative federalism may be losing some ground as a result of the lack of initiative and innovation on the part of state governments and some local governments. Thus the Advisory Commission on Intergovernmental Relations has been looking for "ways in which national power could be wielded to preserve state and city executive leadership and legislative control, and to enhance accountability of governments to voting publics." [11] Unless state governments become more vigorous and more innovative in approaching the problems confronting most Americans, that is, persons living in metropolitan areas, federalism may be kept alive principally through the tolerance and urgings of national government officials. The problem, as seen by many political scientists, has not been one of the Federal government's usurping powers and activities so much as it has been a failure of the states to perform at a level equal to that of the Federal government or of the most modern city governments. The so-called Dirksen Amendment, proposed in 1964 and 1965, which would overrule the Supreme Court decision requiring both houses of a state legislature to be apportioned according to population is another example in a long line of examples of conservatives, who in theory favor the strengthening of state and local governments, acting, in fact, so as to make them less *timely* and hence less appropriate to meet contemporary political demands and to remain active and effective agents for the meeting of contemporary political demands.

In 1965, Congress established an eleventh Cabinet post for the United States with the creation of the Department of Housing and Urban Develop-

[11] Henry Hart, "The Dawn of a Community-defining Federalism," **Annals**, 359:147–156, May, 1965.

ment. This Department absorbed functions from a number of existing agencies, and the Housing and Home Finance Administration became the core of the new department. The Department itself had been urged for many years under one title or another. Opposition to it had centered in the House of Representatives, where congressmen from rural and small-town districts sometimes opposed the measure, probably because the effect of the creation of the agency would be to spend greater amounts of Federal funds in urban areas. Some opposition also came from conservatives who thought that Cabinet status would give the agency greater bargaining power in seeking funds for urban programs. Indeed, proponents of the measure urged the change for the same reason and argued that a Department of Housing and Urban Development would, through giving greater status to its activities, focus more attention on urban problems.

The best friends of state governments over the years have been conservatives. These persons have frequently argued the competitive theory of federalism and have urged that the Federal government remain out of many public policy areas, which they believe should be left to the states. In many cases, these conservatives have favored state control, not because they believed it would be more effective or more representative, but because they believed they had a better chance of dominating state government and their objective was to avoid legislation rather than to improve government or to make it more rational as a system.[12] This negative purpose of many conservatives has had a weakening influence upon state government.

Conservatives, supported by the Council of State Governments, have urged a number of amendments to the United States Constitution which would have the effect of weakening the power of the national government. They are based upon the competitive theory of federalism. One of the proposals would establish a Court of the Union, composed of the chief justices of all the states, with power to review judgments of the United States Supreme Court. A second proposal would set aside the cases which require state legislatures to be apportioned according to population in both houses.

The third proposal would permit greater power on the part of the states over amendments to the United States Constitution. At the present time, the amending procedure is controlled entirely by Congress. It can submit an amendment to the states for consideration by a two-thirds vote in each house. It also controls the situation—never used to date—in which two-thirds of the states could petition for the holding of a national constitutional convention. Although the courts have never ruled, authorities generally agree that Congress could ignore petitions from two-thirds of the state legislatures and that there is no way to force the calling of such a convention. The proposed change in Article V would abolish the never-used convention procedure and establish instead a method which could be controlled entirely by two-thirds of the state legislatures. The proposal provides: [13]

12 See Robert J. Harris, "States' Rights and Vested Interests," Journal of Politics, 15:457–471 November, 1954.
13 Charles L. Black, Jr., "The Proposed Amendment of Article V," Yale Law Journal, 72:958–966 April, 1963.

Whenever applications from the legislatures of two-thirds of the total number of states in the United States shall contain identical texts of an amendment to be proposed, the President of the Senate and the Speaker of the House of Representatives shall so certify, and the amendment as contained in the application shall be deemed to have been proposed without further action by Congress. The proposal would then go back to the state legislatures for approval. The only difference would now be that three-fourths of them would have to approve. In other words, if 34 states were to propose an amendment, it could be adopted by securing only four additional state legislatures' support. If adopted, the proposal would make it possible for the state legislatures to hamstring the Federal government, although there is nothing in the proposal or in the statements of its proponents to indicate that the resulting power vacuum would be filled by the states.

Someone once suggested that with friends like these, the states do not need enemies. But the states do have enemies. At least, some persons doubt that they can any longer perform a meaningful function in our society. The British political observer, Harold J. Laski, reached this conclusion in the 1930s,[14] and his view has been repeated by liberals in the 1960s. One writer has noted that: [15]

Even a casual survey of 20th Century American politics suggests that the major pillars of the *status quo* have been the fifty states. Conversely the major force for innovation and progress has been the Federal government. States have occasionally served as "laboratories of democracy," trying out on a small scale ideas which spread across the country once they prove workable. (California's two-year "community colleges" are an example.) States have also, occasionally, proved more responsive than the Federal government to the needs of their residents. But these are the exceptions. More often, the Federal government, with its vast resources and comparatively innovation-minded officials, has been the sponsor of new and experimental programs. This has been true of almost every scientific and technological area; it has been true in fields like criminal law and penology, in the operation of public parks and conservation programs, and recently in educational research and development.

This writer concludes that the states are hopelessly inappropriate for today and that almost all of them "have proved beyond a shadow of a doubt that they are basically unfit to govern."

It is probably fair to conclude that state governments are not crippled by Federal government action nearly so much as they are by their own failure to modernize: [16]

Certainly the weaknesses plaguing state governments cannot all be traced to one source. Some result from the operation of a federal system. Competition among states tends to drive standards to the level of the lowest common denominator and encourages cut-rate practices such as Nevada's gambling and divorce industries. A good many of the worst weaknesses of state government, however, are unnecessary. These recognized shortcomings, we believe, are traceable to the failure of state governments

[14] Harold J. Laski, "The Obsolescence of Federalism," **New Republic,** May 3, 1939, pp. 367–369.
[15] Christopher Jencks, "Why Bail Out the States?" *ibid.,* Dec. 12, 1964, pp. 8–10.
[16] Charles Press and Charles R. Adrian, "Why Our State Governments Are Sick," **Antioch Review,** 53:100–120, June, 1964.

to reflect the modern viewpoints held by a large majority of their citizens. We charge that ideas dominant among the decision makers for state governments lack *timeliness*. By this we mean that the ideology to which decision makers are beholden is not appropriate as a yardstick against which to judge proposed public policies for today because it is appropriate for a rural, small-town, preindustrial society rather than for our contemporary urban society. Furthermore, it is outmoded because many of its assumptions are based on folk beliefs rather than on the scientific study of psychology, psychiatry, economics, engineering, and other fields that have advanced rapidly in recent decades.

The tendencies of the states to lag behind and for the Federal government to exploit new technological developments has been dramatized many times. One example is in the approach taken to the use of the airplane. The United States War Department announced its intention to purchase airplanes in 1907, only four years after the Wright brothers' famous flights at Kitty Hawk. It was not until the 1920s that state and local governments became seriously interested in furthering aviation.

At one time state governments were known as experimental laboratories in American democracy. Some of them pioneered in a large number of areas, including woman suffrage, child labor, railroad and public-utility regulation, unemployment compensation, old-age pensions, and factory inspection.[17] Some experimentation is still continuing, as in the case of California and higher education, Minnesota and mental-health rehabilitation (in the 1940s), and New York in the support of the arts, but for the most part, the states have reacted to pressures and demands exerted through the Federal government. They have largely ceased to be innovators and, historically, their failure in this respect coincides with the decline in the representativeness of state legislatures of the mainstream of American wealth production and life styles. As a result, the Federal government has adopted legislation or is considering legislation for a vast number of urban problems. It, rather than the state governments, has been seeking to find new approaches to the problem of juvenile delinquency, to remove junk yards and tasteless billboards from along our highways, for slum clearance, for low-income housing, for mass transportation, and for a dozen other serious social problems. Not all these problems could be solved by state action alone, just as the states would not have been able to solve the problem of unemployment compensation, given the competitiveness among states for industry, without some Federal action. But many social problems stemming from an urban way of life could have been met effectively by the state governments, had they been willing to try to meet the challenge.

The Balance of Federalism in Modern Society

The question of the balance of American federalism has long been debated. The controversy involves both the matter of the actual trends in the balance and that of the desirability of trends. Some writers profess to see a constantly declining position of the states and their subdivisions; others see some

[17] James N. Miller, "Hamstrung Legislatures," **National Civic Review**, 54:178–187, April, 1965.

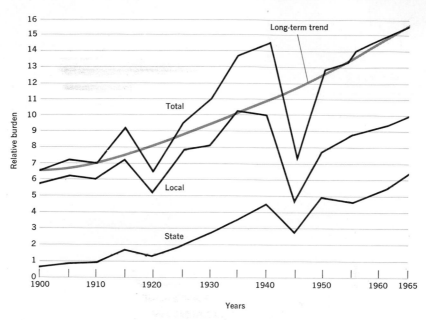

Fig. 3-1   The Burden of State and Local Services.
Relative burden refers to expenditures as a percentage of personal income.
SOURCE: Before 1930, R. W. Goldsmith, **A Study of Savings in the United States,** Princeton University Press, Princeton, N.J., 1956, vol. 3, p. 427. Since 1930, U.S. Department of Commerce.

changes, but with the lesser units retaining their vitality and importance.[18] There are those who bemoan the supposed decline of the states and their subdivisions [19] and others who would gladly see the end of any independence of the states as a supposedly necessary prelude to more effective American government under a central authority.[20] Some empirical evidence exists concerning the current relationship of the Federal government to the states and their subdivisions.

Even before the Constitutional Convention met in Philadelphia in 1787, the maintenance of the balance of federalism was a matter of public discussion. Many ideologies have been involved in the continuing controversy, and the predictions concerning the future of federalism have been varied. Will the state and local governments retain their policy-making powers in the future? Or are they gradually being made administrative units dependent upon the national government for financing and subject to basic policy decisions of Congress and the Federal bureaucracy?

A secondary controversy centers around the nature and effect of Federal grants-in-aid to the states and communities. The argument most commonly presented is that the states cannot remain independent in making policy while becoming financially dependent. On the other hand, the use of Federal grants-

[18] See the bibliography.
[19] Leonard D. White, **The States and the Nation,** Louisiana State University Press, Baton Rouge, La., 1953.
[20] See, for example, Laski, *op. cit.*, and the bibliography.

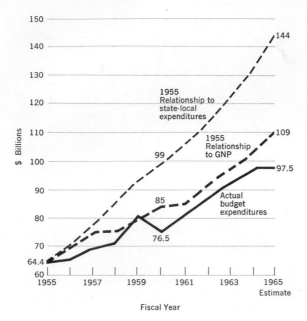

Fig. 3-2   Federal Expenditures Have Been Relatively Less than Those of State and Local Governments.
Shows what Federal expenditures would have been if the 1955 ratio with state-local expenditures had continued.

in-aid is defended, and principally on two grounds: first, the justification is made on the basis that the Federal government's greater taxing resources should be used to help lesser governments, with their more limited resources, to meet the cost of programs for which there is great demand; second, it is held desirable for the Federal government to prod the states and communities into taking action in areas where the latter have not acted for one reason or another, even though they are financially able to provide the service, and society wants the service to be provided. In other words, grants are defended as a means for offsetting alleged unrepresentativeness and irresponsibility in state and local government.

The Increased Number of Federal Grants In 1965, around seventy-one different grants-in-aid were offered by the Federal government to state and local governments. (The total number depended upon the way in which separate programs were defined.) [21] Probably the most important trend in the use of grants-in-aid is toward a proliferation of their number. The bulk of increased grant expenditures have come in the well-established fields of agriculture,

[21] See U.S. Advisory Commission on Intergovernmental Relations, **The Role of Equalization in Federal Grants**, 1964, and **Grant-in-aid Programs Enacted by the 2nd Session of the 88th Congress**, 1965; United States Senate, Committee on Government Operations, **Catalog of Federal Aids to State and Local Governments**, 1964, and **Supplement**, 1965; and United States Senate, Committee on Government Operations, **The Impact of Federal Urban Development Programs on Local Government Organization and Planning**, 1964.

education, highways, public welfare, and housing. The agricultural program increases have been substantial, but they have come largely through expansions in long-existing programs, especially through the 1955 amendments to the Hatch Act, which, beginning in 1887, has provided the basic support for agricultural experiment stations, and through the extensive rewriting in 1953 of the Smith-Lever Act of 1914 providing for the cooperative agricultural extension program.[22]

Housing grants date from 1937, but they were expanded by the Housing Acts of 1949 and 1954. In highways, grants have been a familiar part of the picture since 1916, but the Federal-Aid Highway Act of 1956 provided for a greatly expanded program in the coming years. Pleas for and against the Federal government's "entering" the field of aid to education have tended to obscure the fact that at least twenty-five Federal grant programs were already in existence in 1957 in the field of education. Public-welfare grants have been broadened in scope by frequent new legislation in the years since 1933.

Although these expanding older programs are themselves important, more significant implications for the future may perhaps be seen in the fact that almost every postwar session of Congress has added to the number of grants. In the postwar period, only the Eighty-second Congress, controlled by the Democrats but deeply engrossed in the problems of the Korean fighting and of "McCarthyism," failed to add to the list of grant programs. Even the Eightieth Congress, the leaders of which were committed to a program of retrenchment, passed the National Heart Act, the National Dental Research Act, and the Water Pollution Control Act, all of them in 1948 and all involving new grants-in-aid programs.

Grants as a Portion of State-local Expenditures   Despite the tendency toward an increase in their number, grants have not become a more important portion of total state and local expenditures in postwar years. In fact, up to 1957 they remained an almost stable portion of them, running to about 8.5 percent annually. The prevailing practice has been to spread the grants across the domestic-program panorama in a thin glaze.

Two other tendencies were pointed out by the Eisenhower-appointed Kestnbaum Commission on Intergovernmental Relations. That group noted a postwar tendency for grants "to recognize varying state fiscal capacity,"[23] that is, to make the size of the grant vary inversely with the state's ability to pay. This is in contrast to the almost universal prewar practice of distributing funds according to the amount of service needed and, with equalization as a justifying argument, may offer a basis for additional future grants in many areas. The commission also noted that nearly all grants have some strings attached to them, many of them highly important in their potential effect upon policy. Furthermore, "the conditions attached to grants have not remained mere verbal expressions of national intent; national agencies have generally had funds and staff to make them effective."[24]

[22] Rebecca L. Notz, **Federal Grants-in-aid to States,** Council of State Governments, Chicago, 1956, lists all Federal grants to 1956; Graves, *op. cit.,* Appendix A, lists them through 1962.
[23] U.S. Advisory Commission on Intergovernmental Relations, *op. cit.,* p. 121.
[24] *Ibid.,* p. 120.

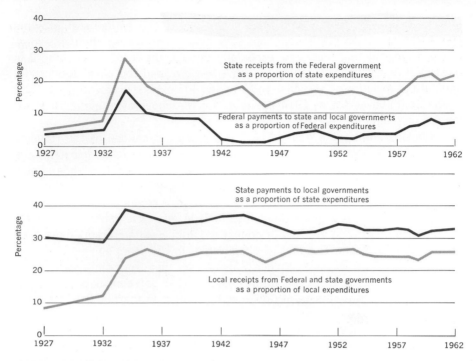

Fig. 3-3   Grants-in-aid as a Proportion of General Expenditures.*
* Years: 1927, even years 1932–1952, annually 1952–1962. Does not include insurance trust funds.
SOURCE: Frederick C. Mosher and Orville F. Poland, **The Costs of American Government**, Dodd, Mead & Company, Inc., New York, 1964, p. 52.

The Impact of Federal Grants   Many a writer has led his readers through a veritable chamber of horrors in discussing the dangers to be found in expanded Federal influence upon domestic programs. The fact is, however, that the specific impact of Federal grants upon policy is not known.

State and Local Expenditure Trends   State payments to local governments have been declining through the last generation. In total dollars, payments have increased, but in terms of proportion of total state expenditures—a more meaningful figure—they have been dropping. The figures are as follows: 1942, 31.1 percent; 1952, 36.8 percent; 1962, 34.9 percent.

State payments to local governments have closely reflected both the traditional American emphasis upon the importance of education and the longstanding domination of state legislators by rural and small-town interests. In 1962, one-half of state payments went to school districts. The counties received 28 percent. Municipalities brought up the rear with 19 percent. Most of the nonschool funds went for aid to public welfare and highways.

State financial aid is not of equal importance to local governments in all states. The states serving most importantly as collecting agents and as influences upon local government policy through grants-in-aid and shared taxes are California, New York, and Pennsylvania. In 1962, aid from these three states to their local governments accounted for 72 percent of the entire total in the United States. Very few states provide financial aid in some of the major areas of Federal activities, areas that involved important social problems for contemporary urban society, such as juvenile delinquency, mass transit, urban renewal, and public housing.

The Financial Balance of Federalism The scope of government in the twentieth century has expanded, but there has been "no substantial shift in such spending among levels of government since World War II."

A detailed study of American public finance found: [25]

In terms of direct domestic spending to the public, the local governments account for about half, the states for about one-quarter, and the federal government for about one-quarter. This has been true ever since World War II. Except for agricultural price support, the federal share in such domestic spending was, in 1962, only slightly higher than it had been in the first quarter of the century.

There has been no significant centralization in the financing of domestic activities of government through grants-in-aid since the Great Depression. Grants received by local governments stand in the same proportion to total local expenditures as they did in the mid-1930s, and there was no substantial change in the proportion during that period. The same was true of state governments until 1957, when the proportion of federal grants to state spending began to rise, principally because of the federal highway program.

Table 6 Expenditures for Selected Program Areas by Level of Government, 1962, percentages

	FEDERAL	STATE	LOCAL
Education	3	19	78
Fire protection	1	1	98
Health and hospitals	29	35	36
Highways	12	53	35
Public welfare	51	25	24
Natural resources	56	19	25
Sewerage and sewage disposal	1	1	98

SOURCE: U.S. Bureau of the Census.

State and local governments spend almost three times as much annually as does the Federal government on domestic programs. The expansion of the national government share of domestic program participation took place principally in the 1930s. Since that time there has been a slight decline in national government participation. At least this is the case in percentage terms.[26]

[25] Frederick C. Mosher and Orville F. Poland, **The Costs of American Governments,** Dodd, Mead & Company, Inc., New York, 1964, p. 66.
[26] James A. Maxwell, **Financing State and Local Government,** The Brookings Institution, Washington, D.C., 1964.

In the years since the Great Depression, state governments have grown more rapidly than has either the national government or local governments by a number of criteria. They have exceeded both national and local governments in terms of revenues collected, expenditures, growth of indebtedness, rate of increase in number of employees, salaries and wages paid, and new activities entered into. These activities represent a reflection of the pressures upon state governments resulting from an emerging urban society and the economic fact that it is easier to raise funds either by taxation or by borrowing at the state level than it is at the local level. These changes have taken place despite the malapportionment of state legislatures (measured in terms of population representation). If state legislatures are substantially reapportioned in the last half of the 1960s, as is generally expected, the states may become increasingly involved in modern serious urban problems. The states may become, in effect, metropolitan-area governments. Their already important function in society will expand as they are called upon increasingly to help meet the expensive and complex problems of an urban, industrial society.[27]

Federal Government Relations with State and Community

States and local governments are increasingly finding it to their advantage to have an ambassador located at the nation's capital. Governors and mayors are called upon to do a great deal of entrepreneurial work, making frequent trips to Washington to try for qualification under some aid program, to seek an atomic energy installation, to keep an Air Force base, and the like. The Council of State Governments and the Federal government provide an information service to state and local governments concerning available assistance and newest regulations. A private weekly reporting service provides information to local area development and renewal officials, community leaders, and public agencies.[28]

The Federal government has a great many nonfinancial contacts with the states and their subdivisions in the administration of governmental programs. Some of these are the result of strings attached to grants-in-aid, others are not. Collectively, they reflect the present-day trend toward the cooperation of administrative officers at all levels of government in seeking to provide socially wanted services despite the arbitrariness of political boundaries and the inappropriate distribution of tax resources among the various units of government.

National Government Advice and Assistance to States   The day-to-day relationships between the Federal government and the states are so many that they cannot be described fully, though the Commission on Intergovernmental Relations made an attempt. The variety of services is indicated by quoting a brief portion of the report of the commission:

[27] Charles R. Adrian, "Public Attitudes and Metropolitan Decision Making," in Russell W. Maddox, Jr., **Issues in State and Local Government**, D. Van Nostrand Company, Inc., Princeton, N.J., 1965, pp. 159–168.
[28] **Area Reports and Record Service**, Washington, D.C., weekly.

The National Government may collate facts about fields of State legislation and publish them. It supplies advisory leadership, as in the drafting of a model milk ordinance by the Public Health Service. It helps to improve local building codes through the technical work of the National Bureau of Standards. It assembles comparative information about State and local governments, as in the Governments Division of the Census Bureau. . . .

Often the National Government trains State and local personnel, and sometimes Federal employees are lent to the local levels. Ordinarily there is no statutory basis for these personnel arrangements. The Natural Gas Act, however, authorizes the loan of rate, valuation, and other experts as paid witnesses to State regulatory bodies. Some types of Federal employees become incidental agents of the States. A Federal law has long provided that Forest Service officials shall "aid in the enforcement of the laws of the States and Territories with regard to stock, for the prevention and extinguishment of forest fires, and for the protection of fish and game." State laws frequently endow Federal employees with the powers of peace officers.

The United States Civil Service Commission furnishes local personnel agencies with information on examination techniques and will furnish testing materials. The Bureau of Standards makes a great deal of technical information available to states and their subdivisions concerning commodity specifications, a valuable service since not many of these governments could afford to operate testing bureaus. The Bureau will make performance tests on all kinds of material and equipment at cost. It also provides communities with model building, fire, plumbing, elevator, and other codes.

The Bureau of Mines gives technical advice on air-pollution problems. The Public Health Service furnishes advice on sanitation problems. FBI agents not only arrest local law violators who have left the state but they testify without charge as experts in handwriting, tire treads, hairs and fibers, and shoe prints.[29] Many other Federal agencies cooperate with state and local officials, giving advice and assistance on everything from how to run a jail to how to care for an elderly elk in the local zoo.

Between 1951 and 1965, the Office of Emergency Planning of the Executive Office of the President provided about $200 million to help in reconstruction following major disasters. These funds and services are immensely varied. They include assistance in the clearance of debris and wreckage; emergency health and sanitation measures; emergency repairs for streets, roads, bridges, dikes, levees, drainage facilities, public buildings, public utilities; temporary housing and emergency shelter, and a variety of other financial aids and services.

Federal Approval of State and Local Activities   Whenever the states or any of their subdivisions are involved in activities over which the Federal government has final jurisdiction, they must conform to Federal regulations. Similarly, they must agree to the strings that are often attached whenever a grant-in-aid is accepted.

Thus, whenever Federal funds are involved in the construction of highways, the plans and technical specifications must be approved by the Bureau

---

[29] See Donald F. Whitehead, **The FBI Story,** Random House, Inc., New York, 1956, chaps. 15–17.

of Public Roads before a grant is made. In effect, this may leave final approval of routes as well as types of materials, and standards of construction to the Federal government. Before a state can receive Federal aid for public-welfare programs, it must establish a merit system for the selection of professional case workers and administrators.

If the state university operates a radio or television station, it must hold a Federal Communications Commission license; if the city or county builds a bridge over a navigable stream, it must have the plans approved by the Corps of Engineers. If a local housing authority accepts a Federal public-housing grant, it must agree to pay wages during construction not less than those provided under the Federal Minimum Wage Act. State-chartered banks may be insured with the Federal Deposit Insurance Corporation, but if they are, they must meet certain conditions of Federal law. Before a hospital can receive Federal funds under the Hill-Burton Act, the state must establish an agency to administer the program within the state, and that agency must prepare an overall state plan, dividing the state into hospital-service areas. Only a hospital fitting into the plan (and meeting certain minimum standards) may receive Federal aid.

The list of Federal supervisory controls is long. However, before reaching the easy conclusion that the Federal government makes all of the rules in modern American society, it should be pointed out that the areas of Federal control are relatively few and that it is not politically expedient for Congress or the Federal administration to seek to impose many effective policy controls upon the states or their subdivisions. But where they do exist, Federal controls are often essential. State and local radio stations, for example, could not operate effectively without being coordinated with commercial stations. Other rules are not viewed with alarm by state and local administrators because their sense of professional standards agrees with the professional standards of the Federal employees with whom they deal. They therefore see themselves as being involved in a cooperative venture to apply professional standards and do not feel coerced. This was the finding, for example, of the Michigan "Little Hoover" commission study in 1950. Furthermore, despite the impression often created, Federal administrators usually try to be reasonable in administering the law and seek to work out problems jointly rather than by fiat. Still, in the event of an unresolved difference between a Federal agency and the state or local government with which it is dealing, the Federal requirements must be met if the state or local government wishes to qualify for Federal aid.

Interstate Relations

The Founding Fathers, writing the Constitution for a nation that was to become "one and indivisible," recognized in the eighteenth century that not all people would remain within their native state. People would want to travel; they would want to do business in other states; criminals would seek to escape across state lines if the act of doing so might give them added protection. All of these possibilities were anticipated, and they were planned for so well that the same basic arrangements which were provided for in the original Constitution are in effect today.

Privileges and Immunities   The Federal Constitution guarantees a citizen of one state the privilege of traveling freely about the country, of moving from one state to another. While he is away from his state of residence, he may actually reside and live in another state, may use its courts, make contracts, marry, own property, or engage in business. He is also entitled to tax equality.

Some effective limits have been placed upon the privileges and immunities clause by the courts. It does not, for example, prevent states from distinguishing between domestic and out-of-state corporations in making regulations or determining fees. It does not guarantee that a person licensed in some trade or profession can practice in any other state. A physician or lawyer moving from one state to another will have to meet the requirements of the second state before he can practice. Unskilled persons or persons whose occupations are not deemed to be closely connected with the health, safety, or welfare of the public are not subject to this kind of limitation, however. A third area of restrictive interpretation of privileges and immunities is the one dealing with the property of the state. Since state universities are maintained in part by tax moneys paid largely by residents and fish and game of the state are fostered and protected by conservation officers, the charge to nonresidents may be, and often is, substantially higher than for residents.

Full Faith and Credit   This clause of the Constitution has been interpreted to mean that the court records, official documents, and vital statistical records of one state must be accepted in all other states. Thus, if the vital statistics of New Hampshire show that Torkelson was born in that state on a certain date, the officials of Oregon must accept that record for, say, the purpose of determining Torkelson's eligibility for old-age assistance.

Extradition   The Constitution provides for the return of fugitives from justice who have crossed state lines: [30]

A person charged in any state with treason, felony or other crime, who shall flee from justice, and be found in another state, shall on demand of the executive authority of the state from which he fled, be delivered up, to be removed to the state having jurisdiction of the crime.

The Supreme Court has ruled, however, that "shall" in the above quotation is permissive in character. The result is that the question of return is one that is settled by the governor of the state in which the person is apprehended. Normally, the fugitive is returned as a matter of routine. Frequently he waives extradition. If he insists, however, he is entitled to a hearing. For this purpose, the governor appoints someone, usually his legal advisor, to act for him. The accused is allowed to state the reasons why he thinks he should not be returned for trial or imprisonment. In some cases, the state issuing the extradi-

[30] Art. IV, Sec. 2.

attract industry, especially from other states, thus providing more jobs and ultimately a stronger tax base. Practices such as this are regarded by economists as unsound, but they are commonplace today and they encourage retaliation. Furthermore, these efforts to rob Peter to pay Paul appear to be largely ineffective, since industries are more interested in the availability of ample, low-cost labor and in proximity to markets than they are in tax patterns.

Interstate Cooperation   Although fears of an eroding economic base cause states to compete with one another, other pressures exist to encourage cooperation. The Constitution permits states, with the consent of Congress, to enter into agreements with one another. The general practice of Congress appears to be to approve these compacts if they do not threaten to reduce the power of the Federal government. In some cases, such as the Interstate Oil Compact, states have acted in order to try to reduce competition. That agreement seeks to prevent the waste of gas and oil through practices that would offer short-range competitive advantages, but would be against the best long-range interests of society, petroleum being an irreplaceable natural resource.

Perhaps the principal pressure for interstate agreements has come from professional administrators anxious to apply to their activities the standards they and their peers regard as desirable. Thus, the Crime Compact of 1934 is now subscribed to by all states, and parole officers are able to cooperate with one another, little hindered by state lines. An exconvict is freer, therefore, to move to a new area where he may be better received, while still subject to parole officer supervision. The Southern Regional Educational Compact permits states with poor professional training schools to send students to other states with the out-of-state tuition being billed to the sending state. A similar arrangement was established by the Western Regional Education Compact for the sparsely settled states of the West, where many of them cannot afford a full set of professional schools at their state university. Other compacts exist in regard to the care of welfare, tuberculosis, and mentally ill patients.

The need to coordinate planning and transportation and to prevent water and air pollution has also caused states to enter into compacts, as in the New York Metropolitan Regional Conference, a permanent organization of New York, New Jersey, and Connecticut local officials for the discussion of problems in the New York metropolitan area. Many agreements will probably result from metropolitan-area problems that spill over state boundaries.

Uniform State Laws   In 1892, the National Conference of Commissioners on Uniform State Laws was established. Since that time, the conference has agreed upon more than 100 proposed laws. The purpose of these is to simplify the conduct of business across state lines. The activities of the conference have been supported by many businessmen and by the American Bar Association, which helps finance it. All of the states have adopted the uniform laws on negotiable instruments, warehouse receipts, and stock transfer. Other uniform laws have been adopted by at least some of the states. In certain cases, a legislature has adopted one of the uniform laws but has modified some portions of it "to fit local circumstances," thus making it nonuniform. Furthermore, the same law has not always been interpreted in the same manner by the courts in various states; still, the work of the conference has helped simplify interstate relations.

The Council of State Governments In order to help state officials to share experiences related to common problems, the Council of State Governments was formed in 1925. Its staff conducts and publishes research valuable to administrators and to persons drafting legislative bills. Its monthly magazine **State Government** helps keep officials and interested persons abreast of developments in other states. The meetings, conducted by its various affiliate organizations—the Governors' Conference, the American Legislators' Association, the Conference of Chief Justices, the National Association of Attorneys General, and others—help to create an awareness of problems and to further interstate understanding. The organization has provided the opportunity for representatives of the various states to join in a search for areas of common interest.

The first governors' conference was called by President Theodore Roosevelt in 1908. A Senate Subcommittee on Intergovernmental Relations was established in 1947. It was allowed to lapse four years later. In 1949, the Commission on Organization of the Executive Branch of the Government (the first Hoover Commission) dealt briefly with the subject of intergovernmental relations. In 1953, a Commission on Intergovernmental Relations was established by President Eisenhower. It gave a report in 1955. In 1959, a permanent Advisory Commission on Intergovernmental Relations was established.

The Advisory Commission on Intergovernmental Relations This Federal agency was established by statute in 1959 as a permanent, bipartisan commission of twenty-six members, "to give continuing study to the relationships among local, state, and national levels of government." The membership of the Commission consists of three officers of the executive branch of the national government, three United States senators, three United States representatives, four governors, four mayors, three county officials, three state legislators, and three private citizens.

State Relations with Local Governments

Local governments are the children of the state. The state has been most unwilling to allow its children to grow up. A theory of perpetual infancy was adopted by nineteenth-century legislatures. Efforts at achieving independence for local governments through the legal device of constitutional limitations have been largely unsuccessful. Cities in most states did achieve more independence and experienced less legislative supervision of their affairs after the first decade or so of the twentieth century, but this seems to have resulted principally from a changing climate of opinion toward cities that accompanied the urbanization of the nation, together with a slight increase of public trust in the politician, both state and local. Other local units of government have been given little additional freedom from state control in recent decades. In the case of school districts, the trend has probably been in the opposite direction: The demand for higher educational standards has resulted in increased state supervision over local school-district activities.

Legislative Oversight of Local Government The traditional pattern of direct legislative supervision of local government administration has declined in the twentieth century. This happened not through accident but for a very good reason. As the twentieth century advanced, government got to be too complicated to be sufficiently understood by amateur legislators meeting for a few weeks annually or biannually as an interlude away from their full-time occupations. Local government, except in the rural and urban-fringe areas, became professionalized and technical; its complex details came to be understandable only to the professional, full-time technician. Flexibility, which legislatures did not possess, was needed. So was continuous, rather than sporadic, oversight. The twentieth century thus represented a period during which state legislators were somewhat reluctantly but inexorably forced to transfer increasing amounts of supervision over local government to the professional bureaucracies of the administrative branch of the state government.

State Judicial Oversight of Local Government Standing behind every local official, looking over his shoulder as the baseball umpire looks over the shoulder of the catcher, is a judge. He is the individual who settles all disputes between the local government and the state, a taxpayer and the local unit, one local unit and another. While he makes a determination only when asked to do so and then upon the basis of laws and ordinances made by other people, he is himself in a real sense a lawmaker, for the judge decides ultimately what the law *means* and hence what the local government can and cannot do. Because a local government is not a sovereign body, its standing at law is approximately the same as that of a private corporation, except when it is acting in the name of the state. Because of this legal position and because it enjoys only those powers granted to it under the principle of Dillon's rule, a local government is constantly faced with the task of proving in court that it has the power to do what it seeks to do.

State Administrative Oversight of Local Governments The administrative branch of state government follows the typically Jacksonian pattern of decentralization. Because of the influence of this frontier ideology, departments of local government, such as the Ministry of the Interior in France or the Ministry of Local Government in Great Britain, are not to be found in the United States. Administrative contacts between the city and the state are characteristically on a *functional* basis. That is, members of the state department of education oversee the activities of the local school district; the state department of health watches the activities of the local department of health; and so on. Canadian provinces, on the other hand, follow British and Continental practices of consolidation for the most part, and perhaps five American states have made some move toward centralized supervision.

Areas of Supervision   Which local government functions are subject to state oversight today? Most of them, might be a brief answer. But the state is especially watchful of local activities that involve (1) the expenditure of state grants-in-aid (e.g., in education, health, welfare, highways); (2) those areas of Federal grants-in-aid which are administered through the states but under conditions requiring state supervision of the expenditures (e.g., the building of airports in some states); and (3) those activities in which the state as a whole has a particular interest (e.g., the spread of communicable diseases, law enforcement, finances).

The degree of state control differs considerably from state to state, and the effectiveness of control by one department as against another may vary a good deal. A Minnesota study, for example, indicated that the department of health's supervision of local agencies was considerably less effective than was that of the division of social welfare.[35] There may also be differences between the law and the practice of state supervision. This results, for example, when administrators feel that they can accomplish more in the long run through cooperation rather than coercion and when public support for firm action is lacking.

The Minnesota study cited above also noted that state supervision had not been very extensive except in situations involving grants-in-aid. In particular, there were two general types of local units that were "supervised even less than others." These were the first-class cities of the state (Minneapolis, St. Paul, and Duluth), which were "often exempt by law or in practice from much of the supervision exercised over other local governments," and the smaller units of government. The smaller and the more rural a unit was, the less state supervision it received: [36]

Rural local health authorities are very seldom visited by the state; such visits require too large a staff and too great an expenditure on the part of the state. Welfare supervision, including relief, is quite effective as concerns the counties. In a few Minnesota counties townships administer relief; here supervision is not effective. . . .

Techniques of Supervision   One popular image of local government sees it as controlled by heavy-handed bureaucrats from the state capital, armed with court decrees and administrative orders. While these devices do play a part, most state agencies try persuasion, education, and other noncoercive techniques wherever possible. The big stick is brought into play principally whenever the state overseers find evidence of incompetence, irresponsibility, or corruption.

State agencies exercising supervision usually start by requiring reports from local communities. This serves the purpose of warning the state agency

[35] Edward W. Weidner, "State Supervision of Local Government in Minnesota," **Public Administration Review**, 4:226–233, Summer, 1944.
[36] *Ibid.*, p. 231.

when trouble spots begin to appear, and it tends to channel local activity, since the reporting official, knowing that he will be judged by his professional peers, will want a good record. Because reports do not necessarily require action, there is the problem of ensuring that they continue to perform a useful function. Some years ago in Minnesota, for example, the regulations of the state board of health required the health officer of each city and village to make an annual sanitary inspection of his community and to send a copy of the report to the state board. Actually, however, the state agency had no idea of how many inspections were being made and no one seemed to know why the information was filed with the state; no action ever resulted from the reports, and the state had no power to abate nuisances or to force local governments to do so. Still, bureaucracy is more self-correcting than the popular stereotype would hold—very few of the local health officers ever bothered to send in the report.[37]

State agencies can furnish advice and information. In the larger states, these services may be nearly as varied as those available from the Federal government. They are especially important for smaller communities, where amateurs may be floundering about seeking to do an adequate job with little experience or where overworked professionals may not have the time to keep up with the latest techniques in their fields. Sometimes the relationship between the state and the technical specialist from the large city or populous county may become strained when the local functionary thinks he is (or in fact is) professionally more competent than is his nominal supervisor on the state level. Is the manager of a large city airport able to get along without advice from the state airports commissioner? He is likely to think so. Sometimes a running feud of many years' duration may color relationships between a department of a large city and the corresponding agency of the state. Usually, however, relations are friendly and cooperative. The smaller cities and counties have technicians who are likely to recognize the genuine need for advice and to seek it. To simplify requests for such help, Tennessee has established a clearing house for information, the Municipal Technical Advisory Service, in connection with the state university, and some other states have municipal research bureaus which may or may not be connected with a state school.

One step beyond advice is technical aid. The state agencies, with (perhaps) relatively larger budgets and more specialized equipment and personnel, are particularly in a position to help out the local amateur or semiprofessional. How effective can the chief of police in a village of 1,500 people be against the professional criminal? And how much experience or scientific equipment can be put to use in the rare event of a murder in his town? What would his colleague, the water commissioner, know about the technical problems of drilling a new deep well for the town? And how much does the overworked local general practitioner really know about public health, even though he may bear the title of health officer? How much special equipment can the town afford when it is needed? The state of Michigan offers its communities technical aids that include assistance in determining which of the local records have histori-

[37] *Ibid.*, p. 230.

cal value and should be preserved, in helping local personnel officers to establish placement examinations, in understanding the complex bond market, in establishing a local traffic safety commission, in designing streets, and in laying out airports, among many others.[38] In many cases, local government services would break down without the help state agencies provide.

Other approaches failing, the state may also make use of its coercive power. Among other things, its agencies can grant or withhold permits for certain things (e.g., to dump raw sewage into a stream under prescribed conditions); or issue orders (e.g., to build a sewage-treatment plant); or issue rules and regulations which are technically called ordinances (e.g., to prescribe the standards for water-supply purification); or withhold grants-in-aid if standards prescribed by state, or sometimes Federal, law are not complied with; or review decisions of local agencies (e.g., the power of the state tax-equalization board to review the determination of local boards and perhaps to order reassessment in extreme situations); or require prior permission from a state agency (e.g., the power of some state health departments to pass upon the qualifications of local health-officer nominees); or appoint certain local officials or remove them (e.g., the local police chief or sheriff). It is even possible in most states, as a last resort, to apply substitute administration. That is to say, in extreme cases the state may suspend local self-government altogether for some or all functions and allow state officials to govern instead. This is particularly true in the fields of finance, public health, and education.[39]

Some states prescribe uniform systems of accounts for municipalities and other local units. About thirty states have some degree of state jurisdiction over auditing of municipal accounts. About twenty-two states require municipalities to submit financial reports to the state periodically. Many states provide budget forms or supervise local debt to one degree or another or even pass on the wisdom of a proposed issue. North Carolina and sometimes Virginia handle the sale of bonds to private investors on behalf of municipalities.[40] In most cases, however, these state activities are carried on in the time-honored decentralized manner.

Organization for Supervision   The increasing tendency in recent years to turn over state supervision to the administrative rather than to the legislative branch of government has probably changed the pattern of state-local relationships to a considerable degree. Local professional technicians feel more at ease and have less of a feeling that they will be exploited when they deal with state professionals rather than with the politicians of the state legislature. A smoother, more confident relationship is the result. The motivation of the

[38] Illustrations are based on two articles on state technical services by Lynn W. Eley, "State Agencies Provide Varied Services," **Michigan Municipal Review,** 29:188–190, October, 1956, and "State Technical Services to Municipalities," *ibid.,* 29:212–215, November, 1956.

[39] This section borrows from Dale Pontius, **State Supervision of Local Government: Its Development in Massachusetts,** Public Affairs Press, Washington, D.C., 1942; and **Report of the Council of State Governments, Committee on State-local Relations,** Council of State Governments, Chicago, 1946, part 2.

[40] F. E. McMillan, Jr., **State Supervision of Municipal Finance,** Institute of Public Affairs, University of Texas, Austin, Tex., 1953, provides details and has several charts showing the practice in various states.

An Office for Local Government was established in New York in 1959. The purpose of the Office was to assist the governor by providing advice relative to policy affecting local governments, to act as spokesman for local governments with regard to state programs, and to provide a service to municipalities through consultation and information.[46]

Many European democracies and all of the provinces of Canada have departments of local government under one title or another. They seek to coordinate the relationships between the central or regional governments and local governments. In some cases, the authority is much broader than it is in others. Because state-local relations have experienced a gradual, unplanned growth on a piecemeal, function-by-function basis, and because few systematic overhauls of local government have been made in this country, state-local relations have, for the most part, been uncoordinated as between functions. For any given function, such as public health or highways, coordination has commonly been effective, particularly through shared professional values, standards, procedures, and goals. But interfunctional coordination has been a problem. What is done by state and local highway departments may have an important influence upon, say, urban planning activities, or upon social welfare activities through the dispersal of welfare clients in the process of putting a freeway through a city. Often, conflicts of jurisdiction occur. For example, juvenile delinquents are of concern to persons involved in social welfare, mental health, and corrections activities at all levels of government. Before the Great Depression, few state agencies coordinated and supervised local governments.

Beginning in about 1957, and coincident with the rising demand for a Federal urban affairs department, state agencies for local government began to be created. These newer agencies have a great variety of powers and are organized in various ways. Quite a number are legislative agencies, designed to assist the legislature in the development of local-government legislation. Some are concerned primarily with finance. Hence, California in 1959 established a local allocation division and office of planning in the department of finance. This agency was oriented toward the approach earlier adopted in New Jersey. In Minnesota, the Municipal Commission, established that same year, is concerned fundamentally with the question of determining local government boundaries in metropolitan areas in a rational and systematic manner. Some are designed principally to provide technical information and assistance to local governments and may be connected with a state university. Thus, in 1959, Maryland established a Municipal Technical Advisory Service as a part of the University of Maryland. This agency was modeled on one by the same name established a decade earlier in Tennessee. Today, much interest centers around the establishment of state planning commissions and state agencies to provide areawide services, particularly in metropolitan areas.

Despite these trends, which are generally in the direction of aid and advice, most states for most purposes still accept the traditional pattern of functional interrelationships between governmental levels. Local governments

[46] **Office for Local Government,** State of New York, Albany, N.Y., 1964.

want help, especially financial help, from state governments. State governments, in turn, want similar assistance from the Federal government. No governmental unit wants to give up more discretionary authority than it must in order to gain the assistance it wants. Integrated departments of municipal affairs, such as those in New Jersey, North Carolina, and Indiana appear to be reasonably successful, in terms of acceptance, but they do not fit the general trend.[47]

Two basic issues are involved concerning the relationship of the state to local administration. One is that of the use of a single state agency over local affairs versus the use of functional relationships;[48] the other centers in the question of the degree of state coercive supervision over local governments, whatever the method of organization. Without much doubt, the overall supervision of local government by a single central department, as in France, results in a high degree of central control, not only over techniques, but over programs and policies. One of the strengths of local government in this country lies in the initiative and autonomy exercised by local officials, in contrast with the French municipal officer, who must get approval of even small decisions from the prefect who represents the Minister of the Interior. Overall supervision may lead to uniformity, which in turn may destroy the opportunity for experimentation. It is likely that in most states, administrative innovations have more often originated in the city hall than in the state capitol. And state services to local governments tend to be mediocre in quality and state departments sometimes have little interest in rendering services to local governments.

In general, technical assistance and advice rather than supervision and control are the ideal sought for in this country by both state and local officials. Although state supervision and control is sometimes used, the extent of state dictation to local officials has been relatively slight, and state officials have applied these sanctions only very reluctantly. In most cases, political expediency dictates this practice even when it is not called for by professional administrative procedure, as it usually is. Local officials are powerful and well organized for political action. The state agency that thoughtlessly seeks to apply pressure may find its appropriation for enforcement purposes reduced the next year. The advancement of standards, education, and techniques is being achieved, in any case, more through voluntary associations of local officials and professional technicians in the same field than through central tutelage of local officers.

The State and the Capital City   A special relationship necessarily exists between the state government and the capital city that houses not only the legislature, during its sessions, and the state officials but also most of the

---

[47] W. Brooke Graves, *op. cit.*, pp. 712–716; John G. Grumm, **A State Agency for Local Affairs?** Bureau of Public Administration, University of California, Berkeley, Calif., 1961.
[48] See **Report of the Council of State Governments, Committee on State-local Relations;** and Joseph E. McLean, "Threat to Responsible Rule," **National Municipal Review,** 40:411–417, September, 1951.

bureaucracy that administers the state's programs. Bitter—sometimes literally bloody—battles have been fought over the location of the state capital. It is regarded not only as a special honor for the community but is also a profitable plum for local businessmen. No doubt, no matter how much local people complain of the crowded public facilities of the city during legislative sessions or of legislative thoughtlessness in imposing costs upon the city, merchants would violently resist any attempt to move the capital elsewhere.

Many state legislators seem to believe that the added value of being the site of the capital is sufficient to offset any extra costs that may result from the state's doing its business. Some acts of the state annoy local residents a great deal, however. For example, in the postwar years the state of New York erected the Alfred E. Smith state office building to house 4,600 state employees—and provided a parking lot to hold exactly six automobiles.[49] Needless to say, Albany, like other American cities, has no surplus of parking spaces. One might wonder which were the more angry, the citizens of the city who worked in the building or those who did not.

In 1956, only three states paid some in lieu taxes on capital-city property. North Dakota pays special assessments only, Oregon pays a symbolic property tax of about $1,000, Pennsylvania pays Harrisburg about $5,000 a year to help fight fires, and six states supply all or most of the support for capital-city airports. There is no general pattern, either among the states, or even within many of the individual states. Legislators decide on an expedient basis whether they should pay something to the capital city, acting whenever outraged cries over some alleged injustice become sufficiently loud. State–capital-city relations and problems are similar to those found wherever the state establishes its institutions.

Interlocal Relations

Changing patterns of transportation and communication, in an age when local government boundaries, considering the total trend, are getting no larger and may even be shrinking, add to the frequency of contacts between local units of government. The increasing complexity of government, together with an expanding population, has also created circumstances which encourage local governments increasingly to work out their problems together.

Cooperative Arrangements   One study, inquiring into the means by which local governments have met service needs which transcend legal boundaries, has reported that: [50]

Informal cooperation among municipalities is one of the least tangible, but undoubtedly one of the most basic approaches to the solution of intermunicipal problems. It requires a language of standard definitions and a setting in which officials and citizens can meet to discuss common problems.

[49] Much of this section is drawn from a series of articles in the **Knickerbocker News**, Albany, N.Y., Aug. 28–30, 1956.
[50] George Goodwin, **Intermunicipal Relations in Massachusetts**, 1956, pp. 3–4. By permission of the publisher, The Bureau of Government Research, University of Massachusetts, Amherst, Mass.

The most significant part of informal cooperation consists of personal contacts among operating officials. State associations of municipal officers, many of which have regional subdivisions, are of great importance. Among others, there are state associations of mayors, managers, selectmen, finance personnel and law officers; and officials concerned with the functions of police and fire protection, public works, planning, health, welfare, education, and libraries.

Just as the Council of State Governments helps to bring state officials together in order to discuss their common problems and to seek to find bases for cooperation, so do these regional and state associations of local government officers and professional employees help to do the same thing on the local level.

Much of this informal cooperation takes place in metropolitan areas, where density of population is at its greatest and the nature of the provision of services is the most complex. For this reason, a discussion of some aspects of interlocal cooperation will be left to the chapter on government in metropolitan areas.[51] But these same general kinds of relationships also take place in relatively rural areas between counties or on a county-village or county-township basis.

For example, in Oregon: [52]

By far the most popular form of cooperation between counties consists of making agreements between adjoining counties for maintenance of border roads and bridges. Mosquito control activity is also the subject of cooperation between counties in a few areas.

County cooperation is facilitated through several voluntary organizations. The Association of Oregon Counties, which consists of the county courts in each county, has an annual convention and several regional meetings throughout the year. Separate organizations of Sheriffs, District Attorneys, Clerks, and other county officials also provide frequent opportunity for inter-county contacts.

Contracts   In addition to cooperative work on an informal basis, local units frequently make contractual arrangements with one another. Again, these arrangements are most likely to be found between a core city and its suburbs, but they also exist in semiurban and rural areas and between counties and the local governments within their boundaries. Some of the contracts are completely informal; some are authorized by statute and are formally drawn agreements. In Massachusetts, such contracts exist for the provision of high school education, for water and sewage disposal, and in the fields of welfare and health.[53] In Oregon, formal and informal agreements exist for the provision of such diverse services as library facilities, rodent- and dog-control programs, recreation programs, water supply, fire protection, sewage disposal, and electrical power.[54]

As the American population increases, urbanized local governmental

---

[51] See Chap. 9.
[52] **Findings and Recommendations,** Oregon Legislative Interim Committee on Local Government, State of Oregon, Salem, Ore., 1956, pp. 113–114.
[53] Goodwin, *op. cit.*, p. 5.
[54] Oregon Legislative Interim Committee, *op. cit.*, pp. 102–104, 114–116.

units will be forced more and more to cooperate. The less populous units will tend to depend upon the state for assistance with services they cannot provide because of their uneconomic size, but some of them will no doubt turn over the administration of some of their programs to other local units on a contractual basis. Hundreds of such arrangements are already in existence in the United States. Many more will follow.

A Closing Note Increasingly, it is true that the major functions of government can be performed only through the joint activity and cooperation of national, state, and local governments. It is not a question of which level is to carry on these functions but rather how all three may effectively aid and participate. This is true in education, highways, health, welfare, housing, airports, law enforcement, and perhaps other functions. The pattern of the future will undoubtedly see more, rather than less, cooperation among the three levels of government in the United States.

SELECTED READINGS

Anderson, William: **The Nation and the States: Rivals or Partners?** The University of Minnesota Press, Minneapolis, 1955. (Statement of cooperative federalism argument.)

————: "Federalism—Then and Now," **State Government,** 16:107–112, May, 1943.

———— and Edward W. Weidner (eds.): **Research in Inter-governmental Relations,** The University of Minnesota Press, Minneapolis, 1950–58.

Armbrister, Trevor: "The Octopus in the State House," **Saturday Evening Post,** Feb. 12, 1966, pp. 25ff. (Muckraking of a high quality—much information on efforts to modify state governments.)

Bennett, Walter H.: **American Theories of Federalism,** University of Alabama Press, University, Ala., 1964. (A study of formal theories of federalism and their relationship to political institutions and public policy.)

Carleton, William G.: "Centralization and the Open Society," **Political Science Quarterly,** 12:244–259, June, 1960. (The liberal argument that federalism is outmoded and the states no longer useful.)

Carper, Edith T.: **Illinois Goes to Congress for Army Land,** The Bobbs-Merrill Company, Inc., Indianapolis, ICP no. 71, 1962. (Sportsmen and businessmen contest for the same piece of land.)

Cohen, Jacob, and Morton Grodzins: "How Much Economic Sharing in Federalism?" **American Political Science Review,** 57:5–23, March, 1963.

Commager, Henry Steele: "To Form a Much Less Perfect Union," **New York Times Magazine,** July 14, 1963. (Denounces the three amendments proposed by the National Legislative Council of the Council of State Governments.)

Fabricant, Solomon: **The Trend of Government Activity in the United States since 1900,** National Bureau of Economic Research, Inc., New York, 1952.

Field, Oliver P.: "States versus Nation, and the Supreme Court," **American Political Science Review,** 28:233–245, April, 1934.

Floud, J. S., Jr.: **Effects of Taxation on Industrial Location,** The University of North Carolina Press, Chapel Hill, N.C., 1952.

Graves, W. Brooke: **American Intergovernmental Relations,** Charles Scribner's Sons, New York, 1964. (An important source book.)

Hein, Clarence J.: **State Administrative Supervision of Local Government Functions in Kansas,** Governmental Research Center, University of Kansas, Lawrence, Kans., 1955.

Highsaw, Robert B., and John A. Dyer: **Conflict and Change in Local Government,** University of Alabama Press, University, Ala., 1966.   (Four case studies of interlocal cooperation in Alabama.)

Kaufman, Herbert: **Gotham in the Air Age,** rev. ed., The Bobbs-Merrill Company, Inc., Indianapolis, CPAC, case no. 10, 1952.   (The decision to turn New York City aviation facilities over to the Port of New York Authority.)

Kilpatrick, J. J.: **The Sovereign States: Notes of a Citizen of Virginia,** Henry Regnery Company, Chicago, 1957.   (A states' rights position.)

Kilpatrick, Wylie: **State Supervision of Local Budgeting,** National Municipal League, New York, 1939.

MacMahon, Arthur W. (ed.): **Federalism Mature and Emergent,** Doubleday & Company, Inc., Garden City, N.Y., 1955.

Mansfield, Harvey C.: "The States in the American System," **The Forty-eight States: Their Tasks as Policy Makers,** Graduate School of Business, Columbia University, New York, 1955.

Martin, Roscoe C.: **The Cities and the Federal System,** Atherton Press, New York, 1965.

McMillan, T. E., Jr.: **State Supervision of Municipal Finance,** Institute of Public Affairs, University of Texas, Austin, Tex., 1953.

Miller, Howard F.: **The Shredded Wheat Property,** The Bobbs-Merrill Company, Inc., Indianapolis, ICP no. 54, 1960.   (A conflict over land use in Niagara Falls, N.Y., between city and state. Who should mediate?)

Mitchell, Wendell: **Relations between the Federal and State Courts,** Columbia University Press, New York, 1950.

Pontius, Dale: **State Supervision of Local Government: Its Development in Massachusetts,** Public Affairs Press, Washington, D.C., 1942.

Report of the Council of State Governments, Committee on State-local Relations, Council of State Governments, Chicago, 1946.

Riker, William H.: **Federalism,** Little, Brown and Company, Boston, 1964.   (A theory of the origin and maintenance of federations.)

The Role of State Aid, New York Department of Audit and Control, Albany, N.Y., 1963.

Schmidhauser, John R.: **The Supreme Court as Final Arbiter of Federal-state Relations,** The University of North Carolina Press, Chapel Hill, N.C., 1958.

Schroth, Thomas N., and others: **Congress and the Nation, 1945–1964,** Congressional Quarterly Service, Washington, D.C., 1965, chaps. 4 and 10.

Services to Local Governments, New York Office for Local Government, Albany, N.Y., 1964.

Stoner, John E., and Catherine F. Siffin: **A Selected Bibliography on Interlocal Governmental Cooperation,** U.S. Department of Agriculture, Washington, 1964, Miscellaneous Publication No. 958.

U.S. Advisory Commission on Intergovernmental Relations: **The Role of Equalization in Federal Grants,** 1964.

U.S. Advisory Commission on Intergovernmental Relations: **A Report to the President,** 1955.

U.S. Office of Domestic Commerce: **Basic Industrial Location Factors,** 1947.

————: **Statutory and Administrative Controls Associated with Federal Grants for Public Assistance,** 1964.

Virginia's Answers to Congressional Questions on State and Federal Authority, The Virginia Commission on Constitutional Government, Richmond, 1963.   (The states' rights, or competitive, view of federalism.)

Wallace, S. C.: **State Administrative Supervision over Cities in the United States,** Columbia University Press, New York, 1928.

White, Leonard D.: **The States and the Nation,** Louisiana State University Press, Baton Rouge, La., 1953.

Wright, Deil S.: "The Advisory Commission on Intergovernmental Relations," **Public Administration Review,** 25:193–202, September, 1965.

Ylvisaker, Paul W.: **The Natural Cement Issue,** The Bobbs-Merrill Company, Inc., Indianapolis, CPAC, case no. 14, 1950. (Pressures on Minnesota decision makers to require a local product to be used in all highway construction in the state.)

4

RULES FOR RULE MAKING

A constitution is a set of rules about rule making. Its principal purposes are (1) to describe the basic structure and decision-making processes of government and (2) to allocate political power. This allocation must be made among levels of government, among branches of government, and between government and the individual. In each constitution, the state government and various types of local governments are established with a statement of their general powers and relationships to one another. Every state government is established with the familiar distribution of authority according to the principle of the separation of powers among the executive, legislative, and judicial branches. And always, some powers are given to government, while others, known as civil rights, are withheld from it to prevent government from encroaching on the rights of individuals.

In addition to the state constitutions, the legal setting of state and local government includes charters and statutes spelling out in greater detail the powers of cities, counties, school districts, and other local units. It also includes the rules which govern the relationship of governments at coordinate levels—intercity or interstate relations, for example—and between general and regional or local governments. This chapter will spell out some of the legal rules that condition the actions of all governments, national, state, and local.

The Content of Constitutions

"We the people of Alaska, grateful to God . . ."

"We the people of Puerto Rico, in order to organize ourselves politically on a fully democratic basis . . ." Thus begin two of the most recent American

attempts at constitution writing.[1] And so begin almost all state and commonwealth constitutions now in effect.

As Americans moved westward, they tended to become more equalitarian
in outlook and new constitutions reflected this fact. This pattern continued all
the way to the westernmost and newest states, Alaska and Hawaii. Each contained the most liberal provisions concerning civil rights and each provided
for a minimum voting age less than that generally prevailing. Hawaii established the voting age at twenty years; Alaska at nineteen.[2]

States have freely borrowed from one another in the writing of their constitutions. In 1777, Vermont depended heavily on the Pennsylvania constitution. The original constitution of Illinois (1818) made generous use of the
constitutions of Kentucky, Ohio, New York, and Indiana. Almost one-half of
the sections in the original constitution of California were borrowed from the
constitution of Iowa and many other sections came from that of New York.
Five other state constitutions were borrowed from by the California convention
delegates.[3] A preamble seems to be a necessary part of each constitution.
Most of the writers of the opening lines, as well as of the other parts of the
document, tend to imitate the language of Gouverneur Morris, chairman of the
famous Committee on Style, which, in 1787, gave the final polish to the United
States Constitution. We assume they intended to imitate. If their hope was to
improve upon his efforts, few if any have succeeded. Some of the state constitution writers, it might be noted, also throw in a few perverted lines from
Thomas Jefferson's Declaration of Independence. The preamble, in any case,
is chiefly a collection of glittering generalities. It conveys no legal powers.

Content   Each state constitution contains a bill of rights. Each describes the
basic structure of state government, sometimes doing so in great detail. Each
provides for the separation-of-powers doctrine, with a system of checks and
balances among the executive, legislative, and judicial branches.

No constitution interprets itself, however. The meaning of terms, even
in the exceptional cases where constitution writers seek to define them, is not
precise. The questions of interpretation that arise must therefore be settled
in one way or another. The usual practice is to leave them to the courts as
cases arise and, barring legislative reinterpretation or constitutional amendment, judicial findings assume the force and effect of constitutional definition.
In some instances, conflicting interpretations cannot be settled by the courts
but must be worked out pragmatically upon the basis of relative political pressure. For example, although the principle of separation of powers is commonly
regarded as a part of the American concept of government, there are in practice
frequent conflicts among the legislative, executive, and judicial branches concerning its meaning in specific cases. Courts jealously guard their "right" to

---

[1] The **Constitution of the State of Alaska** (1958) and the **Constitution of the Commonwealth of
Puerto Rico** (1952).
[2] Paul C. Bartholomew, "A Comparative Analysis of the Constitutions of the States of Hawaii
and Alaska," **Federal Bar Journal**, 22:44–48, Winter, 1962.
[3] Robert B. Dishman, **The Constitutional Document as a Constitutional Problem**, National Municipal League, New York, 1961.

review legislation. Legislators feel keenly the historic trend in favor of the executive at cost to their own branch. Thus, in a 1929 conflict in New York over the question of instituting the executive budget, legislative leaders opposed the proposal and the governor favored it, but each claimed to be doing nothing other than protecting that which "properly" belonged to his own branch of government.

State constitutions specify in some detail the functions and powers of government. Under the federal system, states enjoy all powers not reserved for the Federal government or denied them under the various parts of the United States Constitution known collectively as the Bill of Rights. But because many citizens have long refused to trust their state legislature,[4] they have adopted many constitutional restrictions of legislative powers.

The Amending Process   A state constitution can be amended in a great variety of ways:

1. Like the United States Constitution, it can be changed through executive, legislative, and judicial interpretation. This is, in fact, probably the most common means of changing it. For example, a governor may interpret a vague provision concerning his powers; legislative leaders often give on-the-spot interpretations of the constitution during debates; courts apply the constitution regularly through judicial review.

2. A constitutional convention may recommend changes to be ratified through the regular amending process of the existing constitution. It may also submit an entirely new or largely rewritten document for ratification. Many state constitutions have provisions allowing for a referendum on the question of calling a state constitutional convention. In others, the courts have held that the legislature may submit the question to the voters at its discretion. In about eight states, the question is required to be submitted periodically. Sometimes a "commission," which is a miniature convention, may be appointed by the legislature, the governor, or jointly by both in order to submit proposals. No state constitution authorizes the commission method, but it has been used many times on the basis of legislative establishment. The results of commission deliberations, in the form of successful amendments, have been few.

3. Thirteen states allow voters to propose constitutional amendments through use of the initiative. No action is required by a convention or by the legislature. A petition is circulated stating the proposal. If enough signatures are obtained to satisfy the law, the proposal is placed directly upon the ballot at the next election.[5]

The initiated constitutional amendment is not used widely but it does appear to have an important function where it is authorized. The Michigan experience with this device indicates that its use follows quite a different pattern from that of constitutional amendments submitted by the legislature. Between 1910 and 1955, thirty-four amendments to the Michigan constitution were proposed by initiatory petition. Of these, nine, or 26 percent, were adopted.

[4] On this and other aspects of the development of state government, see above, chap. 3.
[5] For states with the constitutional initiative, see the most recent issue of **Book of the States**.

Over the same period of time, eighty-four amendments were submitted by the legislature, and fifty-three of these, or 63 percent, were adopted. This sharp difference in results may be traced largely to the fact that the apportionment of the Michigan legislature was such as to prevent any proposals other than those enjoying conservative support from being submitted for popular vote. Liberal or extremist proposals would not be submitted to the voters by the legislature. Liberal and extremist proposals are sometimes placed on the ballot by initiative. Examples of the former include two income tax proposals and another calling for the exemption of food from the sales tax. Examples of extremist proposals include two calling for compulsory attendance at *public* schools. The initiative tends to be used especially for proposals of major significance, some of which have been liberal, others conservative. Because so many proposals originating through this device are important, widely publicized, and highly controversial, they are more likely to be defeated than are the less dramatic ones that are typically submitted by the legislature. It seems clear, then, that the initiated constitutional amendment device is an alternative decision-making route to that of the legislature. It may be used to correct situations involving unrepresentative legislatures, as well as to allow dissident groups to blow off steam, thus diminishing the possibility of social disorganization in times of great social or economic unrest. It is worth noting that in the forty-five-year period in Michigan mentioned above, no extremist or "crackpot" amendment was ever approved by the voters, although several that might be so classified were submitted.[6]

    4. The most common means of proposing amendments to state constitutions, by far, is through submission by the legislature. Every state except New Hampshire authorizes this method. It usually involves a resolution by the legislature, commonly requiring two-thirds or three-fifths of the membership to vote in favor. This requirement, of course, makes passage difficult. A few states allow an amendment to be submitted by the vote of a simple majority in each house; but nine states require a majority vote in two successive sessions, and this is often a major obstacle to change. In states with biannual sessions, it may delay amendment for as long as four years.

Ratification of Amendments   Typically, a proposed amendment is adopted by a simple majority vote on the question. This is the case in about thirty-five states. Others require a majority of those voting in the election (failure to vote on the constitutional question is thus an automatic "no" vote) or for candidates for a certain office. Connecticut and New Hampshire ratify through town meetings. Illinois and Rhode Island require extraordinary majorities. In Delaware, the legislature can propose an amendment at one session and adopt it by approving it again at a succeeding session.

    Constitutional amendments proposed by the legislature have a greater chance for ratification than do those proposed by initiative, in part because

6 Research and interpretation by the author. Data from **Michigan Manual,** State of Michigan, Lansing, Mich., 1955–1956, pp. 59–66.

extraordinary majorities are often required for submission of constitutional amendments. If a proposal passes both houses of a legislature, it probably already enjoys a broad consensus.

The Politics of Constitution Writing

Constitutions are political documents. The fact that they help determine the rules of politics would in itself make them the object of manipulation by the various interests of society. Their content is constantly a matter of concern to groups and individuals, and the very fact that constitutions are more difficult to change than are statute laws causes groups to protect their special interests by incorporating them whenever possible into the fundamental law of the state.

Rules can be used for strategical party advantage, as was demonstrated in Ohio in 1965. In the election of the previous fall, Republicans and Democrats each won sixteen Senate seats. The incumbent, lameduck legislature was, however, dominated by Republicans. In December, 1964, a special session was held. It provided that in cases of tie votes, the lieutenant governor—a Republican—would be permitted to cast the deciding vote.

In Georgia, a constitutional revision commission was established in the 1950s in preference to having a constitutional convention meet. A convention would have been more representative of population than was the legislature, and might have weakened rural control of the legislature. In New Jersey, holding a constitutional convention became possible only because party leaders agreed in advance that the convention would not consider the question of legislative apportionment.

Picture of a Convention When the persons who had been selected to write a constitution for New Mexico, which was about to be admitted to the Union, gathered in 1910, they were faced with many of the same practical considerations that their counterparts in other states had known. Their approach to the job was probably not atypical. The convention was organized along strict party lines, even the clerical positions being distributed by the patronage machinery of the Republican party. The rules under which the convention would proceed were designed to minimize the potential influence of the Democratic minority.

In doing their work, the members used earlier drafts of proposed New Mexico constitutions and they referred to the existing constitutions of all other states. Many committees simply copied sections from state constitutions that appealed to them. Partisan conflict centered around the desire of the majority Republicans to write a conservative constitution appealing to the dominant economic elements of the area, including the large ranchers. The Democratic leader was a progressive who wanted to include in the constitution provisions for the initiative and referendum, strict regulation of railroads, the direct primary election, and an easy amending procedure—a rather typical progressive-reform platform of that day. The minority urged that judges be chosen on a nonpartisan ballot, a proposal designed to remove control of choice from the powerful economic leaders who dominated the majority party.

The chief conflict was over the initiative and referendum * (I. and R.). It is not easy today to realize how seriously this conflict was taken. Many liberals saw the I. and R. as the only device that would free the common man from domination by the few. In a sparsely settled area and with property ownership concentrated in a few hands, this seemed like a very real danger. Some conservatives, on the other hand, regarded the I. and R. as subversive of the principle of representative government and viewed the proposal with genuine alarm. The issue was finally compromised. The leaders recognized that popular support was strongly behind I. and R. and that any proposed constitution probably would not be adopted if it did not include a provision for it. They therefore included I. and R., but tied it up with a procedural process which they believed—correctly, as it turned out—would be difficult to put to use. The issues before the constitutional convention in this case, as in most or perhaps all cases, involved a conflict of political, social, and economic interests which were compromised through much the same procedure as they are before any representative body.[7]

* **INITIATIVE. A procedure permitting a specified number of voters to propose changes in a constitution, municipal charter, laws, or ordinances. These proposals are then accepted or rejected by voters at the polls. The REFERENDUM permits voters to accept or reject at the polls changes in a constitution, municipal charter, laws, or ordinances which have been proposed by a legislative body. A referendum follows favorable action by a legislative body; the initiative is designed to operate independently of the legislature.**

Politics and Constitutional Verbiage   The United States Constitution is a brief document, and so were the early constitutions of the states. In 1800, the longest state constitution, that of Massachusetts, contained only about 12,000 words.[8] In 1963, the longest constitution was that of Louisiana, which had at least 200,000 words—or about the number in this book. Some other states were not far behind. The Louisiana constitution of 1921 had 407 amendments in its first forty-two years of existence. More than twelve amendments were proposed each year, on the average, and 79 percent were adopted. This length may be partly the result of the fact that Louisiana uses the civil code, based on French law, rather than the Anglo-American legal system.

Proposals for amendment of the Texas constitution have been submitted by every regular session of the legislature of that state since 1900, and during that time the voters have made at least one change each time they have had choices.[9] In contrast, however, the unusual Tennessee constitution went

[7] Thomas C. Donnelly, **The Government of New Mexico,** The University of New Mexico Press, Albuquerque, N.Mex., 1953, chap. 2, is the basis for this section. A case study for a more recent constitution is found in Bennett M. Rich, **The Government and Administration of New Jersey,** Thomas Y. Crowell Company, New York, 1957, chap. 3.
[8] J. Q. Dealey, **Growth of American State Constitutions,** Ginn and Company, Boston, 1915, p. 39.
[9] James Howard and Bill Henry, "The Texas Constitutional Amendments of 1963," **Public Affairs Comment,** 9:1, September, 1963.

unamended between 1870 and 1953, a period of eighty-three years. Many reasons exist for the expanding length of state constitutions. The fact that American legislatures have never been fully trusted by citizens has encouraged the writing of many rules circumscribing legislative powers. Constitutional provisions are devised to control the legislature or to prevent it from acting in certain areas. This long-standing public attitude has however, in recent decades, tended to come into conflict with the general desire for expanded governmental functions. The Federal government launched the scores of new programs of the New Deal and Fair Deal without once amending the United States Constitution, but a similar feat was not possible in most states where restrictions on governmental powers required changes in the fundamental law before new programs could be established. Thus, constitutions grew in length initially in order to limit governmental power and later to ease existing restrictions.

In the second place, many state constitutions are relatively easy to amend, at least as compared with the Federal Constitution. On the other hand, a few, such as those of Illinois and Tennessee, are very difficult to amend. It is thus often more possible at the state level than at the Federal to appeal from an unpopular judicial interpretation or legislative action by amending the fundamental law.

Lastly, there exists at all times a strong temptation on the part of interest groups to write their most favored policies into the constitution itself, if possible. Since a constitution is fundamental law, it would logically contain only enabling and prohibiting authority, in addition to a description of governmental structure. Upon this base, statute law (i.e., law formally enacted by a legislative body) would be built. In practice, however, groups within society learned in the nineteenth century that there was nothing except custom to prevent the inclusion of statute law in the constitutions themselves. With this understood, they began using constitutions for their own ends. Since these bodies of law are normally more difficult to amend than are statutes, they gave added protection to the pet interests of groups. Furthermore, the fact that any constitutional provision enjoys special legitimacy and sanctity makes it more difficult for another group to mount a counterattack than would be the case if the provision were mere statute law.

It should not be assumed that an interest group, in putting one of its favorite pieces of legislation into the constitution, is seeking to achieve its goals by devious and deceptive means. In many cases, the group believes strongly in the particular piece of legislation and sincerely regards it as having a proper place in the fundamental law. One interest-group spokesman put it simply in justifying a New York constitutional amendment in 1931 involving statute law: He agreed that constitutions should deal with fundamental law, but "in view of the importance of [the particular measure] it seems as if we were justified in making this exception." [10]

Great quantities of statute law have been written into state constitutions,

[10] Bernard Bellush, **Franklin D. Roosevelt as Governor of New York,** Columbia University Press, New York, 1955, pp. 96–97.

especially in the twentieth century. Until the 1950s, the Minnesota constitution included a detailed description of the state highway system. Instead of authorizing the legislature to establish and maintain a highway system (which would have been an example of constitutional law), it gave a detailed description of each route (statute law). This arrangement satisfied both the "good roads" interests which wanted a major construction program to be spelled out in detail and many of the local interests, all of which wanted to be certain that a "hard road" paid for by the state would pass through their counties. The Texas constitution lays out in elaborate detail the powers and duties of the state building commission and provides that "the first major structure erected from the State Building Fund . . . shall be devoted to the use and occupancy of the Supreme Court. . . ." The California constitution concerns itself with the length of wrestling matches; that of Michigan, with provision for an executive mansion; that of Mississippi, with dueling.

A great many interests have contributed to the length and complexity of constitutions. The general distrust of the legislature encouraged conventions from the 1850s onward to spell out state and local government organization in detail. Distrust also caused severe limitations to be placed, in many states, upon powers of taxation and of the incurring of debt. These provisions were a reaction to corrupt legislatures. Today, with many demands for increasing services, they are sometimes major obstacles to public policy making.

The Decline of Constitution Writing   Prior to the second decade of the present century, rewriting state constitutions was part of the American way of life. From time to time, as ecological patterns of economic elites changed, or political values evolved, new state constitutions were written. Over 200 state constitutional conventions have met in our history. There were certain periods of intensive constitution writing, particularly in the 1850s, when the values of frontier individualism were written into state fundamental law, again after the Civil War, and finally during the reform period between the 1890s and World War I. The sacrosanctity which came to be attached to the United States Constitution never was applied to state constitutions. In some states a related phenomenon arose, however. Thus although Massachusetts adopted a new constitution in 1919, the folklore of the commonwealth regards this relatively new document as the constitution of 1780.

Generally the attitude of citizens toward their state constitutions has been one of pragmatism. Yet, after World War I, the old pattern of periodic rewriting of the fundamental law came to an end. Since then, excluding Alaska and Hawaii, only seven constitutions have been adopted. Why this change? The answer is probably to be found principally in the rapid urbanization of the nation since that date and in the clustering of urban populations around a relatively few metropolitan areas. Residents of rural areas, villages, and small cities, who are overrepresented as a result, have recognized that a complete reappraisal of state government by a constitutional convention selected on the basis of population would result in a considerable loss to them of influence in state government. In order to hold on to the disproportionate power they possess through the accident of shifting populations, persons in these areas have opposed constitutional revision. It is also likely that as statute law has accumulated in state constitutions over time, a larger and larger number of groups have come to possess a vested interest in retaining the existing document and in not risking the unknown in a convention.

Even during the second decade reform movement, Governor Frank O. Lowden of Illinois complained of frustrating apathy. He believed a new constitution was badly needed for the state, and he had been elected on a plank calling for "modernizing" state government; but legislators reporting to him after taking soundings in their districts said that they found few ordinary citizens who were dissatisfied with the existing constitution. Lowden noted the same kind of lethargy among his friends in the Chicago business community, and these were people who yearned for "businesslike" state government in Illinois.[11] Of course, it is likely that neither ordinary citizens nor wealthy businessmen knew much about the content of the constitution.

There were probably additional factors involved in the trend away from constitutional revision, too. For example, the proposal to hold a convention in New York State was voted down in 1937, apparently because upstate New Yorkers took the vote as a serious challenge to their control over the legislature, while residents of the city of New York were generally apathetic during the campaign and the subsequent referendum.[12]

Perhaps the nation is about to launch into a new era of constitution writing. After the United States Supreme Court assumed jurisdiction over the definition of fair apportionment of legislatures (see Chapter 14, below), the reason for avoiding conventions was largely eliminated. Michigan held a convention in 1961 and 1962; Connecticut in 1965. Others were likely to follow.

Of the constitutions in effect in 1966, 70 percent were originally written in the nineteenth century, all but five of them after 1850, however. Of the twelve twentieth-century documents, five are the original constitutions of recently admitted states. The average age for constitutions in 1966 was eighty-four years and, hence, the typical state constitution was a product of the last quarter of the nineteenth century. The documents ranged in length from the 200,000 plus words of the Louisiana constitution to the 4,840 words found in that of Vermont. The oldest state constitutions were the shortest and had the fewest amendments. They, like the United States Constitution, were written in general terms, permitting considerable flexibility through judicial interpretation. In general, the constitutions of the newer states reflect a greater degree of innovation than do the revised constitutions of older states.[13]

[11] William T. Hutchinson, **Lowden of Illinois,** The University of Chicago Press, Chicago, 1957, vol. 1, pp. 320–322.
[12] For the issues that might have been considered by such a convention, see V. A. O'Rourke and D. W. Campbell, **Constitution-making in a Democracy,** The Johns Hopkins Press, Baltimore, 1943.
[13] Albert L. Sturm, **Recent Trends in State Constitutional Revision,** Bureau of Government Research, Arizona State University, Tempe, Ariz., 1965.

Fundamental Law for Local Government

While each state has a constitution and is, under our federal system, supreme in every field where it is not limited by the powers of the United States government, local government powers are much more circumscribed. Each unit of local government is essentially an agent of the state government, and its powers are derived either from a charter or from statutory enabling legislation.

The Municipal Corporation   The municipality—the city, village, or borough—is, in lawyer's language, a corporation, an artificial person created by the state. The powers of the municipality are, therefore, derived from the state just as are those of any other corporation, and they are expressed in a charter. A charter is the fundamental law of a corporation which establishes (1) the structure or form of local government, (2) the powers that may be exercised by it, and (3) the general manner in which the powers granted may be exercised. The charter is almost never a single document but includes all state laws and judicial opinions that affect the structure, powers, or manner of exercising the powers of the corporation.

The city, in some respects, has a legal position not unlike that of a private corporation. In fact, it has been only in the last two centuries or so that a definite distinction has developed. The two are still similar in that each has an existence independent of the members of the corporation, may own property, may make contracts, may exist, normally, in perpetuity, and may sue and be sued. They possess very important differences, too. A private corporation is created entirely by the voluntary request of a group of people who wish to form a corporation. They know the corporation law in advance and hence know the conditions under which they will operate. Furthermore, once the corporation charter is granted it becomes a contract which cannot be altered or taken away (except under the rarest circumstances involving a so-called public interest). A public corporation, on the other hand, may be created with or without the consent of its membership (the persons living in the area), the terms of its charter may be quite different from what the people of the community desire, and even more important, the charter is *not* a contract and is hence subject to constant, involuntary, and sometimes arbitrary changes. It can even be taken away without advance notice unless the state constitution specifically prohibits this.

Two other important differences exist between public and private corporations. A public corporation can act only in the public interest and for a public purpose. A private corporation must always have the public interest in mind (one could not long exist, for example, if it were organized for the purpose of robbing banks), but it may also have private interests (such as profit making for the individual owners). The two also differ in the amount of control the state exercises over them. A private corporation can carry on any activities it wishes so long as it does not violate some law; a public corporation can do only those things that it is authorized to do. A corporation producing cigarettes, for example, could take on a side line of producing, say, plowshares without seeking an amendment to its charter or any other kind of permission from the state. (It could not, however, put in a side line of marijuana cigarettes, since this would not be in the "public interest" and could be curbed by the state under its police powers.) A municipal, or public, corporation, on the other hand, could not decide to enter into such side lines as, say, municipal parking lots or a municipal theater, or to adopt a new form of taxation without having first the specific authority to do so.[14]

The Quasi Corporation   Cities, villages, and boroughs (in a few states), and a relatively few counties and school districts operate under written charters and are therefore municipal corporations. There are many other local units of government, however, including most of the counties, townships, unincorporated New England towns, and the so-called special districts such as sewage-disposal, airport, drainage, mosquito-abatement, fire, and irrigation districts. These are known at law as "quasi corporations," that is, bodies that resemble corporations.

So far as the lay citizen is concerned, the principal distinction between corporations and quasi corporations is this: A quasi corporation serves only as an administrative agent of the state, while the true public corporation serves a dual purpose. It acts not only as a local agent for the state, but also performs certain local functions exclusively in the interests of the people living within the boundaries of the corporation.

In legal theory, the city (or other public corporation) acts as an agent of the state whenever it performs a function in which the state as a whole has a certain interest; for example, when it enforces the law or maintains public health standards or collects taxes. On the other hand, the city may perform some tasks purely for the comfort and convenience of the local inhabitants, in legal theory at least, for example, in the operation of a water supply or public transportation system. Quasi corporations, in contrast, perform only such functions of statewide interest as the maintenance of records, the prosecution of crimes, the maintenance of roads, and the education of children.

The Judge Is the Umpire   The subordinate legal status of local governments makes it necessary that the question of whether or not a particular unit of government has the power to perform a particular function in a particular way be decided by the courts. Because the city is merely a creature of the state while the state itself is a sovereign body, the courts have established a rule, Dillon's rule, calling for narrow construction of local powers and broad construction of state powers. To put it another way, the courts say that cities have only those powers expressly granted by, or reasonably implied in, state law.[15]

In 1964, for example, the city of Louisville, Kentucky, was delayed for at

[14] For details, see Eugene McQuillin, **The Law of Municipal Corporations**, 3d ed., Callaghan, Callaghan & Co., Inc., Chicago, 1949, a voluminous commentary.
[15] See John F. Dillon, **Commentaries on the Law of Municipal Corporations**, 5th ed., Little, Brown and Company, Boston, 1911, vol. I, sec. 237. Although Dillon's rule applies specifically to municipal corporations, the same principle applies to the powers of quasi corporations.

least two months in a councilmanic proposal to construct a municipal zoo. After the city announced its plans, two lawsuits were filed. One challenged the right of the city to purchase the proposed zoo site on the technical ground that the city proposed to buy only surface rights and that it could not do so without also buying the mineral rights. Another lawsuit was based on the argument that the city had no authority to establish a zoo. Both suits were lost and the city was able to proceed with its plans, but only after considerable delay. The original plan was for the zoo to be opened to the public early in the summer of 1964. The legal actions delayed opening until almost the end of the summer season.[16]

The New York City Transit Authority, in 1965, faced a typical interest-group ploy, using legal means in an attempt to prevent the execution of policies which the group disapproved of. The Transit Authority proposed to construct a tunnel under the East River at 63rd Street. The Citizens' Budget Commission, a middle-class reform group, preferred a tunnel at 61st Street, arguing that this would permit free transfers for passengers from the Queens and the Bronx to two Manhattan subway lines. The interest group, unable to convince the Transit Authority, challenged its legal right to construct the tunnel at the proposed location, using the legal argument that due process of law had not been observed.[17]

It is Dillon's rule that explains why city officials may have to spend weeks of time and thousands of dollars in actions before the state courts seeking to justify a decision to finance a municipal parking lot from the parking-meter fund rather than from the general-revenue fund; seeking to find some theoretical justification for an FEPC or a smoke-abatement ordinance. That a majority of voters in the community should demand them and that they should be adopted according to democratic procedures is not sufficient. Although the courts seek to apply the principle of *stare decisis* by using one decision as the basis for deciding a later case involving essentially the same question, Dillon's rule in practice allows the judge a good deal of discretion in deciding the powers of local governments. Because Dillon's rule says, in effect, "if in doubt, you do not have the power," local government officials commonly arrange for a friendly lawsuit in the early stages of any new undertaking. This involves expense and delay, but it allows the judges to make their decisions at a time when a negative finding will do less harm and cost less money than would be the case if a disgruntled taxpayer brought a suit when a dam or bridge or parking lot were well under way.

Kinds of Charters   In the United States, local governments may operate under special- or general-act charters, a system of classified general-act charters, optional general-act charters, or home-rule charters. The degree of local control increases roughly in the order they are listed here. Both corporations and quasi corporations may be found operating under any of these systems. Quasi corporations, however, do not refer to their enabling legislation as charters,

---

16 **Louisville Times** (Louisville, Ky.), Oct. 8, 1964.
17 Citizens' Budget Commission, Inc., New York, press release, Aug. 2, 1965.

although the legal effect and status is the same. A city clerk will say, "According to our charter, the city . . . ," but a county clerk will say, "According to state law, the county . . ." The difference is one of tradition and point of view, not of substance. Home-rule cities have a document adopted by the voters and called the city charter, but in other cities, all state laws governing the structure and powers of the city are loosely called the charter.

Special-act Charters The oldest, and at one time the universal, method of granting charters was by legislative act granting a specific charter to a municipality named in the act. This charter could be amended only by the legislature itself. Although quasi corporations were customarily provided for under general acts or the constitution, they were often modified as to detail of organization or powers by special legislation.

Beginning in 1851, when Ohio and Indiana by constitutional provision outlawed all special legislation, attempts have been made to limit the use of this type of legislation. There is no reason why legislatures should necessarily choose to abuse their potential powers of supervision over local government, and they have by no means always done so. Yet, reformers for over a century have held that local governments should not be constantly subjected to legislative control in such a manner that the state governing body could at any moment it chose substitute its own judgment for that of the local governing body. Undoubtedly special legislation simplified interference by the legislature with matters regarded as strictly local. On the other hand, various attempts to prevent the *de facto* enactment of special legislation have been unsuccessful. The degree of legislative activity in dealing with minute details of local government seems to depend more upon tradition in the individual state than upon any other factor.

Despite its unpopularity in urban communities, special legislation continues in use. It is to be found especially in New England and the South, particularly in Alabama, Florida, Maryland, North Carolina, and Tennessee. In Maryland, for example, 70 percent of the bills passed by the 1951 legislature were local in character. About one-half of the states are constitutionally authorized to enact special legislation, and all of them make use of it to one degree or another.

General-act Charters The general-act charter, designed to provide for uniform powers, privileges, and structures for every city in the state,* has not met with much success except where it has been modified by home rule or local option. Since American municipalities vary from hamlets to empires of millions of people, it is unrealistic to expect that every city government should be exactly like every other in powers and structure. Variation is needed. Quasi corporations are often set up with uniform structure and powers, but again the vast differences in size and population commonly impel the legislature to modify the general pattern to fit local needs.

* **CITY.** An urban area of indeterminate population size and density. The term is used in this book interchangeably with *municipality*. Legal definitions of a city differ from one state to another, as do those for a village, town, borough, or other municipal corporations.

enjoy greater powers than do non-home-rule units of government, most of them are potentially just as subject to state control over their affairs. In most home-rule states, the legislature enjoys concurrent or superior power to the local government in matters of local concern. And the legislature is, of course, supreme in those areas that the courts deem to be of state, rather than of local, concern. Normally, general acts of the legislature, or what purport to be general acts, take precedence over local ordinances or charter provisions. Under these circumstances, the question of whether home rule will work and the extent to which it will work is a question, not of law, but of public policy determined by the legislature, at whose sufferance home rule actually exists. Home rule is hence more often an attitude toward local government than it is a legal injunction against legislative action.

Local politicians (who wish to maximize their own autonomy from state control), good-government groups (which believe that efficiency and economy are furthered by local control of government), chambers of commerce (which have similar views), and other interests over the nation continue to press for home rule. They are especially anxious, in many cases, to have the idea applied to county government as well as to cities. Twelve states permit something approximating county home rule, and a mere handful of counties, about a dozen, chiefly in California, have adopted their own charters. Ten states— California, Maryland, Michigan, Minnesota, Missouri, New York, Ohio, Oregon, Texas, and Washington—have constitutional provisions regarding county home rule. In some of these, as in Texas, the provision is, in practice, unworkable. In others, there appears to be relatively little enthusiasm among citizens for county charters. This may be a result of the fact that the county has always been perceived as an agent of the state having few local policy-making powers. Yet, counties are in many states, especially in urban areas, expanding their responsibilities and functions. As they become more and more like municipalities, there may be an expanding need for unique governmental patterns for individual counties. If this is the case, the pressure for county home rule and popular interest in it may well increase in the future.

Local Government Law: An Appraisal   Efforts to prevent or reduce legislative intervention in local decision making have been made through such devices as the constitutional prohibition of special legislation, constitutional control of classification, and the use of the optional-charter plan. These efforts have met with only limited success. The legislature remains paramount, and its members have found it relatively easy to legislate for specific communities whenever they have desired to do so.

But in seeking to grant independence to local government, advocates of general legislation have tended to minimize the fact that local units of government do have unique requirements that must be met by specific legislation. The result is that general legislation must always be modified to meet local needs to one degree or another. The legislatures of an increasing number of states have, as a matter of public policy, given the people a good deal of autonomy in local affairs. In some states, home rule has helped movements in this direction.

Some types of state control and supervision have been helpful to local governments and not restrictive. Furthermore, in many cases, local officials, instead of chafing under the existing degree of state controls, approve of this control or are unconcerned with it. Local units of government will inevitably be subject to a great deal of legislative control. Nearly every function performed by them affects other people of the state. In a day of large economic units and rapid means of transportation and communication, it is impossible for local governments to isolate themselves. Furthermore, there is no natural cleavage between state and local interests and functions. Because one tends to grow out of the other gradually, the state and its subdivisions must work together.

Closing Statement   This chapter has dealt with the skeleton of state and local government, the bones upon which the body of law and policy can be built. The following chapters will develop the political institutions as they exist at the state and local levels.

SELECTED READINGS

Dealey, J. Q.: **Growth of American State Constitutions,** Ginn and Company, Boston, 1915.

Dillon, John F.: **Commentaries on the Law of Municipal Corporations,** 5th ed., Little, Brown and Company, Boston, 1911.

Dishman, Robert B.: **State Constitutions: The Shape of the Document,** National Municipal League, State Constitutional Studies Project, New York, 1960.

Dodd, Walter F.: "The First State Constitutional Conventions," **American Political Science Review,** 2:915–922, November, 1908.

————: **The Revision and Amendment of State Constitutions,** The Johns Hopkins Press, Baltimore, 1910.

Friedman, Robert S., and Sybil L. Stokes: "The Role of Constitution-maker as Representative," **Midwest Journal of Political Science,** 9:148–166, May, 1965. (Constitutional convention delegates were less parochial in views than are legislators.)

Goldbach, John: "Local Formation Commissions: California's Struggle over Municipal Incorporation," **Public Administration Review,** 25:213–220, September, 1965. (Discusses the 1963 provisions for a Local Agency Formation Commission which reviews incorporation proposals and can modify them or even withhold approval of them.)

Graves, W. Brooke (ed.): **State Constitutional Revision,** Public Administration Service, Chicago, 1960.

Keith, John P.: **Methods of Constitutional Revision,** Bureau of Municipal Research, University of Texas, Austin, Tex., 1949.

McQuillin, Eugene: **The Law of Municipal Corporations,** 3d ed., Callaghan, Callaghan & Co., Inc., Chicago, 1949.

Model City Charter, 6th ed., National Municipal League, New York, 1964.

Model State Constitution, 6th ed., National Municipal League, New York, 1963.

O'Rourke, V. A., and D. W. Campbell: **Constitution-making in a Democracy,** The Johns Hopkins Press, Baltimore, 1943.

service of the United States, persons convicted of defrauding the United States or any of the states, or of having offered or accepted a bribe, persons who have voluntarily aided or abetted in an attempted overthrow of the United States government, and persons who have voluntarily borne arms against the United States.[1]

The high level of mobility in the American population makes residence requirements especially significant as factors barring persons from voting. Probably the number disqualified in this manner is high, especially among urban workers and middle-class organization men. Residence requirements are to a degree vestiges of an earlier theory of voting and are not in accord with that of universal suffrage.

Literacy Requirements   In an effort to reduce the once important political influence of the foreign-born, some states imposed English literacy requirements. With the foreign-born often concentrated in cities and belonging to one political party and with the legislature under the control of the opposite party, this kind of requirement might be expected as a product of the struggle for political control of the state. Elsewhere, the same type of literacy test has been used to discourage Negro voting. Some form of the test may still be found in many states for state and local offices.

The Voting Rights Act of 1965 provided that no person could be denied the right to vote if he had successfully completed six grades of education (or more, if applied to all voters in the state) in a school under the American flag even though teaching in that school was not conducted in the English language. This provision protected Puerto Ricans in New York, which had a literacy test. (In 1966, the United States Supreme Court ruled that the New York literacy test could be taken in Spanish as well as English.) The act also suspended literacy requirements in any political subdivision in which the Director of the Census certified that under 50 percent of the persons of voting age were registered to vote.

Restrictions on the Institutionalized   There is a general rule that an individual may not vote so long as he is an inmate of a state or local institution. The rule applies to the mentally ill and to those incarcerated in jails or prisons. Laws vary from state to state, however, as to the conditions under which an individual's voting privilege is restored once he is released from an institution. There is a widespread popular notion that persons convicted of a felony lose their citizenship. This is a misconception, although in some states such persons do lose certain civil rights, including the right to vote, permanently. In other states, however, the individual may vote if he is not actually incarcerated.

Taxpaying Requirements   During the Great Depression, several states provided that only property owners could vote on questions of the direct appropriation of public money or the issuance of bonds. This conservative move was

[1] Earl J. Reeves, Jr., **Kansas Voter's Guide 1962,** Governmental Research Center, University of Kansas, Lawrence, Kans., 1962, pp. 9–10.

dictated by a desire on the part of homeowners to save their property in a day of increased demands for governmental services, especially for public welfare, and of evaporating taxpaying ability. Six states, chiefly in the West and Southwest, retained this requirement in 1959.

Payment of the poll tax, long a requirement in the Southern states as a prerequisite for state and local voting, was a subject of controversy for many years. Through being tied in with eligibility to vote, the tax served as a method for retaining control of governments in the hands of the prosperous, for it disfranchised white and Negro persons alike in the low-income categories in many of the Southern states. The tax was simple enough in concept —a head tax of a few dollars on each adult (or male) within specified age groups. But by various devices—requiring the payment of all past-due taxes in order to be eligible to vote, deliberate failure to send out bills or notices of the tax, making payments of the tax due long before election, for example— the less literate, less politically conscious, and those of low income were easily made ineligible to vote. In the years following World War II, the tax developed a special notoriety that was probably responsible for its repeal in ten states. In 1966, the United States Supreme Court outlawed the payment of such a tax as a prerequisite for voting. Its demise did not, however, necessarily signal a relaxation of resistance to Negro voting—many other devices such as the literacy test or intimidation remained available as weapons in the struggle.

Registration   The practice of requiring individuals to register before they may vote is today a nearly universal practice in the United States, at least in urban regions. Registration is not, in a legal sense, an additional qualification for voting but is only a mechanism for determining that those who cast ballots are actually qualified. The device has been used as a means of reducing fraudulent voting and was especially supported in earlier decades by reformers seeking to control the freewheeling activities of big city machines. In the South, registration has been an effective device for controlling access to the polls, and it is at this point in the process that it can be decided, for example, that a Negro (in former days, not infrequently a poor white, too) could not meet the literacy requirement or could not "correctly interpret" a portion of the state constitution.

An urban, industrial society is also a mobile society. Yet our election laws are based largely upon the more stable population patterns of the nineteenth century. Both the organization man and the hourly rated employee move quite often. The former may be reassigned to a branch of his company in another geographic area, while the latter will tend to move to wherever work is to be found. Some states have restrictions on voting as to the amount of time one must have lived in the county, and sometimes even in the precinct. Even when these restrictions are only for a thirty-day period, they may disfranchise a large number of people, and the restrictions may be for a longer period—up to one year in the election district and two years in the state, as required by Mississippi. Probably more than 8,000,000 people who would otherwise be eligible to vote in a national election are disfranchised each time by residence requirements.[2] The often-publicized low voter turnout in the United States is in part a result of these restrictions. Although only 62 percent of the population of voting age cast ballots in the 1964 national election, a relatively high figure of 82 percent participated if ineligibles are not counted. The Michigan constitution of 1962 attempts to overcome this enforced disfranchisement by eliminating residence requirements for presidential elections and allowing a person who has moved within the state within thirty days of the election to vote in his former precinct.

Negro Voting in the South   In the twenty years following the major Supreme Court decision relative to the right of Negroes to vote in primary elections (normally the critical elections in the south) [3] Negro registrations increased by more than 500 percent. Even so, in 1963, the percentage of Negroes registered in the former Confederate states was only one-half that of whites. Statistically, the most significant factor in helping to determine what percentage of Negroes would be registered was the percentage of Negroes in the total community. The higher the percentage, the less likely that a given Negro would be registered to vote. The more agricultural an area, the less likely were Negroes to be registered, but the effect of this was not great. In general, the increase in Negro registration has been greatest in those areas where white and Negro income is relatively high, where the percentage of middle-class persons is relatively high, and in areas undergoing rapid economic transition, as reflected in an above-average population rate of increase.[4]

One study has indicated that 28 percent of the variation in Negro registration from one area to another in the South can be explained statistically in terms of social and economic variables,[5] another 21 percent in terms of political variables.[6] Although we do not know just what those variables are, it would appear as if differing political styles and traditions from one state to another are extremely important. In other words, ideology and traditional political behavior patterns are almost as important as are social and economic factors.

Voting rights had been granted at differing rates in the South. In Mississippi, around 450,000 Negroes met age and residency requirements in 1965, but only 22,000, or about 5 percent, were registered to vote. (A decade earlier the figure had been 1 percent.) By comparison, about two-thirds of the 500,000 whites meeting the same requirements were registered. But the trend was everywhere the same. In Florida that year, the last two counties having no Negroes on the voting rolls accepted registrations as the result of a drive by the Congress of Racial Equality (CORE). In 1966, a few Negroes were nominated for public office in Alabama counties where no Negroes had previously

[2] Brendan Byrne, **Let's Modernize Our Horse-and-buggy Election Laws,** Center for Information on America, Washington, Conn., 1961, Booklet no. 5.
[3] *Smith v. Allwright,* 321 U.S. 649 (1944).
[4] Donald R. Matthews and James W. Prothro, "Social and Economic Factors and Negro Voter Registration in the South," **American Political Science Review,** 57:24–44, March, 1963.
[5] *Ibid.*
[6] Donald R. Matthews and James W. Prothro, "Political Factors and Negro Voter Registration in the South," *ibid.,* 57:355–367, June, 1963.

been nominated. In one overwhelmingly Negro county, a Negro was elected sheriff.

A new Negro leadership is presenting the voting issue to its followers in simple and straightforward terms. As a Negro spokesman in one Georgia county has said: [7] "If we don't register and vote, we can't get benefits which are comparable to those received by whites—or comparable to our needs."

Prior to 1944,[8] few Negroes were registered in any of the states that had once belonged to the Confederacy, and these were nearly all in the Republican party where they were ineffective and their wants were ignored by a party that had long regarded them as a "captive" vote having nowhere else to go. But in that year, the United States Supreme Court ended the so-called "white primary" by declaring that the primary election was an integral part of the election process that could not be closed to Negroes on the excuse that the party is a private association and the primary a private affair.[9] This rule had the immediate effect of permitting a great increase in the number of Negro registrations in most Southern states.

One writer has found that the remarkable thing about "the political revolution taking place in the South since 1944 is not the white resistance to Negro voting in a few areas but the widespread acceptance of Negro voting by Southern whites. Although many regard it as a 'necessary evil', they see it as an inevitable fact and accept it." [10]

Enfranchisement and the Balance of Power   In terms of political action and its effect upon governmental policy, the question arises, of course, as to the practical effects of increased Negro voting. Does it substantially alter the pre-1944 balance of forces in the settling of public issues? Negroes have been almost totally excluded from participation in the organizations of Southern political parties. The Democratic party, in which Negroes generally registered after the death of the white primary, remains under the control of those who oppose their participation in the election process. And, of course, the Democratic nomination is all-important, since it remains, in most areas of the South, all that is necessary to secure election. Despite such exclusion, Negroes may well influence nominations, even though they can do little within the party itself. They can do this through the use of "political leagues" which have arisen in considerable numbers in the postwar years and which help to secure registrations and voter turnout and, most importantly, act to give support to candidates. The mass meeting has also become important as the percentage of the primary vote cast by Negroes has increased: [11]

[7] Margaret Price, **The Negro Voter in the South,** Southern Education Reporting Service, Nashville, Tenn., 1957, p. 3.
[8] See H. Douglas Price, "The Negro and Florida Politics," **Journal of Politics,** 17:198–220, May, 1955; and by the same author, **The Negro and Southern Politics,** New York University Press, New York, 1957.
[9] *Smith v. Allwright,* 321 U.S. 649 (1944). Various attempts at evasion of this ruling are described in V. O. Key, Jr., and Alexander Heard, **Southern Politics,** Alfred A. Knopf, Inc., New York, 1949, chaps. 25–31, but the courts have continued to rule against these. See *Rice v. Elmore,* 165 F. 2d 387 (1947); *Terry v. Adams,* 345 U.S. 461 (1953).
[10] Price, "The Negro and Florida Politics," p. 207.
[11] *Ibid.,* p. 208. Used by permission.

Segregated rallies have become a common practice. Frequently the county Democratic committee will schedule Negro rallies for the Negro neighborhood. All the Democratic candidates are invited to appear, and most usually do. Negroes regard the segregated rallies as a definite gain even in areas where they freely attend mixed rallies. Facing an all-Negro audience the candidates have to speak on some matters of genuine concern to Negroes. Also, present political mores allow the candidates to take stands at such rallies on many local issues of concern to the Negro, although to give a proportionate amount of time to such questions at a general rally would alienate many white voters. Under such circumstances the candidates are tempted to make, and often do make, promises they would not make before a mixed audience.

If serious candidates for office in the South find it necessary to make direct appeals to Negroes and to make campaign promises to them, we may be sure that the Negro is succeeding in modifying the existing balance of forces in the community. Furthermore, the new pattern of participation has resulted in a decline in the leadership role of the Negro ministers, church organizations, fraternal orders, insurance agents, and community morticians, who were formerly important links between the Negro community and the white political, economic, and social leadership. The new leaders are more issue-oriented and less willing to perform the role of helping to ameliorate potential Negro-white conflict in return for minor concessions in the traditional pattern.

The effectiveness of the new type of leadership is reflected in the way that it has made a subculture, suffering under a tradition almost totally lacking in a concept of political participation, suddenly and significantly aware of the identity of white-supremacy candidates as against those who are more favorably disposed toward Negro interests. Negro sophistication in politics is growing both in the South and in the Northern industrial cities where, in earlier years, the Negro was often a complete pawn to be manipulated by the adroit politician and almost totally without his own political leadership.

Some research [12] seems to indicate that attitudes toward direct Negro participation in the political process are not merely a function of economic concern, but may vary according to different cultural values within the same economic framework. These values, of course, tend to change with time. This offers the possibility that Southern values which seemingly have been changing over recent decades may, through further movement in the direction of permissiveness and tolerance, change enough to permit the development of a genuine universal system of suffrage in the relatively near future.

In every community that has more than a few Negroes, a Negro leadership and power pattern develops, just as is the case in cities which continue to have identifiable ethnic groups. In a study of one Southern city, Negroes rated themselves and were rated by others along a radical-conservative continuum. Negro leaders, as rated by other Negro leaders, were predominantly liberal in their views on public policy questions. There were more conservatives than radicals, but the conservatives, although still considered powerful, were no longer

[12] See John H. Fenton and Kenneth N. Vines, "Negro Registration in Louisiana," **American Political Science Review**, 51:704–713, September, 1957.

important in decision making. Relative to the issue of school desegregation, liberal leaders were found to predominate by a 6 to 1 ratio over conservatives, and by 3 to 1 over moderates. The most powerful Negro leaders, in the view of both minority leaders and the general citizenry, were rated as liberals and were active in all phases of desegregation.[13]

The pattern of Negro leadership has changed greatly since about 1950: [14]

Conservatives are no longer powerful leaders in Crescent City. In the past these compromise leaders often held their positions because they were acceptable to the white community. They believed that the interests of the Negro could best be served by adjusting to the authority of the whites. Some may have feared reprisals if they failed to cooperate with white leaders in controlling the minority community.

They were acceptable to other Negroes, not only because accommodation was regarded as the most practical policy, but because they also had prestige in their own right within the Negro social structure. This type of race leader was powerful in Crescent City through the 1930s and early 1940s. . . .

Today the suggestion that a Negro is unduly susceptible to white influence has meant loss of power. . . .

Conservative leaders still remain the most acceptable to a segment of Crescent City's white leadership. By and large, however, the white leaders by-pass the conservative leader, for they know he no longer wields power in the Negro community.

Table 7   Race-leader Peer-group Classification

TYPE OF LEADER	RADICAL %	LIBERAL %	MODERATE %	CONSERVATIVE %
Power nominees *	6.5	54.8	19.4	19.3
Power leaders *	9.1	72.7	18.2	

* Power nominees were persons believed by three groups of informants to be the most powerful or influential. Power leaders were those individuals who actually played the most active role in community issues.
SOURCE: M. Elaine Burgess, **Negro Leadership in a Southern City,** The University of North Carolina Press, Chapel Hill, N.C., 1962, p. 178.

In a period of rapid economic, political, and social change, the Negro community is badly divided concerning the question of desirable techniques. Older Negro leaders fear that irresponsible individuals may gain power and thus weaken the entire movement toward equality of opportunity and status. Younger Negroes fear that the movement may lose its militant spirit. Similarly, there is no agreement on tactics. Younger activists prefer use of the economic boycott and the sit-in; older, more conservative Negroes, prefer private negotiations, the traditional approach to relations with the dominant white community.[15]

[13] M. Elaine Burgess, **Negro Leadership in a Southern City,** The University of North Carolina Press, Chapel Hill, N.C., 1962, chap. 7.
[14] Ibid., pp. 180–181.
[15] Jack L. Walker, "Protest and Negotiation," **Midwest Journal of Political Science,** 7:99–124, May, 1963.

Apathy and the Duty to Participate   Although the ideal of grass-roots democracy calls for vigorously active participation in the political process and for
the assumption of public office as a duty to the community, in America there
is frequently a great deal of difficulty in getting public positions filled. Not
only is there no competition for some jobs, but sometimes no one will even
allow himself to be drafted for a position.

The small town, the township, the suburb, and the school district often
present scenes, not of strident conflict, but of citizens putting pressure on
other citizens to accept jobs that need to be done. These are positions that
carry some prestige but involve the budgeting of a considerable amount of
what would otherwise be leisure time for the individual.[19] The problem also
exists of filling low-paid but full-time jobs such as those on the county level
and the extremely awkward task, in terms of time allocation, of state legislators
who spend only a few months out of each year, or every other year, at the job
and then must do so at the state capital, which may be a considerable distance
away from their homes.

The lack of attractiveness of the county office has been pointed out with
Iowa as a case study.[20]

In thirty-four counties, there were no Democratic candidates for nomination for
any county office; and in nineteen of these the Republicans presented only one
candidate for each office. In fifty-four counties, there was only one candidate for
nomination for each office on either the Democratic or the Republican ticket. Thus
in more than one-third of the counties of the state [Iowa has 99], there was no contest
for any county office, either in the primary or in the general election. And in well
over half of the counties, there was no contest in the primary for any county office. In
many of the remaining counties, there were contests for only one or two of the
offices available.

Many reasons exist, of course, for the absence of a contest. Some of them
are included in the following:

1. The incumbent is sometimes so popular that other potential candidates have little or no chance to unseat him. He is hence unopposed.

2. In strongly one-party areas, there may be a contest in the primary
election of the major party, but the second party can expect to have difficulty
in getting candidates to run.

3. The formal political process may not be the effective process of decision making. That is, the important decisions affecting the community may
be made outside of government, and public offices are therefore of little importance in the view of the ordinary citizen. There is a long tradition in
America of keeping as many issues as possible "out of politics," because the
political process is not trusted. Furthermore, community leaders may prefer
to negotiate privately among the various interests centering around a controversy, keeping control out of public officials' hands—and outside the reach
of the voter. Thus businessmen may agree among themselves on the amount

[19] See Martin, *op. cit.*, pp. 60–62.
[20] Kirk H. Porter, "The Deserted Primary in Iowa," **American Political Science Review**, 39:732–
740, August, 1945.

of money that is to be devoted to port development and present a packaged plan to the council for its ratification. Land-use policies may be controlled in a similar way.

    4. There may be no contest because voters are generally satisfied—community values are stable and incumbent officeholders reflect them adequately.

    5. The ruling political group may be so strong that no one thinks it worthwhile to oppose it.

    Lack of competition for office reduces the importance of both the primary election or other nominating device and the final election. Absence of genuine conflict is certain to contribute to apathy.

Futility and Nonvoting   Even so, we are justified in asking why voter turnout is so low. Why should 28 percent of the interviewees in a representative sample in the 1952 presidential campaign—one in which interest was generally regarded as having been high by American standards—be willing to state openly that they were "not much interested" in the contest? [21] Why should 32 percent of those interviewed say that it would make no difference whether the Democrats or Republicans won the election and another 40 percent think it would make only a small difference? [22]

    Part of the answer seems to be furnished by a study made in Detroit.[23] A representative sample of persons was asked the question, "Do you feel that there is anything you can do to improve the way the city is run? What do you feel you can do?" *More than one-half the people declared that they could do nothing.* One-third could suggest only voting. Only one person in twelve believed that he could exert influence by means of personal criticism or by joining in group action.

    In another study, one-third of the members of the United Automobile Workers agreed that "people like me don't have any say about what government does." [24] These sentiments were especially strong among persons who had feelings of estrangement from society or feelings of personal futility or who were generally pessimistic. Persons who felt they could not influence governmental policy also, not surprisingly, tended to be nonvoters. On an authoritarian-democratic scale, they tended more toward the authoritarian position in personal values. A similar attitude of futility was to be found before the 1945 election in the city of New York when one-third of those eligible to vote told pollster Elmo Roper that "no matter which of the candidates is elected, the city will be run about the same." [25] They may have been quite right. Elections do not usually decide issues in America; the interaction of interest groups do that, and the election is only one part—perhaps a relatively minor part—of the political process.

[21] Angus Campbell and others, **The Voter Decides,** Harper & Row, Publishers, Incorporated, New York, 1954, p. 34.
[22] *Ibid.*, p. 38.
[23] Arthur Kornhauser, **Attitudes of Detroit People toward Detroit,** Wayne State University Press, Detroit, Mich., 1952, p. 28.
[24] Kornhauser and others, **When Labor Votes,** pp. 198–200.
[25] Elmo Roper, "New York Elects O'Dwyer," **Public Opinion Quarterly,** 10:53–56, Spring, 1946.

How serious is a high percentage of nonvoting? The chances are that its dangers have been greatly exaggerated. Most people who stay away from the polls do so deliberately and by their own choice. They are not interested, and they feel that voting in the particular instance will avail them nothing. The important question is not whether people *do* vote but rather whether they *may* vote if they so choose. Studies made of why people do not vote show that, outside of illness or a broken fan belt on the way to the voting booth, most people stay home because of lack of interest.[26] To most people, choice of candidates is of marginal interest. When something they consider to be truly important comes up, they will appear at the polls. Americans are more interested in voting against candidates than for them.[27] They become excited about elections when they wish to register a protest. The ballot box is the safety valve of democracy.

Nonvoting is sometimes viewed simply in terms of whether or not the individual goes to the polls. It is, however, more complicated than that, for persons who go to the polls vote selectively, commonly disfranchising themselves deliberately in regard to certain offices. For example, in Kansas, about 30 percent of the voters are consistently nonvoters. Another 20 percent vote only in presidential elections, although, once at the polls, they usually vote for other offices as well. About one-half of the eligible voters participate in every general election; but only 30 percent take part in primary elections. In Kansas, the office for which most voters cast their ballot in 1960 was that of President. The office of governor was next, followed by members of the two houses of the United States Congress. After that came eight state offices, ranging from lieutenant governor down to the state printer and the commissioner of insurance. The latter received about 90 percent of the vote cast for President. A supreme court justice received fewer votes than did any of the state officers, but the items on the ballot attracting the least attention were two proposed constitutional amendments. The less interesting of these was voted on by only two-thirds as many voters as those who cast ballots for President.[28] In 1962, the difference was even more dramatic. The office that attracted least interest, that of state printer, received only 65 percent of the number of ballots cast for governor.

Political Participation   Not only do a large number of Americans not vote in elections, and particularly in state and local elections, but another huge bloc of citizens do nothing politically except to vote. In the 1952 presidential contest, 27 percent of the eligible voters said that they talked politics and tried to persuade others to vote for their candidates and 11 percent engaged in

[26] For studies, see Charles E. Merriam and Harold F. Gosnell, **Non-voting,** The University of Chicago Press, Chicago, 1924; Morris Rosenberg, ''Some Determinants of Voter Apathy,'' **Public Opinion Quarterly,** 181:349–366, Winter, 1954–1955; Paul F. Lazarsfeld and others, **The People's Choice: How the Voter Makes Up His Mind,** 2d ed., Columbia University Press, New York, 1948; James K. Pollock, **Voting Behavior,** The University of Michigan Press, Ann Arbor, Mich., 1939; and the Campbell and Kornhauser studies previously cited. These citations are also the basis for the following sections on ''Political Participation'' and ''Who Goes to the Polls?''
[27] The Roper and O'Rourke studies, cited above, lend support to this statement.
[28] Charles Evans, ''Voter Participation in Kansas,'' **Your Government,** 20:1–3, September, 1964.

some kind of organized party activity. In this category, 3 percent said they did some party work such as stuffing envelopes; 7 percent said they attended political meetings, rallies, picnics, and the like; only 4 percent contributed money or bought fund-raising tickets. Some people, of course, were active in all three types of positive activity, and some did not vote either because of ineligibility or for some other reason.[29] In a postelection survey in the same year, 9 percent of the United Automobile Workers' membership claimed (in a sample study) to have been active in the campaign in such things as handing out leaflets, displaying posters, and the like. Another 17 percent said they had talked politics during the campaign, and 73 percent stated that they had done nothing active.[30]

Who Goes to the Polls?   Certain generalizations can be made concerning the qualitative make-up of our voting population. We know that in terms of percentages, more men vote than do women, more whites vote than do Negroes (there is some evidence to indicate that Negroes in some Northern urban areas vote in higher percentages than do whites in the same economic category),[31] more people who are property taxpayers vote than do those who are not, and more conservatives vote than do liberals. Except for persons who must stay at home because of the infirmities of old age, people vote in larger proportions as they grow older. Almost twice as many vote at the age of fifty-one as vote at twenty-one. This seems to support the general theory that people do not vote because they theoretically ought to or because they feel it is a duty or a great privilege, but rather they vote when they feel that they have a direct stake in the outcome.

It should further be noted that there is a direct relationship between size of income and participation in elections and between amount of education and participation. In the postwar years, at least, urbanites have voted in greater proportion than have farmers. The white-collar middle class votes in greater proportion than do nonunion members of the working class.

All of these patterns affect the balance of forces in the political arena. Apathy or a sense of futility within any given category can have the effect of further lessening the strength of the particular interest involved. Each group in society, therefore, has a stake in getting its supporters to the polls, for the vote may be a force in affecting the content of public policy.

The Voters' Information   The lack of information of the typical voter, and even of persons who presumably are above average in information and intelligence, is a favorite subject for editorials, one for which source materials are easily found. The "Ambassador of Hawaii" receives a large number of letters in Washington each year. The post office, which knows that Hawaii is one of the states of the union and not an independent nation, as apparently is the view of the writers, sends the letters to members of the Hawaiian congressional

[29] Campbell and others, **The Voter Decides**, p. 30.
[30] Kornhauser and others, **When Labor Votes**, chap. 1.
[31] *Ibid.*, pp. 49–50.

delegation. A woman in Wisconsin, writing to the "ambassador," said she hoped "that you can read this letter, because English is the only language I know." A writer in Massachusetts wanted "some information about how the people of Hawaii build their houses and what they eat." Another, in Arizona, apparently unaware that Honolulu is a cosmopolitan city of more than 300,000 people, said he was thinking of moving there to "escape the complexities of our modern society." Sometimes people write asking questions about visas and inoculation requirements to enter Hawaii. One schoolteacher offered to exchange United States money for "Hawaiian currency," and another wrote to ask for coins and stamps from this supposedly foreign land.[32]

In 1962, a man was elected to the Massachusetts legislature while in Boston's Deer Island Jail. He was serving a one-year sentence for theft of state funds. The **National Civic Review,** which embraces middle-class reform values, commented in an indignant editorial: "Every political scandal that tends to show a lack of responsibility on the part of our citizens weakens the fabric of our system and our 'image' . . . in the world struggle of ideologies." [33] It seems possible, however, that the voters did not deliberately disregard a conviction for theft. They simply did not know about it. Interviews with those who voted for the man might have shown that the vast majority did not know that this candidate for a rather obscure office had been convicted of stealing state funds or that he was in jail at the time of the election. (Of course, being in jail is not necessarily a basis for rejection by voters. James Michael Curley was reelected mayor of Boston at a time when most of those who voted for him probably knew of his temporary residence, which resulted from a mail-fraud conviction.)

The voter is not merely uninformed. In general, he does not wish to or feel a need to expend time and energy on the complex issues of the day. The "big picture" may seem academic to him. His principal issue concerns, when they exist at all, are usually parochial and self-centered. Thus in the city of New York, "residential rent control has succeeded the nickel fare as the most pervasive and enduring issue in New York City politics. The nickel fare dominated city politics for more than twenty-five years and provided a vehicle in which a succession of Democrats, starting with John F. (Red Mike) Hylan in 1917, rode to power as mayor. All indications are that rent control will provide a similar vehicle for city candidates for at least as long," a **New York Times** reporter observed in 1961.[34]

Generally speaking, the more education a voter has, the more informed he is and the more trust he places in government officials. A study of Cleveland and its suburbs, found that "the higher the income of a ward or town, the more taste it has for public expenditures of various kinds." That the ratio of benefits to costs declines as income increases seems to make no difference.[35] This same tendency of the well-to-do to vote for community "improvements"

[32] United Press-International dispatch, Mar. 14, 1965.
[33] Editorial, **National Civic Review,** 51:536–537, November, 1962.
[34] **New York Times,** Mar. 10, 1961.
[35] James Q. Wilson and Edward C. Banfield, "Public-regardingness as a Value Premise in Voting Behavior," **American Political Science Review,** 58:876–887, December, 1964.

irrespective of prospects of personal gain has also been observed in other studies.[36] Such a behavior pattern may to some extent be a result of the lower marginal sacrifice required by higher-income people—that is, the higher one's income, the less importance an additional cost assumes.[37] Perhaps higher-income people feel that gains in community physical appearance and status are worth the costs, since they are personally identified with the community. But the high relationship between education levels and voting for community improvements seems to indicate that support of local public expenditures is at least in part learned as a behavior pattern that is presumably preferred by groups with which one identifies and hopes, during the course of his professional career, to be associated with.[38]

A study of a bond-issue election in DeKalb County, Georgia, indicated the following: The greatest support came from persons in their years of maximum-earning capacity, the forty- to sixty-year old group. Women were somewhat more favorable in their attitudes than were men. The higher one's income level, the more likely he was to vote in favor of the bond issue. Organization men and professionals and their wives were more likely to vote favorably than were others. Suburban voters were more favorable than were those in the core city or in rural fringe areas. Length of residence in the county or previous residential location was not significant in determining voting patterns. The higher the family income, the more likely it was that voters were aware of information concerning the bond issue that had been published in county newspapers and advocated in pamphlets. Personal contacts were more important and more common than was the influence of the mass media of communication.

The strongest support for the bonds, which were to be used for a number of purposes and had been supported by persons and groups who viewed their adoption as being necessary for the "progress" of the community, came principally from suburbanites, and secondarily from core-city voters, high-income voters, persons who thought of themselves as enjoying above-average status, and from persons whose occupations were of high status.[39]

Appeals in elections are likely to oversimplify complex issues and to portray them in terms of black and white, right or wrong, "good guys" and "bad guys." A study of voting on the question of fluoridating the water of Northampton, Massachusetts, concluded that the opponents of fluoridation made appeals particularly in terms of the invasion of individual rights, a fear of poisoning, and a waste of public funds. The opponents' arguments were found to be easily understood, while the errors in them were often difficult for a layman to understand. In addition, the researchers concluded that the opponents of fluoridation were in part making a symbolic protest against a world that seems

[36] Oliver P. Williams and Charles R. Adrian, **Four Cities**, University of Pennsylvania Press, Philadelphia, 1963, chap. 5; Alvin Boskoff and Harmon Zeigler, **Voting Patterns in a Local Election**, J. B. Lippincott Company, Philadelphia, 1964, chap. 3; Richard A. Watson, **The Politics of Urban Change**, Community Studies, Inc., Kansas City, Mo., 1963, chap. 4; Robert H. Salisbury and Gordon Black, "Class and Party in Non-partisan Elections: The Case of Des Moines," **American Political Science Review**, 57:591, September, 1963.
[37] Robert C. Wood, **1400 Governments**, Harvard University Press, Cambridge, Mass., 1961.
[38] Wilson and Banfield, *op. cit.*, p. 879.
[39] Boskoff and Zeigler, *op. cit.*

to be increasingly menacing and were expressing a popular suspicion of science and scientists. The opponents were "predominately people of the older age groups, people without children under 12, people of the lower income brackets and middle- or lower-class occupation." Support for fluoridation came mainly from the younger groups and those in professional, managerial, and other white-collar occupations. One of the most striking differences was in education. A large proportion of the antifluoridation voters had failed to finish high school.[40] In that election, held in 1953, fluoridation was defeated by a 2 to 1 vote. The fluoridation issue as a symbolic protest has declined in importance since that time, in part perhaps because the obvious evidence is so strongly in favor of fluoridation. For example, a 1965 study by the health department in Baltimore indicated that cavities in the teeth of slum children were one-half as great as they had been in a similar study before the city's water had been fluoridated.

When the stakes of the individual are obvious, his interest level is likely to be relatively high. During a tax crisis in Wisconsin in the early 1960s, a study showed that voters seemed to view tax issues as more salient than other issues. For example, 63 percent of the voters knew the positions of the two major parties relative to a sales tax. A majority of citizens were opposed to raising taxes, but opposition diminished with increase in income, education, and occupational status. A large majority believed the income tax to be more fair in principle than was the sales tax, but the sales tax was viewed as the tax policy most likely to be adopted, despite contrary theoretical principles of respondents. Although many Michigan politicians of the same period believed that factory workers were especially opposed to the income tax, the Wisconsin study showed that preference for the sales tax over the income tax increased with amount of education, income, and job status.[41]

The lack of public attention to state government offices other than that of governor is notorious. The reason appears to be a problem of visibility of the office. Whenever a legislator or other state official gains popular attention, whether as a hero or villain, voters behave differently toward him from the way they did when he was relatively anonymous. Thus in Michigan, a legislator who had been twice elected was discovered to have been using the credentials of a dead man who happened to have the same name as his own. He was also found to have hidden a prison record. When this information was widely publicized through the public press, the legislature refused to seat him in its 1965 session. The ousted candidate then filed for nomination to fill the vacancy in his district, even though both state and Federal charges were pending against him. By this time, however, he was well known to his constituency and he ran fifteenth in a field of seventeen.

Sometimes the lack of information about events and an inability to under-

[40] Bernard Mausner and Judith Mausner, "A Study of the Anti-scientific Attitude," **Scientific American,** February, 1955, pp. 3–7.
[41] Leon D. Epstein, **Votes and Taxes,** Institute of Governmental Affairs, University of Wisconsin, Madison, Wis., 1964.

stand politics leads to cynicism about the political process. After looking at the question of political cynicism, a team of researchers has concluded: [42]

The increasingly widespread distribution of secondary and higher education in society generates a higher level of political trust in the polity. At the same time, there are two counter trends, one minor and one major. The minor trend is due to the relatively few people from well-educated families who do not themselves attain much education and are extremely cynical. The major counter trend is the increasing political cynicism that comes with increasing age. With the aged constituting an increasingly larger proportion of the citizenry the dissipating effect on political cynicism of an increasingly educated citizenry may be effectively offset.

Even among the uneducated and uninformed, the voter is never without some information—and from his point of view, this information is sufficient, for the marginal costs of collecting more are, to him, dysfunctional.[43]

The voter has, as a foundation for decision making, his personal experiences, habits, and personal contacts or reference groups to guide him.

Indeed, the voter early learns his family's general point of view, if it has one, on major issues of the era, and its party affiliation, if any.[44] He is likely either to accept these as basic guidelines or to rebel against them deliberately if he is resentful of parental control. A man who could not identify the party affiliation of Theodore Roosevelt or the approximate period in history when he was President may have a clear recollection of the party allegiance of his mother and father, and their salient life experiences, such as their accounts of the years of the Great Depression. The teachings of one or both parents are often important guides to the voter. Although children, whose life experiences differ from those of their parents, may reject parental teachings, as many young people did during the early years of the New Deal, they are more likely to agree with their parents than with friends.[45]

In addition, each individual has a wealth of personal experiences. He may make a rough correlation between them and political activities. He does not need to rely entirely on the vague promises of politicians. To some degree, at least, he knows of specific kinds of governmental programs or policies that seem to have aided or injured his interests. He may be right or wrong in attributing causes, but he is likely to have some basis for using this relationship in making decisions on voting. He also has his own general feeling of well-being or dissatisfaction.

The voter is ordinarily a member of or able to identify with a number of organizations, and he can take his political cues from these reference groups, or from individuals he respects. He may not know the name of the congressman

[42] Robert E. Agger, Marshall N. Goldstein, and Stanley A. Pearl, "Political Cynicism," **Journal of Politics,** 23:477–506, August, 1961. Quotation from pp. 499–500.
[43] For more on the subject of the voter, see Charles R. Adrian and Charles Press, **The American Political Process,** McGraw-Hill Book Company, New York, 1965, chap. 9.
[44] *Ibid.,* pp. 267–268.
[45] Eleanor E. Maccoby and others, "Youth and Political Change," **Public Opinion Quarterly,** 18:23–39, Winter, 1954–1955; Herbert McClosky and Harold E. Dahlgren, "Primary Group Influence on Party Loyalty," **American Political Science Review,** 53:757–776, September, 1959.

(or legislator) from his district, how he voted on issues, or his party affiliation; but if he is at all interested in the election, he is likely to know which candidate or party his union shop steward or business association secretary is supporting. This information, in itself, may be all he feels he needs to know in order to vote his own interests. Views expressed by such leaders are an important part of the political process, for the cues from trusted interest-group spokesmen are often a substitute for class or even party leadership to Americans. One study of voting found that a number of persons on every level of society, because of their role or as the result of personal motivation, become opinion leaders in politics. Just as women take fashion cues from women who are seen as style leaders, opinion leaders give political cues to other citizens.[46]

In addition, interest-group leaders who are highly visible even to the casually interested may provide the necessary cues for the assumption of a stand on a public issue. When Martin Luther King announces his position on a civil rights measure pending in Congress, both integrationists and segregationists are helped to decide how they stand on the matter. Similarly, although few people have any accurate knowledge of the contents of the Taft-Hartley Act, if Walter Reuther takes a public position on a proposed amendment to it, large numbers of people can instantly make up their minds on their own position and how their own interests would be affected by the proposed change.

Finally, habit is the most important influence of all on voter decisions. In many, perhaps most elections, the individual need only decide whether he is going to continue to support the party or candidate he has been supporting or whether he is going to cast a protest vote. Unless he is consciously dissatisfied, he may also automatically cast his vote in terms of his allegiances.

An alert and informed public is probably an asset to any democracy, but it is not a prerequisite for effective democracy. Democracy does, however, ask for the expenditure of more resources in the political arena than is expected of the citizen in other types of governments. It is the task of opinion leaders to encourage such interest and attention and to secure it despite the competing attractions—personal problems, recreation, sports, hobbies—that constantly lure the citizen.

SELECTED READINGS

Asch, Solomon E.: "Opinions and Social Pressure," **Scientific American,** November, 1955, pp. 3–7.   (Deals with personality types and conformity or nonconformity, and effects of pressures to conform.)

Berelson, Bernard R., and others: **Voting,** The University of Chicago Press, Chicago, 1954.   (An important landmark in the development of voter behavior theory.)

Brittain, J. M.: "Some Reflections on Negro Suffrage and Politics in Alabama," **Journal of Negro History,** 47:127–138, April, 1962.

Burdick, Eugene, and A. J. Brodbeck: **American Voting Behavior,** The Free Press of Glencoe, New York, 1958.   (A series of essays.)

Campbell, Angus, and others: **The American Voter,** John Wiley & Sons, Inc., New

[46] Paul F. Lazarsfeld and others, *op. cit.*

York, 1960. (A report on the 1956 presidential campaign and a theory of voter behavior.)

————— and —————: **The Voter Decides,** Harper & Row, Publishers, Incorporated, New York, 1954. (A report on voter behavior in the 1952 elections.)

————— and R. L. Kahn: **The People Elect a President,** Survey Research Center, University of Michigan, Ann Arbor, Mich., 1952. (The first of the major Survey Research Center studies; covers the 1948 election.)

Harris, Joseph P.: **Registration of Voters in the United States,** The Brookings Institution, Washington, D.C., 1929. (A standard reference.)

Kornhauser, Arthur, and others: **When Labor Votes,** University Books, Inc., New Hyde Park, N.Y., 1956. (A study of voter attitudes among members of the United Auto Workers.)

Lazarsfeld, Paul F., and others: **The People's Choice: How the Voter Makes Up His Mind,** Columbia University Press, New York, 1948. (One of the first voter behavior studies. By social psychologists.)

Levitan, Sar A.: **Federal Aid to Depressed Areas,** The Johns Hopkins Press, Baltimore, 1964.

Merriam, Charles E., and H. F. Gosnell: **Non-voting,** The University of Chicago Press, Chicago, 1924. (A pioneer study.)

O'Rourke, Lawrence W.: **Voting Behavior in the Forty-five Cities of Los Angeles County,** Bureau of Governmental Research, University of California, Los Angeles, 1953.

Pollock, James K.: **Voting Behavior: A Case Study,** The University of Michigan Press, Ann Arbor, Mich., 1939. (An early study.)

Price, H. Douglas: **The Negro and Southern Politics,** New York University Press, New York, 1957.

Price, Margaret: **The Negro Voter in the South,** Southern Education Reporting Service, Nashville, Tenn., 1957.

Rosenberg, Morris: "Some Determinants of Voter Apathy," **Public Opinion Quarterly,** 181:349–366, Winter, 1954–55.

Rowat, Donald C.: **The Ombudsman: Citizen's Defender,** University of Toronto Press, Toronto, Canada, 1965. (The story of the origin, use, and proposed use of the complaint officer. The institution originated in Sweden in 1809 and has been proposed for use in the United States as a means for allowing citizens to have their complaints against administrative decisions investigated.)

Scammon, Richard M.: **America Votes,** The Macmillan Company, New York, 1956.

Sharp, Harold: "Migration and Voting Behavior in a Metropolitan Community," **Public Opinion Quarterly,** vol. 19, Summer, 1955.

Sigel, Roberta (ed.): "Political Socialization: Its Role in the Political Process," **Annals,** vol. 361, entire issue, September, 1965.

6

STATE AND LOCAL POLITICAL SYSTEMS

Elections involve both the process of nomination, or the selection of candidates, and the general elections proper, at which the choice is made of the individual who is to occupy public office. At elections for either purpose, the voters may be called upon to decide by their votes some issues of public policy through the devices often referred to as those of "direct democracy." The basic machinery of elections is today controlled by law in all states. This has evolved gradually, and it has everywhere been subject to manipulation so as to give advantage to the groups which happen to dominate state constitutional conventions, legislatures, and other institutions through which the election procedures can be controlled. Because this is the case, election law varies greatly from one state to another and even from one community to another within a state.

The Machinery of Elections

Methods of Nomination   Before there can be an election, the individuals who are going to make the race must be selected. Numerous ways exist of placing candidates in nomination. The overwhelming majority of nominations in the United States today are by way of either the partisan or nonpartisan direct primary election. There are, or have been, however, numerous other techniques, including caucus or convention nomination, sponsorship, and petition.

   Early Nomination Devices   The caucus, the oldest form of nomination in the United States, consisted originally of an informal meeting to choose candidates deserving of support for the various public offices becoming vacant. But with the growth of cities, the caucus became too large in size and underwent a process of degeneration. To overcome the problem of unwieldiness, the convention method came into use. Under this approach nominations were made at formal meetings with the membership in the convention made up of delegates chosen by caucus at the precinct—or smallest political subdivision —level. But the widespread development of citywide or statewide political machines in the nineteenth century made this method subject to corruption.

The machine controlled the precinct caucus by excluding unwanted persons. This could be done through the trickery of keeping secret the time and place of meetings, by threats, by better strategic planning, and other devices. And whoever controlled the precinct caucuses controlled the convention. Since in most cities, counties, and states, one party is dominant and a balanced two-party system is the exception, the machines often controlled the elective office simply by controlling the nomination process.

Reforms in Nomination   Beginning early in the present century, the reform movement produced a change in nomination procedure. The direct primary election * was substituted for the caucus and convention. It is now almost universal in the United States, although a few states do not use it for important state offices—New York and Indiana nominate gubernatorial candidates by convention—and there are school districts and cities in such populous states as California, Texas, New Jersey, and Massachusetts that do not use it.[1]

* PRIMARY ELECTION. A method for nominating candidates for public office by which voters have a direct choice at an election from among those who wish to be considered for nomination.

A primary election is a nonassembled caucus. In an earlier day every eligible voter was entitled to take part in the selection of candidates. Later, part of this job had to be turned over to those who were theoretically his representatives acting at a convention. When the convention proved to be unrepresentative and class- or boss-ridden, the primary election was devised to return nominations "to the people." The plan in large measure transfers control of the nomination machinery from the party to the state, all parties choosing their candidates on the same day under the supervision of public election officials, with ballots standardized and printed at public expense (except in a few Southern states) and with a secret ballot (in contrast to most caucus and convention systems).

Connecticut, in 1955, adopted the direct primary as the basic nominating device for elections in that state. It was the last state to do so. The method was first used, under Democratic party control, in Pennsylvania in the 1840s, and it gradually spread throughout the country. It began to be used for statewide nominations in the 1890s, and Wisconsin, under the leadership of Governor Robert M. La Follette, was the first state (in 1903) to adopt compulsory statewide primary elections.

Despite the leadership of Wisconsin, which probably can be attributed to

[1] See Spencer D. Albright, **The American Ballot,** Public Affairs Press, Washington, D.C., 1942; Charles E. Merriam and Louise Overacker, **Primary Elections,** The Univesity of Chicago Press, Chicago, 1928; V. O. Key, Jr., **American State Politics,** Alfred A. Knopf, Inc., New York, 1956; or the textbooks on political parties and elections.

the great reform zeal generated by "Fightin' Bob" La Follette, it was in the South that the primary system of nomination first came into general use. This appears to have resulted from efforts on the part of excluded groups and classes to overcome oligarchical potentialities in one-partyism.[2] In rough terms, the primary was adopted first in the one-party states and later in the competitive two-party states. After the South, the West picked up the plan, then the Midwest, and finally the East with its old and well-established party systems.

The Public Attitude   American voters are annoyed by the long "bedsheet" ballot with which they are confronted; they resent the fact that they must usually reveal their party preference in order to vote, and even when the open primary is used, they become incensed to discover that splitting the ticket is not permitted (except in the state of Washington). Yet the primary symbolizes popular participation in the political process, and the device undoubtedly has helped to restore genuine popular competition in the process of selecting public officers after that competition had all but disappeared in many parts of the country as a result of the rise of one-partyism and bossism in the years following the Civil War.

Types of Primaries   Primary elections are of two types, nonpartisan and partisan. The latter is subdivided into two classes, open and closed. In both types, candidates for nomination usually qualify for a place on the primary ballot by securing a required number of signatures of qualified voters on a petition. The nonpartisan ballot is used in seventeen states for some or all of the judiciary. Various local officials are chosen in this manner, including about two-thirds of all municipal officeholders.

The nonpartisan primary is actually an elimination contest. Names appear on the ballot without party designation. The first election, popularly and sometimes legally called a primary, serves to eliminate all candidates except twice the number to be elected. Hence if seven file for the office of mayor, only two will survive the primary—the two with the highest number of votes. If seven councilmen are to be elected, the fourteen highest in the primary are nominated. In some cases, such as in many California cities and in elections for the Chicago city council, if any candidate receives a majority of the vote cast in the primary he is declared elected. This plan is designed to avoid the cost of placing such a candidate on the final ballot, even though in the absence of such a rule, it would be possible for a candidate to receive a majority of the votes in the primary and still lose in the final election.

The partisan primary may be open or closed. An open primary is open to any eligible voter regardless of his party affiliation or whether he is a party member or a confirmed independent. All voters are given the ballots of all parties, though they may vote for the nominees of only one party. In a closed primary, however, the voter must have registered as a member of the party, or

[2] Key, *op. cit.*, pp. 87–97. See also A. D. Kirwan, **Revolt of the Rednecks,** University of Kentucky Press, Lexington, Ky., 1951, chap. 11.

STATE AND LOCAL POLITICAL SYSTEMS 153

declare his affiliation at the polls, and is given only the primary ballot of his party.

The closed primary is more widely used, but in some states one need only declare that he is affiliated with a particular party in order to get its ballot. In some cases, in fact, the election clerk simply inquires, "What ballot do you want?" without even suggesting that allegiance to the party is a technical requirement. In a few states, such as Pennsylvania, transferring from one party to another in the primary is relatively difficult, and a real effort is made to keep the nomination process a membership affair.

About one-fourth of the states use the open primary, which seems to have received a good deal of popular acceptance because one need not reveal his choice of party at any time in the election process and the secret ballot is thus fully preserved. Since nomination is tantamount to election in many parts of the nation—even in two-party states there are many one-party areas—the ordinary citizen regards the primary as an integral part of the election process, the part where very often the real decisions are made.[3] In the state of Washington the voter is not only given a consolidated ballot of all parties before he goes into the polling booth, but he can vote for the candidate of his choice, crossing party lines at will so long as he does not vote for more than one candidate for each office.

The Runoff Primary   The tendency in all states is for popular interest to concentrate in the primary of the stronger party.[4] As the chances for the minority party to win elections decrease, popular participation in that party's primary also decreases, but at a faster rate. In the South, the advantage of the Democratic party is so great that eleven states have tried to assure majority choice for public office by requiring a runoff primary in cases where no candidate wins a majority in the first primary. The runoff is usually conducted between the two candidates getting the most votes in the first primary. This method is used to prevent the manipulation of the results by flooding the ballot with a multiplicity of candidates, something that can be done, for example, through the adroit use of "name candidates." The runoff assures that the candidate who finally wins is acceptable to a majority of those voting, though he may not be the first choice.[5]

Criticisms of the Primary   Although it is the dominant form of nomination for office in the United States, the primary election has always had its critics. They have pointed out, for example, that the primary produces a long ballot, at least in those areas where nominations are genuinely competitive. The long ballot confuses, frustrates, and discourages the voter. The primary election has never enjoyed a large measure of popular participation, if long-run averages are considered. The need to conduct a campaign for the nomination

[3] This was not recognized by the U.S. Supreme Court until the *Allwright* case of 1944, cited above. Earlier, the Court had viewed the primary as an intraparty matter outside the scope of the election process proper.
[4] Key, *op. cit.*, p. 100 and table 9.
[5] On the political patterns in states with the runoff, see V. O. Key, Jr., and Alexander Heard, **Southern Politics**, Alfred A. Knopf, Inc., New York, 1949.

discourages many individuals from entering the lists or even from indicating that they are available for nomination.

The primary is expensive for those who must campaign against competition for a nomination, and the goal of making all interested and qualified persons easily available for the public to nominate is thus frustrated by the fact that only the wealthy or those financed by party or interest group can afford to enter.

Whether financial incapacity or lack of interest is the cause, the fact that so many primary elections have little competition itself indicates a failure on the part of the system to produce the type and number of candidates its originators intended. In many areas, candidates are still determined by the party machinery, and the primary only ratifies the decision.[6]

The primary has not greatly changed the kinds of persons nominated for office, as its originators hoped it would, though it may contribute to the nomination of publicity lovers and demagogues while discouraging less exhibitionistic types. It contributes to the selection of persons with recognizable political names, names that sound like those of persons already widely known in the community and of persons who happen to have a position at or near the top of a long ballot.[7] It discourages party responsibility or the development of slates of candidates who collectively take positions on the issues of the day. It encourages intraparty rather than interparty conflict, thus contributing to the tendency toward one-partyism with its fractional jungles that are so incomprehensible to the typical voter.[8]

However valid these arguments may be,[9] the primary is an entrenched part of Americana and it is and probably will long remain the mechanism through which a great many of the actual decisions in the selection of persons to public office are made. Perhaps changes in it can be devised so as to make it a more effective contributor to the democratic process, but election "reforms" usually come about because a dominant party or faction embraces a reform proposal, seeing in it immediate advantages.[10] The differences in party structure and election machinery from one state to another are in part, at least, a function of the desire of a group in power to strengthen its chances to stay in power. If changes in the nomination process are to be made, they must be made within the political environment as it exists in each state.

Nomination Other than by Primary   Quite a large number of states still make use of the convention system for nomination to some offices. Indiana and New York nominate for statewide office by convention. In Iowa and South Dakota, the postprimary convention is used to choose nominees in cases where no

6 See Kirk H. Porter, "The Deserted Primary in Iowa," **American Political Science Review,** 39:732–740, August, 1945.
7 H. M. Bain and Donald S. Hecock, **Ballot Position and Voter's Choice,** Wayne State University Press, Detroit, Mich., 1957.
8 The arguments for and against the primary are reviewed in the various textbooks on political parties.
9 Key, in **American State Politics,** seeks to test some of them empirically.
10 For a case study in Michigan, see Stephen B. Sarasohn, **The Regulation of Parties and Nominations in Michigan: The Politics of Election Reform,** University Microfilms, Inc., Ann Arbor, Mich., 1953.

candidate receives at least 35 percent of the vote. In Michigan, candidates for governor are nominated by primary, but those for certain lesser state offices are selected by postprimary conventions.

Some California and Wisconsin cities, and school districts in some states, make use of nomination by petition directly onto the final ballot with the candidate who receives a plurality being declared elected. This method saves the expense of primary elections and usually has satisfactory results in small cities, but when the plan was in effect in Boston, it created controversy, because the mayor was sometimes a plurality rather than majority choice, and the machine under James Michael Curley found this useful. Some California cities use the sponsor system, which requires a petition signed by but a few persons. They are listed as sponsors of the candidate. A sum of money must be paid as a filing fee, and it is returned under certain conditions. But in most cases, nominations for office in the United States are through the primary election.

Party Organization

Party structure, like election machinery, is determined in large measure by the desires of the party or faction in power at the time the law is adopted or modified. Seldom are basic theoretical questions regarding what is desirable in the light of our commitment to democracy or the total political picture considered in the making of laws to deal with these matters. Until the reform movement at the end of the nineteenth century began to demand legal requirements for party organization, the structure of each group was determined by its own leadership and varied according to time and party. Today, the parties are controlled as to organizational pattern by detailed state law and informal arrangements established to meet the needs of the moment. The latter may be far different from the former, and detailed state laws probably have not been of much importance in shaping political patterns.

What Is a Political Party? A political party is a group of people banded together for the purpose of seeking to capture elective public offices. As such, it differs from an interest group (or pressure group), which is a group of people banded together for the purpose of promoting or protecting a social or economic interest or set of interests. Of course, a political party may be ideologically cohesive—the members may all have basically the same values and same attitudes toward issues of public policy—and this is generally true in most European democracies. But it is not true in America.

The American Party Pattern In the United States, the following generalizations about parties apply:

Membership Party membership in the United States has a vague meaning, for very few individuals actively participate in partisan campaigning. The term is most useful if we say that a member of a party is anyone who identifies with a particular party label. No one is elected to membership and, except for

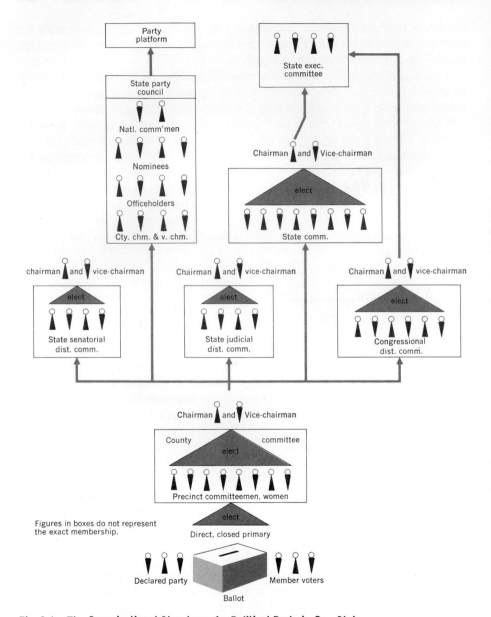

Fig. 6-1 The Organizational Structure of a Political Party in One State.

SOURCE: Earl J. Reeves, Jr., **Kansas Voter's Guide,** Governmental Research Center, University of Kansas, Lawrence, Kans., 1962, p. 28. Chart by M. Meade.

the Communist party, no one carries a party card or is subject to being expelled. Membership varies from confirmed partisans who always vote the straight party or faction line to the independent who reluctantly registers as a party member only because it is necessary to do so in order to vote in the highly important primary election.

Competition and Programmatic Parties   A generation or two ago, reformers commonly demanded increased party discipline. Their assumption was that this would produce a higher level of party responsibility. The assumption was that parties with a high degree of internal control over membership would also become programmatic parties. If this assumption were correct, the two major parties presumably would take different positions and this would permit a real choice by voters. On the other hand, opponents of party responsibility as a basis for political organization "conjure up visions of polarized parties, downtrodden minorities, and multipartyism as the fruits of party responsibility. They are able to make these improbable references by working with an exceedingly simple model, by ignoring the functions of party competition and the complex of factors that seem to shape party systems." [11]

Thomas Flinn, in looking at some of the patterns related to party responsibility, has reached the following conclusions: [12]

1. Although some states, such as Connecticut and New York, have a high degree of party organization and party leaders can establish organizational pressure upon legislators in order to secure cohesion among party members in the legislature, such cohesion also is to be found in states with weak and divided state party organizations, such as in Minnesota and Ohio.

2. Party influence on legislators increases with the size and complexity of districts, and length of term of legislators. Increasing party responsibility also results from this pattern rather than from party support being concentrated in selected, socially homogeneous districts.

3. Officeholders who have won by a wide margin are more likely to be loyal to a party position than are those who suffer the insecurity of a narrow electoral victory. The latter probably attempt to win over independents and weak supporters of the other party.

Issues   Even in the few states where political parties have reasonably identifiable positions on the issues of the day, large numbers of party members do not agree with the party position and probably even more members do not vote for the party because of its stand on issues. Members tend to vote for a party for traditional reasons or as a result of symbolic appeals or dramatic candidates rather than in response to rational arguments.

Factions   There may be two or more, sometimes many more, groups or factions in any state that use the same party label, although these groups may be as competitive with one another for public office as if they bore different labels. Thus many Southern and Border states are made up of factions, each of them a political party within the definition given above but each calling itself the "Democratic party." [13] Similar factions are found in both major parties in all parts of the nation. The primary election process has tended to encourage factionalism, and the result is that the United States does not have two parties but rather dozens of them, perhaps hundreds. Yet we think of there

[11] Thomas Flinn, "Party Responsibility in the States," **American Political Science Review**, 58:60–71, March, 1961.
[12] *Ibid.*
[13] See Key and Heard, *op. cit.*, and John H. Fenton, **Politics in the Border States**, Hauser Press, New Orleans, La., 1957, for descriptions of these factions.

being only two parties because nearly all of them call themselves either Republicans or Democrats. (In this book, "party" will specifically refer to all factions grouped under a single label.)

Party Competition   The real struggle in any given state for control of public office may be between factions rather than between two parties calling themselves Republicans or Democrats. In the mid-1960s, only about one-fourth of the states had genuine competition between the two major parties for state offices, and in less than two-thirds of them did the second party have any real chance of winning control of the governorship or the legislature.

Both political scientists and journalists have long been interested in the question of the effective difference between states with interparty competition and those dominated by a single party. Reformers at the beginning of the twentieth century believed that if political parties could not be eliminated altogether, the next best thing would be to have party competition. The assumption was that one party would tend to "keep the other honest." We have no measure of the relationship of political corruption or of patronage politics to the pattern of two-party competition, but the hope of the reformers probably was not fulfilled. It is true that the states least competitive according to various measurements have not been noted for modern personnel practices while competitive states like California, Michigan, and Minnesota have, in the last generation, had highly developed and pervasive merit systems of personnel administration and relatively little corruption. But Pennsylvania, a highly competitive state, has also been devoted to the patronage approach to personnel administration, while competitive Massachusetts has gained much notoriety for its publicized examples of corruption. It seems likely that local political styles and probably other factors are also relevant.

Following the Great Depression, V. O. Key, and later others,[14] defended the hypothesis that interparty competition tended to increase the size of benefit payments for welfare programs in the state. The assumption was that the more competitive a state, the more each party will tend to offer welfare benefits as an inducement to the "have-nots." Subsequent statistical research has indicated that the hypothesis probably has only a low degree of validity. One study concluded that the level of social welfare programs appears to be more a function of socioeconomic factors than of interparty competition, particularly of per capita income.[15] Another study, using somewhat different techniques, found some validity in the Key hypothesis, but this study did not control for the relative wealth of states. It did show an additional important finding, however: The apportionment of legislatures is not an important factor in explaining social welfare expenditure levels.[16] Finally, another study has concluded that the level of welfare services is related most closely to a

[14] V. O. Key, Jr., and Alexander Heard, **Southern Politics in State and Nation,** Alfred A. Knopf, Inc., New York, 1951, pp. 298–314; Duane Lockard, **New England State Politics,** Princeton University Press, Princeton, N.J., 1959, pp. 320–340.

[15] Richard E. Dawson and James A. Robinson, "Inter-party Competition, Economic Variables, and Welfare Policies in the American States," **Journal of Politics,** 25:265–289, May, 1963.

[16] Thomas W. Casstevens and Charles Press, "The Context of Democratic Competition in American State Politics," **American Journal of Sociology,** 68:536–543, March, 1963.

composite index of industrialization.[17] In this study, industrialization is taken to include patterns of increasing urbanization, rising per capita incomes, some economic dislocations that cause social and political difficulties, increasing education levels, and higher taxes. The argument is that interparty competition tends to increase as the total industrialization pattern, according to these measures, increases in intensity. The various characteristics of industrialization do not all move in the same direction at the same time, however. For example, industrialization often involves the movement of a work force from rural to the new industrial urban complexes. In the case of Florida or Texas, states which have drawn many persons from the North, the effect may be to dilute the dominant position of the Democratic party and to increase competitiveness. But industrialization in Mississippi has largely resulted in migration from Mississippi and Alabama rural areas and hence has not affected the political structure. In Michigan, the cities that have drawn their work force primarily from the South have tended to become Democratic; those that have drawn from their immediate hinterland have remained Republican. The result is a competitive two-party state, but with relatively few competitive counties within it. It seems likely that neither interparty competition nor legislative apportionment is so important in explaining levels of social welfare support as is the degree of industrialization within the state. Robert Wood has reached a similar conclusion relative to expenditure levels in local government.[18] He found that the higher the income level—a factor closely related to the level of industrialization in the area—the higher were government expenditures. This finding can be explained by applying the economic law of marginal sacrifice: It takes less effort in wealthy areas to have a high level of services than it does in less wealthy areas.

These studies still leave the question of the social significance of interparty competition or its absence, or whether any social significance exists at all. As social scientists are fond of saying, "further research is required." [19]

Competition and Rational Strategy   Illinois has a unique system of "cumulative" voting. Its purpose is to secure minority representation and is a rough method of providing for representation in proportion to percentage of electoral strength. Three representatives are elected from each district and each voter has three votes. The voter can distribute his votes in any manner he chooses. That is, he may "plunk" three votes for a single candidate or may distribute them in any other manner. Each party, in turn, can nominate from one to three candidates. In practice, parties always nominate at least one candidate. But 5 percent of the time when they could elect two, they have failed to run a second candidate and 80 percent of the time when they could elect three, they fail to nominate a third candidate. The party committees which make

[17] James R. Elliott, "A Comment on Inter-party Competition," **Journal of Politics**, 27:185–191, February, 1965.
[18] Robert C. Wood, **1400 Governments**, Harvard University Press, Cambridge, Mass., 1961.
[19] See Thomas R. Dye, "The Independent Effect of Party Competition on Policy Outcomes in the American States," a paper read at the 1965 meeting of the American Political Science Association, Washington.

Table 8 Relation between Two-party Competition, Income, and Per Capita
State and Local Welfare Expenditures Less Federal, 1959

INTERVALS OF COMPETITION SCORES	15 HIGH INCOME		15 MIDDLE INCOME		16 LOW INCOME	
	NUMBER OF STATES	AVERAGE PER CAPITA EXPENDITURE FOR WELFARE	NUMBER OF STATES	AVERAGE PER CAPITA EXPENDITURE FOR WELFARE	NUMBER OF STATES	AVERAGE PER CAPITA EXPENDITURE FOR WELFARE
80-100 (strong two-party)	12	$14.24	6	$11.66	1	$8.13
40- 79 (weak two-party)	3	10.01	7	9.01	7	9.32
0- 39 (one-party)			2	6.71	8	6.67

When income is controlled for, party-competitive states spend more than one-party states; when competition is controlled for, income is important. But other factors may be more important. For example, the most competitive states may also tend to be the wealthiest.
SOURCE: By permission of John H. Fenton, from a manuscript.

the decision on the number of candidates to run have been highly conservative. That is, they have concentrated on winning a minimum number of seats and sometimes have feared to nominate the number they might actually be able to elect because they do not want votes distributed broadly. Furthermore, the committees have tended to nominate the same number of candidates in each election, even though important changes in the political environment of the district may have taken place.[20] Custom and interparty agreements may be more important in competition for office than is knowledge of statistical possibilities.

Life Styles and Party Competition   Voting patterns and party allegiance seem to grow more complicated as American life becomes more complicated. According to the assumptions in this book concerning ideological patterns, rural areas of South Dakota should be the most Democratic, cities next, and small towns the least Democratic. In 1960, however, the pattern was for the rural areas to be 44.2 percent Democratic, towns 41.5 percent, and cities 37.7 percent.[21] Obviously, traditions and ethnic patterns must be important in determining the location of persons with predispositions to vote in a certain way.

Before 1936, the two-party vote in Ohio was sharply divided. Beginning in that year, however, the counties in which German ethnic groups were strong became predominately Republican. At the same time, urban industrial counties which had previously been divided between the two major parties, shifted sharply to the Democratic party in support of New Deal policies. Apparently the persons of German descent were, and since have remained, particularly concerned with matters of foreign policy. Other ethnic groups have reflected a greater concern for the "bread and butter" politics of domestic policy.[22]

German immigrants settled particularly in Midwestern rural and small-town areas. Many banks in these areas were run by Germans. Both of these behaviors tended to lead the Americanized Germans toward the Republican party. World War I, coming at a time when many immigrants and their children were not yet fully assimilated into the American culture, probably added to German Republicanism, since the leading anti-German spokesman was President Wilson, a Democrat. Similarly, at the approach of World War II, another Democrat, President Franklin Roosevelt, was highly critical of German policies, beginning in the mid-1930s.

Changes in the Balance of Competition   When the balance of power shifts in a state and a party that has been in the minority becomes the majority party, it may bring with it a new type of politics and a new style of political leadership. The Democratic party, which came into majority status in Michigan

[20] Jack Sawyer and Duncan MacRae, "Game Theory and Cumulative Voting in Illinois," **American Political Science Review,** 56:936–946, March, 1962.
[21] Alan L. Clem, **West River Voting Patterns,** Governmental Research Bureau, University of South Dakota, Vermillion, S.Dak., 1965.
[22] Thomas A. Flinn, "Continuity and Change in Ohio Politics," **Journal of Politics,** 24:521–544, August, 1962.

beginning about 1954, for example, placed great emphasis upon issues as a means of attracting voters and of enticing citizens to become active party workers. A leadership of representatives of organized labor and unaffiliated liberals won control of the Democratic party in 1949 and took five years to bring it into a position of dominance. The task of the new leadership, which it carried out successfully, was to mold together members of organized labor who were whites, either from among recent immigrants or from among Southern migrants, and Negroes, Southern-born, both overwhelmingly labor union members.[23]

Competition and the Time Factor   The pattern in Pennsylvania is indicative of the way in which the party pattern of a state changes through time. Before 1921, the state was overwhelmingly Republican, and it was led from the end of the Civil War until then by three powerful traditional bosses. The last of them, Boies Penrose, died in 1921, and no one was strong enough to replace him. The Republican party continued to dominate the state, however, from then until 1952, but the Democrats, often helped by the fact that they were generally in control of the White House and Congress, made some gains. Both the Republicans and Democrats developed strong state and local party organizations. The Republicans were, however, badly divided by factions. The Democrats finally elected a governor in 1934, but they, too, began to be confronted with factionalism. Neither party has been able to unite on either leadership or ideology. Both parties appear throughout the last century to have been more interested in power, patronage, and welfare politics than in program development.[24]

The More Common Pattern: Factions   Under certain conditions, a faction or coalition may serve virtually as a political party. Thus, a liberal coalition in Durham, North Carolina, served the usual party functions of lining up a leadership elite and separating the "ins" from the "outs." The coalition also recruited candidates for office and these were frequently successful. As in the case of a political party, it recruited some who were members of the coalition, others who were on the fringe, and some who were independent of the coalition but were considered worthy of support by its members and their followers. This coalition was effective in the 1940s and 1950s.[25]

In states where one party dominates, factions grouped under a single party label may be of either like or conflicting views on major policies, or they may compete for office without regard to issues or ideological positions. The histories of many states include tales of politicians of the same party fighting one another bitterly over many years with not a single difference between them involving an issue of policy. They are concerned with winning office, not with

---

[23] Robert L. Sawyer, Jr., **The Democratic State Central Committee, 1949–1959,** Institute of Public Administration, University of Michigan, Ann Arbor, Mich., 1960.
[24] Edward F. Cooke and Edward G. Janosik, **Pennsylvania Politics,** rev. ed., Holt, Rinehart and Winston, Inc., New York, 1965.
[25] Lewis Bowman and G. R. Boynton, "Coalition as Party in a One-party State Southern Area," **Midwest Journal of Politics,** 8:277–297, August, 1964.

selling a program. It is not difficult to construct a party platform vague enough to accommodate the needs of all candidates. Sometimes a single party label may serve as an umbrella for two important factions, one liberal and the other conservative, as has been the case in Minnesota Republicanism since 1938; [26] and among Democrats in the Border states where: [27]

In general, there are two Democratic parties in the Border States. One Democratic party is the party of the Bourbons. This Democratic party is the political vehicle of the gentry, protecting the community from such "evils" as labor unions and "black and tan" rule. It is the party to which a "gentleman" belongs, because only colored people and "hillbillies" belong to the Republican party. The other Democratic party is the refuge of the "Common Man." It is to this political party that the urban Negroes, coal miners, urban workers, and yeoman farmers belong. On general election day both of these Democratic parties are asked to vote for a single candidate.

Few important, and especially controversial, issues are ever decided as the result of political campaigns. This is so because legislators and the many other officers who are chosen by popular vote may come from a variety of different factions within a particular party. Furthermore, politicians seek to broaden their areas of potential support so as to make them as all-encompassing as possible. Under these conditions, political issues involving public policy tend to be settled, not by the public's vote at the general election, but by the balancing off of the various interests in the legislative arena.

The Effect of Gerrymandering In quite a few states, gerrymandering of the legislature—that is allocating legislative seats so as to give disproportionate strength to one party, faction, or geographic region—has operated in such a manner as to guarantee a division of partisan control whenever the minority party succeeds in capturing the governorship. That is, in some states "if the voters want a Democratic governor they are sure to have at least one Republican legislative house; in other, and fewer, states if the voters prefer a Republican governor, they are quite certain to have a Democratic legislature." [28] Majority rule becomes, because of the arrangement of the governmental structure, a practical impossibility. The system also frustrates the desires of the voters if we assume that the majority that wants a governor of a particular party also wants legislators of the same party, which is not always the case, although it apparently generally is.[29]

The Protest Vote Following from the above, the commonplace gerrymandering of legislatures has another important effect in inhibiting the function of party by making it impossible to cast an effective protest vote in times of great political unrest. When the voters wish to express intense dissatisfaction by turning out the normally dominant party, they are frustrated by finding that in "at least one house of the legislature the old crowd simply can-

[26] Ivan Hinderacker, **Harold Stassen and Developments in the Republican Party in Minnesota,** unpublished doctoral thesis, University of Minnesota, Minneapolis, 1949.
[27] Fenton, *op. cit.,* p. 208. By permission of the Hauser Press, New Orleans, La.
[28] Key, *op. cit.,* p. 64. See also V. O. Key, Jr., and Corinne Silverman, "Party and Separation of Powers," **Public Policy,** Harvard University Press, Cambridge, Mass., 1954, vol. 5, pp. 382–412.
[29] Key concluded that deliberate choice of divided partisan control by the electorate is "rare." *Ibid.,* pp. 64, 73.

not be ousted." [30] In the case of city councils, school boards, and some other local bodies, the same type of frustration results, not from gerrymandering, but from the use of the nonpartisan ballot which makes it difficult for the voter even to identify the majority group.[31]

The Long Ballot   Most of the states, and a great many local governments, continue to use the long ballot, the origin of which was discussed in Chapter 2. In relation to the development of collective responsibility through the party, this practice has several effects. For one thing, it means that when a protest vote is cast, it will often affect only the chief executive, the mayor or governor, with the lesser elective administrative officers remaining with the dominant party. For another, the lesser offices become a base from which one party seeks to sabotage the efforts of the chief executive, resulting in the potential detriment of effective government and perhaps a blocking of the popular will. The lesser offices are filled either on the basis of political expediency by a convention or by the chance results of a long-ballot primary election.

Some mediocre individuals have gotten into office through the accidental results of the long ballot; yet "such officers, even when they are only most moderately endowed, often begin to picture themselves as statesmen or great tribunes of the people and become formidable, even successful, aspirants for senatorial or gubernatorial nominations." [32] The long ballot also tends to cause the public to vote into office name candidates; that is, persons with the same names as, or names very similar to, those of the persons the voter *thinks* he is voting for are elected.[33]

The effect of all these factors is to confuse the voting public and to reduce the chances for the selection of public officials representative of the popular mood. In times of protest, in particular when the general public sentiment is in favor of change, the long ballot prevents or at least retards the realization of such change. The periods of serious protest voting are so widely separated in time, however, that this very fact could be the reason why the typical voter is not greatly concerned with the way in which the system occasionally frustrates his political wishes. Indeed, the typical voter apparently still accepts the Jacksonian notion of the intrinsic value of the long ballot as a device for keeping government "close to the people." [34]

State and Local Party Structure

Even though American political parties are tents to cover a great variety of persons, they may be badly divided by factions, and although the primary election opens the doors to all well-financed comers, the party is conceived of legally as a cohesive unit. In each state a party structure exists at the state

[30] *Ibid.*, p. 75.
[31] Charles R. Adrian, "Some General Characteristics of Nonpartisan Elections," **American Political Science Review**, 46:766–776, September, 1952. Reprinted in many readers.
[32] Key, *op. cit.*, pp. 212–216.
[33] Sarasohn, *op. cit.*, analyzes "name candidate" voting in Detroit elections; see also Donald S. Hecock, "Too Many Elective Officials?" **National Municipal Review**, 41:449–454, October, 1952, for effects of the long ballot.
[34] See Hecock, *op. cit.*

level as well as at the county, town, or township and, in some of the larger cities, even at the ward, precinct, and block levels. Most of this structure is explained in some detail in the statutes of each state.

Nonpartisan Elections: The Prevailing Urban Pattern   Early in the twentieth century, many members of the reform movement began to advocate the use of nonpartisan elections. The nonpartisan ballot is today widely used and is particularly popular in the Midwest and the area west of the Mississippi, especially in municipal elections. The device is also used for school, township, county, and other elections.[35]

Nonpartisanship has various meanings. Sometimes it is used, especially in newspapers, when bipartisanship is meant; sometimes in connection with elections in areas that are overwhelmingly dominated by a single party and the party label, in effect, becomes meaningless; sometimes as part of the political ideology of the middle-class suburbanite, which emphasizes rational discussion toward consensus on "the best man." Finally, it is used to refer to an election system in which no party labels appear on the ballot, although political parties may, in fact, be involved in the election campaign. An added characteristic is that the ballot is generally a long one, with many candidates to be selected. Because of this, nonpartisan elections in the United States are to be distinguished from ordinary partisan elections in most of the British Commonwealth countries, where the party of the candidate does not appear on the ballot, either, but his party identification is easy to determine, because the ballot is brief.

When progressivism and urban reform were at a peak, many states adopted the nonpartisan ballot for municipal, judicial, and school elections. Three states, California, Minnesota, and North Dakota, made county offices nonpartisan. The Minnesota legislature was placed on the nonpartisan ballot in 1913, and that of Nebraska in 1935. In the mid-1960s, probably more than one-half of all elections to public office in the United States were being conducted using the nonpartisan ballot, although it was less popular in large urban places than elsewhere. The ballot was being used for at least 85 percent of all school elections and 65 percent of municipal elections, including almost all of suburbia, except where state law did not permit it.

In large cities, political organizations may be characterized as machines, factional alliances, or nonpolitical elites. A machine is "a political organization which attracts and holds the loyalties of its workers primarily (although not entirely) through the distribution of tangible rewards." This involves what is popularly called patronage. Few machine cities now exist in America, although they were once common. A factional alliance is "a coalition of groups, none of which can impose its will on the other members of the coalition." In the mid-1960s, a number of communities in the Midwest and the East were

[35] For the effects of nonpartisanship, see Charles R. Adrian, "A Typology for Nonpartisan Elections," **Western Political Quarterly,** 12:449–458, June, 1959, and citations there; J. Leiper Freeman, "Local Party Systems," **American Journal of Sociology,** 64:282–289, November, 1958. On the nonpartisan legislature in Minnesota, see Charles R. Adrian, "The Origin of Minnesota's Nonpartisan Legislature," **Minnesota History,** 33:155–163, Winter, 1952.

dominated by factional alliances. In addition, some of the large cities traditionally dominated by machines were moving toward factional politics. This
was true of both New York and Philadelphia.

Cities characterized by nonpolitical elites were dominated by "persons
wielding substantial influence over the selection of public officials and the
determination of public policy who are themselves not occupants of political
posts or leaders of political organizations." [36]

Some evidence indicates that partisan and nonpartisan politicians are
not insulated into two separate compartments. If this was once true, as seems
to have been the case,[37] it is probably less the case today.[38] In such cities as
Minneapolis, Milwaukee, and Detroit, as well as some cities in California, persons who begin their careers in the nonpartisan arena move into candidature
for offices on partisan ballots. In a few cases, the opposite career pattern has
appeared. It seems likely that the following generalization is valid: The more
visible the office, the greater the options available to the incumbent officeholder as he seeks career advancement, regardless of whether the office is
partisan or nonpartisan.

A study of nonpartisan municipal elections in California indicated a considerable degree of competition for office and considerable opportunity for
dissent and for casting a protest vote. On the other hand, Republicans were
found to have a considerable advantage in nonpartisan elections in the state,
which has a majority of Democratic voters. Councilmanic elections were found
to be as competitive as the partisan elections for the state legislature. The two
major political parties had little formal relationship to local nonpartisan campaigns, but nonpartisan officeholders were found quite commonly to compete
for partisan office, often successfully. Most incumbents and most Republican
county chairmen wanted to continue nonpartisan elections, but 60 percent of
the Democratic chairmen favored a change to the partisan ballot. In elections,
Republicans and conservatives exercised greater influence because of their
higher propensity to vote. The larger the city, the more likely the political party
organizations were to be formally involved in campaigns; the larger the city,
the more influential the role of the local press was considered to be in influencing voter decisions.[39]

Nonpartisanship at the state level also seems to be breaking down in
those areas where the usual public expectation is for party activity. In Minnesota, a two-party state, the liberal and conservative legislative caucuses have
been associated with the two major parties, at least since the late 1930s. In
1965, the liberal caucus dropped all pretense of nonpartisanship and began
to call itself the DFL (Democratic-Farmer-Labor) caucus. Both major parties
now recruit and endorse candidates for the Minnesota legislature.

[36] James Q. Wilson, "Politics and Reform in American Cities," **American Government Annual,**
Holt, Rinehart and Winston, Inc., New York, 1963, pp. 37–52.
[37] **Adrian,** *op. cit.*
[38] A. Clarke Hagensick, "Influences of Partisanship and Incumbency on a Nonpartisan Election
System," **Western Political Quarterly,** 17:117–124, March, 1964.
[39] Eugene C. Lee, **The Politics of Nonpartisanship,** University of California Press, Berkeley, Calif.,
1960.

Experiments in Direct Democracy

The Initiative and Referendum   The decline in the prestige of governing bodies in the last half of the nineteenth century was accompanied by a decline in faith in representative democracy. As a consequence, reformers proposed what were then considered radical solutions. They renovated and reorganized some old American institutions, introduced some new ones, and offered techniques for direct democracy as a check upon excesses and incompetence. The idea of permitting the electorate to vote on constitutions and amendments dated almost from the beginnings of state government, and referendums on bond issues were also established at an early date. The innovation of the reformers was to extend the referendum to ordinary legislation and to authorize the initiative.

The initiative permits a legally defined number of voters to propose changes in the constitution, charter, laws, or ordinances which are then accepted or rejected by the voters at the polls. This device permits legislation to be effected with no reliance on the legislative body. The referendum permits the voters to accept or reject at the polls changes in the constitution, charter, laws, or ordinances which have been proposed by the legislative body. The referendum differs from the initiative in that it *follows* favorable action by the legislative body, whereas the initiative takes place independently of the legislative body.

The Procedure   An initiated proposal is normally drafted by the attorneys for the particular interest group seeking the legislation. Petitions to put the proposal on the ballot are then circulated, either by volunteers or by persons hired for the purpose, often at the price of a certain amount per signature. The total signatures required may be a specific number or a certain percentage of voters (registered or voting for a certain office at the last general election or some other formula). Where such a percentage is used, it is generally from 5 to 10 percent but may be higher. In most instances the proposal is adopted if supported by a majority of those voting on it, although in some cases a majority of those voting in the *election* is required (this means that if a voter ignores the proposal, he in effect votes "no"), or some special formula may be used. Often, an initiated item may not be amended or repealed by the legislative body, at least within a certain prescribed time limit.

The initiative and referendum (I. and R.), particularly the latter, date from early times in America and elsewhere. Antecedents are to be found in the direct democracy of ancient Greece, the ancient tribal governments of Germany, the right to petition the king in medieval England, the town meeting of colonial New England, and the direct democracy of Switzerland.[40] As early as 1825, the Maryland legislature provided for a referendum on the question of establishing a public school system. It later became commonplace to hold referendums on liquor questions, charter amendments, public-utility fran-

[40] See William B. Munro (ed.), **The Initiative, Referendum and Recall,** The Macmillan Company, New York, 1913.

chises, bond issues, and other matters. California, Iowa, and Nebraska in the late nineteenth century authorized the use of the initiative and referendum by cities. The San Francisco home-rule charter of 1898 was the first such document to provide for them. The movement then spread rapidly, and is today widely authorized.

Around the beginning of the century, when many governments adopted the initiative and referendum, proponents made greatly exaggerated claims of their merits. Opponents were equally vociferous, viewing with alarm the potentiality for hamstringing of the governmental process by their use. The results have not borne out the claims of either side.

The first state to adopt the initiative and referendum was South Dakota. It was only slightly ahead of other states where members of the Progressive movement demanded it. The I. and R. resulted from a lack of trust in state legislatures and a popular view that legislatures were either too conservative to meet the demands of the times, or were corrupt, or both.[41] Within about ten years or so, about twenty states adopted I. and R. Then the drive seems to have spent itself. After 1917, only Alaska, upon its admission to statehood, made constitutional provision for the initiative and referendum.

The initiative and the referendum are each divided into two types. Under the *direct initiative*, if the required number of signatures are obtained on a petition, the proposed law is placed on the ballot for a vote. Twelve states have such provisions today. All of them are west of the Missouri River, except for Arkansas and Missouri. Under the *indirect initiative*, petitions with the required number of signatures must be submitted to the legislature in order to give it an opportunity to enact the proposed measure, or a substantially similar substitute. If the legislature fails to act within a stipulated period of time, the question of the adoption of the proposed law is placed before the voters. Six states have this type of initiative—Maine, Massachusetts, Michigan, Nevada, Ohio, and South Dakota.[42]

Two types of referendums are in use. One, the *petition referendum* (in use in fourteen states), provides that before a proposed law may go into effect, it must be approved by voters according to some formula. These states include all of the states having the direct initiative, plus Maryland and New Mexico.

A second type, the *optional referendum*, is provided for by more than one-half of the states with a petition referendum. An optional referendum is one in which the legislature itself may order a referendum on any measure it has passed, requiring that a specified majority of voters approve before the proposed law may go into effect. The optional referendum is used in eleven states, all of which, except for Maine and Michigan, are west of the Mississippi River.

On referred matters, particularly relative to bond issues, it is quite common to require more than a simple majority for adoption. In California, local bond issues require a two-thirds majority. One study indicates that if the present extraordinary majority requirement were reduced to a simple majority,

---

[41] Hugh A. Bone, **The Initiative and Referendum,** National Municipal League, New York, 1959.
[42] *Ibid.*, pp. 1–2.

a substantial increase in the number of bond-issue proposals accepted would result. Even if the two-thirds majority were reduced to 60 percent, the increase in the number to survive would be substantial.[43]

Table 9   Selected California Local Bond Issue Results

TYPE OF LOCAL GOVERNMENT	APPROVED UNDER RULE REQUIRING TWO-THIRDS VOTE, %	WOULD HAVE BEEN APPROVED:	
		UNDER A 60 PERCENT RULE, %	UNDER A SIMPLE MAJORITY RULE, %
County	67.1	85.7	94.3
City	53.2	69.8	84.6
School district	82.7	92.8	94.3

Supermajority rules have serious impacts on bond-election results.
SOURCE: Frank Marini, **Local Bond Elections in California,** Institute of Governmental Studies, University of California, Berkeley, Calif., 1963, table 1.

Arguments Concerning I. and R.   Proponents of direct democracy argued that corrupt and incompetent governing bodies made it necessary for voters to have a check upon the government. Reformers also took note of the trend toward a concentration of authority in government and a breakdown of the traditional check-and-balance system. The initiative and referendum could serve to replace some of these disappearing checks. It was argued that the use of these devices strengthened popular control over government by giving voters "a gun behind the door" which could serve as a means of requiring greater alertness, honesty, and responsiveness on the part of legislators.

Reformers believed that the I. and R. would protect the people from political tricks and thefts from the public treasury. Some argued that it would encourage voters to become better informed on issues because they would have to vote on so many of them directly and they could have a chance to influence policy making directly. The I. and R. were adopted at a time when Populism was in vogue and its leaders demanded "more democracy" so that "the people" could "govern themselves."

Opponents of the system argued that the initiative and referendum confused legislative responsibility, lengthened an already overly long ballot, created a bad psychological effect upon governing bodies, expected more than was reasonable from an uninformed and uninterested electorate, would promote radicalism and disrespect for property rights, was opposed to the principles of Americanism (since the Constitution is based upon representative, and not direct, democracy), and would allow well-organized pressure groups representing a minority of the population to exercise an inordinate advantage.[44] Wherever conservatives controlled legislatures, charter commissions, and constitutional conventions, they either sought to prevent the adoption of I. and R.

[43] Frank Marini, **Local Bond Elections in California: The Two-thirds Majority Requirement,** Institute of Governmental Studies, University of California, Berkeley, Calif., 1963, table 1.
[44] Extensive arguments on the pros and cons are presented in Munro, *op. cit.,* chaps. 1–11.

or they deliberately established very cumbersome machinery for their operation, as was done by the New Mexico convention of 1910, which provided for
a referendum procedure in the face of seemingly irresistible public demand,
but made it so complicated that it has been used successfully only a few times
in the history of the state.[45]

I. and R.: An Appraisal   The debate over the use of I. and R. has subsided
in recent years, though the use of these devices is, if anything, increasing.
Perhaps it is necessary here to make only two points without discussing the
merits of the arguments briefly outlined above.

First, I. and R. seem to carry the implicit assumption that the individual
voter is always informed and rational in his choices. Actually, of course, this
assumption is false. The voter in a democracy is not asked to rule, but merely
to choose those who are to rule. He is not asked to vote rationally, but only
according to his state of satisfactions. However, I. and R. ask more than this
of the voter. They ask him to help rule himself and to make policy decisions
on questions that are often complex, technical, and minutely detailed.

There is reason to believe that even highly publicized I. and R. questions
are not well communicated to those who are asked to make the decisions. Thus,
the United Automobile Workers' leadership took a strong stand in 1952 in
favor of a reapportionment proposal that would have based representation in
both houses of the Michigan legislature on population. The proposal was regarded by the leadership as of prime importance, and their proposal was
given much publicity. Passage might have been to the immediate advantage
of rank-and-file UAW members. Yet, just before the election, only 56 percent
of the *registered* UAW members in a sample had even so much as heard of the
proposal, and only 23 percent could show that they knew something about it
which could serve as a basis for an informed vote.[46]

Yet, studies in California by Winston Crouch indicate that the I. and R. in
state elections have not upset the continuity of governmental policy and that
the outcome of votes generally conforms to what appears to be the prevailing
values of society. This is true even though thirty to fifty propositions may be
on the ballot at a single election.

The thirty to fifty propositions on the ballot in a California election do
not necessarily refer to matters proposed by initiative. The great majority of
them are legislative proposals to amend the constitution or to float bond issues.
Usually, only one or two initiative proposals are on the ballot in California in
any given election.

Second, opponents of I. and R. are wont to overlook the fact that the
American political structure is pluralistic and not neatly integrated and that
the American political process is typically based upon the interaction of pressure groups. American political subdivisions, for the most part, do not have
responsible political-party structures. Cities, for example, seldom have a two-
party system of any kind regularly competing for voter support. State legisla-

---

[45] Thomas C. Donnelly, **The Government of New Mexico,** The University of New Mexico Press,
Albuquerque, N.Mex., 1953, pp. 110–111.
[46] Kornhauser and others, **When Labor Votes,** p. 71.

tures have been gerrymandered against urban interests—and may continue to be conservative even if apportioned by population. Because this pattern may result in governing bodies that are neither responsible nor representative of a cross section of the population, the I. and R. may well be used as a check, a gun behind the door.

The Recall   The third member of the triumvirate that was to produce popular control of government was the recall. This is a device allowing any elective officer to be removed from office by a popular vote prior to the expiration of his term. The recall may exist independently of the initiative and referendum. It was brought into extensive use by reformers who argued that a faithless or incompetent public servant should not be inflicted upon the people for the duration of his term—that he should be removed as soon as his shortcomings are discovered. Again, Jacksonians who were displeased with the increasing popularity of the four-year term as against the traditional two years found it easier to accept the longer term if "continuous responsibility" were maintained through the availability of the recall. The mechanism was probably first provided for in the Los Angeles home-rule charter of 1903. It was first authorized on the state level in Oregon in 1908.

The Procedure   In order to recall an official, a petition must be circulated. Because a large number of signatures is usually required—such as 15 to 25 or even as much as 55 percent of the vote cast for the office of the individual under attack or for some other office (such as that of mayor or governor) in the last election—an organized group with high motivation and a sizable treasury is usually required. After sufficient signatures are procured and certified by the appropriate official, an election becomes obligatory. Several variants of the recall ballot exist, and its form may itself serve either to aid or discourage the prospects for removal of the official.

Arguments Pro and Con   The principal argument for the recall is that it provides for continuous responsibility, so that the public need not wait in exasperation and frustration until an official's term comes to an end. It is also argued that with a sword constantly hanging over his head, the public official will tend to remain alert at all times.

Opponents of the recall point to its costliness. A special election is imperative for its use, since it would be unfair to conduct such an election in connection with other questions (although this is sometimes done). A second objection to the recall is that it is not an attempt to prove charges against an officeholder but is merely an attempt to persuade the electorate—by whatever means, to remove the incumbent. A third objection is that the recall is unnecessary. In all states, improper conduct by public officials is grounds for removal by judicial, legislative, or sometimes gubernatorial action.

A final objection to the recall centers in the assertion that it serves as a tool for well-organized groups and for political recrimination. Similarly, it is said that the threat of the recall is a constant and legal means for intimidation of public officials who must, in order to defend themselves against its use, follow public whims and sentimentality. A strong leader with a positive program may find that some interest group will stand in his path, threatening him with a recall action if he seeks to carry out a program, even if it is the one upon which he was elected.

There is a trend away from the recall, and it has never been widely used. Few new adoptions of it have taken place since 1920, but it is authorized for some or all state officers in twelve states—none of them in the East—and for some or all local officers in twenty-eight states, all outside the East except New Jersey. But the question of the use of the recall is no longer very important.

The Public Hearing Another important American device for involving the citizen in decision making is the public hearing. This institution is unusual in Europe, but is well established in America where tradition requires the general public to be consulted, or at least informed, about almost every public policy decision. Public hearings generally involve a rather informal procedure at which every person present is allowed to speak if he cares to do so. They are commonly held prior to the making of decisions concerning the zoning of land, the location of taverns, the moving of highways, the changing of public utilities rates, the exempting of certain property from the tax rolls (as in the granting of a permit for a cemetery), the location of a new school, and for dozens of other purposes.

Political neophytes sometimes find the hearing procedure puzzling because nearly all persons expressing themselves are opposed to the proposal which is the subject of the hearing. The official or public body conducting the hearing does not, of course, take a vote at the hearing and dispose of the issue on that basis. Instead, the hearing is used as a safety-valve device for allowing disapproving persons to vent their feelings. These people thus gain a feeling of having had their "day in court," and they may succeed in having the proposed policy modified somewhat so as to meet at least partially some of their objections. The hearing also allows officials to judge the political climate in advance of decisions. They may learn something that will suggest to them the language in which to couch the announcement of a decision so as to minimize the number and intensity of unfavorable responses.

Citizens advisory groups execute some of the same functions for the political system as do public hearings. These types of groups have become increasingly common in recent years. In some cases legislation requires that they be established, as is true for urban renewal activities. Advisory bodies may be constituted of representatives of various interest groups, or they may be appointed for the special purpose of ratifying and hence legitimizing policies desired by a governor, mayor, or manager, or they may be used for the actual purpose of developing a public policy in relation to some specific problem.

These advisory groups are characterized by slow action and noninnovation, that is, a general acceptance of administrative goals, established and accepted methods, and reliance on the advice of experts, as well as a lack of realism concerning the financial and political aspects of the problem they are considering. Although these groups improve the communications network between the decision makers and citizens who are affected by decisions, they do not solve the problem of avoiding a sense of alienation on the part of the citizen, and they are not representative of a cross section of the community, for they are usually chosen from among higher-status persons, representatives of interest groups, and persons who are particularly concerned about the problem or function involved.[47]

Closing Statement   This chapter has examined the nature of the electorate and of those who participate in elections, the process of nomination and the machinery of election, and something about political party structure in American government. Chapter 7 will deal with the nature of political power and the interaction of interest groups upon one another in the political process. Chapter 8 will discuss the way in which ideologies, election machinery, and group interests are involved in the pattern of political structures, which influences and is influenced by elections and public policy. The patterns cannot be fitted together into a total process except as the material in these chapters is considered as a description of interrelated parts.

SELECTED READINGS

Adrian, Charles R.: "The Origin of Minnesota's Nonpartisan Legislature," **Minnesota History**, 33:155–163, Winter, 1952.

————: "A Typology for Nonpartisan Elections," **Western . Political Quarterly**, 12:449–458, June, 1959.

Albright, Spencer D.: **The American Ballot**, Public Affairs Press, Washington, D.C., 1942.

Alexander, Henry M.: **The Little Rock Recall Election**, McGraw-Hill Book Company, New York, 1960, Eagleton Institute case no. 17. (Story of attempt to recall the "moderate" on the Little Rock, Arkansas, school board in a school integration dispute.)

Bain, H. M., and Donald S. Hecock: **Ballot Position and Voter's Choice**, Wayne State University Press, Detroit, 1957.

Banfield, Edward C.: **Big City Politics**, Random House, Inc., New York, 1965.

Blair, George S.: **Cumulative Voting**, The University of Illinois Press, Urbana, Ill., 1960. (A study of the unique system of voting for legislators in Illinois.)

Bollens, John C.: **Special District Governments in the United States**, University of California Press, Berkeley, Calif., 1957.

Brucker, Herbert: "Mass Man and Mass Media," **Saturday Review**, May 29, 1965, pp. 14ff. (Is the nation's press becoming despotic rather than a guarantee against despotism?)

Eldersveld, Samuel J.: **Political Parties**, Rand McNally & Company, Chicago, 1964. (A theory of parties and an empirical testing in a single county. The theory relies on contemporary concepts of political behavior.)

[47] Lyle E. Schaller, "Is the Citizen Advisory Committee a Threat to Representative Government?" **Public Administration Review**, 24:175–179, September, 1964; Roberta S. Sigel, "Citizen's Advisory Groups and their Role in the Decision-making Process," a paper read at the 1965 meetings of the Midwest Conference of Political Scientists.

Fenton, John H.: **Midwestern Politics,** Holt, Rinehart and Winston, Inc., New York, 1966.

——: **Politics in the Border States,** Hauser Press, New Orleans, Louisiana, 1957.   (A study of Maryland, West Virginia, Kentucky, and Missouri.)

Flinn, Thomas A., and Fredrick M. Wirt: "Local Party Leaders: Groups of Like-Minded Men," **Midwest Journal of Political Science,** 9:77–98, February, 1965.

Freeman, J. L.: "Local Party Systems," **American Journal of Sociology,** 64:282–289, November, 1958.

Gilbert, Charles E.: "Some Aspects of Nonpartisan Elections in Large Cities," **Midwest Journal of Political Science,** 6:345–362, November, 1962.

Goldman, Ralph M.: "The Advisory Referendum in America," **Public Opinion Quarterly,** 14:303–315, Summer, 1950.

Gottfried, Alex: **Boss Cermak of Chicago,** University of Washington Press, Seattle, Wash., 1962.   (A study of the rise to power of an ethnic group leader, Chicago's only foreign-born mayor. Makes use of psychiatric analysis of motivation.)

Greene, Lee S. (ed.): "City Bosses and Political Machines," **Annals,** 353:entire issue, May, 1964.

Harris, Joseph P.: **California Politics,** Stanford University Press, Stanford, Calif., 1955.

Heard, Alexander: **Money and Politics,** Public Affairs Press, Washington, D.C., 1956.   (By the leading authority on the subject.)

Janowitz, Morris, and Dwaine Marvick: **Competitive Pressure and Democratic Consent,** Bureau of Government, University of Michigan, Ann Arbor, Mich., 1956.

Jennings, M. Kent: **Community Influentials,** The Free Press of Glencoe, New York, 1964.   (Atlanta about a decade after Hunter.)

Jonas, Frank H.: **Western Politics and the 1956 Elections,** Appendix to the **Western Political Quarterly,** vol. 10, 1957.

Kelley, Stanley, Jr.: **Professional Public Relations and Political Power,** The Johns Hopkins Press, Baltimore, 1957.

Key, V. O., Jr.: **American State Politics,** Alfred A. Knopf, Inc., New York, 1956. (A theory of parties and state politics.)

—— and Alexander Heard: **Southern Politics,** Alfred A. Knopf, Inc., New York, 1949.   (A classic study.)

—— and Corinne Silverman: "Party and Separation of Powers," **Public Policy,** Harvard University Press, Cambridge, Mass., 1954.

Kirwan, A. D.: **Revolt of the Rednecks,** University of Kentucky Press, Lexington, Ky., 1951.   (A study of Populism in the South.)

Lancaster, Lane W.: **Government in Rural America,** 2d ed., D. Van Nostrand Company, Inc., Princeton, N.J., 1952.

Liebling, A. J.: **The Earl of Louisiana,** Ballantine Books, Inc., New York, 1960. (A sympathetic study of Earl Long and the legacy of Populism.)

Lockard, Duane: **New England State Politics,** Princeton University Press, Princeton, N.J., 1959.

Martin, Roscoe C.: **Grass Roots,** University of Alabama Press, University, Ala., 1957.   (Description of the rural boss and machine.)

Marz, Roger H.: "The Democratic Digest: A Content Analysis," **American Political Science Review,** 51:696–703, September, 1957.

Merriam, Charles E., and Louise Overacker: **Primary Elections,** The University of Chicago Press, Chicago, 1928.

Michener, James A.: **Report of the County Chairman,** Bantam Books, Inc., New York, 1961.   (An account of his political activity, by a famous novelist.)

Munro, William B. (ed.): **The Initiative, Referendum and Recall,** The Macmillan Company, New York, 1913.

Overacker, Louise: **Money in Elections,** The Macmillan Company, New York, 1932.

Pitchell, R. J.: "The Influence of Professional Campaign Management Firms in

Partisan Elections in California," **Western Political Quarterly,** 11:278–300, June, 1958.

Ranney, Austin, and Willmoore Kendall: "The American Party Systems," **American Political Science Review,** 47:337–358, June, 1953.

Reichley, James (ed.): **States in Crisis,** The University of North Carolina Press, Chapel Hill, N.C., 1964.   (An impressionistic study, by newspaper reporters, of politics in ten states.)

Roady, E. E.: "Florida's New Campaign Expense Law and the 1952 Democratic Gubernatorial Primaries," **American Political Science Review,** 48:465–476, June, 1954.

Sarasohn, Stephen B.: **The Regulation of Parties and Nominations in Michigan: The Politics of Election Reform,** University Microfilms, Inc., Ann Arbor, Mich., 1953.

Schlesinger, Joseph A.: "The Structure of Competition for Office in the American States," **Behavioral Science,** 5:179–210, July, 1960.

Schubert, Glendon: **The Michigan State Director of Elections,** The Bobbs-Merrill Company, Inc., Indianapolis, ICP no. 23, 1954.   (A study in election administration.)

Shannon, Jasper B.: **Money and Politics,** Random House, Inc., New York, 1959.

Simon, Herbert A., and Frederick Stern: "The Effect of Television Upon Voting Behavior in Iowa in the 1952 Presidential Election," **American Political Science Review,** 49:470–477, June, 1955.   (Television did not tend to increase voter turnout.)

Thompson, C. A. H.: **Television and Presidential Politics,** The Brookings Institution, Washington, D.C., 1956.

Wilson, James Q.: **Negro Politics,** The Free Press of Glencoe, New York, 1960. (A major source book.)

7

INTERGROUP ACTIVITY AND POLITICAL POWER

The long life of American political institutions in comparison with those of most other countries in part can be explained by the attitudes most Americans express toward conflict. The common notion in Europe that conflict is the result of incompatible goals and life styles has not been accepted by most persons in this country, not even by most of the persons of the extreme left and right in their frequently intolerant behavior patterns and pressure tactics. Instead, "conflict is assumed to be neither irrevocable nor irreconcilable, and does not necessarily lead to a revolutionary end; nor does social class constitute an inherently unbridgeable social cleavage in the society. Conflict, instead, is evidence of solvable social problems." [1]

Furthermore: [2]

Assumptions such as these necessarily presume a model of man as actor in conflict situations. He is expected to be moderate, reasonable, willing to compromise, in short, a negotiator or bargainer. And, indeed, the model of role behavior created by the bargaining situation in labor negotiations has become somewhat a generalized model in our society in recent years for indicating an acceptable pattern of behavior. And it is more than a model of role behavior—there is expected to exist in the relevant persons attitudes and values that provide a readiness to accept compromise and to seek the basis for agreement.

[1] James B. McKee, "The Ideology of Moderation," Provost Lecture, Michigan State University, East Lansing, Mich., 1964.
[2] *Ibid.*

The Nature of the Political Process

Politics as Demand and Supply   The political process is a by-product of the struggle for individual power, prestige, and security. Some people, in their search, become part of the relatively small group of the politically active.[3] The general public, politically passive though it may be, becomes a collection of clientele groups seeking services from government in order to help themselves, in turn, achieve these same ends. Or they seek to prevent government from launching certain types of services if they believe their goals can be reached by some alternative, nongovernmental type of activity.

In order to achieve his desired objectives in public policy, the individual may choose to work through a political party. If the party stands for a definite set of principles, this approach is worthwhile and is the common one used in European democracies. In the United States, however, political parties are loose coalitions, each covering a great variety of political viewpoints. This is often the case even at the local level. The individual belongs to a political party for a variety of reasons connected largely with economic status, geographic location, and family tradition. He can, however, seldom go to the polls and vote for a set of policies.

He may choose to become active in a political party, of course, and seek to influence its policies. But by the simple act of voting for the slate of a particular party, he will not be able to select a group of public officials who are ideologically in accord with himself. If he wishes to influence public policy, therefore, he will usually find it more expedient and fruitful to join forces with like-minded persons in an interest group. In fact, the individual normally belongs to a number of such groups, not all of which have like views toward the same questions of policy. It is this overlapping of membership in groups which helps to mitigate their conflicts and to enable a stable system to develop.

What Is an Interest Group?   An interest group differs from a political party chiefly in that it does not seek to capture offices for its members but rather attempts to influence public policy. It also differs from most political parties in the United States in that it is made up of persons with basically the same interests and viewpoints—it is normally much more ideologically cohesive than is a political party in this country. Much has been said of the evil influences and dangers of pressure groups in politics. It has even been suggested by some critics that they be legally abolished or stringently controlled. Most such suggestions are, however, naive. If we had a system of two or more political parties, each standing upon a definite platform of proposed action to which the parties could be held, interest-group lobbying * activities would take place largely within the party structures, since it would be important to control

[3] See the writings of Harold Lasswell, especially **Psychopathology and Politics,** The University of Chicago Press, Chicago, 1930, and **Power and Personality,** W. W. Norton & Company, Inc., New York, 1948.

platforms and policy directives. Such is not the case in the United States, however. Neither is it practical to say that a public official can determine the viewpoints of a cross section of the citizenry simply by noting the comments of those who contact him personally—not in any but the smallest villages, at any rate. And only the naive or foolhardy would suggest that the officeholder should be elected with no promises to the public and then be entrusted to use his own free will and best judgment in doing as he sees best "for all the people" while in office. He must constantly be reminded of the nature of the shifting viewpoints of his constituents.

* LOBBYING. Lobbying, often performed by professionals, consists of seeking to influence legislative and administrative officials in a variety of ways so that their actions will be favorable to the group doing the lobbying. Lobbyists are also frequently in charge of the dissemination of propaganda to the general public. In this book "propaganda" is used to mean any communication designed to create a desired effect, impression, or opinion.

An interest group is not only not an evil, it is a necessity in a modern democracy. It serves the purpose of marshaling individual opinions, organizing them, and presenting them in a skillful way to the proper governmental officials. While individual pressure groups no doubt do sometimes go beyond the bounds of the mores of society, do fail to give an accurate picture of the interests, desires, and aspirations of their individual members, and do act otherwise irresponsibly, most of them are kept in check quite automatically by the fact that for nearly every pressure group that comes before government, there is a counterpressure group. In this fashion, most of the potential dangers of the organized power of such a group are neutralized by the watchful eye of an opposing group. And each watcher is also watched. In fact, "public policy" might be defined as the end result of the interaction of the various interested interest groups upon one another. It is the sum of the vector forces, where each vector represents the total force and direction of each group as determined by its age, respectability, size of membership, wealth, ability of leadership, skill at lobbying, inside connections, intensity of interest, and other pertinent factors.

Even though Americans are joiners, it is easy to exaggerate the extent to which they belong to organized interest groups which can represent them in the decision-making centers of government. Fewer than one-half of all adult Americans belong to voluntary organizations, if we except churches and church-sponsored groups. Of those who do belong to groups, relatively few belong to more than one.[4] In at least one case where middle-sized communities were to be studied, it was necessary to abandon an original attempt to observe their politics from the perspective of group participation because the groups were too few, too ephemeral, and too vague as to membership and strength of support in the community.[5]

[4] Charles R. Wright and Herbert H. Hyman, "Voluntary Association Memberships of American Adults," **American Sociological Review,** 23:284–294, June, 1958.
[5] Oliver P. Williams and Charles R. Adrian, **Four Cities,** University of Pennsylvania Press, Philadelphia, 1963.

The ability to influence government through membership in interest groups reflects the advantages of higher-income (and thus usually of higher-educated) persons. About 60 percent of the persons in lower-income brackets do not belong to any groups, as compared with only 20 percent among high-income persons. Furthermore, one-half of those with eight years or less of education do not belong to any organization, as compared with about 20 percent of those who have attended college.[6]

What Is an Interest?   An interest may be interpreted in many different ways. In this book, it is assumed that an interest may be economic, but it may also be ideological. Furthermore, an interest may be conceived of in either short- or long-run terms. The importance of ideology may vary from one socioeconomic group to another. This may also be true of willingness to consider long-term factors, that is, the rate at which the future is discounted. Similarly, an interest may be viewed in highly parochial or neighborhood terms, or it may be viewed in a socially and spatially broader context. Thus, "voters in some income and ethnic groups are more likely than voters in others to take a public-regarding rather than a narrowly self-interested view of things—i.e., to take the welfare of others, especially that of 'the community' into account as an aspect of their own welfare." [7] It seems probable that each subculture "has a more or less distinctive notion of how much a citizen ought to sacrifice for the sake of the community as well as of what the welfare of the community is constituted; in a word, each has its own idea of what justice requires and of the importance of acting justly." [8]

Characteristics of Interest Groups   Interest groups are organized interests. Some of them are especially created for the single purpose of lobbying, while for others lobbying is only a sideline. Some are temporary organizations created for a special problem, while others are permanent groups. Some, in large cities and at the state and national level at any rate, are always present and lobbying at the seat of government, while others lobby only when a matter of particular interest is under consideration. The Anti-Saloon League, for example, was created with political action to prohibit the sale of intoxicating beverages as its purpose; lobbying is only one of many activities of the AFL-CIO. Temporary organizations are often created to campaign on a single matter as, for example, a new school bond issue. A large labor union or manufacturers' association would have enough interests involved to be on hand constantly, at least when the legislative body is in session, but a group such as the motion-picture-theater operators might not engage in lobbying until a measure affecting its members is under consideration.

Groups constantly realign their forces as expediency demands. It should not be assumed that politics is simply business versus labor, though that is a part of the story, or that businessmen always work together, or that various groups

---

[6] Data from Survey Research Center, University of Michigan, Ann Arbor, Mich.
[7] James Q. Wilson and Edward C. Banfield, "Public Regardingness as a Value Premise in Voting Behavior," **American Political Science Review**, 58:876–887, December, 1964. Quotation from p. 885.
[8] *Ibid.*

operate in fairly permanent alignments. The fluidity of the pressure-group system is one of its greatest advantages. To take an example, we might find a lobbyist for the state AFL-CIO organization lined up in bitter opposition to the lobbyist for the American Legion in a committee hearing before a state senate dealing with the proper manner of handling potential subversives and of giving them access to conventional civil rights. But when the hearing adjourns, it might not be unusual to find these same two lobbyists crossing over to the lower house side of the capitol and both testifying on the same side of a question dealing with appropriations for meeting the problem of juvenile delinquency or of mentally retarded children. Businessmen often line up on opposite sides of an issue. Downtown merchants might lobby before a city council for one-way streets, for example, since this would help hurry traffic to the place where their stores are located, but neighborhood shopping area merchants oppose one-way streets, since they feel that it reduces accessibility to their locations. Downtown and neighborhood-shopping-area merchants alike may favor municipally owned parking lots, but realtors are quite likely to oppose them. Labor unions frequently come into conflict with one another before legislative or administrative bodies. Jurisdictional disputes and the long-standing conflict of interests between the railroad brotherhoods and the teamsters' (truckers') union are examples. Businessmen and labor leaders work together on many matters. Ours is a dynamic system.

The example of the AFL-CIO and the American Legion given above also brings out the breadth of interests often encompassed by pressure groups. Organized labor wanders over almost the entire public-policy panorama in its legislative programs. The American Legion, controlled by conservatives from the time it was first incorporated, has never limited its lobbying activities to veterans' affairs but has taken stands on civil rights, labor, taxation, and other legislation in great variety. The same broad scope may be included by business, church, fraternal, and other groups.

Pressure-group membership and interest orientations may change over time. As a result, the kind of lobbying that a group does and the positions it takes on issues may change. Thus, the leadership of the Woman's Christian Temperance Union (WCTU) during its heyday came from the socially dominant classes. The leaders took a *noblesse oblige* attitude toward the drinking problem. They thought of themselves as a humanitarian group that would solve the problems of the underprivileged by removing from them the temptation created by the saloonkeepers' trade. Since repeal, however, the group has drawn its membership from the lower middle class, and it now concentrates upon criticism of upper-middle-class morality rather than upon that of the working class. As a result, it has become far less influential before legislatures.[9]

Organized and Unorganized Groups   If all groups in society were equally well organized and equally effective in presenting their sides of issues, the process of determining public policy through compromise among the various interests

[9] Joseph R. Gusfield, "Social Structure and Moral Reform: A Study of the Woman's Christian Temperance Union," **American Journal of Sociology**, 61:221–232, November, 1955.

involved would be highly satisfactory, indeed nearly as perfect a device for democratic policy making as human society could achieve. It happens, however, that not all groups have their interests equally well protected. The less verbal members of the working class are not so likely to have their views expressed before legislative bodies as are members of the most prestigeful groups in society. They are certain to be accorded less deference when they speak. In terms of status, inside connections, funds for spreading propaganda, and other factors, there are vast differences in the relative power of groups.

It should not be assumed, however, that a group is necessarily strong because it is well organized or weak because it is unorganized. A well-organized and vigorously active group may, for example, have its relative strength reduced through the gerrymandering of city councils or legislative bodies. Organized labor, with its strength concentrated in small geographic areas, is subject to this kind of control. Some unorganized groups are very weak politically (e.g., ex-convicts); others are very strong (e.g., the elderly). In a democracy, virtually all groups are free to organize and to lobby, but the ability of the members of a group to understand the techniques of doing this vary greatly, and the result is a weakening of the representativeness of a politics based upon the summation of vector forces.

The relative strength of an interest group in terms of numbers or by any other single measure of power is not necessarily proportional when compared with other groups. The ability to use potential political resources depends to some extent upon the ideological acceptability of the particular interest as well as of its particular potential resources. This is true of the political system just as it is true that in the human physiological system the efficiency with which caloric inputs are utilized depends upon the metabolism rate of the individual system.

An example of a large group, highly restricted in political influence in relation to its size, is the Latin Americans of El Paso, Texas. According to one study: [10]

El Paso was predominantly Latin until the 1950's. Many Latin families have lived in or near the city since the 16th century. About 12 per cent of the city's population was born in Mexico; the parents of another 30 per cent were born there. The Latins' influence is not in proportion to their numbers, however. Usually there is only one Latin on the city council and one on the school board. None of El Paso's five state representatives is a Latin. Only one mayor in recent history has been a Latin. Although their votes have often been decisive in city and county elections, the Latins have very little to show for it.

This large group of citizens has relatively little education and a high rate of illiteracy, and many of its members cannot understand English. They come from a subculture highly different from the American mainstream. Not only are the values they learn from that culture different from that of the dominant political leaders of El Paso, but the group itself suffers from a relatively low-status position in the value system of the community leaders.

[10] Edward C. Banfield, **Big City Politics**, Random House, Inc., New York, 1965, p. 76.

The Techniques and Motivation of Groups   Not only do groups vary according to their degree of organization, but they also vary according to the techniques they use and the level of motivation they have for political participation.

Techniques might be said to vary according to the way in which the group fits into the system of cultural values. One group may be able to "get away" with something that would produce highly unfavorable publicity for another. The medical association feels impelled to act within the public image of dignity which it has created for itself; a labor union can safely be more free-swinging in its behavior. A conservative group may be able to make recommendations concerning the election of nonpartisan judges with newspaper approval; a liberal group may be criticized by the same newspaper for "interfering" if it does the same thing.

There are many bases for the political motivation of groups. Many organizations, for example, seek to use the sanctions of the state to support their own battles against other interests. Either labor or management can benefit in their struggles by having governmental officials or legal provisions supporting one side. In other cases, one might make the generalization that *the political activity of any group is proportionate to its stake in the marginal definition of legality and of law-enforcement levels.* Thus, the middle-management bureaucrat in private industry is not intensely involved in politics, except by choice, because his job and his way of life are well within the bounds of accepted behavior. He is not likely to be in trouble with the law, or his welfare especially dependent upon its decisions. Similarly, the professional bank robber is not politically active because his job is so far outside the law that he cannot possibly hope to secure governmental sanction for his activities. But those on the edge of legality where economic survival depends on marginal definitions are the ones with the greatest stake in political definitions and decisions, and they make the maximum investment in the political process. Thus, a racetrack owner must be politically active because his business is just barely acceptable as legitimate by American values. The electric-utilities executive is similarly highly motivated because his rate structure is determined through the governmental process. The corner druggist is deeply concerned over traffice-flow patterns. A decision to prohibit parking near his store may wipe out his margin of profit.

The pattern of marginality varies over time. Prostitutes and public servants holding office by political appointment were once highly active in politics. Neither group is apolitical today, but their activities have diminished as the prostitute has moved outside the pale, while the merit system, by extending protection to civil servants, has moved public employees away from the margin, toward stability and acceptance. On the other hand, Negroes who once thought they could not make economic or social progress through political action now find that they can. As a result, they have changed their behavior pattern from almost total political apathy to intense activity. Americans vote, lobby, issue propaganda, or otherwise take part in the process of politics according to their level of motivation. This, in turn, varies according to whether the individual's activities are well within the norms of society and of established public policy, or whether decisions on public policy that may affect the individual are of a sort that are unpredictable but of immense importance to his social or economic welfare.

Groups and the Public Interest   When any group announces a policy position, it seeks explicitly or implicitly to associate its stand with the public interest. In fact, virtually every politically active individual or group claims—sincerely, no doubt—to be acting in the name of the public interest. Critics of the stand taken by a particular group, on the other hand, not uncommonly complain that pressure groups are selfish and that they ought to act in the public interest. With everyone thus using the term, it becomes useless as an analytical tool. Yet, it is a basic part of the myth of democracy to say that public policies as they are adopted are, or ought to be, in the public interest. As such, the concept may serve a useful function in encouraging compliance with the law, which in turn is an important device for achieving a stable society. It is also useful as a symbol to remind legislators and administrators that no matter how many groups they may have listened to before making a decision, other groups and citizens who are unrepresented or underrepresented before them will also be affected by the decision.

As one writer on the subject has said: [11]

Instead of being associated with substantive goals or policies, the public interest better survives identification with the process of group accommodation. The public interest rests not in some policy emerging from the settlement of conflict, but with the method of that settlement itself, with compromising in a peaceful, orderly, predictable way the demands put upon policy.

The Complexity of Interests: An Illustration   "There are two sides to every question," all of us learn at an early age. Actually this worthy proverb is quite untrue. There are many sides to every question. The following description of the diversity of interests found in the Minnesota legislative session of 1931 relative to a single economic activity is illustrative: [12]

The [motoring] public wanted to reduce highway hazards by putting specific limitations on the length, width, height, and load capacities of motor vehicles. The large trucking firms wanted legislation to curb wildcat operators engaged in cut-throat competition. The railroads professed to work for the reduction of truck competition and the recapture of less than carload business, although they are actually playing a deeper game. Organized labor was chiefly interested in regulation of the wages, hours, and working conditions of truck drivers, while [unions representing] railroad workers carefully checked all proposed transportation legislation to determine its possible effects on the security of their jobs.

[11] Frank J. Sorauf, "The Public Interest Reconsidered," **Journal of Politics,** 19:616–639, November, 1957. Quotation from p. 638. See also Glendon A. Schubert, Jr., **The Public Interest,** The Free Press of Glencoe, New York, 1960, and E. P. Herring, **Public Administration and the Public Interest,** McGraw-Hill Book Company, New York, 1936. The way in which administrators and judges view the public interest is discussed below, chaps. 15 and 17.
[12] George H. Mayer, **The Political Career of Floyd B. Olson,** 1951, p. 74. Olson was Governor of Minnesota, 1931–1936. By permission of, and copyright 1951 by, The University of Minnesota Press, Minneapolis.

This variety of viewpoints toward the same governmental activity, the regulation of the trucking industry, must be multiplied by the number of potential and actual governmental activities considered by a legislative body in order to get some approximation of the staggering complexity of the total forces operating in the political process.

Types of Interest Groups

Interest groups operate in basically the same pattern whether on the national, state, or local level. To be sure, there may be differences in the relative balance of power of the various groups. On the national and state level, for example, agricultural groups tend to be powerful, while in cities they have but a small support group. Liquor lobbyists tend to be more powerful before state and local bodies than before the national government. Real-estate groups and downtown merchants tend to be extraordinarily powerful in city politics.

The relative strength of any give lobby probably varies over time. Thus, in prosperous times, people may accept much leadership from, and make many concessions to, the business community. In a depression, business groups fall into a spot of lower esteem and hence lower political strength. Both liquor lobbies and their temperance opponents have relatively less political strength today than they once had, probably because public values change over time and the resultant change in attitudes affects their lobbying strength.

The pattern of interest-group strengths varies from state to state. In some places, a single group seems to dominate the scene, but the group may be different in each state. In others, two very strong groups may be closely balanced and the pattern of conflict on many issues may reflect the struggle between these groups. In still others, many groups may be closely balanced with hegemony depending upon the nature of the issue.

In some states no sharp interest differences may exist, and state government has considerable difficulty in securing public visibility. In some states, governments deal with "*micro-decisions,* involving highly specific conflicts of localized interests." Thus: [13]

A starting point for an understanding of Missouri politics is the recognition of the fact that not only is there no pervasive rural-urban conflict but there are really *no* basic economic and social interests in conflict in the Missouri political arena. Business corporations do not seriously combat organized labor in the state capital. Broad social groupings are not engaged in efforts to secure advantage or to block opponents through the medium of state politics. The rudimentary class conflict which has appeared in areas of the United States with extensive heavy industry and large "late immigrant" groups have turned some states into meaningful political battle grounds. . . . But Missouri has little heavy industry, relatively few immigrants striving to achieve status, and the state has not experienced rapid growth with the accompanying social strains.

[13] Robert H. Salisbury, "Missouri Politics and State Political Systems," **Research Papers**, 1958, Bureau of Government Research, University of Missouri, Columbia, Mo., p. 17.

Some Types of Group Patterns   Intergroup relations may be extremely complex. For example, in Hawaii for many years, middle-class Republicans joined with old-time oligarchs, also Republicans, in their attitudes toward legislation controlling labor unions, particularly the International Longshoremen's and Warehousemen's Union (ILWU), controlled by Harry Bridges. But middle-class groups opposed the spokesmen for the wealthy descendants of the missionary families on matters of land-policy reforms. Most of the land in Hawaii is owned by trusts established by the old families and it is difficult for persons to secure title to land, as is common in the rest of the United States, except for Manhattan and a few other areas. The old families, furthermore, were joined by politicians of Polynesian (Hawaiian) descent in opposing land reform, since Hawaiians gain from the income left by one of the great estates, that of Bernice Bishop. Furthermore, leaders of the ILWU, who are Democrats, have often also joined with the old oligarchs, who are Republicans, on matters of land reform. But independent Democrats have joined with middle-class Republicans on this crucial issue.[14]

Some contemporary conflict before legislatures and state administrative agencies centers around rural and urban differences (over the distribution of the local share of the state gasoline tax between rural and urban units of government, for example). Sometimes it is a split between a huge metropolis and the rest of the state, as between Chicago and downstate, or New York City and upstate.

Conflict between the conservative, properous Bourbons and the small farmers is common in the South, as in Mississippi in the historic struggle between the planters of the delta and the "red-necks" of the hills. In Minnesota, the pattern is varied to one in which many issues center around a split between the conservative and prosperous corn-hog farmers of the southern part of the state and the less well-endowed, liberal-to-radical wheat and potato farmers of the Red River Valley. In New Mexico, both cultural and economic interests may be symbolized in the friction between "Anglos" and Spanish Americans, in Louisiana between Catholic French and Protestant Anglo-Saxons, in Massachusetts between late-immigration Catholics and old-family Yankee Protestants, or in New Hampshire between Yankee Protestants and Catholic French-Canadian newcomers.

Iron and sugar interests are powerful in Colorado; gas and oil companies in Texas; truckers and loan sharks in Missouri.[15] The education lobby in New York is reportedly as strong as that of the great insurance companies of that state. In Michigan, where automobile manufacturers and automobile unions often clash, the most powerful set of pressure groups may well be that of public education. The pattern varies over the country and may be vastly different even as between adjoining states.

[14] Lawrence Fuchs, **Hawaii Pono**, Harcourt, Brace & World, Inc., New York, 1961, p. 347.
[15] According to Lester Velie, **The Great Unwatched**, 1953, a pamphlet reprinting a series of five articles from the **Reader's Digest**. John Gunther, **Inside U.S.A.**, rev. ed., Harper & Row, Publishers, Incorporated, New York, 1951, lists the principal pressure groups in several states as he saw them immediately after World War II.

It is not possible here to give a summary of the interests of even the most common and powerful groups. But a few examples may be mentioned to indicate the types of interests that exist.

Business Groups   There are so many business groups exerting pressure upon government that they would probably overshadow and overpower all of the others if it were not that they spend so much of their time opposing one another. The enormous variety of these groups can be inferred from the following list of business activities that registered lobbyists with the Michigan legislature for the 1958 session: there was the Watchmakers' Guild, the Upper Peninsula Dairy Manufacturers Association, the Society of Architects, the Council of Painting and Decorating Contractors of America, the Independent Accountants Association, the Beauticians' Aid Association, the National Association of Margarine Manufacturers, the Funeral Directors' and Embalmers' Association, the Cash-and-carry Milk Dealers' Association, the United Commercial Travelers of America, the Institute of Dry Cleaning, the Association of Private Driver-training Schools, the Trailer Park Association, and the Association of Civil Engineers and Land Surveyors in Private Practice. These are but a few. The total number of business pressure groups before almost any legislature would run into the hundreds.

An organization is equipped to lobby for every business interest in the city, county, or state. The pattern is so complex that a particular business may be represented by an elaborate combination of groups, some with broad interests that include those of a specific calling, others dealing with a particular type of business, and the individual businessman may himself lobby before council or legislature. A supermarket chain may, for example, have its interests represented generally by the state chamber of commerce, but the company may also belong to an association of chain stores (which must parry the thrusts of the corner-grocers' lobby), to a retail-food-dealers' organization, to the package-liquor-dealers association (if some of the stores have permits to sell it), and the company may itself register a lobbyist. In addition, if the chain is encountering labor problems, it may contribute to a "right-to-work" committee which lobbies against the union shop, and the executives of the company may choose to help support the state taxpayers' league. If the company owns its own fleet of semitrailer trucks or leases them, it may be represented by a company of additional groups dealing with the interests of this part of the business. A pluralistic society is simple in neither theory nor practice.

The Goals of Labor   Organized labor has a whole list of wants it desires from government, and a large number of them result in conflicts with other interest groups. Labor expects that the many services it demands should be financed on an ability-to-pay theory of taxation rather than on a benefit theory. This brings labor into conflict with those who are expected to foot the bill. Labor is more interested in services than in the tax rate. It is, however, very much interested in the tax *structure*. Generally, labor opposes the municipal payroll tax as being regressive and hence a greater burden upon its membership than upon higher-income persons. It prefers a state corporate income tax to a personal income tax, but the latter to the sales tax, since this is the inverse of the order of burden upon the working man, in the opinion of union economists.

Among the interests of labor are such items of direct concern as the specific provisions of workmen's compensation and unemployment compensation acts, rules concerning picketing, various right-to-work laws, labor mediation requirements, and the like. In addition, labor often favors such things as expanded public housing, housing for the aged, and expanded public-health program, liberalized welfare rules, low tuition rates in public universities, a strong fair-employment-practices commission for intergroup relations, and high wages for public employees. Labor also is interested in the manner in which laws are administered, which gives it a reason for political activity in connection with the election of governors, mayors, and judges. Control of the executive branch is especially important, since it helps to ensure that state or local police will be sympathetic in the event of strikes or other labor disturbances.

Despite this list of interests involving all levels of government, one study has concluded that: [16]

> Labor evidences almost no desire to have a distinctive community program. Traditional labor goals in the community are given at best a secondary priority and management's objectives are generally endorsed. Labor's ideology is essentially one of cooperating with other groups in conserving and improving the present community organizations. Although it sees few allies, labor assesses itself as a potentially powerful organization. What it wants most is to be consulted in community problems from the beginning.

Organized labor has, thus, concentrated on national and state politics, and on private collective bargaining. Its political power at the local level has lagged behind its economic power,[17] probably because organized labor, actively in the political arena for the most part only in the last generation, prefers to expend most of its resources at the state and national levels in election campaigns and in lobbying. In the mid-1960s, despite the general acceptance of organized labor as a legitimate institution in the American social system, labor leaders still were not generally accepted as having a legitimate place in the community power complex. Respondents to questions concerning the identity of persons who held power in particular communities tended to discount the power and the right to power of labor leaders.

Group Variety   A list of the major types of interests that are usually represented before state and local governments would include the following: chambers of commerce and manufacturers' associations, banks, downtown-merchants associations, public utilities, railroads, truckers, taxicab companies, insurance companies, general contractors, the professions (lawyers, physicians, dentists, teachers, and others), realtors, liquor and racetrack interests, newspapers, general labor-union organizations and their various sub-

[16] William H. Form and Warren L. Sauer, "Organized Labor's Image of Community Power Structure," **Social Forces**, 38:332–341, May, 1960.
[17] William H. Form, "Organized Labor's Place in the Community Power Structure," **Industrial and Labor Relations Review**, 12:526–539, July, 1959.

divisions, racial, ethnic, and religious group organizations, public employees, government officials, veterans, groups representing agricultural, conservation, and highway interests, and good-government and reform groups.

In addition to the groups representing the major pressures, legislative bodies are intermittently subjected to the idiosyncratic behavior of the extreme left and right fringes of the political continuum and to the loud and insistent demands of crackpots, faddists, zealots, headline grabbers, representatives of unusual businesses, and inventors of schemes and machines. Colorful California has such lobbies as those of the Antivivisection League, the Dancing Masters of California, the Dog Defenders League, the Pines to Palms Wildlife Committee, the State Council of Trail Hound Clubs, and the Western Nudist Conference.[18]

State capital reporters are an important, if not popularly recognized, interest group. In one study by a veteran reporter, it was found that reporters "are guided by editorial policy in covering and writing political stories." Furthermore, reporters believe that newspapers should and do attempt to influence legislators. Legislators, in turn, attempt to influence the views of reporters, hoping to affect the way in which their stories are written. Press association reporters make less of an attempt to influence the legislative process than do the reporters for daily newspapers. Certain norms were found to exist among the reporters concerning what was proper for them to comment upon. In particular, they considered it improper to report concerning the personal behavior of legislators. The legislators did not generally resent reportorial influence upon the political process and, indeed, some legislators asked reporters for advice on public policy questions and such advice had an impact on legislative decisions. Reporters often make news themselves by developing ideas for stories or for legislative investigations and use friendly legislators to give stories an official flavor. Legislators, although suspicious of reporters, not only ask them for advice but deliberately leak stories to them.[19] There appears to be an inexhaustible supply of voluntary groups in America, and each seems to have an interest in affecting public policy.[20]

The Power Structure and Group Leadership

"In all societies," a famous sociologist once wrote,[21] "two classes of people appear—a class that rules and a class that is ruled. The first class, always the less numerous, performs all political functions, monopolizes power and enjoys the advantage that power brings, whereas the second, the more numerous class, is directed and controlled by the first."

[18] Joseph P. Harris, **California Politics,** Stanford University Press, Stanford, Calif., 1955, p. 18, and California State Assembly, **List of Legislative Advocates and Organizations,** State of California, Sacramento, Calif., 1957. For another list, see Earl Latham, **Massachusetts Politics,** Citizenship Clearing House, New York, 1956, pp. 68–70; also various references to pressure groups in the states visited just after World War II by Gunther, *op. cit.*

[19] Albert Kaufman, "The State Capitol Political Reporter," unpublished M.A. thesis, Michigan State University, East Lansing, Mich., 1964.

[20] For additional material on interest groups, see the bibliography.

[21] Gaetano Mosca, **The Ruling Class,** English trans. by Hannah D. Kahn, McGraw-Hill Book Company, New York, 1939, chap. 2.

Today, social scientists know that political organization is not so simple as all that. The ruled do not accept uncritically the orders of a ruling class, at least not all of the time. Group leadership is actually as variegated, complex, and filled with crosscurrents as are the interactions of the groups to which the leaders belong. The notion that the exercise of power is a conspiracy against the common people is still to be found in some writings,[22] but it is probably much more realistic to view political power as a tool of social organization rather than a weapon of oppression.

To talk of "power relationships" is not to imply sinister evil doing. The term does not contain any value implications. The possession of power—the ability to manipulate social institutions toward desired goals—is vested in individuals and groups in society because, in practical terms, power is necessary to perform the vital function of establishing and maintaining an ordered society. The particular type of political structure or process through which social order is achieved is determined by the values which are dominant in a particular society at a particular time. Whether the exercise of power by specific individuals or groups is good or bad, therefore, is decided by the citizenry on the basis of whether or not individual actions are in accord or discord with the values of society.

The Power Structure   Not enough is as yet known about those who are discovered in studies to be the "leaders" of the community. It is possible, for example, that persons who appear to be policy leaders, even to the extent of seemingly dominating the decisions of those holding public office, are really only verbalizers. That is, they merely say, as symbolic leaders of the community, the things that are already widely believed in the community. If this is the case, the same policies could have resulted whether or not these persons had taken any action in seeking to have policies developed. Leading bankers, merchants, realtors, and chamber of commerce secretaries are certain, in small towns or middle-sized cities, to have their remarks given considerable publicity through newspapers, radio, and television and may thus seem to be real leaders. Merchant princes and bankers are sometimes listened to because they are natural leaders or because of the deference they receive as a result of their prestigeful positions. But their preferences as to public policy may be forestalled, for example, by implacable resistance from workingmen responding to a labor leader. This leader's own status position will probably be a modest one, and his technique not one of oppressive coercion but merely of pointing out to the union membership the consequences for them of a proposed line of action.

Yet leadership is an intrinsic part of group existence, and leaders make decisions. Furthermore, group action generates power. Those who take a positive interest in any problem are likely to have a considerable advantage over those who are passive and apathetic. And, of course, those who feel they

[22] C. Wright Mills, **The Power Elite**, Oxford University Press, Fair Lawn, N.J., 1956, is an example, although Mills denied using a conspiracy theory. An implicit conspiracy hypothesis seems to underlie the work in Floyd Hunter, **Community Power Structure**, The University of North Carolina Press, Chapel Hill, N.C., 1953, and some other writings in the field.

have the most at stake are also likely to be the ones who become the most active in political decision making.

The following points might be kept in mind in regard to the political power structure as it exists or is supposed to exist:

1. Some economically powerful leaders, in particular the managers and top executives of local plants of nationwide corporations, may refuse to become involved in community activities of any kind not directly affecting the company, lest enemies be unnecessarily made. Thus some of the persons who, because of great economic power, might be expected to be important decision makers exert little or no influence on decisions regarding community public policy.

2. Power structures may not necessarily be constructed in the shape of pyramids, although some studies have found such shapes. It is quite possible, at least in theory, to have power structures that do not lead to a few top leaders but instead have a polynucleated structure with various leaders, each of whom is powerful in some particular area of public policy but not in all such areas. In other words, there may be functional specialization, so that a man who is very influential in deciding questions dealing with, say traffic-flow patterns, may have much less to say about housing policies and may not be consulted at all relative to the introduction of a new recreation program.

3. Some studies show that a few people are very much interested in and influential over virtually all important decisions made in regard to public policy. These are the top members of the power elite. It is possible, even probable, that no such small clique of general leaders exists in the largest cities or in relation to state government because of the great complexity of social organization that exists in such large governmental units. In general, it appears that the economic elite is more likely to control community decisions and the power structure more likely to take on a pyramidal shape in communities where the major economic units are home-owned.[23]

Some evidence indicates that community power complexes were once more nearly monolithic than they are today. With the decline of home-owned industry and the entrance into political activity on an effective basis of racial, ethnic, and labor groups, the community power complex has become increasingly competitive in character.[24]

4. Policy leadership should not be confused with policy invention. The studies made so far tend to show that leaders need not themselves be creative in finding solutions to social needs. Their job is to assess proposals as to their degree of adequacy as solutions and then to push for the adoption of those found most acceptable. New ideas in meeting problems are most likely to come from persons with exceptional technical knowledge of a particular subject, persons who may be in the bureaucracies of private business, government, the universities, or elsewhere. Their names are commonly little known to the general public and sometimes even to the person who serves as sym-

[23] Williams and Adrian, *op. cit.;* and Robert E. Agger, Daniel Goldrich, and Bert E. Swanson, **The Rulers and the Ruled,** John Wiley & Sons, Inc., New York, 1964, pp. 680–681.
[24] Ruth McQuown and others, **The Political Restructuring of a Community,** Public Administration Clearing Service, University of Florida, Gainesville, Fla., 1964.

bolic leader for the promotion of the ideas they have put forth. Thus, it should be remembered that when the headlines read "Banker Lauded in Presenting New Parking Plan" or "Governor Zilch Announces New School-aid Idea," the prestigeful persons mentioned in the stories are merely playing out their particular social roles. The anonymous men who actually thought up the plans in the first place will probably not even be mentioned in the story.

5. Governmental officials may once have been tools of the economic leadership group, but they are becoming increasingly important centers of power in their own right; and this is especially true as government plays an ever greater role in the lives of citizens. In earlier times, government was simple and performed few functions. With business institutions overwhelmingly important by comparison, business leaders sometimes used officeholders as their front men. This is less likely to happen today, and many important community leaders now themselves become councilmen, mayors, and governors.

6. The top members of the power structure may be powerful because they come from high-status families to whom deference has always been paid by the other residents of the community or because they are newspaper editors. But they are most likely to be powerful because they are spokesmen for interest groups and have ability to bring some of the weight of the group to bear upon political institutions. One's place in the power structure reflects, except perhaps in small cities and towns where individuality remains especially important, the relative overall strength of the group for whom the leader is a spokesman.

7. Members of what has been called the community power complex, do not necessarily make up a monolithic power group.[25] They may, in fact, be badly divided internally into two or more factions. In some cases, the editor of the local newspaper, the real-estate board, and commercial and industrial leaders, may be arraigned against racial, ethnic-group, and organized-labor leaders. As the middle class moves out of the core city into the suburbs, the latter grouping is likely to increase in power, thus encouraging a split between the community economic and political leadership.

The exodus of the middle class to the suburbs in the last generation has altered the power structure of core cities. In one city: [26]

The top leaders of 1954 or their immediate successors in the same positions continued to dominate decision-making in 1961. However, the top group was no longer monolithic, but more variegated than was the case seven years before. Also, given roles appeared, in some cases, to be more important than the particular incumbent. . . .

A further conclusion is that decision-making in the community is shared between two antagonistic groups, neither in complete control. The dominant group in the power structure cannot legitimize its decisions on public policy without the approval of an electorate-based veto group in the council, a group with only small membership in the top power complex.

[25] Delbert Miller and William H. Form, **Industry, Labor and the Community,** Harper & Row, Publishers, Incorporated, New York, 1960.
[26] David A. Booth and Charles R. Adrian, "Power Structure and Community Change," **Midwest Journal of Political Science,** 6:277–296, August, 1962.

8. Community power cannot be considered independently of power at the state and national levels. The important decisions affecting communities are not made in the community alone. All three of the traditional levels of government and all three of the traditional branches of government are involved in policy development. A prosperous community in which most persons are employed in locally owned industry may be relatively more independent than is the community which has most of its labor force employed in absentee-owned industry and business.[27]

9. Many vital decisions are not made by government at any level. Furthermore, "a comparatively small portion of the attention and involvement of most Americans" is devoted to governmental activities.[28] This means not only that many decisions are made by power structures of nongovernmental social institutions, but also that those who feel strongly enough about the desirability of achieving a particular public policy and who are willing to invest time, money, social capital, and other resources are likely to find that they are not challenged by other citizens.

In a study by Robert Presthus, 52 percent of the organizations identified in one community and 28 percent of those in another participated in the major decisions of the community; however, 90 percent of these organizations had been active in only one decision each.[29]

In a small industrial city, politics was commonly viewed as being of less importance than other activities, particularly business. Political leaders were found to be selected from the middle level of economic positions. Persons of higher economic status felt that the political game was not worthwhile, and persons in lower positions did not possess enough information to play the game effectively.[30]

10. Professional administrative specialists and "influentials" are both necessary for decision making. In a study contrasting professional administrators with members of the community power structure not associated with bureaucratic positions in city government (influentials), the influentials ranked higher in socioeconomic status, were involved in more policy issues, and were far more willing to be involved in taking positions in local elections. Even so, the two groups were frequently involved in close working relationships and hence were interdependent to a considerable degree.[31]

11. In early community power studies, the assumption seemed to be made implicitly that power was inexhaustible in the hands of those who, for one reason or another, held it. More recent studies seem to imply that the use of power is costly, that is, that power is one form of social capital and can be exhausted if used improvidently. Because power is exhaustible, those who

[27] See Robert V. Presthus, **Men at the Top,** Oxford University Press, Fair Lawn, N.J., 1964; and city "Alpha" in Williams and Adrian, *op. cit.*
[28] York Willbern, **The Withering Away of the City,** University of Alabama Press, University, Ala., 1964, chap. 5; Robert A. Dahl, **Who Governs?** Yale University Press, New Haven, Conn., 1961, chaps. 24–26.
[29] Presthus, *op. cit.*, pp. 432–433.
[30] Paul A. Smith, "The Games of Community Politics," **Midwest Journal of Political Science,** 9: 37–60, February, 1965.
[31] M. Kent Jennings, "Public Administrators and Community Decision Making," **Administrative Science Quarterly,** 8:18–43, June, 1963.

hold it probably choose not to make use of it unless they believe that the input-output ratio is efficient, that is, unless they believe the payoffs are worth the costs.

12. One of the difficulties in identifying a power structure results from the fact that participants in community decision making may be involved either overtly or covertly. Those who are openly involved are relatively easy to identify, but some may be powerful figures, even though they are not actors on the community stage. These may be individuals who enjoy high status in the community or who, because of their economic or political positions, are feared by others. This results in *anticipatory behavior*. That is, the decision makers *assume* that these persons are potentially actors in the decision-making process and that it is necessary to accommodate to their particular interests, as the other leaders view them, if they are not to become active in the process and veto proposed policies of other actors. The "richest man in town," or a leading banker, or a major manufacturer, or any other person viewed as potentially powerful may, hence, remain out of the political arena by having his expectations discounted in advance. The possibility always exists that they are overdiscounted and, for the researcher, it is extremely difficult to determine who such actors are and whether the allowance made for their potential power is exaggerated or not.

13. The community roles that are viewed by the culture as being important and hence deserving of a place in the community power complex are well known as the result of the large number of studies by sociologists and political scientists. Almost all power structure studies include the following leaders: the editor or publisher of the local newspaper, a leading banker or two, the heads of the two or three largest manufacturing firms, the heads of the major central business district retail firms, the manager of the local chamber of commerce, the mayor, and one or possibly two councilmen, but never a majority of the council. In addition, the head of the realty firm that handles most of the central business district property will often be included.

Among those who are seldom mentioned in a study of reputational elites are ethnic and racial leaders, the manager of the leading television or radio station, and labor leaders. These persons probably are not included in the reputational power elite because they lack legitimacy, that is, the respondents do not view them as having a *right* to be included in the community power structure and hence they are not listed.

In an attempt both to simplify the determination of local power elites and to overcome the prejudice against persons who are not viewed by the upper middle class as having a right to a place in the power structure, two sociologists have developed a simplified method of determining the local power leaders.[32] They have assumed that the actual leaders in a community cannot be hidden from knowledgeable people, an assumption also made by the political scientist, Robert A. Dahl. Using this assumption, they have found it possible to construct a profile of the local power elite by asking any two leaders in the following seven areas to list the persons whom they regard as

[32] Miller and Form, *op. cit.*

having most power and influence: persons from business, the clergy, the communications media, education, financial institutions, organized labor, and the Negro community.

Public Awareness of the Political Power Structure   In both the small town and middle-sized city evidence indicates that many citizens are not aware of the identity of the most influential persons in the community when it comes to policy leadership. The extent of this specific problem was inquired into in a study made in Detroit. (Keep in mind that the small Oregon town referred to above contained many people who could not identify the informal leaders —possibly size is not too important a factor in relation to this matter.)

Before answers are given to the question, Who runs Detroit? it should be pointed out that Detroit city government has been dominated almost without interruption from the time of World War I by the businessmen of the community: members of the board of commerce, the downtown merchants, and the real-estate groups in particular. This is accomplished through a community of interests with the daily newspapers, whose control of the principal means of local communication is all-important in a system of nonpartisan elections. Detroit political parties are weak, and there are no political bosses in the traditional sense. The labor unions, despite the huge membership of the United Automobile Workers, have been very weak in local politics. Jews and Negroes have had little representation in either the legislative or the administrative branch of city government (the first Negro was elected to the council in 1957). Organized racketeering has not been influential in Detroit government for many years.

The answers to the question, Who runs Detroit? were classified as follows: [33]

Answer	Percent
No special group: "the public," don't know, etc.	42
Special groups named:	
Businessmen, industrialists, the rich	18
Labor unions, organized labor	11
Politicians, political bosses	11
Jews	6
Negroes	5
Racketeers, gamblers, underworld	2
Others	5
Total	58

The survey showed interesting variations of response among different population groups. The better educated were most convinced that special

[33] Arthur Kornhauser, **Attitudes of Detroit People Toward Detroit,** Wayne State University Press, Detroit, Mich., 1952, pp. 13–15. This is a summary of a longer, more technical study, **Detroit as the People See It,** Wayne State University Press, Detroit, Mich., 1952. By permission of the Wayne State University Press.

groups "really run the city." Only 30 percent of those who went beyond high school named no groups that had most influence, while 50 percent of people with eighth-grade education or less named no particular groups. High school and college graduates and the upper socioeconomic groups almost never named Jews or Negroes. It is significant that the more education a person had, the more likely it was that he would be able to name the influential groups. Although this particular survey did not attempt to measure the ability of respondents to name specific individual leaders, it does give some idea of the relative ability of citizens in a large city to assess the actual power relationships that exist as against the tendency that exists in some personality types to ascribe power to those who are distrusted or feared.

Closing Statement   This chapter has served to introduce the concept of power and the political role of the intergroup process, both of which have leading parts in the American political drama. The techniques used by lobbyists in representing interest groups will be developed in Chapter 12, while Chapter 8 will round out an exposition of the political process by discussing the formal structure in which it operates.

SELECTED READINGS

Agger, Robert E., Daniel Goldrich, and Bert E. Swanson: **The Rulers and the Ruled,** John Wiley & Sons, Inc., New York, 1964.   (A major theoretical and empirical study of community power and politics.)

Anton, Thomas J.: "Power, Pluralism, and Local Politics," **Administrative Science Quarterly,** 7:425–457, March, 1963.   (Discusses various approaches to study of community decision making.)

Bachrach, Peter, and Morton S. Baratz: "Two Faces of Power," **American Political Science Review,** 56:947–952, December, 1962.   (Argues that findings of centralized or diffused power bases miss the point; that the important question is who is advantaged or disadvantaged by particular community ideologies.)

Booth, David A., and Charles R. Adrian: "Power Structure and Community Change," **Midwest Journal of Political Science,** 6:277–296, August, 1962.   (A replication after a seven-year period of the study of a middle-sized city reported in George M. Belknap and Ralph H. Smuckler, "Political Power Relations in a Mid-west City," **Public Opinion Quarterly,** 20:73–81, Spring, 1956.)

Carper, Edith T.: **Illinois Goes to Congress for Army Land,** The Bobbs-Merrill Company, Inc., Indianapolis, ICP no. 71, 1962.   (Sportsmen and businessmen contest for the same piece of land.)

Daland, Robert T.: **The County Buys Dunwoodie Golf Course,** The Bobbs-Merrill Company, Inc., Indianapolis, ICP no. 61, 1961.   (Interest groups and land-use conflicts.)

David, Henry: "One Hundred Years of Labor in Politics," in J. B. S. Hardman and M. F. Neufeld (eds.), **The House of Labor,** Prentice-Hall, Inc., Englewood Cliffs, N.J., 1951.

Farris, Charles D.: "Prohibition as a Political Issue," **Journal of Politics,** 23:507–525, August, 1961.   (Support for prohibition is still a local-option issue in some states. It is positively correlated with dogmatism [measured by Rokeach scale], fundamentalism, and lower-class status.)

Freeman, H. E., and M. Showel: "Differential Political Influence of Voluntary Associations," **Public Opinion Quarterly,** 15:703–714, Winter, 1951–52.

Fuchs, Lawrence H.: **The Political Behavior of American Jews,** The Free Press of Glencoe, New York, 1956.

Garceau, Oliver, and Corinne Silverman: "A Pressure Group and the Pressured," **American Political Science Review,** 48:672–691, September, 1954. (A study of a manufacturer's association and the Vermont legislature.)

Herring, E. Pendleton: **Public Administration and the Public Interest,** McGraw-Hill Book Company, New York, 1936.

Hofferbert, Richard I.: "Classification of American State Party Systems," **Journal of Politics,** 26:550–567, August, 1964. (Offers a flexible, useful method for calculating party competitiveness by states.)

Hogarty, Richard A.: **New Jersey Farmers and Migrant Housing Rules,** The Bobbs-Merrill Company, Inc., Indianapolis, ICP no. 94, 1966. (Should the state require New Jersey farmers to provide hot water for migrant laborers? Involves ideology and tactics of leaders on each side.)

Hunter, Floyd: **Community Power Structure,** The University of North Carolina Press, Chapel Hill, N.C., 1953. (A pioneering study. The method used has since been refined.)

Jennings, M. Kent: **Community Influentials: The Elites of Atlanta,** The Free Press of Glencoe, New York, 1964. (Finds that, a decade after Hunter's study, the elite of Atlanta is not homogeneous or dominant in all fields of community decision making.)

Kammerer, Gladys M., Charles D. Farris, John M. DeGrove, and Alfred B. Clubok: **The Urban Political Community,** Houghton Mifflin Company, Boston, 1963. (Eight case studies of council-manager government in Florida.)

Kaufman, Herbert, and Victor Jones: "The Mystery of Power," **Public Administration Review,** 14:205–212, Summer, 1954. (Two political scientists criticize Hunter.)

Lane, Robert E.: **Political Life: How People Get Involved in Politics,** The Free Press of Glencoe, New York, 1958.

Lasswell, Harold: **Power and Personality,** W. W. Norton & Company, Inc., New York, 1948.

————: **Psychopathology and Politics,** The University of Chicago Press, Chicago, 1930. (An early attempt to apply Freudian theory to political behavior.)

Latham, Earl: "The Group Basis of Politics: Notes for a Theory," **American Political Science Review,** 26:376–379, June, 1952. (A brief statement of group theory.)

Long, Norton E.: "The Local Community as an Ecology of Games," **American Journal of Sociology,** 64:251–261, November, 1958. (A classic article borrowing from systems theory.)

Lynd, Robert S.: "Power in American Society as Resource and Problem," in Arthur Kornhauser (ed.), **Problems of Power in American Democracy,** Wayne State University Press, Detroit, Mich., 1957. (A conspiratorial analysis.)

Mills, C. Wright: **The Power Elite,** Oxford University Press, Fair Lawn, N.J., 1956. (Nonempirical theory.)

Munger, Frank J., and others: **Decisions in Syracuse,** Indiana University Press, Bloomington, Ind., 1961. (A study of community decision making.)

Parsons, Talcott: "The Distribution of Power in American Society," **World Politics,** 10:123–143, October, 1957. (A criticism of Mills by a famous sociologist.)

Press, Charles: **Main Street Politics,** Institute for Community Development, Michigan State University, East Lansing, Mich., 1962.

Presthus, Robert: **Men at the Top,** Oxford University Press, Fair Lawn, N.J., 1964. (A comparative study of two small cities, using both reputational and decision-making research techniques.)

Rossi, Peter H.: "Community Decision-Making," **Administrative Science Quarterly,** 1:415–443, March, 1957.   (A review of the literature.)

Salisbury, Robert H.: "Urban Politics: The New Convergence of Power," **Journal of Politics,** 26:775–797, December, 1964.   (Concludes that the views on community power by both the Dahl and Hunter schools are correct part of the time.)

Schubert, Glendon: **The Public Interest,** The Free Press of Glencoe, New York, 1961.

Schulze, Robert O.: "The Role of Economic Dominants in Community Power Structure," **American Sociological Review,** 23:3–9, February, 1958.

————, and Leonard U. Blumberg: "The Determination of Local Power Elites," **American Journal of Sociology,** 63:290–296, November, 1957.

Sorauf, Frank J.: "The Public Interest Reconsidered," **Journal of Politics,** 19: 616–639, November, 1957.   (The public interest is found in the *process* of decision making.)

Stedman, Murray S., Jr.: **Religion and Politics in America,** Harcourt, Brace & World, Inc., New York, 1964.   (Religion is usually a negative pressure, opposing rather than proposing public policy.)

Truman, David B.: **The Governmental Process,** Alfred A. Knopf, Inc., New York, 1951.   (The detailed statement of the interest-group theory of politics.)

"Unofficial Government: Pressure Groups and Lobbies," **Annals,** 319:entire issue, September, 1958.

Vidich, Arthur J., and Joseph Bensman: **Small Town in Mass Society,** Princeton University Press, Princeton, N.J., 1958.   (An anthropological study of a New York village.)

Walker, Robert S., and Samuel C. Patterson: **Oklahoma Goes Wet: The Repeal of Prohibition,** McGraw-Hill Book Company, New York, 1960, Eagleton Institute, Case no. 24.   (A study of conflicts of interest groups and of ideologies.)

Wasserman, Paul, and F. S. Silander: **Decision-making: An Annotated Bibliography,** Graduate School of Business and Public Administration, Cornell University, Ithaca, N.Y., 1958.

Wells, Richard S.: "The Legal Profession and Politics," **Midwest Journal of Political Science,** 8:166–190, May, 1964.   (The profession is segmented and hence does not exert the monolithic power often attributed to it.)

Wildavsky, Aaron: **Leadership in a Small Town,** The Bedminster Press, Englewood Cliffs, N.J., 1964.   (A study of Oberlin, Ohio, finds a pluralistic pattern of leadership and that this is desirable in a democracy. As a "how to influence" suggestion, it recommends that persons who want to be effective concentrate in a particular issue area.)

Williams, Oliver P., and Charles R. Adrian: **Four Cities,** University of Pennsylvania Press, Philadelphia, 1963.   (A comparative study of community politics in four middle-sized cities.)

Wood, Robert C.: **Suburbia—Its People and Their Politics,** Houghton Mifflin Company, Boston, 1959.   (A theory of suburban politics.)

8

FORMS OF GOVERNMENT

The forms of government are important because they affect the pattern of influence of various groups upon government. Yet Americans have been obsessed with the idea of a relationship between structure and effectiveness of government. Many advocates of reform have been guilty of overstatement in this direction. Much literature may be found urging the council-manager form of city government or the strong-governor type of state government, for example, on the ground that these plans follow the organization form of the business world, the corporation. The implication is that the success of the one should ensure the success of the other.

The "one grand solution" approach contrasts with the views of such persons as the Minneapolis alderman who once said that forms of government have nothing at all to do with the effectiveness or honesty of government. He believed that Minneapolis, which has a nineteenth-century form of government, operates as well as it could under any of the newer forms often advocated by reformers. The viewpoint was not new with him, however; similar expressions have come from Alexander Pope, Edmund Burke, and Lincoln Steffens.

Political scientists are now reasonably certain that: [1]

the governmental structure affects in crucial ways the manner in which . . . interests will be articulated into political parties, and in so doing it plays an important role in determining the scope and intensity of political conflict in the community. It seems doubtful whether one could say that a particular structural form would in every case bring about a particular party system or give a particular shape to the conflict, since the structure and the interest configuration interact in each case.

[1] Robert H. Salisbury, "St. Louis Politics: Relationships among Interests, Parties, and Governmental Structure," **Western Political Quarterly**, 13:498–507, June, 1960.

Structural arrangements have an effect upon the quality of government, but they neither guarantee good government nor prevent it. The structure of government helps to establish behavior patterns and attitudes toward power and the exercise of power that definitely affect the process whereby decisions are made. In a weak-governor state, a department head may present a program to the legislature without having cleared it with the governor—the governor may first learn of it in the newspapers, in fact. This program may be pushed with a vigor at least equal to that behind the governor's own competing program. Such behavior would be considered contemptuous—and would probably have disastrous consequences for the department head—in a strong-governor state. But in a weak-governor state, the department head not only can get away with it, but the fact that he does further weakens the governor's position as an administrative leader by creating a climate of opinion that discourages consultation or coordination between agency heads and the governor. The very nature of the supervisor system of county government is such as to encourage a "you scratch my back and I'll scratch yours" attitude; the same temptation exists but is not so definitely built in, in the commissioner system. The councilmen in council-manager cities probably feel less of an imperative to serve as policy innovators than do their counterparts in weak-mayor cities. A study of the relationship of attitudes of officeholders toward one another would probably reveal considerable variation according to the structure of government.

State Government Organization

The distrust of the chief executive of the colony during Revolutionary times helped to establish a general climate of opinion toward state government that was favorable to the legislature and less favorable to the governor. As was seen in Chapter 2, the conservative interests that provided for strong administrative powers in the office of the President of the United States were less powerful in the individual states, and the same philosophy was not applied in these areas. Indeed, the Jacksonian movement took hold in state government before the governor was restored to his prewar dignity and power. As a result, certain values of that period were rooted into state constitutions, particularly during the orgy of constitution writing of the 1850s, and these values became the basis of a persistent attitude toward state government that still dominates contemporary practice.

The Weak-governor System   The pattern of state government organization that arose in the nineteenth century and that remains powerful today is analogous to the weak-mayor system (discussed below) which is also a product of the Jacksonian period of frontier individualism. It called for many elective officers, each independent of the others; for the provision of much of the detail of government organization in the constitution itself; for the control of many agencies by boards and commissions, chosen for overlapping terms of office and with members almost unremovable by the governor or, in practice, by any-

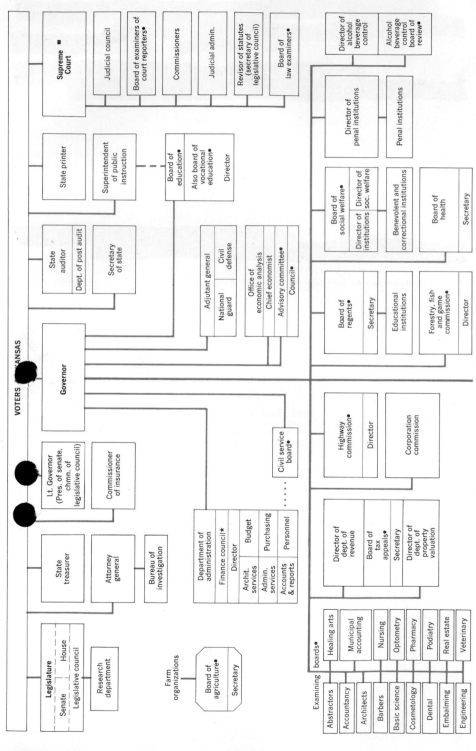

VOTERS KANSAS

Legislature
Senate
House
Legislative council
Research department

State treasurer
Attorney general
Bureau of investigation

Lt. Governor (Pres. of senate, chmn. of legislative council)
Commissioner of insurance

Governor

State auditor
Dept. of post audit
Secretary of state

State printer
Superintendent of public instruction

Supreme Court
Judicial council
Board of examiners of court reporters●
Commissioners
Judicial admin.
Revisor of statutes (secretary of legislative council)
Board of law examiners●

Board of education●
Also board of vocational education●
Director

Adjutant general
National guard
Civil defense

Office of economic analysis
Chief economist
Advisory committee●
Council●

Farm organizations
Board of agriculture●
Secretary

Department of administration
Finance council★
Director
Archit. services
Admin. services
Accounts & reports
Budget
Purchasing
Personnel

Civil service board●

Director of alcohol beverage control
Alcohol beverage control board of review●

Director of penal institutions
Penal institutions

Board of social welfare●
Director of institutions
Director of soc. welfare
Benevolent and correctional institutions
Board of health
Secretary

Board of regents●
Secretary
Educational institutions
Forestry, fish and game commission●
Director

Highway commission●
Director
Corporation commission

Director of dept. of revenue
Board of tax appeals●
Secretary
Director of dept. of property valuation

Examining boards●
Abstractors
Accountancy
Architects
Barbers
Basic science
Cosmetology
Dental
Embalming
Engineering
Healing arts
Municipal accounting
Nursing
Optometry
Pharmacy
Podiatry
Real estate
Veterinary

200

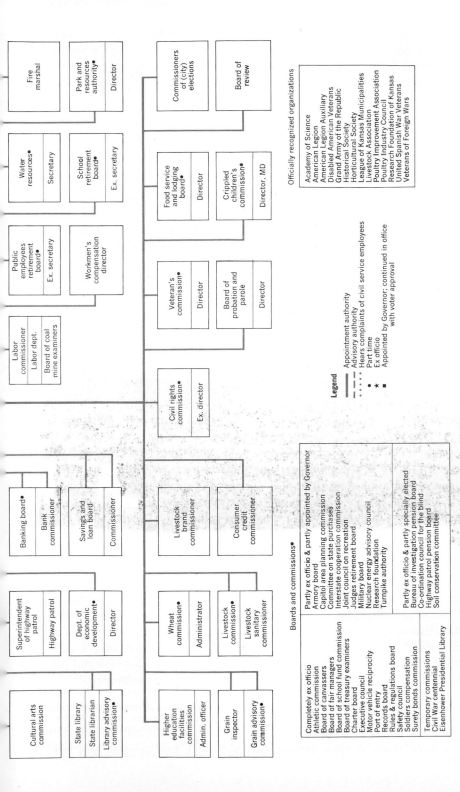

Fig. 8-1 State Government Organization Is Complex.

SOURCE: Governmental Research Center, University of Kansas, Lawrence, Kans. Data as of Jan. 1, 1966. Chart by J. W. Drury.

with its strong commitment to Jacksonian traditions, has helped to slow down change.

Yet, changes are taking place. There is now evident a slow but perceptible movement toward an increase in the governor's powers. Legislators have reluctantly acceded to pressures for an executive budget; they have increasingly supported the merit system of personnel administration with all its threats for erosion of the patronage base; they have even in a few cases given the governor power to rearrange and combine agencies and their administrative assignments, subject only to legislative veto. Although the typical legislator probably views—perhaps correctly—every increase in gubernatorial powers as a loss in his own and although department heads often share this view with him, pressures for change have been great because of the need to place competent individuals in charge of the carrying out of ever-expanding programs. They have generally been coupled with demands for increased powers in the hands of the governor and of persons directly responsible to him.

The Patchwork of Local Government

Much has been written over many years concerning the irrational pattern—or lack of pattern—to be found in American local government. Most of these criticisms center on two points: (1) that local government boundaries drawn up to suit a nineteenth-century pattern of transportation and communication are inappropriate for the twentieth century and (2) that technological and social change, as well as changes in the role of various units of government, makes the traditional units and their structural form unsuited for contemporary government, especially from a point of view of cost considerations. Both of these criticisms seem plausible. It is possible—though by no means certain—that local government boundaries would have been much larger in size and population if America had been settled under conditions including present-day technology. The frontiersman not only distrusted controls from a remote city and preferred grass-roots controls, he also treated the local unit of government as a social community. Its problems and activities helped create a set of common interests and goals for the area and reduced some of the psychological problems of isolation that were chronic on the frontier.

In cities, boundaries were drawn according to the limits of the built-up area, for technology did not permit urban services to be offered outside the city limits. In rural America, the local governing unit encompassed an area not greater than that which would place the town hall within approximately an hour's buggy ride from the farthest corner; the county was an area where (east of the Missouri) no one was more than a day's buggy or horseback ride from the county seat. It was thus not illogical for the 6- by 6-mile Congressional township originally established for survey purposes to become the unit of local government in the Midwest. And ninety-two counties were not "too many" in Indiana in the 1840s.

Yet, in the latter half of the twentieth century, a township may be traversed in ten minutes by an automobile traveling at a side-road pace. A county courthouse 20 miles away can be reached in less than half an hour. Local services, which once had to be supported by a sparse population existing at a low standard of living, now have behind them a much greater earning capacity and a much larger number of persons. Are the old boundaries still appropriate? Many students of government say that they are not.[5] They seem inefficiently small by modern standards. They are not structured with modern service requirements in mind. They do not meet the needs of the technical characteristics of administration today and of the larger units of government required for adequate service by contemporary standards. The loyalties that supposedly exist toward traditional units are not proved and may well be exaggerated in the claims made by local politicians. Yet efficiency cannot be the only criterion used in drawing boundaries. It seems likely the average citizen is more concerned with psychological identification with the local unit of government, and especially, with the representative character of government than he is with efficiency; that the average citizen is especially interested in the question of whether or not he has access to the decision-making personnel of local government and whether or not that government seems to represent his interests and values. In this sense, drawing anew "logical" or "efficient" local boundaries may seem to the local citizen both illogical and unreasonable. Yet in a society where a sense of isolation from fellow men is strong and a sense of community is weak, man feels the need to believe in something. He needs, among other things, a sense of political community.[6]

The Number of Local Units   Local government changes "have occurred on the basis of step-by-step, incremental, *ad hoc* adjustments made to answer specific needs and forces and demands, and not on the basis of adherence to any general doctrine." [7] Over the nation as a whole, local units of government are declining in number. More than 40 percent of the units in existence in 1942 had disappeared by 1962.[8] Most of the decline occurred, however, as a result of the consolidation of school districts, but quite a few towns and townships were abolished, too (see Table 10). Special districts (e.g., for sewage disposal, fire protection, or mosquito abatement) have continued to increase in number. Between 1942 and 1962, such districts increased by 120 percent.

The largest number of local units of government are to be found in the Midwestern states where the township and the one-room-school district have been traditional. Almost one-half of the total number of units of government in the United States are to be found in eight states: Illinois, Kansas, Michigan, Minnesota, Missouri, Nebraska, Pennsylvania, and Wisconsin. All of these are

[5] See, for example, William C. Havard and Alfred Diamant, "The Need for Local Government Reform in the United States," **Western Political Quarterly**, 9:967–995, December, 1956; William Anderson, **The Units of Government in the United States**, rev. ed., Public Administration Service, Chicago, 1949; and Alvin H. Hansen and H. S. Perloff, **State and Local Finance in the National Economy**, W. W. Norton & Company, Inc., New York, 1944. Each of these emphasizes efficiency considerations in determining boundaries.
[6] Sebastian de Grazia, **The Political Community**, The University of Chicago Press, Chicago, 1948.
[7] York Willbern, **The Withering Away of the City**, University of Alabama Press, University, Ala., 1964, p. 106.
[8] See U.S. Bureau of the Census, **Governments in the United States**, 1962.

in the Midwest, of course, except for Pennsylvania, which uses the township system and also has the largest number of school districts outside the Midwest.

Table 10   Number of Local Governments in the United States, by Type

TYPE OF GOVERNMENT	NUMBER OF UNITS				CHANGE IN NUMBER	
	1962	1957	1952	1942	1957–1962	1942–1962
Total	91,236	102,328	105,743	155,116	−11,092	−63,880
U.S. government	1	1	1	1		
States	50	48	48	48	2	2
Counties	3,043	3,047	3,049	3,050	−4	−7
Municipalities	17,979	17,183	16,778	16,220	796	1,759
Townships and towns	17,144	17,198	17,202	18,919	−54	−1,775
School districts	34,678	50,446	56,346	108,579	−15,768	−73,901
Special districts *	18,323	14,405	12,319	8,299	3,918	10,024

* Increase from 1957 to 1962 partly a result of reclassification.
SOURCE: U.S. Bureau of the Census, Governments in the United States, 1962.

The fewest governmental units are to be found in the geographically small states of Rhode Island, Delaware, and Maryland, and in the sparsely settled states of Nevada and New Mexico. In the South and West, where the township system was never established and where school districts have always covered more territory than in the Midwest, governments are relatively few in number.

The County

Counties—in Louisiana they are called parishes—are to be found in every state except tiny Connecticut and Rhode Island, and sparsely populated Alaska. The average state has sixty-three counties, but the pattern varies greatly according to region. In the South, where there were never any townships, the county is relatively small in size. In the West, where distances are vast, it is quite large. The number in each state varies from none to 254 in Texas.

With a few areas excepted, county boundaries are drawn irrespective of whether the area enclosed is rural or urban territory or a combination of the two. As a result America's population is distributed unevenly over the 3,043 counties of the nation. More than one-fifth of the population is concentrated in sixteen counties. On the other hand, one-fourth of the counties of the nation are organized to serve 3.5 percent of the population. It may be assumed that even though they may provide only minimal services and receive a fairly large amount of state financial aid, these counties are expensive to operate and have a low efficiency rating.

But efficiency may not be the prime consideration in evaluating a unit of

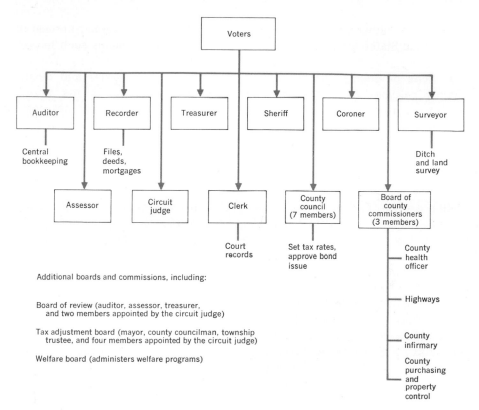

Fig. 8-2   County Government Is Usually Not Centrally Controlled.

SOURCE: Bureau of Government Research, Indiana University, Bloomington, Ind.

government. Except in New England, where it has never been important, the county has served from earliest times as a basic unit of grass-roots government. Until the advent of the auto and the telephone, the county was the largest government with which the citizen could hope to have direct, personal contact. Especially in rural areas, a legion of social organizations were established using the county as the area of focus. It became a center for the administration of health, welfare, and educational programs, for the dispensing of justice, for the paying of taxes (even state taxes), for the election of legislative representatives, for the agricultural extension program, for voluntary social agencies, for such colorful bits of Americana as the county fair, for the keeping of vital statistics and of land ownership and debt records, for the maintenance of roads, and for a thousand other things, governmental and otherwise. The county seat was a prize sought, sometimes in bitter fashion, by every community. The winning community became a trade center, the seat of the local bureaucracy, the home of governmental hangers-on such as lawyers and members of abstract companies, the location for the county fair (usually), the recreation and business center, and the home of retired farmers. The county was not an impersonal administrative unit of the state with arbitrary boundaries. It was rather a real, an important, social and political center. In most of the United States, despite changes in our way of life, it remains such today.[9]

The Form of County Government   In response to local values and needs, county governments developed great organizational variety in the United States. As people moved westward, they brought with them to the new territories the traditions already established in the East. But mutations of structure, of nomenclature, of powers took place everywhere.

In general, county government is organized around a governing board and a greatly varied and often complex array of individual officers, boards, commissions, and ex officio bodies. The pattern is not uniform, usually, even within a state. Part of the structure and even many details of organization may be set out in the state constitution. The remainder is usually determined by state law. Traditionally, county governing bodies have had little direct control over structure of government.

The variation in county governments is indicated by the great variety of names that have been given to governing bodies. Although most of them are referred to by titles similar to either board of commissioners or board of supervisors, those in Delaware are called levy courts, in several states county courts, in Kentucky fiscal courts, in Texas commissioners' courts, in most of Georgia commissioners of roads and revenue, and in Louisiana parish police juries.

Despite the variety, a few generalizations can be made about county government, including the following:

1. With the exception of a very few urban counties, there is no chief executive officer for the county. A group of coequal, elected administrators is the common pattern.

2. County government grew unsystematically and has rarely been deliberately revised and altered as has been the case with municipal government in most states.

3. The separation-of-powers principle has not been important in county government. Executive, legislative, and judicial powers are often to be found in the same person.

4. County government structure falls generally into two types, the commissioner and supervisor forms. The former centers around a small governing board directly elected by the voters either at large or by districts and with the board members being concerned primarily or exclusively with county government duties. The latter has a governing board, often of much larger size, some or all of whose members serve ex officio as county board members by right of holding some other office, usually as judicial, township, or municipal officers.

The Commissioner Form   About two-thirds of the counties of the nation have governing boards made up of persons elected specifically to serve on

[9] For details on county government and for its history, see Lane W. Lancaster, **Government in Rural America,** 2d ed.; D. Van Nostrand Company, Inc., Princeton, N.J., 1952; or C. F. Snider, **Local Government in Rural America,** Appleton-Century-Crofts, Inc., New York, 1957. The county as an urban unit is discussed in Victor Jones, "Local Government in Metropolitan Areas," in Coleman Woodbury (ed.), **The Future of Cities and Urban Redevelopment,** The University of Chicago Press, Chicago, 1953, part IV.

those bodies and with no duties at other than the county level.[10] The board of county commissioners (in some states, such as Iowa, called the board of county supervisors) is usually small in size, commonly having three or five members. It may be elected by districts or at large or may be nominated by districts and elected at large.[11] The area from which commissioners are chosen (called "districts" usually, but "beats" in Mississippi and "wards" in Louisiana) is commonly much larger than a town or township. Typically, the board has both legislative and administrative powers. Although the commissioners still have, in some states, the remnants of the judicial powers their historical predecessors held, in most cases these are now of little practical significance.

The commissioner form was developed in Pennsylvania and spread westward, as did American frontier migration typically, along the lines of parallel. Thus Ohio, Indiana, southern Illinois, Iowa, and the Western states generally follow the Pennsylvania tradition.

The Supervisor Form   The state of New York, which adopted some of the tradition of the New England town but modified it and gave greater emphasis to the county, served as the breeding ground for another kind of county government, the supervisor form. This method of governing the county is to be found in about one-third of the states. Again, the migrants carried the old form of government with them in a westerly fashion, so that the supervisor form is found, in addition to New Jersey, in Michigan, Wisconsin, and northern Illinois. The pattern of settlement ended it there, however, and Minnesota adopted the commissioner plan (its sparsely settled northern areas were not divided into townships).

This form historically was characterized by a governing body made up of persons who were originally elected as township supervisors and who sat on the county governing board in an ex officio capacity. The size of the board was determined by the number of townships in the county, although in most states the cities were also entitled to representation on the board according to a formula determined in state law. The largest such governing body was in Wayne County (Detroit), Michigan, which had a 1966 membership of over 115. A more typical board of supervisors would have around twenty members, although quite a few were larger than that, and some had less than ten.

Because of the ex officio character of board membership under the supervisor form, citizens in these states seem to have been less aware of county government than were citizens in commissioner-form states. Furthermore, the large size of boards of supervisors encouraged the use of the committee system for getting the board's work done, and this removed county government still more from citizen oversight.

In addition to the conventional (New York-type) supervisor structure of county government, there were several variations which might be subsumed under this form, since they depended wholly or in part upon ex officio governing boards. In some states a judge, usually a judge of probate, served both as

---

[10] See U.S. Bureau of the Census, **County Boards and Commissions,** 1947.
[11] On the political significance of commissions, see Bertil Hanson, "County Commissioners of Oklahoma," **Midwest Journal of Political Science,** 9:388–400, November, 1965.

chairman of the county board and as a judicial officer. Other members of the board, usually called commissioners, functioned primarily as members of that body. In most of Kentucky and Tennessee, the other members were the justices of the peace of the county, an arrangement that made for a large governing board. In Arkansas, and in a few counties elsewhere, a single judge acted both in his judicial capacity and as the lone legislative officer of the county.[12]

The traditional supervisor system may soon be eliminated. In 1965, the courts in both Wisconsin and Michigan ruled that the Supreme Court decision in *Reynolds v. Sims* concerning equal representation in state legislatures also implied that county governing boards would have to be apportioned according to population or elected at large. (Presumably the same rule would also apply to city councils.) If these decisions are upheld, states using the New York system will have to make drastic modifications in their systems of choosing county boards.

Prior to the decision of the United States Supreme Court requiring legislative bodies to be apportioned on the basis of population, numerous efforts had been made in the counties using the New York supervisor system to amend the rule concerning county representation.[13] In other cases, efforts had also been made to centralize the administrative structure, which in the typical county is made up of a number of independently elected officials. Reformers have often called for county home rule, which would permit choice of a county executive, a centralized administrative structure, and a governing body based on population.[14] Change may be slow in coming, however. In Wisconsin, for example, in the first sixty years of this century, 101 unsuccessful attempts were made to amend the state constitution to permit structural changes in county governments.[15]

County Administrative Officers   Although the tasks of executive officers will be examined more closely in Chapter 10, a few remarks about county administrative officers would be appropriate here. As it has been noted above, county government is characterized by the use of the long ballot. Each of the elected officials is independent, by and large, of the county board. The original Jacksonian theory called for coordination through the political party, but the party does not perform this function effectively in the typical county today. The legislative body usually has few, if any, coordinating powers over elective officials. The powers of each officer and board are carefully described in state law, and there is no person who could be classified as the chief executive officer in the typical county.

The American county is descended from the English county, which in turn

---

[12] In a few states and in scattered counties in states having predominantly one of the forms already mentioned, governing boards did not fit into either the commissioner or supervisor types. See U.S. Bureau of the Census, *op. cit.*

[13] Ruth Bauman, **The County in Wisconsin,** Bureau of Government, University of Wisconsin, Madison, Wis., 1962. A pamphlet.

[14] W. Brooke Graves, **American Intergovernmental Relations,** Charles Scribner's Sons, New York, 1964, pp. 700–712.

[15] Bauman, *op. cit.*

stems from the Anglo-Saxon shire. Thus, county offices have a great deal of tradition behind them. Sheriffs' offices stem from the shire-reeve, which originated in the ninth century. Similarly long history is a part of the offices of clerk, coroner, and treasurer. In addition to those named above, more than one-half of the states have elective county officials in the following posts: recorder or register of deeds, superintendent of county schools (an office of declining importance in most states), assessor, attorney or solicitor, and surveyor or engineer. Although no county actually elects a dogcatcher, some of them do elect public weighers, drain commissioners, and officers with such strange-sounding titles as those of surrogate (in New York, an officer who probates wills) and prothonotary (in Pennsylvania and Delaware, the clerk of the court of common pleas).

In addition to elective officers, many officers and boards and commissions are appointive or ex officio in their makeup. The right of appointment usually rests with the county board, but sometimes it belongs to a judicial officer or to one of the elective administrative officers. Boards and commissions may be found for a great variety of different county functions: for the county fair, airports, elections, roads, health, welfare, hospitals, libraries, schools, and dozens of others.[16] It is through the use of these boards that county government achieves the ultimate in decentralized and uncoordinated operation. Even the county governing board, which may formally make the appointments, is likely to lose effective supervision over the various boards and commissions. Each function of government operates on its own, often without relationship to other functions and far below the level of perception or oversight of the average citizen.[17]

Trends in County Government   Perhaps three trends can be delineated in county government in the 1960s.[18]

1. Counties are performing an increasing number of functions of government, particularly counties that contain a large proportion of urban residents. The traditional functions—law enforcement, judicial administration, road construction and maintenance, public welfare, the keeping of records, and, in some states, school administration—have been augmented both through the assumption of new services and through the transfer to the county of services once provided by other local governments, particularly the townships.[19] Many functions once considered properly those of municipal corporations are now performed by counties, even in rural areas. In fact, some counties in some states are today performing all of the functions of the municipality, although the number and variety of functions varies from one county to the next. Despite

[16] U.S. Bureau of the Census, *op. cit.*
[17] See Edward W. Weidner, **The American County: Patchwork of Boards**, National Municipal League, New York, 1946.
[18] See Clyde F. Snider, "American County Government: A Mid-century Review," **American Political Science Review**, 46:66–80, March, 1952; Public Administration Service, "The Changing County," **National Municipal Review**, 45:433–437, October, 1956; William N. Cassella, "County Government in Transition," **Public Administration Review**, 16:223–231, Summer, 1956.
[19] Snider, **American County Government**, pp. 73–74.

talk about the trend toward centralization, the fact is that "functionally, the county is of greater importance today than a generation ago, and expansion of the services provided by its government appears likely to continue." [20]

2. The cost of county government is becoming increasingly burdensome, even allowing for increased returns to the citizen in the form of more and better services. This is so because, in some urbanized areas, the county has become a unit of government partially duplicating urban services with core-city taxpayers often being called upon to help pay for elaborate services provided by both the city and the county. At the same time, about one-half the counties in the United States are losing population, and the residents of these rural counties are increasingly feeling the burden of a government which seeks to achieve modern service levels but is faced with a declining population and an eroding tax base.

3. The number of counties has remained almost constant during the twentieth century, and their structure has changed but little. Still, some reorganization is taking place, and: [21]

Whenever the structure of county government has been modified to meet new demands it becomes increasingly similar to that of cities, with particular emphasis placed upon a strengthened executive and a more adequately representative legislative body.

A handful of counties have adopted the manager plan; a few others have chief administrative officers with some managerial powers, the best-known example being that of Los Angeles County. Quite a few counties have been reorganized with elective chief executives, including Cook County (Chicago), Illinois, Nassau and Westchester counties in New York, and St. Louis County, Missouri. In some states, one of the traditionally elective offices has been selected, in recent years, for the assignment of increasing amounts of supervisory powers. Examples include the county clerk in Wisconsin, the auditor in Indiana, the county ordinary in Georgia, and the county judge in Arkansas.[22]

Because of the slowness with which counties have been reorganized, the trend has been toward the use of functional consolidation (such as city-county or bicounty health departments) and of formal and informal contractual and cooperative arrangements. Although this approach has not helped in making county government more representative—an area in which it has had notorious failings—it has helped to provide services of a higher caliber than would otherwise be possible.

One student has described the present condition of the county government as follows: [23]

County government in South Dakota is confronted by many of the problems facing county government generally in the United States. County government was

[20] *Ibid.*, p. 78.
[21] Cassella, *op. cit.*, p. 224.
[22] Snider, *op. cit.*, p. 71. See Abraham Holtzman, **Los Angeles County Chief Administrative Officer: Ten Years' Experience**, Bureau of Governmental Research, University of California, Berkeley, Calif., 1948.
[23] William O. Farber, "Improving County Government," **Public Affairs**, 14:1, Aug. 15, 1963.

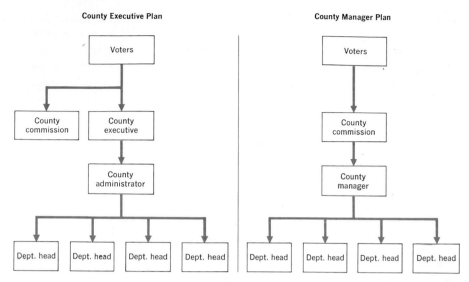

Fig. 8-3   Executive Leadership Proposed for Urban Counties.
SOURCE: C. J. Hein, **The Stake of Rural People in Metropolitan Government,** U.S. Department of Agriculture, 1961, p. 7.

established when transportation and communication systems were far different from those today. The average citizen now knows more about government in Washington than he does about government in his county courthouse. As governmental problems have grown in scope and complexity, personnel needs have changed, demanding public servants trained in the administration and conduct of public welfare, highway planning and construction, assessment procedure, law enforcement, and numerous other technical activities. While the burdens imposed on county government have grown, the capacity of county government to do the job has been questioned, for counties vary greatly in area, population, and financial resources. States have found it increasingly necessary to regulate county activities and to aid counties by various grant-in-aid systems.

The more sparsely settled states have problems in county administration because population is pyramiding in cities and simultaneously is dropping in rural areas. For example, in 1940, only ten South Dakota counties out of sixty-four had a population of less than 5,000. By 1960, this number had doubled. For every county service, the per capita cost was higher in these small counties than it was in the state's most populous counties. It is also likely that for some functions, at least, the quality of service was lower even though the price was higher.[24]

The county, then, is becoming an increasingly important unit for the provision of social services wanted by the public, but only very slow change can be noted toward making its government more responsive to popular control. Because so many of its activities are carried on below the level of perception of the average citizen, the "courthouse gang" has been highly successful in

[24] Farber, *op. cit.,* tables 2 and 3.

preventing changes in governmental structure, in the use of the spoils system (not less than 90 percent of the counties still use it), or in the method of selection of the governing body which is thought by specialists to be either too small (one to five persons) to be representative of the various interests in the county or too large and too indirectly selected (in the supervisor-type and similarly structured counties) to be held responsible to the voters. The county is today much more than a mere administrative subdivision of the state performing routine functions involving little or no policy making. Yet state legislatures and county officials persist in treating the county as if this were the case. And an apathetic public, trusting to pressure groups to look out for its interests, pays this unit of government perhaps less attention than any other save the special districts.

Towns and Townships

The county is an intermediate unit of government for the most part. In the East and Midwest, as well as in some other parts of the country, there is normally a local unit of government closer to the people than is the county. The oldest of these is the New England town, a unit of government unique to its part of the nation. Despite the fact that it has been greatly admired by Thomas Jefferson and other philosophers as the ideal form of direct democracy, the town government idea did not spread to other parts of America, although elements were borrowed from its structure as New Englanders left their rocky, forested lands and moved westward.

The Town   Faced with severe winters and potentially hostile Indians, the New England colonists settled in small villages and farmed the land surrounding them. These self-contained units, each of which constituted a church congregation, was a natural governmental area. The term "town" came to mean the entire community, rural and urban land alike. Although the towns were not incorporated, they were recognized by the legislature as having a right to exercise certain powers which elsewhere came to be associated with the municipal corporation. Later, when New England counties were established, they served principally as judicial districts. As some areas became increasingly urbanized, the town continued to serve as the basic unit of local government. At the time of the War of Independence, there was not a single municipal corporation in New England. Even today, though some modification is taking place, the town remains the common unit of local government in New England. (In Maine, a similar unit is called the "plantation," but its government is now essentially the same as the town.) [25]

Town Government   The town is governed by a meeting of all the qualified voters, who choose officers and make basic policy. There is an annual meeting, traditionally in March, with as many other meetings as may be necessary. After making basic policy, the people choose a board of selectmen, usually

[25] On the historical evolution of "plantations," see Snider, **Local Government in Rural America**, pp. 213–214.

three but in some places as many as nine. A fairly large number of other officers—a clerk, treasurer, assessor, overseer of the poor, constable, school committee, and fence viewer—are either elected or appointed by the selectmen. The selectmen and elective officers are then entrusted with carrying out the basic policies established by community action.[26]

The urbanization of many towns has been accompanied by a sharp decrease in attendance at town meetings and a consequent decline in the democratic effectiveness of this form of government. In fact, even in rural towns, attendance is often poor, and finding persons willing to serve in town offices is likely to be a problem.[27] In many areas of New England, a *representative* town meeting plan has been developed. Under this plan, the voters choose a large number of citizens, perhaps a hundred or more, to attend the meeting, represent them, and vote. Any citizen can attend and take part in debates, but he no longer has a direct vote. This plan is used in such large urban places as Brookline, Massachusetts (1960 population: 52,300).

Town government, outside of the meeting feature, resembles the weak-mayor or, more particularly, the American village form except that there is no mayor at all, only a president of the council, and no one has a veto power. It is becoming more and more common for the selectmen to choose a manager and turn actual administration over to him. This is particularly the case in Maine and Vermont and is to be found in all New England states. The New England legislatures have been under constant pressure to alter the traditional town government in order to help meet contemporary needs. They have created new offices and commissions such as those of aviation commissioner, planning boards, civil-service commissions, library trustees, and finance committees, the last in order to help provide for better planning in budget making so that this document is not pieced together in haphazard fashion at the public meeting. (Titles vary by states and even towns, of course.)

Townships   In the Middle Atlantic states and in the Midwest, townships (in some states, officially called towns) developed as basic units of rural government. In the East townships were irregularly shaped, as they were in New England, but the tendency in the Midwest was to follow the lines established by the surveyors who laid out this vast area on Congressional order beginning in 1787, using a 6- by 6-mile basic unit of measure called the "Congressional township." A great many townships are, therefore, square in shape and enclose an area of 36 square miles.

In addition to those in the Middle Atlantic states, townships still remain active for all or major portions of Illinois, Indiana, Kansas, Michigan, Minnesota, North Dakota, Ohio, South Dakota, and Wisconsin. A few townships also remain in Missouri, Nebraska, and Washington.[28] Iowa and Oklahoma once had viable townships, but they have been deactivated.

[26] See *ibid.*, chap. 8, and his bibliography.
[27] See Roscoe C. Martin, **Grass Roots**, University of Alabama Press, University, Ala., 1957, pp. 60–62.
[28] **Municipal Year Book**, International City Managers' Association, Chicago, 1965.

Township Government   Township government is organized much along the lines of the New England town, many of the states even retaining the town meeting which the early settlers carried with them. The annual meeting, which is poorly attended today unless an unusually important issue is on the agenda, has fewer powers than is the case in New England, but it does usually have the right to levy taxes, approve a budget, adopt such ordinances as state law permits, and, to a lessening degree today, elect officers. The states which follow the New York plan of organization generally adopted the use of the annual meeting (though New York itself abolished it in the 1930s), while those following the Pennsylvania pattern of local government have never had annual meetings. Details of organization vary widely.

The Decline of the Rural Township   The township was designed to serve a purpose in a society based on slow communications, primary social relationships, and the general property tax. In contemporary society, with its high labor and operations costs and with a great deal of specialization in personnel and equipment, the township is less and less suitable as a unit of government, particularly in sparsely settled areas. The decline of the township may be noted both in the transfer of its traditional functions to the county and in the failure of residents of townships (and New England towns) to fill many of their offices.

The Pattern in Urban Townships   In many parts of the nation, the township remains in existence largely because it serves as a district for election administration, performs the assessment function, or is a unit for representation on the county board. Its traditional justice, welfare, health, and road functions are largely gone or are disappearing. In rural areas, the township seems to be definitely dying.

But the pattern is different on the fringes of cities. In several states, urbanized townships are increasingly performing urban functions. In New Jersey, townships serve as municipal corporations and in that highly urbanized state are, except as to flexibility of governmental organization, virtually indistinguishable from cities. The same is true of first-class townships in Pennsylvania (those with a density of over 300 persons per square mile) and to a lesser degree in New York. Attempts have been made to fit the township form of government, which was designed for rural government on the frontier, to modern urban society. In Pennsylvania, townships have been classified by size, and since about the beginning of the present century, the first-class townships have been important units of local government in metropolitan centers. Nearly all such townships are wealthy, suburban, and generally populated with middle- and upper-middle-class citizens. The legislature has gradually given them greater powers so that they can today do practically everything of importance that can be done by a borough or city.[29]

Urbanized townships in Kansas have many municipal powers. The fate of the township has varied from one state to another. Townships have almost disappeared in Iowa, but remain important in Michigan. Township boundaries in Pennsylvania are about the same today as they were in the eighteenth cen-

[29] Letter from William D. Monat to the author, Dec. 7, 1961.

tury, but they have changed radically in neighboring New Jersey. In that state, there were then only thirty-two townships in southern New Jersey. By 1960, this number had increased to more than twice that, to seventy-one townships.[30]

Michigan townships have nearly all of the powers of cities, and many fringe areas are satisfied to remain organized in this fashion even though it gives them little flexibility in organizational structure. The only important local function, in terms of potential policy controversies, not controlled by Michigan townships is roads. The state-shared tax system is such as to make it financially advantageous for urbanizing areas not to incorporate.

In fringe areas where the township remains a vital social force and performs essentially urban services, it is in essence a special type of city government, existing through historical accident. Its strengthening trend should not be confused with that of the rural township toward moribundity.

Forms of Municipal Government

Three basic forms of city government are used in the United States, the mayor-council, commission, and council-manager plans. Many variations of the mayor-council plan exist and important differences are found between so-called strong-mayor and weak-mayor plans of this type.[31]

The structure of city government has been deliberately planned to a considerably greater degree than is the case with state, county, town, or township government, but few cities fit the ideal of the general plan they follow. Probably no two cities in the United States have exactly the same structure of government. Nearly every charter commission or state legislature, in considering structure, finds it politically expedient to add its own improvisations on the given theme. For example, the strong-mayor–council system calls for the appointment of department heads by the mayor; yet many such cities have elective clerks and treasurers. Dozens of such cases could be cited.

The Mayor-Council Plan   During nearly all of the nineteenth century, American cities operated with the weak-mayor–council (or weak-mayor) system. Near the end of that century, what is now called the strong-mayor system gradually evolved. In recent years a third principal derivative of the plan, the strong-mayor–council plan with chief administrative officer (or strong mayor with CAO) plan has been developed in order to correct a major weakness of the strong-mayor system in large cities.

The various types of mayor-council cities taken collectively make up more than one-half of all cities of the nation under any form of government.[32] Fifty-one percent of American cities of over 5,000 population are of the mayor-council types. So are most smaller cities, except in New England, where the town remains the governing body in smaller urban areas. All but one of Amer-

[30] Pennsylvania Economy League, **Citizen's Business**, Apr. 8, 1963.
[31] For greater detail than is here presented, see Charles R. Adrian, **Governing Urban America**, 2d ed., McGraw-Hill Book Company, New York, 1961, chap. 8.
[32] **Municipal Year Book**, International City Managers' Association, Chicago, 1958, p. 62.

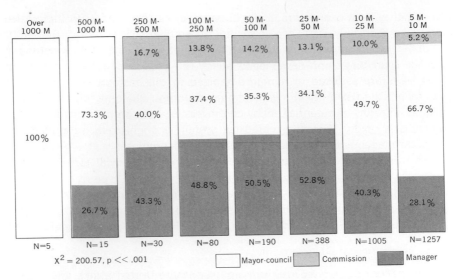

Fig. 8-4   **Governmental Structure Varies with Community Size.**
The mayor-council plan is most popular in large and small cities.
SOURCE: John H. Kessel, "Governmental Structure and Political Environment," **American Political Science Review**, 56:615–620, September, 1962.

ica's cities of over one-half million inhabitants use the mayor-council plan, usually of a strong-mayor type. Sixty percent of the small cities of 5,000 to 10,000 people have the mayor-council form, usually of a weak-mayor type.

The Weak-mayor–Council Plan   In the early decades of the nineteenth century, America's budding cities borrowed from rural government certain essential concepts. Today we call it the weak-mayor–council plan.

(1) **Characteristics**   The weak-mayor plan is a product of Jacksonian democracy. It reflects the spirit of the frontier, with a skepticism both of politicians and of government itself. It grew out of a time when the functions of city government were few, when local officials were coordinated through the political party, and when people were afraid to give powers to a single executive. Implicit in the weak-mayor plan is the belief that if a politician has few powers and many checks upon him, he can do relatively little damage and that if one politician becomes corrupt, he will not necessarily corrupt the whole government.

The council is both a legislative and an executive organization under the weak-mayor plan. In small cities, the council is small—five or seven members —but in larger cities it is usually a fairly large body of perhaps eleven to fifty members. At one time councils might be as large as 200. Members are (except in small cities) ordinarily elected by wards on a partisan ballot.

In addition to making policy, the council appoints several administrative officers, such as the city engineer and the city attorney. Councilmen (often called aldermen if they represent wards) may serve on several ex officio boards and commissions. A committee of the council usually prepares the budget and may even appoint the controller, who administers the expenditure of the budget.

The mayor is not "weak" because he lacks policy-making power—he normally has a veto, can recommend legislation, and may even preside over the council. He is "weak" because he lacks administrative power. There is, in fact, no single individual charged with the responsibility of seeing to it that the laws and ordinances are properly carried out or that the city administration proceeds in accord with an overall plan. The mayor has very restricted appointive powers; even when he is allowed to make appointments, he may not be able to remove those he places in office, so that he is deprived of any real control over them or responsibility for them.

Ordinarily several of the principal city offices are filled by direct election—the long ballot is characteristic of the weak-mayor plan. There are also likely to be a large number of boards and commissions, some filled by appointment by the council or the mayor, some ex officio, some elected.

(2) **Appraisal** The weak-mayor plan was a product of a different world from that which Americans occupy today. It was never intended to serve large, impersonal urban communities. The arguments for the plan are based upon the precepts of Jacksonianism. Many of these ideas are still popular with a large number of American people. For example, Americans may not know which officers are elected and which are appointed or what the requirements are for, say a good city clerk or city controller, but they are likely to insist that those who are elected should continue to be elected. They will also argue that an elective official, no matter what his duties, is more responsible to the public in all cases than is an appointive official.

The strongest argument for the weak-mayor plan rests upon the fact that, with many elective officers and with a fairly large council elected by wards, it offers the ordinary, noninfluential citizen the best chance for access to the decision-making centers of government. Yet, ironically, the very clumsiness and lack of coordination of the plan in an impersonal urban society makes it the least likely to be "visible" to citizens who want to know what it is doing. It, therefore, also provides the best chance for corruption to creep in unnoticed.

The plan is today generally thought to be unacceptable for any but small communities, where government is on a neighborly basis, because of the lack of provision for political and administrative leadership. There is no officer or—generally—party to coordinate the multifold activities of a complex, modern city, no one to balance off the demands of the parks department against those of public works. Each functional agency gallops off in its own direction, spending money with little oversight and causing an excess of wealth in one department while another one struggles in poverty.

The weak-mayor system is characteristically found in small cities and villages. In the case of the latter, there is no separation of powers and the mayor or president merely presides over the council, having no veto power. In this form, the weak-mayor plan is close to the townships, towns, and traditional English forms of local government.

There are still quite a few cities of considerable size with relatively weak mayors, especially in the South, though they may be found in all parts of the nation. In cases of communities where the simple, primary relationships of rural society are replaced by the impersonal urban way of life, this plan has definitely been found wanting. The trend away from it in such cities has been pronounced in the twentieth century.

The Strong-mayor–Council Plan   The development of the strong-mayor system of government in the last two decades of the nineteenth century was a gradual one. The plan differed only in degree from that of the weak-mayor system. It was not conceived of as a distinctly new form of government, nor was it one. Actually, the weak-mayor form resembled the structure of most state governments of that day and this. The strong-mayor system, on the other hand, was modeled on the national government with its integrated * administrative structure under the control of the President.

* By an INTEGRATED administrative structure, political scientists mean one in which all administrative authority and responsibility is theoretically in the hands of a single individual or body. The administrative structure is arranged so that each employee or officer is formally responsible to some one superior who in turn must answer to his superior, until ultimately department heads are each responsible to a single chief executive.

1. **Characteristics**   Most mayor-council cities represent a compromise between the very weak- and the very strong-mayor plan. This should be kept in mind in considering the description below.

In the strong-mayor–council city, administrative responsibility is concentrated in the hands of the mayor, while policy making is a joint function of the mayor and the council. The plan calls for a short ballot with the mayor as the only elected administrative officer. He in turn appoints and dismisses department heads, preferably without councilmanic approval. The mayor thus becomes the officer responsible for the carrying out of established policy and for coordinating the efforts of the various departments. The mayor is also responsible for the preparation of the annual budget and for the administration of the budget once it is adopted by the council. This allows the whole financial picture and the needs of the various departments to be compared in financial policy making. This is in contrast to the piecemeal methods by which these things are approached under the weak-mayor plan.

The mayor's legal position allows him to exert very strong political leadership in addition to his powerful administrative leadership. Not only does he have the veto power and the right to recommend legislative policy to the council, as is the case under the weak-mayor system usually, but his complete control over administration gives him constant oversight of the needs of the city as a whole and furnishes a vantage point from which to recommend policy. His strong position puts him constantly in the limelight, his actions and recommendations get generous news-source play, and his budget is normally so obviously based upon his day-to-day knowledge of governmental affairs that the burden of proof for any change rests upon the council.

The council plays a definitely subordinate role in a strong-mayor city. It does not, as in the weak-mayor city, share in the performance of administrative duties. Its functions are limited to the exercise of legislative policy making, and even this role must be shared with the mayor. The council is likely to be small (typically seven or nine members) and elected at large on either a partisan or nonpartisan ballot. Unless the city is very large, members are likely to serve on a part-time basis. Four-year terms for both mayor and councilmen are the most common. This term, longer than was the case on the frontier, is the result of the reform-movement belief that public officials should be given time enough in office to prove themselves.

2. **Appraisal**   Because of its provisions for vigorous political leadership, the strong-mayor plan seems especially adaptable for use in large cities, where the complexities of government require someone to give firm leadership and direction. Most of the nation's largest cities, in fact, do have versions of this plan. The plan has the advantage of allowing for the pinpointing of responsibility and for overall policy planning and permits the coordination of administration.

Disadvantages that seem to go with the plan include the fact that it expects too much of the mayor—few persons of the caliber the job requires are willing to run for the office. Furthermore, few men combine the talents of the adroit politician with those of the expert administrator. The plan also permits deadlocks between a strong mayor and a council that may occasionally refuse to allow itself to be dominated. The result of such stalemates is not likely to be to the advantage of society.

3. **The Strong-mayor–Council Plan with Chief Administrative Officer**   The chief executive in a strong-mayor city may well recognize his shortcomings as an administrator and attempt to do something about them. The most common method of buttressing his position is to appoint an able, professionally experienced administrator to the position of chief fiscal officer, usually called the controller. He may act as something of a deputy mayor and attend to many details of administration.

But the typical politician-mayor is not always willing to choose professional deputies. To remedy this weakness of the strong-mayor plan, a recent trend has been one toward establishing by charter or ordinance an official known by various titles but perhaps best called a chief administrative officer (CAO). His powers vary considerably from one city to another, and sometimes he can scarcely be differentiated from the chief budget or fiscal officer; but according to the theory of the position he should be appointed by the mayor and should perform, in general, such functions as the supervision of heads of various departments, preparation of the budget, and personnel direction. It is his task to correlate the various departments in the important routine of day-to-day administration, to give technical and professional advice to the political mayor, and hence to free the mayor for his other two major jobs of serving as ceremonial head of the city (greeting the governor, laying cornerstones, and crowning the latest beauty queen) and of proposing and launching broad overall policy.

The CAO plan probably originated in San Francisco in 1931, although other cities have some claim to the honor. In the period after World War II it spread to many of the nation's largest cities, including New York, Philadelphia, Honolulu, and New Orleans.

The Commission Plan   During the period of rebuilding Galveston, Texas, after it was struck by a hurricane in September, 1900, the legislature suspended local self-government in the city and substituted a temporary government of five local businessmen—-the Galveston "commission," hence the name for the system. The commission, working with great zeal under extraordinary conditions, accomplished much more at less cost than had its almost bankrupt predecessor government.

After the emergency, the plan was retained permanently in Galveston, and the publicity it had received attracted much interest. It was hailed as a "businessman's government," and ten years after its accidental creation, it was in use in 108 cities. The number increased to at least 500 by 1917. Then a reversal took place. Municipal reformers lost interest in the commission plan and began to advocate the council-manager plan as the true embodiment of a business form of organization. The number of cities using the plan (there were less than 300 of over 5,000 population in 1965) has declined steadily since the time of World War I.

Characteristics   The commission plan's outstanding feature is the dual role of the commissioners. Each of them serves individually as the head of one of the city's administrative departments, while collectively they serve as the policy-making council for the city. There is no separation of powers. The commission performs both legislative and executive functions.

The commission is always small, usually consisting of five members, but varying from three to seven. There is a mayor, but he has no powers beyond those of the other commissioners, except that he performs the ceremonial duties for the city and presides over council meetings. He has no veto power. He is usually specifically elected to the office, but in a few places, the person who happens to receive the highest number of votes among all candidates becomes mayor.

Commissioners are usually elected on a nonpartisan ticket, at large, and for four-year terms. The ballot is short, especially since terms of office of the commissioners are staggered with only two or three members of a five-member commission elected at one time.

Appraisal   The commission plan provided for a more modern approach to administration than did the weak-mayor systems at the turn of the century. It concentrated responsibility in the hands of a few men so that the interested citizen could assess credit or blame for municipal activities. It shortened the ballot and allowed voters a chance to know something about the character and qualifications of the candidates. Furthermore, only the principal officers of the city were chosen by election.

The commission plan had, however, too many disadvantages to make it workable. For one thing, it was not possible to get the quality of personnel needed through election, especially in smaller cities. Successful citizens of the community were not willing to give up their own businesses and run for an office that paid a low salary. The plan also encouraged amateur administration, for many of the persons chosen to the commission had little or no administrative experience. In this respect, there was little change from traditional Jacksonian practice.

The plan had other weaknesses, and they were of a serious nature. The commission was so small that there was no provision for the function of criticism. The mayor-council plan at least allowed the council the negative role of critic of the mayor in all cases. Under the commission plan, a fraternity of tolerance was more likely the result. Often the mutual hands-off policy meant that there were really several different city governments, each operating independently of the others, with an occasional five-power conference being held to satisfy the demands of the charter. And, finally, the plan made no provision for overall policy or administrative leadership. With each commissioner jealously guarding his control over his own department, the top of the administrative pyramid was sawed off. Each department moved in its own direction.

That plan was quickly outmoded with the development of the council-manager and the modern strong-mayor plans. The inherent weaknesses in the commission plan have made it more anachronistic than are some of the older forms of government which still thrive in America.

The Council-Manager Plan   The origin of the idea for the council-manager plan is not known with certainty. It seems that one of the first instances in which it was urged was in an editorial in the August, 1899, issue of **California Municipalities.** Haven A. Mason, editor of the magazine, urged that there should be "a distinct profession of municipal managers." [33] In 1908, Staunton, Virginia, by ordinance hired a "general manager" to serve as a full-time administrator under an old-fashioned weak-mayor and bicameral-council system. A few years later, Richard S. Childs, a businessman who was at that time secretary of the National Short Ballot Organization and who later was to become president of the National Municipal League, drew up a plan which embodied the basic characteristics of the council-manager plan as we know it today. His plan was adopted by Sumter, South Carolina, in 1912 and spread with great speed thereafter. By 1915, there were 49 manager cities and five years later, 158. The number has increased uninterruptedly ever since. On January 1, 1966, more than 2,000 manager cities and other local governments existed in the United States and Canada. Nearly 50 percent of the cities of between 10,000 and 500,000 had managers.

The council-manager form of government was most likely to be used in cities having a young, mobile, white, middle-class, rapidly growing population.[34] Working-class cities usually have some version of the mayor-council

---

[33] The editorial is reprinted in John C. Bollens, **Appointed Executive Local Government: The California Experience,** Haynes Foundation, Los Angeles, 1952, appendix III.
[34] Leo F. Schnore and Robert R. Alford, "Forms of Government and Socioeconomic Characteristics of Suburbs," **Administrative Science Quarterly,** 8:1–17, June, 1963.

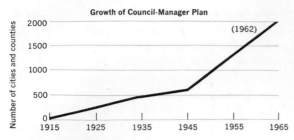

Fig. 8-5   The Council-Manager Plan Is Popular Today.
The spurt in the number of adoptions of the council-manager plan since 1945 stems from its compatibility with suburban values.
SOURCE: International City Managers' Association.

form. The socioeconomic character of a city has a bearing on the governmental structure of the city.

Of the twenty cities in the United States having a population of more than 500,000, four have the council-manager plan: Cincinnati, Dallas, San Antonio, and San Diego. Of these, all except San Antonio have used the plan for more than thirty years. In addition, Dade County, Florida, with a population of about one million, has a manager, and Los Angeles County, California, with a population approaching seven million, has a chief administrative officer with many of the powers of a manager.

One study has shown that rapidly growing cities in the United States are the most likely to have the council-manager form. Three-quarters of the cities which had a growth rate of over 80 percent between 1950 and 1960 used the plan. In contrast, cities showing a loss in population during that decade were the least likely to use the plan. This is probably explained by the popularity of the council-manager plan in the suburbs and the fact that losses in population were to be found principally in small cities and the core cities of metropolitan areas, neither popular locations for the manager plan, historically. The same study found that the higher the percentage of foreign-born in a city, the more likely it was to use the mayor-council form, while the council-manager plan was found most commonly in cities that were overwhelmingly of native-born population. Once again, the relationship is probably in large measure a function of the contrast in the socioeconomic characteristics of the suburbs and the core cities. Cities whose economic base was principally that of personal service and retail trade were the most likely to have the manager plan, while cities with a manufacturing base were the least likely. This reflects both the difference between the bedroom suburb and the core city and also the fact that the council-manager plan has always been more attractive to members of the middle class than to those of the working class.[35]

In most cities where the plan is in effect, the city manager has emerged as a major, sometimes *the* major, community leader, and "the manager's job in

[35] John H. Kessel, "Governmental Structure and Political Environment," **American Political Science Review**, 56:615–620, September, 1962.

the complex affairs of tomorrow will probably not be vastly different from that of the elected executive. Like the mayor, he too must court favor with his council, and like the mayor, he can be far more effective if he has a strong following of civic groups, newspapers, and the public to support him. . . . If he serves the community as prime mover and star salesman of forceful governmental action, he will build up his own clientele—a clientele which the council will antagonize only at its peril." [36]

Once a city or county has adopted a council-manager plan, it seldom abandons it. The plan is, however, frequently challenged, even in cities that have long had the plan. Thus, fifty years after it went into effect in Dayton, Ohio (1913), a referendum vote on abandonment was held. It was defeated by a margin of 6 to 1.

Characteristics The outstanding identifying marks of the council-manager plan include a council of laymen responsible for policy and a professional administration under a chief administrator responsible to the council. The theoretical structure rivals that of the British parliamentary system in its simplicity.

The council is small, five to nine members, and is commonly elected at large, on a nonpartisan ballot, often for four-year staggered terms. It is theoretically responsible to the public for all policy making and ultimately for the overall character of administration. Under the model charter,[37] members of the council are the only officers who are popularly elected. The intended purpose of the short ballot is to concentrate responsibility upon these people and to ask the voters to fill only those positions in which they can reasonably be expected to take an interest.

There is no separation of powers or checks and balances. There is a mayor or president of the city or village, but he normally performs only ceremonial functions and presides over council meetings. He has no administrative powers, except in the case of an emergency, and has no veto. In more than one-half of the manager cities over 5,000 population, the council chooses the mayor from among its own membership. In most other cities he is directly elected, although a few give the post to the person with the most votes in the councilmanic race.

The administration of the city is integrated under the control of a professional manager, who is hired by the council. He serves, in the model plan, for no definite term of office but rather at the pleasure of a majority of the council.

Not only is the manager a professional person, but he is expected to hire professionally competent technicians to run the various departments of the city. The lower administrative positions, roughly those below the department heads, are also filled with persons who are technically competent. They are usually chosen by civil-service merit examination.

Appraisal Municipal reformers have tended to accord to this plan inordinate praise, often attributing to it miraculous powers to bring about effi-

[36] Edward Sofen, "Problems of Metropolitan Leadership: The Miami Experience," **Midwest Journal of Political Science**, 5:18–38, February, 1961, p. 37.
[37] See the **Model City Charter**, 6th ed., National Municipal League, New York, 1963. The manager plan has been endorsed by the League, a good-government organization, since 1916.

cient and economical city administration regardless of the traditions of city government, the kind of personnel which it employs, and the existence or lack of public understanding and support of the basic principles of the plan. These exaggerated claims for the plan, as well as some of the specious arguments used against it, should be discounted by the sophisticated student of government.

The general political climate in which the council-manager plan exists and the tradition against more than token pay for councilmen help assure a council of laymen who are amateur politicians uninterested in making a living out of whatever is available from the public treasury in the style of the old-fashioned machine politician. The manager plan places heavy emphasis upon professional and technical competence from the manager to the lowest-paid position, an appropriate characteristic in a complicated modern society. There is adequate provision for criticism in the system, since the legislative branch has no reason not to feel free to comment on the quality of the work of the manager and his staff.

Although the manager plan is simple in mechanism, it is sometimes misunderstood. It has been called "dictatorial" or "un-American" because the chief administrative officer is not elected—a violation of Jacksonian traditions. But the argument is invalid, since there is full responsibility for administration. Some people argue that the plan costs too much for smaller cities, but it is actually in use in a large number of cities of under 5,000 population, apparently successfully. The public sometimes does not understand the theory of the plan and, therefore, does not support it.

A more valid criticism of the plan centers around the question of the competence of some managers, a problem that has been complicated by the number of adoptions of the plan outrunning the supply of trained and experienced persons to serve. In some cities, managers have had the status of an errand boy. The council cannot lead collectively. The lay, part-time council looks to the professional, full-time manager for policy recommendations. The manager is nearly always in a better position to make recommendations than is the council.[38] If the council accepts the recommendations of the manager with regularity, it does not necessarily mean that it is a rubber stamp; it may mean that the council has hired a competent manager who is sensitive to local values. The function of the council has emerged, not so much as the idealized one of the original plan, but as a reviewing and vetoing agency, checking upon the manager more than leading him in policy making.

Other failures in the carrying out of the original plan include these: The mayor may seek to challenge the manager for control of policy; or the council may seek to continue the traditional practice of entering into administrative oversight at the lower levels, bypassing the manager and undermining the confidence of his underlings in his authority. City employees may be of low competence. There is also a good deal of feeling, especially among working-

[38] Clarence E. Ridley, **The Role of the City Manager in Policy Formulation,** International City Managers' Association, Chicago, 1958; and Charles R. Adrian, "Leadership and Decision-making in Manager Cities: A Study of Three Communities," **Public Administration Review,** 18:208–213, Summer, 1958.

class voters and their opinion leaders, that the manager-plan councils are too small to be representative of a cross section of the population and that electing persons to councils by the at-large system results in "an overrepresentation of business and professional interests and an underrepresentation of labor, ethnic, and other lower-class interests." [39] But there can be no doubt of the expanding popularity of the council-manager plan.

Special Districts

"Special districts," one observer has noted,[40] "are the least known and least understood units of government in the United States. Yet, paradoxically, more than 58 percent of all governments in the nation are special districts."

A special district is an organized unit of government, having substantial autonomy from other governments, its own taxing and, usually, its own bonding authority.[41] In particular, since it has its own fiscal authority and a separate governing body, it exists as a separate unit of government performing some public service. Districts exist for such varied purposes as recreation, sewage disposal, airports, planning, parking, and mosquito abatement. They may have boundaries coterminous with another unit of government, such as a city or county, or they may overlap other units. They exist in both rural and urban areas and are to be found in every state in the union, though 60 percent of the national total are located in ten states: California, Illinois, Kansas, Pennsylvania, Missouri, Nebraska, New York, Oregon, Texas, and Washington.

The use of special districts is usually defended using one or more of the following arguments: (1) It makes it possible or at least easier to finance a particular function because bonds can be floated and taxes levied in the name of the special district, rather than in the name of some county or municipality already heavily burdened; (2) agencies involved in a single function regarded as important in the community will draw greater support from professionals in the field and higher-status members of the community; and (3) special districts, being wholly dependent upon their own resources, must be "business-like" and must avoid politics. In addition, it is argued that special districts need not be concerned with the parochial demands of a narrow constituency and may concentrate on efficiency, and lastly, that the special district has greater flexibility concerning boundaries, that is, that it is more able than other units of local government to fit its boundaries to the area actually in need of the particular service.[42]

Growth of Special Districts The general trend of special districts has been one of steady increase in number since the end of World War II. This is true even though the most common form of special district, the school district,

[39] Charles D. Goff, "The Politics of Council-manager Plan Adoption and Abandonment in Wisconsin," a paper presented to the Midwest Conference of Political Scientists, Ann Arbor, Mich., 1958.
[40] W. G. Thrombley, "Texas Special Districts," **Public Affairs Comment,** 4:1, March, 1958.
[41] U.S. Bureau of the Census, **Governments in the United States,** 1957, p. 9.
[42] Robert G. Smith, **Public Authorities, Special Districts and Local Government,** National Association of Counties Research Foundation, Washington, 1964, chap. 7.

decreased by 53 percent between 1942 and 1957,[43] and by another 30 percent in the next five years. This countertrend was the result of special factors, however, and nonschool special districts continue to increase in numbers. In 1962, there were six times as many nonschool special districts as there were counties. The total of such special districts nearly equaled the total of municipalities in the nation. These same districts had nearly twice as much debt as counties and half as much as the state governments. Despite all the vast amount of school construction that has taken place in the postwar years, special districts other than for schools have debts 73 percent the size of those for schools—a reflection of the fact that the functions generally assigned to special districts are of a high-cost, capital-outlay type.

Most nonschool special districts are in rural areas, particularly those for fire protection, soil conservation, and drainage, which together make up about one-half the total districts. But quite a few are in urban areas, especially fringe areas, as are many cemetery districts and most housing authorities. These five types taken together make up about two-thirds of the number of special districts.

Ad hoc districts may be governed by a body appointed by the state, one appointed by officials from the local governments overlaid by the district, with members being either appointed especially for the position or in ex officio capacities, one appointed by a judge, or, sometimes, one elected by the voters of the area. The variety is almost endless, but since the last possibility is not the usual one, special-purpose districts ordinarily do not come within the direct oversight of the voting public.

Reasons for Postwar Trend   The need for an areawide approach to problems exists in rural areas, as in the case of drains that cross township and county lines, as well as in urban areas. Problems requiring such an approach have increased as urban populations have increased. Other solutions failing or seeming to be politically impossible, the special district has been turned to. It has been very popular in many rapidly urbanizing states and has, as in California, served as a substitute for incorporation or for a fringe government of less area than the county.

Often districts are the only means by which added services can be supplied in a metropolitan area. The pattern of use for the special district seems to depend upon local customs and perhaps upon the accident of the gradual accumulation of rigid constitutional and statutory restrictions controlling general governments and discouraging the use of the existing units for newer services. For example, one might expect special districts to be used especially in states not having townships, but six of the ten states with the most special districts also have townships in all or part of the state. Special districts are very popular in the West, where they are especially used for the procurement, distribution, and allocation of scarce water supplies. But they are found in every part of the land.

Several factors account for the trend toward special districts. Citizens

43 See below, Chap. 18.

learn that their state or other states authorize districts to perform certain services. The approach usually has strong appeal. Citizens do not resist this approach as they do attempts at governmental consolidation, since they expect it to be less expensive and to preserve the independence of their local government. Interest groups that may want services performed by government (amateur pilots wanting an airport, physicians wanting a hospital), together with the professional administrators of particular functions, characteristically want their special problems handled in a special way by a special organization.[44] School administrators have long ago convinced the American public that they should be independent of the rest of local government, and the school district is at once the most common and the best-known special district. Others have followed the lead of the educators and the pressure groups supporting them. The special district has also had great appeal to the wistful who would take their pet governmental function "out of politics."

Pros and Cons of Districts   The advantages of special districts are said to include the following: They make possible the provision of needed governmental services when and where they are most needed, and they limit the financial burden to residents most directly benefited, while at the same time they skip lightly over the myriad local government boundaries which otherwise stand in the way of making these services available. Other units of government frequently cannot or will not supply these services. Consolidating local units is often politically unfeasible. By leaving the political *status quo* undisturbed, the social need is met with a minimum of resistance; political loyalties are not disturbed, jobs are not threatened, property taxpayers need have little fear of being assessed for someone else's benefit. Usually, the debts and costs of special districts do not count in determining debt and tax limits of regular local governments, and the bonds of such districts are sometimes more easily marketed than are those of other local governments.

Disadvantages of special districts, it is argued, include the fact that the behind-the-scenes way in which they generally operate helps to make them especially profitable for lawyers, engineers, bankers, bonding houses, and salesmen of equipment, services, and real estate. They are often designed to meet short-range needs and not only do not consider more permanent solutions, but by taking the urgency out of the situation for at least a considerable portion of a community, serve to forestall efforts toward long-range, rational governmental organization.

Special districts have often done very good jobs in construction and engineering and sometimes in management. They do not necessarily eliminate political patronage, however, do not guarantee professional administration of functions, and do not remove from the arena of politics governmental functions that involve issues of policy. Special districts often result in increased costs of local government because of the duplication of personnel, the inefficient utilization of equipment, and inability to save through centralized purchasing and other centralized housekeeping activities. They do not balance the vari-

[44] As Jones has pointed out in Woodbury, *op. cit.*, pp. 527–528.

ous needs for services of a community, do not recognize the interdependence of various functions, and are not usually provided with a method for coordinating their activities and budgets with those of the other governments in the area in which they exist. If the governing board is elective, the ballot is made longer and voters are asked to fill offices in which they have little interest or competence. If the governing board is indirectly chosen, as is usually the case, there is no real responsibility to the public for the function performed. Victor Jones has concluded: [45]

A corporate form of metropolitan government in which the selection of the authority or district commission members is once or more removed from the electoral controls may give us efficient and effective government but it cannot give us good government. It is not necessary, nor is it desirable, for all policy-making officials to be directly elected by popular vote. They should, however, be subject to the budgetary control of popularly elected legislators and their policies should be subject to debate and discussion.

Of course, any legislative body, whether it have jurisdiction over the matter or not, may debate anything it wishes. The object, however, is not futile and irresponsible talk. Our uneasiness should not be allayed by saying that the ordinary municipal governments are frequently corrupt, irresponsible, ineffective, and inefficient. Our job is to make them responsible and efficient. This cannot be done by slicing off the most important functions of local government and handing them over to one or several autonomous bodies.

Concluding Statement   Structures of government are tools. They are important, but like other machinery they may be modern or antiquated and are hence not all equally suited for present-day government. A tool will not operate itself, however, nor will the same one be equally effective in various kinds of soils. Local cultural circumstances will determine the type of structure that is needed and the quality of government that will be produced from any chosen form.

SELECTED READINGS

Booth, David A. (ed.): **Council-Manager Government, 1960–64: An Annotated Bibliography,** International City Managers' Association, Chicago, 1965.

Buck, Arthur E.: **The Reorganization of State Governments in the United States,** Columbia University Press, New York, 1938.   (The standard statement of efficiency-and-economy values and goals.)

Cassella, William N.: "County Government in Transition," **Public Administration Review,** 16:223–231, Summer, 1956.

Childs, Richard: **Civic Victories,** Harper & Row, Publishers, Incorporated, New York, 1952.   (A statement of efficiency-and-economy values and goals.)

Dye, Thomas R.: "Urban Political Integration," **Midwest Journal of Political Science,** 8:430–446, November, 1964.   (Discusses some of the conditions under which core-city annexation is possible.)

Garceau, Oliver, and Corinne Silverman: "A Pressure Group and the Pressured,"

[45] Jones, *op. cit.*, pp. 585–586. By permission of the publisher.

American Political Science Review, 48:672–691, September, 1954.   (A study of a manufacturers' association and the Vermont legislature.)

Hansen, Alvin H., and Harvey S. Perloff: **State and Local Finance in the National Economy,** W. W. Norton & Company, Inc., New York, 1944.

Havard, William C., and Alfred Diamant: "The Need for Local Government Reform in the United States," **Western Political Quarterly,** 9:967–995, December, 1956.

Jones, Victor: "Local Government Organization in Metropolitan Areas," in Coleman Woodbury (ed.), **The Future of Cities and Urban Redevelopment,** The University of Chicago Press, Chicago, 1953.

Kammerer, Gladys M., Charles D. Farris, John M. DeGrove, and Alfred B. Clubok: **The Urban Political Community,** Houghton Mifflin Company, Boston, 1963.   (Eight case studies of council-manager government in Florida.)

Lancaster, Lane W.: **Government in Rural America,** 2d ed., D. Van Nostrand Company, Inc., Princeton, N.J., 1952.

Model State Constitution, 5th ed., National Municipal League, New York, 1948.

Porter, Kirk H.: "A Plague of Special Districts," **National Municipal Review,** 22: 544–547, November, 1933.

Public Administration Service: "The Changing County," **National Municipal Review,** 45:433–437, October, 1956.

Ridley, Clarence E.: **The Role of the City Manager in Policy Formulation,** International City Managers' Association, Chicago, 1958.

Salisbury, Robert H.: "The Dynamics of Reform," **Midwest Journal of Political Science,** 5:260–275, August, 1961.

Smith, Lincoln: "The Manager System and Collectivism," **American Journal of Economics and Sociology,** 24:21–39, January, 1965.   (The council-manager plan is seen as having the effect of promoting municipal ownership of utilities and other enterprises.)

Smith, Robert G.: **Public Authorities, Special Districts and Local Government,** National Association of Counties Research Foundation, Washington, 1964.   (Discusses special districts as they affect other local governments.)

Snider, Clyde F.: **Local Government in Rural America,** 2d ed., Appleton-Century-Crofts, Inc., New York, 1965.

————: "American County Government: A Mid-century Review," **American Political Science Review,** 46:66–80, March, 1952.

Stone, Harold A., Donald K. Price, and Kathryn H. Stone: **City Manager Government in the United States,** Public Administration Service, Chicago, 1940.

Wager, Paul W. (ed.): **County Government Across the Nation,** The University of North Carolina Press, Chapel Hill, N.C., 1950.

Weidner, Edward W.: **The American County: Patchwork of Boards,** National Municipal League, New York, 1946.

Williams, J. D.: **The Defeat of Home Rule in Salt Lake City,** McGraw-Hill Book Company, New York, 1960, Eagleton Institute Case Study no. 2.

Wood, Robert C.: **Suburbia—Its People and Their Politics,** Houghton Mifflin Company, Boston, 1959.   (A theory of suburban politics.)

9

GOVERNMENT IN METROPOLITAN AREAS

A favorite European stereotype sees Americans as holding efficiency to be a value second in importance only to the possession of material things. The organization of the metropolitan community in this country effectively refutes that notion, however. Our metropolitan areas are inefficient in dozens of ways, particularly in land usage and in governmental organization and operation, if measured in terms of costs alone. Furthermore, the fragmented metropolitan area is not a result of accident or apathy (although both of these are contributing factors) so much as it is of deliberate choice by the contemporary urban dweller.[1]

The American city today is more than a legal entity existing within carefully described boundaries and headed by a single government. It is actually a sociological complex consisting of a downtown sector, a blighted and decaying older portion, newer sections of a principally residential character, and, outside the legal limits but an intrinsic part of the community, the suburbs. A suburb may be defined as a community beyond the legal boundaries of the core city but lying within its economic and sociological limits and with a population at least partially dependent for a livelihood upon the core city. The pattern of movement is from the center toward the periphery, and this applies to residences, business, and industry. But the problems of government stretch across it all.

[1] On this point, see Robert C. Wood, "Metropolitan Government, 1957: An Extrapolation of Trends," **American Political Science Review**, 52:108–122, March, 1958; and his **Suburbia: Its People and Their Politics**, Houghton Mifflin Company, Boston, 1959.

The Movement toward the Suburbs

Who Lives in the Suburbs?   According to the census of 1960, nearly two-thirds of the population of the United States lived in 212 metropolitan areas, but only 20 percent of the local governments of the nation were located within these areas. On the other hand, more than 70 percent of all local taxes and revenues were collected within their boundaries and they were responsible for over 70 percent of all local government expenditures.[2]

The pattern of suburbia within these metropolitan areas differs markedly from one state to another, depending on local traditions and existing statutes. Many of these statutes date from the nineteenth century and fortuitously contribute to the pattern of government found in metropolitan areas. In California, a state without townships, the large suburban population outside of incorporated areas has only the county as its local government. This unit may seem relatively distant to the citizen, and one which he cannot directly influence in elections because the county commissioners are voted upon by persons living in both corporate and unincorporated areas of the county. A similar situation exists in Delaware, where almost two-thirds of the population of New Castle County (the Wilmington area) lives outside of incorporated areas. People in this area are governed by a three-man body called the levy court, which acts as both a legislative body and an administrative committee. It has not changed in fundamental pattern since colonial times and was designed for a frontier society.[3] Pennsylvania, on the other hand, has townships and has classified these. First-class townships in that commonwealth have become virtual municipalities and, furthermore, they have served to prevent extreme fragmentation into dozens or hundreds of separate municipalities around the Pennsylvania metropolitan areas. This is so because residents have generally chosen to remain a ward within a first-class township rather than to incorporate separately.

Why Move to the Suburbs?   The postwar rush to the suburbs ranks in American history with the move across the Appalachians, and the later migrations to Oregon, Utah, and California, as one of the great mass migrations of a historically restless people (see Figure 9-1). What is behind the centrifugal force that is pushing our urban population toward the periphery of the community? No doubt the increasing size of urban population—resulting from higher birthrates and rural-to-urban migration—is itself an important factor, for additional urban population is likely to require increasing area. But this alone is not a sufficient reason to explain the great suburban movement.

Rather, we should ask, what do most American people want out of life? Where and under what conditions can their desires best be fulfilled? The answer seems to rest in the fact that Americans wish to combine what they like about the large city with their parents' teachings concerning the ad-

[2] U.S. Advisory Commission on Intergovernmental Relations, **Metropolitan Social and Economic Disparities,** 1965, chap. 1.
[3] Governor's Committee on Reorganization of the Government of New Castle County, **Report and Proposed Legislation,** State of Delaware, Dover, Del., 1964, p. 3.

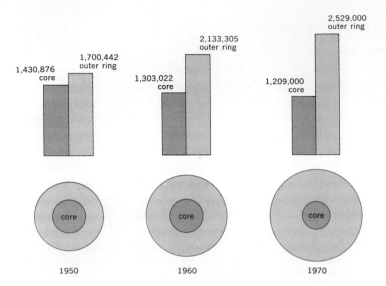

Fig. 9-1   The Suburban Movement Continues.
SOURCE: Municipal Manpower Commission, **Governmental Manpower for Tomorrow's Cities,** McGraw-Hill Book Company, New York, 1962.

vantages of the small town. People want the friendships and convenient access to economic and governmental establishments as found in the small town. They want at the same time the variety of activity, the wide choice of occupations, the chance to avoid the extreme personal scrutiny of the small community, and the great potential for a better income and better chance for advancement that exist in the large city.[4]

The suburb seems to be widely regarded as the best available compromise, especially if the medium-sized city is not a possible choice. In addition to allowing the urbanite to keep some of the best of both the large city and the small town, there are other subjectively determined values held by Americans today that add to the attractiveness of the suburb. Studies show that people want to own their homes, that they want single-family dwellings, and that they want more space than is available within built-up cities at a cost they can afford. They want to avoid, or at least reduce, dirt, noise, congestion, traffic, and taxes. They want vegetable gardens and rosebushes. They want a private play yard for the children.

People want better government than they think they are getting in the core city. They want "services without politics." A "better, more honest" government is something that many think is available in the suburb. The core city is regarded as "politics-ridden" with a great amount of chronic conflict. Neighborliness, the reestablishment of some of the primary controls of the

[4] See William L. Slayton and Richard Dewey, "Urban Redevelopment and the Urbanite," in Coleman Woodbury (ed.), **The Future of Cities and Urban Redevelopment,** The University of Chicago Press, Chicago, 1953, part III. The empirical research justifying the above statements is there summarized and cited.

rural and small-town society is something that many yearn for. A suburban address may also carry more prestige than a core-city address, especially in a rapidly growing city, and this fact is important as a source of recognition in an impersonal society.

The suburb keeps one within hailing distance of the variety of scene and activity, of job opportunities, and of accessibility to multiple and specialized services that people want from the large city. Most people would like to have nearby, at walking distance—even in the suburbs—a small grocery for last-minute shopping, a drugstore, a playground, and a grade school. Other services, the supermarket, the high school, entertainment media, and places of work may be considerable distances away, for the automobile, people believe, will take them there within the limits of a tolerable amount of sacrifice. The commuting time and effort, within present value systems, is not too great a price to pay for the advantages of not living near the crowded parts of town.

What Makes Suburban Living Possible?   A brief answer might be simply this: modern techniques of transportation and communication. To the extent that a decentralization of industry is also a factor, the availability of highly mobile sources of power in the form of electricity has also been important. Together with prosperity after World War II, the Federal government's policy of aiding purchasers of new homes through a loan guarantee to the mortgage holder has been another important factor. The Veterans Administration and the Federal Housing Authority have thus been substantial contributors to the suburban movement by making low-interest mortgages and low down payments a possibility for large numbers of families who could not otherwise have afforded homes of their own. Advances in water and sewage technology have also contributed to the flexibility of living patterns.

World War I brought an acceleration in the rate of urbanization in the United States. People began to look for additional space to occupy. They found it outside the city proper. They also found that a prewar novelty, the automobile, had now become commonplace. In fact, it had become a necessity for members of the middle class, and Henry Ford was building a "poor man's car" in the famous Model T. There were suburbanites and commuters before the 1920s, to be sure, for those were the days of the electrified interurban lines, and there were commuter trains operated by the railroads out of the largest cities; but it was the coming of the automobile that made suburban living as it is known today a possibility.[5]

Modern methods of communication are also contributors to the suburban movement. Without the effective, inexpensive telephone service of today, few would isolate themselves from the core city. The telephone is used to obtain services rapidly, for the employer in town to contact his employee in his suburban home, for the husband at work downtown to "check on things back

[5] The early movement toward the fringe is discussed in H. Paul Douglass, **The Suburban Trend**, Appleton-Century-Crofts, Inc., New York, 1925. See also Frederick Lewis Allen, "The Big Change in Suburbia," **Harper's Magazine**, 208:21–28, June, 1954; Leo F. Schnore, "Metropolitan Growth and Decentralization," **American Journal of Sociology**, 63:171–180, September, 1957; Wood, **Suburbia**, chaps. 2 and 3.

at the house," and for all to keep in contact with relatives and friends in other parts of the city even when many miles of crowded highways separate them.

In the postwar period, mass-produced housing in the suburbs proved to be the manner that best suited American needs during a period of high marriage rates and birthrates. Finally, business and industry followed the crowd. Partly it did so in order to be nearer to customers and labor supply but perhaps chiefly in order to build modern one-story plants with adjacent parking lots on land less expensive than that in their older locations. The suburb then became a location for factory, branch stores, business headquarters of all sorts, and shopping centers.

Problems of the Core City

The centrifugal movement of population and industry to the periphery of the urban area is causing a multitude of problems for both the core city and the suburbs. Some of these problems are severe and appear to be chronic.

Loss of the Tax Base   While the cost of operating municipal governments has increased along with almost everything else in the postwar years, the movement toward the suburbs has seen the core cities lose more and more of their tax base. Industries tend to move to the suburbs when they build new plants, retail stores expand by building suburban branches, the people best able to pay property taxes on their homes are the first to move into the suburbs.

As an example of the decline of the core-city tax base, the ratio of the tax base of Syracuse, New York, to that of Onondaga County has been declining at a faster rate than the population decline in the last generation. Assessable industrial property has been growing at a faster rate in the suburbs than in the core city. The same pattern, although less important for tax purposes, is probably also to be found relative to residential housing.[6]

To heap trouble upon trouble, as the prosperous citizens move out, part of the population loss is made up by the rural-to-urban migration that supplies the extra manpower to cities, but the newcomers to the core city are likely to be a financial liability rather than an asset. The majority of migrants will settle first in the city, probably in the decaying zone of transition. Because they are culturally marginal people—that is to say, they live in the culture of a large city but still have many of the values they earlier received from a quite different rural culture—they are likely, in their isolation, resentment, or economic desperation, to create police and juvenile problems. They are insecure and confused people. They are unlikely to be homeowners, and those who own their blighted dwellings do not pay so much in taxes as the city must spend in the area. Furthermore, as the density of population in the core city decreases, the value of homes also decreases, since demand for them becomes less. The eroding of the tax base is therefore a cumulative phenomenon.

[6] Roscoe C. Martin and others, **Decisions in Syracuse**, Indiana University Press, Bloomington, Ind., 1961.

Subsidization of the Suburbs   In addition to its decreasing tax base, the core city has been forced, in most states, to subsidize the suburbs. As the tax base declines, the amount and number of subsidies increase. There are at least two ways in which the core city is forced to help the suburbanite pay for his governmental services: by furnishing services of the city free or below cost and by paying a disproportionately large share of state and county taxes in return for a disproportionately small share of their services.

The core city furnishes free services to suburbanites by providing them with roads and traffic control devices during their journey to work. It usually permits suburbanites to use libraries, parks, and recreational facilities free, although quite a few suburbs restrict their own facilities to residents. The city must expand its public-health department in order to inspect the restaurants where the noontime hordes of suburbanites eat—blissfully unaware that it costs other people money to see to it that they are not poisoned. Public-welfare costs hit the core city especially hard, although the cost of unemployment is a social one logically distributable among all members of society and not among core-city residents alone.

The core city also normally pays a disproportionate share of the county taxes, both because it contains much or most of the industrial valuation and also because its assessors are likely to place values closer to true value than are assessors in the suburbs. Furthermore, in many states the county performs almost no functions within the core city: the county collects most of its taxes within the core city and spends them in the outlying part of the country.

The large cities also pay most of the state taxes since, in spite of losses to the suburbs, they remain centers of concentration of wealth. Yet the state tends to spend most of its money in the rural and suburban areas expecting the large cities to finance most of their functions themselves. The state police, for example, will often lend assistance to the amateurish efforts of suburban policemen but seldom operate within the core city. Health, education, highway, welfare, and other state functions may be provided more generously outside the large cities than inside them. Grants-in-aid by the state usually give preference to the lesser populated local governments.

Americans have traditionally developed an area, used it for individual and social profit, and then as the efficiency of the area declined, abandoned it with its problems and moved on to newer, more promising places. Such, to a considerable degree, has been the fate of the core of our metropolitan areas. Yet, the core cities and the central business districts within them still serve a useful social purpose.

The Core City's Future   One assumption frequently made by both journalists and political scientists concerning the future of the core city in large metro-politan areas is that the style of central-city politics will change as the middle-class leaves for the suburbs. The assumption has been that politics will lose its middle-class orientation and, as a result, will become increasingly corrupt and oriented toward the neighborhood and ethnic or racial group, rather than toward a broader community. An evaluation of government in nine of our large cities—necessarily highly subjective in character—has concluded that: [7]

> The quality of city government has been improving despite the departure of the good government'-minded middle class for the suburbs and its replacement by Negro and Southern white migrants who, because of the backwardness of the rural places they come from, are in general far from civic-minded. One would expect that as the lower-class tide rises in the central cities the governments of these cities would get worse. Perhaps they will when it has risen far enough. But, as several notable examples—St. Louis, Boston, and Philadelphia, among others—show, so far at least the quality of government has been getting better, not worse.

This same observer concluded that the quality of the mayors in these cities was high. He added that because "city politics is rarely a route to high state and national office, the wonder is that so many men of first-rate ability devote themselves to it." [8]

Problems of the Suburbs

The politically atomized pattern of contemporary American suburbia results from the fact that this was a rural nation in the days when laws of annexation and attitudes toward large cities were developing. Rural-dominated legislatures have for the most part kept the traditional legal situation unchanged. As a consequence, the boundaries of a city are almost always artificial and arbitrary and have nothing to do with economic and social realities.

One study of the outer fringe of suburbs of a metropolitan area found that the first settlers who began to convert the area from agriculture to suburban residence patterns themselves had in most cases, some farm background. The earliest nonfarm residents tended to be blue-collar workers who worked with their hands and many of them built or extensively improved their own homes. The outer-fringe dwellers viewed urban development as inevitable, but hoped that it could be controlled in such a way as to preserve the rural atmosphere of the area. After the first wave of urban-employed persons, came other suburbanites. The later ones were less likely to be looking for a place where they could build a home on a do-it-yourself basis. They were more often white-collar workers and persons who had, on the average, higher incomes, more education, and were less likely to have farm backgrounds. The result of the coming of this group, sometimes supported by, but sometimes opposed by the early residents and the farmers, was a demand for stricter zoning regulations and building codes, and for the improvement of schools. [9]

The entire community is an organic whole, despite its artificial compartmentation, and most suburbs, if they were moved fifty miles away, would wither and die. The prevailing pattern produces independent suburbs that, be-

[7] Edward C. Banfield, **Big City Politics**, Random House, Inc., New York, 1965, pp. 11–12.
[8] *Ibid.*, p. 11.
[9] Charles Press and Rodger Rice, **Rural Residents and Urban Expansion**, Economic Research Service, U.S. Department of Agriculture, 1963.

cause of their extravagant use of the resources of government, are expensive. Yet, most suburbanites wish to retain the present system. Some of their reasons are based upon important psychological factors; others stem from ignorance and misinformation.

The Demand for Independence   Not only has the population of the fringe area grown rapidly, but the number of suburbs has been increasing at a great pace. In 1911 there were eight incorporated municipalities in St. Louis County. In 1935 the number had increased to twenty-five. The postwar expansion raised the total to ninety-six by 1956.[10] A similar pattern is to be found around most metropolitan areas. These figures would indicate not only that the population is expanding in many directions from the core cities but also that there is a tendency toward a governmental fragmentation of the fringe area. As each group of subdivisions becomes partially populated, it tends to seek incorporation for itself rather than annexation to another suburb or to the core city.

Why do people want "their own" little suburb? A major reason is surely a desire to own their own homes, however heavily mortgaged. Because the cost of home ownership is increased by core-city taxes levied in order to provide urban services, suburbanites hope to be able to afford to own a home by keeping taxes low. Since many suburbanites may feel that they literally cannot continue to afford a home in the price category they are in if costs increase, they will fight anything that threatens higher costs, including taxes. This attitude, therefore, produces hostility toward annexation. It may also produce opposition to the incorporation of the suburb, for incorporation symbolizes increased taxes and the threat of being required to accept urban service costs.

Another significant reason deals with the common belief that the core city is run by professional politicians, is expensive to operate, and is strife-ridden. The first of these is regarded as bad because it violates the Jacksonian value of government by neighbors. The second runs counter to the citizen's use of his home as a status symbol which causes him to prefer a larger home to additional services. The last violates a desire for a sense of community, a consensus of values such as existed in rural areas of an earlier day. The core city consists of many ethnic and racial groups, a variety of subcultures. The one-class, one-culture, one-group tendency of individual suburbs appeals to the desire of the citizen to minimize social tensions and conflicts.

Government in the suburb is also likely to be more personal. One may easily come to know the suburban officials personally or by reputation. The city hall is more personalized and humanized than in the core city. All of these features are regarded as desirable by the typical suburbanite.[11]

One study found that even when suburbanites were dissatisfied with the level of governmental services, they believed that a satisfactory level of effi-

[10] John C. Bollens and others, **Background for Action**, St. Louis Metropolitan Survey, St. Louis, Mo., 1957, pp. 30–34.
[11] On the general subject, see Wood, **Suburbia.**

ciency could be achieved without having to give up their most valued asset, that of governmental autonomy.[12]

The Desire for Access A psychological factor that has contributed to the balkanization of the suburbs is the desire of citizens to have access to the decision-making centers of local government. As urban life became more impersonal with the growth of population and as the old-fashioned political machine, which had served as an access point to great numbers of citizens, declined, the feeling of isolation and of frustration on the part of the urbanite must have increased. The reform-period practice of electing all councilmen at large contributed to the barrier between the ordinary citizen and those who decide things that matter. But in the suburb, he found a reestablishment of those close relationships that symbolized democracy on the frontier, and he regained the comfortable feeling that goes with confidence in the thought of having influence over government decisions and of having officeholders who share one's social values.

The feeling that the sense of community is being lost is common in metropolitan America. One observer has seen three efforts to find again a sense of community. One is to use planning and the power of the state in an effort to slow down the process of change. A second is to seek community in suburbia. A third is to try to find its modern equivalent in metropolitan government.[13] Yet the urbanite feels only the most tangential loyalties to the metropolitan area as a whole. There are few regional institutions. To the typical citizen, the only reality is the family and the neighborhood, so "regional problems find no vehicle for their solution and the capacity to look ahead, to plan rationally, to awake a regional consciousness is lost." [14]

Because of his narrow scope of vision and narrow loyalties, the typical suburbanite knows little of the structure or physical limits of his local government, to say nothing of the metropolitan area as a whole. He does not know what legal powers it possesses, what it is prohibited from doing by state law, how services can be provided, what a reasonable cost for them would be, or why they cost what they do.[15] The local government to him is good, not because he has an emotional loyalty to it, but because through it he has influence and access in relation to governmental services while through any type of regional government he does not.

In the Philadelphia metropolitan area, 82 percent of the chief elected officers agreed that "some problems facing local officials are just so big that they cannot adequately handle them without assistance or aid." However, 89 percent of these same officials also said that "local communities should get

[12] Charles Press, " 'Efficiency and Economy' Arguments for Metropolitan Reorganization," **Public Opinion Quarterly,** 28:584–594, Winter, 1964.
[13] York Willbern, **The Withering Away of the City,** University of Alabama Press, University, Ala., 1964, p. 70.
[14] Wood, "Metropolitan Government," p. 111. On this section, see also his **Suburbia,** and Edward C. Banfield and Morton Grodzins, **Government and Housing,** McGraw-Hill Book Company, New York, 1958.
[15] Basil G. Zimmer and Amos H. Hawley, "Local Government as Viewed by Fringe Residents," **Rural Sociology,** 23:363–370, December, 1958, provides partial verification.

together and solve their own problems instead of letting the county and state governments take control." And 41 percent agreed that "county and state officials just cannot understand the problems faced by local officials." [16]

The Desire for Local Control Over which governmental functions does the suburbanite wish to retain control for himself and his neighbors? In which service areas is diversity positively preferred to uniformity? An attitude study would probably show that suburbanites feel that some services are more important than are others in terms of the way in which policies will affect the character of their neighborhoods. Among the most important areas where local retention of control is most wanted would probably be the following: land use, garbage and rubbish collection, maintenance of residential streets, and education.

Local wishes may call for luxury services, for minimal services, or for some level in between. Wealthy people do not want to be forced into a single mold, by the creation of one legal entity for the whole area, for they can afford and often wish to have luxury services (in one Cleveland suburb, members of the police department deliver the milk) which core city government would not be likely to provide. Paradoxically, wealthy suburbanites sometimes want fewer services than they might have to take from the core city. For example, they may not want their streets paved (the cost in an area of two-acre estates would be very high and the result would be to destroy the pristine rural charm of the area and to encourage through traffic and the curious) or lighted (they prefer their own ornamental lighting using "carriage lights" and flood lamps).

In contrast, one finds in modest suburbs a violent dislike and fear of the core city. In these areas, residents can barely afford to own their homes. They want minimal services because they fear that even a small increase in costs such as through "unnecessary" services might force them out of the home-owning category with all of its prestige and psychological satisfaction. To these people, joining the core city would mean buying a package of services that they feel they can do without and cannot afford. People in between these two extremes recognize that additional services are symbols of prestige and that they cost money. They are usually willing to pay extra taxes for extra services, but they generally believe that these services can be secured more cheaply by incorporating the area than by becoming annexed.[17]

It should be clear why residents of different types of suburban areas would want to control the above functions. Low-income neighborhoods may want to haul their own rubbish to the dump. Well-to-do people may prefer twice-a-week collection from the back door while the core city offers only once-a-week service from the front curb. Local control of educational services is desired because of the great expense of this item and because of the im-

[16] James V. Toscano, **The Chief Elected Official in the Penjerdel Region,** Penjerdel, Philadelphia, 1964, table 38.
[17] For partial verification of this paragraph, see three articles by Basil G. Zimmer and Amos H. Hawley: "Home Owners and Attitude Toward Tax Increase," **Journal of the American Institute of Planners,** 21:65–74, Spring, 1956; "Property Taxes and Solutions to Fringe Problems," **Land Economics,** 32:369–376, November, 1956; "Approaches to the Solution of Fringe Problems," **Public Administration Review,** 16:258–268, Autumn, 1956.

portance of the school plant as a status symbol. Parents want to control the social environment of their children in grammar school and high school, just as they later may want them to go to the "right" college and join the "right" fraternity. Low-income areas and areas of older people may want minimal services in education out of cost considerations. Higher-income areas use the school to indicate their relative status. The automobile and the wife's wardrobe are important devices for displaying pecuniary emulation (in Thorstein Veblen's term), but the size and luxury of the school auditorium and, especially perhaps, of the swimming pool (if any) have become equally important symbols in contemporary suburbia. To have decisions about these policies left to the impersonal bureaucracy of a large-city school system would be undesirable to all suburbanites, of low and high income alike. Land-use policies, which by the logic of the planning profession are the most region-wide in character of all policies, are vitally important to the suburbanite. The ethnic, industrial, and commercial balance is of the greatest concern to him. He wants races, classes, and occupations segregated. He wants to be personally acquainted with, or to feel that he can influence, those who sit on the planning commission so that they will not change the land use in his area (except to his advantage). The professional bureaucracy of the core city with its impersonal dedication to the principles of planning does not spell an improved community to him; it spells loss of control and potential disaster for him as a homeowner.

The Control of Functions of Marginal Importance   In addition to the services named above, certain other services are regarded by the suburbanite as being important enough that the local retention of control over their policies is preferred. These include police, fire protection, mass transportation, and public housing. To the suburbanite, police protection has a highly elastic demand curve.[18] He does not view it as being vitally important. In a suburb that has never had a case of murder, rape, or arson, arguments for a metropolitan police force make little sense indeed. And if a difficult case should come along, the county sheriff or the state police, both heavily subsidized by the core city, would provide the needed extra help. Fire protection costs can be reduced in the suburbs by using volunteer help (there is usually a waiting list of persons wanting to join the company) and people seem not to mind paying higher fire-insurance premiums than do core-city residents. Furthermore, by avoiding a metropolitan fire-protection system, the suburbanite can avoid helping to pay for the expensive equipment needed to guard the high-rise buildings and warehouse areas of the core city. Suburbanites, with one, two, or more cars in the family would rather not help subsidize a public transportation system designed primarily for the lower-income residents of the core city. And to the suburban homeowner, public housing is regarded with suspicion and as something that might better not exist at all, especially in his part of the urban scene.

There are certain areas where the suburbanite might not object strongly

[18] So it would seem from the figures in Seymour Sacks and others, **Metropolitan Cleveland—A Fiscal Profile,** Metropolitan Services Commission, Cleveland, Ohio, 1958.

to region-wide administration of services. These would probably include those functions where professionals in the field make basic policy, and the average citizen therefore views the function as not involving policy making or "politics," at all. Examples include public health and welfare, garbage and sewage disposal, and water supply. In these areas, the suburbanite feels no strong need to control policy, but he is not willing to spend more than a minimum amount, in the typical situation, for the service. With few multifamily dwellings, restaurants, or public assembly places, he is likely to think of health as a matter for the family physician (many suburbs spend nothing on public health); he will favor disposing of sewage in the raw state into the nearest stream if no one stops him; and he will insist that a well is cheaper than a municipal system, so long as the pump brings forth water.

Duplication of Services   The social waste of a legally atomized urban area is great. With the community broken up into a series of small units, it becomes difficult to make use of the advantages of specialization of personnel and mechanization of equipment. For example, sewage-disposal and water-filtration plants require such large capital investments that they are not economical unless they are in constant use. Small plants are expensive either because they are inefficient or because they do an inadequate job. Yet these plants are to be found in great numbers in any metropolitan area. Suburbanites may favor them through deliberate choice ("We don't want to depend on the city for our water"), or through ignorance, or because the cost of the inefficiency is widely socialized (as when a suburb dumps partially treated sewage into a river which then flows through the core city).

Amateurism   In the midst of specialists of every type, many of the suburbs try to get along with untrained amateurs. Businessmen who would hire nothing but qualified specialists in their businesses permit amateurs to furnish services to their suburban homes. On the other hand, the governmental operations of suburbs are simpler than are those of large cities, and fewer skills are required. The suburbanite avoids some of the increasing costs of scale that characterize urban government.

Lack of Services   "Taxes are lower in Perambulator Park," the real-estate advertisements proclaim—they are less likely to mention that they are lower because almost no services are provided. The absence of many services which are usually thought to be characteristic of urban life may be accounted for in a variety of ways, some of which have been mentioned earlier in this chapter. Suburbanites may think they cannot afford the services and thus deliberately refuse to institute them. They may prefer to perform the service individually for themselves. They may regard the services as not worth the cost. Many services are more expensive in the suburbs than in the core city because of the lesser density of population. This applies particularly to sewage, storm drainage, street paving and maintenance, street lighting, water supply, garbage collection, and sewage disposal.

The lack of services in suburban areas is felt most keenly by residents in relation to schools. As a result, this is the governmental function on which interest is concentrated, the tax rate increases the most rapidly, and the largest proportion of tax funds are spent. For example, in the Milwaukee metropolitan area, the core city spends 54 percent of its property taxes on schools, the inner ring of suburbs, 76 percent, and the outer ring, about 92 percent.[19]

Lack of Cooperation   Suburbs tend to become intensely jealous of their independence, and—egged on by local officeholders—they attribute ulterior motives to all suggestions of cooperation with the core city or even with another suburb. This attitude is likely to increase the lack of coordination and inefficient use of equipment.

Unequal Tax Bases   The accident of boundary lines contributes to the creation of suburbs with highly unequal financial facilities for supporting local government. There may be very wealthy suburbs alongside of a core city that is desperately in need of more taxable wealth to support its services—which are used by residents of that suburb. Other suburbs may be very poor even though they are located in the heart of a prosperous urban area. This is true, for example, of middle- or lower-income suburbs with no industry. Often the suburbs most needing services are the least able to afford them.

There is some evidence that these inequities are being relieved to some extent by the transfer of some functions to special districts, the county, or the state; by increasing use of state and federal grants-in-aid with built-in formulas to consider relative need or by state-shared taxes; by forcing the commuter to pay some of the cost of his use of other local units of government through the application of earnings taxes or through his payment of state and local taxes; and by a broadening out of the tax base so that even poor suburbs that have not attracted industry are having their property-tax income increased somewhat through the diversified location of offices, salesrooms, medical clinics, supermarkets, shopping centers, and other commercial establishments.[20] But these trends are being partially offset by the lowering in the relative average value of new construction in suburbs as they become increasingly the home of all classes.

Rising Costs   Fringe-area taxes may start at what appears to be a much lower level than those of the core city, but the suburban buyer can be assured that they will increase at a rapid pace. The major portion of one's property-tax bill goes toward the support of schools, and in contemporary suburbia one school-bond issue has followed another with regularity. Each issue raises taxes. This matter will be discussed further in Chapter 18. As population density increases, furthermore, the need for other urban services increases. Each new service must be paid for by additional taxes.

[19] Citizens' Governmental Research Bureau, **Report**, 53:1, Apr. 15, 1965.
[20] Wood, "Metropolitan Government," pp. 113–115.

Water and sewerage systems must be installed. Soon neighbors want to have their street paved and a storm sewer laid. Street lights become desirable. Fire and police service may have to be expanded. The sewage-disposal problem, enormously expensive and nearly always ignored as long as possible, must be solved.

All of these problems fall upon the mortgage- and debt-ridden suburbanite. Many of them were never faced by the subdivision developer. He has, in any case, long since disappeared from the area. In desperation, the citizens seek solutions through special districts, incorporation, new state legislation, or, more rarely, annexation to an existing municipality.

Problems of the Metropolitan Area

The problems listed above generally are those of either the core city or of the suburbs. But there are matters of concern to the metropolitan area as a whole. Unsafe sewage-disposal practices in any part of the area may endanger health in another part. Economics may dictate a collective effort to secure additional water supplies from a distant lake or mountain stream. Traffic-flow patterns for the entire area are necessarily interrelated. Land-use practices in any one section will affect those in other sections. Smoke and noise nuisances pay no more attention to legal boundaries than do disease germs.

Even where structural reorganization of the metropolitan area is a matter that may be accepted for placement on the community agenda, existing legal arrangements may make it unfeasible. The core city may be completely surrounded by incorporated municipalities and state law may be forbiddingly complex so far as consolidation of such areas is concerned. State law may make easy the incorporation of small suburbs that have inadequate tax resources and cannot benefit from *economies of scale* (the efficiencies that result from specialization of personnel and equipment in a large organization).

These are some of the collective problems. Little agreement exists as to which are the most important, and they probably differ from one metropolitan area to another according to local values and existing service levels. The greatest problem of all, perhaps, is "the inability of metropolitan residents to reach any substantial degree of consensus as to what should be done . . . about the generally recognized issues of their common life—government organization, finance, blight and redevelopment, schools, race relations, land use control, and so on." [21]

The problems of the metropolis, as of the state, are probably complicated by the low level of attention given by most voters to their problems of public policy.[22] When residents of the Dayton metropolitan area were asked what in the area they were most proud of, more than one-half of them referred to the cleanliness and beauty of the area. Some of this beauty—such as wide streets —resulted from the efforts of their local governments, but apparently these

[21] Coleman Woodbury, "Great Cities, Great Problems, Great Possibilities?" **Public Administration Review,** 18:332–340, Autumn, 1958. Quote from p. 339.
[22] See Charles R. Adrian and Charles Press, **The American Political Process,** McGraw-Hill Book Company, New York, 1965, chap. 9.

agencies were not credited. Only 5 percent of the respondents mentioned local government or public services and only 2 percent spoke of citizen interest and participation in community affairs. People of the area thought of it principally "in terms of a physical place to live or work. For residents of this particular metropolis (and there is no reason to believe them atypical), local government and its operations do not form an important part of the total image of their community." [23] In the 1957 vote to form a metropolitan government for the Miami area, an issue of intense interest to local politicians and newspapermen, only 26 percent of those eligible voted.

The problems confronting large and relatively small metropolitan areas are similar. Demands for change are much stronger in larger areas, however. This is so for a variety of reasons. In the first place, the very size of a problem makes a difference. The larger the number of persons affected, the more dramatic the situation. Second, the larger the area, the more likely that there will be a political constituency organized around each critical problem. Similarly, the larger the community, the more likely that a particular function or concern about a function will result in the making of policy relevant to it. A village, for example, "may appropriately deal with street paving in a particularistic manner because the issue comes only once in ten years. A large city must have universal rules [policy] about street paving because this activity is continuous." Finally, the larger the metropolitan area, the more likely it is that professionals will be organized and articulate. And by training, professionals are problem-oriented. The result is that large urban areas are under greater pressure to accept professional norms concerning procedures and goals than are the less populous areas.[24]

Metropolitan-area Government Proposals

Numerous proposals have been made over the years in seeking solutions for metropolitan government. Up to the present time, however, each of these has nearly always proved to be either unsuccessful as a permanent solution or politically inexpedient. At present there is no trend toward the adoption of a particular approach to the problem, nor has anyone been able to devise a plan that would be both practical and successful. Some isolated exceptions are to be found and some makeshift and temporary devices have been put to use in various places.

Two specialists in metropolitan-area government have summarized the factors that militate against governmental reorganization in metropolitan areas. These include: "the established bureaucracy, the favored tax position of various units, central city-suburban antagonisms, political differences among sections of the area, and the general lack of community bonds." [25] In addition to this, they recall the observation by Robert Wood that the dominant

[23] John C. Bollens and Henry J. Schmandt, **The Metropolis,** Harper & Row, Publishers, Incorporated, New York, 1965, p. 217.
[24] James G. Coke, "The Lesser Metropolitan Areas of Illinois," **Illinois Government,** 15:1–5, November, 1962.
[25] Bollens and Schmandt, op. cit., p. 581.

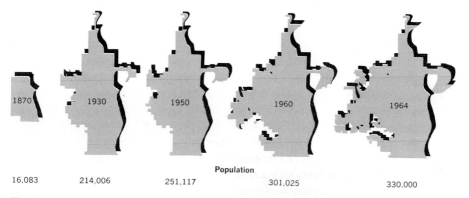

			Population	
16,083	214,006	251,117	301,025	330,000

Fig. 9-2   In a Few States, Annexation Has Paralleled Growth.
The city boundaries of Omaha, 1870–1964.
SOURCE: Omaha City Planning Board, **Annexation**, City of Omaha, Nebr., 1965.

preference in metropolitan areas is for "fraternity" rather than "democracy." [26]
Most people, in other words, prefer social segregation to the tensions created
by attempts at social heterogeneity and racial integration·in living areas.

Annexation   Superficially, the most obvious method of keeping the sociological and legal cities identical would seem to be for the core city to annex fringe
areas as they become urbanized. Formerly this method was widely used, but it
has become increasingly unsatisfactory. As industry, commerce, and higher-
cost houses move outward to get at undeveloped land, demands in the core
city for annexation increase. Indeed, a considerable number of annexations
take place each year in both large and small cities, but they seldom succeed in
equating the political with the sociological city, because laws in nearly all
states provide that outlying areas may be annexed only after a referendum has
been held and the annexation is approved by the voters of the outlying areas
as well as those of the core city. And annexation is nearly always unpopular in
the fringe areas. Only in a few states, notably in Missouri, Texas, and Virginia,
is the core city relatively free to expand its boundaries as the surrounding unincorporated area becomes urbanized.

Many cities are faced with a seemingly unending debate as to whether
they should annex additional territory. Usually, as the community grows older
or as industry begins to prefer the periphery to the central part of the city, the
"expand or die" ideology of the chamber of commerce becomes dominant.

[26] Robert C. Wood, **Suburbia**, chap. 7.

The question also arises in relation to policy concerning the supplying of municipal services outside municipal boundaries. Some communities refuse to extend services to any area not annexed to the city. This type of coercion is resented, of course, by many suburbanites. Large cities sometimes must supply services to suburbs in order for their own utilities to be profitable. Sometimes they cannot annex new territory because they are already surrounded by incorporated territory and they may find it profitable to sell services in order to help defray their own costs.[27]

In 1959, the Minnesota legislature established a Municipal Commission. It was given authority to hear petitions for incorporation, detachment, and annexation of land within the state. On the basis of certain criteria, the commission was authorized, after hearing, to decide on questions of proposed incorporation of villages or cities within the three most populous counties of the state. In the other counties of the state, the county governing board was authorized to decide the same questions, using the same criteria. A similar law, also designed to provide a more rational and systematic procedure for incorporation and annexation, was adopted in Wisconsin that same year.[28]

In 1963, the California legislature provided for a Local Agencies Formation and Annexation Commission for each county. The purpose of this legislation was not only to require some kind of systematic study of proposals to create additional special districts in the state (at the time California had 1,962), but also to provide a more rational approach to incorporation and annexation. The commission consists of two county officers appointed by the board of supervisors, and two city councilmen, appointed by all of the mayors of the county meeting as a committee. These four persons choose a fifth member. On the basis of criteria prescribed in the statute, they decide whether or not to permit the creation of a new special district, the incorporation of a new city, or the annexation of territory to an existing city or special district.[29]

It seems unlikely that annexation to the core city will be the approach used in many areas in the foreseeable future. There is no trend toward revising existing laws so as to make annexation easier.[30]

Special Districts   If annexation becomes impossible, the next solution that might suggest itself would be to take those functions for which a particularly evident need for metropolitan-wide administration is seen and create one or more special districts to administer them. This approach is, in fact, an increasingly common one, and covering all or part of a metropolitan area, there might be park, sewage, water, parking, airport, planning, or other districts. Districts may be authorized to perform more than one function. Their general characteristics were discussed in Chapter 8. Although some observers have

[27] William R. Gable, "Outside Extension of Municipal Services," **Michigan Municipal Review**, 38:216ff., July, 1965.
[28] Kenneth G. Bueche, **Incorporation Laws: One Aspect of the Urban Problem**, Bureau of Governmental Research and Service, University of Colorado, Boulder, Colo., 1963.
[29] *Ibid.*, pp. 200–201.
[30] John C. Bollens and others, **Background for Action**, St. Louis Metropolitan Survey, St. Louis, 1957, pp. 25–52; Wood, **Suburbia**, pp. 76–78.

supported the use of single-purpose special districts partly on the assumption that they will lead to general-purpose districts for metropolitan government, there appears to be no trend in that direction.[31] Special districts are often used for areas of less than the total metropolitan area.

City-County Consolidation   Until recent years, reformers have felt that consolidating the city with the metropolitan county was a desirability second only to annexation and a truer and more permanent solution than the use of the special district. This plan (there are dozens of possible variations of it) calls for an integration of the functions of the core city with the county. The county may retain a partial identity, and incorporated municipalities may remain independent for local purposes.

At least fifteen attempts at city-county consolidation have been made in the twentieth century, and only the combination of Baton Rouge with East Baton Rouge parish in 1947 succeeded. Attempts of this type usually require state-wide approval on a constitutional-amendment referendum, or legislative approval, or a majority vote on referendum in both the core city and in the portions of the county outside. Such approval is not easy to secure. Not only is city-county consolidation almost impossible politically, but it does not guarantee that the city-county will have sufficient powers to meet all metropolitan problems, and it causes even greater political difficulties if the metropolitan area expands beyond the county limits.[32]

City-County Separation   Core-city dwellers, watching the county snowplows at work in the unincorporated reaches of suburbia and remembering that the core city bears most of the cost of county government while securing few services from it, are likely to be intrigued with the idea of separating the city from the rest of the county. This plan is not far different from the preceding one except that, instead of integrating the offices and leaving the county boundaries as they are, separation would create a city-county of the core city and create a new county of the outlying areas.

San Francisco, Baltimore, St. Louis, Denver, and all cities of over 10,000 in Virginia are separate city-counties and have been for a long time. Except in Virginia, there have been no separations in nearly half a century. The plan encounters many of the same problems as does city-county consolidation and is no more practical politically. Furthermore, it is not likely to be satisfactory since it traps the city within its own walls (except in Virginia) instead of treating metropolitan problems on an area-wide basis.

Metropolitan Federation   There are strong arguments, based upon efficiency, economy, and equity, that call for functions of government to be integrated throughout the metropolitan area. At the same time there is merit in keeping

[31] Victor Jones, "Local Government Organization in Metropolitan Areas," in Woodbury, *op. cit.*, pp. 582–583, and Bollens, *op. cit.*, pp. 117–126.
[32] For the successful Baton Rouge attempt, see Thomas H. Reed, "Progress in Metropolitan Integration," **Public Administration Review**, 9:1–10, Winter, 1949; R. G. Kean, "Consolidation That Works," **National Municipal Review**, 45:478–485, November, 1956.

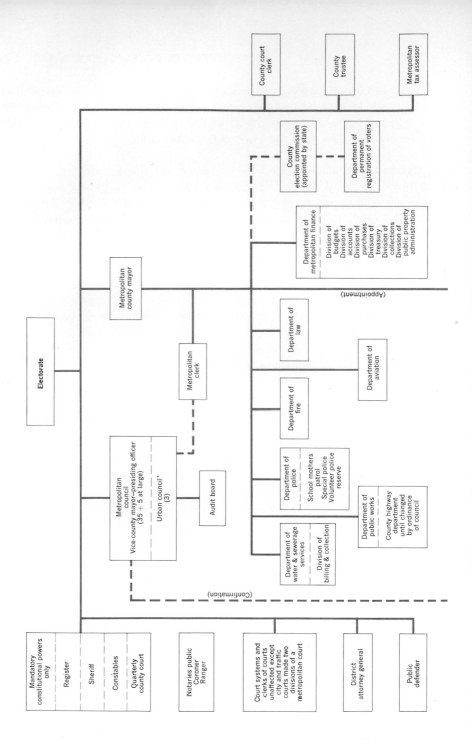

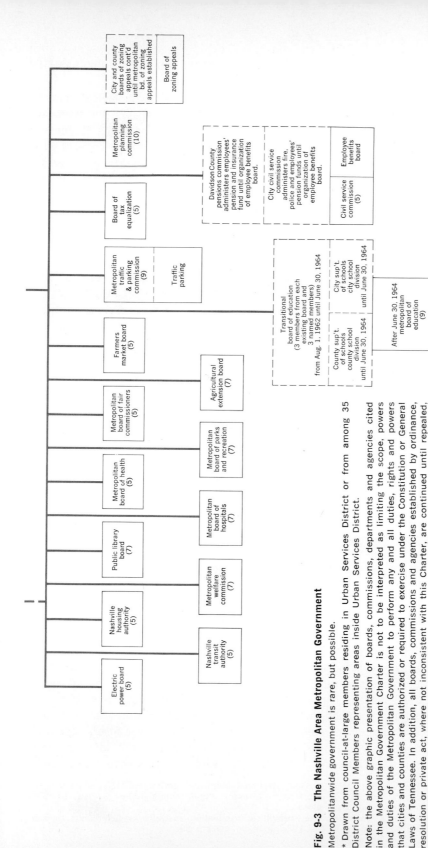

Fig. 9-3   The Nashville Area Metropolitan Government

Metropolitanwide government is rare, but possible.

* Drawn from council-at-large members residing in Urban Services District or from among 35 District Council Members representing areas inside Urban Services District.

Note: the above graphic presentation of boards, commissions, departments and agencies cited in the Metropolitan Government Charter is not to be interpreted as limiting the scope, powers and duties of the Metropolitan Government to perform any and all duties, rights and powers that cities and counties are authorized or required to exercise under the Constitution or General Laws of Tennessee. In addition, all boards, commissions and agencies established by ordinance, resolution or private act, where not inconsistent with this Charter, are continued until repealed, modified or amended as provided in this Charter or by subsequent action of the Metropolitan Government.

SOURCE: Beverly Briley, "The Davidson County Story," **The County Officer**, September, 1962, pp. 406–407.

government as close to the people as possible and a psychological value in retaining the community spirit of the smaller suburb as against the impersonality of the core city. Because of the dilemma thus created, some students of the problem have suggested that a federal plan of government be applied to the metropolitan area with two tiers of government, one areawide to perform functions fitting into that classification and another for the local community to handle functions of a more parochial interest. It is sometimes suggested, for example, that such things as sewage disposal, water supply, police protection, and planning should be area-wide, while perhaps garbage collection and local street maintenance would be appropriate for the lower-tier government.

This plan has been used in London, England, and Toronto, Ontario. Perhaps half a dozen American communities have considered it, but all such attempts to this writing have been defeated. The adoption in 1953 of the Toronto plan by action of the legislature of the province divided authority between the Municipality of Metropolitan Toronto and the thirteen local governments of the area. This experiment has received a great deal of attention. The principal difficulties to be encountered in adopting the plan center around the problems of determining the distribution of powers between the lower and upper tiers of government and in establishing the formula for representation on the governing body for the metropolis.[33]

In the relatively few cases where some form of metropolitan government has been enacted in the United States, the process has been slow and complicated. Thus, a proposal for the consolidation of Nashville and Davidson County, Tennessee, had to "run the gamut of a dress rehearsal in 1958, a reprise that involved the two local legislative bodies, the state legislature, an advisory vote by the electorate, and the drafting of a new proposal, a bitter campaign, and the adoption of the charter at the polls," and still was faced with judicial challenges in the lower courts and the state supreme court. Persons who had favored metropolitan government in 1958 did not achieve success until 1962 and those who had voted for consolidation on June 28 of that year did not learn until October 5 whether the plan they supported, which had received a majority of the votes, was successful.[34]

The County as a Metropolitan Unit   Since about two-thirds of the standard metropolitan areas are located in single counties, it is sometimes suggested that the already existing county governments might be used as a basis for forming supergovernments. There are, however, several handicaps to such a plan. In the first place, the county may be a poor profile of the metropolitan area. The core city may be tucked off in the corner of a county that is in large part basically rural, or the metropolitan area may extend over several counties. Second, in most states, there are many legal obstacles to the county's acting as a municipality. Third, the traditional structure of county government, under

[33] See Eric Hardy, "Progress in Toronto," **National Municipal Review,** 47:445ff., October, 1958; W. W. Crouch, "Metropolitan Government in Toronto," **Public Administration Review,** 14:85–95, Spring, 1954; Bollens, *op. cit.*, pp. 86–104.
[34] David A. Booth, **Metropolitics: The Nashville Consolidation,** Institute for Community Development, Michigan State University, East Lansing, Mich., 1963, p. 88.

either the supervisor or commissioner system, is unsatisfactory for urban government, especially because of the absence of a chief executive officer.

A very few urban counties have been given powers and governmental structures that enable them to act as supergovernments. One example is Los Angeles County, which has a chief administrative officer and furnishes many urban services to unincorporated areas as well as, by contract, to incorporated municipalities. Westchester County in New York has, in effect, the strong-mayor plan of government with an elective chief executive. Several counties have the council-manager form. Dade County (Miami), Florida, has adopted it, although the "Miami plan" absorbed some of the features of the federated plan, with twenty-six municipalities retaining their identities and some powers.[35]

Other Arrangements In order to help meet the problems of furnishing services to a complex metropolitan area, some legislation short of "master-solution" proposals has been adopted. In some cases, cities are permitted to own and control land outside their boundaries. Extraterritorial powers may be given a city to help control nuisances, to secure a water supply, for recreation purposes, and to control subdividing of land, among others. The approach is helpful but is not a permanent solution to metropolitan problems. It is often resented by the fringe areas.[36]

The most common means of attacking joint problems and needs is to make use of formal or informal devices of cooperation and of agreements. Thousands of agreements exist, for example, for the disposal of sewage, garbage, and rubbish; for the sharing of such facilities as those of police radio networks; and for the supplying of services of all types, but especially of water supply.

Two specialists on metropolitics have suggested that the cooperative approach to metropolitan decision making is showing promise of meeting the problems of metropolitan areas for several reasons. First, metropolitan decision makers are under pressure from both national and state governments to face up to their problems. Increasingly, their financial assistance is coupled with requirements of planning and coordination. Second, local officials recognize the possibility that the decision will be taken out of their hands and moved to higher levels of government if they fail to act. Third, the concept of cooperative federalism, with decisions resting in the hands of specialists and political leaders at various levels of government, with the decision shared and not made unilaterally, is now widely accepted as it was not when the early studies advocating metropolitanwide government were made.[37] American political decision making is furthermore, characteristically, one of incremental change. Through cooperation in the solving of the most pressing problems, that is, those receiving the most public attention, metropolitan decision makers know they can effectively reduce pressure for drastic governmental reorganization.

[35] Gustave Serino, **Miami's Metropolitan Experiment,** Public Administration Clearing Service, University of Florida, Gainesville, Fla., 1958.

[36] See Russell W. Maddox, **Extraterritorial Powers of Municipalities in the United States,** Oregon State College Press, Corvallis, Ore., 1955.

[37] Bollens and Schmandt, *op. cit.*, pp. 588–589.

In every metropolitan area, a vast and complex communication network exists among the professions in various fields. Frequently formal organizations exist for such professionals as highway engineers, public health officers, and sanitary engineers. At their regular meetings, they informally discuss mutual problems. In addition, countless informal contacts are made as occasions arise. Sometimes leading political or professional persons involved in a given function will call a meeting or conference which will permit informal discussion by representatives of all interested communities.[38]

Metropolitanwide action, according to one study, takes place only within a narrowly defined frame of reference. Such action normally takes place only in response to some particularly difficult problem in the community and not as a result of any particular ideology. Furthermore, action usually comes only after extensive discussion and sometimes a number of failures to launch proposals. Skilled and experienced political leaders must succeed in convincing the general public to accept the proposal. Amateurs have little chance of success without the backing of the professionals. Although the public must be convinced of a need for change, proposals for metropolitan action usually evoke relatively little citizen interest. Because they result from negotiations, proposals almost always reflect numerous compromises. They must be accomplished within the limits of state law and must have the acquiescence of important state decision makers. Finally, the Federal government has increasingly played a part in the metropolitan decision-making process in recent years and is likely to do so more in the future.[39]

There has been an increasing interest in the use of metropolitan councils in recent years. These are made up of representatives of the principal governments in an area and they "seek to identify area-wide problems and to arrive at negotiated agreements." Hence, the Association of Bay Area Governments, (A-BAG) in the San Francisco area, the mid-Willamette Valley Council of Governments, and the Regional Conference of Elected Officials in the Philadelphia area.[40]

Metropolitics   A vast literature has been accumulated on metropolitan areas and the difficulties of supplying urban services to them. Well over 100 surveys have been conducted. Yet, despite the reams of paper devoted to the subject, most of the proposed solutions had been based upon a priori reasoning rather than empirical data; few studies have been made concerning the climate of opinion existing in metropolitan areas or of the limits of tolerance within which proposed approaches might be feasIble; little work has been done concerning the levels of awareness which metropolitan residents have of their community and its problems; no rank order of values has been worked out; few studies have been made as to why integration proposals fail.

[38] **Alternative Approaches to Governmental Reorganization in Metropolitan Areas,** U.S. Advisory Commission on Intergovernmental Relations, 1962, chaps. 4 and 5.
[39] See Roscoe C. Martin, **Metropolis in Transition,** U.S. Housing and Home Finance Agency, 1963, which presents nine case studies.
[40] *Ibid.,* p. 27.

Perspectives on the Metropolis   Interpretations of metropolitan-area politics depend in part upon one's perspective of the metropolitan area. Several perspectives have been, or might be, used in interpreting this aspect of American politics:

1. The traditional, reform-movement emphasis was upon a search for *solutions*, with an emphasis upon efficiency-and-economy goals rather than upon problems of securing access and representation. The emphasis was on structural reform, with the implicit assumption that, given metropolitanwide formal institutions, metropolitan areas would be well governed. These reformers generally assumed that other citizens in the area were as well informed as they, or at least adequately well informed to react favorably to their arguments. Because they themselves had no problems of access and representation—being overwhelmingly upper middle class—they failed to observe this central problem.[41]

2. The metropolitan area may be viewed as a problem in diplomacy. That is, decision making in the metropolitan area may be seen as resembling that of the diplomatic community more than that of the political. When it is, relative size of communities, although a factor, is not so important as that of securing unanimity in decisions, as is required for agreement in diplomatic negotiations. Viewing the area as a diplomatic problem also permits us to analyze it in terms of alliances of various groups. These alliances are not always so simple as one of the core city against the suburbs. They may involve groups of suburbs against other groups, or alliances may be formed on the basis of particular functions, rather than for all purposes of negotiation.[42]

3. The metropolitan area may be viewed as a market for services. In this sense, it can be analyzed in economic terms.[43] In large metropolitan areas, many or at least several suppliers of services may exist. The core city, plus the county government, plus some of the larger suburbs may all, for example, compete for customers among suburbs for the distribution of water, or for sewage disposal, or for some other function. Cooperative arrangements involving buying from the lowest bidder are possible where both the purveyor and the consumer of services feel that they gain through the transaction—the fundamental requirement for an exchange in economic theory. The concept of the market also applies to the fact that residents of the area appear to choose their place of residence in terms of the amenities they desire and can afford.

4. The dozens, sometimes hundreds, of governmental units in a metropolitan area make it especially appropriate to view the metropolitan area as a part of the system of cooperative federalism. Shared decision making involves not only the traditional three levels of government, but a great amount of interlocal cooperation. To the extent that this is the case, the emphasis in

---

[41] See Paul Studenski, **Government of Metropolitan Areas,** National Municipal League, New York, 1930.
[42] Matthew Holden, Jr., "The Governance of the Metropolis as a Problem in Diplomacy," **Journal of Politics,** 26:627–647, August, 1964.
[43] Vincent Ostrom and others, "The Organization of Government in Metropolitan Areas," **American Political Science Review,** 55:831–842, December, 1961; Thomas R. Dye, "Metropolitan Integration by Bargaining Among Sub-areas," **American Behavioral Scientist,** 5:11, May, 1962.

cooperative federalism upon shared values and goals by professional administrators in various areas of government is especially appropriate. If the theory
of cooperative federalism is reasonably satisfactory as an explanation of how
decisions are made relative to American domestic policy today, the implication
is that metropolitan areas will be able to operate satisfactorily (though certainly not ideally) through the use of negotiation and shared decision making
and financing.[44]

5. The metropolitan area may be viewed as a complex of local governments which, if combined into a single unit, would no longer be a local government, but which through county and state governments, might be able to
provide those services that strictly local governments cannot provide by themselves. Although one-third of the metropolitan areas cover more than one
county—and these are generally the largest such areas—the other two-thirds
may increasingly find the county a useful unit of metropolitan government. In
these areas as well as in those that cover more than a single county, the state
is likely to provide metropolitanwide services in future years. Reapportionment
is especially likely to encourage the use of the state as an instrument for
meeting metropolitan problems. In such areas as air and water pollution, highway systems, health services, welfare services, urban renewal, and areawide
planning, the state is particularly likely to be able to serve as a metropolitan
unit of government.[45]

6. The metropolitan area can also be viewed as a set of competing and
sometimes conflicting ideologies. Perhaps this view has been least investigated, but we may in the future find research relative to it important in developing public policy in metropolitan areas, where some residents are committed
to the urban industrial liberalism of organized labor, others are representative
of the middle-class oriented ideology of the organization man typically found
in the suburbs, and a small but sometimes politically important minority remains committed to the small-town ideology of the nineteenth century.[46]

The Failure of Integration   The value patterns of those who support plans for
metropolitan supergovernments are not dominant in the community, and the
leaders of integration movements characteristically do not give adequate consideration to other values. The result is that proposals for reorganization of
metropolitan governments are rarely implemented.

Upper-income business and professional people tend to favor metropolitan government for a number of reasons. Some are concerned lest as a result
of the middle-class exodus to the suburbs the political control of the core city
be lost to low-income groups with little education. Some believe that governmental consolidation will reduce costs through economies of scale. Low-income
groups tend to oppose metropolitan government for a number of reasons.
Negroes fear that such a government will weaken their political power, since

[44] See citations for Chap. 2.
[45] Charles R. Adrian, "Public Attitudes and Metropolitan Decision Making," in Russell W. Maddox, Jr. (ed.), **Issues in State and Local Government,** D. Van Nostrand Co., Inc., Princeton, N.J.,
1965, pp. 311–321.
[46] Adrian and Press, *op. cit.,* chap. 7.

Negroes are concentrated in the core city of the metropolitan area. Labor leaders sometimes oppose consolidation because business leaders favor it and they assume it must therefore be to the advantage of the business leaders. Labor leaders or working-class people sometimes also oppose metropolitan plans because they include proposals for a short ballot and professional leadership. That is, they fear a loss of access and representation. Some low-income persons fear that metropolitan government would be more expensive to them, that is, that it would result in more rapid tax increases than would otherwise be the case. The question of whether or not to have metropolitan government is not, therefore, simply a question of efficiency and economy as the reformers of a generation ago believed, but is a political question closely related to costs and to perceived abilities to influence policy making.[47]

Suburban officeholders and the entrenched bureaucracy of the area will almost always oppose metropolitan government and reformers seldom pay enough attention to their values and interests or show any imagination in compromising with them. They fail to recognize that *representativeness* of government and *access* to the decision makers are likely to be more important considerations for the typical citizen than are questions of efficiency and economy. Rarely does a metropolitan-area study even mention these two psychologically important factors, to say nothing of adequately providing for them.

Negro voters, in particular, have been suspicious of proposals for metropolitanwide government. In Cleveland, on ten issues submitted to referendum between 1933 and 1959, the level of support for metropolitan government steadily declined, but it declined much more rapidly among Negro voters than it did among whites. The percentage of positive vote among Negroes declined from 79 percent in 1933 to 29 percent in 1959, while the vote in predominantly white wards declined from 69 percent to 46 percent.[48]

Reformers tend to forget that the symbols—efficiency, a bigger and better Zilchville, and the like—that they respond to with enthusiasm ring no bells for *hoi polloi*. It is the latter, of course, which dominates the decision when a proposal is put to a popular referendum. The ordinary citizen is characteristically apathetic. If water flows from the tap and the toilet flushes today, he is not likely to ask whether it will do so tomorrow.

Yet, votes against metropolitan government are not necessarily votes in favor of the *status quo*. They may be votes in favor of gradual or incremental change rather than revolutionary change.[49]

Communicating a concept of future needs on a realistic basis is seldom done by groups organized to support metropolitan governmental reorganization. Furthermore, the reformers tend to put their arguments on a theoretical plane, discussing efficiency ("We have sixteen different fire departments in the metropolitan area!") without translating it into concrete terms as it affects the ordinary citizen. Examples are often not made meaningful. It makes little impres-

[47] See Richard A. Watson and John H. Romani, "Metropolitan Government for Metropolitan Cleveland," **Midwest Journal of Political Science**, 5:365–390, November, 1961.
[48] *Ibid.*, table 2.
[49] Robert Warren, "Political Form and Metropolitan Reform," **Public Administration Review**, 24: 180–187, September, 1964.

sion on the suburbanite to be told that his police force is amateurish and inferior if, in practice, his community has little crime and the state police take care of the arterial highway traffic.

One review of metropolitan government in the 1960s concluded that: [50]

It would be difficult today to find an American metropolis in which the governmental system is in danger of breakdown. Despite dire predictions, disaster had neither struck nor even appeared imminent. The basic public needs of metropolitan residents, whether in an area of 100,000, or 10 million, are being provided for in one fashion or another. Lives and property are being protected, goods and people transported, sewage and garbage disposed of, water supply and general order maintained.

This same review notes, however, that the fact that failure has been avoided in the past is not necessarily an indication that we have done as much as we might in meeting the expectations of the contemporary metropolitan resident or that collapse may not take place in the future. It also notes that the metropolitan resident will probably settle, in the future, for a satisfactory rather than an ideal environment, just as he has in the past.

Concluding Statement   Each device so far tried for the government of metropolitan areas either is basically unacceptable politically to groups powerful enough to block adoption or has proved to be inadequate as a solution. Any proposal that does not meet the requirement of responsibility and responsiveness to the general public must be dismissed—as it will be by the electorate—as lacking accord with our basic concepts of democratic theory. Victor Jones believes that only some system based upon the federal principle has a chance of lasting success. And to date, that principle has proved politically inexpedient. Jones concludes: [51] "If the government of metropolitan areas is to be a local government, we still have before us the job of devising acceptable and effective ways of organizing it."

SELECTED READINGS

Allen, Frederick Lewis: "The Big Change in Suburbia," **Harper's Magazine,** 208: 21–28, June, 1954.

Banovetz, James M.: "Metropolitan Subsidies—An Appraisal," **Public Administration Review,** 25:297–301, December, 1965.   (The question of subsidy of core city or suburb is not important—the amount is not consequential, but metropolitan consolidation would increase subsidies, with net balance in favor of suburbs.)

Bollens, John C.: **Special District Governments in the United States,** University of California Press, Berkeley, Calif., 1957.

————: **The States and the Metropolitan Problem,** Public Administration Service, Chicago, 1956.

———— and others: **Background for Action,** St. Louis Metropolitan Survey, St. Louis, Mo., 1957.

[50] Bollens and Schmandt, *op. cit.,* p. 580.
[51] Jones, *op. cit.,* p. 605. See also Arthur W. Bromage, "Political Representation in Metropolitan Areas," **American Political Science Review,** 52:406–418, June, 1958.

——— and Henry J. Schmandt: **The Metropolis,** Harper & Row, Publishers, Incorporated, New York, 1965. (A major study of metropolitan politics, ecology, and economics. Includes fine bibliography.)

Bromage, Arthur W.: "Political Representation in Metropolitan Areas," **American Political Science Review,** 52:406–418, June, 1958. (The problem of representation for metropolitan governments.)

Chinitz, Benjamin (ed.): **City and Suburb, the Economics of Metropolitan Growth,** Prentice-Hall, Inc., Englewood Cliffs, N.J., 1964.

Chute, Charlton F.: "The Honolulu Metropolitan Area: A Challenge to Traditional Thinking," **Public Administration Review,** 18:36–47, Winter, 1958.

Dobriner, William M. (ed.): **The Suburban Community,** G. P. Putnam's Sons, New York, 1958. (A series of readings.)

Douglass, H. Paul: **The Suburban Trend,** Appleton-Century-Crofts, Inc., New York, 1925.

Dye, Thomas R., and others: "Differentiation and Cooperation in a Metropolitan Area," **Midwest Journal of Political Science,** 7:145–155, May, 1963. (The social and economic differences among communities are a factor discouraging metropolitan government integration.)

Freeman, Linton C., and others: **Metropolitan Decision-making,** University College, Syracuse University, Syracuse, N.Y., 1962.

Glazer, Nathan, and Daniel Patrick Moynihan: **Beyond the Melting Pot; the Negroes, Puerto Ricans, Jews, Italians, and Irish of New York City,** The M.I.T. Press and Harvard University Press, Cambridge, Mass., 1963. (A refutation of the "melting pot" theory. The larger ethnic groups in New York, and in other large cities, do not become assimilated into a distinctive American culture, but often remain clustered in self-segregated neighborhoods.)

Government Affairs Foundation: **Metropolitan Communities: A Bibliography,** Public Administration Service, Chicago, 1956.

Greer, Scott: **Metropolitics: A Study of Political Culture,** John Wiley & Sons, Inc., New York, 1963. (Examines a referendum campaign in the St. Louis metropolitan area.)

Grumm, John G.: **Metropolitan Area Government: The Toronto Experience,** University of Kansas Press, Lawrence, Kans., 1959.

Gutman, Robert, and David Popenoe (eds.): "Urban Studies," **American Behavioral Scientist,** 6:entire issue, February, 1963. (Useful bibliography.)

Hanson, Royce: **The Politics of Metropolitan Cooperation,** Metropolitan Washington Council of Governments, Washington Center for Metropolitan Studies, Washington, D.C., 1964.

Havard, William C., and Floyd L. Corty: **Rural-urban Consolidation: The Merger of Governments in the Baton Rouge Area,** Louisiana State University Press, Baton Rouge, La., 1964. (Consolidation does not bring cheaper government; benefits of better services is the main payoff.)

Hudson, Barbara J.: **The Urban Fringe Problem: A Bibliography,** Bureau of Public Administration, University of California, Berkeley, Calif., 1952.

Jones, Victor: "Local Government Organization in Metropolitan Areas;" in Coleman Woodbury (ed.), **The Future of Cities and Urban Redevelopment,** The University of Chicago Press, Chicago, 1953.

Metropolitan Area Problems. (A bimonthly publication of the Graduate School of Public Affairs, State University of New York, supplying news and a digest of research reports relative to metropolitan affairs.)

Meyerson, Martin (ed.): "Metropolis in Ferment," **Annals,** 314:entire issue, November, 1957.

Press, Charles: "The Cities Within a Great City," **Centennial Review,** 7:113–130, Winter, 1963. (Metropolitan federation should start within the core city itself.)

Sacks, Seymour, and others: **Metropolitan Cleveland—A Fiscal Profile,** Metropolitan Services Commission, Cleveland, Ohio, 1958.

———— and William F. Hellmuth: **Financing Government in a Metropolitan Area,** The Free Press of Glencoe, New York, 1961.

Schmandt, Henry J., Paul G. Steinbicker, and George D. Wendel: **Metropolitan Reform in St. Louis: A Case Study,** Holt, Rinehart and Winston, Inc., New York, 1961.

Schnore, Leo F.: "Metropolitan Growth and Decentralization," **American Journal of Sociology,** 63:171–180, September, 1957.

Senate Subcommittee on Intergovernmental Relations, United States, **Metropolitan America: A Selected Bibliography,** United States Government Printing Office, Washington, D.C., 1964.

Simon, Herbert: **Fiscal Aspects of Metropolitan Consolidation,** Bureau of Public Administration, University of California, Berkeley, Calif., 1943. (A classic study, still valuable. Shows that with metropolitanwide government, consolidation would result in higher taxes if services were made uniform.)

Slayton, William L., and Richard Dewey: "Urban Redevelopment and the Urbanite," in Coleman Woodbury (ed.), **The Future of Cities and Urban Redevelopment,** The University of Chicago Press, Chicago, 1953.

Tableman, Betty: **Governmental Organization in Metropolitan Areas,** The University of Michigan Press, Ann Arbor, Mich., 1951.

U.S. Advisory Commission on Intergovernmental Relations: **Reports,** continuing from 1960.

Warner, Sam B., Jr.: **Street Car Suburb,** Harvard University Press and The M.I.T. Press, Cambridge, Mass., 1962. (A study of the Boston area.)

Whyte, William H., Jr., and others: **The Exploding Metropolis,** Doubleday & Company, Inc., Garden City, N.Y., 1958. (Essays on metropolitan government.)

Wood, Robert C.: **Suburbia—Its People and Their Politics,** Houghton Mifflin Company, Boston, 1959. (A theory of suburban politics.)

Zimmer, Basil G., and Amos H. Hawley: "Approaches to the Solution of Fringe Problems," **Public Administration Review,** 16:258–268, Autumn, 1956.

———— and ————: "Home Owners and Attitude Toward Tax Increase," **Journal of the American Institute of Planners,** 21:65–74, Spring, 1956.

———— and ————: "Local Government as Viewed by Fringe Residents," **Rural Sociology,** 23:363–370, December, 1958.

———— and ————: "Property Taxes and Solutions to Fringe Problems," **Land Economics,** 32:369–376, November, 1956.

10

EXECUTIVE OFFICERS

In colonial times, governors were distrusted by the people because they represented the Crown rather than the colonists. This same attitude of skepticism lived on after the War of Independence was won, and it was reenforced by the individualism of the frontier. Throughout the nineteenth century, the powers of executives in public office were carefully circumscribed and balanced with a system of checks.

One of the characteristics of American government in the twentieth century has been the increasing authority and influence of the chief executive. This has not been true at the national level alone. Through statutes, constitutional amendments, and new state constitutions, the powers of the governor have been increasing. The same has been true of mayors and managers at the local level, and a slight trend toward this exists even in counties. For example, a few counties now have elected or appointed chief executive officers. In some other counties, the clerk or some other administrative officer has assumed these responsibilities. Often they are established by informal arrangement.

Of course, this tendency toward a shifting of authority and influence has caused some unrest. To most political scientists, however, there is no sign that the executive will move beyond his traditional functions in a democratic system. The chief executive still is enormously hampered by the rules and customs of the system. This has been pointed out by Richard Neustadt relative to the Presidency,[1] by practically all books and articles discussing the powers of state

[1] Richard E. Neustadt, **Presidential Power,** John Wiley & Sons, Inc., New York, 1960.

governors, and by Edward Banfield relative to the mayor of Chicago,[2] as well as by Wallace Sayre and Herbert Kaufman in relation to New York.[3]

Banfield notes, for example, that "in Chicago as elsewhere the formal centralization of executive power is much greater than it was a decade or two ago. It seems highly unlikely, however, that this strengthening will go far enough in the foreseeable future to change the essential character of the system." He also notes that "Mayor [Richard] Daley, despite his great power as boss, can do little even in the city proper without at least tacit support from the governor." The chief executive, at any level, is primarily a negotiator, diplomat, needler, or mendicant; he is one who marshals public support or opposition, who activates latent interests and focuses public attention. But he seldom gives direct orders. He is expected to lead, but not to command.

The Conflict over Centralized Leadership

The issue over the question of how much power to give to the chief executive has historically been intertwined with the conflict between the elements of society, especially commercial interests, which stood to profit from central regulation, and other people whose interests were best served by the maximization of government at the local level. The yeoman farmer disliked central government whether it was in the hands of the king or of business leaders. He correctly perceived that executive power may be an instrument for centralization. Only with the advent of the social service state, as discussed in Chapter 2, did the strengthening of the executive become a generally popular cause, and even then it was the result of desperation.

Although the Jacksonian period saw some increase in the status of chief executives and a rise from the low esteem of the period just after the War of Independence, those dominant in politics during the first half of the nineteenth century also kept executives weak by favoring rotation in office, many elective positions, and a romantic view of grass-roots government. The Jacksonians represented the worker and the yeoman farmer, not the commercial interests of the day, and they reflected the values of these groups.

Following the Civil War, party responsibility, which had served to coordinate elective officers, broke down, but most Jacksonian traditions, including those of rotation in office, amateurism, the long ballot, and others, remained. The result was a highly diffused executive power. During this period, the general values of business—every man for himself—that existed at the time permitted corruption to become widespread. When reformers made their influence felt beginning in the 1870s, they favored the establishment of many government activities outside the regular political structure. The result was an increase in the number of independent boards and commissions. By the beginning of the twentieth century, the typical state or local chief executive was

[2] Edward C. Banfield, **Political Influence,** The Free Press of Glencoe, New York, 1961, esp. p. 325; also his earlier work with Martin Meyerson, **Politics, Planning, and the Public Interest,** The Free Press of Glencoe, New York, 1955.
[3] Wallace Sayre and Herbert Kaufman, **Governing New York City,** Russell Sage Foundation, New York, 1960.

administratively impotent, unless as boss or through the party machine he could achieve the powers the law denied him.

After about 1910, a move for increasing the powers of the chief executive began to have some effect. The reasons for the development include the trend toward increasing complexity of government, making coordination more urgently necessary; the high cost of modern government which encouraged many citizens to grasp at any possibility for cutting down expenses; and an increasing prestige of executives together with a growing conviction that the people could elect some who would act, not for the leaders of industry, but for the common man. The increased administrative and legislative influence of the governor in turn produced greater visibility which helped attract a great variety of persons to the job. This acted reciprocally to increase the status of governors. Modern techniques in the art of administration made it possible to bring the efforts of a vast number of people to a single focus in the office of the chief executive. Urbanization had an effect upon the governor and his office, for he became increasingly the spokesman for the cities, protecting the urbanite from the potential hostility of rural-dominated legislatures. The Great Depression, finally, helped add to the prestige of executives at all levels of government when citizens turned to firm leadership in a social-service state as the best hope for a cure to their personal economic problems and insecurities.[4]

In the South, where a one-party system existed almost continuously for more than a century, where most of the governors are not eligible constitutionally to succeed themselves, and where Jacksonian traditions have long been strong, the reform doctrine of a strong administrative leader in the governor with an integrated administrative structure under him has never been popular. The assumption has been that the legislature and, through referendums, the voting public must check the administrative powers of the governor. In recent years, the legislature has often failed to perform this function effectively, but two other checks have arisen to maintain something of a balance: Arbitrary action by the governor is discouraged by (1) the increasing professionalization of the bureaucracy with its characteristic set of professional values and standards, and (2) the increasing importance of standards imposed by Federal legislation in connection with grants-in-aid.[5]

Of all executive officers, short of the President, perhaps the public pays most attention to its governors. This chapter will concentrate on that office, but not to the exclusion of other executive offices.

The Office of Governor

"The governor is not the executive; he is but a single piece of the executive," Woodrow Wilson, who was to become Governor of New Jersey, once complained.

[4] See, generally, Allan R. Richards, "The Traditions of Government in the States," **The Forty-eight States: Their Tasks as Policy Makers and Administrators,** The American Assembly, Graduate School of Business, Columbia University, New York, 1955; Leslie Lipson, **The American Governor: From Figurehead to Leader,** The University of Chicago Press, Chicago, 1939; Richard S. Childs, **Civic Victories,** Harper & Row, Publishers, Incorporated, New York, 1952.
[5] Robert B. Highsaw, "The Southern Governor—Challenge to the Strong Executive Theme," **Public Administration Review,** 19:7–11, Winter, 1959.

He was quite correct, at least for the majority of states in his day and ours. But the governor is also more than the executive. And his office is more than a single individual. The governorship is an institution; to the people, it is a symbol of the unity of society within the state; to the governor, his staff, and his many advisors, it is an image to be carefully constructed and then disseminated through the mass media of communication until it influences every politically conscious person in the state. The governorship is many things, as is the Presidency, and the governor must play many roles and must learn to help the public to keep them individually identifiable. The governor is chief of state, the voice of the people, chief executive, commander-in-chief of the state's armed forces, chief legislator, and chief of his party.[6] No one man acting alone could play so many roles.

There is a good deal of truth in the popular perception that the "men around the executive" really run the state. The executive process in any large city or state is a collective process, producing a collective product, much as does management in big business.

The Governor's Staff   The governorship is an institution and its brain center is his personal staff. The staff in many states consists of no more than an executive secretary and clerical help, though in an increasing number of states it is made up of several professional-level persons in addition to stenographers, receptionists, file clerks, mail clerks, police aides, and telephone operators. The immediate staff is augmented by the person in charge of the executive budget (controller, budget director, commissioner of administration, or otherwise) and by political party leaders and the few paid members of the party staff.[7]

In the more populous states, the governor is likely to have an executive secretary, a press secretary, a legal advisor, a legislative secretary, perhaps a speech writer, and such additional administrative assistants as money can be found for. The Governor of California has a staff of more than fifty persons.

The size of the staff of the Governor of Michigan approximately doubled between 1943 and 1963. Not all of the positions were paid for by public funds. Governor George Romney had five professional staff persons paid from private —that is, political—funds.

Staff members must be persons of considerable ability who are willing to serve as the alter ego to the governor. Normally, they will be as anonymous— and just as important to the total effort—as the offensive tackles on a football team.

The extent to which the staff can project a desired image of an executive is limited. A member of the staff of Governor Mark Hatfield of Oregon has noted: [8]

[6] These categories follow those in Clinton Rossiter, **The American Presidency,** Harcourt, Brace & World, Inc., New York, 1956.
[7] See Coleman B. Ransone, Jr., **The Office of the Governor in the United States,** University of Alabama Press, University, Ala., 1956; Homer E. Scace, **The Organization of the Executive Office of the Governor,** Institute of Public Administration, New York, 1950.
[8] Conrad Joyner, "The Governor's Staff: Its Role in Image Projection," a paper read at the 1961 meetings of the American Political Science Association, St. Louis, Mo.

The staff cannot build a strong man; they cannot become his spokesman. Yet, within their areas of specialization they must be sufficiently proficient to provide him with a constant flow of ideas and materials necessary to make decisions. They may have reservations about some of his statements and decisions, but they do not second guess. Once the decision is made they move on to the next problem. They acknowledge and accept his role as decision-maker. But more important, they relate their activities to his concept of the governor's role.

In the assembly of a staff for the governor, we see dramatized one of the major difficulties involved in being a political executive. One observer has commented: [9]

Little, if any, advance planning normally goes into selection of top personnel for an administration prior to the day of the election. The press of the campaign usually requires that such matters be deferred until a later date, and that date never seems to arrive until the candidate finds himself a governor-elect. Then the impact of personnel recruitment becomes so sharp that the campaign staff—in moments of retrospection—wonders why adequate time was not spent during the campaign on this phase of the post-election requirements. The reason is apparent to any participant in the political process: total commitment is first to win the election and then to worry about forming an administration.

Assignments within the staff group will vary, but their general responsibilities will usually include the following:

1. The development of policy recommendations to be presented to the voters during campaigns and the legislature during sessions. The governor must appear to be wise, aware of all issues and problems in the state, and have a suggestion in response to every inquiry. Because the staff can, at any time and in the name of the governor, gather information from state agencies and private persons throughout the state, it can provide the governor with more information than is to be had by legislative leaders or the governor's political opponents.

2. General responsibilities for public relations. Although the press secretary—usually an experienced journalist—will frame the governor's words for all important press releases, each staff member with a responsibility for certain subject-matter areas will watch for warning signs of possible political hot water, for developments that the governor can claim credit for, and otherwise keep his eye peeled for pegs upon which to hang news stories favorable to the governor.

3. Liaison with the various state, local, and Federal government agencies. The governor cannot personally know all that is going on in various agencies, and what is going on may have an enormous bearing upon his political future. For that reason, staff members are assigned to serve as liaison with various agencies. It is their job to know what difficulties an agency is experiencing, what goals it is pursuing, who are its friends and enemies among the interest groups and their lobbyists, what ideas for legislation their staffs are developing that the governor might endorse, their budgetary situation, and any other in-

[9] David J. Allen, **New Governor in Indiana,** Institute of Public Administration, Indiana University, Bloomington, Ind., 1965, p. 27.

formation that the governor might ask for in a staff meeting, or the press secretary might need to know in order to frame a well-informed story.

4. Answering most of the governor's mail and deciding which pieces of it should go to the governor personally. Governor Franklin D. Roosevelt of New York "never permitted a letter to go unanswered [thus] strengthening his contact with men and women from all walks of life. . . ." [10] Every wise governor follows the same policy.

Answering the Mail   The governor's mail includes the greatest possible variety, of course. He is sent complimentary copies of periodicals including everything from highbrow "little magazines," to scurrilous hate-peddling tabloids, to such intriguing items as the *Pretzel Baker*. A staff member scans them for possibly useful material. He receives letters from "crackpots," some of whom are paranoid and blame public officials for all their troubles; others have the world's greatest invention which, if the governor would lend assistance, would produce a fortune for both; some offer cures for the troubles of mankind; quite a few are religious fanatics. Every governor's office has a list of these correspondents; they are the only ones whose letters are not answered.

Many letters contain complaints, and these are not answered over the governor's signature unless they come from prominent persons or the complaint can be rectified. The others are answered over a staff member's signature or are referred to a state agency for reply. (The agency may be able to mollify the citizen, but if it cannot, this technique allows the complainant's displeasure to be projected upon the anonymous staff member or agency bureaucrat, thus often preserving undamaged the perception of the governor held by the disturbed citizen.)

Most of the governor's mail comes from ordinary citizens in need of help of some kind. Typically, these are people who do not know the ins and outs of the bureaucracy, who have been frustrated in their other efforts to get satisfaction concerning some real or fancied problem, and who do not have connections through the party organization, the government bureaucracy, or the business world. Having nowhere else to go (they often state this explicitly in their letters), they turn to the chief executive of the state, asking his intercession. The request may deal with an agency over which the governor has jurisdiction, and the complaint may be a valid one deserving of correction; but more often it will concern a state agency over which the governor has no control, or it will involve a matter falling within the jurisdiction of some local or Federal agency. Every request is given consideration and a reply. Contrary to popular impression, little attention is paid to party membership or activity, and the governor's staff will ordinarily not seek preferred treatment but only fair treatment for those who complain. In the great majority of cases, the governor is helpless to act. People write for jobs when there are none to be had, seek the release of felons over whose sentence the governor has no control, and ask for additional welfare aid even though the eligibility requirements are spelled out in detail in state and Federal law and the governor cannot modify

[10] Bernard Bellush, **Franklin D. Roosevelt as Governor of New York,** Columbia University Press, New York, 1955, p. 33.

them. The author, having read many thousands of such letters, would make this generalization: It is easier for well-adjusted, well-educated people in a state of detachment to admire the process of democracy than it is for people in trouble to do so. People write to the governor, asking him to overrule the workmen's compensation board, to set aside the deliberations of the state supreme court, to waive legislation and ordinances which have been set up to assure equity, and even to defy the President of the United States. In their desperation, they are not interested in justice or equity. Often they seek neither. They want their personal problem taken care of, and nothing else matters. The governor may be able to help them—and so to him come daily hundreds of pieces of mail. He never sees most of them, but his staff plods through them, seeking to avoid making him enemies and where possible making him friends. Many an injustice has been avoided, many a piece of red tape has been cut in this way. Often, the problem is no more complicated than that of putting the individual in touch with the public or private agency that can help him. The "errand boy" function of the governor's staff is a time-consuming one —in 1956, Governor G. Mennen Williams of Michigan received 219 pieces of mail, on the average, every day, seven days a week—but it undoubtedly performs a useful social function.

Liaison with the Legislature   The governor will have a staff member assigned to work with the legislative members, although all staff members deal with legislators in their own areas of specialty and responsibility. The governor's program, once it is developed, must be interpreted to members of his party in the legislature and support from these members must be secured to the greatest extent possible. The legislative secretary attends party caucuses, provides information to legislators concerning the implications of pending legislation, and keeps track of all pieces of major legislation as well as of all administration bills. The legislative secretary must be able to brief the governor at any time on the status of his program and of political assets and liabilities to be found in legislation presented by the opposition. He must try to placate members of the governor's party in the legislature, for they will be sensitive about being "dictated to," and he must try to win over the support of wavering members. During a legislative session, he will be the busiest man on the staff.

Liaison with the Party   Some staff members will be expected to keep in touch with party officials and their paid staff (if any). The person, most likely the executive secretary, who handles clearances for appointments to state offices, boards, and commissions, is the one who will have to spend most of the time at these assignments. Each proposed appointment must be cleared through party channels to see if strong objection is raised to the individual. Perhaps the executive secretary does not know, for example, that the man intended for appointment to a state commission had supported the governor's opponent in the last election. Since there are probably quite a few persons capable of serving on the commission, party workers will prefer that a party active or at least a supporter of the governor get the assignment. This applies even to seemingly unimportant, unpaid jobs—in states with strong merit systems, most of the gubernatorial appointments are likely to be to unpaid jobs—for to the persons involved, these carry a good deal of prestige.

The staff member in charge of patronage will have another task, a most difficult and an almost thankless one—almost, because the governor will appreciate what he does. That is the job of informing unsuccessful candidates that the governor has had to pass them over. The really skilled person at this assignment can let the person down so gently that he scarcely knows he has been refused. And if the disappointed person must blame someone, the staff member must see to it that it is not the governor or the state chairman. This job is not only difficult, but it entails the expenditure of a great amount of time of the "hand holding" sort. Furthermore, the assistant for patronage will use up even more time chatting with county chairmen and other important politicians who inevitably stop at the governor's office when they visit the capital. The use of this time may seem inefficient, but it is necessary in order to support the governor's role as party leader.

The Governor's Callers   There are a great number of personal callers—famous, obscure, important, psychotic, desperate, or curious persons—who come to the office of every governor: [11]

> In the office [of Governor Franklin D. Roosevelt of New York], day in and day out, there were streams of visitors, some on state business, some from other parts of the country . . . some who simply wished to see a governor and prominent political leader. [Personal Secretary, Guernsey Cross] turned away most of those whose business was not definite, and could not guarantee that many who came without appointments could get in. Usually when Roosevelt went home there were still ten or fifteen disappointed ones left in the anteroom. . . .

Who Are the Staff Members?   They vary a great deal as to background. A few are professional politicians perhaps, others are lawyers (especially in the South, for some reason), an occasional college professor on leave will be found, others are bright young men who hope one day to launch their own political careers. They have in common the fact that the governor places trust in them and delegates to them a great deal of responsibility, for they must do things the governor would do himself if he had the time. This being the case, the wise governor staffs his office without considering the patronage factors that are usually so important. He does not care about size of political contributions in the past, degree of party activity, geographical section of the state where the individual lives, and the like. The vital question is whether or not the man can fill the job assigned him with vigor, imagination, and a devotion to anonymity. The staff member who wishes to place his personal stamp on his work or is unwilling to accept a policy decision from the governor once it is made is not qualified for this type of work. It might be added that, as in the case of the White House staff, opportunities and pressures for performing favors beyond what the public regards as proper may be great and corruption occasionally appears. In 1958, a former administrative assistant to Governor

[11] Frank Freidel, **Franklin D. Roosevelt: The Triumph,** Little, Brown and Company, Boston, 1956.

George N. Craig of Indiana was convicted of bribery and conspiracy charges in planning to profit from the sale of supplies to the state highway department.

Perhaps the two principal members of a governor's staff, more important even than the budget officer and the legislative aide, are the press secretary and the executive secretary. The press secretary, almost always a newspaperman or public relations counselor, is responsible for creating and maintaining a favorable image of the governor, and he must try to control the timing and the content of news stories in which the governor has a direct interest. In a day when the voter knows the politician only through the mass media of communication, a politician's professional life may well lie in the hands of his press secretary.[12] The same might be said, too, of his executive secretary, who not only must keep the staff functioning smoothly but must serve as the man who absorbs much of the pressure directed against the governor. Vince A. Day, a Minneapolis lawyer who served as executive secretary to Governor Floyd B. Olson in the 1930s, possessed the needed qualities: [13]

Not only was he tactful, efficient, and loyal, but he cheerfully carried a heavy administrative burden. . . . A quiet, reflective man who loved to close the office door and hold long intellectual discussions with a few cronies, Day was a sharp contrast to the aggressive back-slapping politician. Small stature, unobtrusive manners, and a genuine desire to avoid the limelight partially concealed his fanatic devotion to Farmer-Labor principles and his penetrating insight into party problems. As a clearinghouse of information for the governor, he exhibited good judgment, candor and unselfishness.

Gubernatorial Roles

We have seen, then, that the governorship must be viewed as an institution. It is created through a formula, the individual ingredients of which become integrated. The governor loses, during much of his official day, his individual personality and becomes part of the total institution—the governorship—which consists of, in addition to himself, his personal staff, certain other high government officials (which may be organized as a cabinet), and the principal members of his political party. The governor may or may not be the actual leader of the team. Publicly, of course, he is the entire institution. His constituents are unaware of most of the other members.[14]

Chief of State   Like the President, though in a much more modest way, the governor serves as the living symbol of the state. In this role, he is not a representative of a political party. He is not seen as the man who controls patronage or struggles with the legislature over a new state school-aid formula. Instead, he is the representative of all of the people of the state and perhaps

[12] For a case study, see Lawrence S. Hobart, **Governor's Press Secretary: A Profile of Paul Weber,** Bureau of Public Administration, University of Michigan, Ann Arbor, Mich., 1958.
[13] George H. Mayer, **The Political Career of Floyd B. Olson,** 1951, pp. 57–58. By permission of, and copyright 1951 by, The University of Minnesota Press, Minneapolis.
[14] For a typical day in the life of Governor Franklin D. Roosevelt of New York, see Bellush, *op. cit.,* pp. 34–35. Any good biography of a governor will help the reader with an understanding of gubernatorial roles.

of all society, as he dedicates a new highway, or opens the state convention of the Sea League of America, or throws out the first baseball of the season, or attends the funeral of a prominent physician, or crowns the cherry queen, or sends greetings to the Western Bohemian Fraternal Association, or proclaims February 16 as Lithuanian Independence Day.

He is called upon to shake hands with thousands of convention members as they visit the state capital, and he shakes still more thousands of hands as he travels about the state by automobile and airplane. He allows thousands of school children to go through his office each year, none of them of voting age, but each anxious to get home to tell mother, father, uncle, and aunt, who are, that he shook the hand of the governor. Though much of the work—the proclamations, the letters, the speeches—can be taken care of by the staff, the rituals, both sacred and profane, which the governor is expected to take part in require a great bit of his personal time. He avoids them at great peril to his political career; he accepts them instead, perhaps with reluctance, more likely with considerable enthusiasm, for most governors genuinely like people. Even those who do not, find that the ceremonial functions allow them to make contact with constitutents under very favorable conditions and with a minimum of the tension and conflict that accompany appearances in the political role. Through them, a governor can keep his physician's finger on the public pulse while allaying suspicion by appearing in his priestly garb.

The governor is asked to send a letter of greeting to every kind of meeting, from the sheet-metal workers' anniversary ball to the state well drillers' association assembled in annual convention. Of course, the governor cannot spend the necessary time to write such letters or to find out what it is that the Beta Chapter of the Order of Ahepa might recently have done that is deserving of compliment. In addition to letters of greeting, the governor will be asked to issue 50 to 100 proclamations each year. These vary from a proclamation to support a worthy charity drive, such as the March of Dimes, to the bizarre and improbable. A few years ago, governors' staffs across the country were confronted with the problem of what to do with requests to issue "National Laugh Week" proclamations. They knew whom the laugh would be on if they obliged—newsmen dislike handouts announcing yet another special day, week, or month under the best of conditions. Yet, some long-suffering member of the governor's staff must find nice things to say about Plumbing, Heating, Cooling Week, or Good Posture Month. The assignment may pain him, but the letters and proclamations are vitally important to the people requesting them, even though the staff member may sometimes have to check to make sure that no one is trying to make a fool of him. The job, furthermore, cannot be turned over to a clerk, since many requests involve subtle policy questions (should the governor praise the state board of realtors just after it has succeeded in helping to kill his public housing bill?); or may easily involve the governor in political hot water (he must not take sides between feuding professional organizations; or lend his endorsement to a fraudulent charity drive). Neither the governor nor his staff ordinarily originates proclamations and greetings; they are requested by individuals or groups and those making the requests frequently furnish a draft of what it is they want said. Sometimes people unknown to the governor or the party write in asking that they be publicly congratulated, perhaps upon a fiftieth-wedding anniversary or election to a lodge office. Ignoring the lack of modesty, the governor, through his staff, will oblige. The important thing in these time-consuming ceremonial functions is that the letter or proclamation appear to be drafted by the governor himself and signed by him. (Most governors have a staff member or two authorized to sign the governor's name to certain documents and letters.) Persons who would never consider voting for the governor will leave no telephone call unmade in their efforts to get a letter of greetings from the governor for the annual convention of their favorite organization. The governor is, after all, the living symbol of the state.

The ceremonial functions of the chief executive may involve a certain amount of adolescent horseplay. At the 1963 dedication of a municipal swimming pool in Boulder, Colorado, for example, Scott Carpenter, an astronaut, was tossed in the pool by the mayor when Carpenter dedicated the pool. The mayor, in turn, was then tossed in by others. Ceremonial duties can be trying.

Voice of the People   Just as "The President is the American people's one authentic trumpet," [15] so is the governor the spokesman for the morality, the higher aspirations, and the conscience of all the citizens of the state. While he is able to command but a small portion of the prestige and attention of the President, he is still the only person in a position to speak of the ideals of the people of his state in a sense that is accepted as being above politics. He becomes something of a father image, and in this role he talks of the need for "education for all," for the protection of the young and old, the dependent mother, the mentally ill. No matter what his policies may be, he is expected to present the higher values of society and to defend them—even though his means of implementing specific programs may belie his true interest in, say, the mentally ill, and his specific proposals become items of intense controversy.

As an individual, the governor portrays not only the state government, but the state itself. This is, however, a two-edged sword politically. The governor, rather than the legislature, is often credited with almost everything that is perceived by the voters as an advancement in state government. This principle has been recognized by all able and successful governors, and they often play upon it as Governor Franklin D. Roosevelt of New York did. When he first became chief executive with a legislature controlled by the opposition party he announced that "about 90 percent of the legislation ought not to be taken up from a partisan point of view." [16] From such an approach, a governor goes on, aided by his favorable image as voice of the people, to create the impression that his program is the nonpartisan one symbolizing the higher aims of the state, and legislative opposition is a devilish thing designed to thwart the will of the people. Sometimes this gambit is successful. But, unfortunately for many a governor, the public also blames him for anything that goes wrong dur-

15 Rossiter, *op. cit.,* p. 23.
16 Freidel, *op. cit.,* p. 15.

ing his administration, no matter where the responsibility in fact lies. Thus, public relations men specializing in political campaigns hold widely to the view that any new tax added during a governor's tenure in office will be blamed upon him, even though it may not have been of his making and he may indeed have opposed it or favored major changes in the version which he finally and reluctantly signed.

Chief Executive Although few governors have the legal powers necessary to make them masters over the way in which state agencies are administered, they do have quite a few powers. Symbolically, they are regarded as head of the administration, and the governors' mail certainly indicates that they are so viewed by the public. As a political leader and as voice of the people, the governor may be able to exert influence over administration where his legal powers fail him. In many cases, however, the governor lacks both power and effective influence over the administration of some (perhaps many) departments, both because of the means by which department heads are selected and because of legislative provisions designed to insulate certain agencies from gubernatorial influence.

Appointments Appointments made by the governor are subject to approval by the state senate (or by the governor's council in a few New England states). Sometimes he can appoint, but cannot remove, an official—the latter power being vested in the civil service commission, state supreme court, or some other agency. Some department heads are chosen by boards or commissions appointed for staggered terms so that the department may remain in the hands of the political enemy unless the governor remains in office for many years. In a few instances, department heads are civil servants. The administrative structure is so complex that gubernatorial staffs have difficulty in keeping up with changes that take place. Thus Governor John Lodge of Connecticut once appointed a dead man to a judgeship, and Governor G. Mennen Williams of Michigan named a man to a commission that no longer existed.

   Some governors have power to remove local officials after notice and hearing, though this power is seldom exercised because, from a political viewpoint, it is likely that either (1) a local politician who has violated the local mores will be removed through other means before the governor need act or (2) removal of a local politician would be unpopular and hence politically damaging.

Budget Control During the 1920s and 1930s, economy pressures were so great that several state constitutions were amended to give the governor the power of the item veto and many legislatures surrendered part of their traditional power of control over the purse. They permitted the establishment of all or part of the executive-budget system which divided up the financial process so that the executive branch makes a recommendation for revenues and expenditures in the form of a systematic, comprehensive statement of income and outgo. The legislature then adopts this budget, nearly always with some, and perhaps with many, modifications. The executive branch next oversees the expenditure of the appropriations by the various departments, requiring them to spend at a rate that will not exhaust their appropriations prematurely and keeping expenditures within the requirements of the law. Finally, the legislative branch, through its auditors, checks to ascertain whether or not its instructions have been carried out and whether or not appropriate provisions of the state law have been followed by the executive. The power of the chief executive, through his budget officer, is potentially very great, both in preparing the budget itself—the document is, of course, a major policy statement, explaining how the governor would spend moneys—and in controlling its expenditure after the legislature votes the funds. The budget officer is, therefore, one of the governor's chief aides today. He and his budget examiners serve to advise both the governor and legislators, reviewing appropriation requests and preparing evidence in support of the position on policy finally taken by the governor. He often controls the conditions under which appropriations may be spent.[17]

Clemency   The pardoning power of the governor stems from the fact that he inherits some of the authority of the king in England. The monarch ultimately owned all of the land in feudal theory, and the law was his too; he could, therefore, pardon offenses against it. Until after the nineteenth century, the pardon was almost the only device whereby a convicted person could be released from prison short of the full term of his sentence. Once nearly 50 percent of all prisoners were pardoned before the expiration of their sentences.

The pardoning power was, and still is, sometimes abused. Governor Len Small of Illinois was so generous with pardons that his 1924 opponents commissioned and used against him a song, "Oh, Pardon Me." Governor John C. Walton of Oklahoma freed 693 prisoners in eleven months and was impeached and convicted for having taken bribes for some of the pardons. Governor Miriam "Ma" Ferguson of Texas pardoned 3,700 prisoners in two years—and some of the state's newspapers derisively ran daily pardon columns. But most governors have probably disliked the responsibility for acting on pardons and paroles.

Today, fewer than 2 percent of prison sentences are commuted and very few are outright pardons, although in some states governors continue the tradition of granting a few pardons at Christmas time, a practice designed to help maintain morale among long-termers. Executive clemency now serves to correct miscarriages of justice and is given once in a while for other reasons, but it has been largely replaced by use of parole, probation, and the indeterminate sentence; and these devices have been turned over for administration to agencies of the state with final decision in the hands of a parole board on which the governor may or may not sit and over which he has no veto.

The Executive Potential   A governor who possesses considerable administrative skill can wield a great deal of influence over the way in which a state

[17] See Frederick C. Mosher, "The Executive Budget, Empire State Style," **Public Administration Review**, 12:73–84, Spring, 1952.

government operates, even in the absence of complete statutory power to act as a chief executive. In Kentucky, a study concluded that "the problem is to persuade governors to maximize for the general improvement of state administration the power governors often fail to realize they possess."[18] The observation would no doubt apply equally well in other states.

Commander-in-chief   The governor serves as commander-in-chief of the National Guard (state militia) when it is not called into national service, as it is in times of emergency or war. The Guard, which is largely supported by Federal funds, has today apparently outlived its traditional function, but it is protected by powerful pressure groups made up of members of the Guard and veterans' organizations. Prior to World War II, the Guard was available on call of the governor to handle large disturbances, such as prison riots, race riots, and strikes. On these occasions, "Lapses of gubernatorial discretion . . . were not infrequent."[19] To be more specific, the Guard sometimes was used ruthlessly and brutally in putting down prison riots; it sometimes added to, rather than relieved, tensions in race disturbances; it often served, especially in the 1930s, as a management tool in breaking up industrial strikes. Sometimes in cases of civil disturbance the assistance of the Guard was needed and was used with discretion, of course.

Since World War II, from "an embodiment of force," the Guard has become largely an instrument of "rescue and relief." Guard units have become community service organizations. Instead of using them in emergencies, governors now prefer, for the maintenance of order, to rely upon the professional peace officers in the state police or highway patrol. This is possible as a result of the growth of these forces, from 8,400 in 1938 to around 35,000 in 1966. Since 1945, the use of the National Guard for police work has become a rarity, and almost every instance has provoked controversy.

The most important activity of the National Guard since World War II has been in aid and rescue work in connection with disaster relief, particularly in the wake of tornadoes, hurricanes, and floods. In the five years following 1947, the Guard was called out a total of 387 times, about 95 percent of the cases fitting into the community service category. When difficulties arose in Little Rock, Arkansas, over a school integration issue, Federal troops were used during the period of greatest tension and the National Guard was called into Federal service before it was used. The National Guard as a military establishment seems outmoded. In its new role, it continues to serve a useful function. But it is an expensive luxury for the states to afford.

Chief Legislator   The public has never paid much attention to the pleas of reformers for an integrated administrative structure under the governor. This is so not only because the public is well grounded in the Jacksonian myth

[18] Gladys M. Kammerer, "The Governor as Chief Administrator in Kentucky," **Journal of Politics,** 16:236–256, May, 1954. See also Ransone, *op. cit.*
[19] Bennett M. Rich and P. H. Burch, Jr., "The Changing Role of the National Guard," **American Political Science Review,** 50:702–706, September, 1956. See also William H. Riker, **Soldiers of the States,** Public Affairs Press, Washington, D.C., 1957.

which holds that any office is more responsible if it is elective but probably also because the public thinks of the governor primarily as a policy leader and not as an administrator. The governor has, in fact, become so important as a policy leader that the legislature's role has become one essentially negative in character. The legislature vetoes, modifies, or perhaps enlarges upon gubernatorial recommendations, but it is not likely to provide policy leadership or innovation. The public does not seem to expect more than a negative role from the legislature. There are some exceptions to this, however. In a few states, governors have traditionally not been much concerned with issues of policy.

The governor is in a position to influence the legislature as well as the public and to serve as a leader of policy as a result of his right to submit a comprehensive executive budget and messages to the legislature and of his power to veto bills. Legislative leaders often resist gubernatorial leadership and resent it, regardless of whether the governor is of the same party or of another one. Yet, the governor has the capacity to rally public opinion and to attract a great deal of publicity in support of his recommendations. The very fact that he has superior public relations power will be resented, however, as will the fact that he will often have an imaginative, varied program to present. Thus, the Republican majority in the New York legislature [20]

adopted the policy that anything desired by [Governor] Al Smith was evil, extravagant, radical, or unscientific, despite the fact that many of the views of the Tammany Governor had been evolved from studies made by eminent Republicans.

The approach was spectacularly unsuccessful. By the time Governor Smith left office he had accumulated one of the most impressive lists of accomplishments of any governor in any state. Similarly, the persistent political unwisdom of the legislative leadership in New York did much to enhance Governor Franklin D. Roosevelt's public image as a man of creativity who developed workable ideas in relation to public problems, a man of action. On many occasions, Roosevelt's sails could have been trimmed by imaginative action and effective reactions by legislative leaders.[21]

For purposes of policy innovation, the governor has great resources. He can call upon any of the state agencies for ideas and data, and even those in enemy or neutral hands cannot afford to refuse to give him the information he requests. He can also call upon knowledgeable people in private life for help. A favorite device is the study commission, often made up of persons who are politically inactive or of the opposite party or faction, in addition to his own stalwarts. The legislature will sometimes refuse to appropriate any money for such groups, but because of the prestige of a governor's study commission and of their interest in the subject matter, these people will often work hard without so much as being paid their expenses. The ideas they develop are

[20] Bernard Bellush, *op. cit.*, p. 29.
[21] See Freidel, *op. cit.*; Bellush, *op. cit.* On Smith's accomplishments while in office, see Freidel, *op. cit.*, p. 11.

often immensely valuable to the governor and his staff in putting together a program.[22]

In presenting a program to the legislature, the governor may include some spectacular items which are too costly for the state to afford without additional taxes. He may well pass along to the legislature the politically thankless task of telling this to the people. He may recommend items that are to be found in the party platform, knowing that the less practical ones will be killed in the legislature. The items he really wants, he may present in moderate tones, leaving the door open for compromise and giving the legislators a chance to work out some of the detail for themselves in a face-saving manner. But if the legislature is seriously out of step with the times, it may be stampeded by the force of the governor's popular appeal and attention-getting ability.

The politician may be a forceful leader on behalf of the demands of effective interests. He is not unwilling to make decisions where social conflict exists, as he is sometimes accused of being. Nearly all of his decisions on policy involve conflicts of interest among the public; some are happy with his proposals, some unhappy. The politician's task is to assess the balance of interests revolving about an issue. If he fails to act, it is often because he does not feel confident of having adequately evaluated the situation. At this point he needs help from his staff, interest groups, appropriate department heads, and citizens who are specialists in a particular subject. Once a strong governor can evaluate the desires of society, he is willing to act, even though his proposals are controversial.

In addition to the pressure the governor can exert through his use of the budget and his messages to the legislature, he can invite key legislators to breakfast or afternoon conferences where he can force them into serious arguments over the things he wants out of a session. In addition, he can resort to other pressure techniques, such as in the use of the patronage or in arranging for "spontaneous" public rallies on the capitol steps. The governor cannot expect to get all that he asks for (many of them would be appalled if they did), but he does serve as a major policy leader. And by claiming credit for everything adopted by the legislature that he approves of and chastising it for not adopting the rest of his program, he can advance his own career.

The Veto   The power to veto is a great weapon in the hands of a governor. It is important both as a threat and in actual use. The veto is, incidentally, one of the few powers possessed by governors that are broader in scope than is the equivalent power of the President. The latter can veto whole bills as presented to him, but governors in thirty-nine states can also veto single sections of appropriation bills, the so-called item veto.[23]

The Governor of North Carolina is the only one not possessing a veto power. In other states, the strength of the veto power varies a great deal. The number of days which the governor is allowed before returning a vetoed bill

[22] Elizabeth M. Scott, "State Executive Departments Play Growing Part in Law Making," **National Municipal Review,** 32:529–534, November, 1943.
[23] See Frank W. Prescott, "The Executive Veto in American States," **Western Political Quarterly,** 3:98–112, March, 1950, for a general discussion.

is different from state to state. In South Carolina, the governor has only two days in which to act on a bill. In some states, the governor may use the "pocket veto" by refusing to sign a bill after the legislature has adjourned; in others, the bill becomes law if the governor fails to act in such instances. There are also differences in the degree to which the veto is actually used. Thus, New York governors between 1927 and 1952 vetoed 26 percent of the bills presented to them—and when the governor was a member of the same party as the majority group in the legislature, more bills were vetoed than when he was of the opposite party. Pennsylvania governors between 1939 and 1946 vetoed over 10 percent of the bills reaching them. But Governor G. Mennen Williams of Michigan, between 1949 and 1955, vetoed only 2.5 percent of the bills sent to him by a legislature dominated by his political opposition.[24] Governor Williams thought legislative action should be challenged only under unusual conditions. He considered it politically inexpedient to veto most measures with which he disagreed. In fact, political advantage seemed to be with him when he accepted bills "reluctantly" and then carried the campaign for his own program to the voters. The legislature, in turn, did not expect him to veto many measures.

While Governor Williams returned about six bills per session, Governor Thomas E. Dewey of New York averaged about 365. Obviously, their attitudes toward the use of the veto and the legislative expectation of gubernatorial behavior were quite different from those in Michigan. In New York, many bills of local interest but expensive or unpopular as statewide policy are killed, not in committee as in Michigan, but by gubernatorial veto. Conventional behavior patterns in politics differ from one state to another.

In the 1960s, the authority of the gubernatorial veto was questioned in several states as to its application to issues of reapportionment. Because governors are generally oriented toward their metropolitan constituencies, small-town legislators have sometimes argued that apportionment legislation was not subject to veto. In 1965, the Minnesota Supreme Court upheld the authority of the governor to veto reapportionment legislation.

The reasons given for a veto vary both within and between states. Of the 194 vetoes in Massachusetts between 1939 and 1963, nearly 75 percent were for the stated reason of policy differences between the governor and the legislature. Relatively few vetoes were for the stated reasons of bills' being unconstitutional, defective, or unnecessary. To some extent, this probably was a reflection of competent bill drafting. Almost all financial differences were settled by negotiation between the budget commissioners and the legislative committees. During the twenty-five-year period, vetoes averaged 8.4 per year.[25]

The likelihood of a veto's being sustained varies from one state to another. Not a single gubernatorial veto was overridden in Minnesota between

[24] Belle Zeller (ed.), **American State Legislatures,** Thomas Y. Crowell Company, New York, 1954, p. 167; M. Nelson McGeary, "The Governor's Veto in Pennsylvania," **American Political Science Review,** 41:942, October, 1947; Peter J. Turano, "The Use of the Veto by Michigan's Governor Williams," a paper presented to the Michigan Academy of Science, Arts and Letters, Ann Arbor, Mich., 1956.
[25] Joseph F. Zimmerman, "Rationale of Veto Use in Massachusetts," **Social Science,** 39:204–207.

1858 and 1935. Only one was overridden in Pennsylvania in the first half of the twentieth century, and but four in Iowa in over a century after the granting of statehood. In contrast, twenty-eight vetoes were overridden in California between 1933 and 1949. Even this is not a very large number, however, and the usual expectation is that a gubernatorial veto will kill any measure. It is a powerful threat.

Chief of Party   As at least the nominal, and frequently the real, head of his political party, the governor must spend a good deal of time attending party activities—barbecues, dances, picnics, rallies, and conventions. He must try to iron out disputes between rival factions within the organization or rival members of the legislature. He must dispense patronage in a manner that preserves a reasonable level of satisfaction among the party rank and file while at the same time securing persons sufficiently competent for public office that they will not embarrass him. A good appointment strengthens the hand of the governor and the standing of the party, but the low salaries that generally prevail make this a difficult assignment.

In each election at the state, and sometimes the local, level the governor must campaign for party candidates whether or not he is himself a candidate. As he travels about the state, he must make sure the local county chairman knows of his coming, or that chairman may sit on his hands during the next campaign. When a United States senator dies or resigns, the governor must choose a man who will be honored by party workers but who will not become a Frankenstein, stronger than the governor himself. He is expected to support the party platform, whenever he can determine what it means, and his voice in messages to the legislature is at once that of the governorship and of the party. His role as party leader, in fact, becomes intertwined with virtually everything he does, either explicitly or as a hidden purpose while he carries out his other duties.

The Governor in a Crisis   While items of grave concern and great importance to the welfare of citizens are everyday matters in the governor's office, there are certain situations that arise which call for emergency action by the governor. He and his staff ordinarily make plans for such circumstances, often in cooperation with the state police and other officials and agencies likely to be involved. Crises that may arise for the most part fall into the following categories:

1. A natural disaster, prison break, race riot, or other serious disorder. In the event of a flood or tornado, the governor will probably cancel his schedule and go immediately to the scene. He may be needed in order to call out the state police or National Guard. As a symbol of the state, people will be reassured by his presence. And it will not hurt him politically to be photographed, tired and disheveled, gazing upon the ruins. A race riot or labor disturbance is an emergency that may result in bloodshed and property damage as well as in a serious deterioration of intergroup relations if prompt

action is not taken. If the governor does not have a plan and does not act with decisiveness in such a situation, his political career may be ruined. This is especially true in the event of a prison riot or mass break, a possibility that governors fear, perhaps above all other disturbances, so far as its potential political effects are concerned. Governor Adlai Stevenson interrupted his 1952 campaign for the Presidency in order to take personal charge during a prison riot.

2. Political crises of various sorts. A sudden, unexpected political maneuver by the opposition in the legislature, discovery that a trusted lieutenant has been receiving kickbacks on contracts, a charge that a mental hospital patient has been abused, or a dozen other matters dealing with party morale or the governor's own political future may require the cancellation of other plans and immediate work on the crisis situation. If the afternoon papers contain headline announcements of some particular stratagem by an opposition leader, or of some charge of misfeasance or failure to act, or of a grand plan to solve the state's financial problems, the governor and his staff will immediately have to go into damage-control operations. The objective will be to minimize the propaganda advantage gained by the opposition and to regain the initiative as quickly as possible. The general rule is to decide first whether an overt defense of any kind is to be offered (sometimes the best defence is silence). If one is to be made, it is considered important by veteran politicians to release a partial answer as quickly as possible and then to develop the theme preferably with new material which will help both to distract the public from the opposition's main point and to regain the initiative. Under such circumstances, the press secretary becomes a key man, though only the governor can make the ultimate decision. Not infrequently he must do this in the face of conflicting advice from his staff and party leaders, for veteran politicians by no means always agree on what should be done at such times.

The Big Decisions While in a sense every decision made in the governor's office has important implications both for his political future and for the welfare of citizens and while the most innocent-appearing problems may suddenly become headline matters, there are of course some decisions that are of special importance both to the governor and to the public. Basic changes in existing public policy, new state programs, major alterations in the tax structure, all are critical in nature. How are such decisions made? The answer probably varies with the personality of the governor, the political structure of the state, the alignment of interest groups, and other factors. The governor is likely to seek a wide range of opinions on the subject. If time permits, he may appoint a citizens' study committee to look into the matter and advise him. The press secretary will spend a good deal of time considering the public relations implications of various alternatives and toying with various ways to release the final decision to the press. The budget officer will be asked to bring in detailed reports on the fiscal implications of various possibilities, and his figures may be checked against independent sources. A meeting of the governor's staff will be held, possibly many meetings, at which the alternatives will be discussed and staff members may be encouraged to think of every possible argument the opponents might use and of every possible question the governor might be asked by the press. The press secretary will try to anticipate the "newspegs" that the opponents will use and the way in which the opposition press will handle the story once a policy is announced. The assistant in charge of patronage will be asked to evaluate possible alternatives in terms of rank-and-file party reaction. Department heads concerned with the policy, and their staffs, will be brought in for consultation.

The state party chairman and other important party figures will be consulted and they will be tipped off in advance of the press release as to what the decision is and what the public and private reasons were for it, so that these persons will take the same position as the governor. Interest-group leaders who were instrumental in getting the governor nominated and elected and who helped finance his campaign will either be consulted or will volunteer suggestions, and these will not be taken lightly.

Finally, the governor alone, or perhaps with a very small group of advisers, will make the decision. It will be announced in a carefully timed and carefully worded press release. Political supporters will then be assisted in writing letters to the editor in defense of the decision. Legislative leaders will be briefed—few of them, if any, will have been on the inside in the making of the decision—so that they may use the appropriate arguments. Reams of statistical evidence in support of the position will come from the budget office. Party chieftains will publicly praise the "courageous, imaginative leadership" of the governor. Ultimately the results, or what appear to be the results of the decision, will help to determine the political fate of the governor and of his party or faction. He cannot afford to be wrong often.

Legal Considerations

In every state, usually in the constitution, rules prescribe qualifications for the governorship. A person must be a citizen of the United States. He must be of a certain age, usually at least thirty. He must have lived in the state a certain period of time, usually at least five years, and he must be a qualified voter. These legal qualifications are generally far less important than are considerations of "availability"—the right man in the right place at the right time, politically speaking, to be selected.

Term of Office   The early state constitutions commonly provided a one-year term for governors, but the historical trend has been toward lengthening the tenure. Massachusetts in 1920 was the last state to give up the one-year provision; and by 1966, thirty-six states had four-year terms, the others electing for two years. In fifteen states (mostly in the South) a governor cannot succeed himself; in seven others he can serve no more than two terms consecutively.

The lengthening of the term seems to stem from the complexities of modern campaigning and the time involved in the task. Governors generally have

lieutenant governor. In states which have no lieutenant governor, or if that office is vacant, a designated administrative or legislative officer succeeds to the office of governor in case of a vacancy. Unlike the practice in the Federal government, the designated successor acts for the chief executive whenever the latter leaves the state.

The practice of permitting the governor to exercise the powers of his office only when physically present within the state's borders is probably an anachronism in today's world of telephones and jet airplanes. Acting governors have, on some occasions, used the opportunity of the momentary absence of the governor to take actions directly antithetical to the policy positions or career interests of the governor.

How to Become Governor   In the period between 1870 and 1950, 995 different individuals were elected governors of states. Of these, 45.8 percent were practicing lawyers.[27] One need not be a lawyer to win in politics, but being one helps, principally because of the lawyer's "legal skills which give him a monopoly of offices related to the administration of law in the court system." Nearly all judges and prosecutors, in addition to principal law-enforcement officers, are lawyers, and it is through these offices that lie most of the paths of advancement to higher political office including the governorship.[28] The pattern of advancement to the governorship varies from state to state. In Massachusetts, Vermont, and Iowa, promotion often runs from the legislature to the speakership, to the lieutenant governorship, to the top office. In Mississippi and Georgia, a legislator not infrequently goes directly to the governorship. In the states bordering the Deep South, a man chosen governor has usually had at least two judicial or law-enforcement posts previously. And in the West, governors are often selected from among persons holding nonelective administrative offices. The pattern that one follows to the top seems to depend upon the traditions and political systems as they exist in the individual states.

Other State Executive Officers

In most states, many executive officers are elected in addition to the governor. In Jacksonian theory, these men were to work together as a team, with the party serving to coordinate their otherwise independent status. But with today's loose party arrangements, they are often of differing political parties or factions and thus may work against one another. Sometimes, as in Iowa, Michigan, Oregon, and West Virginia,[29] they are organized for certain statutory purposes into a board and become a plural executive with many powers vested in the body by law, powers that in other states belong to the governor acting alone.

The officer most commonly elected is the lieutenant governor (thirty-eight

27 Joseph A. Schlesinger, "Lawyers and American Politics," **Midwest Journal of Politics,** 1:26–39, May, 1957.
28 Joseph A. Schlesinger, **How They Became Governor,** Bureau of Social and Political Research, Michigan State University, East Lansing, Mich., 1957.
29 See W. W. Kaempfer, **The Board of Public Works: West Virginia's Plural Executive,** Bureau for Government Research, West Virginia University, Morgantown, W.Va., 1957.

states), who most often serves ex officio on a variety of boards and commissions.

The office of lieutenant governor originated in colonial America. It has been supported through the popular preference for elective office and for having the governor be succeeded, if necessary, by someone also elected by the public. It also reflects the example of the vice presidency at the national level.[30]

Others elected often include the secretary of state, attorney general, treasurer, auditor, and members of various boards and commissions, especially for highways, public instruction, and higher education.[31] These officers, although many of their duties are routine, are often of considerable influence in policy making. The attorney general has an opportunity to gain headlines by investigating irregularities, graft, and corruption. He can decide, often, what he is going to investigate and hence whose ox is to be gored. The secretary of state may be able to expedite or delay special elections as political considerations dictate.

In Oregon, the secretary of state determines who is a "serious candidate" and hence eligible to enter the presidential preference primary, one that has long been among the most important along the road toward nomination.

If his staff is large enough only for spot checks, the auditor general may be able to select the local governments whose books he is going to inspect, and he may try harder to find irregularities when inspecting in the camp of the enemy. The treasurer can decide which bankers are to profit from being allowed to receive state bank deposits.

The ordinary duties of the secretary of state include the keeping of the official records. He is something of a glorified county clerk. He also generally acts as the keeper of election records and may have some supervisory powers over elections. The treasurer is the keeper of the funds. Normally he can pay out no money except on a warrant signed by either the controller or the auditor or both. He has no discretion in the matter. He may also administer the floating of state bond issues. The attorney general is the chief interpreter of the law and chief law-enforcement officer of the state. Legislative acts are not completely self-defining, and his office spends a great deal of time preparing opinions concerning the powers of various state agencies and local units of government—opinions which sometimes come out of the process with interpretations quite favorable to the political interests of the attorney general.

The auditor is supposed to check up on the administrative branch of government. Sometimes he has only the power of postaudit; that is, he reviews *after* the money is spent to see if it was spent according to "legislative intent" and without corruption or undue waste. He (or the controller) may have the power of preaudit, or the right to approve expenditures *before* they take place. This enables him to interpret "legislative intent" and thus often to decide

[30] Byron R. Abernethy, **Some Persisting Questions concerning the Constitutional State Executive,** Governmental Research Center, University of Kansas, Lawrence, Kans., 1960, p. 18.
[31] See the latest volume of the **Book of the States,** published by The Council of State Governments, Chicago, for details.

whether an agency is to be allowed to spend money for a certain purpose or in a certain way—a most influential power. Students of administration often bemoan the fact that the preaudit and postaudit are commonly intermingled and confused at the state level, since this mixes up the control function of the executive budget with the audit function. In a few states the auditor is selected by the legislature and performs only postaudit functions. Accounting and expenditure control (preauditing) is usually given to the executive in cities with the strong-mayor or council-manager plans, while postauditing is done by an auditor appointed by the council or popularly elected. The distinction is important, since the preauditor determines whether any unusual expenditure or new or unique interpretations of the law are to be permitted. An unimaginative or reluctant auditor with preaudit powers can effectively block important parts of an executive's program at times.

The Office of Mayor

The mayor of today's American small town is commonly a moderately successful small businessman, long active in local politics and civic affairs and well liked by his neighbors. In the large city of an earlier day, the mayor was often corrupt and incompetent—although there were outstanding exceptions. Today our large cities seem to be producing an increasingly large number of capable chief executives. Still, many contemporary mayors are amiable mediocrities, lacking in ability and imagination and under obligation to a few interest groups that put them in office.

The dominant figure and chief negotiator among ideological and economic interests in the large city of today is the mayor. His position has been described as follows: [32]

He presides over the 'new convergence,' and, if the coalition is to succeed, he must lead it. More than anyone else he determines the direct action of urban development; yet his sanctions are few, his base of support insecure. The mayor is both the most visible person in the community and, on questions of public policy, probably the most influential. Yet his is a classic example of the separation of influence and power. Few big-city mayors have significant patronage resources. Even fewer use their appointments to give themselves direct leverage over policy. Although the mayor in a partisan city is necessarily elected through processes that involve the ward organizations, no big-city mayor, not even [Richard] Daley, can be regarded as the creature of the machine. Rather the mayor is an individual who has 1) sufficient mass appeal and/or organizational support to win an election, 2) enough awareness of the complexities of urban problems to rely heavily on a professional staff for advice and counsel, and 3) the ability to negotiate successfully with economic notables in the city to mobilize both public and private resources in efforts to solve core city economic and social problems.

An impressive list of public servants can be made up from among the names of men who have served as mayors of American cities, especially since

[32] Robert H. Salisbury, "Urban Politics: The New Convergence of Power," **Journal of Politics,** 26:775–797, November, 1964. Quotation on p. 787.

the early 1900s. The problem of securing able men as mayors of large cities is particularly complicated, however, by the fact that men who seek these offices are likely to have to place themselves under obligation to interest groups with specific political goals. This is so because someone must furnish the money for the expensive large-city campaign. While a mayor so obligated could in theory be representative of a substantial portion of the population, could be imaginative and aggressive in meeting problems, and could be responsive to changing demands of the people of the city, in practice it appears that often he is not. This general problem applies also to the governorship and other positions of influence, of course, but the political environment in which the large-city mayor finds himself—surrounded by public apathy, well-organized business groups, and labor groups which concentrate upon the state and national scene—offers few incentives for the mayor to seek to represent a broad electorate.

Powers of the Mayor   The powers exercised by the mayor vary widely throughout the United States. The person called the mayor in a commission or council-manager city normally has few powers other than those of presiding over the council and performing the ceremonial role for the city. The mayor in a mayor-council city may have a great many powers, or he may be merely one of many virtually collegial members of the city administration, as is the case in a very weak-mayor city.

In general, the powers of the mayor for the city are similar in kind to those of the governor for the state government. In larger cities, especially, the mayor is likely to play a role similar to that of a governor and his staff as described above. In mayor-council cities, the tendency is for the mayor to have greater administrative powers than those commonly given to a governor. In smaller communities, the values, interests, and personality of the mayor have a good opportunity to be made known. The office is administered more as an individual than a staff operation as it would be in states or large cities.

Mayors possess legislative powers similar to those of governors and also perform administrative and ceremonial functions that are similar.[33] They are so powerful in some strong-mayor types of cities that it is not uncommon to find that the council does not attempt to make policy independently of the mayor. In these kinds of cities, the mayor is in fact the chief administrative officer, in possession of supervisory and coordinative powers over the activities of the various departments that very few governors have been granted.

Legal Considerations   The mayor of the city may be selected by the voters directly, as he is in nearly all mayor-council cities, or he may be chosen by the council. In a few cities, the person who gets the largest number of votes in the election for councilmanic seats becomes mayor. The pay of the mayor varies according to both the size of the city and the structure of its government. In general, his salary is higher in mayor-council cities than in other

33 For details, see Charles R. Adrian, **Governing Urban America**, 2d ed., McGraw-Hill Book Company, New York, 1961, chap. 9.

types.[34] The pay is typically modest and some of the subordinate officers with professional skills (e.g., the health officer and city engineer) are likely to be better paid than is the mayor.

The trend is toward a four-year term for mayors, although it varies from one to six and is likely to be shorter in weak-mayor cities than in other types. Removals and succession follow much the came pattern for mayors as for governors.

Despite the vast legal powers they often possess, the mayors of large cities, like governors,[35]

frequently must mediate between the claims of contending groups, no one of which is dominant in the community. In such instances their role as decision-makers assumes greater importance. Holding the balance of power, they occupy a strategic position of influence which they can exploit to further their total program and objectives. The mayors of large cities, particularly, enjoy such opportunities. It would be grossly misleading, however, to assume that men who have reputations as strong mayors, such as Daley in Chicago, Lee in New Haven, or Tucker in St. Louis, rule by fiat or by arbitrary exercise of their official prerogatives.

Robert Dahl made a similar observation relative to New Haven. He found that the mayor "was not the peak of a pyramid but rather at the center of intersecting circles. He rarely commanded. He negotiated, cajoled, exhorted, beguiled, charmed, pressed, appealed, reasoned, promised, insisted, demanded, even threatened, but he most needed support from other leaders who simply could not be commanded. Because the mayor could not command, he had to bargain." [36]

The City Manager

It is a basic part of the theory of council-manager government that the entire administration of the city or other unit of government should be professionalized. Managers are supposed to be trained to use the tools of administration and, especially in smaller cities, to possess a technical skill, such as engineering, as well. The manager must be a diplomat, for his job is dependent upon his ability to get along with the council. He must be a politician of a special sort, too, for his job calls upon him to give advice on matters of public policy but to avoid involvement in controversial campaign issues.

Managers play important roles in policy innovation and leadership,[37] in public relations, and, in a role secondary to that of the mayor, in ceremonial functions. Although they do many of the things an elected officeholder would

[34] For details, see the most recent edition of the **Municipal Year Book,** published by The International City Managers' Association, Chicago.
[35] John C. Bollens and Henry J. Schmandt, **The Metropolis,** Harper & Row, Publishers, Incorporated, 1965, p. 208.
[36] Robert A. Dahl, **Who Governs?** Yale University Press, New Haven, Conn., 1961, p. 204.
[37] See Clarence E. Ridley, **The Role of the Manager in Policy Formation,** International City Managers' Association, Chicago, 1958; and Charles R. Adrian, "Leadership and Decision-making in Manager Cities: A Study of Three Communities," **Public Administration Review,** 18:208–213, Summer, 1958.

otherwise do and although they act very much as politicians act in many of their roles, managers think of themselves, and are probably perceived by the public, as being professional administrators possessing special qualifications for their position. Undoubtedly they enjoy widespread respect and higher prestige than would be accorded an elected official in a similar role.[38]

Selection and Tenure of the Manager   Managers, like school superintendents, are often chosen from among persons living and working outside the local unit of government doing the hiring. Charters or the law commonly permit this because the governing body is looking not for a deserving local politician but for a professionally competent administrator. The legislators may get ideas for candidates from the state league of cities, from the International City Managers' Association, which is the managers' professional organization, from the retiring manager, or from the universities where recent managers of the community studied. Sometimes a department head of the hiring community or of another one is chosen. Most managers today are college graduates and often have advanced degrees in public administration, engineering, or some other appropriate field.

The manager is normally selected by the governing body by majority vote and is dismissable by that body at any time by the same method. For the plan to work successfully, it is essential that the governing body be allowed to remove the manager at any time and for any reason that the majority of the body thinks sufficient. Otherwise, the administration of the city becomes autonomous and irresponsible. Generally, the manager is paid a salary higher than an elective chief executive would receive for a similar position.[39]

The Duties of the Manager   While charters vary widely, the manager is the chief administrative officer of the city and has all or most of the following responsibilities:

1. Overseeing enforcement of all laws and ordinances

2. Controlling all departments, with power to appoint, supervise, and remove department heads and bureau chiefs

3. Making recommendations to the council on such matters as he thinks desirable

4. Keeping the council advised of the financial condition of the city and concerning future needs and trends

5. Preparing and submitting to the council the annual budget

6. Preparing and submitting to the council reports and memoranda such as are requested

7. Keeping the council, and indirectly the public, informed concerning the operations of all aspects of government

[38] On the manager generally, see above, Chap. 8, as well as Adrian, **Governing Urban America,** pp. 219–225; Harold A. Stone, D. K. Price, and K. H. Stone, **City Manager Government in the United States,** Public Administration Service, Chicago, 1940, and the periodical **Public Management,** which is published by The International City Managers' Association, Chicago.
[39] For salary ranges, see the most recent issue of the **Municipal Year Book.**

8. Performing such other duties as the governing body may legally assign to him

The manager thus has full responsibility to the governing body for the conduct of the administration of the city, county, or other unit of government.

In most cases, the manager presents significant matters to the governing body for consideration. Since such items are not initiated by legislators these men are normally free to consider them on the merits of the question, having no vested interest in them. New business coming before the governing body is usually first referred to the manager for a report at a future meeting. The manager, in making his report, is in a position to consider the effect of possible forms of action upon all departments. No legislator making the report could do this so well. Furthermore, by leaving the report to the manager, the legislators remain free to criticize it and to judge it.

A study of the office of city manager in Florida produced the following findings: [40]

1. If the mayor was directly elected, he tended to develop a separate power base from that of the rest of the council. This tended to bring him into conflict with the city manager and the length of tenure of a manager in such cities was shortened.

2. No relationship existed between the rate of population growth in a city and the tenure of the manager. However, if a city tended, through growth, to attract a different class- or income-level of people, this might have an effect upon the tenure of the manager. In other words, a change in dominant life style in the community might produce a demand for a change in the manager.

3. Local residents and amateur managers tended to have longer average tenure than did professional managers. A local amateur may "have had little formal education, but he frequently has acquired some factional or clique ties that impart political strength." He is in a much stronger position as a rule to contend with council opponents than is a professional manager brought in from the outside.[41]

4. Manager tenure is longer in cities with little conflict within the community power complex and with a low level of interest conflict. In other words, manager tenure is longest in cities with a high level of political consensus.

5. Managers usually play a major part in policy development and in the making of the principal decisions in their cities. "Therefore, they were right in the heart of politics, in the broadest sense of that term, to the extent that certain interests might well be alienated as a result of actions taken by the council on manager recommendations. Such alienated persons might and sometimes did seek political retaliation." [42]

Managership is today an important profession in America. The attitudes of those who follow it have a profound effect upon the kind of government that local communities experience today and will experience in future years.

[40] Gladys M. Kammerer and others, **City Managers in Politics**, University of Florida Press, Gainesville, Fla., 1962, chap. 5.
[41] *Ibid.*, p. 81.
[42] *Ibid.*, p. 83.

Other Elective Offices

For counties, townships, and cities, there is a variety of elective officials performing for their level of government many functions that parallel those of that state executive officer discussed above. In cities there has been a pronounced decline in the number of administrative officials who hold office by election. In 1936, 70 percent of American cities over 5,000 population elected one or more officers other than the mayor (particularly, the treasurer, clerk, assessor, auditor, attorney, controller, police chief, or public-works director). This figure has since dropped steadily, and in 1956 stood at 52 percent. For some kinds of offices, the drop has been especially sharp. In 1936, for example, the police chief was elected in 240 cities; in 1956, in only 101 cities.[43] A similar trend may be found for counties and townships, but at a much slower pace. At the same time, there has been a trend toward the development of a chief executive office in the nonmunicipal units of local government.[44] For these units of government the structure is often in part spelled out in the state constitution, making change difficult, and it remains common for all department heads and officers (as distinguished from employees) to be elected in local units of government outside of cities.

The trend for local elective officials is toward longer terms in office. In twenty-five states, most or all of the county officials serve four-year terms; in fifteen states, two-year terms; in others, a variety of provisions exists.[45]

Minor Officials as Policy Makers   Elected administrative officers perform a great many routine duties, such as recording titles to property, keeping the records of board meetings, paying out money in a manner prescribed by law, and auditing expenditures. But they also have considerable policy-making influence. A county or village clerk may become a veritable manager. The auditor sometimes exercises considerable influence over county policies.[46] The village attorney, often possessing a monopoly of legal skills, may by that fact do much to steer the policy-making activities of the council. The sheriff, being elected and with little supervision or accounting to either the county board or state officials, may decide almost alone what the policies in the county will be relative to liquor law enforcement. The county prosecutor, in the same position, may be able to determine specifically which cases are to be prosecuted, which will be dropped after an investigation of some sort, and which are to be ignored. The assessor may choose to award his friends and punish his enemies; he may leave a large, profitable business firm at a low assessment, or off the books altogether, or he may levy an assessment at more than market value. In some states, no effective appeal can be made from an assessor's decision.

[43] **National Municipal Review,** 46:393, September, 1957.
[44] See above, pp. 210–214.
[45] John Wood and Clayton L. Ringgenberg, **Terms of Office of Elective County Officials in the 48 States,** Iowa Legislative Research Bureau, Des Moines, Iowa, 1954.
[46] For a case study, see A. A. Mallas, Jr., and others, **Forty Years in Politics: The Story of Ben Pelham,** Wayne State University Press, Detroit, Mich., 1957. Pelham was the nonelective Wayne County, Michigan, accountant for many years and became virtually a county manager.

The local police chief or constable may set up a profitable speed trap in cooperation with the justice of the peace. The latter remains one of the most arbitrary officials in American government. On a minor charge before a justice, there is often virtually no chance of defending oneself, especially in traffic cases, and although appeal in theory lies to a higher court, in practice this is usually considered too expensive and time-consuming.

We are often told that local officials in the lesser offices perform no policy-making functions and for that reason should not be selected by popular ballot. In fact, however, it is because they *do* perform policy-making functions that there is danger in the office's becoming lost in the jungle of names on the long, or "bedsheet," ballot. The threat to democracy is not so much in the inability of the citizen to identify the function of the office as it is in his inability to hold a long list of independent officers responsible for their acts. A student of rural government has commented: [47]

It is necessary to remember that those in office have in their charge large amounts of public property and the disposal of large sums of public money. With the best of intentions and the greatest ingenuity the controlling state legislature could not enact laws which the local "ring" with more or less ease could not circumvent or turn to its own benefit. Moreover, officials must be given some discretion in performing their duties, and once this discretion is granted, the honest enforcement of law is left as a precarious hostage to those in office.

A shorter ballot does not necessarily make law enforcement less of a hostage in the hands of officeholders, but to the extent that it gives the citizen a greater opportunity for oversight and for identifying those responsible for policy decisions, it makes the position of the hostage less precarious.

SELECTED READINGS

Carleton, W. G.: "The Southern Politician, 1900 and 1950," **Journal of Politics,** 13:215–231, May, 1951.

Derthick, Martha: **The National Guard in Politics,** Harvard University Press, Cambridge, Mass., 1965. (A study of the National Guard Association as an interest group.)

Fannin, Paul, and others: **The Office of Governor in Arizona,** Bureau of Government Research, Arizona State University, Tempe, Ariz., 1964. (A conservative governor views the task.)

Flinn, Thomas: **Governor Freeman and the Minnesota Budget,** The Bobbs-Merrill Company, Inc., Indianapolis, ICP no. 60, 1961. (The budget as a political resource.)

Garceau, Oliver, and Corinne Silverman: "A Pressure Group and the Pressured," **American Political Science Review,** 48:672–691, September, 1954. (A study of a manufacturers' association and the Vermont legislature.)

Golembiewski, Robert: **The Trenton Milk Contract,** The Bobbs-Merrill Company, Inc., Indianapolis, ICP no. 50, 1959. (Some of the problems of the department head depending upon staff members. He is a prisoner of their advice and data.)

Hamburger, Philip: "The Mayor," **The New Yorker,** Jan. 26 and Feb. 2, 1957. (A profile of Robert F. Wagner of New York.)

[47] Lane W. Lancaster, **Government in Rural America,** rev. ed., D. Van Nostrand Company, Inc.. Princeton, N.J., 1952, p. 58.

Herzberg, Donald G., and Paul Tillett: **A Budget for New York State, 1956–1957,** The Bobbs-Merrill Company, Inc., Indianapolis, 1962. (Executive-legislative relations.)

Hoan, Daniel W.: **City Government: The Record of the Milwaukee Experiment,** Harcourt, Brace & World, Inc., New York, 1936.

Hobart, Lawrence S.: **Governor's Press Secretary: A Profile of Paul Weber,** Bureau of Public Administration, University of Michigan, Ann Arbor, Mich., 1958.

Hofstadter, Richard: **The American Political Tradition,** Alfred A. Knopf, Inc., New York, 1948.

Isom, W. R.: "The Office of Lt. Governor in the States," **American Political Science Review,** 32:916–933, October, 1938.

Johnson, Tom L.: **My Story,** The Viking Press, Inc., New York, 1911.

Kinnard, William N., Jr.: **Appointed by the Mayor,** rev. ed., The Bobbs-Merrill Company, Inc., Indianapolis, ICP no. 63, 1961. (Study of influence of a "weak" mayor on appointments in a small Eastern city.)

Lipson, Leslie: **The American Governor: From Figurehead to Leader,** The University of Chicago Press, Chicago, 1939. (Historical coverage.)

Lowi, Theodore J.: **At the Pleasure of the Mayor,** The Free Press of Glencoe, New York, 1964. (A study of patronage patterns in the city of New York over a sixty-year period.)

MacDonald, Austin F.: "American Governors, 1900–1910," **National Municipal Review,** 16:715–719, November, 1927.

McGeary, M. Nelson: "The Governor's Veto in Pennsylvania," **American Political Science Review,** 41:942, October, 1947.

Mills, Warner E., Jr.: **Martial Law in East Texas,** The Bobbs-Merrill Company, Inc., Indianapolis, ICP no. 53, 1960. (The problem of use of the National Guard by a governor.)

"New York City: Is It Governable?" **Newsweek,** May 31, 1965. (An article cataloging some of the great numbers of fantastically difficult problems the mayor of New York must cope with as a policy leader.)

Perkins, John A.: "American Governors, 1930–1940," **National Municipal Review,** 29:178–184, March, 1940.

Prescott, Frank W.: "The Executive Veto in American States," **Western Political Quarterly,** 3:98–112, March, 1950.

Ransone, Coleman B., Jr.: **The Office of the Governor in the United States,** University of Alabama Press, University, Ala., 1956.

Rich, Bennett M., and P. H. Burch, Jr.: "The Changing Role of the National Guard," **American Political Science Review,** 50:702–706, September, 1956.

Riker, William H.: **Soldiers of the States,** Public Affairs Press, Washington, D.C., 1957.

Scace, Homer E.: **The Organization of the Executive Office of the Governor,** Institute of Public Administration, New York, 1950.

Schlesinger, Joseph A.: **How They Became Governor,** Bureau of Social and Political Research, Michigan State University, East Lansing, Mich., 1957.

———: "Lawyers and American Politics," **Midwest Journal of Politics,** 1:26–39, May, 1957.

Sherwood, Frank P.: **A City Manager Tries to Fire His Police Chief,** The Bobbs-Merrill Company, Inc., Indianapolis, ICP no. 76, 1963. (Conflict in Southern California city. Question of professional evaluation of the manager and conflict of management and police values.)

——— and Beatrice Markey: **The Mayor and the Fire Chief,** The Bobbs-Merrill Company, Inc., Indianapolis, ICP no. 43, 1959. (Attempt by Mayor Norris Poulson to get fire department to desegregate. The chief feared desegregation would damage morale and efficiency.)

Solomon, S. R.: "American Governors since 1915," **National Municipal Review,** 20:152–158, March, 1931.

————: "United States Governors, 1940–1950," **National Municipal Review,** 41:190–197, April, 1952.

Steiner, Gilbert Y., and others: **The Office of Governor,** Institute of Government and Public Affairs, University of Illinois, Urbana, Ill., 1963.   (Articles by eight political scientists and politicians.)

Whitlock, Brand: **Forty Years of It,** Appleton-Century-Crofts, Inc., New York, 1925.   (The autobiography of a noted reformer.)

Williams, G. Mennen: **A Governor's Notes,** Institute of Public Administration, University of Michigan, Ann Arbor, Mich., 1961.   (Interesting to contrast with Fannin, above.)

Wood, John, and Clayton L. Ringgenberg: **Terms of Office of Elective County Officials in the 48 States,** Iowa Legislative Research Bureau, Des Moines, Iowa, 1954.

Zeigler, Harmon: **The Florida Milk Commission Changes Minimum Prices,** The Bobbs-Merrill Company, Inc., Indianapolis, ICP no. 77, 1963.   (Executive efforts to influence a regulatory agency dominated by a single interest group.)

11

ADMINISTRATION

Administration is a part of the political process. The term generally applies to that process of government that is involved in the application of general policies to specific cases. One specialist in the field, after much effort, has produced the following summary of what administration is: [1]

> *Administration* is cooperative human action with a high degree of rationality. . . .
> The distinguishing characteristics of an administrative system, seen in the customary perspective of administrative students, are best subsumed under two concepts, organization and management, thought of as analogous to anatomy and physiology in a biological system. *Organization* is the structure of authoritative and habitual personal interrelations in an administrative system. *Management* is action intended to achieve rational cooperation in an administrative system.

Developments in Administration

The Growth of Administration To have an understanding of the great size and influence of modern public management, it is necessary to compare the functions of state and local government today with those of, say, two generations ago. In 1913, all state governments taken together spent only $297 million. In 1957, however, the states spent over $388 million *each month for payroll alone*. Their expenditures totalled $16,924 million for that year. Local units of government spent $1,960 million in 1913, most of it for schools. In 1957, they spent $30,710 million. Even allowing for the declining value of the dollar, state expenditures increased twentyfold and local expenditures nearly sixfold in two generations.

[1] Dwight Waldo, **The Study of Public Administration,** 1955, pp. 11–12. By permission of the publisher, Random House, Inc., New York. Copyright 1955.

In 1913, states spent little money for schools, except for higher education. And relatively few persons went to college in those days. Local governments provided much of the education of the day through the one-room school, offering minimal programs taught by poorly trained and largely inexperienced teachers who received low pay. Roads, another major expenditure program today, were largely cared for by the local unit two generations ago. They were often unsurfaced and required little care in that preautomobile age. Most states had little to do with highways before the beginnings of the good-roads movement and the adoption of the first Federal-Aid Highway Act. The mentally ill received no rehabilitative treatment in those days. They were given custodial care in ramshackle asylums run by untrained persons who received patronage appointments from the city, county, or state. Some patients were housed in the local jail. Welfare was a local function provided reluctantly and at the bare subsistence level; the states kept out of the field except for some institutional care. In general, state government functions were minimal, centering around the regulation of utilities and other businesses, control over the state colleges and universities, enactment of the laws governing business transactions and the criminal statutes, and supervision over local government powers and activities. State government was distant and had few direct contacts with the ordinary citizen. Local government was more active and spent more —about 6.6 times as much—than state government but was a thin shadow of its present-day self as a supplier of services to the citizen. The growth in the activities of state governments has been the more spectacular, but both the state and local governments have become vitally important social institutions affecting the daily lives of each citizen.

The Historical Trend   Some of the developments in administrative organization have been noted earlier in this book.[2] We have seen that the legislatures at first dominated government at both the state and local levels. As legislative bodies and city councils declined in prestige and importance during the nineteenth century, they were replaced both by the direct democracy of the initiative and referendum and by a large number of elective administrative officials. Both of these trends contributed to the development of the long ballot.

As the number of governmental functions increased, the number of governmental agencies increased, too. Each new function tended to be established as a separate agency, usually in order to give it protection against the competing fiscal demands of the older, better-established functions. The interest groups which secured the adoption of new programs and policies generally preferred this arrangement. As a result, by 1950, Colorado had 140 state agencies, Connecticut 172, and Texas 124. The typical state, such as Tennessee or Iowa, had around eighty-five. The more populous cities had once been similarly departmentalized, though reorganizations resulting from the adoption of the strong-mayor, council-manager, or commission forms had gen-

[2] See Chap. 2. A summary of the subject may be found in York Willbern, "Administration in State Governments," **The Forty-eight States: Their Tasks as Policy Makers and Administrators,** The American Assembly, Graduate School of Business, Columbia University, New York, 1955, chap. 5, from which this account borrows.

erally decreased the number of separate municipal agencies.[3] The rising number of agencies resulted after a while in a problem of communication. It became highly difficult for the governor, the legislator, or the citizen to know what was being done in the agencies or who was responsible for their activities.

One possible result of having a large number of agencies in state government is that the governor may be forced by pressure to devote time disproportionate to the apparent social importance of an agency because of low morale within it, a feud between two clientele groups of the agency, or simply the forceful and aggressive personality of the department head. One of the agencies that plagued former Governor G. Mennen Williams of Michigan for many years was the state Board of Cosmetology. Williams later commented:[4] "I don't know why it is, but there seems to be a greater tendency for this Board to have more difficulties among its members than any other, and when the fur flies there is trouble all over. . . . The number of times this agency blew its top in my early years was too great to remember with any pleasure. We eventually got it into somewhat normal control, but even then there were occasions which demanded an inordinate amount of time." The Governor, apparently, missed the opportunity to note that it was hair rather than fur that flew and that it probably blew its well-combed wig, rather than its top. In any case, this board was enough to convince the Governor that having more than 120 state agencies was "complete idiocy."

Administrative Developments   The municipal-reorganization movement began in the 1890s and, to a degree, even earlier. It was concerned with both the eradication of corruption and the stopping of administrative sprawl. Administrative reorganization of counties and other nonschool local units followed along at a much slower pace. At the state level, reform at first concentrated upon the reshuffling of agencies so as to group them into a more manageable number and to concentrate responsibility for their operation in the governor. This movement gained headway after about 1910. The reorganization in Illinois under Governor Frank Lowden attracted a great deal of attention. While few comprehensive reorganizations have taken place over the years since, there has been a gradual evolution in state administration, highlighted by expanding staff services, greater professionalization of personnel, more effective administrative planning, the development of the executive budget, and firmer executive leadership within departments and over departments.

The first state commission on administrative reorganization was appointed in Wisconsin in 1911. It was followed by similar groups in Massachusetts and New Jersey the next year. The action in Wisconsin, a part of the progressive movement in that state, took place in the same year that President William Howard Taft appointed the Commission on Economy and Efficiency for the national government. The movement gained great momentum with a general reorganization in Illinois in 1917 under Governor Frank Lowden. Re-

[3] See Chap. 8.
[4] Undated memorandum, Governor G. Mennen Williams of Michigan to his Citizens' Advisory Committee on Reorganization of State Government, Summer, 1960.

formers during the 1920s spent a good deal of time in talking about and urging the administrative integration of state governments. A majority of the states took some kind of action, but few of them came anywhere near adopting the set of recommendations of the efficiency-and-economy movement listed below.

In the period following World War II, beginning with the first Hoover Commission at the national level and spreading to the states, there was a revival of structural reorganization effort. Most states established "Little Hoover" commissions in the years following 1949. At least thirty-two states had such commissions, some appointed by the governor, some by the legislature, some consisting partly of state officials and legislators and partly of private citizens.[5] Some changes resulted from the reports of these groups, but there was relatively little support for drastic overhauls of state structures. Administrative reorganization is, after all, a political question and changes in it are likely to take place in the same general fashion as do changes in substantive public policy. That is, adjustments are made on the basis of small increments of change. The efficiency-and-economy movement did, however, establish a kind of liturgy for reform and this received or benefited from a certain sense of legitimacy accorded to it by many educated, middle-class citizens interested in politics and government generally.

The Assumptions of the Reform Movement   Nearly all the reform efforts at the state and local levels have concentrated upon making administrative changes that have been based upon the following assumptions: [6]

1. Authority and responsibility should be concentrated in the chief executive officer by placing the heads of agencies under his authority and subject to his appointment, removal, and control. This was perhaps the most basic assumption and proved to be, especially outside of cities, the most difficult to achieve. Interest groups wishing to dominate the governmental administration of their interests have feared, probably with justification, that executive unity would increase the executive's power at the expense of their own. In cities, the dominant groups were more unified than at the county or state levels, and they wanted what they considered businesslike efficiency. As a result, strong mayors and city managers, generally, were given wide (but rarely complete) administrative powers, but governors were not; and counties remained without a chief executive of any kind.

2. Related functions should be integrated into single departments and the number of departments should be few enough to permit the executive to require direct accountability from the department head. Reformers complained that there were often many agencies performing functions in the same general field with little coordination, effective planning, or responsibility.

3. Boards and commissions might effectively be used for advisory, but not for administrative, purposes. Boards sometimes serve as quasi-legislative or quasi-judicial bodies; that is, they act much as legislative or judicial bodies.

[5] Roscoe C. Martin, **The Cities and the Federal System,** Atherton Press, New York, 1965, chap. 3.
[6] Arthur E. Buck, **The Reorganization of State Governments in the United States,** Columbia University Press, New York, 1938, gives a complete statement of the orthodox view.

This type of activity arose, for example, in the case of public-service commissions which had to establish rates for public utilities and was considered acceptable. In most states, and in weak-mayor cities, these boards were and still are common devices for administration. As an indication of the extent of their use, the "Little Hoover" commissions found about seventy of them in Nevada and fifty in Mississippi.

4. Budget control should be centralized under the direction of the chief executive with auditing under the legislative body. Some characteristics of the executive budget were discussed in Chapters 8 and 10. This administrative device has had widespread acceptance in principle and has had perhaps the greatest effect of any single development upon executive control over agencies. Budget staffs, in the larger jurisdictions at least, have become the general management arm of the chief executive, not only reviewing the budget estimates of the agencies, but also aiding in coordinating their activities. Budget offices have become important agencies for administrative supervision, though they generally have only a limited amount of control over expenditures by the departments. They apportion funds over the fiscal year and exercise certain minor controls, but they are not usually in a legal or political position to claim sweeping jurisdiction over detailed expenditures. The check-and-balance tradition has been maintained through the establishment of an independent audit —independent, that is, of the executive branch.

5. The staff services of administration should be coordinated, usually through central agencies, to serve all of the operating departments. This "principle" has received more acceptance than the others. The reason is to be found in the fact that the centralizing of housekeeping functions has been thought to be a means of saving money without the loss of policy control by the interest groups watching over the individual agency. As a result there has been a strong trend toward the central purchasing of materials and supplies (large-volume buying brings lower prices); the operation of central warehouses, records archives, motor pools, and mailing and telephone services; and the central maintenance of buildings and grounds. Personnel recruitment has also been centralized to a considerable degree.

6. An executive cabinet should be established as a device for the coordination of governmental agencies. Cabinet members should be appointed by the chief executive, rather than elected, so that he may hold them responsible for their acts.

Forces for Separatism   Many forces have discouraged reorganization, including the following:

1. Agencies prefer a maximum of autonomy. A department head feels that he will lose status if his agency becomes merely one of many bureaus in a larger department. He is likely to argue, often from conviction, that his agency is unique both as to function and to the process by which it performs its service. He may claim, with interest-group representatives shouting "amen" in the background, that the integration of his agency with another will result in a lower level of service to its clientele groups.

2. A strong tradition exists for separate responsibility to the electorate for many functions of government. Generally the public prefers to elect an officer who has traditionally been elected, even when the functions of the officer are obscure. Many voters believe that direct election is more democratic than appointment by the chief executive. Party leaders like to have several elective offices on the ballot, since this enables them to develop a slate with widespread racial-ethnic or geographic appeal.

3. The cleanup campaigns that follow scandals often result in recommendations that encourage separatism. The usual suggestion is that the tainted function should be separated from the rest of government, given autonomous status, and "taken out of politics."

4. Clientele and interest groups normally prefer to have the function of their special concern separated from the rest of government. This preference also encourages the use of separate or "dedicated" funds. Sportsmen prefer a small agency for fish and game to a vast agency including conservation, agriculture, and economic-development functions. Their interest groups can more easily dominate policy under the former structure, while the department head or the governor is more likely to do so under the latter. Temperance groups will similarly prefer to have education on the dangers of alcoholism handled by a separate agency rather than to have it a part of the department of public health where its program might receive a lower priority and be less subjected to temperance-group direction (and perhaps more to influence by the medical profession). Citizens are often in favor of the principle of "improved administration" but opposed to specific proposals that would alter the existing pattern of operation of governmental functions in which they have interests.

5. Professional groups prefer separate organization for the functions that they regard as being a part of their profession. These groups have "organized bodies of knowledge, generally available only to members; group standards of training and performance; codes of ethical conduct; and, particularly, close group ties and associations." [7] Under these circumstances, they believe that their goals, procedures, and knowledge can best be organized to benefit their clientele groups if their function is not commingled with others. Librarians do not want libraries to be administered by the education department; lawyers do not want their profession controlled by a state agency that licenses and examines all professional persons; penologists do not want their function administered by the same agency that handles social welfare or mental health.

6. The strings attached to Federal grants-in-aid encourage a link between Federal and state administrators of functions, but they discourage the association of various state programs into a single agency. In some cases, Federal grant conditions require the establishment of earmarked or dedicated funds, which in turn encourages separate organization.

7. Citizens and legislators often believe that certain special programs should be placed "above politics" and hence in a separate agency. This has been true of civil-rights agencies, liquor control, and education, among others.

[7] Willbern, op. cit., p. 116.

8. Legislators are reluctant to give greater power to the chief executive. Not only are they jealous of his glamour, political power, and policy leadership potential, but they often view him as the spokesman of the state's largest cities. Urban chief executives have been less subjected to this kind of suspicion, partly because councilmen in cities where the reform movement has been influential do not want to become involved in the details of administration and partly because of the widespread use of the council-manager plan, which keeps the manager always potentially subject to control by the council, since he is not an independent agent with a direct popular mandate.

9. Americans have generally been skeptical of strong administrative leaders and have been more concerned with specific functions than with the abstract principle of efficient, well-coordinated government in general. Many people from rural areas and small urban places are skeptical of turning over power to a governor who—to their detriment, they fear—will administer programs with a political eye on the large city vote. Other persons believe that governors are not usually elected on the basis of issues and that turning full administrative power over to the governor is uncomfortably akin to the signing of a blank check.

Separatism of agencies remains the rule in state and county government because of the diversity of interests and forces involved in the political arena. In cities, the dominant groups have generally preferred integration and, with some qualifications, have been able to achieve it through the strong-mayor and council-manager plans. Groups for separatism have seldom been strong enough to prevail.

The Arguments for Integration   Persons supporting reorganization movements have used two principal arguments to support their cause: that integration will produce coordinated governmental activities and that responsibility to the public will be increased. It is sometimes held that there is really not much to coordinate in government. How much coordination, it is asked, is needed between those who work in the departments of highways and public health? The concept of coordination, it is held by others, goes beyond this, however. It involves more than the bringing about of cooperation between, say the psychiatric social workers in the public-welfare department and the psychiatric social workers in the adult mental-health clinic of the public-health department or the juvenile section of the probate court. Coordination also makes possible the economies of joint housekeeping activities and of the balancing off, in the executive budget, of the relative priorities of various functions of government. The chief executive is the only feasible person available to perform the role of coordinator.

The argument on responsibility is based upon the assumption that there should be but a single legitimate source of authority, the chief executive, and that his lieutenants should receive their authority from him. If this is the case, authority and accountability are equal to one another. Authority cannot be exercised, in the words of the Hoover Commission, unless there is a "clear line of command from the top to the bottom and a return line of responsibility and accountability from the bottom to the top." [8]

Government, its services, and its many clientele groups are all too complicated for a simple, single line of responsibility, of course. Most of those who would reorganize government recognize this, but they argue that "a general responsibility to the general public interest may be better achieved through the main line of political responsibility, focused on the legislature and the governor, than through the limited, specific, hidden responsibilities involved in some of the other relationships." Government, it is held, becomes more visible, and hence more subject to public scrutiny, if there is a single elective officer, the chief executive, to be held accountable.

The Middle Ground   Once again, it is necessary to remember that things are never completely black or white in politics. Total integration is probably never possible, and not even the most enthusiastic reorganizer could argue that separatism is the equivalent of anarchy. As York Willbern has said: [9]

Separatism and integration are not opposites without middle ground. Neither is ever absolute. Even with an agency that appears completely independent, the governor may have much influence simply because he has produced a majority of the popular votes, has influence with the legislature, and has public prestige and constitutional responsibilities. And even in an agency over which the governor appears to have complete control, the influence of a special clientele, of the group connections and thought habits of employees, of interested legislators and legislative committees, and of intergovernmental relationships all will be of incalculable importance. Agencies will be grouped all along the spectrum from nearly complete independence to nearly complete subordination to central political control. . . .

The precise details of agency organization differ according to such things as historical accident, the wants and needs of the clientele of a particular agency, the desires of interested groups, and the personal idiosyncrasies of transient administrators, chief executives, and legislators. Because differing points of view are often held by the various interested parties, questions as to whether an agency will be headed by a board or by a single administrator, the manner in which board appointments, if any, are to be made, who is to be represented on the board, the internal structure of the agency, and other such considerations are a matter, not so much of deliberate planning, as of negotiation among the interested parties.[10] The politics of the organization of an agency, in other words, follows the same pattern as that by which the policies of the agency are determined.

Decision makers in government as well as elsewhere have been urged, at least since the time of the scientific management movement of more than fifty years ago, to make decisions more systematically and to make greater use

[8] Quoted in *ibid.*, p. 120.
[9] *Ibid.*, p. 121.
[10] On this point, see Robert A. Dahl and Charles E. Lindblom, **Politics, Economics and Welfare,** Harper & Row, Publishers, Incorporated, New York, 1953.

of data. To some extent, the coming of the computer, which can calculate at such incredible speeds that it can deliver in seconds or minutes data that might otherwise take years to gather, has added to the emphasis upon more scientific decision making. The administrator must, however, always combine factual information with ethical values in making decisions.[11] When those decisions are complex, the administrator has neither the time, the information, nor the resources to make the decision highly scientific in character. He does, of course, make use of such data as are available when the decision must be made, but beyond that he counts on "muddling through." In a famous essay by the economist, Charles E. Lindblom, the process is described as follows: [12]

The administrator focuses his attention on marginal or incremental values. Whether he is aware of it or not, he does find general formulations of objectives very helpful and in fact makes specific marginal or incremental comparisons. Two policies, X and Y, confront him. Both promise the same degree of attainment of objectives a, b, c, d, and e. But X promises him somewhat more of f than does Y, while Y promises him somewhat more of g than does X. In choosing between them, he is in fact offered the alternatives of a marginal or incremental amount of f at the expense of a marginal or incremental amount of g. The only values that are relevant to his choice are these increments by which the two policies differ; and, when he finally chooses between the two marginal values, he does so by making a choice between policies.

The American art of "muddling through" carries with it a number of advantages to democracy, as Americans see it. It helps to prevent control of our political system by subject-matter experts, by giving nonprofessional values a chance to be heard and considered in the legislative branch of government. It helps preserve access to government by the ordinary citizen and to assure that his uninformed opinion may have some influence upon decisions affecting public policy. But our chronic tendency to take the short view and let tomorrow take care of itself is a luxury that probably can be afforded only in an enormously wealthy nation. Each year, it results in millions of dollars of waste. For example, although state highway departments know for years in advance the general route for a new highway, and probably know for a year or two the precise route, they are generally unable to prevent real-estate operators from building directly in the path of proposed highways, and this lack of influence is made more serious because of the unwillingness of legislatures to appropriate funds for purchase except immediately prior to time for construction. The result is that the state, instead of buying vacant fields, must pay the full value of new homes. This enormously increases the cost of a new highway, it inconveniences the often unsuspecting buyer who purchases a home which must be moved a year or a few years later, and it probably does not benefit financially either the home owner or the real-estate dealer, since the state need not pay more than the actual market value for land purchased. The social waste is enormous, but it is the cost of "muddling through."

[11] Herbert A. Simon, "Decision-making and Administrative Organization," **Public Administration Review**, 4:16–30, Winter, 1944.
[12] Charles E. Lindblom, "The Science of 'Muddling Through,' " *ibid.*, 19:79–88, Spring, 1959. Quotation from pp. 82–83.

Reorganization of government may be stimulated by the rise of new governmental functions, or by new ways of financing old ones. The increasing importance that cities, especially core cities in metropolitan areas, have placed upon urban renewal in the years since about 1955, has encouraged extensive shuffling of agencies. The objective, in such cases, is to organize government in such a way as to make easier some particular process, such as the renewal of cities, or to make a highly valued goal more likely to be achieved. In 1961, for example, Milwaukee established a Department of City Development. It placed under a single administrator public housing, redevelopment, planning, all real-estate functions, and the coordination of building codes enforcement. Where such reorganizations take place, the person who formerly headed the most important agency in the new coalition is frequently named the head of the new agency and that was true in Milwaukee, where the executive director of the Milwaukee Housing Authority was made executive director. About the same time, Boston created the Boston Redevelopment Authority, abolished the city planning board and put its functions under the new authority, enlarged the powers of the renewal administrators, and created the new post of Development Administrator. Syracuse created a Department of Urban Improvement, responsible for urban renewal, building code enforcement, and licensing. Syracuse chose to keep public housing and urban planning outside the new office, but the trend is to lump these together in order to increase the ability of related administrators to cooperate toward the major task of urban renewal.[13]

Administration and Ideology

Administration cannot be wholly scientific or neutral. It must be related to the prevailing ideology. The manner in which a social-welfare, prison, or educational system is administered will depend upon cultural values of the contemporary society. There is no "one best way" to care for people on welfare, for example. The level of assistance they get, whether the needs of children or of old people are emphasized, the amount of outside income that is permitted by overlooking the precise requirements of the law, the amount of training which social workers are expected to have, the philosophy of social workers toward society, government, and in particular, toward those at the lower end of the social scale—all of these things will be conditioned by the culture in which the program exists.

The Administrative Process   Administration is a part of the political process, not an activity fundamentally different from it. The determination of policy in the legislative body will at the same time inevitably involve questions of the means of carrying out policy. Similarly, the execution of policy always involves modification of the policy and its selective application to actual circumstances as they arise.

The degree of specialization of equipment, training of personnel, or types

[13] **Journal of Housing,** October, 1961, pp. 410–412.

of organizational structure employed in a governmental unit are important variables in determining the level and cost of services, no doubt, but the kinds of equipment used, the training expected of personnel, the organizational structure, and the level of service itself that exists in connection with a given governmental function are a result of a balancing off of public attitudes, the values of those who are involved in the decision making within the legislature and the administrative organization, and the expectations and goals of interested groups. It will probably never be possible to eliminate these political considerations and to replace them with objective criteria as to how an agency should be organized and operated.

Organization

State or local government agencies may be organized in a great variety of ways. Some of them are headed by an elective officer. Some have a single administrator appointed by and responsible to the chief executive. In other cases, the administrator may be chosen by the chief executive but may be removable only by a complicated process involving perhaps the civil service commission or the courts. In a fourth category are the agencies headed by boards or commissions. (The two terms mean the same.) Board members are usually appointed for long, staggered terms, and the chief executive may find members to be irremovable for practical purposes. When a board controls, an agency may be administered in a variety of ways. The chairman of the board may also serve as the chief administrator of the agency; the board may choose an executive secretary or a director, with its own powers reserved in law or practice to broad policy making; the commission may be advisory only, with the chief executive appointing the administrative head; but the most common arrangement has been for the board to divide up its work among its members, each exercising considerable autonomy. Each of these structures is likely to produce a different pattern of administration.

Organization and Ideology   Allowing always for some time lag, it seems probable that state administrative structures tend to reflect contemporary ideological concerns in society. In the period between 1915 and 1930, for example, the problem of road building was considered to be important by the common man, who could now afford an automobile. Highway agencies were established on a semiautonomous basis and the highway departments were generally given preferential treatment by legislators and governors. Today, because of their high rate of expenditures, highway departments are still important, but they have faded somewhat into the background. The emphasis is now likely to be on a separate department for the administration of matters related to civil rights.

Many governmental functions could be established in any one of a large number of departments. A current social problem, for example, is that of alcoholism. If this social problem were viewed principally as a matter of public health, it could be in a department of health; if the problem were seen primarily as one of educating people concerning the characteristics and dangers of alcoholism, it could be in a department of education; if it were viewed as principally a problem that occurs in poverty and broken homes, it might be in a department of welfare; or if it were seen as being principally a disease related to certain types of emotional difficulties, it might be in a department of mental health. Current ideology as well as scientific knowledge classifies it principally in the last category and, hence, the logical place for an alcoholism program might be argued to be that of a department of mental health.

The pattern of organizational structure also tends to shape to some degree the amount of emphasis that will be given a particular function by government. When functions are lumped together, they tend to lose some of their public visibility. Where a function of government operates under conditions involving substantial social consensus, this creates no particular political problem. On the other hand, the political leader who wants to increase public interest in and visibility of a particular function will tend to want to place that function in a separate agency.

The values, standards, and goals of various professions also have an influence upon the way a particular function of government is administered. As a result, the allocation of a function to a particular agency may have an important bearing upon the way in which that function is administered. For example, persons convicted under the criminal statutes are likely to be treated differently in a separate department of corrections if that department is dominated chiefly by the custodial values of the professional peace officer. On the other hand, rehabilitative programs are likely to be emphasized if prisons are under the control of a department of social welfare dominated by the professional values of social workers. Similarly, the prisoner who is extremely neurotic or psychotic will be treated differently if he is in an institution subject to the custodial values of the police rather than the rehabilitative values of professionals in the field of mental health.

The Choice of Organization: A Problem   It is difficult to determine the preferred organizational structure, or to determine the allocation of functions within agencies. For example, in the 1950s, many state officials became interested in the establishment of programs dealing with the problems of the aged. These problems cut across traditional department lines, for they deal with housing, welfare, health, employment, and many other things. How should the program be established in order to minimize conflict with existing programs and organizational patterns? What organizational pattern would best fit the needs of the aged and be most acceptable to their interest groups? The answer is not easy to find. A strong tendency exists, however, to establish new programs as separate organizations. This usually best suits the interests involved and seems to give the new program its best chance for survival.

Single Agency Head   As compared with other types of organizations, where an individual serves as head of an agency and is appointed by the governor, the agency programs are likely to be more diversified, more related to the overall balance of needs in the annual budget, less able to avoid cuts during an economy drive, more involved in the decisions that are important to the political future of the governor and his party, less dominated by a single-interest group, and more easily shaken out of bureaucratic lethargy by a chief executive who is necessarily concerned with public reactions to governmental programs.

Independent Head   When the head of an agency is independent of the chief executive because he is elected to office, because he cannot easily be removed, or because he is a civil servant, the agency is likely to develop a strong ingroup sense against the rest of the government, professional standards are likely to be the criteria used as the measuring stick in making decisions, and bureaucratic inertia, if it becomes very great, cannot easily be overcome because of the difficulty of exerting pressure from outside. The agency becomes largely insulated from ordinary controls, although it will usually have to seek to maintain good relations with the legislative body unless it can find some means of obtaining an independent budget. Agencies with independent heads may include state or city police, social-welfare, or public-health departments, although other examples also exist.

Boards and Commissions   The use of boards and commissions became widespread after the Civil War. This marked a transition from control of departments by legislative committees to control by the chief executive—a transition more nearly completed in cities than in other state or local units of government. It also reflected a desire to take government "out of politics." Boards were either bipartisan or, later, nonpartisan in structure, members were usually appointed for long and overlapping terms, and their removal from office was normally difficult.

Librarians, educators, and other professional people strongly favor independent boards over their departments. Powerful and vociferous groups often wish to take functions under their wings and protect them as infants that should not be exposed to the rigorous and competitive circumstances of the ordinary governmental agency. An attempt to make the agency autonomous almost always exists in the case of public health, public transportation, airports, parks and recreation, art galleries, and museums.

Boards and commissions seem inappropriate for the direct administration of any agency, and the tendency to organize in this fashion is declining. On the other hand, a board chairman, if he possesses administrative skill, can sometimes serve adequately as the agency head. It is not uncommon in agencies which have boards as policy-making bodies for most of the policies ultimately adopted to be generated within the bureaucracy of the agency and to be adopted by the commission. In some cases, as with the various examining boards which control qualification for licensure (e.g., boards of cosmetology, medicine, dentistry, law), the board views its principal job as being that of preserving orthodoxy and preventing the administrative head, who may be a layman, from doing something the profession would not approve of.

Many boards and commissions are established by law in such a way as to require interest-group representation upon them. In other cases, it is a firmly established custom for certain groups to be included in the membership. The idea of group representation seems antithetical to the traditional American skepticism about "the interests" and "special privilege," but it is very much in harmony with the concept of a pluralistic society that is a basic part of our culture and one which is accepted by most Americans.[14]

Characteristics of Boards   Boards and commissions as the operating heads of agencies have certain characteristics:

1. Like all committees, the board must find a position on any controversial issues that at least a majority of the members will agree to. This tends to discourage innovation, which can be significant especially in times of rapid social change. The lowest common denominator on a board is more likely to represent the *status quo* than anything else.

2. Boards are usually small, ordinarily having fewer than fifteen members and quite often fewer than ten. This produces a small-group situation in which persons who are members of the board are also members of a little informal club. The pressure, therefore, is for the group to seek unanimity rather than to make decisions by majority vote. This pattern, in turn, discourages innovation. As with city councils, which are also small-group organizations, the tendency is to allow the initiative to pass to the executive.

3. Sometimes the director of an agency prefers to pass along to the board politically sensitive problems that he would rather not settle himself. This means that the questions the board does receive for its own determination —that is, questions not accompanied by a recommended answer by the director—are likely to be difficult questions, ones on which the board members cannot make political gains.

4. Members of boards frequently see their role as passive, rather than active. That is, they do not believe it proper or perhaps even possible for them to initiate policy suggestions. They serve as judges in acting upon matters brought to them by the operating department head or director.

5. Sometimes the operating head or director will exploit factional differences on the board, thus giving him even greater personal control. The threat of such exploitation again tends to force the board members together and to try to find unanimity. This is not always possible, especially in cases where the board is made up of members of more than one political party.

An Evaluation of Boards   Millions of man-hours are probably spent in the United States each year by unpaid citizens serving on advisory and policy-controlling boards at the state and local levels of government. What do they accomplish? These were the findings of a study in Pennsylvania: [15]

1. Boards "study complex problems to which the elected body cannot devote enough time."

2. They insulate the legislative body and executive from certain types of political pressures. Since the members are (usually) nonelective, they can more easily do things that are thought necessary and desirable but which, in the short run at least, might be politically unpopular.

3. They do not "take politics out of important areas" of government.

[14] See Alfred de Grazia, **Public and Republic**, Alfred A. Knopf, Inc., New York, 1951.
[15] **Horizons**, 5:1, April, 1958.

4. The effectiveness of the boards depends upon the quality of the members "and not upon the advisory commission device itself."

5. They provide, especially at the local level, a great amount of staff work which, if paid for, would be very expensive. They, in other words, serve to socialize some of the cost of government.

6. Members perceive their jobs rather narrowly, tending to avoid performing a function about which they are in doubt. That is, they do not engage in "empire building."

7. Members often feel that they are not consulted frequently enough, that their advice is too freely ignored, and that they are not informed of the disposition made of their recommendations.

8. For things requiring decisive action and, outside of the work done by boards of adjustment, civil service commissions and planning commissions, the professional administrative staff of a department works more "efficiently" than can boards.

9. "Citizens' boards and commissions can still offer effective and useful aid to officials and the community."

10. State agencies for which the department head is elected or appointed by the governor tend to have a larger share of the state budget than do agencies headed by boards or commissions.[16]

The larger a city is, the more likely it is to use boards and commissions.[17] This is probably also generally true of other local units. State governments make wide use of them. At the state level and in weak-mayor cities, they are especially likely to have formal policy-making powers that exceed mere advisory status.

The reason for the existence of advisory boards in the structure of the more populous units of government stems from the old problem of citizens having less opportunity to know their officials personally when population density is high. There is, at the same time, less opportunity to participate directly in policy making. The citizens group serves in lieu of the direct consultation between officeholder and constituent that is typical in the small suburb or the rural township. It provides a measuring stick by which public reactions to programs can be gotten—and a more gentle stick it is than the one that may otherwise rap the politician's knuckles at the next election. A cross section of ideas and of opinion can be furnished to those whose political life depends upon a proper assessment of community attitudes.

Simple Structures   In small cities, towns, and townships, administrative structure is likely to be simple and rather informal. Elaborate departmentalization is not necessary. In such communities, the success of governmental operations may depend upon having two key administrators, one an "outside" man and the other an "inside" man. The former may have such a title as "director of public works" but may handle many matters including roads, parks, building

[16] Joseph A. Schlesinger, "The Politics of the Executive," in Herbert Jacob and Kenneth N. Vines (eds.), **Politics in the American States,** Little, Brown and Company, Boston, 1965, chap. 6.
[17] R. B. Richert, "How Michigan Cities Make Use of Lay Citizens in Government," **Michigan Municipal Review,** 26:33ff., February, 1953.

inspection, water supply, and planning. The latter may be called the "clerk" or perhaps the "director of finance" and may handle finance, personnel, purchasing, and routine office duties. Of course, the greater the population, the more that specialization is indicated.

The Importance of Professionals   In contemporary society: [18]

The more complex the governmental arrangements, the greater the influence and [importance] of governmental professionals, of experts, of career bureaucrats, whether within government or as staff members of interest groups. The more complicated the maze, the more expertness, the more experience, the more constant attention is required to thread a path through it. The involvement, for example, of several levels of government in public welfare programs or in urban renewal programs has helped produce a system of regulations and policies and understandings which can be negotiated only by professionals, or by those whose interests are so directly involved that they must invest the time and effort necessary to learn their way around.

The Concept of Adequate Standards

The political process would be much simpler if we had objective criteria for measuring adequate standards both of service and of performance levels in government. But we do not. These standards are culturally determined and as such vary over time and geographic location. The people of a small, rural county may not—probably do not—expect the civil servants in the courthouse to be selected by a merit system, and they probably do not expect them to have a great deal of training for their jobs. In most cases, public employees probably meet community expectations as to standards. Similarly, the level of services wanted or expected will vary according to the economic conditions, local value patterns, density of population, and other considerations.

Professional Standards   Because of their vested interest, professional organizations set standards for their areas of governmental activity. These standards are often spoken of as being "optimum"—a word that somehow has come to be used in newspaper editorials and political speeches as if it meant "minimum acceptable" instead of "best." Psychiatrists prescribe standards both for service levels and for administrative organization of mental hospitals; educators, for public schools; social workers, for public welfare; and so on. The goal is usually set so high that few governmental units can claim to meet them. Thus in the postwar era, public-health administrators established standards for a health unit that could operate effectively in furnishing primary services. Yet, in 1948 a survey showed that only forty-seven counties and seventeen cities in the entire United States met the standards.[19] The citizen might well wonder how realistic they were and what reasonable standards might be.

Politicians often use the optimal goals of professional organizations for

[18] York Willbern, **The Withering Away of the City,** University of Alabama Press, University, Ala., 1964, p. 218.
[19] National Health Assembly, **America's Health,** Harper & Row, Publishers, Incorporated, New York, 1949, p. 61.

their own political propaganda. So do nonelective administrators, who are often themselves members of such groups. Legislators frequently find it difficult to defend themselves if they do not provide a full program or meet the standards, since neither the politicians nor the public can judge the fairness of the criteria used or whether they provide for minimal or ultimate goals. Furthermore, of course, each professional organization deals only with goals in its own area of governmental service while the beleaguered legislator must balance off one such demand against another, and all of them against what the public seems willing to pay.

The Concept of the Public Interest

Theorists writing about administrative behavior have used a great many words in seeking to develop a notion of what would be accepted as the public interest in the decision-making process.[20] Public administrators are supposed by citizens to be serving the public broadly and not a minor portion of it. The typical citizen probably thinks that the duty of the government is to serve the public interest. He does not define it. Certainly he is not likely to view government, as political scientists tend to, as serving a large number of clientele groups rather than a single public at large.

Administrators themselves probably are not much interested in, or aware of, what philosophers say about the public interest. To the extent that they consider the concept consciously or subconsciously, their implicit assumptions concerning its nature seem to include such items as the following: [21]

1. The administrator tends to identify the public interest with the expectations of his professional peers. If he is a physician, a social work administrator, a school superintendent, or other professional person, he is likely to think that the standards established and the administrative methods approved by his profession are both right and in the public interest.

2. He tends to accept the expectations of his administrative superiors and to view them as representative of the public interest. This is the road to both convenience and security. It is a simple and effective rationalization.

3. He identifies his personal value system with the public interest through the process psychologists call "projection." His views quite surely are held by a large number of persons in the general public, but he has no way of knowing what proportion of the public. In any case, this approach minimizes personal psychological strain. Of course, an administrator is often called upon to do things that do not fit his personal values; in such cases, the more easily he can accept his superior's position as the public interest, the easier it is for him.

4. He tends to reach a decision—as do elective politicians—that will minimize interest-group pressures upon himself and his agency. It is not difficult to identify in one's mind the views of the most interested persons or

[20] A summary is provided in Glendon A. Schubert, Jr., " 'The Public Interest' in Administrative Decision-making," **American Political Science Review**, 51:346–368, June, 1957.
[21] Based upon the author's observations while serving as administrative assistant to the Governor of Michigan.

groups in relation to a particular policy or program with the general good. The tendency is in this respect to identify the public interest with the wishes of the interested publics.[22]

Red Tape

Red tape—strict adherence to the forms and routine of office—is to be found in private and public bureaucracies everywhere. In part, it is a result of the desire of the members of a large, impersonal organization to protect themselves by making sure that their actions are in accord with established policy. If in doubt, the safest course is to apply as literal an interpretation of the rules as is possible and to keep a written record of every move. One is less likely to get into trouble by doing so and it also provides a framework within which to make decisions.

In a democracy, officials must account to the people for governmental actions. This accounting may be clumsy and at times obscure, but the requirement that bureaucrats follow the law as closely as possible stems from the notion that government cannot do that which it is not authorized to do. Furthermore, Americans have never trusted their governments very far, and the state constitutions, statutes, and city charters have long been filled with minute detail designed to limit the freedom of action of administrators. The result is an increase in the amount of red tape.[23]

The Chief Executive

One scholar has seen the "most essential and characteristic functions" of the executive to be the following: First, he must make value judgments. He translates the overall mission of the organization into specific goals and redivides these, in turn, into immediate objectives and targets. He also decides what kinds of compromises are acceptable if compromises must be made. Second, he makes moral judgments. He shapes the organizational image, decides what the fundamental duties of the organization are and how its activities must relate to what society regards as right and legitimate. Third, he makes estimates about probability. He makes medium- to long-range plans concerning what the organization should be doing in what he thinks is the probable future. He makes estimates of how opinion will react to various possible developments and makes estimates of the capability of his own organization and of its members. Finally, he engages in long-range planning and the encouragement of innovation. He encourages the development of ideas concerning future courses of action and means of dealing with problems.[24]

The chief executive is important in the administrative process, not alone

[22] On this, see Avery Leiserson, **Administrative Regulation,** The University of Chicago Press, Chicago, 1942, p. 14.

[23] For more on bureaucracy, see Charles R. Adrian and Charles Press, **The American Political Process,** McGraw-Hill Book Company, New York, 1965, chap. 17.

[24] Edward C. Banfield, "The Training of the Executive," in Carl J. Friedrich and Seymour E. Harris, **Public Policy,** Graduate School of Public Administration, Harvard University, Cambridge, Mass., 1960, pp. 27–28.

because he may have the power to hire and fire department heads, but also because he is the coordinator of a variety of different programs and interests, the principal architect of policy, and the liaison between the agencies that provide services and the clientele groups that receive them. His role is so crucial that a portion of Chapter 10 is devoted to it.

The Department Head

Beneath the chief executive, but above middle management and the clerical and minor employees, is the principal administrator—the agency head or head of a large division. He plays a vital role in policy formulation because he is likely to know his particular governmental activity better than does the chief executive or the legislators. If he does not, he has easy access to those who do. He advises the chief executive who wants ideas on a program; he testifies before the legislative body or its committees, telling them what he wants them to know and often demonstrating great skill at withholding information unfavorable to his point of view.

The Agency Head as a Symbol   The agency head, like the chief executive and members of the legislative body, spends a great deal of time in symbolic activities. While matters requiring his decision pile up on his desk, he trudges from one meeting to another, often spending an afternoon in the governor's office, or in an interdepartmental meeting, or as an ex officio member of some board, or at a convention of a professional group with which his agency has important relations, making a comment here and there or perhaps a platitudinous speech of welcome. In this way his activities follow much the same pattern as do those of principal executives in large private corporations.

From a rational or "efficiency" point of view, this activity may seem enormously wasteful. Yet it is most important, for at the top level, the administrator (often he has worked his way up and knows the tasks of the lesser positions within his agency) leaves to trusted aides much of the actual work that goes out over his signature, and he spends most of his own time in molding the agency members into an effective working unit, reassuring them of their importance by expressing their values in public speeches and by awarding a pin to the clerk-stenographer of the motor pool who has just completed thirty years of service, and in seeking to maintain smooth relationships between the agency and its clientele groups, its interest-group support, the chief executive, the legislative body and potential friends and enemies of all kinds. His principal job is to understand and to communicate to others the values, loyalties, and goals of his organization.[25]

The informed citizen should understand, too, that in the process of seeking to placate their various publics, the personnel in the various departments often come into conflict with one another. They compete over budgetary matters and in seeking status in the community. Some department heads feud

[25] In this connection, see Philip Selznick, **Leadership in Administration,** Harper & Row, Publishers, Incorporated, New York, 1957.

publicly with other department heads—with resultant damage to all of government, since the citizen is likely to believe the worst that each official says about other officials.

Because the status and even the survival of a government agency may depend upon the way it is perceived by the public, large state and local agencies maintain their own public relations staffs. These may not often be large —the legislative body will generally see to that—but they are important.[26]

Bureaucracy and Democratic Government

The problem of bureaucracy in contemporary America is essentially this: citizens want many services from their governments, but the values of the culture imply that there is a danger of losing democratic control over policy making if professional bureaucracies grow large.

Not all citizens are in favor of the expansion in the size and number of governmental services that has taken place since the beginning of the Great Depression (1929). Probably no citizen favors having his governments furnish all of the service they do. But many citizens give support to each of the services. At the same time, regardless of whether a bureaucracy is developed and selected through merit system examinations or purely on the basis of patronage appointments, today's jobs are technical and complicated. They, by their nature, indicate the necessity for the use of qualified specialists. And qualified specialists do not speak lay language. The result is a desire for service, coupled with a popular suspicion of bureaucracy, and no little fear of the implications for democracy in its growth. People like the product of government; they do not like the means that seem necessary in order to deliver the product.

Bureaucracy as Antithesis   Keeping in mind the ideologies that have guided Americans in evaluating politics,[27] it is understandable that bureaucracy should come to be regarded as the antithesis of democracy. When the proponents of a professional bureaucracy, several decades ago, also gave support to the concept of integrated administrative control under the chief executive, they reinforced one popular fear with another. There has further been a tendency both in conventional wisdom and in some academic writing, to romanticize the representative character of legislative bodies, national, state, and local. Furthermore, this same combination of forces has been lined up at times in support of the idea that "whatever the people want is right, and they should have it." Hence, if the people want a chaotic pattern of government, it must be right; if they prefer amateur legislative opinion to that of professional bureaucratic opinion, the former must be better. These ideas are similar to Rousseau's romantic notion of the "general will" and is reflected in the Latin inscription found somewhere in most capitals, though usually beyond the ken of tourists and legislators alike: *vox populi, vox Dei*—the voice of the

[26] On the attitudes, role perceptions and problems of high level administrators, see C. H. Coates and R. J. Pellegrin, "Executives and Supervisors," **American Sociological Review**, 22:217–220, April, 1957.
[27] See Chap. 2.

people is the voice of God. The difficulty with this self-congratulatory notion is that the *vox populi* can be interpreted in a great many ways by legislators, bureaucrats, chief executives, and editors. And what seems to be the voice of the people today is viewed by those same people as a horrible mistake tomorrow. The legislator who must perforce take the short view and the bureaucrat who is sometimes permitted the luxury of the long view may both speak the voice of the people—if the problem is viewed from the vantage of the historian.

We may assume that it is difficult at times to turn the bureaucratic troops around or to divert their path, that red tape and literal interpretations of the rules are endemic to bureaucracy, that mature bureaucracies tend to resist innovation and lack initiative, and that trained specialists are sometimes impatient with unknowing laymen, without assuming that bureaucrats wish to destroy the system in which, as citizens, they too live.

One political scientist, pointing out that bureaucrats need not be anti-democratic tyrants, has put the matter this way: [28]

It is not by any means sure that the people think that what they want is the same as what [the legislative body] wants. . . . Given the system of parties and primaries, rural over-representation, seniority rule, interest-dominated committees, and all the devices that give potent minorities a disproportionate say, it should occasion no surprise if [the legislative body's] claim exclusively to voice what the people want be taken with reservations. Skepticism of the exclusiveness of the claim, however, is no warrant for denying the vital contribution of the representative legislature to the maintenance of constitutionalism. Without it bureaucratic absolutism would be well-nigh unavoidable.

If one rejects the view that election is the *sine qua non* of representation, the bureaucracy now has a very real claim to be considered much more representative of the American people in its composition than the [legislative body]. This is not merely the case with respect to the class structure of the country but, equally significantly, with respect to the learned groups, skills, economic interests, races, nationalities, and religions. The rich diversity that makes up the United States is better represented in its civil service than anywhere else.

Bureaucracy and Democracy The problems of bureaucracy in a modern society are more complex than the question of public acceptance of the bureaucrat or the problem of retaining democratic control over a bureaucracy. Some possibility exists that the bureaucratic system, in itself, contributes to contemporary personality problems and conflicts may exist between expected bureaucratic behavior and expected behavior of the individual as a citizen.

One study, for example, has found conflicts between the needs of mentally healthy individuals and the demands of formal organization. Mental health in our society is dependent in part upon relatively independent activity by the individual, and a certain creativeness by him. The culture, furthermore, urges him to make the fullest possible use of whatever abilities he has. But

[28] Norton E. Long, "Bureaucracy and Constitutionalism," **American Political Science Review,** 46:808–818, September, 1952. Quotation from pp. 813–814. Used by permission. Long was referring to the Federal bureaucracy, but his observations probably apply generally at the state and local levels, too.

at the lower echelons in a bureaucracy, the work situation calls for the individual to be dependent upon his supervisor, to passively accept orders, and to use few and relatively unimportant skills. The result of the incongruence between psychological needs (which, of course, vary with the individual) and social expectations on the one hand, and bureaucratic expectations on the other may result in feelings of frustration, failure, an emphasis on short-term considerations rather than broader organizational or social problems, and an internal sense of conflict. These characteristics, in turn, may cause the members in the lower reaches of the bureaucracy, and perhaps at any level, to come into conflict with one another, for as they attempt to advance they will find fewer positions available at each higher level and themselves in mutual competition. Hostility toward the supervisor, or "boss," may also develop and the individual may tend to focus upon only some small part of the function of the organization and never take an interest in the total operation.

In some, "this dilemma between individual needs and organization demands is a basic, continual problem imposing an eternal challenge to the leader. How is it possible to create an organization in which the individuals may obtain optimum expression and, simultaneously, in which the organization itself may obtain optimum satisfaction of its demands?" [29] Bureaucracy is essential in our society, but it poses problems both to the democratic system of government and to the emotional well-being of members of society.

Americans probably have reason to be on guard against an irresponsible autocratic, muscle-bound bureaucracy. But there is no evidence to indicate that the danger from this direction is any greater than is the danger from an irresponsible legislative body, an autocratic chief executive, or a muscle-bound court system. Each contains its dangers; each must in turn be watched.

SELECTED READINGS

Altshuler, Alan: **The Ancker Hospital Site Controversy,** The Bobbs-Merrill Company, Inc., Indianapolis, ICP no. 82, 1964.   (Problems involved in contradictory technical information reflecting different professional values—in this case medical administrators and urban planners.)

Appleby, Paul H.: **Big Democracy,** Alfred A. Knopf, Inc., New York, 1945.

————: **Morality and Administration in Democratic Government,** Louisiana State University Press, Baton Rouge, La., 1952.

————: **Policy and Administration,** University of Alabama Press, University, Ala., 1949.

Banfield, Edward C.: "The Decision-making Schema," **Public Administration,** 17: 278–285, Autumn, 1957.   (A criticism of Simon.)

Bart, Peter, and Milton Cummings, Jr.: **The Transfer of the Kansas State Civil Service Department,** The Bobbs-Merrill Company, Inc., Indianapolis, ICP no. 31, 1955. (Conflicting pressures involved when a civil service board is transferred from independent status to that of an agency within a department responsible to the governor.)

Bosworth, Karl A.: "The Politics of Management Improvement in the States," **American Political Science Review,** 47:84–99, March, 1953.

[29] Chris Argyris, "The Individual and Organization: Some Problems of Mutual Adjustment," **Administrative Science Quarterly,** 2:1–24, June, 1957. Quotation from p. 24.

Buck, Arthur E.: **The Reorganization of State Governments in the United States,** Columbia University Press, New York, 1938. (A statement of efficiency-and-economy values and goals.)

DeGrove, John: **The Florida Flood Control District,** The Bobbs-Merrill Company, Inc., Indianapolis, ICP no. 58, 1960. (Conflicts between executive officials and a governing board appointed for staggered terms by several governors.)

Earle, Chester B., and Valerie A. Earle: **The Promotion of Lem Merrill,** The Bobbs-Merrill Company, Inc., Indianapolis, ICP no. 20, 1960. (A study of a battle in which a city councilman sought to secure the promotion of a city employee to the position of Superintendent of Streets and Garbage.)

"Electronic Data Processing Systems for State and Local Governments," **SDC Magazine,** 7:entire issue, November, 1964.

Eliot, Thomas H.: **Reorganizing the Massachusetts Department of Conservation,** rev. ed., The Bobbs-Merrill Company, Inc., Indianapolis, ICP no. 14, 1960. (The politics of reorganization.)

Foss, Phillip O.: **Reorganization and Reassignment in the California Highway Patrol,** The Bobbs-Merrill Company, Inc., Indianapolis, ICP no. 75, 1962.

Gallagher, H. R.: "State Reorganization Surveys," **Public Administration Review,** 9:252–256, Autumn, 1949.

Gouldner, A. W.: "Red Tape as a Social Problem," in H. D. Stein and R. A. Cloward, **Social Perspectives on Behavior,** The Free Press of Glencoe, New York, 1957.

Graves, W. Brooke: "Some New Approaches to State Administrative Reorganization," **Western Political Quarterly,** 9:743–754, September, 1956.

Hyneman, Charles S.: **Bureaucracy in a Democracy,** Harper & Row, Publishers, Incorporated, New York, 1950.

Joiner, Charles A.: **Organizational Analysis: Political, Sociological and Administrative Processes of Local Government,** Institute for Community Development, Michigan State University, East Lansing, Mich., 1964. (The application of organization theory to local political systems.)

Kaufman, Herbert: "Emerging Conflicts in the Doctrines of Public Administration," **American Political Science Review,** 50:1057–1073, December, 1956.

————: **The New York City Health Centers,** rev. ed., The Bobbs-Merrill Company, Inc., Indianapolis, ICP no. 9, 1959. (Problems of organization within an agency, especially those of field agency organization.)

Leiserson, Avery: **Administrative Regulation,** The University of Chicago Press, Chicago, 1942.

Long, Norton E.: "Bureaucracy and Constitutionalism," **American Political Science Review,** 46:808–818, September, 1952.

Mosher, Frederick C.: **Reorganization of the California State Personnel Board,** rev. ed., The Bobbs-Merrill Company, Inc., Indianapolis, ICP no. 32, 1961.

Parkinson, C. Northcote: **Parkinson's Law and Other Studies in Administration,** Houghton Mifflin Company, Boston, 1957.

Presthus, Robert: **The Organizational Society,** Vintage Books, Inc., Random House, Inc., New York, 1965. (Studies the effects of large organizations on individual behavior and personality.)

Rich, Bennett M.: "Administrative Reorganization in New Jersey," **Public Administration Review,** 12:251–257, Autumn, 1952.

Sayre, Wallace S.: "Premises of Public Administration: Past and Emerging," **Public Administration Review,** 18:102–105, Spring, 1958.

Selznick, Philip: **Leadership in Administration,** Harper & Row, Publishers, Incorporated, New York, 1957. (Describes the function of top, as distinguished from middle, management.)

Sherwood, Frank P.: **A City Manager Tries to Fire His Police Chief,** The Bobbs-Merrill Company, Inc., Indianapolis, ICP no. 76, 1963. (Conflict in a southern California city. Emphasizes a conflict between management and police values.)

Simon, Herbert: **Administrative Behavior,** 2d ed., The Macmillan Company, New York, 1957.   (A major theoretical work.)

Stein, Harold (ed.): **Public Administration and Policy Development,** Harcourt, Brace & World, Inc., New York, 1952.   (Readings.)

Stout, Ronald M.: **The New York Farm Labor Camps, 1940–1946,** The Bobbs-Merrill Company, Inc., Indianapolis, ICP no. 12, 1953.   (The political agency head as innovator.)

Waldo, Dwight: **The Administrative State,** The Ronald Press Company, New York, 1948.   (Readings.)

————: **The Study of Public Administration,** Random House, Inc., New York, 1955.   (A brief introduction to the major schools of thought on the subject.)

Willbern, York: "Administration in State Governments," **The Forty-eight States: Their Tasks as Policy Makers and Administrators,** The American Assembly, Graduate School of Business, Columbia University, New York, 1955.

12

THE BUREAUCRACY

About one out of every eight employed persons in the United States is a civilian government worker. Despite newspaper editorials which create the impression that public employees are nearly all located within telescopic range of the top of the Washington Monument, most of them work for state or local governments. In fact, about 75 percent of them do. These people occupy positions which include virtually all of the occupations that also exist in private employment, and others besides. They are school teachers, firemen, chemists, dietitians, glass blowers, stenographers, film editors, and crime-laboratory technicians. They are a cross section of the American population, even though this fact may be disguised by gobbledygook which defines their jobs by such terms as Economic Research Assistant II, Property Appraisor III, Psychometrist I, or Child Therapist A-1.

Table 11   Government Civilian Employment and Payrolls, October, 1964

	NUMBER OF EMPLOYEES (THOUSANDS)	MONTHLY PAYROLL (MILLIONS OF DOLLARS)
Total	10,064	4,572
Federal (civilian)	2,528	$1,475
State and local	7,536	3,097
State	1,873	761
Local	5,663	2,336
Schools	3,674	1,604

SOURCE: Statistical Abstract of the United States, 1965.

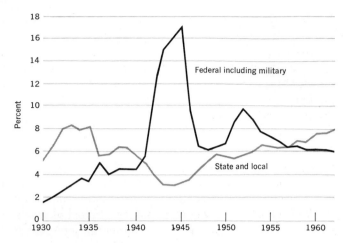

Fig. 12-1   State and Local Payrolls Continue to Increase.

As a percentage of personal income, California state and local government payrolls have increased faster than those of the Federal government since 1945.

SOURCE: Orville F. Poland, **Public Employment in California,** Institute of Governmental Studies, University of California, Berkeley, Calif., 1964.

In the sixteen years preceding October, 1962, Federal civilian employment increased by 4.3 percent, but local government employment increased by 87 percent. And state government employment during the same period increased by 209 percent. During this same postwar period, Federal civilian monthly payrolls increased by 236 percent, those of local governments by 435 percent, and those of state governments by 496 percent.[1] In other words, state governments are growing faster than other levels of government in the United States, and local governments trail behind them. The national government has expanded the least in the postwar period, so far as domestic programs and civilian employment are concerned.

Contemporary Personnel Practices

In 1940, there were about 3.3 million state and local government workers. By 1964, this figure had climbed to 7.5 million (though about 20 percent of these were part-time workers). Three-quarters of these were employed at the local level.

Efficiency and Status   It is difficult to make comparisons of efficiency as between local units or between states because the allocation of functions and the level of services performed fluctuates from one government to another. It does appear, however, that the highest ratio of public employees to population is to be found in states with low densities of population, including Nevada,

[1] U.S. Bureau of the Census, **Census of Governments,** 1960, 3, table 2.

Montana, Oregon, Vermont, and New Hampshire.[2] In these states, the sparseness of the population makes the operation of state government relatively expensive.

Increased state and local employment in the years after World War II is a result of many factors, some of which include rising standards in education, mental hygiene, conservation, state police, and other functions as well as in the introduction of new programs at both the state and local levels.

A great many people still believe, as they believed in the mid-1930s according to a survey and as Andrew Jackson believed well over a century ago, that government jobs are so "simple that men of intelligence may readily qualify themselves for their performance."[3] Of course, this is no longer the case. Government now performs a great many, rather than a few, functions. In the last century or so, the performance of most of man's activities has become specialized and mechanized. Governmental activities are no exception. Since the early twentieth century, government employment has become increasingly specialized and increasingly performed by professionally trained personnel with professional attitudes toward their work.

The typical citizen still has reservations about the worth of employment by government, but seems to be giving ground in recognition of the changing position of government in our society. The prestige value of government jobs has increased markedly since before the Great Depression, and this is especially true among working-class, lesser-educated persons, that is, among the persons most benefiting from the availability of governmental services and from the increased security that they provide.[4]

Patronage was a basis for building a strong political organization in the great city machines of the nineteenth and twentieth centuries, but it had its origins in rural America and is still important there.[5] In Indiana, for example: "Party machines in the poor farm lands of southern Indiana are oiled by patronage far more than their counterparts in the prosperous rural north and the industrial urban areas." In a major struggle for control of the Indiana Republican party, "the dynamic element in intra-party politicking in Indiana was not issues or ideology, but patronage."[6]

Civil Service and the Merit System   The term "civil service" refers to civilian employees of government. In practice it is often used interchangeably with "merit system." The latter properly refers to a method of choosing government employees on the basis of examinations demonstrating the technical or professional competence of the applicant. The beginnings of state and local civil

[2] U.S. Bureau of the Census, **1950 Census of Population: Detailed Characteristics for the 48 States,** table 79.
[3] See Commission of Inquiry on Public Service Personnel, **Better Government Personnel,** McGraw-Hill Book Company, New York, 1935, and Andrew Jackson's first message to Congress (1829).
[4] See Morris Janowitz and Deil Wright, "The Prestige of Public Employment: 1929 and 1954," **Public Administration Review,** 16:15–21, Winter, 1954.
[5] Roscoe C. Martin, **Grass Roots,** University of Alabama Press, University, Ala., 1957.
[6] Frank Munger, **The Struggle for Republican Leadership in Indiana, 1954,** McGraw-Hill Book Company, New York, 1960, Eagleton Institute Case no. 23, p. 28–29.

service based on the merit system appeared in 1884, but the principle did not become widely accepted until the 1930s. The national government, through its insistence upon professional competence of administrators for some programs receiving Federal grants-in-aid, prodded many cities and states along in this direction.

The Patronage-merit Dichotomy Since reformers began to campaign for a merit principle of hiring administered by a civil service commission, the American public has been bombarded with propaganda seeking to establish a dichotomy between the merit system and the patronage system of personnel administration. This painting of simple blacks and whites was originally an attention-getting device designed to help eliminate corrupt patronage practices. But the campaign, which played upon our well-rooted skepticism concerning government, was so successful that a great many Americans apparently believe that the friends of every politician are either thieves or idiots. The merit plan, furthermore, was in its early days always based on the control by a civil service commission of detailed examinations, promotions, dismissals, and other factors. This was thought necessary in order to prevent sabotage.

Today, an informal system of personnel administration may produce a competent civil service or a corrupt one, just as is the case with a formal system. Either may produce qualified persons with high or low morale. Conditions vary in government employment according to social and economic conditions and to the prevailing political value system.

Patronage and Quality About one-half of the states have no merit system except one applying to a few agencies, generally those where Federal grant programs make a merit system a condition of eligibility. Other states have merit systems for a considerable portion, but not all, of their employees. Several states have comprehensive merit systems, as do many cities and some urban counties. Few other local units do.

We find, for example, that the Texas state government [7]

is one of the great strongholds of the spoils system, which is open, unabashed, and unashamed. The best way to get a job in a state department or agency is to support the successful candidate or be a friend of a political ally of the appointing authority. . . .

Patronage in Utah involves, on the other hand, a system with a relatively low turnover of state employees and a genuine effort to get qualified personnel, though no formal merit system exists.[8]

This situation may well be typical. Except in times of high unemployment, the jobs of specialists may be difficult to fill because of low public salaries, and a new administration will be glad to keep those already employed. The

[7] Stuart A. MacCorkle and Dick Smith, **Texas Government,** 3d ed., McGraw-Hill Book Company, New York, 1956, p. 135.
[8] Frank H. Jonas and G. N. Jones, "J. Bracken Lee and the Public Service in Utah," **Western Political Quarterly,** 9:755–765, September, 1956.

same applies to positions occupied by persons with special skills or intimate knowledge of the operations of an agency. The unskilled positions are likely to be hard to fill, because unskilled workers can earn more in a factory than on a road gang or in sweeping out the courthouse or capitol.

In areas retaining a patronage system of personnel administration, it has been necessary to turn some positions over to technicians chosen on a merit basis, for competent people cannot otherwise be recruited for the complex jobs of contemporary government. The parallel existence of these two approaches to personnel is sometimes a confusing matter to observers. Hence, in Delaware: [9]

New Castle County is fortunate in having a hard core of very competent and loyal civil servants. This circumstance exists despite the almost rampant political patronage considerations which are widely acknowledged to be a principal, if not, indeed, the principal consideration in the recruitment, retention, promotion, and discipline of public personnel.

According to a study of the use of patronage in the administration of Governor Averell Harriman of New York, patronage was of little use as a means of winning voters. Few jobs existed in relation to voters to use it for this purpose. Harriman and his staff were, furthermore, interested in using patronage chiefly to satisfy party leaders rather than to reward party workers. The Governor appears to have been most interested in using patronage as an instrument for increasing his chances of putting into effect the policies he advocated in his program and of achieving a record of efficiency in government. Patronage was a relevant, but not an overwhelmingly important, factor in achieving these goals.[10]

Relatively few "fat jobs" exist, therefore, and patronage is more likely to consist of piecework assignments against which the merit system is no defense. For example, a county probate judge must often appoint appraisers for estates when an individual dies and leaves real property with no fixed market value. Appraisers' fees, which come from the estate, are set by the judge, and he appoints the appraisers. He may well appoint his friends. In fact, he may appoint members of the county board to do the job. There is nothing necessarily wrong with this. His friends may be competent appraisers. So may county board members. The "bcodle" aspects of such activities become evident when one considers that the extra income from such assignments may be considerable and the work may be conducted while the appraiser is supposed to be doing a public job for which he is already being paid. It is noteworthy that where the probate judge appoints members of the county board to these assignments, he may be appointing the men who also determine his own salary. This type of patronage is probably quite common; the kind that involves throwing out the current employees for the friends of the newly elected party or faction is probably much less common.

[9] Governor's Committee on Reorganization of the Government of New Castle County, **Report and Proposed Legislation,** State of Delaware, Dover, Del., 1964, p. 5.
[10] Daniel P. Moynihan and James Q. Wilson, "Patronage in New York State, 1955–1959," **American Political Science Review,** 58:286–301, June, 1964.

Patronage Systems in Practice   The dispensing of patronage is supposed to strengthen political parties and ensure a continued organization for the next campaign. Probably to some extent it does do this. But patronage is also a headache for the persons responsible for passing it out. They find either that they cannot fill jobs at prevailing pay rates or that the few really lucrative or attractive positions produce so many applicants that the governor or other responsible officer is likely to make one friend and twenty enemies. Competent persons must be found for the important jobs, or the party will be headed for difficulties.

In patronage-system states, someone in the governor's office is likely to act as chief personnel officer, but much of the responsibility for filling jobs is passed along to county chairmen. In some states, a representative of the governor is named in each county. He handles patronage and hears complaints which he sends along to the governor's office. This "man to see" is, in Kentucky, called the "administration man" and in West Virginia, the "state house man." [11] Usually he is the county chairman or a high-ranking county elective officer, but if the local organization is not of the same faction as the governor, some other individual may be chosen.

The Case of Pennsylvania   The largest state depending primarily upon the patronage system is Pennsylvania. When Governor George M. Leader took office in 1955, he found that he had 40,000 patronage jobs at his disposal. He controlled more positions than did the President. He also found that the task of filling the jobs was time-consuming and one that caused many problems. Partly for this reason, partly perhaps in order to prevent a recapture of many of the positions by Republicans if the state returned to its normal gubernatorial pattern (Republicans had controlled patronage for sixteen consecutive years before Leader), he urged that the state adopt a comprehensive merit system. This the Republican legislature refused to do, but the number of classified (merit system) employees was increased from 21.5 percent of the total to about 37 percent.[12] The number of agencies serviced was increased from eleven to thirty-five. Even so, the governor and his faction were left with an enormous number of jobs to fill.

How does this patronage, when it is distributed to the local area, affect a small, rural county of Pennsylvania? It accomplishes a number of purposes: [13]

It serves a limited function as a political reward and stimulus, particularly in the more desirable caretaker positions [foremen in the highway work forces within the county]. It serves also as an *ad hoc* merit system, whereby skilled and experienced men are recruited by superintendents and caretakers and then given even a semblance of tenure regardless of political changes. At another level the party simply runs an employment and recruitment agency, staffing the highway crews and trying

[11] John H. Fenton, **Politics in the Border States,** The Hauser Press, New Orleans, La., 1957, pp. 19–22, 87–88.

[12] R. D. Tive, "Pennsylvania Begins to Rejuvenate Its Civil Service," **Good Government,** 74:48–49, September–October, 1957.

[13] Frank J. Sorauf, "State Patronage in a Rural County," **American Political Science Review,** 50:1046–1056, December, 1956. Used by permission.

to keep them at full strength. Finally, patronage may gratify the egos of local party functionaries and supervisory highway employees by permitting them to dispense political largesse to friends and acquaintances in the community. What political strength the local party does gain from its appointments may, therefore, be partially offset by the need to attend to the non-political uses of patronage.

Merit System States   In sharp contrast to Pennsylvania is Michigan, which along with California, New York, New Jersey, Wisconsin, and a few other states has a comprehensive merit system. The civil service commission in Michigan is constitutionally independent. It can increase salaries of civil servants without consulting the governor or legislature and, in 1966, controlled 97.5 percent of all state jobs. Only four nonclassified positions are allowed in each department. Members of boards and commissions, legislative and judicial employees, and the staff and employees in higher education are the only other exemptions.

The overwhelming majority of Michigan state employees probably make no campaign contributions to either party, although they are permitted to do so. Opinion polls indicate that they are about evenly divided between the parties in voting habits. The civil service commission permits no overt political activity by employees—even though a highly politics-conscious governor appoints all of the commission members—and a sharp letter will go to any department head who allows a subordinate to transgress.

A highly competent bureaucracy has flourished under the Michigan system, though it cannot be said with certainty that the independent commission is responsible for creating it. Neither party appears to suffer from the lack of the promise of patronage that results, and the commission has been cooperative in permitting flexibility in reassigning persons at the higher positions when a change of administration takes place. The bureaucracy has, however, become a source of frustration to both the governor and legislators because of its independence, especially in regard to basic policy development and interpretation. The ability of the bureaucracy to remold a gubernatorial or legislative policy directive to suit its own values and purposes is impressive.[14]

Personnel Administration

The Civil Service Commission   The acts establishing civil service merit systems in 1883 (Federal) and 1884 (New York and Massachusetts) provided for a semi-independent civil service commission and began a pattern that is still typical. It is common to have a three-member civil service commission appointed (usually by the chief executive) for overlapping terms, not more than two of the members being of the same political party. An executive secretary is normally hired to handle the actual administration, and he may be highly influential in the determination of policies.

The commission makes rules respecting examinations, classifies positions,

14 In this connection, see York Willbern, "Professionalization in the Public Service: Too Little or Too Much?" **Public Administration Review,** 14:13–21, Winter, 1954.

administers service (quality-of-performance) rating plans, conducts examinations, and keeps a list of eligible appointees. In some states and communities it establishes uniform wages, hours, and conditions of labor (so that two clerks doing about the same job, but in different departments, will receive the same pay). It makes rules on transfers and promotions and may review cases involving the disciplining or dismissal of employees. It may, especially in larger systems, conduct training programs. It certifies the payrolls so as to discourage payroll padding. It may have other functions too.

The Personnel Director   In recent years, students of public administration have often criticized the use of the civil service commission to head personnel recruitment. It is argued that the commission competes with the chief executive for control over employees. The resultant conflict is thought to be harmful to administration and morale. Personnel control is now believed to be inherently a function of management and hence one to be handled as a part of the chief executive's office—as it is in patronage systems.

The commission system was probably necessary in the early days of civil service reform because the administrative branch of government was opposed to the merit principle. Today, however, a chief executive who wants to run a smooth, effective administration desires competent personnel. He dare not resort to spoilsmanship; if he tried to do so, he would in any case be detected immediately.

There is a trend, therefore, toward the establishment of a personnel department under a single head, the personnel director, who is responsible to the chief executive. (There may be an *advisory* civil service commission.) Personnel administration becomes an executive function and responsibility. This form of organization has been used most often in council-manager cities, where it began. It is more easily accepted in such cities than elsewhere, because the manager is himself a professional careerist.

The Merit System and the Culture   Many artificial safeguards have been established in the past in attempts to require use of the merit system. These have included the independent commission, elaborate rules concerning tenure and dismissal, detailed examinations, complex position classification systems, and the like. All are inadequate protection, and many devices exist for evasion of the merit principle if that is the officeholder's desire. Yet, the professional, career approach to personnel administration does work in many communities because it has become a part of the local political style. And in England, where there are no formal safeguards at all against making every appointment a political one, the system works very well indeed. The voters would not allow it to be otherwise.

The spirit, rather than the letter, of the merit system is the important thing. Many small and middle-sized local units of government cannot afford to employ professional personnel directors and staffs. The mayor, manager, clerk, or some other official may act as personnel officer. Yet in many communities that have no organized merit system existing policy is to get the best

available man for the job. It should also be remembered that the personnel
methods used in any community are not likely to be more modern in character
than are those used in private enterprise in that community and that the major
personnel problem in state and local government is likely to be, not spoils, but
low pay, particularly in smaller communities.[15]

Position Classification   In the establishment of a merit system of civil service,
the various jobs are categorized. Position classification consists of determining the duties and responsibilities of each individual job, whether occupied
or vacant, and the assignment of that position to a class together with other
positions of similar or related duties and responsibilities. Thus positions may
be classified, for example, as junior clerk-typist, senior budget analyst, patrol-
man, chauffeur, or personnel director. Accurate and meaningful classification
of positions is a technical and difficult job and can be done properly only by
persons with training in personnel-administration techniques. Furthermore, we
now know that it cannot be done in so scientific a fashion as was once hoped
and believed.

Once the duties of each position have been described, the number and
type of classes needed are determined, classes are given descriptive titles, and
positions are assigned to classes. This last activity may create a good deal of
controversy. Since it is a part of a supervisor's duty to look after the welfare
of his subordinates, a bureau chief may well engage in a bitter controversy
with the personnel agency over whether his best stenographer fits the job
description of junior stenographer or senior stenographer.

Although a position-classification plan may be considered red tape by the
general public and governmental employees alike, it performs many useful
functions. Classification raises employee morale by standardizing job titles.
Employees in the public-works department who are referred to on the payroll
as "bookkeepers" are not happy if persons doing the same job in the department of water supply are called "accountants." Morale drops if the mayor lists
his favorite stenographer as an "office manager." Classification of positions
prevents this sort of thing.

Classification permits the use of a uniform pay plan so that all persons
doing approximately the same work receive the same pay. In an earlier day,
the pay of employees depended largely upon the ability of the department
head as a lobbyist before the chief executive, the controller, or the legislative
body. Even today, of course, much pressure may be brought to bear against
standardization of salaries, and legislators may refuse to base salaries upon
the position classifications established by the personnel agency. Established
procedure, however, calls for the coordination of classifications and salary
scales.

If salaries are standardized, classification permits periodic uniform pay
raises. These may be based on the employee's increased value and faithful
service over a period of time or on his receiving additional training. Often,
however, they are based almost entirely on the length of employment. Since

[15] On rural personnel administration, see Martin, *op. cit.*, pp. 33–41.

the opportunities for promotion are necessarily limited, it is important to the morale of employees that they may be advanced in pay up to a maximum limit while continuing to perform the same type of duties. Such a policy may be systematically incorporated into a classification plan.

Classification allows for the transfer of employees among departments on the basis of their job descriptions. It simplifies recruitment, since a single standard examination may be given for a class, even though many positions in that class are to be filled.[16]

Types of Examinations   Unlike the civil service examinations in most other countries, those in the United States tend to be specific, technical, and designed to test a person for a single position. The practice of the national government in this regard has been copied by most of the cities and states. In recent years, however, there has been somewhat of a change in the type of examination used. Newer ones follow some of the elements of the British system and some taken from American business practices. Education is given more importance. So is the record of previous employment. Intelligence tests and adaptability or aptitude tests are used to a greater extent, as are personal interviews to determine personality traits.

The Requirement of Local Residence   Except for teachers and city managers, it is a common rule established by state law, city charters, or civil service commissions that employees must reside within the boundaries of the employing governmental unit. This rule is an anomaly in a contemporary personnel system. It is based upon a spoils, rather than a merit, concept. The old idea held that government jobs should be reserved for local people. The present-day need for qualified persons is creating increasing pressure to waive residence requirements in recruiting persons for positions requiring technical and administrative training and experience. Yet, the old view remains powerful. In 1957, for example, Ohio voters turned down a proposal to waive the residential requirement for state employees.

Pay Scales and Politics

Salaries in Public Employment   The total monthly payroll for state and local governments in 1957 averaged about $1,615 million or around 45 percent of their budgets. Obviously wage and salary levels are major factors in determining government costs. Their relative burden differs, however, by type of governmental unit.

The lesser-skilled and unskilled employees in large cities and states receive pay that tends to run somewhat above the average for comparable private employment. In smaller cities, rural counties and townships, and many states, pay is likely to be no better or less than private employment, although there is considerable variation. The higher pay in larger cities probably reflects the

---

[16] Ismar Baruch, **Position-classification in the Public Service**, Civil Service Assembly, Chicago, 1942, is a standard reference.

generally higher cost-of-living in those areas, as well as the trend toward the organization of public employees into trade unions and employee associations for collective bargaining. At least some employees in all of the largest cities in the United States are members of labor unions. The smaller the city, the less likely the employees are to be organized; but four out of five cities even in the 25,000 to 50,000 class have employees belonging to unions.[17] In small cities, in rural areas, and in predominantly rural states, employee organizations are less common because trade unions are not an established social institution as they are in cities. Whether trade unions exist or not, however, the sheer numbers of governmental employees, their families, relatives, and friends are enough to exert considerable pressure upon legislative bodies to provide pay scales at a high level.

Salaries at the lower levels tend to be fairly good, but pay for top government technicians and administrators is usually below the average paid similar employees in private industry. There is no labor union to protect the salaries of the county attorney or the chief engineer at the city power station. Furthermore, persons in positions like these have, because of fewer numbers, far less political influence in getting pay increases.

When the rank-and-file workers in the mass transit or public-works departments of a city ask for a raise, councilmen will consider the possible repercussions in the next election if they are refused. No such fears need sway the councilmen when it is suggested that $9,000 is an inadequate salary for the city attorney in a city of 150,000 people. Quite to the contrary, the Jacksonian tradition lends public support in opposition to an increase. Since the average citizen is making less than the present salary of the attorney, psychologically he is unsympathetic to arguments for an increase. A suggestion of $12,000 or more as being a necessary salary to get an able man will be greeted with jeers, for even today that is an income beyond the aspirations of the average citizen. Councilmen and other legislators can thus make friends by refusing a raise to chief administrators and technicians. In the years after World War II, however, there has been a trend toward paying salaries at the higher levels that are equal to those on private payrolls. The very top positions have not been included in this trend.

Salary is not, and never has been, the major determining factor in attracting professional people into governmental service. Although salaries have been increasing, those at the professional level are generally less than they are in private employment. In 1965, the mean *maximum* salary of a state director of an employment service was less than $13,000, or only about as much as a rookie baseball player or a slightly above-average insurance salesman receives. The typical maximum salary for a local office manager was $7,600, or only slightly more than would be paid for a clerical position not requiring a college degree. The director of child welfare in a typical state—a critically important position—was worth only $11,500. In general, the most urban states paid the highest salaries, while those of rural New England and

17 See the current **Municipal Year Book**, International City Managers' Association, Chicago, for the most recent data.

the states of the plateau region were the lowest paid. In other words, there seemed to be a definite relationship not only between ideology and salary, but also between ability to pay and salary.[18]

Retirement Provisions   In 1964, almost all of the 7.5 million employees of state and local governments enjoyed the advantage of a retirement system. Of these, about 1.4 million had only the protection of social security. Another 2.0 million were not under social security, but were covered by state and local retirement systems. The others were under both systems. Mobility of state and local employees was still severely hampered, however. Only eleven (22 percent) of the states had retirement systems on an integrated basis, so that an employee at a state, local, or school district level could move to another jurisdiction while preserving his full benefits under the retirement plan. About one-half of the states permitted no reciprocity when an individual moved from one governmental jurisdiction to another within the state.

School teachers enjoy more flexibility than do other governmental employees. About one-half of all teacher retirement systems permit transfer from one state to another through the purchase of credit in the state's system into which the individual moves. Although some efforts have been made to permit greater mobility of state and local employees without loss of retirement credits, most still lack privileges of transfer and this serves to reduce mobility among civil servants at these levels.

The Problem of Recruitment   In 1916, just after his election, Governor Frank O. Lowden was "so beset by place-seekers that he disliked to go to his office in Chicago or even to venture on the streets. His telephone rang almost continuously and his mail overflowed with envelopes made weighty by dozens of letters of endorsement attached to applications from working citizens anxious to render public service in well-paying positions." [19] This general situation continued through the Great Depression, but since that time, except during periods of relatively high unemployment, and despite some increase in the prestige of public employment, the recruitment of able personnel has become a major problem of both state and local governments.

It is difficult to get people to take the higher administrative positions in government because qualified persons can get higher paying and more prestigeful jobs elsewhere. If the top positions are unclassified and the chief executive is not of the same party or faction as the dominant group in the legislative body, as is not uncommon, pay may deliberately be kept low so as to embarrass the chief executive and reduce his patronage potential. Many conscientious citizens have allowed themselves to be persuaded by a mayor or governor to accept a public position at less than current income, only to be refused clearance for the post by an influential interest group or party organization on what he considers picayunish grounds. Or a person may be

[18] Salaries are available in the current **Municipal Year Book** and the **Book of the States.**
[19] William T. Hutchinson, **Lowden of Illinois,** The University of Chicago Press, Chicago, 1957, vol. 1, pp. 302–303.

cleared by the party or interest group only to be humiliated and bullied in a hearing before a senate or council committee when the appointment is submitted for approval. Publicity connected with such occurrences discourages the next citizen to be approached from accepting a position about which he already has misgivings and which would result in a loss of income for him.[20]

Governmental agencies at all levels have generally had difficulties in competing effectively with private business organizations. The national government has less difficulty than do governments at the state and local levels. It is likely that state governments have the most difficulty of all, yet the problems at the municipal level are severe and are likely to become greater in the future. The Municipal Manpower Commission, with a grant from the Ford Foundation, issued a report that included the following findings: [21]

First, the Commission noted there was a national shortage of administrative, professional, and technical personnel for local governments and that the rate of training was inadequate and would not close the gap. Secondly, it found that current personnel practices were not sufficiently designed or directed in recruiting and keeping competent persons in local government positions. Thirdly, it concluded that the selection, promotion, and disciplining of personnel was largely separated from control by the chief executive at the local level and that this was undesirable in terms of contemporary personnel practices in business.

In addition, the Commission concluded that recruitment, compensation, and career development practices in most local governments were insufficient to attract and retain the necessary number of specialized personnel. Finally, the report concluded that even today—without even considering the future—local government personnel in the professional and technical areas were unable to cope satisfactorily with metropolitan problems.

In general, state governments cannot attract civil servants equal to those of the Federal government. Local governments are usually in an even less favorable position. A study of professional personnel in New York City has indicated that professional, technical, and managerial personnel serve either because of their dedication to a particular program or to the city, or they are attracted by the factors that, in the stereotype, are a basis for criticism of government employees—that is, pensions, security, and fringe benefits.[22]

Yet, despite unfavorable factors, with the decline of spoilsmanship and the development of modern personnel policies, it has been increasingly possible to appeal to persons to make a lifetime career of government service, and the possibilities for successful recruitment have been aided by the adoption of retirement systems for state and local employees. Nearly all cities of over 10,000 and many other local units of government have such systems. Larger units may operate their own retirement machinery, but many belong to state-administered systems. Smaller units, in particular, are aided in maintaining solvency by being banded together with others in a state system. Most

[20] See Paul T. David and Ross Pollock, **Executives for Government,** The Brookings Institution, Washington, D.C., 1957, which deals with the Federal government, though the subject matter also applies to the larger state and local units.
[21] Municipal Manpower Commission, **Governmental Manpower for Tomorrow's Cities,** McGraw-Hill Book Company, New York, 1962.
[22] David T. Stanley and others, **Professional Personnel for the City of New York,** The Brookings Institution, Washington, D.C., 1963.

state and local employees are also eligible for coverage in the Federal Old Age and Survivor's Insurance Program (popularly called social security).

State and local governments are increasingly recruiting college graduates, not only for professional jobs, such as those of the lawyer, physician, engineer, social worker, and chemist, but also for administrative careers for which opportunities are becoming increasingly attractive. Good possibilities, in terms of pay and advancement, exist for example in the ever-growing number of council-manager cities. Not only is the manager normally a career person, but he usually has an administrative assistant, often fresh out of college; and if the community is large enough, it will also have line department headships to be filled by career administrators. The same is true in the budget, personnel, and planning offices. The largest states have generally followed the pattern of cities into career employment patterns, and the trend is toward an increasing number of them looking in this direction in preference to the use of patronage recruitment. Regular management-trainee programs are now to be found in many state and larger city governments as well as in some other local units. The complexity and expense of government alone today makes it necessary to look for qualified personnel with long tenure opportunities. Changing value patterns of society, however, also support this trend.

Concluding Statement   In recent decades, Americans have expected more and more services from government. As a result of this, the public employee has perforce become a technical specialist, skilled in his task. In order to obtain such persons for the public service, the elaborate art of modern personnel administration and management has been applied to governments. Public employment can no longer serve as a reward for faithful political effort. The similarities between public and private employment are greater than are the differences, and a discernible distinction, except for the quasi-military police and fire functions, is becoming increasingly harder to find.

SELECTED READINGS

Baruch, Ismar: **Position-classification in the Public Service,** Civil Service Assembly, Chicago, 1942.

Bell, James R., and Lynwood B. Steedman: **Personnel Problems in Converting to Automation,** The Bobbs-Merrill Company, Inc., Indianapolis, ICP no. 44, 1959. (Study of California Department of Employment—problems of transitions and of layoffs as result of automation.)

Gibb, Cecil A.: "Leadership," in Gardner Lindzey, **Handbook of Social Psychology,** Addison-Wesley Publishing Company, Inc., Reading, Mass., 1954, chap. 24.

Lowi, Theodore J.: **At the Pleasure of the Mayor,** The Free Press of Glencoe, New York, 1964.   (A study of patronage patterns in the city of New York over a sixty-year period.)

Municipal Manpower Commission: **Governmental Manpower for Tomorrow's Cities,** McGraw-Hill Book Company, New York, 1962. (Current personnel situation and future needs.)

Wager, Paul W. (ed.): **County Government Across the Nation,** The University of North Carolina Press, Chapel Hill, N.C., 1950.

See also bibliography for Chap. 11.

13

LEGISLATIVE ORGANIZATION AND FUNCTIONS

"A member of the legislature," said one who was serving in Oregon, "assumes reality in the eyes of a constituent when he does something which touches that constituent personally." [1] And because this is so, a legislator is given little room to strive for greatness, to look at the larger picture, or to apply broad general principles to the major issues of the day. Constituents do not expect their legislators to be statesmen, or geniuses, or authorities on the law. They do expect them to care for the little, individual problems that confront the citizen in his day-to-day living.

The legislative body at all levels from the state on down spends most of its time dealing with subjects that indirectly affect all people but directly are the interest of relatively few. Thus, when the legislator quoted above was first elected: [2]

I arrived at our new marble Capitol expecting to spend most of my time considering momentous issues—social security, taxes, conservation, civil liberties. Instead we have devoted long hours to the discussion of regulations for the labeling of eggs. We have argued about the alignment of irrigation ditches, the speed of motorboats on mountain lakes, the salaries of justices of the peace, and whether or not barbers and beauty parlor attendants should be high school graduates. For two days we wrangled about a bill specifying the proper scales for weighing logs and lumber.

None of these questions concerns large numbers of people. Yet each question concerns a few people vitally. Two or three poultry raisers told me that a change in the labeling of fresh and cold storage eggs would put them out of business. . . .

It is because most legislative bills do not concern many people directly and because they do concern a few vitally that the legislative climate is what

[1] Richard L. Neuberger, "I Go to the Legislature," **Survey Graphic**, 30:373ff., July, 1941.
[2] *Ibid.*, p. 374.

it is. This situation is, in fact, an important consideration in the determination of the caliber of legislative personnel, in the tendency of interest groups to bypass the legislature on the most important issues, in the general lack of policy leadership to be found among legislators, and in the general status level of legislatures as social institutions.

The legislative body, once viewed as the very symbol of representative democracy, has gradually lost status through the last century or so, as the judicial and executive branches have increased in importance. Publicity concerning malapportionment has probably further damaged the legislatures' images. In an attempt to improve its image, the California Legislature in 1965 authorized the production of a promotional film about the legislature, to be shown to service clubs, schools, and church groups.

This chapter will describe the general structure, organization, powers, and behavior patterns of legislatures and legislators. Concentration of attention will be at the state level, but other governing bodies will also be given consideration.

The Legislative Function

The modern function of the legislature in the governmental process, that of declaring and thus legitimatizing the law, is a relatively recent one in Western civilization. Traditionally, it belonged to the courts. The oldest functions of legislative bodies in our civilization are those of debate, criticism, modification, information, and investigation.

Development of Assemblies   To understand the trend in the use of legislative bodies as a part of the total process of policy making, it is necessary to place these institutions in their historical context. Representative assemblies originated in Europe about the thirteenth century out of the feudal obligation of vassals to provide counsel to the sovereign. At first, these early assemblymen served chiefly to petition the king and to enter formal complaints against him and his bureaucracy. Later, especially in England, they developed the right, on behalf of the influential classes, to give or withhold consent when the king proposed unusual expenditures or risky undertakings. Under the colonial-frontier influence, American legislative bodies, even before the War of Independence, began to develop a positive voice in decision making, although in most colonies the governor was very powerful. With the fall from favor of executives during that war, the new state legislatures became highly influential, as did city councils. The frontier influence of egalitarianism encouraged this trend and for much of the nineteenth century the governors and mayors tended to pass into eclipse as molders of policy. This same period was also the golden age of parliamentary power generally in the European democracies. Though they were powerful in policy making, early assemblies were, as a result of restricted suffrage along class lines, less representative than are American assemblies of today.

With the rise of a complicated, technological society and with the in-

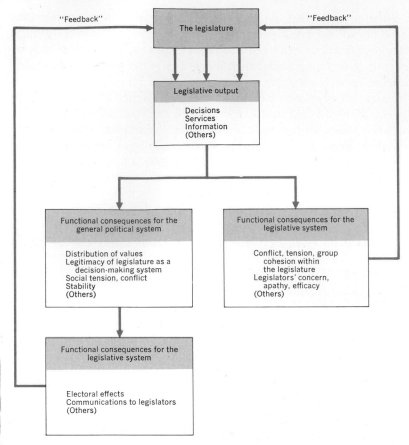

Fig. 13-1   The Legislative System.
SOURCE: John C. Wahlke and others, **The Legislative System,** John Wiley & Sons, Inc., New York, 1962.

crease in governmental functions that accompanied urbanization, the executive was turned to for policy leadership.[3] As a result, the popular assembly began to return to its historic function. But because Americans do not remember this agency in that role, there has been much criticism of executive "usurpation" and of the "bureaucracy's taking over." The essentially negative function of the legislature as a check upon the executive represents, then, the reestablishment of the traditional pattern rather than of the relegating of the legislature to a lesser role.

As this change in function has taken place, there has been an increasing expansion and exercise of the old power of investigation by the assembly. There has, however, also been some delay in the development of procedures by which the power of inquiry can be exercised in a responsible manner consistent with the liberty of individuals. The development of such procedures is

[3] See chap. 10.

a matter of prime importance to the legislatures of our time and its solution seems necessary for the preservation of effective democracy. The only democratic alternative, that of returning policy leadership to the assemblies, seems unrealistic. European history in the twentieth century is a continuous record of the failure of assemblies to develop procedures by which they might exercise a significant role in the process of government. The record is an ominous one, indicating the urgency attached to the need for working out a modern function of assemblies at all levels in the United States.

Legislatures and the Purse   The central struggle between modern legislatures and executives has been concerned with control over policies in the raising and spending of money, just as it was in the Middle Ages. As a logical and perhaps necessary part of the increasing power of the executive, fiscal policy making has shifted from the legislature to the executive, as was discussed in Chapter 10. As a result of the change, responsibility for the innovation of taxation and appropriation proposals is placed in the hands of the executive, with the legislative body serving to review them. This represents a return to medieval practice. A major task of the assembly, traditionally, was to approve or disapprove proposed executive fiscal policies.

By the mid-1960s, most states had some kind of executive budget, though in a few the legislature was attempting to retain control, and at the rural local level, relationships between members of the representative body and administrators are close enough for the former to retain many powers of direct oversight and of initiating policy.

In a few states and weak-mayor cities, there is a budget board with the chief executive as chairman, other members being from either the legislative body, other elective administrative posts, or both. In North Carolina, it is customary for the chief legislative committee heads to work with the governor's budget officer throughout the process of putting the budget together. In Texas, two budget bureaus exist, one headed by the governor's budget officer, the other being the Legislative Budget Board. Each prepares a document for public and legislative consideration. In most states, however, the proposed budget is that of the governor and his staff. The same pattern is generally found in council-manager and strong-mayor cities.

In the days of legislative supremacy, members of the tax, appropriation, and budget committees in each house made up the budget, working out differences among themselves on an informal basis. Today, these committees continue to work, dissecting the executive budget, listening to interest-group representatives and agency personnel, bringing to bear their own often considerable interest and store of information, and helping to center the spotlight of publicity upon the process that determines the public's tax load. The policy-making initiative has been lost by the representative assemblies and nothing is more indicative of this than the trend toward the executive budget. But through its actions in reviewing the tax and spending proposals of executives and administrators, of modifying them, and of withholding approval in many cases, the assemblies continue to perform an ancient function.

Representativeness

The Concept of Representation   Except for the limited use of the initiative and referendum,[4] modern democracy is of the representative type. It is therefore necessary to gain some idea of what is meant by representation. One authority has described it as "primarily a frame of mind, reflecting a process of social communication that often changes in important respects without disturbing the outward appearance of political institutions . . . it concerns the agreement prevailing between the ruler and ruled."[5]

Who represents the individual in the making of public policy? Possibly a person voted for a liberal governor of one party, a middle-of-the-road representative for the lower house of the legislature from another party, and a conservative member of the state senate from the governor's party. Can all of these represent him? Suppose that he belongs to a powerful labor union which lobbies for a particular program regarding state grants-in-aid to public schools but that his representatives on the local school board (for whom he voted) oppose this program, his church takes still another position, the governor (for whom he also voted) has a plan of his own, and his favorite digest-type magazine urges legislators to abandon grants-in-aid altogether. Just who is representing this individual's interests?[6]

Society and its government are able to operate because, although within each individual rests a degree of antagonism, conflict, and competition with every other individual, there is also a degree of common purpose. In relation to every other individual, therefore, a combination of shared interests and potential conflicts exists. The intensity of the relationship varies greatly among persons, and in modern society, each of us is handicapped because we do not know personally the others with whom we are in agreement or conflict. To make the situation even more complex, within each individual is a felt conflict between his specialized interests and his community interests.[7] His representatives—lobbyists and elected officials—must try to reflect both of these interests.

The idea of representation is a complicated one. The "problem of reconciling unity and diversity is always present"[8] in society and the success of democracy depends to a large extent upon providing adequate representation for the carrying out of the agenda where unity exists and in reconciling the conflicts where they exist.

---

[4] See chap. 6.
[5] Alfred de Grazia, **Public and Republic,** Alfred A. Knopf, Inc., New York, 1951, p. 3.
[6] Discussion of the relationship of the individual and the community to its public representation may be found in John Dewey, **The Public and Its Problems,** Holt, Rinehart and Winston, Inc., New York, 1927, and David Truman, **The Governmental Process,** Alfred A. Knopf, Inc., New York, 1951.
[7] Avery Leiserson, **Administration Regulation,** The University of Chicago Press, Chicago, 1942, p. 251.
[8] *Ibid.*

State Legislative Structure

States show their individuality in the varied nomenclature of their legislative bodies. What is called the Legislature in most states is called the General Assembly in several and is known by a variety of other terms, including the General Court in Massachusetts and New Hampshire. But in quite a few states, the term "assembly" applies to the lower house, which may also be called the House of Delegates or House of Representatives. In New Jersey, for example, the lower house is called the General Assembly, but in North Carolina this term refers to the entire legislature. The upper house is called the Senate—a symbol of prestige dearly loved by all who can claim membership in it.

Sizes of Legislative Bodies   There is no generally accepted basis for representation in American legislatures, and the size of each house seems to have depended originally upon expedient considerations at the time the constitution was drafted; and subsequent changes have depended upon similar factors whenever legislatures have been reapportioned. It is significant that a reapportionment is likely to result in an increase in the size of at least one house. The membership in the upper houses of legislatures varies from 17 in Delaware and Nevada to 67 in Minnesota. The lower houses have an even greater range: from 35 in Delaware to 400 in New Hampshire. The enormous size of the lower houses in New England, relative to population, results from the fact that the town is there used as the representative unit. Legislative houses tend to be quite small, commonly under 100 members, in the West.

Terms of Office   The term of office for legislators seems to be equally as haphazard as is the size of legislative bodies. Generally, members of the upper house enjoy a longer term than do their colleagues in the lower house. About two-thirds of the senates have four-year terms; the others are for two years. The overwhelming majority of lower houses have two-year terms. (Forty-five of forty-nine in 1965.) In some legislatures, the four-year terms are staggered so that part of the membership comes up for election every two years.

Prerequisites and Perquisites   Like governors, certain qualifications are usually required of legislators. They must be citizens, have resided in the state a certain length of time, have reached a certain age (senators usually have a higher minimum-age requirement than representatives), and be registered or eligible voters.

The pay for legislators at one time was small. The task of representing one's friends and neighbors was thought to be a patriotic duty. Seats were usually occupied, in pre-1850 America, either by well-to-do persons with a sense of social obligation (and a desire to protect their wealth) or by farmers who had a minimum of chores around the place after harvest and before spring planting. Social changes have since brought demands for higher pay for legislators, however. Working-class representatives can ill afford to become legislators unless the pay is good or they are paid by a trade union while attending sessions. Merchants can less well leave the shop today, given present competitive conditions. The general emphasis upon getting ahead makes legislative service a liability rather than a business asset for all but a few types of persons, such as members of the legal profession. Most lawyers, especially relatively young ones, find it good, ethical advertising to serve a few terms at the state capital. Similarly, some organization men are encouraged to seek legislative seats by their firm. Governor Sherman Adams of New Hampshire got his political start when he ran for the legislature at the behest of the quarrying firm that employed him. For generations, the Proctor family, which controlled the Vermont Marble Company, sent its sons to the legislature. Some firms have a policy of granting a leave of absence during sessions to any salaried employee who is elected to the legislature.

With the pressure for higher salaries, there has been a tendency to remove from state constitutions the severe restrictions on pay that once were common. Until after World War II, legislators were frequently limited to $3 or $4 a day, and the number of days this could be drawn was also limited. The argument was often presented that these rules made legislators easy victims of the old-fashioned lobbyist whose little black bag carried many tempting items such as bourbon whiskey and unmarked $20 bills. On the other hand, no evidence shows that increased pay has improved the caliber of legislators. It is true, however, that overt bribery has declined, but whether this is the result of better pay or of changing social conditions is not known. Salaries and allowances range from $5 a day in North Dakota and Rhode Island to $15,000 a year in New York. In addition to base pay, legislators may get extra compensation for special sessions and are commonly given travel allowances. Additional allowances are commonly made for stationery, postage, telephone, and "expenses."

Legislators in those states where they are constitutionally permitted to do so tend to raise their salaries and to vote themselves increased expense and travel allowances. Yet, some reformers have argued that the only way to "raise the quality" of a legislative body is to provide salaries that will attract persons from a higher income bracket, presumably, then, persons of higher quality. Both of these arguments probably miss the point. No evidence exists to indicate that increases in salaries produce any substantial effect upon the recruitment process, except perhaps to encourage more candidates to enter the primaries. The educational and occupational backgrounds of legislators do not appear to vary much according to salary paid. Furthermore, the question of quality—whatever that may mean—in a legislative body is probably a relatively unimportant one. The forces affecting legislative voting patterns are the same irrespective of the education of legislators. The strongest argument for raising legislative salaries is not related to quality or whether the legislator, indeed, earns more than he receives. Rather, it is that unless legislative salaries are increased from time to time, legislators will be reluctant to increase bureaucratic salaries. And it is in the area of competition for professional and technical personnel that state governments are most vulnerable.

In Texas, to use an example of the cost of being a legislator, members receive a maximum of $3,000 for a regular session. By one estimate the typical member can just meet his expenses at this figure, assuming that the campaign that resulted in his being elected cost him nothing and his business losses were zero. Neither assumption is, of course, often realistic.[9]

Sessions   After the corn was picked, Christmas reverently observed, and the New Year boisterously brought in, the squires of nineteenth-century rural America took off for the state capital, where they could, with reasonable convenience, remain until spring planting time. Beyond then, however, they would stay with great reluctance. In those simpler days, legislative sessions were brief.

The length of sessions is still constitutionally limited often to sixty or ninety days in some states, but the demands of contemporary government are such that, in practice, the work of the legislature can usually not be completed in so short a time. Several devices have been developed to circumvent the limitation. One used in Georgia and Minnesota, for example, is that of "covering the clock," thereby pretending that the legislators are not aware that the time limit has expired. In this fashion, it is possible to extend the session to an amount of time equal to that of the legal session plus the number of days the governor, who cannot, in practice, use this subterfuge, has to consider a bill before signing or vetoing it. Another device is to adjourn and go immediately into special session. In some states, the constitutions have been amended to extend the time limit or to do away with it.

Traditionally, regular sessions met in odd-numbered years only, but this pattern is changing along with the trend toward longer sessions. Quite a few states have formally amended their constitutions to provide for annual sessions. In others, even in such relatively sparsely populated states as Wyoming, annual sessions exist in fact because a special session is called for January of each even-numbered year. Only four state legislatures met annually in 1941. In the mid-1960s, more than twenty were, in practice, doing so. In some states, the governor alone can determine the subject matter that may be considered at a special session; in others, the rules of the legislature alone control this.

Bicameralism   Several colonial legislatures consisted of but one house, although most of them were bicameral. In the nineteenth century, however, the two-house system became universal in the United States, partly in imitation of the Federal government, partly because it permitted the constituencies to be divided according to two different methods. It fitted in well with the politician's constant desire to please everyone if possible, to strike a compromise. The chances are that representation under a two-house system will satisfy everyone somewhat, and this is more important politically than satisfying a relatively few completely. The usual pattern was, and remains, one of basing one house largely on area, the other largely on population.

9 Texas Legislative Council, **Compensation of Legislators and Frequency of Legislative Sessions,** State of Texas, Austin, Tex., 1956, chap. 3.

The fashion of the reform movement several decades ago called for the adoption of unicameral legislatures. It was argued that the two-house system allows for passing the buck, that it obscures responsibility for legislative decisions, that it encourages deadlocks, and that it offers an additional excuse for gerrymandering, since there will be efforts to find a basis other than population for representation in one house in order to help justify the existence of bicameralism.

Under the leadership of an outstanding reformer, Senator George Norris, Nebraska adopted unicameralism, and the plan went into effect there in 1937. In this one-party, overwhelmingly rural, socially homogeneous state, the plan appears to have worked satisfactorily.[10] There has been relatively little interest in it elsewhere, however, though it is still strongly supported by some reformers. Buck-passing, the obscuring of responsibility, and other alleged weaknesses in the bicameral system could easily be transferred to unicameralism by willful legislators. Reformers who look to structural change as a means for overcoming behavior patterns they find offensive give too little credit to the imaginativeness and creative ability of the American politician.

Legislative Organization and Procedure

State legislatures follow generally the organizational and procedural patterns of Congress. While there are some differences among the states as to detail, the basic pattern of decentralized policy making through the committee system is the characteristic one.

Presiding Officers   In the lower house, the speaker presides. He is, in form, elected by the entire membership. In practice the choice is normally made in a caucus of members of the majority party or faction. Sometimes the actual selection is made by a relatively few top leaders. The vote on the speakership is commonly a mere formality, but it is usually the one test of party loyalty that must not be failed. A legislator may defect on an important roll call later in the session without losing status as a party member. But if he does not support the party candidate for speaker, he will not get majority party assignments to committees and will probably not be invited to caucuses. In this sense, it is the key vote of the session.

The speaker may be a powerful member in his own right, or may simply serve as a satrap for the leadership group. In states having a lieutenant governor, that official presides over the senate. Since he is not a member of the body, he does not have a vote except sometimes in case of a tie. Furthermore, he usually has little influence over policy formulation, and this is true whether or not he is a member of the same party as the majority in the senate.[11] While the speaker of the lower house appoints the standing committees in most states, this power less often goes to the lieutenant governor in the

10 See Adam C. Breckenridge, **One House for Two,** Public Affairs Press, Washington, D.C., 1958.
11 Francis J. Coomes, "The Role of the Lieutenant Governor in the Legislative Process in the United States," unpublished master's thesis, Michigan State University, East Lansing, Mich., 1956.

senate. Rather, committees in the upper house are often named by a committee on committees which is normally made up of the most powerful members of the majority group in the senate.[12] When there is no lieutenant governor, the senate chooses its own presiding officer.

In many legislatures, two of the committees are often more important than the presiding officers. One is the committee on committees, mentioned above. The other is the rules committee. It is powerful, not because the permanent rules of a legislative body are changed very often, but because it is this group that can grant a bill a special order or special rule, thus giving it a privileged position on the calendar of the house. In the rush of bills toward the end of the session, sometimes the only way a bill can get before the house is through such action by the rules committee. This group, thus, may in practice be able to decide what is to be permitted to become law, a question that in theory belongs to the house as a whole. In some states it is traditional to permit only members of the majority party or faction to sit on the rules committee, thus permitting the inner circle to keep its tactical plans secret.

Other Officers and Employees   The various sergeants-at-arms, clerks, secretaries, and typists who make up the work force for the legislature hold posts that represent important patronage for the membership. The majority party or faction parcels these out, often on a rough geographic basis. They are commonly given to persons who cannot get jobs in the regular market, to retired people, and to the wives of needy party faithfuls. The doorkeeper is frequently an ex-legislator in need of a little extra income—the sense of fraternity in a legislative body is strong.

The importance of the positions that are usually viewed as being minor was indicated by a powerful California lobbyist, "Artie" Samish, who called the engrossing and enrolling clerk "the key figure in the Assembly." He pointed out that if it can be "arranged" for this obscure functionary to misspell a word or mislay a bill, an important measure can be killed in the rush late in the session or a stall can be effected which will give a group time to rally its forces.[13]

The Committee System   Because legislative houses are normally made up of a large number of persons and because the floor of such houses is not the most effective place for serious decision making or for political horse trading, American legislatures traditionally do most of their work through committees. The committee system seems to be necessary where the deliberative body is large, but the approach used in state legislatures has been widely criticized because the system obscures the nature of the work of the legislature, confuses responsibility to the public, and frequently allows a minority of the house (the committee majority) to determine policy. Standing committees, as in city and county governments where they are used, tend to take over administrative functions or at least to become involved in them.

[12] Details on legislative membership and organization may be found in the most recent volume of the **Book of the States,** published by The Council of State Governments, Chicago.
[13] See Lester Velie, "The Secret Boss of California," **Colliers,** Aug. 13 and Aug. 20, 1949.

The committee system in legislatures works basically the same as it does in Congress or in local governing bodies that use them (many small governing boards and councils do not). The legislative house as a whole becomes chiefly a ratifying body for the actions of the committees. Even if the house can override a committee recommendation or relieve the committee of further consideration of a bill, these things are not likely to happen, since each legislator —like each congressman—will tacitly agree to allow other legislators to be supreme in their committee areas if they will extend the same privilege to him. The committee is the key group in the legislature.

There are some advantages to the committee system. Legislative bodies, to provide adequately for representativeness, must be fairly large. If they are to get their work done, the committee system is a logical means by which to expedite the job. Members of committees often become specialists in their fields, knowing much more about a specific subject than does the average legislator. They may learn enough to make knowledgeable recommendations to their colleagues concerning programs and budgets.

The committee system provides a means of specialization of effort within the legislature. Similar policies of specialization are followed in the executive and judicial branches. In our complicated contemporary world, we should have to attract into the legislature persons of a high level of training and intelligence indeed to serve as general overseers of those who carry out policy. The committee system, therefore, permits the legislature to carry on one of its most vital democratic functions, that of criticism and review.

Seniority   Although it is not observed so rigidly in most legislatures as it is in Congress, the seniority system of assigning committee seats is important. Perhaps it is somewhat less observed because until recent decades legislative turnover was very high, but the idea of "wait your turn" is an important one in many of our social institutions, beginning with the play group, and it is common for ranking members to want, and to receive, the most desirable assignments. Committee chairmanships are often assigned exclusively on the basis of seniority, and it is frequently almost impossible to remove an incompetent from such a position if he outranks other party members in years of service.

There are usually a large number of committees in each house—they range from less than ten to more than sixty in various legislatures around the country. Exceptions to the general pattern are to be found in Connecticut, Maine, and Massachusetts, which depend wholly or partly upon joint committees, with membership from both houses sitting together. Although reform efforts in recent decades have aimed at reducing the number of committees so as to encourage more concentration on the important bills, legislators like the prestige of serving on many committees. Having a large number of committees is also convenient because it provides handy places into which to shunt new members as well as potentially influential members of the minority party or faction. Thus, committees were once so specialized in the Minnesota House of Representatives that there was a committee on binding twine and another on (railroad) sleeping cars. When Alfred E. Smith, a minority Democrat, was in his second year in the New York Legislature, he was appointed to two committees: one on banks and the other on public lands and forests. These assignments were not based on any consideration of his knowledge or talents. As Smith himself later said, "I had never been in a bank except to serve a jury notice and I had never seen a forest." [14] Being buried alive in this fashion is not necessarily fatal, however; six years later, Smith was chairman of the powerful ways and means committee which controls taxation, and in a few years more, he was governor of the state.

Party Organization and Discipline   No thorough study of the function of the political party in state legislatures has been made,[15] but it varies a great deal. An "Artie" Samish could quite easily achieve great power in California with its weak-party system,[16] but would find this much more difficult in New York, where party discipline in the legislature has been strong for decades.[17] In New York, the political party itself to a large extent finances legislative campaigns; in California, the candidate gets much of his support from interest-group representatives. Groups also pay directly into the party treasuries and hope thus to be influential, but the impact is likely to be weaker through this approach.

In Vermont, legislation results from the balancing off of interest groups or of negotiated compromises between them. There is no party line because, as in the Southern states and in some others elsewhere, nearly all the legislators are of the same party.[18] This stands in contrast to Connecticut, a state with a two-party system. Issues there tend to be divided along urban-rural or urban-suburban lines. Since most of the Democrats are from urban areas, and Republicans from suburban and rural areas, a natural cleavage is produced on many issues. Under these circumstances, party control is meaningful, and: [19]

As a final resort, party leaders in Connecticut will at times discipline legislators either because of factional shifts which cut the ground from under the individual or because of disloyalty to the party program. Discipline can extend to a denial of renomination for the General Assembly and, of course, denial of higher offices on the state level, but in more subtle ways it can make the individual very ill at ease while in the legislature, both through social pressures and through refusal to grant legislative time for pet projects which the legislator wants to enact for his home town.

[14] Emily Smith Warner, **The Happy Warrior,** Doubleday & Company, Inc., Garden City, N.Y., 1956, p. 52.
[15] See William J. Keefe, "Comparative Study of the Role of Political Parties in State Legislatures," **Western Political Quarterly,** 9:726–742, September, 1956, and his citations.
[16] Velie, *op. cit.*
[17] A. Lawrence Lowell, "The Influence of Party upon Legislature," **Annual Report of the American Historical Association for the Year 1901,** American Historical Association, New York, 1901, vol. 1, pp. 319–542; Warren Moscow, **Politics in the Empire State,** Alfred A. Knopf, Inc., New York, 1948.
[18] For a case study, see Oliver Garceau and Corinne Silverman, "A Pressure Group and the Pressured," **American Political Science Review,** 48:672–691, September, 1954. G. Y. Steiner, **Legislation by Collective Bargaining,** Institute of Labor and Industrial Relations, University of Illinois, Urbana, Ill., 1951, offers a case study of legislation involving compromises negotiated directly between interest groups.
[19] W. Duane Lockard, "Legislative Politics in Connecticut," **American Political Science Review,** 48:166–173, March, 1954. Quotation from p. 173. Used by permission.

Disciplinary action . . . remains a fearsome weapon and its ominous existence in the party armory is not easily forgotten.

This pattern of control is probably not to be found in many legislatures. In states with the one-party system, party caucuses would be meaningless, and the quasi nonpartisanship of the legislature in such states results in turn in encouraging parties to break up into factions.[20] In states with strong two-party systems, there is considerable voting along party lines, and the amount of this "appears to be significantly higher in those two-party states which are larger and more urban." [21] In the large, two-party, industrial states, "a high level of party voting in the legislature results from party alignments which have largely followed the liberal-conservative, urban-rural pattern of national politics."

In such states, however, each party tends to move toward a moderate position, and representatives from districts that are atypical of the party not infrequently show independence of party discipline.[22] Furthermore, a great many legislative roll calls are unanimous, and the number of cases of clear alignment of one party against another are relatively few. In one session of the Pennsylvania General Assembly, only 4.7 percent of the Senate roll calls and 10.7 percent of the House votes showed such alignment.[23]

The Formation of Law   The pattern of introduction, hearings, floor debate, and rules on passage varies somewhat from state to state, but in general it follows that used in Congress. Figure 13-2 outlines the passage of a bill according to the rules in Illinois. Bills may be drafted by the attorney general's office at the request of some state agency, or of the governor; they may be written by a lobbyist or by an attorney for an interest group; or they may be drawn up, in some states, by the legislative bill drafting service at the request of a member.

The number of bills introduced annually in each legislature and the trend in the number introduced seems to vary greatly from one state to another and probably depends not so much on the importance of the issues of public policy confronting state decision makers or their complexity as it does on differing political styles and formal rules. Before World War II, for example, more than eleven hundred bills were normally introduced in each session of the Kansas Legislature. Since 1947, the average has declined to only 883. In contrast, the number of bills introduced into the Illinois Legislature between 1943 and 1961 increased from 1,501 to 2,680. In both states, the percentage of bills passed in relation to the number introduced has increased. Between 1901 and 1947, only about 27 percent of the bills introduced in Kansas be-

[20] On this general point, see V. O. Key, Jr., "The Direct Primary and Party Structure: A Study of State Legislative Nominations," **American Political Science Review**, 48:1–26, March, 1954.
[21] Malcolm E. Jewell, "Party Voting in American State Legislatures," **American Political Science Review,** 49:773–791, September, 1955.
[22] Duncan Macrae, Jr., "The Relation Between Roll Call Votes and Constituencies in the Massachusetts House of Representatives," **American Political Science Review,** 46:1046–1055, December, 1952.
[23] William J. Keefe, "Parties, Partisanship, and Public Policy in the Pennsylvania Legislature," **American Political Science Review,** 48:450–464, June, 1954. See, also, by the same author, "Party Government and Lawmaking in the Illinois General Assembly," **Northwestern University Law Review,** 47:55–71, 1952; and Belle Zeller (ed.), **American State Legislatures,** Thomas Y. Crowell Company, New York, 1954.

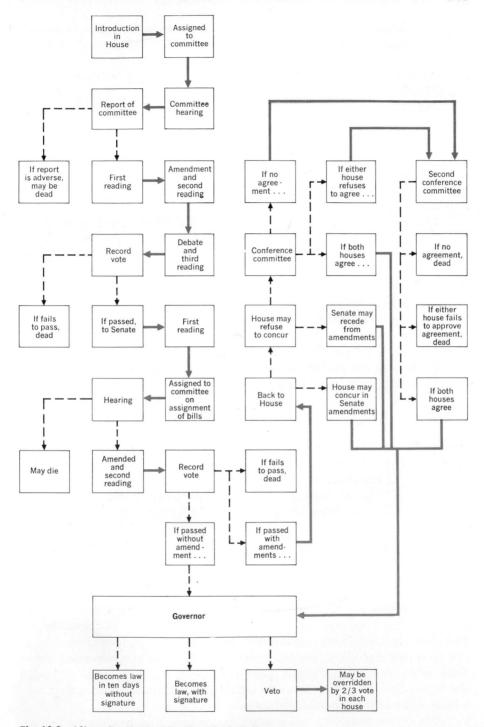

Fig. 13-2   Life or Death of a Bill: The Illinois Pattern.
Dotted lines indicate alternative possibilities.
SOURCE: Based on **Legislative Manual and Fiscal Facts: 1957,** Taxpayers' Federation of Illinois, Chicago, 1957.

came law. Since 1947, the average has been 55 percent of the total. In Illinois, the percentage increased from 41 percent in 1943 to 45 percent in 1961. Since 1947, the Kansas Legislature has adopted about 485 new laws each year. In Illinois, a much larger, more urbanized state, 1,205 bills became new law in 1961.[24]

The key to the fate of a bill may rest with the committee to which it is assigned. The presiding officer or the committee that has the power to decide which committee should receive the bill may sometimes by the decision made determine the fate of the measure. One committee chairman may view the bill with definite favor; another may be determined to kill it and may be influential enough to do so even though he believes the bill would pass if it reached the floor of the house.

Procedures as to public hearings vary from state to state and according to the assumed importance of a bill. In some states, the capitol has few hearing rooms adequate for public hearings. Sometimes, tradition does not support the demand for public hearings and few are held, even on matters of great moment.

If bills pass the two houses in even slightly different form, they must go to a conference committee which is usually made up of equal representation from the two houses, but the presiding officer or committee that has the power to decide who is to sit on the conference committee again is often in a position to expedite or to impede the passage of the bill. It is easy to stack the conference committee with friends or enemies of the bill. In some states, however, it is customary for the originating house to accept the amendments of the second house without holding a conference.

Once a bill is passed, some kind of waiting period commonly ensues before it goes into effect. For example, in New Mexico, laws go into effect ninety days after the adjournment of the legislature, except general appropriation bills, which go into effect as soon as approved by the governor or when passed over his veto. Any act "necessary for the preservation of the public peace, health, or safety" also takes immediate effect, providing that two-thirds of the members of each house agree to it.

In a sense, a new law still must go through a further process of refinement before it becomes binding as a part of the rules that control the actions of people. The legislature could not be specific enough in its language, even if it tried, to make the meaning of every part of the law completely clear. A new act must, therefore, often be "interpreted" by rulings of the attorney general which have the force and effect of law unless overruled by the courts. Important laws, especially if they venture into new areas of governmental activity or prescribe new procedures, are often tested finally in the supreme court of the state before their full meaning is clarified. Occasionally, a state law will go to the United States Supreme Court for interpretation if it seems to conflict with a Federal law or the Federal Constitution.

One of the problems facing state legislatures that has received much attention in the press has been the one that results when legislators attempt
[24] **Your Government,** Oct. 15, 1963.

to determine how to vote on issues raised in bills that are presented to them in a final, last-minute rush. Some kind of Parkinson's law has probably always applied to legislatures. That is, they tend to take up in talk the amount of time available, irrespective of the number or importance of issues before them. Then, in a desperate lurch to meet a constitutional deadline or one established by the leadership, they pass most of the major acts of a session in a short period of time. For example, during seven regular sessions of the Kansas Legislature, it passed, on the average, 41 percent of its legislation during the first *three months* of the session; and 59 percent during the last *three days.* Given the increasing complexity of issues facing legislatures and the increasing conflict in the political arena, it is perhaps understandable that most legislative sessions have grown longer. But the overall pattern has not changed. One observer, looking at the Kansas Legislature and its history in the twentieth century has noted: [25]

On the whole the Kansas legislature over the years reflects little obviously significant change in its work load patterns. Although sessions are getting longer, more laws are being enacted, and members are becoming more inclined to remain in office [in 1960 and 1962 fewer senators and representatives retired than ever before], the legislative approach to processing bills undergoes little alteration.

Legislative Powers

In addition to its powers of lawmaking, the state legislature has ceremonial, constituent, executive, administrative, and judicial functions.

Ceremonial Functions   Although the legislative body acting collectively, or the members individually, are not called upon so often as is the governor to perform ritualistic functions, they do spend much of their time on this sort of thing. As with the governor, such activity is important to the legislators' political future.

Constituent Functions   Legislatures have the power to submit proposals for constitutional amendment to the voters, as was discussed in Chapter 4. This, together with the power to submit the question of calling a constitutional convention, is known as the "constituent power" of the legislature.

Executive Powers   A great many appointments are made by governors to administrative positions, to boards and commissions, and, in some states, to judicial posts. These appointments are generally subject to approval by the Senate. That body, in granting its approval, is exercising an executive function that stems from the days when the upper house in some of the colonial legislatures served as the executive council, advising the governor. In a few states in New England and in the South, the legislature elects some of the judges as well as some of the administrative officers. Thus, the New Hampshire Legis-

[25] *Ibid.*

lature elects the secretary of state and the treasurer. The insurance commissioner is chosen by the legislature in South Carolina.

Legislatures also commonly prescribe detailed organizational structure
for each state agency and may also spell out quite specifically the administrative procedures that they are to follow in performing their functions.[26]

The power to investigate is a traditional legislative function. Legislatures
generally have extensive powers in this field, though they do not ordinarily use
them to the extent that Congress does. Investigations may deal with suspected
corruption, mismanagement, or "inefficiency" in an agency. Potential headlines can be seen by the imaginative legislator in an investigation into the
"morals of state employees." In the early 1950s, legislative committees joined
their congressional counterparts in searching for subversives. The Tenney
committee became well known for this in California. The Georgia Legislature
searched its state government for many months; it failed to turn up a single
Communist.

If the governor or other elected official is not of the same party or faction
as the majority in one house, an election year usually produces a rash of
investigations of the administration. Sometimes these fishing expeditions find
cases of popularly unacceptable behavior; at other times they only appear
to do so. In either case, the material is generally useful against the party in
power or the particular candidate for office.

Quite a few committee investigations are aimed at exploring areas where
new legislation may be needed. In the short, hectic sessions that are characteristic of most legislatures, little opportunity exists for careful study or
extensive hearings. Between-sessions investigations help to overcome this
deficiency. When used for its intended purpose, the legislative investigation is
an important device for making it more difficult for the executive and judicial
branches to become dishonest, inefficient, autocratic, or unresponsive to
society's values and wants.

Judicial Powers   As in the case of Congress, legislatures are the judges of
the qualifications of their own members. Usually, they can determine whether
or not they will seat a member whose claim by right of election is clouded for
some reason. They can also sit in judgment of a member who is accused of
wrongdoing and may expel him. The impeachment powers possessed by legislatures are also judicial in nature.

Legislative Staff Assistance

In 1956, a legislative resolution in Texas submitting a constitutional amendment to provide state aid for the permanently disabled was carelessly worded
to provide for a referendum by the voters to be held on "the second Tuesday in
November," when it should have been worded "the Tuesday after the first
Monday." As a result, on November 13, a special election had to be held to

[26] See Gladys M. Kammerer, "Legislative Oversight of Administration in Kentucky," **Public Administration Review**, 10:169–175, Summer, 1950.

vote on the amendment, even though a general election had been held a week earlier. The cost to the taxpayers of this blunder amounted to about $250,000. In 1965, Nebraska passed a new weed-abatement act, designed principally to reduce the number of noxious weeds in rural areas. The act made elaborate provision for the administration of the program, even including the *election* of weed commissioners. But apparently no one thought to exempt Douglas County (the Omaha area), where the ground is covered mostly with concrete, asphalt, and well-tended, almost weed-free lawns. The county was faced with a mandatory requirement for providing an unneeded and ineffective service. These incidents illustrate the need for careful bill drafting and the expensive results of its absence.

Legislators in quite a few states, in an attempt to improve their work and to relieve themselves of their dependence upon lobbyists and the administrative bureaucracy, have employed staffs to assist them. In other states, however, they have persistently refused to do this, even though the cost would be relatively small and the result would considerably improve their public image concerning performance. It is likely that many legislators do not understand the nature of staff work or conceive of the benefits it can produce. In the many states where the governor is often of a different party from that of the legislative leadership, the latter would be in a much stronger position to fend off the governor's criticisms and to improve the party's chances in the next election if a staff were available to do research and to generate ideas. The use of legislative reference bureaus is expanding. In a large state, such a bureau is today likely to consist of at least fifty persons, including attorneys, researchers, and clerical employees.

Legislative assistance is usually centered, when it exists, in a legislative reference bureau, or a bill-drafting service. Most states have legislative councils consisting of selected legislators together with, sometimes, a research staff. This group works between sessions, investigating or drawing up legislation and perhaps preparing programs and making recommendations for their colleagues' consideration at the next session. Generally these councils have greatly improved the spadework that is done prior to the enactment of legislation and they have freed the legislator from his otherwise total dependence upon the interest groups and the administration. But legislators who are not named to the council may be jealous of its status and power. They may resent the fact that it sometimes presents to them at the beginning of a session a completely prepared policy proposal, with council members primed with answers to questions the nonmembers have not yet even had a chance to formulate.[27]

The Kansas Legislative Council, the oldest one in the country, has an image that is favorable; "it seems to be accepted by most legislators and the

[27] See the appraisal of legislative councils and other staff operations in Karl A. Bosworth, "Lawmaking in State Governments," The Forty-eight States: Their Tasks as Policy Makers and Administrators, The American Assembly, Graduate School of Business, Columbia University, New York, 1955. Also, Gladys M. Kammerer, "Advisory Committees in the Legislative Process," Journal of Politics, 15:171–196, May, 1953; H. W. Davey, "The Legislative Council Movement in the United States," American Political Science Review, 47:785–797, September, 1953.

general public as a relatively objective, fact-finding agency." In Kansas, bills prepared by the Council are usually not introduced unless a majority on a standing committee in one of the houses is willing to introduce it as a standing committee bill. Occasionally a member will introduce a Council bill in his own name. In either case, the bill is subject to amendment or defeat. In the twenty-five-year period following 1935, only 52 percent of the Council bills were adopted as written or in an amended form. This figure was not much higher than the 47 percent acceptance for all bills.[28]

The legislative-council movement did not gain much momentum until after World War II. Since 1945, thirty-two states, or 64 percent of the total number, have adopted legislative councils. By 1965, forty-two of the states (84 percent of them) had such agencies.[29]

Legislatures in the larger and more prosperous states are beginning to make use of computers. A computer can do in seconds (or in minutes, if it must print out the relevant laws verbatim) what would otherwise take months by a staff member. The state of New York, for example, has put all of its compiled laws on tape for use in a computer memory bank. The computer can quickly find all the laws relating to, say, the regulation of insurance companies. This is especially important in trying to find laws that are not in the major acts on the subject. The computer can also help in codifying the law by locating duplications and obsolete provisions. It can also do rapidly the enormously complex task of compiling into logical order a set of laws on a given subject. In minutes, the computer can put together the various provisions in a preprogramed standard legal coding system.

Lobbying

The old-style professional lobbyist, working simultaneously for several interest groups and carrying a black bag filled with temptation, is a passing character on the political scene. Today, the most effective lobbyists are generally officers of influential organized groups, respected citizens, careful of their facts, and persons whose sense of ethics is in accord with the society in which they live. The term lobbyist continues to carry the old evil connotation; but influence is now exerted on a different plane, and inducements are usually much more subtle.

The Gourmand and Government   Thick steaks and expensive liquor still have their place when lobbyists seek to explain their position on a subject to members of a committee. Overt bribery is uncommon today but probably is not rare. On important legislation, pressure groups may offer or imply the offer of campaign contributions for the next election. Sometimes, they do something that

[28] William H. Cape and John P. Bay, **An Analysis of the Kansas Legislative Council and Its Research Department,** Governmental Research Center, University of Kansas, Lawrence, Kans., 1963, p. 109.
[29] Frederic H. Guild, **Legislative Councils after Thirty Years,** Public Affairs Research Bureau, Southern Illinois University, Carbondale, Ill., 1964.

legislators respond to even more surely: they threaten to run a well-financed candidate against the reluctant legislator in the next primary election. Some legislators—probably a very small minority of them—still work the ancient shakedown by introducing nuisance bills which are withdrawn if the proper campaign contribution is made. Thus, one legislator introduced a bill that would prevent hotels from charging for telephone calls. The problem with such bills is in trying to determine the motive of the author. Was he angered that the hotel at which he was staying during the session made a profit on each of his telephone calls? Or was he working a shakedown? [30]

Methods of Lobbying   The lobbyist is likely to be an attorney or the executive secretary or some other officer of an interest group. Often he has himself served in the legislature. Even if he has not, he is likely to have been frequenting legislative sessions for a longer time than have most of the members of the body. He knows his way around. And some lobbyists are also members of the legislature.

Lobbyists do much of their work by giving formal testimony before legislative committees and by deluging legislators with propaganda or with letters which they outline and arrange to have mailed to legislators by the membership of their interest groups. They write bills or suggested amendments to bills. They hold dinners at which they can discuss their position on matters. But lobbyists spend most of their time in the capitol or hotel lobby engaging in light banter with legislators and other lobbyists. In the course of some of these conversations, the point of view of the lobbyist's employer will be presented, often fleetingly and unsystematically. The object of the lobbyist is to use the technique of projection; by creating a favorable image of himself, he hopes to encourage a similar one for his employer. At the same time, he engages in as much serious talk as the patience and interest of the particular legislator will permit.

The number of lobbyists is considerable. In California, there may be four times as many lobbyists as there are members of the legislature; in Michigan, about twice as many. Lobbyists, being important to the welfare of the groups they represent, are generally well paid. "Artie" Samish, when he was the most powerful lobbyist in California, received $50,000 a year from the Santa Anita Race Track, and this was but one of his clients. The typical lobbyist probably receives a salary of $15,000 a year or less—and this will usually be in payment for many other activities in addition to his work at the capitol.

A study of lobbyists in Oklahoma concluded that most of them were more than forty-five years of age and lived in the state capital. No women were registered as lobbyists. The typical lobbyist was a professional staff member of some interest group who usually spent less than one-half of his time as a lobbyist and the rest in other activities for his group, perhaps as executive

[30] Other examples may be found in Lester Velie, **The Great Unwatched,** Reader's Digest Association, Inc., Pleasantville, N.Y., 1953, a pamphlet reprinting a series of five articles which appeared in the **Reader's Digest.** Velie exaggerates, however, and thereby does a disservice to the typical legislator.

secretary or as the executive secretary's assistant. Most lobbyists had never held any political party or public office. In general, they were well educated, with the highest percentage of those with college education representing business and professional groups. Nearly one-half of them, 47 percent, had an income of more than $10,000 a year in 1962. The role of lobbyist was not perceived in the same way by all persons performing that function. They were classified as contact men, informants, or watchdogs. The *contact man* sees his job as one of building personal acquaintanceships with legislators and serving as a communication link between his interest group and legislators. The *informant* sees his task as that of effectively presenting the case of his group through carefully prepared information for legislators, including frequent formal presentations to legislative committees. His lobbying, in other words, is likely to be public rather than private and to concentrate more on formal testimony than on light chatter over a cup of coffee or a highball. The *watchdog* sees his job as being one of keeping a careful eye on the legislative calendar and floor debates. He serves mostly as a communicator, telling his group when danger or opportunity is observed, so that it may bring pressure upon legislators by whatever approaches his employers consider appropriate.[31]

At the 1961 session of the Illinois Legislature, 485 individuals registered as lobbyists. This was a decrease from the 541 registered in 1959. In the latter year, lobbyists representing governmental agencies had been required to register. The difference gives some—but only a rough—idea of the number of governmental employees who act as lobbyists before the legislature. Of those registered in 1961, 49 represented trade unions, 115 business and trade associations, 48 civic groups (such as chambers of commerce), 72 specific industries, 30 utilities, 27 insurance groups, 26 financial groups, 37 professional groups, 37 local governments, and 35 public-employee groups. The others represented agricultural, educational, church, fraternal, welfare, and other groups.[32]

Lobby Registration and Control   In efforts at the regulation of lobbying, the states once again present the enigmatic character that has so long puzzled observers. Although little systematic evidence exists, it is widely believed that the states are frequently the scene of flagrant abuses of lobbying, with many tactics commonly employed that would not be tolerated if they were attempted in relation to Congress. Yet, the states, or some of them, began to attempt to regulate lobbying as long ago as the Civil War period, while there was no regulation of the Federal lobby before 1946. One observer has commented: [33]

In the strictest sense, [lobby regulation laws] are not solutions at all. At bottom, state lobbying laws involve no more than the casual application of a wholesome general principle to some of the more visible aspects of group-legislative relationships— primarily those that can be described as "lobbying." This principle has been called

[31] Samuel C. Patterson, "The Role of the Lobbyist: The Case of Oklahoma," **Journal of Politics**, 25:72–92, February, 1963.
[32] Samuel K. Gove, "The Business of the Legislature," **Law Forum**, Spring, 1963, pp. 53–54.
[33] Edgar Lane, **Lobbying and the Law**, University of California Press, Berkeley, Calif., 1964, p. 15.

"disclosure." It rests on the old-fashioned belief that, in a democracy, the public interest is always served by the widest possible diffusion of information about matters of public consequence or interest. It further holds that when such information is wanting, withheld, or otherwise unavailable, government should require that it be disclosed. The disclosure principle is as simple as that. It assumes no benefits or uses in advance. It assumes only that if men had access to the facts, they will seek them out and put them to whatever use their preferences and needs dictate.

Professional lobbying began in the state capitals and later spread to Washington. The constitution of New Hampshire in 1792 prohibited legislators from accepting fees for their support or opposition to bills pending before the legislature. Other states later placed similar prohibitions in their constitutions. Alabama was the first state to attempt to control lobbying through constitutional provision. This was done in 1873 in the post-Civil War constitution of that state. The Georgia constitution of four years later actually declared lobbying to be a crime and the state legislature promptly passed an act virtually prohibiting it. It was in vogue for state legislatures to pass legislation to regulate lobbying. Massachusetts, in 1890, adopted a new approach, requiring systematic disclosure of lobbying activities. This subsequently became the most popular form of lobby legislation. In 1965, thirty of the states had legislation which was little changed from that of the Massachusetts act. In the various states, the legislation to require disclosure was generally written hastily, borrowed from a neighboring state, and usually at a time when charges were being made that legislators had been unduly influenced by lobbyists, or were in danger of being subverted. Edgar Lane has concluded that: [34]

There is, in sum, no reason to assume that disclosure laws alone can bring about significant alterations in the shape and texture of the [political] system. They have appeal as low-key reminders that a bias for open dealing is part of the American political tradition.

County and Township Boards

Some attention has already been given in Chapter 8 to the size and patterns of local governing boards. The detail concerning these various bodies is too complicated to summarize it here. In fact, it is doubtful if the reader could profit much from such a summary. An inquiry at the county, town, or township clerk's office should produce detailed information concerning any specific local unit of government.

Virtually all local governing bodies are now unicameral. The meeting pattern is different from that of the state legislature in that local bodies usually meet once a week or once a month, rather than in the periodic long session that is dictated for legislatures by the great distances some members live from the capitol.

Governing bodies with large membership, especially county boards under the supervisor system, are likely to use the committee system. Some smaller bodies do so too, but these boards are likely to operate in an even more in-

[34] *Ibid.,* p. 188.

formal manner than does the state legislature, and the close ingroup relationship that springs up in bodies of under, say ten persons, is likely to be the dominant consideration in law making. Relationships are personal rather than party or constituency oriented.

Some board members, especially in counties under the commissioner system, are likely to be professionals making a career of membership. Otherwise, members may be drawn from almost any walk of life. The chances are that the typical member is a person of relatively good standing in his neighborhood, performing a task that he interprets as a civic responsibility. He seeks to carry to board deliberations what he takes to be the consensus in his neighborhood.

City Councils

The pattern of councilmanic functions varies with the forms of city government. In weak-mayor cities, for example, each alderman, in addition to sharing in policy-making duties, often serves as a ward foreman supervising administrative functions. On the other hand, in council-manager cities the councilman normally has only policy-making duties.[35]

Structure of the Council Councilmanic salaries are generally fixed at a low rate, perhaps a few hundred dollars a year or nothing at all, in order to discourage candidates who are interested in the salary. In the largest cities, councilmen may be paid up to $12,500 per year, though this is highly unusual. Pay is likely to be highest, other conditions being equal, in commission-type cities. In these cities, councilmen are also administrators.[36]

Councilmanic terms range from one year to six years. The four-year term has become the most common and is more likely to be found in larger than in smaller cities. The size of councils ranges from two members in several cities to Chicago's fifty. Roughly, the size of the council increases with the city's population, though the form of government is also a factor. Small cities are likely to have councils of five members or less; large cities not uncommonly have no more than nine, however. Weak-mayor cities have larger councils than other types. Virtually all councils are now unicameral in character, although at the turn of the century, about one-third of the cities of over 25,000 had bicameral councils. The change is indicative of the much greater rate of change that has taken place in city as compared with state government.

Nineteenth-century city council members were commonly elected by wards, but well over one-half of the cities of more than 5,000 population now elect at large, and a much greater percentage of the smaller cities do so. In large cities, serious questions of representativeness have been raised by the practice of electing but a few councilmen, and all of them at large. The individual citizen has, in these cities, lost his traditional direct contact with

35 For details, see Charles R. Adrian, **Governing Urban America,** 2d ed., McGraw-Hill Book Company, New York, 1961, chap. 10.
36 For pay in specific cities, see the most recent issue of the **Municipal Year Book,** The International City Managers' Association, Chicago.

his representative. About two-thirds of American cities now elect councilmen on a ballot without party designation. This practice is especially common in council-manager cities.

Occupations   In the vast majority of American cities, the typical council member is a local businessman, well respected in the community, active in civic organizations, and often a college graduate. He runs for the council because of the prestige and power the position affords. He may believe that the prominence of the position will help his business, but often he is merely acting out of a sense of community responsibility. He is usually not among the top of the businessmen in his earnings and standing, but generally he is prosperous. Typically, he is above average in intelligence, but it is not necessary for the council to consist of a group of intellectual giants or the leading men of the community; if it has a few able leaders, that is enough, for there is need also for the plodding type who will accept and follow that leadership.

Generally, the smaller the city, the more likely it is that council members are chosen from among the most prestigeful citizens of the community. As cities increase in size, the professional prominence of councilmen, in general, tends to decrease. In the largest cities, councilmen may well devote full time to the work at the city hall and may have run for the office partly because of the salary involved. Although venal and corrupt councilmen were once commonly found in these large cities, they are now a rarity. The greatest sins of the councilmen of the metropolis today are likely to be in their allegiance to particular pressure groups—a real-estate board, a labor union, a group of builders, the liquor dealers, the downtown merchants. They are likely to view their function as that of protecting these particular pressure groups, although they invariably claim to act "for all the people." In varying degrees, this same pattern may be found as cities decrease in size, but the value consensus that generally exists in smaller communities makes loyalty to pressure groups a less important factor: nearly everyone agrees on what is right and wrong and on the general limits within which public policy should be established, and there is little room for manipulations of policy to favor particular interests.[37]

Concluding Statement   Legislative bodies represent a basic part of the process of public policy formulation. But their function is only one in the total. Along with the chief executive, interest groups, the administrative hierarchy, and the courts, they share the important task of changing, within achievable limits, wants into policy. Later chapters will add to the discussion in this and earlier chapters in seeking to show that policy making is a continuous, many-faceted process. Yet, the adequacy of the law in meeting social needs and the quality of its enforcement cannot be expected to be better than that of the legislative body, for it, in a democracy, is said to speak for the people.

[37] Not much has been done in research on city councils. A good introduction to the general subject is Arthur W. Bromage, **Councilmen at Work**, George Wahr Publishing Co., Ann Arbor, Mich., 1954. On consensus politics and a small village council in upstate New York, see Arthur J. Vidich and Joseph Bensman, **Small Town and Mass Society**, Princeton University Press, Princeton, N.J., 1958, chap. 5.

SELECTED READINGS

Allen, Don A.: **Legislative Sourcebook,** California State Assembly, Sacramento, Calif., 1965.   (Appendix D has an extensive bibliography on apportionment; generally much information on the California legislature.)

American Legislatures: Structure and Procedures, Council of State Governments, Chicago, 1955.

Blair, George S.: "Cumulative Voting: Patterns of Party Allegiance and Rational Choice in Illinois State Legislative Contests," **American Political Science Review,** 52:123–130, September, 1958.

Bosworth, Karl A.: "Lawmaking in State Governments," **The Forty-eight States: Their Tasks as Policy Makers and Administrators,** The American Assembly, Graduate School of Business, Columbia University, New York, 1955.

Bromage, Arthur W.: **Councilmen at Work,** George Wahr Publishing Company, Ann Arbor, Mich., 1954.

Buchanan, William: **Legislative Partnership: The Deviant Case of California,** University of California Press, Berkeley, Calif., 1963.

Childs, Richard: **Civic Victories,** Harper & Row, Publishers, Incorporated, New York, 1952.   (A statement of efficiency-and-economy values and goals.)

Davey, H. W.: "The Legislative Council Movement in the United States," **American Political Science Review,** 47:785–797, September, 1953.

de Grazia, Alfred: **Apportionment and Representation Government,** Frederick A. Praeger, Inc., New York, 1963.   (A conservative view.)

————: **Public and Republic,** Alfred A. Knopf, Inc., New York, 1951.

Derge, David R.: "Metropolitan and Outstate Alignments in Illinois and Missouri Legislative Delegations," **American Political Science Review,** 52:1051–1065, December, 1958.

Dewey, John: **The Public and Its Problems,** Holt, Rinehart and Winston, Inc., New York, 1927.

Eulau, Heinz, and others: "The Political Socialization of American State Legislators," **Midwest Journal of Political Science,** 3:188–206, May, 1959.

Garceau, Oliver, and Corinne Silverman: "A Pressure Group and the Pressured," **American Political Science Review,** 48:672–691, September, 1954.   (A study of a manufacturers' association and the Vermont Legislature.)

Garfinkel, Herbert, and Leibel Fein: **Fair Apportionment,** Bureau of Social and Political Research, Michigan State University, East Lansing, Mich., 1961.

Graves, Brooke W. (ed.): "Our State Legislators," **Annals,** 195:entire issue, January, 1938.

Guild, Frederic H.: **Legislative Councils after Thirty Years,** Public Affairs Research Bureau, Southern Illinois University, Carbondale, Ill., 1964.   (Observations by the first and long-time director of the Kansas Legislative Council.)

Hamilton, Howard D. (ed.): **Legislative Apportionment,** Harper & Row, Publishers, Incorporated, New York, 1964.   (A reader.)

Havens, Murray C.: **City versus Farm?** Bureau of Public Administration, University of Alabama, University, Ala., 1957.

Hyneman, Charles S.: "Tenure and Turnover of Legislative Personnel," **Annals,** 195:21–31, January, 1938.

Jewell, Malcolm E. (ed.): **The Politics of Reapportionment,** Atherton Press, New York, 1962.   (A study concentrating on reactions to *Baker v. Carr* in a number of states.)

————: **The State Legislature: Politics and Practice,** Random House, Inc., New York, 1962.   (Study summarizing Jewell's own vast knowledge and many empirical studies.)

Kammerer, Gladys M.: "Advisory Committees in the Legislative Process," **Journal of Politics,** 15:171–196, 1953.

Karsch, Robert F.: **The Standing Committees of the Missouri General Assembly,** Bureau of Governmental Research, University of Missouri, Columbia, Mo., 1959.

Keefe, William J.: "Parties, Partisanship, and Public Policy in the Pennsylvania Legislature," **American Political Science Review,** 48:450–464, June, 1954.

————: "Party Government and Lawmaking in the Illinois General Assembly," **Northwestern University Law Review,** 47:55–71, 1952.

Kilpatrick, James J. (ed.): **One Man, One Vote,** Virginia Commission on Constitutional Government, Richmond, 1965. (Comments and documentary material very critical of the Supreme Court decision in *Reynolds*.)

Lamb, Karl A., William J. Pierce, and John P. White: **Apportionment and Representative Institutions,** Institute of Social Science Research, Washington, D.C., 1963. (A historical account of apportionment in Michigan.)

Lane, Edgar: **Lobbying and the Law,** University of California Press, Berkeley, Calif., 1964. (A history of lobbying and lobby regulation.)

Lee, Eugene C.: **The Presiding Officer and Rules Committee in Legislatures of the United States,** Bureau of Public Administration, University of California, Berkeley, Calif., 1952.

Littlewood, Thomas B.: **Bipartisan Coalition in Illinois,** McGraw-Hill Book Company, New York, 1960, Eagleton Case Study no. 22. (A study of a factional struggle over the speakership in the Illinois House in 1959. For a similar struggle in New York, see the **New York Times** for January and February, 1965.)

Lowell, A. Lawrence: "The Influence of Party Upon Legislature," **Annual Report of the American Historical Association for the Year 1901,** American Historical Association, New York, 1901.

Macrae, Duncan, Jr.: "The Relation Between Roll Call Votes and Constituencies in the Massachusetts House of Representatives," **American Political Science Review,** 46:1046–1055, December, 1952.

Mann, Dean E.: "The Legislative Committee System in Arizona," **Western Political Quarterly,** 14:925–941, December, 1961.

Neuberger, Richard L.: **Adventures in Politics: We Go to the Legislature,** Oxford University Press, Fair Lawn, N.J., 1954.

Parsons, Malcolm B.: "Tension and Conflict in a One-party Legislative System," **American Political Science Review,** 56:605–614, September, 1962.

Perkins, John A.: "State Legislative Reorganization," **American Political Science Review,** 40:510–521, June, 1946.

Schubert, Glendon (ed.): **Reapportionment,** Charles Scribner's Sons, New York, 1965. (A reader.)

Shils, Edward A.: "The Legislator and His Environment," **University of Chicago Law Review,** 18:571–584, 1951.

Siffin, William J.: **The Legislative Council in the American States,** Indiana University Press, Bloomington, Ind., 1959.

Smith, T. V.: **The Legislative Way of Life,** The University of Chicago Press, Chicago, 1940. (By a philosopher who served in the Illinois Legislature.)

Sorauf, Frank J.: **Party and Representation: Legislative Politics in Pennsylvania,** Atherton Press, New York, 1963.

Steiner, Gilbert Y.: **Legislation by Collective Bargaining,** Institute of Labor and Industrial Relations, University of Illinois, Urbana, Ill., 1951.

———— and Samuel K. Gove: **Legislative Politics in Illinois,** The University of Illinois Press, Urbana, Ill., 1960.

———— and ————: **The Legislature Redistricts Illinois,** Institute of Government and Public Affairs, University of Illinois, Urbana, Ill., 1956. (The principal interest when the legislature redistricts itself is that of the members themselves.)

Tucker, William P.: "Characteristics of State Legislators," **Social Science,** 29:94–98, April, 1955.

14

LEGISLATIVE BEHAVIOR AND APPORTIONMENT

This chapter is concerned with the way in which legislators are chosen, where they come from, how they perceive their jobs, and how they behave in relation to one another while performing their jobs. Our concerns are with apportionment, with the behavior of legislators as members of a very special kind of social club, and with social roles as they are interpreted by legislators.

Legislative Apportionment

"Many factors have conspired to produce the low status of the American state legislature," V. O. Key once pointed out. "Yet," he continued, "among these factors, its unrepresentative character must be assigned a high rank. . . . A body that is condemned by its constitution to the defense of a partial interest in the state becomes, if not a council of censors, something other than a representative body in the conventional sense." [1]

The number of seats in each house of the legislature is usually, but not always, determined by the constitution or by constitutional formula. The creation of legislative districts and assigning seats to them is called "apportionment," and it is over the apportioning of the legislature that a great many political battles have been fought and will be fought in the future.

The basic quarrels over reapportionment result from the fact that the nation has urbanized rapidly, while most states continue to be governed by constitutions drafted prior to World War I. Rural areas, if we consider population as the basis of representation, have been disproportionately strong in legislative bodies; the urban voice, far weaker than its numbers of people allow it to be.

[1] V. O. Key, Jr., **American State Politics**, Alfred A. Knopf, Inc., New York, 1956, pp. 76–77.

Efforts to Involve the Judiciary   In 1926, an effort was made to get the Illinois Supreme Court to order the Illinois Legislature to reapportion itself in compliance with the state constitution. The court refused to act by using the separation of powers doctrine, claiming that it had no right to order the legislature to do anything.[2] The ruling in this case was widely supported in the judiciary and advocates of legislative reapportionment were forced to concentrate their pressures on generally unwilling legislators. The picture remained unchanged until well after World War II.

The *Magraw* case of 1958 was a landmark decision, even though it did not reach the United States Supreme Court.[3] It was significant in that a Federal district court judge accepted jurisdiction in a case involving the apportionment of a state legislature. Previously, state and Federal courts avoided the question either by arguing that the separation of powers doctrine prevented the courts from imposing their will upon the legislature, or by arguing that the apportionment of a legislature was a "political question" for which there were no judicial guidelines and hence no justiciable controversy, as it did in the *Colegrove* case.[4]

The next major case was *Baker v. Carr*,[5] in 1962. In this case the United States Supreme Court for the first time accepted jurisdiction in a reapportionment case. The Court then went on to rule that lower courts should consider whether the Tennessee Legislature had violated the equal protection of the laws clause of the Fourteenth Amendment, by failing to reapportion itself as required by the constitution.

The *Baker* case was significant because the Court had accepted jurisdiction in apportionment cases and because it had ruled that failure to apportion might deprive a citizen of his constitutional right to equal protection of the laws. Beyond this, all it did was to remand the case with instructions that the lower court take jurisdiction and to call upon the court to enforce the provisions of the Tennessee constitution. The direction in which the Court would move had been indicated, however. The next year, 1963, it ruled that the Georgia county-unit system of voting in primary elections for the governorship and for congressmen, a system under which the person who carried a majority of counties would win irrespective of his cumulative vote, also deprived citizens of their right to equal protection.[6] This case made it clear that by equal protection the court was talking about total population or total potential votes, in other words, "one man, one vote."

The next year, the Court went the full distance to the logical conclusion. In February, it ruled that when legislatures determine the boundaries of congressional districts they must make sure "as nearly as practical, one man's vote in a Congressional election must be worth as much as another's." [7] And in June, 1964, in the *Reynolds* case, the court ruled that both houses of a

2 *Fergus v. Marks*, 321 Ill. 510 (1926).
3 *Magraw v. Donovan*, 163 F. Supp. 1589 (1958); dismissed after legislature reapportioned, 177 F. Supp. 803 (1959).
4 *Colegrove v. Green*, 328 U.S. 549 (1946).
5 *Baker v. Carr*, 369 U.S. 186 (1962).
6 *Gray v. Sanders*, 371 U.S. 821 (1963).
7 *Westberry v. Sanders*, 376 U.S. 1 (1964).

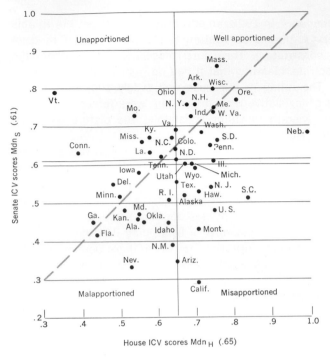

Fig. 14-1 Apportionment Patterns before Judicial Action.

Diagram shows the degree to which legislatures were apportioned according to population on March 26, 1962, the date of the *Baker v. Carr* decision.

SOURCE: Glendon Schubert and Charles Press, "Measuring Malapportionment," **American Political Science Review**, 58:302–327, June, 1964; as modified in *ibid.*, 58:970, December, 1964.

state legislature must be apportioned as strictly as possible according to population.[8] The Court did not indicate how much of a margin of variation it would permit, but it held again that the equal protection clause applied to apportionment. In this historic case, the Court also dealt with two touchy arguments, arguments upon which the opponents of straight population representation had based their hopes. It held that the pattern of representation in the United States Congress, in which no state can be deprived of its equal representation in the Senate without its own permission, did not apply. The Court specifically pointed out that the Senate apportionment was the result, not of the estimate by the Founding Fathers of what was equitable, but of a political deal necessary in order for the United States Constitution to be politically acceptable to the less populous states. The Court also ruled that popular votes relative to apportionment were not relevant to the case, that is, that one's civil rights cannot be voted away by popular majority. The majority opinion, written by the Chief Justice, said that, "a citizen's constitutional rights can hardly be infringed upon because a majority of the people choose to do so."

The *Reynolds* case actually involved six cases. One justice dissented from

[8] *Reynolds v. Sims*, 377 U.S. 533 (1964).

the entire decision and two others dissented in part. The sweeping decision promptly produced a wave of proposals to set it aside. A number of bills and resolutions were introduced in Congress. The one receiving the most support was that by Senator Everett Dirksen of Illinois, who proposed a constitutional amendment which would permit the states to have one house based on something other than straight population. Many state legislatures—still unapportioned—petitioned Congress either to submit a constitutional amendment similar to the Dirksen proposal, or to have Congress call a national constitutional convention, at which such a proposal could be considered.[9] In 1965, the Dirksen proposal narrowly missed securing the two-thirds vote needed in the United States Senate and the issue of reapportionment remained very much conflict-ridden. In the meanwhile, state and Federal courts both began issuing rulings pressuring states to comply with the *Reynolds* decision.

Illustrations of Malapportionment   At the time of the *Baker* decision, each town in Vermont was entitled to a representative. As a result, the smallest town, with a population of 38, had one member in the lower house of the legislature, and so did the largest city in the state, Burlington, with a population of 35,531. In the California Senate the three largest counties had 7.5 percent of the representation, but these three counties had 51 percent of the population of California. In Vermont, a majority of the members of the lower house could be mustered from among representatives of only 12 percent of the state's population. In California, senators representing less than 11 percent of the population could control a majority of the votes. In Tennessee, districts with 27 percent of the state's population elected a majority of the senators and districts with 29 percent elected a majority of representatives. In Florida, 15 percent of the population could elect a majority of the members of the lower house. In Florida, Kansas, New Mexico, Oklahoma, and Tennessee, districts with less than 30 percent of the state's population could elect a majority in both houses of the legislature. Nevada, which consists largely of cities and empty deserts, seemed to hold the record. There only 8 percent of the state's population could elect a majority of the members of the Senate.[10]

A generous way for measuring malapportionment would be to note the number of percentage of districts that are either more than 25 percent under or 25 percent over the average population size for the state. While the average in probably all states varies through time, it has generally become greater since about World War I. In Michigan, for example, only 3 percent of the Senate seats—actually only one seat—varied from the average by more than 25 percent in 1907, but by 1952 the percentage of Senate seats varying by more than 25 percent was 76 percent. In the Michigan House of Representatives, only 14 percent of the seats varied by more than 25 percent from the average after the census of 1910. After the census of 1940, the percentage rose to 57. After reapportionment following the 1950 census, this figure dropped to 25 percent. The greatest range in the Michigan Senate in the nine-

[9] E. W. Kenworthy, "Dirksen Hopeful on Apportioning," **New York Times,** May 23, 1965.
[10] George B. Merry, "A Closer Look," **Christian Science Monitor,** Boston, Mar. 14, 1963.

teenth century was found in 1891, when 28 percent exceeded the 25 percent range, compared with 76 percent in 1952. In the Michigan House, the greatest range in the nineteenth century was 49 percent of the seats falling outside the 25 percent range in 1849 as compared with 57 percent in 1943 as the greatest twentieth-century range. The 1841 figure is misleading, however. After a reformulation, the range in the Michigan House dropped to 9 percent in 1846. Between 1838 and 1890, the Michigan House usually had under 20 percent of its seats falling outside the 25 percent range.[11]

The Meaning of Judicial Involvement   In assuming jurisdiction over reapportionment cases, the courts did so reluctantly and after a number of cases in which jurisdiction was refused. But as in the question of school desegregation, the courts acted to accomplish change where great pressures for such change had built up and both the legislative and executive branches had failed to take remedial action. In the period immediately after the *Baker* case, the state courts continued to avoid assuming jurisdiction and relatively few did so. The lower Federal courts, however, were faced with the need for action, but with the problem of how to proceed unresolved. As a result, they decided to "speak sternly, assert power, show extreme reluctance to intervene, but grave concern, and, above all, provide an actual order which allows plenty of time for political forces to act, hoping the while that you will never have to face the problem of positive relief. The assumption underlying this strategy is that urban political forces are generally powerful enough to drive a legislative bargain, once they are armed with a judicial declaration of rights. The corollary is that in this way the courts will be spared the necessity of a showdown." [12]

   Although the state supreme courts were reluctant to become involved in questions of apportionment, nearly one-half of them accepted cases at one time or another prior to the *Baker* case. They usually limited themselves to declaring a specific apportionment act unconstitutional, although in some cases they did change the boundaries of legislative districts to conform to the constitution and, in a few cases, even threatened to apportion according to the provisions of the constitution if the legislature failed to act.[13]

Consequences of Reapportionment   One possible result of widespread reapportionment of state legislatures will be for state governments in the South to accept racial integration rather than to stage a bitter-end fight. The fact that rural legislators are more segregationist than are urbanites has been noted by journalists as well as political scientists.[14] Two political scientists have noted that "the urban areas have no special stake in the perpetuation of racial dis-

[11] John P. White, "Legislative Apportionment Under Three Michigan Constitutions," in Karl A. Lamb, William J. Pierce, and John P. White, **Apportionment and Representative Institutions,** Institute of Social Science Research, Washington, D.C., 1963, pp. 140–141.
[12] Jo Desha Lucas, "Of Ducks and Drakes: Judicial Relief in Reapportionment Cases," **Notre Dame Lawyer,** 38:413–414, June, 1963.
[13] Anthony Lewis, "Legislative Apportionment," **Harvard Law Review,** 71:1057–1070, December, 1958.
[14] Murray C. Havens, **City versus Farm?** Bureau of Public Administration, University of Alabama, University, Ala., 1957.

Table 12   States Are Pressured to Reapportion

STATE	POPULATION PLAN USED IN LAST ELECTION *	NEW PLANS ADOPTED FOR NEXT ELECTION *	UNDER ORDERS TO CHANGE AND TAKING ACTION	CHALLENGE NOW IN COURT	NO SUIT FILED
Alabama		✔			
Alaska		✔			
Arizona		✔			
Arkansas		✔			
California		✔			
Colorado	✔				
Connecticut		✔			
Delaware	✔				
Florida		✔			
Georgia	✔				
Hawaii			✔		
Idaho		✔			
Illinois		✔			
Indiana		✔			
Iowa	✔				
Kansas			✔		
Kentucky	✔				
Louisiana				✔	
Maine					✔
Maryland		✔			
Massachusetts	✔				
Michigan	✔				
Minnesota			✔		
Mississippi				✔	
Missouri			✔		
Montana		✔			
Nebraska		✔			
Nevada		✔			
New Hampshire		✔			
New Jersey	✔				

Table 12   (*Continued*)

STATE	POPULATION PLAN USED IN LAST ELECTION *	NEW PLANS ADOPTED FOR NEXT ELECTION *	UNDER ORDERS TO CHANGE AND TAKING ACTION	CHALLENGE NOW IN COURT	NO SUIT FILED
New Mexico		✔			
New York	✔				
North Carolina			✔		
North Dakota		✔			
Ohio		✔			
Oklahoma	✔				
Oregon	✔				
Pennsylvania			✔		
Rhode Island			✔		
South Carolina			✔		
South Dakota		✔			
Tennessee		✔			
Texas		✔			
Utah		✔			
Vermont	✔				
Virginia	✔				
Washington		✔			
West Virginia	✔				
Wisconsin	✔				
Wyoming		✔			
Totals	15	24	8	2	1

Most states have acted to reapportion their legislatures. This was the situation on January 1, 1966.
* Includes some states where further changes are necessary.
SOURCE: **State Legislatures Progress Reporter**, 1:2, January, 1966.

crimination; indeed, the tensions and conflicts it produces can only harm them. Thus, while the urban counties particularly in southern Florida do not actively *want* integration (many individuals certainly oppose it), neither will they act affirmatively to prevent it." [15]

The full effect of the *Reynolds* case upon the function of state government and its position in the Federal system cannot be known at this time. It is safe,

[15] William C. Havard and Loren P. Beth, **The Politics of Mis-representation**, Louisiana State University Press, Baton Rouge, La., 1962, p. 244.

given the incremental nature of change in the American system of government, to predict that the result of apportionment strictly by population—if this is maintained as the rule—will not accomplish so much as its proponents hope or undo so much as its opponents fear. It does seem likely, however, that the rule will produce a gradual shift toward urban-oriented state legislatures. It will encourage the states to become concerned about urban problems, to spend money on them, and to become increasingly governments which will seek to meet some of the problems created by metropolitan areas and which cannot be handled by local governments alone in those areas.

One observer, going further, has commented: [16]

The urbanization of state legislatures will be a relatively slow process. It will involve much litigation and conflict. It will involve the courts directly; it will lead to efforts to revamp state constitutions; it will be fought out in the polls as the prime political issue it promises to become. And it will be accompanied by the urbanization of state politics.

The ultimate effect of this shift will be to weight the party system toward the urban-national side as against the state-local side and this is a necessary condition for the emergence of a national party system. To augment an already developing bypass of the state the direct national-metropolitan relationships with a national party system that is built upon an urban basis must mean a fundamental restructuring of our formal system of government. *Baker v. Carr* is a decision on the functional merits of federalism; it does strike deep into its heart.

Rural-urban Conflict How important is the question of whether a legislator comes from an urban or a rural area? How badly will rural areas fare in an essentially urban state? We do not yet have enough studies to tell the answer to this question. In a study of the Indiana General Assembly, however, the question of political party affiliation was far more important than the question of where the legislator came from.[17] In Michigan, the lobbyist for the American Farm Bureau Federation, after the first session in which the legislature was apportioned in both houses on the basis of population, concluded that farmers had fared well and had gained from several pieces of legislation adopted by the legislature which had been urged for several years by the Farm Bureau. It is difficult to generalize about the effects, however, for several other changes had taken place simultaneously. The legislature that year was under Democratic control for the first time in a generation. It is also possible that the urban-dominated legislature, knowing that it was being watched fearfully by rural observers, made a special effort to allay rural fears. Whether it would do so in future years could not be known, of course.[18]

The consequences of malapportionment apparently vary from one state to another. While reapportionment in 1964 strongly affected party balance and legislative leadership, a study of the Texas Legislature has shown that reap-

[16] Martin Landau, "Baker versus Carr and the Ghost of Federalism," in Glendon Schubert (ed.), **Reapportionment**, Charles Scribner's Sons, New York, 1965, p. 247.
[17] Howard D. Hamilton and others, "Legislative Reapportionment in Indiana," **Notre Dame Lawyer**, 35:368–402, May, 1960.
[18] **State Journal**, Lansing, Mich., Aug. 25, 1965.

portionment would apparently make very little difference in the policy product. In that state, during the 1961 and 1963 sessions, more than one-half of the legislative districts differed by more than 15 percent from the average district population. In the two sessions, urban legislators were not more cohesively liberal and more labor-oriented than were rural legislators in comparisons of districts having cities of 100,000 or more against those with no city so large as 10,000 population. A majority of the urban legislators were on the winning side in all but five out of forty-five bills on which questions involving liberal-conservative, rural-urban, or organized labor questions were involved. The study concludes that "it seems likely that the rural voters have as little to fear from the urban areas as the cities have to fear from the rural areas." [19]

A study in Alabama examined the effect of the urban movement upon the legislation of that state.[20] It found that the majority of roll-call votes do not result in an urban-rural alignment but that a significant number of them do. Questions dealing with race relations and reapportionment especially tended to be structured along urban-rural lines. There were other types of substantive legislation that revealed this kind of split, however—types that are indicative of the variety of conflicts of interest that exist between the producers and consumers of foods and fibers. A bill to give added protection to the state's dairy industry from outside competition had almost unanimous support from rural legislators, with those from urban areas less enthusiastic. Rural legislators wanted a prohibitive tax on trading stamps. Small-town merchants regard them as unfair competition; urbanites generally favor the stamps.

A labor-supported amendment to the state open-shop bill received significantly more support from urban as compared with rural representatives. Another split occurred in connection with a bill to create an Alabama Turnpike Authority—urbanites want high-speed highways connecting cities; farmers view them as being of relatively little use to them since access is limited; small-town merchants see them as spelling a loss of trade. Rural legislators also split with their urban colleagues over a bill providing for the employment of depositions in judicial proceedings. The bill would, in essence, have applied Federal court procedures in this respect to the courts of Alabama. City lawyers generally saw this as a step toward improved judicial procedure, but many "rural lawyers, having less experience with the new system than most of their urban colleagues, opposed the new method." There were several bills involving race relations during the session, and each of these brought sharp urban-rural clashes, with considerably more tolerance indicated by the urban representatives. Urban-rural conflict was not the dominant theme of the session, but it was an important one.

The degree to which a rural-urban split exists in legislative bodies is a matter of dispute. Where it does happen, however, it is not simply a Democratic-Republican conflict. In the 1965 South Dakota Legislature, for example, thirteen of the twenty-two legislators from rural senate districts were Demo-

[19] Clarice McD. Davis, "State Legislative Malapportionment and Roll-call Voting in Texas," **Public Affairs Comment**, 11:1–4, May, 1965.
[20] Havens, *op. cit.*, p. 7.

crats. In the House, twenty-four of fifty were Democrats.[21] In Iowa, a small-town Democrat, reflecting the small-town ideology more than that of urban society, became something of a thorn in the side of Democratic leaders and of the Democratic governor in the 1965 session. In particular, he seemed to resent the influence of organized labor leaders upon urban legislators. But his protests extended beyond labor measures. He viewed himself as an independent Democrat. One day, late in the session, he noted in his diary: [22]

This morning we got into [a dispute over] a bill which will levy a service tax on Iowa barbers, beauty shop operators, garage mechanics, etc.

Shortly after I made a strongly worded protest against this bill our Democratic leaders called a recess and asked for a caucus.

Here we were told that this was a pet measure of Governor Hughes, that the $2 million plus it would raise was badly needed in the state funds, and that we must support it!

I'm getting tired of being told what I must support, and so are many others.

Opposition to taxes on small businessmen and on services is in accord with small-town ideology.

Apportionment and Policy Payoffs   Thomas Dye, after comparing a large number of state expenditure patterns with their degree of wealth and relative apportionment of legislatures has concluded: [23] "On the whole, the policy choices of malapportioned legislatures are not noticeably different from the policy choices of well-apportioned legislatures. Most of the policy differences which do occur turn out to be a product of socioeconomic differences among the states rather than a direct product of apportionment practices. Relationships that appear between malapportionment and public policy are so slight that reapportionment is not likely to bring about any significant policy changes." A projection into the future of this finding, is, however, based upon the assumption that what has happened in the past will continue in the future. This is by no means certain to be the case. For example, the function of state governments in the political system of the United States is based upon tradition and ideology. Urbanites have neglected state governments as a possible source of assistance with their problems in both well-apportioned and malapportioned states. If the attitudes of political leaders and opinion molders in society toward state governments were to change, the result might be a substantial increase in the importance of state government and the extent of apportionment on the basis of population could become significant. As Dye has noted, "The consequences of reapportionment may be so subtle and diverse that they defy quantitative measurement. Perhaps the consequence in each state will vary so much that direct interstate comparisons are inappropriate." In any case, the rural-urban split in legislative bodies, although probably based upon ideological differ-

[21] George M. Platt, "South Dakota's 1965 Legislative Session," **Public Affairs,** May 15, 1965, table 1.

[22] Richard Radl, "Diary of an Iowa Legislator," **Mount Vernon Hawkeye-Record** (Mount Vernon, Iowa), June 3, 1965.

[23] Thomas R. Dye, "Malapportionment and Public Policy in the States," **Journal of Politics,** 27:586–601, August, 1965.

ences, is only one of many possible divisions within a legislature. Furthermore, it is possible that the tradition in legislatures of recognizing the need
to assist individual members with particular problems in their own constituencies has tended to mitigate the effect of malapportionment in the legislatures. Furthermore, small-town and suburban ideologies, although they conflict,
are not necessarily represented by persons from constituencies that are literally small town or suburban in nature. A legislator with an orientation toward
the values of the "typical" suburbanite may be found in a relatively small
county seat town. A conservative legislator oriented toward the values of nineteenth-century industrial individualism may come from a sophisticated, well-
educated, upper-income suburb of a metropolitan area. Finally, the question
of actual payoffs in terms of governmental policy is independent of the question of the ethical imperative of equal representation. Advocates of reapportionment have generally emphasized that population is the only "fair" basis
for apportionment. The argument that it would result in a legislature more concerned with contemporary urban problems has generally been secondary. Even
so, research to date—none of which includes a study of policy payoffs before
and after reapportionment—indicates that the residential location of the legislator may be considerably less important than has previously been assumed
to be the case. A major reason for local governments' turning to the Federal
government for financial assistance is economic rather than ideological. That
is, more money can be raised at less effort from the Federal government than
from the states. Reapportionment will not change economic facts of this sort
and the pressures for "going to Washington" will be as great after reapportionment as they were before.

Footnotes on Apportionment   Here are some factors relevant to the controversy:

  1. Original Practice   In the original constitutions of the fifty states,
thirty-two of the upper houses and twenty-six of the lower houses were based
on something approximating a straight population principle.[24]

  2. The Conservative Position   At the time of the *Baker* decision, it was
common for conservatives to argue in favor of a "balanced" legislature, that
is, one in which one house was based fundamentally on population and the
other gave some (though a varying) amount of credit to area. This was not
actually the case, however. In practice, the tendency in many states was to
apportion both chambers in about the same way. Overall, however, the lower
houses of the legislatures tended to be based more on population than were
the senates. At the time of the *Baker* decision, the Ohio Legislature was closest
to apportionment on a population basis, followed by Oregon, New Hampshire,
Nebraska, and Massachusetts. The legislatures that least reflected the equal
representation principle were those of Alabama, Oklahoma, Kansas, Minnesota,

[24] Robert G. Dixon, Jr., "Reapportionment in the Supreme Court and Congress," **Michigan Law Review,** 63:209–242, May, 1965. Data from p. 239. The figure of thirty-six states using population as a base is given in a less-carefully prepared study by the U.S. Advisory Commission on
Intergovernmental Relations, **Apportionment of State Legislatures,** 1962, table 2.

and Georgia. Thirty-six of the states were apportioned more closely on a population basis than was the United States Congress.[25]

To those opposed to the theory of majoritarianism implied in equally weighted votes for the legislature, the most common positive argument is that the majority may be tyrannical in its treatment of the minority.

Although any form of apportionment not based strictly on population tends to emphasize the power of the small-town ideology, the conflict to some extent is also one involving political parties. Because the Democratic party in the urban, industrial North had its power concentrated in relatively few counties, reapportionment on a strict population basis in these areas would mean a weakening of the Republican party in the state legislature, even though it might make little or no difference in policy payoffs. In Indiana, for example, only seven out of the total of ninety-two counties would be able to control a majority of the state Senate under the 1965 apportionment and only nine counties could control the lower house. These were, of course, the most urban and most Democratic counties.[26]

3. The Party Interest   The pattern of apportionment of legislatures is directly related to the relative strength of political parties and, sometimes, factions. In the Michigan constitutional convention of 1961–1962, political party interest was dominant in decisions on legislative apportionment.[27]

4. The Effect of Multimember Districts   Historically, part of the problem of drawing legislative district boundaries has been simplified by the use of multimember districts. A 1954 study showed that about one state senator in nine and nearly one-half of the lower house members were elected from multimember districts.[28] When simple plurality voting is used, the party getting more votes than any other carries all of the seats in a multimember district. Illinois has attempted to overcome this mathematically unfair result by a rough use of proportional representation in a cumulative voting system. Republican leaders in the Michigan constitutional convention of 1961–1962 argued successfully for a constitutional requirement of single-member districts, particularly in order to increase their chances of getting a proportionate share of the seats in the Detroit metropolitan area.

Actually, 46 percent of the members of lower houses of legislatures came from multimember districts in 1954. This figure was virtually unchanged in 1962. During that same time, the percentage in the upper house increased from 12 percent to 16 percent.

5. Sectional Rivalries and Reapportionment   Part of the conflict over reapportionment results from sectional rivalries within states and fear concerning a shift in relative political power. After a Federal court ordered the California Legislature to be reapportioned, the California Senate, one of the

[25] Havard and Beth, *op. cit.*, p. 244.
[26] John S. Waggamen, "Reapportionment in Indiana—A Continuing Struggle," **Public Affairs Notes**, 7:1–6, July–August, 1965.
[27] Theodore R. Ervin, **Concurrents of Influence**, Institute for Community Development, Michigan State University, East Lansing, Mich., 1964.
[28] Maurice Klain, "A New Look at the Constituencies," **American Political Science Review**, 49: 1105–1119, December, 1955; Paul T. David and Ralph Eisenberg, **State Legislative Redistricting**, Public Administration Service, Chicago, 1962, table 2.

nation's most malapportioned legislative bodies, voted twenty-seven to twelve to divide the state at the Tehachapi Mountains. This would create a Southern California of seven counties and 10.3 million people, and a Northern California of fifty-one counties and 7.8 million people.[29] The Senate action was a symbolic protest. Even if Southern Californians were to agree to this division, which they would not, the obstacles to the division of a state are so formidable as to be virtually impossible, save under the circumstances of mutual consent of the two areas, as happened in the separation of Maine from Massachusetts in 1820, or under Civil War conditions, as happened in the separation of West Virginia from Virginia in 1863.

6. Reapportionment and the Republican Form of Government   Future reapportionment cases may raise the question of a "Republican form of government," as well as of "the equal protection of the laws." [30] The argument could be made that the phrase in the Constitution refers to *fair representation,* and hence to representation by equal population districts.

7. Reapportionment and Population Concentration   Apportionment on a straight population basis would mean that in fifteen states, or about one-third of the total, two or three counties would have a majority of the legislators.[31]

8. Reapportionment and Negro Political Power   Reapportionment is certain to have some effect upon the opportunity for Negroes to be represented in legislatures. After a court-order reapportionment of Georgia in 1965, eight Negroes were elected to the state lower house. They were the first Negroes to sit in that body since 1907. The Senate had gained its first Negro representation since postreconstruction days in 1962. Two Negroes were elected at that time, not as the result of reapportionment, but rather because of increasing Negro voter registration and participation in Georgia. Incidentally, in this same special election for the Georgia House, Republicans increased their representation from four to seventeen. All of the Negroes elected were Democrats.[32]

Automatic Reapportionment   As urban pressures for periodic reapportionment have increased and as it has become increasingly clear that the legislature is not in a position to reapportion itself, pressure has increased to provide for some kind of system by which the legislature is regularly reapportioned through a process not involving that body itself. In 1963, however, this was the case in only fourteen states, and not always in both houses in those. The tendency to remove the task from the legislative bodies, where it had almost always been found painful, was clear, however.[33]

Future Guidelines   If reapportionment difficulties are to be avoided in the future, four guidelines should be followed, according to one scholar: First, the

[29] Associated Press dispatch, June 5, 1965.
[30] Arthur E. Bonfield, "Baker v. Carr: New Light on the Constitutional Guarantee of Republican Government," **California Law Review,** 50:245–263, May, 1962.
[31] Charles Press, "One Man-One Vote and the Farmer," **Farm Policy Forum,** 17:9–14, 1964–1965.
[32] **Newsweek,** June 28, 1965, pp. 24–27.
[33] U.S. Advisory Commission on Intergovernmental Relations, **Apportionment of State Legislatures,** 1962, chap. 4.

method of apportionment should be provided for in the state constitution. The assumption should be that future changes will be necessary and the procedures for making those changes should be specified. Second, clear standards should be specified concerning the limits of variation in size and perhaps shape of districts. Third, the system should be automatic, so that the legislature would be reapportioned after every United States census. Lastly, the provisions for reapportionment should be enforceable. This would probably mean that the legislature should not have any responsibility for reapportionment, but that it should be done by some kind of commission, with provision for appeal to the courts.[34]

Apportionment and Local Governing Boards   The decision in the *Reynolds* case caused many lawyers to conclude that the rule in that case will probably also be applied to local-government governing boards. In other words, city councilmen elected partly or completely by wards or districts will have to represent roughly equal numbers of people. The same thing will be true of county and other local governments. The problem is likely to be most serious in states using the New York supervisor system of county governments. Only eight days after the *Reynolds* decision, a case was filed to declare unconstitutional the means by which the board of supervisors of Kent County, Michigan (which includes Grand Rapids), is selected. Evidence was presented to show that a suburb of Grand Rapids, which was the most underrepresented local government, had a supervisor who represented sixteen times as many people as did a supervisor from a township in the northern part of the county. A supervisor from Grand Rapids represented approximately nine times as many people as the supervisor from the least populous township. The court ruled the Michigan formula for reapportionment unconstitutional, retained jurisdiction in the case, and gave the legislature one session to provide a constitutional formula.[35] In 1966, the legislature enacted a county apportionment formula in accord with the court decision.

The problem of malapportionment in terms of equal population does not exist only in states using the supervisor system. Even under the commissioner system, where a county board typically consists of only three or five members, malapportionment is quite common. For example, South Dakota law does not permit a city to have more than two representatives in counties with three. The result in many counties has been a serious departure from the "one man, one vote" principle. When the 1964 legislature failed to provide a new formula for choosing county boards, a circuit judge ruled the law in conflict with the "equal protection" clause. He said that if the legislature did not provide a formula in conformity with the Supreme Court ruling, he would order that the commissioners be elected at large.[36]

Although the Supreme Court has not yet ruled concerning the meaning

[34] James D. Barber, **Legislative Malapportionment,** Center for Information on America, Washington, Conn., 1962, pp. 10–11.
[35] *Brower v. Bronkema,* Kent County Circuit Court (Mich.), No. 1855 (1964).
[36] Alan L. Clem, "Distorted Democracy: Malapportionment in South Dakota Government," **Public Affairs,** November, 1964.

of equal protection relative to the election of city councils, it did hold in 1960 that boundary lines cannot be drawn in such a way as to discriminate or deprive a citizen of the right to vote on the basis of race. In a case involving Tuskegee, Alabama, the Court voided a plan designed deliberately to eliminate the possibility of Negroes' being elected to the city council.[37]

The Legislature and Political Parties

In the typical legislative session, few issues are decided fundamentally along party lines, but in many legislatures, the most important issues tend to be shaped by party differences and the more urbanized a state is, the more this is likely to be the case.[38]

The Importance of Party Competition   Party competition makes a difference in the degree of party discipline in the state legislature and the degree to which party pressures are significant in the decisions of individual legislators. "When there is little or no competition in general elections, parties are usually an inadequate substitute because the choice means less to the voter than the choice between Democratic and Republican candidates. Frequently, there are no factions to take the place of truly competitive parties; where there are, these factions seldom extend to legislative primaries; where they do, the voters are unlikely to perceive that the factional candidates stand for significantly different policies." [39]

Characteristically, "in a large majority of the states, between one-third and two-thirds of the legislators are serving their first terms. . . . Since most of those who serve one or two terms are not defeated but retire voluntarily, the voter often loses his chance to pass judgment on the incumbent legislator at the polls. . . . One cause of this high turnover is that in many multi-county districts the rotation principle is followed. The legislator's job is rotated evenly among the counties, so that no incumbent serves more than two or four years. Rotation may be based on tradition and practice or may result from a formal intra-party agreement in one or both parties. It not only causes turnover, but it may easily cause capable candidates to be passed over in favor of others from another county." [40]

Party responsibility is meaningful when the voters have a choice of candidates, a chance to understand what programs the candidates support, and an opportunity to defeat those candidates who have not fulfilled their promises.[41]

Although the number of one-party states is declining, in those that remain, "party responsibility is meaningless and factional responsibility is rare." Furthermore, in states with competitive politics, "many voters live in one-sided

[37] *Gomillion v. Lightfoot,* 364 U.S. 339 (1960). The story is told in Bernard Taper, **Gomillion versus Lightfoot,** McGraw-Hill Book Company, New York, 1962. In paperback.
[38] Malcolm E. Jewell, "Party Voting in American State Legislature," **American Political Science Review,** 49:773–791, September, 1955; William J. Keefe, "Parties, Partisanship and Public Policy in the Pennsylvania Legislature," *ibid.,* 48:450–464, June, 1954.
[39] Malcolm E. Jewell, **The State Legislature: Politics and Practice,** Random House, Inc., New York, 1962, p. 45.
[40] *Ibid.,* p. 46.
[41] *Ibid.,* p. 6.

districts. If so, the voter may find that only one party runs a candidate, and that he has no vote unless he joins the majority party in order to make a choice in the primary among several candidates, all of whom repeat the same cliches or ignore issues entirely." [42]

In a few states, voting behavior on most issues can be explained by party affiliation. In some others, parties, "though evident on only a fraction of the roll calls, appear to be the most significant factors." In still other states, party is rarely significant in legislative voting. The party is most likely to be significant when it is "relatively homogeneous and policy-oriented, where there is a political bi-polarization along urban-rural lines. This tends to occur in the more industrial states. It may also be significant, at least temporarily, where the second party is rebuilding and challenging the majority party." If party is unimportant in voting, factional, regional, or urban-rural patterns are likely to be highly varied and highly transient.[43]

The Case of Kansas   As an example of the importance of parties in legislatures, in the Kansas Senate, party membership was the most important indicator of probable voting behavior. Democrats voted together as a group more consistently than did Republicans. A party vote was found most commonly in matters of taxation, election law (which directly affects the fate of a political party), state civil service, and the appointive powers of the governor. Republican senators—they were in the majority—were more closely related to the Republican voting bloc if they came from basically Republican districts. The higher the Democratic percentage in the district and the higher the percentage of workers engaged in manufacturing, the less was the likelihood of the Republican senator's voting the party line. In other words, the legislator from a politically marginal district tended to crowd into the middle of the road and to feel constituency pressures more than party pressures. There was a significant tendency for senators from rapidly growing districts, in terms of population, to vote together and for senators from districts of declining population to do so. A rural-urban voting split also existed, although this factor was weaker than the other two. A fourth voting bloc pattern was weak. What held the bloc together was obscure, but it appeared to be related to liberal and conservative ideologies.

In the Kansas House of Representatives, voting patterns were not so clear cut as in the Senate. The state at the time had a Democratic governor and a much larger share of the House than of the Senate. In the Senate, therefore, the Democrats could all vote together in order to indicate disapproval or to embarrass the Republican leadership. In the House, however, it was possible for the Democratic minority to sustain a veto by voting together. As a result, the Republican leadership had to consider their positions. With additional power, therefore, the Democrats had to be more than simply obstructionists and "the more positive role they had to play in the House oriented them in a direction somewhat different from that of the House Republicans but not

[42] *Ibid.*, p. 47.
[43] *Ibid.*, p. 75.

diametrically opposed to them." A rural-urban split in the House was related to party membership, but was not identical with it.[44]

The Case of Florida   As another example, in Florida, "the alleged independence of candidates, the emphasis in the campaign on personal characteristics which may have little relation to fitness for legislative service, the complete subordination of statewide issues to local issues in the election literature and speeches, and the absence of acknowledged party or factional stands on issues are barriers against the possibility of responsibility to the electorate." [45]

A study of the Florida Senate indicated that, even though it was a one-party body, the pattern of conflict approximated that of a two-party system. Such conflict was to be found particularly in relationship to the determination of officers and of committee assignments. On controversial roll calls, the divisions tended to follow a two-faction pattern. One faction tended to be made up of Democrats who lived in or represented districts of rapid social change where the Republican party was emerging, while the other represented constituencies where neither factor was apparent. The factional split was in evidence on more than one-half of the controversial roll calls, a significantly higher percentage than is found on party splits in Congress on controversial roll calls.[46]

The sharp factional break in the Florida Legislature between rural and urban Florida may, however, have been not so much "a result of rate of growth or of rate of Republican increase in power, as it was the sharp conflict between [Governor] Leroy Collins (1955–1961) and the North Florida group, known in the local press as 'the pork-chop gang.' " [47]

Party Importance through Time   The political pattern within a state legislature varies through time. Before the 1950s, California state politics was so overwhelmingly Republican that the legislature became essentially a nonpartisan body, with few votes showing any important correlation with party membership. In the 1950s, however, the California pattern changed rapidly. With the great influx of urbanites from all over the country and, especially, with the rise of amateur clubs, the Democratic party enjoyed a revival which shortly produced a pattern of competition between the parties within the legislature as well as for statewide offices. These amateur clubs were policy rather than patronage oriented and reflected the middle-class values of honest, efficient, "businesslike" politics.[48]

[44] John G. Grumm, "A Factor Analysis of Legislative Behavior," **Midwest Journal of Political Science,** 7:336–356, November, 1963.
[45] Havard and Beth, *op. cit.,* p. 244.
[46] Malcolm B. Parsons, "Quasi-partisan Conflict in a One-party Legislative System," **American Political Science Review,** 56:605–614, September, 1962.
[47] Hugh Douglas Price, "On Parsons on Florida Politics," *ibid.,* 56:974–975, December, 1962.
[48] Jewell, **The State Legislature,** pp. 130–131. Also Francis Carney, **The Rise of the Democratic Clubs in California,** Holt, Rinehart and Winston, Inc., New York, 1958; William Buchanan, **Legislative Partnership,** University of California Press, Berkeley, Calif., 1963; James Wilson, **The Amateur Democrat,** The University of Chicago Press, Chicago, 1962.

Another study of the California Legislature reached a number of conclusions, including the following: [49]

1. There are no internal legislative operations which only a political party can perform. The functions parties ordinarily do perform (calendaring, staffing, screening) may be performed by the chamber as a whole or by the speaker on behalf of the chamber.

2. The nonpartisan system is not adapted to communication between the legislature and the public, primarily because of an information blockage. Nonpartisan legislatures are comprehensible only to close observers.

3. Size of chamber, legislative pay, rules for electing leaders, office space, and other constitutional, legal, and physical requirements made upon a legislature are substantial factors in determining its performance.

Factionalism in the Legislature   In one-party states, patronage is likely to be more important as a device for gubernatorial leadership over the legislature than it is in competitive states. Because he cannot rely on party loyalty or party pressure, the governor will often use patronage as a weapon. Such patronage historically and, apparently, even today is more likely to be effective when used to secure the votes of rural and small-town legislators than those of large cities. The promise of a new bridge on a state highway in one county, or the expansion of a mental hospital in a small county-seat town of another, or the promise to appoint to a salaried position a constituent of a legislator in a third county may produce the necessary votes to secure adoption of an item important to the governor. In rural areas such patronage is likely to be more visible and is more likely to be noticeably supportive of the economy than is the case in a city. A legislator who can show his constituents that he can "bring state money into the district," gains in popularity. The use of patronage by the governor in this fashion in one-party states tends to weaken further the already weaker party. Minority party members, of course, are likely to come from districts that receive few patronage benefits. Under these circumstances, "the more patronage they can get, the less incentive they have to gain majority status; the more often they support the governor, the fewer issues their party has for the next campaign. When a recent Kentucky Democratic governor needed Republican votes for his program, he told the Republican members in a caucus that voting support was the price for roads and parks in their districts." [50]

Something resembling factional patterns also exists in two-party states. The Illinois Legislature, for example, has long had two parties but three separate power blocs, each with a different perspective on legislative behavior: [51]

The Democratic bloc which makes peace within itself when necessary, values Democratic cohesion highly, considers interparty logrolling an obvious fact of legislative life, and changes its legislative spokesman in both chambers without concern

[49] Buchanan, *op. cit.*, p. 150.
[50] Jewell, **The State Legislature**, pp. 126–127.
[51] Gilbert Y. Steiner, "Legislative Power Blocs," **Illinois Government**, October, 1963, p. 1.

for the presumed advantages of seniority; the House Republican bloc with a roughly similar [ideology] of legislative behavior save for somewhat less emphasis on cohesion; the Senate Republican bloc which tends to be monolithic and thus avoids internal dissension, recognizes and utilizes its effective veto over legislation, disdaining interparty logrolling, and magnifies its appearance of firmness by presenting an unchanging leadership group session after session.

Footnotes on the Legislature and Parties   Here are some additional notes:

1. Party Competition and District Characteristics   Even in states with highly competitive two-party systems, most legislative districts are not two-party competitive and the degree of competition changes only slightly through time. In the vast majority of legislative constituencies in the United States, competition for the office takes place within a single political party. Furthermore, the incumbent has a very considerable advantage and even in those districts with a relatively high degree of competitiveness in the primary election, the incumbent seldom loses. The typical state legislator is quite secure in his job as long as he wants it.[52]

2. Factional Struggles and the Legislature   Factional struggles within a state political party may carry over into the legislature and may become extremely bitter. In 1965, after the Democrats had captured both houses of the New York Legislature for the first time in many years, the Democrats could not agree on selections for the speakership or the Senate majority leadership. One set of candidates was supported by persons allied with Mayor Robert F. Wagner of New York, while another was allied with Senator Robert F. Kennedy. After a month-long struggle, during which the Democrats were widely ridiculed in the newspapers and state legislatures generally received damaging publicity, the Republican minority broke the deadlock by siding with the Wagner faction.

3. The Party and Interpersonal Relations   The behavior of the individual legislator may be the result of a variety of political party influences. "Personal convictions can often result from party influence processes; for example, through the recruitment by parties of candidates with certain viewpoints and background characteristics, or the socialization of new legislators into the norms of the party." [53] The party even influences the interpersonal relations and friendship patterns within the "club." Personal friendships tend to be formed most commonly within the individual's own party. Furthermore, the legislators with the greatest number of friends are the party leaders, although this conclusion involves the characteristic chicken-and-egg or causal relationship problem that plagues the social sciences. Are legislative leaders in their positions because they have many friends? Or do they have many persons who claim to be their friends and whom they claim as friends because they are leaders?

4. Visibility of Legislative Contests   The office of legislator has a relatively low level of visibility on the ballot of most citizens. Unlike the highly visible governor's office, that of legislator tends to reflect quite sharply changes

[52] Robert W. Becker and others, "Correlates of Legislative Voting," **Midwest Journal of Political Science**, 6:384–396, November, 1962.
[53] Greenstein and Jackson, *op. cit.*, p. 161.

in overall electoral swings. In particular, this is true in urban areas, where the legislator is even less visible than in the small town, and shifts in the vote for President are particularly important in the outcome of legislative contests. In the anti-Goldwater landslide of 1964, for example, the Democrats witnessed such previously rare events as seeing their party take control of both houses of the legislature in Indiana, Iowa, Maine, New York, Utah, and Wyoming. In Michigan, the Democrats were advantaged by reapportionment, but their control of the Senate could almost certainly be traced to the national presidential voting pattern. On the other hand, in the Deep South, where Goldwater generally made his best showing, the Republicans gained representation in the legislatures of Georgia, South Carolina, and Tennessee. Yet, local issues can sometimes be dominant and override even the crest of a large presidential wave. In 1964, the Oregon House of Representatives went Republican for the first time in many years. Republicans also made net gains in seats in Arizona, California, Idaho, and New Mexico.[54]

Informal Patterns of Organization

Certain functions must be performed in every legislative system, but these functions need not all be performed by the same institutional devices. Furthermore, nomenclature within the legislative body differs, just as it does for legislative bodies themselves, from one state to another.

The Unwritten Rules The formal organization of a legislature may have little meaning. Thus, "there is often a paper caucus that meets only biennially. There are frequent committees that do not receive bills on the subjects implied by their titles or that rubber stamp those bills they do receive. A lieutenant-governor may be powerful in one state and a figurehead in the next."[55]

As in the case of the community, power is not evenly distributed among members of a legislative body. "In a strong two-party state, they are most likely to be party leaders; elsewhere leaders of factions or representatives of the governor may stand out. In any state legislature, but particularly where the parties are weak, lobbyists may be strong."

The institutional structure of a legislature is such that actual leaders are also likely to occupy the formal positions of power, but there is no necessary rank ordering of their relative power. For example, in one state the speaker of the house may be the most powerful leader, while in another state the speaker may be someone who has been "kicked upstairs," while the majority floor leader or some other person actually is the dominant leader. Leaders gain power through control over procedure, committee assignments, and their influence with the governor. They may use various techniques—the caucus, a rules committee, or the standing committees (bills may be arbitrarily assigned to committees controlled by dependable legislators).

Malcolm Jewell, a specialist on state legislatures, has observed that while most bodies are organized for strong leadership, they are not usually organized

54 **National Civic Review**, 53:600–601, December, 1964.
55 Jewell, **The State Legislature**, pp. 103–104, is the basis for this section.

"to provide careful deliberation on legislation. Usually the sessions are too short, and the legislators too poorly staffed, to permit that." Because of their weaknesses as innovative bodies, leadership often comes not from within the body, but from the governor's office.

The unwritten rules of the legislative process are important to the maintenance of the political system and to the institution itself. They add support to and often modify the formal rules. In this sense, the unwritten rules "fill in the chinks" in the structure that is the legislative institution. Indeed, "they are directly relevant to and supportive of the purposes and functions of the legislature as these are conceived of by legislators: they maintain the working consensus essential to legislative performance." [56]

As with the formal rules, the unwritten rules are enforced through sanctions, which are understood and can be anticipated by members. Both formal and informal rules are enforced primarily, of course, not through threat of punishment, but rather through consensus on the proposition that they are useful and in some cases essential to making the legislature functional. A legislator is judged by his colleagues in part by his understanding and acceptance of the unwritten rules of the game. A legislator is more effective to the extent that he demonstrates such understanding, not only to the leaders of the body, but also to the rank and file members. Indeed: [57]

The maintenance of group norms which constitute the working consensus appears to be independent of the power or influence acquired through holding formal office. Rules of the game are the property and the creature of the group membership at large, not a reflection of requirements set by either personal or formal leadership. Formal leadership operates within the working consensus provided, in large part, by legislators playing their consensual roles.

Formal and Informal Leaders   In a study of four state legislatures, those of California, New Jersey, Ohio, and Tennessee,[58] the presiding officer was the most important formal authority figure. He is expected to contribute to "a climate of impartiality, stability, and predictability," and to preside in such a manner that the losers, when a particular issue is finally acted upon, feel that they have had fair treatment and have been able to present their best possible case. Committee chairmen are expected to behave in a similar manner, but in their case the formal rules are generally less specific and the role calls for the chairman to demonstrate fairness and decisiveness. Although he may have a great deal of control over the agenda of his committee and what is sent on to the floor of the House, he is expected to be fair in his treatment of the minority. If he is a specialist in some substantive area of legislation, as is often the case because of his seniority and tenure on the committee, he is expected to use that information.

The third type of legislative leader, the party leader, performs the function of coordination and liaison. He does this in relation to members of his party

[56] John C. Wahlke, Heinz Eulau, William Buchanan, and Leroy C. Ferguson, **The Legislative System,** John Wiley & Sons, Inc., New York, 1962, chap. 7. Quotation from p. 168.
[57] *Ibid.*, p. 169.
[58] *Ibid.*, chap. 8.

in the legislature, to leaders of opposition parties, to the governor, and to the party machinery. The party leader also provides useful cues. His position on matters, as interpreted by anything from subtle hints to blunt comments, is helpful to other legislative leaders as they seek to make up their own minds on a particular matter. If the party leader indicates support for a particular item, for example, this indicates to the party regulars the position they should logically take. To party mavericks, it indicates whether or not their positions are going to produce further abrasions as the result of conflict with the leadership or not, and to members of the opposition party, the cues are useful both in determining their own positions and in giving leads as to optimal strategies to be pursued.

The Subject-matter Specialist as Leader   Even though the principal task of the legislator is to bring grass-roots opinion into the total policy-making process, and even though legislators are constantly faced with technical problems beyond the ken of most of them as individuals, legislators do serve as subject-matter specialists. The new legislator is encouraged to specialize and to find some area in which his expertise, when developed, can be of particular use, especially to the committees on which he serves. Specialization in some particular aspect of state public policy is particularly important because "legislatures are perennially confronted with decisions where a technical minutia of no obvious significance to the laymen may be the precise point on which policy, broad or narrow, turns. The effect on highways of an increase in the truck weight limit, how much paregoric may safely be dispensed without a prescription, the size of a standard prune crate, the limit on balloon payments to second mortgages, the effect on sanitation of fishing in reservoirs, the closing date of the squirrel season, the relation of attorney to physician in private adoptions, the impact of oil severance taxes on petroleum production, salaries of beginning teachers versus experienced ones—something more than a coherent political [ideology] is required to take a comfortable position on such matters." [59]

Probably the most important function of the subject-matter specialist in the legislature is his task of translating the technical information given by bureaucratic and interest-group specialists into language that the layman can understand. He is also useful in explaining the implications, if not the technical complexities or complications, of the reasons why certain proposed policies will produce certain results. In other words, he can help to explain to the uninformed legislator that policy A or B, as proposed, will not have the effect of preventing highways from breaking up in the spring or of increasing the size of the deer herd, or whatever the goal may be.[60]

Legislators generally become recognized as influential in a given policy area before they achieve more general influence. Those that do achieve more general influence seem to do so as the result of organizational skills.[61]

[59] *Ibid.*, p. 214.
[60] *Ibid.*, chap. 9.
[61] Wayne L. Francis, "Influence and Interaction in a State Legislative Body," **American Political Science Review**, 56:953–960, December, 1962.

Social Interaction and Informal Organization   Social relationships between legislators, in practice, seldom bring together persons of highly divergent ideological positions. Social contacts, in other words, are most likely to occur between members with similar social, economic, and educational backgrounds. Where this is not the case and friendships are formed, the inner action of the two different legislators may have some effect upon their voting behavior, but it is "almost negligible." The structural characteristics of the legislature do have some effect upon the formation of friendships and of social linkages. Persons of long tenure are likely to form friendships with one another as are freshman members and committee chairmen. These are "horizontal" linkages. On a vertical basis, party or factional membership is likely to be an important factor in the formation of friendships. In general, however, the political role of a legislator is far more important as an influence upon his behavior and voting record than are his social roles.[62]

Legislative Membership

Few legislators serve reluctantly; they want their jobs. But in other respects they differ widely, and they are of all personality types. When James J. Walker was in the New York Legislature, where he served for fifteen years before becoming mayor of the nation's largest city, "He always voted for the machine and he made a host of warm personal friends. He dressed boldly, drank gaily, and fought for the freedom of sports." [63] In contrast was the rather dour, conservative leader of the Minnesota Senate who led the opposition to Floyd B. Olson, the Farmer-Labor Governor. A. J. Rockne "had risen to the top through seniority, persistence, and hard work rather than any special ability." [64]

To some legislators, the job is a career; they combine their salary with pay they receive from some corporation, labor union, or local unit of government. Others see the job as a stepping stone to higher—and better paying— executive, judicial, congressional, or even large-city councilmanic offices. To some it is a consolation prize for those who wanted to achieve greater success and failed.[65]

About two-thirds of all legislators are businessmen, lawyers, and farmers. Very few skilled craftsmen or hourly rated employees of any kind are members. But "occupational data must be used with caution, for members may have, or have had, several occupations and their choices of which they will list may reflect their political calculations." A favorite device is for a man who owns a farm to list himself as a farmer, though a tenant may do the work and the "farmer" may live in the city.

Since the beginning of the present century, occupational patterns of

[62] Wahlke and others, *op. cit.*, chap. 10.

[63] Bernard Bellush, **Franklin D. Roosevelt as Governor of New York,** Columbia University Press, New York, 1955, p. 270.

[64] George H. Mayer, **The Political Career of Floyd B. Olson,** The University of Minnesota Press, Minneapolis, 1951, p. 130.

[65] See Karl A. Bosworth, "Lawmaking in State Governments," **The Forty-eight States: Their Tasks as Policy Makers and Administrators,** The American Assembly, The Graduate School of Business, Columbia University, New York, 1955, p. 99. Quotation below from same source.

legislators appear to have changed little; but the average age of incumbents has increased somewhat, there has been a steady increase in the average amount of education, and the average amount of legislative experience in each session has been increasing, although legislative turnover remains high.[66] Lack of an adequate number of experienced legislators remains a problem in many states. It is difficult to generalize much more about legislators, however. Incumbents in any given legislature are likely to range in age from under thirty to over eighty, from a few years of school to advanced degrees, from the loud-mouthed, back-slapping type to the quiet reflective type, from those who regard it as a lark to be away from the family and its responsibilities, to those who find absence from family, friends, and the everyday habits of life a painful thing. Some are hard drinkers, some are teetotalers; some are stupid, some are brilliant; some are lazy, some hardly ever relax from their work. Most fit somewhere into the middle range. In many ways, they are not particularly different from a cross section of the people they represent.

Table 13   Occupation of Legislators, South Dakota, 1963 and 1965

| | 1965 | | | 1963 |
	REP.	DEM.	TOTAL	TOTAL
Agriculture	25	28	53	47
Business	21	12	33	38
Attorneys	11	3	14	13
Other professions	6	3	9	11
Labor	1	0	1	1
Total	64	46	110	110

SOURCE: George M. Platt, "South Dakota's 1965 Legislative Session," **Public Affairs**, May 15, 1965, table 2.

Lawyers dominate as the single most common occupation of legislators. In one study, the conclusion was that legislative lawyers were about equal to other lawyers in ability. (However, about 90 percent of the lawyers in eleven state legislatures studied in the West were found to have received their legal training in relatively low-status law schools within the state in which they served.) [67] Lawyers tended to seek public office as part of their career planning. That is, they thought a term in the legislature would be helpful in the advancement of their careers as attorneys. In general, service in the legislature was believed to be most helpful to an attorney early in his career and, indeed, lawyers did tend to be younger than nonlawyers when first elected to the legislature and were also younger at retirement. They were more likely than non-

[66] See William P. Tucker, "Characteristics of State Legislators," **Social Science**, 29:94–98, April, 1955; Edward A. Shils, "The Legislator and His Environment," **University of Chicago Law Review**, 18:571–584, 1951; Charles S. Hyneman, "Tenure and Turnover of Legislative Personnel," **Annals**, 195:21–31, January, 1938, and other turnover studies by Hyneman; Heinz Eulau and others, "The Political Socialization of American State Legislators," **Midwest Journal of Political Science**, 3:188–206, May, 1959.
[67] David Gold, "Lawyers in Politics," **Pacific Sociological Review**, 4:84–86, Fall, 1961.

lawyers to retire voluntarily. After retirement, lawyers did not necessarily leave politics. Indeed, they were more likely than nonlawyers to remain in politics. As legislators, lawyers did not usually vote as a bloc on policy matters.[68]

The Social Role of the Legislator

Legislators have changed in recent decades in many ways. The membership is far less venal than it was in former times. Training and education are more extensive than they once were. Average years of service have increased. Rules have been simplified in many cases and inappropriate limitations on length of session removed. Electrical voting devices have speeded up procedure, as have other changes.

Perceived Roles and Tasks   One of the tasks of the legislature is to referee the struggle between and among interest groups. Legislators may consider their standing with the group or groups that are most important to their constituency as more significant than political party allegiance or other factors. Indeed, "a central function of the American state legislature is the accommodation of interest-group demands in the legislative process." [69]

Legislators tend to perceive their roles in terms of being a trustee, a delegate, or a politico. The trustee insists that he rely on his own conscience and his estimate of the relevant "facts" concerning an issue. The delegate believes he should represent the interest of his constituents or his clientele groups, as he sees them. The politico says that he will adopt either one of these two orientations, depending upon circumstances, and that he believes he must balance one against the other.[70]

Public opinion polls in the 1940s indicated that nearly two-thirds of the public believed that a legislator should perform the role of a delegate.[71] However, a study about a decade later indicated that nearly two-thirds of all state legislators in a four-state sample saw their role as that of trustee, that is, that the legislator believed he was elected by his constituents with a responsibility to use his own best judgment on their behalf and on that of the "public interest." [72] In a more recent study, only 47 percent of the respondents in a sample supported the delegate role and findings indicated that "there is as much public tolerance of the functionally necessary trustee role as for the less realistic delegate role." [73] It was also found, however, that in the complex everyday life of a legislator, it was necessary for him to fluctuate between these two roles. This type of behavior has been called the *politico* role, one which, in the opinion of many legislators, cannot easily be explained to constituents with-

[68] David R. Derge, "The Lawyer in the Indiana General Assembly," **Midwest Journal of Political Science,** 6:19–53, February, 1962; Leon D. Epstein, **Politics in Wisconsin,** The University of Wisconsin Press, Madison, Wis., 1958, pp. 111–115.
[69] Wahlke and others, *op. cit.,* p. 342.
[70] *Ibid.,* chap. 11.
[71] Hadley Cantril (ed.), **Public Opinion, 1935–1946,** Princeton University Press, Princeton, N.J., 1951, p. 133.
[72] Heinz Eulau, John Wahlke, William Buchanan, and Leroy Ferguson, "The Role of the Representative," **American Political Science Review,** 53:742–756, September, 1959.
[73] Carl D. McMurray and Malcolm B. Parsons, "Public Attitudes Toward the Representational Role of Legislators and Judges," **Midwest Journal of Politics,** 9:167–185, May, 1965.

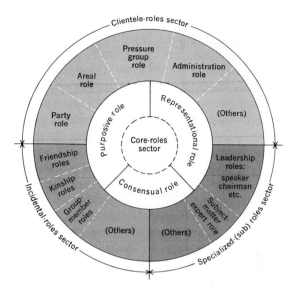

Fig. 14-2   The Role of the Legislator.
SOURCE: John C. Wahlke and others, **The Legislative System,** John Wiley & Sons, Inc., New York, 1962.

out risking loss of status.[74] In order to protect himself, therefore, the legislator is likely to express in public a verbalization of either the delegate or trustee role.

Another Set of Role Types   In a Connecticut study, a considerable number of legislators were found to be in a category known as Spectators. In general, these persons attended sessions regularly, but did not introduce many bills or participate in debate. They found the legislative sessions "fascinating" and entertaining. Many of them appeared to find it a diverting experience from the humdrum of everyday life.[75]

In general, Spectators differed from other legislators in that they had made considerably less personal effort to get nominated, attended far fewer meetings during the campaign, were less sought after for advice, had a lower opinion of themselves as to their ability as legislators, viewed themselves less as "politicians," were less interested in leadership positions, had fewer relatives who were active in politics, and were less likely to be under forty years of age, to have education beyond the high school, to have an income over $10,000 a year, to come from larger communities, or to expect income to increase in the following decade. Spectators were more willing to run for reelection than were other legislators and, in fact, did run for reelection more often than did others in the two elections following the study.[76]

Another group of legislators, the Advertisers, seeks to make contacts and to publicize their businesses. About one-half of the Advertisers among the freshman legislators studied by Barber were attorneys. The others were dis-

[74] Eulau and others, **The Role of the Representative,** pp. 750ff.
[75] James D. Barber, **The Lawmakers,** Yale University Press, New Haven, Conn., 1965, chap. 1.
[76] *Ibid.,* chap. 2.

Table 14   Activity and Willingness to Return, Ninety-six First-term Representatives, Postsession Questionnaire

WILLINGNESS TO RETURN THREE OR MORE TIMES	ACTIVITY		
	HIGH %	LOW %	TOTAL %
"Definitely" or "probably would"	34	31	65
"Definitely not" or "probably would not"	17	18	35
Total	51	49	100
			(N = 96)

SOURCE: James D. Barber, **The Lawmakers,** Yale University Press, New Haven, Conn., 1965, table 1, p. 20.

tributed among many occupations, almost all of them depending, however, upon individual advisory or sales relationships with clients and customers. As one of the Advertisers put it, "if I get active enough in the public eye, and politically, maybe I could get myself a ten or fifteen thousand dollar job one of these days." [77] Unlike the Spectator, who is looking for entertainment and fellowship, the Advertiser sees the job of legislator as a stepping-stone in a professional career. Advertisers, as a group, were more likely than the average legislator to have originated the action to secure nomination, to introduce themselves and seek to become well known to other legislators, to offer and be sought after for advice, to seek and secure important committee assignments, and to consider themselves to be superior or excellent as legislators. In general, the Advertiser expects to secure enough publicity in one or two terms in the legislature to satisfy his purposes.

A third type of legislator includes the Reluctants. These legislators are serving under protest and, if they can be said to be serving willingly, it is only because of a sense of obligation to their community and to society. Often they are older persons who have achieved a considerable degree of success in some nonpolitical calling. They are not highly aggressive, but bring to the legislature a great deal of experience. The position is not particularly prestigeful so far as they are concerned and offers no direct economic payoffs in terms of professional advancement.

Usually the Reluctant found that he liked campaigning more than he expected to and more than the typical freshman legislator, but once in the legislature, he quite certainly did not assume a leadership position or accept an important committee post. As a person of experience in a position of some importance to society in the past, he realistically tended to consider himself as being less influential than the average legislator and graded himself as being less effective than the average.[78]

A fourth category of legislators are called Lawmakers. These are the ones who concentrate on the real work of the legislature. They, "in comparison with other new members, . . . appear to devote an unusual amount of attention and energy to the formulation and production of legislation. . . . On both

[77] *Ibid.,* chap. 3.
[78] *Ibid.,* chap. 4.

sides of the aisle, these were the new members who came to grips with the substantive problems of the legislature and contributed considerably more than their share, proportionately, to the final result." [79] Most Lawmakers were responsible for originating action in order to get their nomination, they campaigned hard and attended many meetings during the campaign. They were anxious to become known to other members of the legislature, were often sought out by members seeking advice, and had a high opinion of themselves as legislators. They regarded themselves as "politicians," for the most part, and were far more interested in seeking leadership positions than were typical freshman legislators. They were also more willing to run for three or more future sessions of the legislature and a disproportionate number of them did, in fact, run for reelection the next time, although in the election next following fewer than average ran for reelection to a third term. However, this was in part a result of the fact that they moved into other governmental positions; in fact, 94 percent of them sought some governmental office, including that of legislator, after their first session. In some cases, the Lawmaker probably did not run for reelection because he was promoted to a more important and more time-consuming position in his own (nonpolitical) profession.

The Legislator and His Constituency   In relation to his district, the legislator is likely to see three different possible roles for himself. These have been named by Heinz Eulau, errand-boy functions, communications functions, and mentor functions. The *errand boy* sees his task as that of helping constituents with their particular problems and defending the interests of his district. This probably applies at the local as well as the state level.

Some legislators see their principal job as keeping people informed. Like the errand boy, the *communicator* is oriented principally toward his district. He sees his most important activities as being those of promptly answering all mail addressed to him, making frequent speeches in his own district, and appearing in the press, and on radio and television, as often as possible.

The *mentor* sees the job of the legislator principally in terms of his responsibility to explain events and policies to his constituents. The mentor differs from the errand boy and the communicator in the same way that the cosmopolite differs from the localite at the local level.[80] He tends to be oriented toward the problems of the state as a whole, as he sees them, rather than toward those of his particular district. He sees his job as one of explaining to his constituents why "what is good for the state is good for the district." [81] Each of the three role concepts is probably relevant to the function of the legislature in the total political system.

SELECTED READINGS

See bibliography for Chapter 13.

[79] *Ibid.*, chap. 5. Quotation from p. 164.
[80] Robert K. Merton, **Social Theory and Social Structure**, rev. ed., The Free Press of Glencoe, New York, 1957, pp. 71–81.
[81] Wahlke and others, *op. cit.*, chap. 13.

15

LAW AND THE JUDICIARY

The adjudication of disputes among members of society in a manner that is relatively undisruptive of the smooth operation of that society is a common objective of social control. As governments became more complicated, part, though by no means all, of the responsibility for this function was turned over to the state and came to be administered through its judicial system. In time, certain acts by one person against another were thought of as being damaging primarily to society at large and thus to the state. These were called "crimes." Other similar acts remained classified by the culture as being primarily wrongs against the interests, rights, or person of the second party and not of society as a whole. But even these cases came to be settled through the machinery of the state as civil actions before the courts. In contemporary society, the judicial branch of government, through an elaborate set of rules, administers both criminal and civil law in the name of society and largely in accord with the dominant values and interests in the community.

The Nature of Law In all but the simplest societies, law performs certain functions. The first of these is to define relationships among members of a society. The law explains which activities are permitted and which are prohibited. Second, law serves to control behavior and to maintain order in a society. It specifies who may exercise sanctions against other members of society on a legitimate basis. "Law is distinguished from mere custom in that it endows certain selected individuals with the privilege-right of applying the sanction of physical coercion, if need be."

Third, the law disposes of troublesome cases as they arise. Although a case may be unique, it is expected that the law will apply existing legal norms to the case and to dispose of it in a manner that will seem to be normal to members of the society. Lastly, the function of the law is to redefine relationships among individuals, organizations, and groups as technology and life styles change.[1]

A few points should be made concerning the nature of law and the way it is administered:

1. Law is only one of the devices for social control. In both primitive and complex societies, values are important. Violation of the mores is always serious in the eyes of society and is often made a crime (e.g., "Thou shalt not kill"), while violation of the (less important) folkways is more likely to be controlled by gossip or ridicule, though some folkways are reinforced by law (e.g., the requirement of driving on the right side of the road).

2. The law has its own logic, its own value system, its own devices for providing it with protective coloration and for justifying its immense power to maintain social equilibrium. One of the most important of such concepts is the one which holds that justice is distributed impartially to all. In our society, the symbol of justice is a woman (gentle protectiveness), blindfolded (so as to ensure impartiality) and holding a balance scale (upon which to determine objectively the merits of the case). Justice is not actually dispensed equally and impartially to all who come before the courts, as will be discussed below, but the concept is an important part of the myth system, of the mechanism for making the actions of the courts legitimate in the eyes of citizens.

3. Crime, justice, equity, and other such terms are all social concepts. What is a crime in one society, is not in another. A crime in one American state is not always a crime in another. The harsh "justice" of class-structured England was rejected on the American frontier for a more egalitarian, but sometimes equally harsh, "justice." Each represented the adjustment of a social institution to its particular environment. The notion of what is fair punishment for a crime or the conditions under which a crime may be overlooked by the prosecutor or may result in a "not guilty" verdict from a jury, even though the alleged act was obviously committed, are determined by the values of society and not by objective standards for measuring an impartial law, as the myth portrays the system. Similarly, judicial organization and administration reflect the values of society. The institution of the jury, providing as it did judgment by one's social equals, was vital under a feudal class system but is less important under the American fluid class system. The English culture provides a system that makes it seem natural for judges to be appointed for life; the American makes it seem natural for them to be elected for a period of years.

4. Because the law and its administration are of vital importance to social control in a complex society and because law is a symbol of stability in a nation historically undergoing constant social change, great deference is paid to the courts, and particularly to the law, in the United States. It is well for the student of social institutions to recognize that this is a part of the method for securing compliance to the law and that an examination of the judicial process

[1] E. Adamson Hoebel, **The Law of Primitive Man,** Harvard University Press, Cambridge, Mass., 1954, chap. 2.

requires a look at it from outside of this framework if we are to understand how it operates.[2]

The Meaning of Justice   Justice is a cultural concept and the procedure by which it is pursued and accomplished is a reflection of the belief systems of a particular society. Justice may be viewed as a process by which a person wronged (by cultural definition) is able to right that wrong. In primitive societies, he may be expected to be able to do this by securing a settlement against the person or the family or clan of the person who wronged him. In seeking justice, he may have the support of his own family and clan. The wrong may be righted in these cases through the payment of a fine by the family of the wrongdoer, or a blood feud may result which continues until the wronged party believes that a redress of grievances has been secured. In primitive societies, government as an institution may not be involved in the process at all.

Where government is involved, the process by which justice is secured may vary enormously, depending upon the cultural concept of what is fair and who is able to bestow justice or to make a decision determining it. In medieval times, for example, justice was sometimes secured through trial by combat or trial by ordeal. The former involved a physical battle between the person who believed himself wronged and the alleged wrongdoer. Medieval citizens believed that God would ensure that the proper person would win the battle. It was not even necessary for the actual litigants to be involved in the battle. The belief was that their representatives would win or lose just as readily as might the principals. Trial by ordeal involved exposure to various forms of torture that could not ordinarily be endured by an individual. An accused wrongdoer, for example, might be called upon to walk across a bed of red-hot coals, or be dunked in a tub of boiling water. If he could survive the ordeal without physical damage, this was viewed as a sign from God that he was innocent.

Trial by jury, a more modern approach to justice, had its beginnings in the twelfth century under the great English judicial reformer, King Henry II.

The Jurisdiction of State Courts   The great bulk of judicial proceedings in the United States are handled by state and local courts. In most states, local courts are viewed as branches of state courts. The state courts can handle almost all of the cases that may be brought before Federal courts and a large number of others besides. This is the case even when Federal questions are involved, if the proceedings are not of a criminal character or, in civil cases, the amount is not more than $10,000. The Federal court system has about 400 judges. About eight times that many judges sit in New York State alone, although about one-half of these are justices of the peace and hence for the most part not professional attorneys. The annual budget of the courts of the state of New York is greater than that of the entire Federal system of courts. Contrary to popular belief, decisions in state courts are *not* ordinarily subject to appeal to the Federal courts. The only point at which the two systems meet

[2] On this section generally, see Thurman Arnold, **Symbols of Government,** Yale University Press, New Haven, Conn., 1935.

is in the United States Supreme Court, and even it can review state court decisions only after all state judicial remedies are exhausted and then only in cases where a "Federal question" is involved, that is, where it is argued that state law or judicial procedures contravene Federal statutes or the provisions of the United States Constitution.[3]

Organization of State Courts

Because of our federal system, Federal courts and state courts have simultaneous jurisdiction over the same territory, people, and corporations. Despite this, the ordinary citizen is likely to have contact only with the latter, for the great bulk of domestic law, both criminal and civil, is based upon state statutory or common law, or local ordinances. Cases that result are normally tried in state courts. The typical criminal is likely to be tried in state rather than in Federal court, although he is sometimes tried in both for the same offense.

The Justice of the Peace   The traditional institution for community justice is that of the justice court. This court originated in England and has existed in this country almost without change since colonial times. The justice of the peace (JP) is not usually an attorney and probably knows little law, but he is authorized to hear and settle civil actions involving small amounts of money (up to a limit of, say $500), hold preliminary hearings for felonies, and try minor criminal cases. The JP was once a man of considerable prestige in his neighborhood, but this is not likely to be the case today. Instead of being a country squire whose "father image" allowed him to dispense a rule-of-thumb justice in neighborhood disputes in an agrarian society with a relatively simple legal system, he is now likely to be some minor local politician of modest social standing.

Normally, JPs are paid through fees assessed against the losing party in each case, and they do not receive salary. The justice thus profits from each case that comes before him, and he may engage in advertising and in agreements with local peace officers in order to increase his volume of business.

The office of the justice of the peace has been criticized a great deal in recent decades. The fact that the JP is elected by a small constituency, often the township, gives him an opportunity to profit from nonresidents who come before his court, and he may do so with no fear of electoral recrimination. Although appeal lies from all justice court decisions to the major trial court of the area, in practice the delay and cost involved in appeals usually leave the citizen at the mercy of the justice. Yet this officer is commonly untrained in the law, responsible to no one for his acts (the professional lawyer-judge is embarrassed if he is criticized or overruled by a higher court, but the typical justice is not), and has a financial interest in the outcome of each case.

Under pressure from the law profession, efforts have been made to eliminate the justice court, but its presiding officer is normally influential in local politics, especially in those states where he sits as a member of the county or

[3] Delmar Karlen, **The Citizen in Court**, Holt, Rinehart and Winston, Inc., New York, 1964, chap. 1.

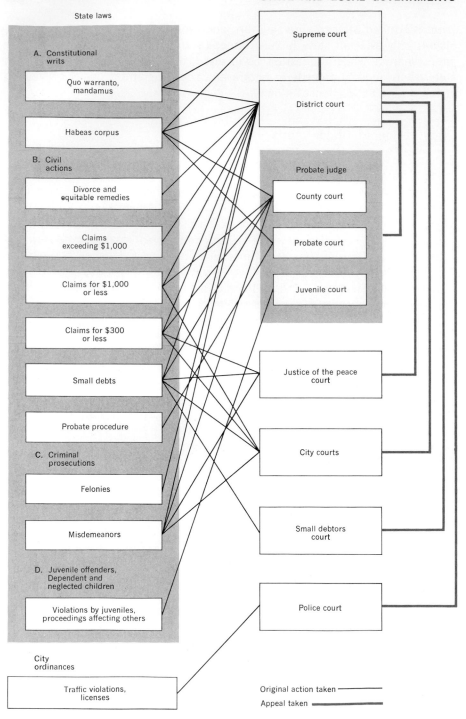

Fig. 15-1   A State Court System: Kansas.

SOURCE: Derived from **Your Government,** Governmental Research Center, University of Kansas, Lawrence, Kans., Mar. 15, 1948.

township governing board, and the justices frequently have powerful statewide organizations to protect their interests before the legislature. Despite this, in recent years the character of the office has been changing. In some states, it has lost some of its powers. In many parts of the country, justices are largely inactive and many do not even bother to qualify for office once elected. In 1957, Ohio abolished the office of justice of the peace, substituting for it a system of county courts and municipal courts with expanded jurisdiction.[4] Michigan did so in 1962, and Oregon has abolished the office in most counties.

Other Minor Courts   Although justice courts continue to exist in some urban and especially suburban communities, the tendency is for cities to have their own court systems, generally under names such as "magistrates court," "traffic court," "court of common pleas," or "police court." These urban courts are usually made up of salaried judges who have legal training and devote full time to the job. The pay is likely to be poor, however, the courts undignified, and the judges not eminent lawyers in the community, though there are probably many exceptions. The person of influence is usually treated far differently from a low-status person.

These courts deal particularly with traffic cases, but also handle such things as lawsuits or contract violation claims involving a few hundred dollars, violations of building codes, and landlord-and-tenant statutes; family disputes, alcoholics, prostitutes, and feuding neighbors; or complaints from mentally disturbed persons who fancy that they have been wronged. In some cases, the judge's ability to serve as a counselor or lay psychiatrist may be more important than his knowledge of the law.[5]

General Trial Courts   The principal courts for hearing both civil and criminal cases "in the first instance" are the backbone of the American judicial system. Most cases that the typical citizen is concerned with will come before them. The quality of justice the individual receives and his image of the court system will depend largely upon the way in which these courts are administered. In most states, they are known as county courts, district courts, or circuit courts, although other names are also used and the nomenclature may not be uniform throughout a state. The larger cities, in particular, are likely to have their own court systems, parallel to, but independent of, the rest of the state courts and often with a different nomenclature.

In these courts, the criminal cases presented by the prosecutor or grand jury are tried (often before a jury) for the first time, as are all but the most minor civil actions (except cases involving the probating of wills). Appeals taken from the minor courts to the general trial courts are also really heard "in

[4] On the justice of the peace, see Lane W. Lancaster, **Government in Rural America**, 2d ed., D. Van Nostrand Company, Inc., Princeton, N.J., 1952, pp. 175–180; Clyde F. Snider, **Local Government in Rural America**, Appleton-Century-Crofts, Inc., New York, 1957, pp. 305–317; and their citations.
[5] See George Warren, **Traffic Courts**, Little, Brown and Company, Boston, 1942; Morris Ploscowe, "The Inferior Criminal Courts in Action," **Annals**, 287:8–12, May, 1953, and other articles in the same volume; and H. H. Curran, **Magistrates Courts**, Charles Scribner's Sons, New York, 1942.

the first instance," since they are started over again from the beginning (tried *de novo,* the lawyers say).

Permanent records are kept of the proceedings of these courts, and they are therefore sometimes referred to as "courts of record." Except in unusual circumstances, one judge presides over the courtroom (several judges may serve a single district if it is populous enough). In most cases, the decision of the trial court is final. Although in theory appeal can almost always be taken to a higher court, in practice this is done only in unusual circumstances: for example, in civil cases where a great amount of money is involved or a well-to-do person or corporation wishes to test the constitutionality of a law; in criminal cases where the defendant is well-to-do, or a defense fund has been collected for him, or his case has become a test case and is being financed by some group interested in civil liberties, such as the American Civil Liberties Union. Most litigants and criminal defendants must accept the findings of the trial court.

The Importance of Trial Courts   Justice, in the United States, is not only defined essentially by state courts, but primarily by the trial courts. Appeals in criminal convictions are rarely taken, and this tendency for trial court decisions to be final has been increasing in the current century. In a study of all the decisions of the Wisconsin Supreme Court between 1839 and 1959, it was found that criminal appeals showed an increase equal to the rate of population increase until around the beginning of the present century. Except for appeals on cases involving the prohibition statutes of the 1920s, criminal cases coming before the supreme court dropped in proportion to population after 1900. By 1961, fewer criminal cases were decided by that court, in actual numbers, than had been the case in 1867.

During the period as a whole, only 5 percent of the cases before the court were criminal appeals. By comparison, 12 percent of the cases coming before the circuit court in Chippewa County over the period of a century were criminal in nature. Of the 20,000 cases, civil and criminal, decided in Chippewa County in a 100-year period, only 1.5 percent were appealed to the state supreme court. Most of the criminal cases that did come before the state supreme court did not involve the substantive concept of criminal law or the penalty imposed upon those found guilty, but rather centered around questions of procedural regularity on the part of the police, the prosecutor, and the trial court.

This study concluded that: [6]

Convictions involving reversible error might never be appealed because the accused feared what other charges the prosecutor might bring against him later, because the accused was resigned to the sentence imposed, or because he expected early admission to parole.

The study also concluded that:

With rare exceptions the appellate cases only dimly reflected the great economic,

---

[6] Edward L. Kimball, "Criminal Cases in a State Appellate Court: Wisconsin 1839–1959," **American Journal of Legal History,** 9:95–117, April, 1965. Quotations from pp. 116–117.

social and political changes in the society. For example, the labor movement, the automobile, the insurance industry, and the credit economy produced so few criminal appeals distinctively identified with the phenomena that one could not see their tremendous importance to the community through this window alone.

Courts of Appeal   The most populous states usually have a court of appeals above the trial courts and below the state supreme court. These courts do not hear cases over from the beginning but rather receive written and oral arguments concerning points of law that were made a matter of dispute at the trial. Questions of fact are not reviewed ordinarily by appellate courts. Since law and not fact is being considered, there is no jury in appeal courts and a multiple bench—from three to nine judges—is used.

In some states, the decision of these intermediate courts is final unless a constitutional question is involved, in which case appeal can be made to the state supreme court. This arrangement frees the highest court for intensive consideration of the most important cases. In some populous states no intermediate court of appeal has been established, with a result that the supreme court is the only appellate court and it is therefore forced to consider cases in large number, hurriedly, and with a chronic backlog on the docket.

These courts sometimes are organized separately for criminal and civil appeals; they may be established on the basis of appellate judicial districts, or there may be only one such court for the entire state. Titles vary, but they are usually known by such names as the "court of appeals" or the "superior court." Under customary procedure, decisions are reached by a majority vote of the judges who hear the case, and one of the judges writes a formal decision explaining the facts of the case briefly, setting out the legal reasoning used (or said to have been used) by the judges in reaching their decision and stating the ruling of the court and the disposal of the case. The latter will usually involve either sustaining the findings of the lower court or reversing them. In the latter case, the defendant in a criminal case may be freed, but the usual order is for another trial in conformity with the findings of the decision.

State Supreme Courts   The general function of the state supreme court (in New York, Kentucky, and Maryland called the "court of appeals") was indicated above. Like other appeals courts, it consists of from three to nine judges and follows the same general procedure. The principal difference is found in the fact that the supreme courts are the courts of final decision from which there is no appeal on any ground except for those rare instances where a case in state jurisdiction can be held to involve a Federal question or the state court procedure can be held to violate the United States Constitution. In these unusual circumstances, it is possible to appeal from the state supreme court to the United States Supreme Court. Such cases are heard by the highest court in the land only at its own discretion, and it accepts only cases involving basic questions.

In unusual cases, a state supreme court hears cases in original jurisdiction—the case is tried initially before the court. In some states it offers ad-

visory opinions at the request of the governor, some other state official, a legislative house, or a legislator, but in most states this function is reserved for the
attorney general, and the court hears only those cases in which a real issue at
law in a specific case is involved.

The state high courts do not slavishly imitate the United States Supreme
Court. In one-half of them, dissents occur in only 5 percent of the cases. In
contrast, more than two-thirds of the cases decided by the United States
Supreme Court in recent years have had at least one dissenting opinion. In the
high courts of California, Louisiana, Michigan, Pennsylvania, and Texas, dissent is a common and expected pattern of judicial behavior. But even in these
states, dissenting opinions occur only about one-half as often as they do in the
United States Supreme Court.[7] In some states, court routine discourages dissent. For example, in Maryland, the high court has a tradition of rotating
assignments for the writing of opinions and judges who do not agree are expected to accept the majority viewpoint without dissenting.[8]

Another reason for the paucity of dissenting opinions may well be related
to the fact that the United States Supreme Court handles only the most difficult cases, while quite a few state high courts serve routinely as appellate
courts and even when there is an appellate level between the trial courts and
the state supreme court, its cases are generally heard within a more definite
frame of legal reference than is the case with the Federal high court. Furthermore, the state supreme court justices do not, for the most part, enjoy the
extreme independence which is guaranteed to members of the United States
Supreme Court.

Four of the five courts in which dissent was most common in 1961 had
relatively high levels of political party competition. In Michigan, in particular,
differences in viewpoint were likely to be along party lines, and this was probably because the parties themselves were ideologically divergent in that state.[9]

All courts, but especially courts of final jurisdiction, have great public
policy-making powers. They must give the fine edge of meaning to legislative
acts and administrative orders since they apply these general policies to specific cases. They also decide the meaning of the state constitution and apply
it to cases. Although decisions are stated in the ritualistic language of the
law, the court in such cases is actually serving as a political body; that is, it
makes policy that has the force and effect of law.

Throughout our history, conflict, tension, and competition have existed
between the state supreme courts and the only judicial agency that may review
their decisions, the United States Supreme Court. No judge likes to be reversed on appeal. Perhaps he likes to be reversed least of all on questions
involving basic social values; yet these are the very kinds of cases that are
most often taken to the nation's highest court. Some of these involve interpretation of state statutes and constitutions by the Federal high court, and this is

[7] In a majority of the state high courts (twenty-seven) in 1961, decisions were unanimous at
least 90 percent of the time.
[8] Robert J. Sickels, "The Illusion of Judicial Consensus," **American Political Science Review**,
59:100–104, March, 1965.
[9] **The Workload of State Courts of Last Resort**, Council of State Governments, Chicago, 1962.

especially galling to state judges. Furthermore, the long-range trend has been for the United States Supreme Court to permit expansion of Federal activities, bringing about additional jealousy from the state judges.

In 1958, the Conference of Chief Justices of state supreme courts adopted a resolution censuring the United States Supreme Court for making "hasty, impatient" decisions, for not using "proper" judicial restraint, and for acting as a "maker of policy in many major social and economic fields." [10] The complaint came after a series of important Court decisions over several years dealing with state laws on segregation, crime control, subversion control, labor relations, and procedural rights in state courts. It reflected both the traditional antipathy between the state and Federal high courts and the ideological conflicts involved in the state-national contest for power.

Special Courts   Special-purpose courts exist in many states. Perhaps the most common is the probate (or surrogate) court which has the principal responsibility for the probating of wills and the settlement of estates. Juvenile courts and domestic-relations courts are sometimes established as branches of probate courts, or they may be organized separately.

All state legislatures have given some recognition to the argument that juvenile offenders should be treated differently from adults. Some states have rather elaborate systems of juvenile courts. Others have makeshift arrangements. For example, in Indiana two counties have full-time juvenile courts and two other counties assign special responsibility for juveniles to the probate courts. The law provides that courts are to be regarded and formally known as juvenile courts whenever the circuit or superior court judge is hearing a case involving a juvenile.[11]

The first of the juvenile courts was established in 1899. Their fundamental purpose has been to emphasize rehabilitation rather than punishment, and the approach is based on the demonstrated fact that young criminals have better prospects for rehabilitation than do older ones.

When a youth (typically an individual under the age of sixteen) violates the law, the objective of the juvenile court is to preserve his social utility. Therefore, a juvenile "is not accused of a crime, not tried for a crime, not convicted of a crime, not deemed to be a criminal, not punished as a criminal, and no public record is made of his alleged offense." [12]

Juvenile courts have assumed a major position in the total judicial system. In 1962, persons classified as juveniles were the subject of 62 percent of the arrests for auto theft, 51 percent of those for larceny, 49 percent for burglary, 25 percent for robbery, 19 percent for rape, 13 percent for aggravated assault, and 8 percent for murder. In total, almost one-half of the arrests for crimes in these categories involved juveniles. One psychologist has identified at least four principal causes of juvenile delinquency. In at least one-fourth of the cases, those arrested had serious neurotic problems, mental

[10] Associated Press dispatch, Aug. 23, 1958.
[11] Henry J. Merry, "The Court System of Indiana," **Public Affairs Notes**, 6:1–6, January, 1964.
[12] **Publicity and Juvenile Courts**, Freedom of Information Center, University of Missouri, Columbia, Missouri, 1965, Publication No. 140.

deficiency, psychoses, or organic brain damage. Second, many juvenile delinquents belong to a "delinquent subculture." That is, they secure most of their recognition in the world through the deliberate flouting of the law. These youngsters are frequently social rejects and have not done well in school. Many of them have dropped out of school. A third factor is really an accumulation of many factors. The individual may have come from a broken home, or may have neurotic problems. At some point, he is faced with a particular problem that seems minor to other people, but is the "final blow" to him. This may be when the only teacher in the school system that understands him resigns, or he fails a particular course, or he is involved in an automobile accident, or one of his parents dies, or his parents are divorced. Finally, he may simply come from a family in which he is neglected. His parents do not perform the task expected of them both by society and by the child. In many such cases, the father and mother are separated. In others, the mother is the boss or the father rejects his parental responsibilities. In some cases the father is himself a law violator, or he or the mother may be an alcoholic. In the great majority of homes from which juvenile offenders come, one or more of these pathogenic situations is to be found.[13]

Judicial Reorganization Court structure and procedures are highly traditional. Only on rare occasions in the history of Anglo-American jurisprudence have the courts been drastically overhauled as institutions and even in these cases, the changes have been relatively slow, as was the case of changes made by Henry II of England in the twelfth century and the establishment of an elective judiciary on the American frontier. One observer has noted that "while courts are asked to solve litigation generated by the Space Age, they operate in almost the same manner as during the wagon-trail era. The only technological innovations evident in courtrooms are stenotype machines, typewriters, and occasional tape recorders."[14]

Courts have resisted change for a number of reasons. For one, ordinary reform movements do not usually affect the courts, which are protected by elaborate traditions, rituals, and the "cult of the robe." In folklore, the courts are independent and the judges are expected to dispense justice impartially. Thus President William Howard Taft vetoed a bill to admit Arizona to the Union on the ground that the state's proposed constitution would threaten judicial independence by providing for the popular recall of judges. Yet, as Herbert Jacob has pointed out, at this very time the courts were deeply involved in public policy formation, particularly through decisions weakening the organizing ability of labor unions and setting aside state welfare legislation. Second, the complex, ritualist characteristics of court procedures discourage change. Judges must be aware of the danger to the magic touch of legitimacy that could be found in a modern court procedure or language. The ancient tradi-

[13] Nick J. Colarelli, "The Adolescent and His Need for Control," in **Juvenile Delinquency Prevention and Control,** Governmental Research Center, University of Kansas, Lawrence, Kans., 1965, pp. 13–21.
[14] Herbert Jacob, "The Courts as Political Agencies," in Herbert Jacob and Kenneth N. Vines (eds.), **Politics in the American States,** Little, Brown and Company, Boston, 1965, p. 48.

tions of the courts and of the law, in general, discourage change. All lawyers are taught these traditions and respect for them in law schools. The assumption that legitimacy rests with the *status quo* is particularly powerful in the legal profession. Finally, the courts have tended to be individualistic, with each judge responsible for his own courtroom. Effective administrative leadership within the judiciary has for the most part arisen only in recent years. Without such leadership, change is unlikely to take place. Furthermore, the most innovative and imaginative lawyers—that is, those with least respect for rules and traditions—are also those least likely to get support for judgeships.[15]

Pressures for reorganization of court systems in the United States have tended to concentrate upon four objectives.[16] One of these is to take judges "out of politics" and give control over standards, if not selection, to the state or local bar association. The second goal is to secure a coordinated system of state courts under the control of the chief justice. The first of these goals is perhaps exemplified in the Missouri Plan for selection of judges. The second is found in New Jersey, where the chief justice has administrative responsibility for the entire system and can send judges wherever they are actually needed, thus increasing the rate of decision making at lower cost. The third objective is a unified court structure. The objective is to secure a unified trial court as in Illinois, eliminating the welter of municipal, justice, probate, juvenile, and other specialized courts. Finally, reformers urge that judicial districts be redrawn to recognize modern methods of transportation and ecological patterns. The objective is to eliminate such illogical and often inequitable situations as those in Iowa where some judges serve as few as 22,000 people and others serve 50,000; some judges try more than 140 cases annually, others less than 30. Minnesota, on the other hand, has reorganized its trial court system into ten districts for the entire state. The objective is, of course, to secure professional judges and other court officers.

Judges who identify with a particular political party are likely to reflect the ideological leanings of that party. One study found that in nonunanimous decisions of state supreme courts, Democratic judges were more likely to take a liberal view on civil rights and liberties and to be less sympathetic to the claims of businessmen. Similarly, they lean toward the claims of working men in actions against corporations and in favor of tenants as against landlords. They also tended to side with the injured person in automobile accident cases against insurance companies.[17]

The Mystery of Nomenclature   The citizen who wishes to be informed about his government must dig in order to learn the functions and responsibilities of various governmental agencies, including the courts. Kentucky offers a good example of the need to learn local nomenclature and to avoid hurried conclusions concerning the function of the various courts. In that state, the supreme

[15] *Ibid.*, pp. 48–49.
[16] Harvey Uhlenhopp, "The Job Still Ahead in Court Reform," **The Iowan**, Winter, 1964–1965, pp. 2ff.
[17] Stuart Nagel, "Political Party Affiliation and Judges' Decisions," **American Political Science Review**, 55:843–851, September, 1961.

court is called the "court of appeals." The principal trial courts are called "circuit courts," and probate courts are called "county courts."

Judges and Juries

The Function of the Judge   What does the judge do for society? The popular impression is that he, like the legislator or bureaucrat, acts to protect the public interest. And, unlike the bureaucrat or even the legislator, the judge feels impelled to consider what is meant by the public interest in many of his decisions.

Some judges and judicial writers view the law as a value-neutral technical process. They hold that what they would consider the proper decision will be made if the system is free from interference by laymen.[18] This view was once widely held, but it does not conform to reality. Some advocates of the Platonic concept of the philosopher-king have viewed the judge as a wise, highly moral person standing above the storms of social conflict, correcting errors by legislators, and in general, serving as a social engineer, making the world a better place to live in despite the machinations of politicians. A realistic view indicates, however, that judges are not that qualified or that noble. They have high prestige and the best of them are very intelligent, but they do not stand above the cultural pressures that affect us all.

Judges on the bench tend to reflect, to a degree at least, their personal ideologies. These preferences are restricted in scope by the expectations of the judicial role and by the ideology of the profession, but they are still to be found. In one study, judges of identifiable ethnic backgrounds tended more frequently than did Anglo-Saxon judges to find for the defense in criminal cases, to support civil rights and liberties claims, and to find for the wife in divorce cases. Catholic judges tended more than did non-Catholic judges to find for the defense in criminal cases, for the wife in divorce cases, for the debtor in conflicts with creditors, for the employee in industrial accident cases, and for the governmental administrative agency in conflicts with business concerning regulation. Ethnic and Catholic judges were, in other words, generally more liberal and working-class oriented than were Anglo-Saxon judges.[19]

Perhaps every state supreme court includes persons with differing life experiences and differing perspectives on the law. These differences are present even though the judges may secure their offices from a political machine and even though all of the judges may be strongly committed to the values, standards, and goals of the legal profession. In Louisiana, for example: [20]

The seven judges of the Court have much in common; their education, methods of recruitment and interests are those of local politicians born and raised in the same state of Louisiana, educated in the schools of the state and exposed to similar

[18] Glendon A. Schubert, Jr., **The Public Interest,** The Free Press of Glencoe, New York, 1960.
[19] Stuart Nagel, "Ethnic Affiliation and Judicial Propensities," **Journal of Politics,** 24:92–110, May, 1962.
[20] Kenneth N. Vines, "Political Functions of a State Supreme Court," in Jacob and Vines, *op. cit.,* p. 69.

bodies of law and to similar political experiences in their elections as Supreme Court judges. But there are also some important differences among them. They come from different sections of the state and from different types of rural/urban environments; they have been exposed to some differing interests, and finally their loyalties and experiences may be with different political factions in the state. We may expect that the judges embody both those values which are common to the social life of political Louisiana as well as those differences which are part of the structure of political life.

The judge serves primarily, it would seem, as a referee or perhaps as a catalytic agent who balances off the various interests involved in each case coming before him. In the individual case, the philosophy of the judge, short-range social conditions (indignation over a particular crime, a vast depression), and other factors may affect the outcome. In the long-range view, the basic values of society are closely reflected in the decisions of judges.

How Judges Are Chosen The public simultaneously wants public officials, and perhaps especially judges, to be "free from political pressure to insure that their decisions are impartial," and at the same time wants them to be "accountable to the people for their official actions." [21] The expectations are not entirely compatible and an ambivalent attitude results.

Because of early nineteenth-century efforts to bring government closer to the people, judges were commonly made elective, and their terms were kept to relatively short duration, two or four years. Only in the East, where the pattern of government was well established before the full impact of Jacksonian democracy was felt, was a different method adopted. In those states—and for some courts in other states—judges are appointed by the governor or elected by the legislature.

Reformers of the early twentieth century thought that the practice of electing judges was detrimental to the interests of society. The argument ran that judges should not only be lawyers but should be especially good lawyers, that they should have a good understanding of sociology, and that voters were ill-equipped to select them because voters cannot evaluate the qualifications of the candidates. Appointment by the governor was commonly proposed as a substitute for election.

We now know that no simple formula exists for choosing the best way by which to select judges. Some governors make most of their appointments from among the outstanding attorneys available; others appoint men of no distinction among their professional colleagues. Where judges are elected, various devices have been developed to help put in office persons who are qualified, at least by the standards of the local bar association. In some cities and states, the bar association makes endorsements or takes a poll on the relative qualifications of various candidates. These endorsements are given wide publicity and are influential in filling positions, particularly if there is no incumbent. Incumbent judges who seek reelection are normally chosen over their challengers because of the greater familiarity of names—and a judge

21 Carl D. McMurray and Malcolm B. Parsons, "Public Attitudes Toward the Representational Role of Legislators and Judges," **Midwest Journal of Political Science**, 9:167–185, May, 1965.

whose incompetence has become notorious risks losing his seat in the next election by that very fact.

Some states have what is nominally an elected, but is virtually an appointed, judiciary. Because of the tendency of judges to stay in office until death or until the infirmities of old age force them to retire, they seldom fail to run for reelection. The result is that the governor, when authorized to do so, fills most judicial vacancies by appointment. And because the incumbent normally has a great advantage in elections, the new judge is then elected and reelected until he dies, when the governor again fills the post. It is possible for a majority of the judges in a state to have been originally appointed to their posts by the chief executive; the theory thus provides for an elected judiciary, but the practice is for virtually an appointed one with periodic review by the voters.

States today use a variety of methods by which to select judges. In the 1960s, the overwhelmingly popular method was that of election. In nineteen states, all or most judges were chosen by election using a partisan ballot, in eighteen other states all or most judges were chosen on a nonpartisan ballot. Four states, two in New England and two in the South, had judges chosen by the legislature. In eight others, judges were appointed by the governor. These states included Delaware, Maryland, New Jersey, Hawaii, and four states in New England (including Connecticut, where formal selection was by the legislature, but actual choice was by the governor). Missouri used its own plan of selection (one which was also used for certain positions in at least six other states), but even in that state some judges were chosen by election.[22]

Although most state judges are elected, they seldom face opposition when running for reelection and are rarely defeated. Insecurity of tenure seems to increase, however, as political party competitiveness increases, at least in those states where judges can be identified by party membership or support.[23]

The political party may be important in shaping the behavior of elected judges. The party affiliation of a judge may have a significant bearing upon his votes, at least in states where some identifiable ideological difference exists between the two major parties. In the Michigan Supreme Court, for example, 65 percent of the workman's compensation cases coming before the court between 1958 and 1960 were settled by a unanimous vote. In the remaining 35 percent, or in ten cases, the vote in each case was 5 to 3 in favor of the compensation claim. In every case, the five majority votes were from Democratic judges and the three dissenting votes from Republicans.[24] A pattern almost as clear-cut was found in the analysis of unemployment compensation claims coming before the court during that same period.

The Missouri Plan for Appointments   Since 1937, the American Bar Association has advocated a plan whereby the chief executive appoints each judge

[22] **State Court Systems,** Council of State Governments, Chicago, 1962.
[23] William B. Fenton, **District Courts in Kansas,** Governmental Research Center, University of Kansas, Lawrence, Kans., 1964, pp. 42–49.
[24] S. Sidney Ulmer, "The Political Party Variable in the Michigan Supreme Court," **Journal of Public Law,** 11:352–362, Fall, 1962.

from a list prepared by a nominating panel composed of judges and lay persons. At the end of a year or at the next election and periodically thereafter the judge's name would appear on the ballot with the question, Shall Judge Jones be retained in office? If the vote is unfavorable the chief executive must appoint someone else from the nominating panel's list. This plan would likely have the effect of giving control over judgeships to the state or local bar associations.[25]

In Missouri, this tendency has been strengthened by the tactics of the nominating panel, which has sometimes offered to the governor one name from the opposing party, one probably unacceptable to him for one reason or another, and a third wanted by the nominators. The governor thus has no real choice in the matter. This plan has been in effect in Missouri since 1940. (Unsuccessful efforts were made in 1941, 1944, and 1955 to force abandonment of the plan.) Plans somewhat similar to it are in effect in all or parts of Alabama, Alaska, California, Illinois, Iowa, Kansas, and Nebraska. The California approach is not so much influenced by the bar association. The California governor is not restricted to a list of nominees. His appointments, by law, must be reviewed by a judicial qualifications commission consisting of two judges and the attorney general. In practice, the report of this commission has usually been quite perfunctory.

Removal of Judges As with other public officials, means exist for the removal of judges, but some are seldom used or even attempted. The following are available:

1. Rejection at the polls. This is perhaps the most common method, though even a judge with a bad reputation sometimes encounters little difficulty in securing reelection. Although one might expect that judges would occasionally have to defend specific decisions at election time, this appears to happen rarely. In fact, the public pays little attention to judicial elections.

2. Impeachment. This elaborate device is generally available, at least for judges of the principal appellate courts, but it is rarely used.

3. Removal by the governor upon request of the legislature. This method is found in a few states. It is not often used, though it is simpler than impeachment since it does not require a formal trial.

4. Removal by joint resolution of the legislature. Similar to the above, but the governor does not participate.

5. The recall. In several states, the recall applies to judges as well as to other elective officials. It is probably used even less often than it is against other officeholders.[26]

Tenure and Qualifications Most states require that judges be "learned in the law," that is, that they be lawyers. This does not apply to the justices of the

[25] Jack W. Peltason, **The Missouri Plan for Selection of Judges,** University of Missouri Press, Columbia, Mo., 1945; William J. Keefe, "Judges and Politics," **University of Pittsburgh Law Review,** 20:621–631, March, 1959.
[26] On the recall generally, see above, pp. 171–172.

peace, who may be barbers, factory workers, housewives, or almost anything else, including lawyers. North Carolina requires judges to "believe in God"; some other states hold that they be "of good character"; but most make no formal requirement. Terms of office vary from election for two years in the case of some trial courts and of the supreme court in Vermont to appointment for life in Massachusetts.[27]

Unlike the Federal court system, each state court is usually autonomous and is coordinated with others only by the general laws of the state and the procedural rules laid down by the state supreme court. The latter may have specific powers of this kind, or it may have influence only through the effect its decisions have upon the lower courts. Frequently one state trial judge works hard while another loafs; one follows a set of procedures that would not be accepted by the next. New Jersey has a unified court system, and the American Judicature Society has long urged that all inferior courts become branches of a single statewide court system with unified administrative supervision. Under such a plan, the state supreme court would have broad rule-making power that would make it more possible for the law to be administered uniformly throughout the state. A director of court administration under the chief justice would have power to move judges about the state from one district to another in order to meet varying peak loads and help clear up the docket in courts where it becomes overcrowded.

The Jury   In difficult cases, a well-known judge has said, "The Greeks went to the oracle at Delphi. We go to the jury. . . ." [28] In traditional legal practice, it has been the task of the judge to decide questions of law, the jury to decide questions of fact. The way in which juries do this in practice has been condemned by both lawyers and laymen who say that these bodies behave with startling inconsistency, that they sometimes free persons who have obviously broken the law, that the process is cumbersome and expensive, that jurors are not typical citizens but often ne'er-do-wells picked because they need the extra income, that jurors cannot understand the technical testimony frequently presented in court, and that juries generally do not act very rationally.

Some of these criticisms are probably valid, especially as to the means by which jurors are selected. But the desirability of eliminating the jury because its procedures are not very rational is questionable. Although the method by which the jury "unravels truth from fiction, with all the shadings of both, is a mystery around which we reverently draw a curtain," [29] it plays an important part in bringing the values of the culture to the judicial process. Undoubtedly jurors sometimes view certain kinds of criminals as heroes, and their attitudes differ with the type of charge. They sometimes are harsh with one

[27] Qualifications for office, length of term, and salaries of judges are reported in detail from time to time in the **Book of the States,** Council of State Governments, Chicago. On judges and courts in general, see A. T. Vanderbilt, **Judges and Jurors,** Boston University Press, Boston, 1956, which gives a well-known judge's viewpoint on judicial organization, and Francis R. Aumann, **The Instrumentalities of Justice,** Ohio State University Press, Columbus, Ohio, 1956, which is a general introduction to the American legal system.
[28] Curtis Bok, "The Jury System in America," **Annals,** 287:92–96, May, 1953.
[29] *Ibid.,* p. 94.

who murders during a family argument—a type of criminal who rarely repeats his crime and is not likely to be dangerous to society—but sympathetically free a dangerous psychopath. Certainly jurors are likely to be swayed by their emotions and prejudices and may ignore all of the competent technical testimony in favor of these considerations. Yet, in doing this they help keep the law in step with changing values in society.

Selection of Jurors About 1.5 million persons serve on juries in the United States each year. Usually the individual is called upon only to spend a few days, or even only a portion of one day, but sometimes a complex case may keep him involved for several months.

Persons to be called for service on both grand and petit juries are chosen in a variety of ways, depending upon state law. A panel of names of prospective jurors may be drawn from the property tax or voters' lists by the judges, court clerks, jury commissioners, or sheriffs. Although in theory a "jury of one's peers" should contain a broad cross section of society, law and the practice of those making selections are such as to exclude many citizens from service, particularly persons who have had an above-average amount of education. In North Carolina, for example, "druggists, telegraph operators, printers, millers, radio announcers, and optometrists are among those exempted." [30] It is also commonplace to exempt or excuse physicians, lawyers, teachers, and college professors. The nonrepresentative character of the jury is one of the most telling criticisms against it.

In trials before a petit jury, the prosecutor, defense attorney, and judge each have an opportunity to challenge and reject persons whose names are pulled from the "jury wheel" if the person is thought to be prejudiced or to have formed an opinion. The judge may also exclude persons who present a plausible excuse for being "unable" to serve.

Folk Myth and the Jury Judges and attorneys sometimes try to create an almost supernatural image of the court system and its procedures. The courts are, however, only another set of institutions in the governmental decision-making process. As Delmar Karlen has pointed out: [31]

Decisions in court are not greatly different from those made outside the court; in that they concern, for the most part, familiar day-to-day happenings; that they involve the same kind of mental operations as are used in solving problems that arise in business or housekeeping; and that they can be and frequently are made by ordinary citizens without special training—namely, jurors.

Several years ago, the University of Chicago Law School undertook a study of the way in which the jury system operates in the United States. [32] One hope had been to be able to observe juries in action, unknown to the members

[30] Robert S. Rankin, **The Government and Administration of North Carolina**, Thomas Y. Crowell Company, New York, 1955, p. 166.

[31] Karlen, *op. cit.*, p. 118.

[32] D. W. Broeder, "The University of Chicago Jury Project," **Nebraska Law Review**, 38:744–760, May, 1959.

of the jury, and to determine how, in general, a jury reaches its verdict. This produced such criticism and was seen as such a threat to a major symbolic institution in American jurisprudence, that the project had to be aborted.[33]

The Grand Jury   This body in common law consisted of from twelve to twenty-three property owners—today it is sometimes smaller—"to which is committed the duty of inquiring into crimes committed in the county from which its members are drawn, the determination of the probability of guilt, and the finding of indictments against supposed defendants." [34] Traditionally, the grand jury has had two functions: (1) to decide whether persons brought before it by the prosecutor should, according to the evidence presented, be held for trial and (2) to conduct investigations into the existence of a crime, or of crime generally, and to hold for trial, through a "presentment," * persons it believes may be guilty of crimes, even if the prosecutor has not acted.

* **PRESENTMENT. An accusation made by a grand jury, after investigation and independently of any recommendation by a prosecutor. A charge made against a person on recommendation is called an INDICTMENT, or the grand jury is said to have returned a TRUE BILL.**

For the purpose of returning indictments, the grand jury is falling into disuse and about one-half the states place little or no dependence upon it for this purpose. In its native England, the grand jury has been virtually abolished. The indictment was never anything more than a finding by the jury that there was enough evidence to make it probable that the accused is guilty and should be held for trial. Replacing the use of the grand jury in deciding this today Is another ancient procedure whereby the prosecutor himself, occasionally in some states and frequently in others, simply files an "information" * with the appropriate court saying that he is holding John Soandso for trial, specifying the charge. This method is faster and less expensive than the grand jury method. Prosecutors much prefer it. They dislike having to face two juries, and they prefer not to reveal any of their evidence before the trial, as is necessary to get a grand jury to indict. Although one of the functions of the grand jury is disappearing, that body continues occasionally to perform a vital service as a citizen's investigating body. Whenever the prosecutor is lazy, incompetent, or corrupt, a grand jury may be the only means by which the suspected existence of crime may be inquired into, although sometimes the state attorney general may act where the local prosecutor has failed to do so. Any investigating grand jury can hold persons for trial. It has the power to require the appearance of witnesses, to punish for contempt, and to grant immunity in exchange for testimony that may be self-incriminating.

* **INFORMATION. A charge made by the prosecutor on his own responsibility and without grand jury action. In most American states, this is the common procedure by which a charge is formally made.**

[33] Harold Kalven, "Jury, the Law, and the Personal Injury Damage Award," **University of Chicago Law School Record,** 7:6–21, February, 1958.
[34] "Grand Jury," **American Jurisprudence,** Lawyers Co-operative Publishing Co., Rochester, N.Y., 1939, p. 832.

The Trial Jury   The common-law trial jury consisted of twelve persons and a unanimous verdict was required for it to bring in a verdict. It is called the petit (i.e., small) jury to distinguish it from the grand (i.e., large) jury. There is today a tendency to use the jury in fewer and fewer cases, turning the more complex ones over to the judge, especially in civil actions. In some states a criminal defendant may waive jury trial, and the defendant is not in all cases entitled to a jury trial. Other trends include one toward the use of a body smaller than twelve and toward a dropping of the requirement for a unanimous decision. The latter is thought by some law specialists to give the defendant an undue advantage and to increase delays and expenses because it encourages hung juries.

Officers of the Court   In addition to the judge, who in theory represents the interests of society at large, the court of record has a clerk who prepares the technical documents used in the legal process, keeps the transcript of the court proceedings, and calls witnesses by subpoenas and jurors by summonses. In some states, he has the imposing title of prothonotary. Often he is elected, and he may be on a fee, rather than salary, basis. The bailiff, commonly a deputy sheriff, serves legal court papers made out by the clerk, has custody of prisoners during trial, and keeps order. Other actors in the courtroom, although they are not officers of the court, include the prosecuting attorney (his title varies from state to state), who presents the case on behalf of the state; the sheriff, the traditional law enforcement officer of the county; and the coroner, who investigates deaths under unusual circumstances and decides, sometimes with the help of a jury, whether a deceased died a natural, suicidal, or accidental death or by the "hands of a person or persons unknown."

All of these officials are usually elected to office. Because of the technical job he must perform—involving as it does both medical and legal knowledge—there is a trend toward the abolition of the coroner's office and toward turning its functions over to a medical examiner on the prosecutor's staff. There is no trend toward a basic change in any of the other offices.

The Public Defender   California is one of a number of states having the position of public defender. This officer takes over the defense of any accused person who, in the judgment of the court, cannot afford legal advice. The largest operation in the state is in Los Angeles County, where the office has about seventy full-time trial lawyers on its staff. They serve under merit system civil service rules and are paid by the county.

The Court in Action

Criminal Procedure   Criminal procedure varies somewhat, depending upon the nature of the case and upon state law. In simplified form, however, a case begins with a complaint filed by the prosecutor. This officer has the power, anytime before the indictment, to nol-pros the case, that is, to discontinue it. This discretionary authority is enormously important, and the prosecutor's good judgment, integrity, energy, and ability to reflect the expectations of the community are important considerations in the way in which it is used. Warrants for search and arrest are secured and served as follows: [35] A complaint is made to a judge who is authorized to issue a warrant. The complaint is made under oath and alleges that a crime has been committed and that the complainant has reason to believe that "fruits or instrumentalities" are concealed in a particular place or vehicle. If the judge considers the complaint to be justified, he issues a warrant which directs a law-enforcement officer to seize the allegedly incriminating evidence. In order to be legal, the warrant must describe adequately the place to be searched and the contraband to be seized. Whatever property is seized must be brought before the judge who issued the warrant.

If the accused is not already in custody, apprehension by municipal, county, state, or, sometimes, Federal law-enforcement officers is the next step. Then comes an examination, or preliminary hearing, before a judge or justice of the peace, to determine whether there is evidence to justify holding an individual in custody. This step is often waived by the accused. It is followed by extradition to the state where the crime was committed, if this is necessary. The individual is then bound over to the grand jury, or if the information device is used, is held for trial. He may be released on bail if this is permitted by law and the opinion of the judge. Indictment by the grand jury follows, if this step is required in the case. This is a hearing at which the only question is whether the prosecutor has enough evidence to warrant holding the accused for trial. Formal arraignment on the charge follows, and the defendant enters a plea. In the great majority of cases, a guilty plea is made and no trial is necessary, excepting in a few circumstances such as when the crime may carry the death penalty.

At the trial, the defendant may hire his own attorney (60 to 80 percent of persons accused of crimes cannot afford to do so), have one assigned by the court (usually from among the inexperienced or incompetent members of the profession), or be defended by the public defender. The latter operates an office exclusively for this purpose. He is usually able to offer more competent assistance than is furnished by a court-appointed attorney. The jury (or sometimes the judge) renders a verdict. If the individual is found not guilty, he is released unless another charge is pending against him. If he is found guilty, the bailiff returns him to the jail, or he is delivered to a state penal institution, unless at his sentencing (usually sometime after the verdict), he is placed on probation, a conditional release that may require periodic reporting to a probation officer or court officer who may or may not be trained and competent in rehabilitative techniques. Appeal of the conviction can be taken to higher courts, and the governor may be requested to commute (reduce) the sentence or pardon the convicted person. Imprisonment, except of course in cases involving the death penalty, is usually followed eventually by parole (conditional release) or discharge.

[35] Paul E. Wilson, **Basic Rules of Arrest, Search and Seizure**, Governmental Research Center, University of Kansas, Lawrence, Kans., 1964, p. 22.

The only reason contemporary courts can keep reasonably up to date on their dockets is that the great majority of criminal cases are quickly settled through a plea of guilty, and most civil actions are settled out of court or are defaulted. Both procedures help to clear court dockets, but they do not necessarily aid in the furthering of justice. Not only are most cases not actually tried in court, but even among those that are, the great majority are not appealed. That is, the decision of the original trial court is final. It is true that a statutory provision for appeal to a higher court exists for almost every type of case whether civil or criminal, of major importance or trivial, but the typical participant in a case does not know this or, if told by his attorney, does not believe he can afford the cost of appeal which, indeed, is often extremely high. More than 90 percent of the cases in which a legal right to appeal exists are settled at the trial court level.[36]

Conflicting Professional Concepts and the Law   Many conflicts arise between the legal and other professions in the interpretation of criminal behavior. Medical and legal approaches to the same problem may differ sharply, for example. In crimes of violence, it is quite common for the defendent to plead innocent by reason of insanity. Most states do not define "insanity" as a sufficient defense against an alleged criminal act. They have rules concerning conditions under which an individual may or must be committed to a mental institution, but these criteria do not necessarily apply to responsibility for criminal acts. In criminal cases, forty-three states in 1966 applied the so-called M'Naghten rule. This rule was first established in a British court in 1843 when one Daniel M'Naghten was acquitted of murder on grounds of insanity. The decision was based on the conclusion that the defendant was not, at the time, able to distinguish between what society regarded as right and what as wrong. If he did not know "that he was doing a wrong or wicked act," the judge said, he could not be held guilty.

The difficulty with this interpretation of behavior is that the rule was devised long before the development of contemporary theories of psychiatry and psychology. In fact, psychologists point out, it is uncommon for persons who are clinically diagnosed as psychotic, which is roughly equivalent to the legal concept of insanity, not to know the difference between social concepts of right and wrong, even though they may not themselves necessarily accept the distinction. Psychiatrists have argued that the old rule should be abandoned and a more practical one, in terms of modern psychiatric knowledge, should be applied, namely, that an individual should not be held criminally responsible for an unlawful act if it is the result of the individual's being mentally ill or mentally deficient. A few state courts have moved somewhat in this direction.

Civil Procedure   Civil procedure begins when an attorney for the plaintiff files a complaint with the clerk of the court, stating the facts of the alleged wrong. A copy of this is served on the defendant, who may file an answer with the

[36] Karlen, *op. cit.*, chap. 7.

court. The case is then, as in a criminal case, put on the docket for trial. The case may be heard by a jury, though it is increasingly the practice for civil cases to be heard by the judge alone. Witnesses are used much as they are in criminal cases, and their attendance may be required by the court. The judge or jury renders a verdict and in appropriate cases determines the amount of damages that must be paid if the finding is for the plaintiff. The judge generally has more discretion in civil than in criminal cases, even when a jury is used. He may direct a verdict, thus telling the jury what it must decide, or he may set aside the verdict, under some circumstances. Appeal in civil cases follows much the same lines as in criminal cases. The kinds of civil actions that are possible are enormously varied and technical and cannot be discussed here.

Political Questions before the Courts   When judges fear that a question put to them is dangerous politically, or the procedures of the courts are ill-adapted to the settlement of the case, or there are no judicial standards upon which to base a decision, they may refuse to hear the case on the grounds that it involves a "political" rather than a judicial question. The numbers of such cases apparently are not large. During a sixteen-year period in Louisiana, only two cases were rejected by courts as political questions. Such cases, although not large in numbers, may be extremely important to the persons raising the question, however.[37]

Justice in Myth and Practice

Scene: A courtroom.

Said the arresting officer: "He was 'plastered.' "

Said the handsome professional football star: "I would say I had about six drinks, but I was not under the influence to the point where it hurt me."

Said a woman juror: "He ought to give us women a big kiss for letting him off." [38]

The same edition of the newspaper that carried the above story also told of the case of a nineteen-year-old girl who was fined $10 and sent to the county jail for a day for running a red light—no accident was involved. On the same day, in the same county, in a different courtroom, a twenty-one-year-old boy who pleaded guilty to negligent homicide—he had driven through a stop sign and caused an accident in which a girl was killed—was neither fined nor jailed. He was placed on probation for two years and ordered to pay court costs.

The Concept of Justice   Justice is a relative thing. And in the individual case it depends upon the ideology, attitude, diligence, interest, and other considerations of the police officer, the prosecutor, the judge, the jurors, the defense attorney, the probation officer, and every other person who comes in contact

[37] Kenneth N. Vines, "Political Functions of a State Supreme Court," in Jacob and Vines, *op. cit.*, p. 58.
[38] Quotations from the **State Journal,** Lansing, Mich., Dec. 7, 1957.

with the case. It also makes a difference who you are. The jurors were very much aware of the identity of the famous athlete mentioned above. A police officer will often take one view of a man in greasy overalls who stumbles out of a working-class tavern and another of a man dressed in a well-tailored suit who stumbles out of the bar of the most expensive hotel in town. The former may spend the night in the "drunk tank"; the latter may be helped to his room.

Culturally inspired deference of this type is not the same, however, as the tendency of a jury to apply cultural values or the popular sentiment of the moment to a particular case. A jury will often refuse to convict a woman who kills her unfaithful husband, for example. In the South, the mores may prevent a jury from finding a white man guilty of a crime against a Negro. If the jurors believe the penalty is too severe for any crime, they will not convict regardless of the evidence, and the result sometimes is that the legislature must modify the law to suit the jurors' concept of justice.

The judicial process as it exists in practice is often criticized ("the jury was made up of corner loafers"; "it took two years to collect sixty bucks"; "I needed a witness, and ten people saw the accident, but not one of them stopped"). Yet, the people who make unfavorable comments may well be the same ones who dodge jury duty (it is easy to do so) or refuse to testify even though they suspect their testimony is needed by the plaintiff or the prosecutor.[39] Certainly both of these acts are common on the part of Americans.

There are often great delays before cases, either criminal or civil, come to trial, especially in more densely populated areas. "Justice delayed is justice denied," is a cliché, but it is often true. Witnesses die or disappear; the jury discounts an old wrong more than a recent wrong; evidence cannot be kept intact. The woman whose purse is stolen becomes more angry with the police if the purse is locked in a safe as evidence for a year than she was with the thief.

Justice is also a costly thing. Some efforts are being made to overcome this problem. The office of the public defender is becoming a more common institution to assist the person accused of a crime. Legal-aid bureaus have become common in cities as a source of information in some kinds of cases, at least, for the low-income person. These bureaus are run by incorporated charities, bar associations, social agencies, and other organizations. Yet even the middle-income person finds legal procedures a heavy financial burden, and the law, which grows ever more complicated, is totally unfathomable to the layman. It is significant that the number of lawsuits is decreasing, despite our population growth and the increasing complexity of our society. Appeals to higher courts are expensive, and few appeals are therefore taken, although failure to carry the case above the decisions of an incompetent or indolent trial judge may well result in the denial of justice. In contrast, the large corporation can afford to keep a case in court for years on appeals, not only to win a particular case, but to discourage other actions against the company. (The large corporation has its own cross to bear: juries tend to award generous

[39] A. S. Cutler, "Why the Good Citizen Avoids Testifying," **Annals,** 287:103–109, May, 1953. This entire volume on "Judicial Administration and the Common Man" deals with some of the issues discussed in this section.

judgments against it and sometimes to regard the person who defrauds it as something of a hero.) And the wealthy person or corporation that hires a former state supreme court justice to argue its appeal before the supreme court or an incumbent legislator to argue its case before an administrative tribunal such as the liquor-control commission is certainly "one up" on a less well-to-do opponent or on the prosecutor in a criminal case.

The law is slow to change, and many of its rules, particularly its rules of evidence, may permit injustice. The legal concept of insanity, for example, differs widely at times from scientific knowledge gained from a study of psychosis. The courts may refuse to admit evidence which, to the layman, seems to be highly relevant—sometimes because the advancement has come too recently to be recognized. Just as the lexicographer seems to be the last person to learn about a new word usage, the judge seems to be the last person to learn of scientific advancements. Much of the work of crime laboratories is now admissible evidence, however.

The courts have always had something of the circus about them, and they hold a hypnotic attraction for people who find murder or rape trials exciting and a welcome change from their own dull lives. In the nineteenth century: [40]

People came from miles around and hung on every syllable while the lawyers talked for days. Happy was he who could sit in the jury box and be directly thundered at. The resulting public hangings drew huge crowds, with choice seats going at fancy prices. Court term in country districts brought in the neighbors to see the artful lawyers and hear the speeches even for the ordinary calendar. . . .

This pattern may be changing, and some courts are dignified today. Certainly the United States District Courts fit this category, and their enormously prestigeful judges will ordinarily not permit the court to become too much of a theater. But judges are sometimes careless about the appearance of the courtroom, they hesitate to clear it of spectators during spicy testimony lest they be reversed on appeal (one's civil rights guarantee a public trial), and newspaper editors attract crowds to the more spectacular trials as a result of their financial interest in dramatizing them. The theatrical setting in such cases probably does not contribute to a disinterested review of the evidence by either the judge or the jury. And, of course, the fox-and-hounds nature of criminal trials will probably always keep them something of a show.

Trends in Judicial Administration   Serious efforts are being made by bar associations, legislatures, judges, social service agencies, and others to keep judicial administration abreast of the times. Many changes have taken place; others seem to be on the way. Juries are less used; judges are more specialized; witnesses are more often sought as experts than as persons who observed, supposedly, certain activities; nonlawyer specialists (clinical psychologists, social workers, and others) make an increasingly large portion of the major decisions.

Law and the judicial process, then, are parts of the total culture in which
[40] Bok, *op. cit.*, pp. 92–93.

they exist and are subjected to the same kinds of pressures that affect other institutions. In a day when most of our socially useful activities are dominated by the expert and the pattern of specialization, our courts are also coming to be dominated by the expert and to conform to the pattern of specialization.

SELECTED READINGS

Arnold, Thurman: **Symbols of Government,** Yale University Press, New Haven, Conn., 1935. (A landmark study of the symbolic roles of governmental officials and symbolic functions of institutions.)

Aumann, Francis R.: **The Instrumentalities of Justice,** Ohio State University Press, Columbus, Ohio, 1956.

Berle, Adolph A.: "Elected Judges or Appointed?" **New York Times Magazine,** Dec. 11, 1955.

Beutel, F. K.: **Some Potentialities of Experimental Jurisprudence as a New Branch of Social Science,** University of Nebraska Press, Lincoln, Nebr., 1957.

Cook, James M.: **Texas Corporation Courts,** Institute of Public Affairs, University of Texas, Austin, Tex., 1961.

Courts of Last Resort in the Forty-eight States, Council of State Governments, Chicago, 1950.

Curran, H. H.: **Magistrates Courts,** Charles Scribner's Sons, New York, 1942.

Frank, Jerome: **Courts on Trial,** Princeton University Press, Princeton, N.J., 1949.

Jacob, Herbert: "The Effect of Institutional Differences in the Recruitment Process: The Case of State Judges," **Journal of Public Law,** 13:104–119, January, 1964.

———— and Kenneth E. Vines: "The Role of the Judiciary in American State Politics," in Glendon Schubert (ed.), **Judicial Decision-making,** The Free Press of Glencoe, New York, 1963, pp. 245–256.

Keefe, William J.: "Judges and Politics," **University of Pittsburgh Law Review,** 20:621–631, March, 1959.

Mitchell, Wendell: **Relations Between the Federal and State Courts,** Columbia University Press, New York, 1950.

Peltason, Jack W.: **The Missouri Plan for Selection of Judges,** University of Missouri Press, Columbia, Mo., 1945.

Ploscowe, Morris: "The Inferior Criminal Courts in Action," **Annals,** 287:8–12, May, 1953.

Pound, Roscoe, **Criminal Justice in America,** Holt, Rinehart and Winston, Inc., New York, 1945.

Rosenblum, Victor G.: **Law as a Political Instrument,** Random House, Inc., New York, 1955.

Schmidhauser, John R.: **The Supreme Court as Final Arbiter of Federal-state Relations,** The University of North Carolina Press, Chapel Hill, N.C., 1958.

Schubert, Glendon: **The Political Role of the Courts: Judicial Policy-making,** Scott, Foresman and Company, Chicago, 1965.

Scigliano, Robert G.: **The Michigan One-man Grand Jury,** Social Science Research Bureau, Michigan State University, East Lansing, Mich., 1957. (Contains history of the grand jury and of the variant of it in Michigan by which a single circuit court judge performs the jury's function.)

Strodtbeck, Fred L., and others: "Social Status in Jury Deliberations," **American Sociological Review,** 22:713–719, December, 1957.

Talbott, Forest: **Intergovernmental Relations and the Courts,** The University of Minnesota Press, Minneapolis, 1950.

Trial Courts of General Jurisdiction in the Forty-eight States, Council of State Governments, Chicago, 1951.

Vanderbilt, Arthur T.: **Judges and Jurors: Their Functions, Qualifications and Selection,** Boston University Press, Boston, Mass., 1956. (By a lawyer, famed for judicial reform advocacy.)

———— (ed.): **Minimum Standards of Judicial Administration,** Law Center of New York University, New York, 1949.

Vanderzell, John H.: "The Jury as a Community Cross-Section," **Western Political Quarterly,** 19:136–149, March, 1966. (By no known empirical measure is the jury a community cross section.)

Vines, Kenneth N., and Herbert Jacob: **Studies in Judicial Politics,** Tulane University Studies in Political Science, New Orleans, La., 1963.

Warren, George: **Traffic Courts,** Little, Brown and Company, Boston, 1942.

Younger, Richard D.: "The Grand Jury on the Trans-Mississippi," **Southwestern Social Science Quarterly,** 36:148–159, September, 1955.

————: **The People's Panel: The Grand Jury in the United States, 1934–1941,** Brown University Press, Providence, R.I., 1963.

16

CIVIL RIGHTS AND LIBERTIES

The protection of an individual's civil rights and liberties is, in the first instance and in the final result, usually, the responsibility of state and local governments. The dramatic legislation and United States Supreme Court decisions, especially of the 1960s, in these areas have resulted from the same kinds of pressures that have brought the Federal government into other aspects of domestic public policy. Legislation and litigation have resulted both from the failures of state and local governments to meet the expectations of large blocs of persons and from widespread demand for more uniform, nationwide policies.

All state constitutions make some provision for the protection of civil rights and liberties, but interpretations of these have varied widely from one state to another. Traditional concepts of justice, and its principal components, due process of law and the equal protection of the law, have varied greatly by states and regions of the nation. Recent pressures from all branches of the Federal government have been designed to narrow the range of differences.

The attitude of Americans toward civil rights is probably well expressed by the writers of the perennial television favorite, "Gunsmoke." Through the years, the program has consistently failed to show respect for the fundamental traditions of Anglo-American jurisprudence. Individual civil rights and liberties are frequently violated. This was probably the actual practice on the frontier, but the point is that the program reflects *contemporary*, as well as frontier values. The stereotypic hero of the program, instead of being concerned with the bill of rights, applies a rule-of-thumb equity to the criminal cases he confronts. In Anglo-American jurisprudence, of course, equity applies only to civil actions. Its equivalent in criminal cases is found in the pardoning power of the chief executive and the latitude often given the sentencing judge, but in theory, it is never delegated to a mere United States marshal, not even Matt Dillon.

The States' Attorneys

The Prosecutor   The prosecuting attorney, known by a variety of titles, holds an office of great discretion. To a considerable extent, he decides which laws are to be enforced, how vigorously they are to be prosecuted, and in some states how heavy a penalty is to be demanded or at least requested of the trial judge in sentencing. Characteristically, in the American system the prosecutor, as a key decision maker, is generally an elective official. In all but four Eastern states this is the case. The political system is therefore designed to provide for a method by which local values are maximized in the interpretation and prosecution of the law.

As a result of this pattern, bootleggers during the prohibition era were not proceeded against, or were treated lightly by prosecutors in areas where there was little "dry" support. Similarly, in the 1950s and 1960s, many prosecutors in the rural South concluded that their constituents did not want laws or court interpretations on desegregation vigorously enforced. As a result, enforcement came to depend primarily upon action by Federal agencies.

Prosecuting attorneys with political ambitions may seek to gain publicity and public approval through their actions. Local prosecutors may go on to the state legislature, to Congress, to the office of state attorney general, or they may become governor. Of course, many who hope to have a political career are frustrated and fail despite their ambitions. On the other hand, it appears that quite a large number of prosecutors do not have in mind a political career,[1] but rather hope to use the office for the sake of publicity and to establish contacts which will later be helpful in the development of a career as a practicing attorney. In addition, of course, we may assume that some prosecutors are interested primarily in public service as a temporary civic responsibility. In some sparsely settled areas, attorneys are so few in number that they may, in turn, be virtually drafted for the office.

The use of the "information," rather than the cumbersome traditional grand jury, is commonly favored by prosecutors, for the approach adds still further to his power of discretion as to the type and vigor of law enforcement. A former Governor of Michigan has commented: [2]

Personally, I believe Michigan should have a system of regular periodic grand juries similar to the federal system. I have always felt that law enforcement in several communities was retarded because there was no regular grand jury.

The Attorney General   The attorney general is the legal officer of the state, but he is severely restricted in his powers relative to the enforcement of criminal law. In Missouri, for example, he normally enters a case only at the

---

[1] Herbert Jacob, **Justice in America,** Little, Brown and Company, Boston, 1965.
[2] G. Mennen Williams, **A Governor's Notes,** Institute of Public Administration, University of Michigan, Ann Arbor, Mich., 1961, p. 32.

direction of the governor, although he could enter at the request of the local prosecutor, if the trial judge agrees. Under the law, he is authorized to act on his own initiative only to enforce the provisions of the Liquor Control Act.[3] It is probable that small-town legislators, fearful that urban counties might be lax in enforcement of liquor regulations, made this special exception, but are unwilling to have the attorney general looking over the shoulder of the prosecutor in their own districts. In any case, he is permitted under the law only to assist in the prosecution of a case. Excepting where the local prosecutor is incapacitated or disqualified, he cannot take over actual prosecution. The local prosecutor "is in a position to restrict the role of the Attorney General in the case to a *pro forma* one." During the period between 1953 and 1960, the attorney general was involved in criminal cases on the average of only about four a year. Most of these involved delicate political situations affecting public officials or important persons. The local prosecutor, in such cases, probably preferred to leave the case to an outsider. He also was involved in some cases in counties with few attorneys, where the prosecutor found himself barely out of law school but responsible for a major felony case. In other instances, the local prosecutor was disqualified because he had a direct interest in the case.

Richard Watson has concluded that "the role of the Attorney General in criminal law enforcement in Missouri, while undoubtedly important on occasion, is too sporadic and limited to be of any real significance." [4]

One of the most important duties of the attorney general is to interpret the law. These rulings generally have the force and effect of law unless overruled by the courts. In Michigan, requests for opinions must come from county prosecuting attorneys, state officers, and legislators. Individuals in these positions can, however, make a request on behalf of someone else. The pattern of opinion development is probably somewhat different in Michigan from most states, because the assistant attorneys generally are all civil servants. Under these circumstances, the values and goals of the legal profession itself probably tend to dominate.

A request for an opinion goes to the deputy attorney general, who is an appointee of the elected attorney general. If he believes the request is legitimate, it is assigned by him to specialists in the area of law concerned. Political interests are probably maximized at this point, since it is possible for the deputy attorney general to find a reason for not making a finding in favor of an opinion and he has some discretion in the division of the department to which the request is to be sent. The group of specialists in the division which receives the request prepares a draft of the opinion. If this is approved by the division head, the proposed opinion goes to an opinion review board. All members of the board are civil servants. The board may return the opinion for further work, may make modifications which are noted in a memorandum, or may approve it as it is presented. The deputy attorney general then reviews it and, if he approves, sends it to the attorney general for signature. If either the

[3] Richard A. Watson, **The Office of the Attorney General**, Research Center, University of Missouri, Columbia, Mo., 1962, chap. 6.
[4] *Ibid.*, p. 36.

deputy or attorney general disapproves, the opinion is recirculated through the procedures. The results are not always to the liking of the attorney general or to the governor, even if he is of the same party, but they are usually found acceptable to leading members of the legal profession.

Attorneys general have, in the present century, been among the foremost prospects for advancement to the office of governor. Perhaps for this reason, attorneys general in the South, following the 1954 decision of the United States Supreme Court requiring the desegregation of schools, were among those most insistent upon preserving the *status quo* and resisting the effort of the Court to impose a national policy.[5]

Procedural Due Process

In 1965, James J. Kilpatrick, chairman of publications for the Virginia Commission on Constitutional Government, complained somewhat bitterly that: "the whole drift of our law, these days, is toward the absolute prohibition of all ideas that diverge in the slightest form from a Federal standard. The entire field of criminal law, which the Constitution reserved almost exclusively to the States, rapidly is becoming subject to increasing scrutiny by the United States Supreme Court. And once the Court scrutinizes, the Court is reluctant not to impose Federal standards upon a State's administration of criminal justice." [6]

The Police and Civil Rights   The task of state and local law-enforcement officers is always difficult. They frequently must make quick decisions and these decisions may directly affect the civil rights and liberties of citizens. If a policeman lacks zealousness in seeking to enforce the law, he will be criticized. If he is overly zealous, he may not encounter criticism from local newspapers or his professional colleagues, but he may do great damage to the peace, property, and psychological well-being of private citizens.[7]

Due Process and Arrest   Until the nineteenth century, responsibility for bringing violators before the courts was essentially that of the individual citizen. The professional police officer did not appear in England until the early nineteenth century and in the United States until later than that. In an earlier period, a "citizen's arrest" was common and perhaps the most customary means of apprehending a criminal. As organized professional police forces have developed, participation by the citizen has become less common. Indeed, today a citizen's arrest is a dangerous move, in the view of many persons, for they fear the possibilities of lawsuits for false arrest. The tendency of the contemporary American is to argue that he does not "want to become involved." As a result,

[5] Samuel Krislov, "Constituency versus Constitutionalism: The Desegregation Issue and Tensions and Aspirations of Southern Attorneys General," **Midwest Journal of Political Science**, 3:75–92, May, 1959.
[6] James J. Kilpatrick, **Nor Cruel and Unusual Punishments Inflicted**, Virginia Commission on Constitutional Government, Richmond, 1965, p. 31.
[7] For an example of poor judgment by law-enforcement officers, see H. Frank Way, Jr., **Liberty in the Balance**, McGraw-Hill Book Company, New York, 1964, pp. 119–120.

arrest is today almost exclusively an activity of persons holding a formal warrant as peace officers.[8]

Under normal circumstances, an arrest cannot be made in the absence of a warrant. A warrant is a command issued by a judge or other magistrate ordering the arrest of the person named in the warrant. An arrest may be legally made, however, without a warrant in emergency situations. These must be defined in statute or by precedent. When an arresting officer acts in the course of carrying out an order provided in a warrant, he is safe from any charge of misfeasance, but if he makes an arrest without a warrant, he is personally responsible for his act and may be sued for false arrest under some circumstances. Even so, illegal arrests in the United States probably exceed by far the legal ones.[9]

The law enforcement officer does not merely arrest an alleged offender. He is also expected to produce for use in court the articles and documents that may be used in evidence. Because this is his responsibility, he has a right to search the person of an individual arrested and also the premises on which the arrest takes place, if he can reasonably believe that evidence is located there.[10] In many states, it was customary for courts to admit evidence without inquiring as to the method by which it was obtained. Until 1961, states could determine for themselves whether evidence was admissible. In that year, however, the United States Supreme Court abandoned its laissez-faire attitude, and ruled that no evidence could be admitted in state or Federal court proceedings unless it had been lawfully obtained.[11] The practical effect of this decision is to require persons to be acquitted if prosecutors do not follow precisely the requirements of the law.

Search and seizure regulations are complicated and technical. They vary from one state to another. As is characteristic of the complex law of the modern era, these laws and judicial interpretations cannot be easily understood by the layman and his full protection is not possible except through the help of a competent attorney.

Due Process and Confession   State and local police formerly could use fear, threats, or promises in seeking confessions. Thus, "the police might strongly hint that unless a confession is made, they will arrest close members of the accused's family or that unless the accused confesses the police will be unable to protect him from the awaiting mob." But the United States Supreme Court has held that confessions secured through force, fear, threats, or promises are illegal. The Court has also insisted that state courts apply in general the same rules that must be followed in the Federal courts, that is, that the accused must be advised of his legal rights, that arraignment must not be unduly delayed, and that an accused is entitled to counsel and must be advised of this

[8] Paul E. Wilson, **Basic Rules of Arrest, Search and Seizure,** Governmental Research Center, University of Kansas, Lawrence, Kans., 1964.
[9] Marshall Houts, **From Arrest to Release,** Charles C. Thomas, Publisher, Springfield, Ill., 1958, p. 24.
[10] Wilson, *op. cit.*
[11] *Mapp v. Ohio,* 367 U.S. 643 (1961).

right before interrogation. Confessions obtained prior to advice that the accused is entitled to an attorney were ruled inadmissible in court by a 1966 ruling.

Despite the criticisms of those who have argued that the rulings of the Supreme Court make the task of state and local law-enforcement officers extremely difficult, the Court reviews only a miniscule portion of the criminal cases of the land. Even if it wanted to, it could not hear many more such cases than it does at the present time. As a result, its influence upon state courts on matters of the behavior of law-enforcement officers and of judicial proceedings is very small. Indeed, it is not difficult for a prosecutor or judge at the state level, if he is intelligent and informed concerning prior Supreme Court decisions, to avoid successful appeal to the United States Supreme Court.[12]

Police officers and prosecutors complain that it is becoming increasingly difficult to use a voluntary confession on the part of the accused as a basis for securing a conviction in court. In 1964, by a 5 to 4 vote, the United States Supreme Court reversed the conviction of an alleged murderer, not because they questioned his guilt, but because the police had refused to let the subject consult a lawyer until after they had finished questioning him. During the questioning, the suspect made an incriminating statement and this was a fundamental basis for his conviction in state court. The Supreme Court, however, held that this was not a voluntary confession and could not be admitted in evidence. Justice Arthur J. Goldberg, for the majority, argued that it is the responsibility of the prosecutor to find his own evidence, rather than to rely upon a confession, whether or not it was completely voluntary.[13]

Ample evidence exists to show that a "confession" is not necessarily proof that the accused has committed a crime. In the case of a murder committed in New York City in 1964, the police arrested a young Negro and secured a confession from him. Later, it was proved that he was innocent of the crime. At the time of the subject's release, a member of the staff of the district attorney said he was "positive" that the police had actually prepared the confession the suspect had signed.

In 1965, former New York Police Commissioner Michael J. Murphy, in a talk before judges of United States courts, criticized a decision of the United States Supreme Court which extended to the state courts a rule making inadmissible evidence that had been illegally seized. He also complained that: "It has been our experience that if suspects are told of their rights they will not confess." [14]

In response, Yale Camisar, a law professor, said:

Fighting crime is a difficult, frustrating business. When you cannot handle it, the easiest and most politically attractive device is to blame it on the courts. It is a lot more popular than raising taxes to increase the police force.

[12] Way, *op. cit.*, chap. 5. See, for example, *Collins v. Texas*, 352 S.W. 2d 841 (1961).
[13] *Escobedo v. Illinois*, 378 U.S. 478 (1964), further restricted in *Miranda v. Arizona*, 16 L. Ed. 2d 7 (1966).
[14] United Press-International dispatch, Sept. 10, 1965. The case referred to was *Mapp v. Ohio*, 367 U.S. 643 (1961).

A Jury of One's Peers   The United States Supreme Court has attempted, in many ways, to impose upon the states obligations to observe procedural civil rights where the state government officials have themselves failed to do so. Thus, the Court has ruled that Negroes and minority ethnic-group members cannot be systematically excluded from jury duty.[15] This decision has had little practical meaning, however, for many techniques exist for the actual exclusion of such persons from juries, in fact.[16] First, most jury lists include only a token representation of Negroes or unwanted minority-group members. Second, it is common in the South for the defense and prosecuting attorneys to agree not to accept Negro jurors. Third, an attorney has a certain number of peremptory challenges to which he is entitled. Furthermore, Negroes often ask to be excused on the grounds that jury duty would be an economic hardship.[17]

The Right to Counsel   In 1963, the United States Supreme Court ruled that every state must provide counsel to persons accused of felonies and serious misdemeanors if, in the judgment of the trial judge, the defendant is not able to pay for such advice. The case involved an ex-convict, Clarence Gideon, who had been accused of breaking into a poolroom. He asked the judge to appoint a defense attorney, but the judge refused, pointing out that under Florida law the government did not have to pay for legal counsel except in murder cases. Gideon was sentenced to five years in the state prison, but largely through his own efforts to learn the law and to bring his case directly to the attention of the United States Supreme Court, he was able to secure a retrial at which he was found innocent. His case was responsible for putting pressure once again upon the states to bring their criminal proceedings up to standards required in the Federal courts.[18]

As a result of this decision, the Florida Supreme Court immediately provided a framework for handling appeals from other persons in the state penal institutions. A few months later, the Florida Legislature created the office of public defender in each of the state's judicial circuits. He was assigned the task of representing any person accused of a felony who, in the opinion of the judge, was not able to pay the fees of an attorney.

Florida officials accepted the decision of the United States Supreme Court and attempted to comply with its ruling, at considerable cost to the state and with many resulting problems. After the decision: [19]

The Florida Division of Corrections had to provide additional notary service, arrange to transport prisoners, recompute sentences and perform a host of other related tasks for its inmate population. Evidence seems to show that this has been accomplished with more than reasonable dispatch.

[15] *Hernandez v. Texas,* 347 U.S. 475 (1954); *Eubanks v. Louisiana,* 356 U.S. 584 (1958); *Swain v. Alabama,* 380 U.S. 202 (1965).
[16] Way, *op. cit.,* chap. 5.
[17] See, for example, *Avery v. Georgia,* 345 U.S. 559 (1953).
[18] *Gideon v. Wainwright,* 372 U.S. 335 (1963). See Anthony Lewis, **Gideon's Trumpet,** Random House, Inc., New York, 1964.
[19] David G. Temple, "Facing up to Gideon," **National Civic Review,** 54:354ff., July, 1965.

At the time of the *Gideon* decision, fifteen states did not provide a guarantee of the right to counsel for indigent defendants in all felony cases.[20] In those states where right to counsel did exist, it was common for the judge to name as attorney for the defense an inexperienced newcomer to the bar. Even in the case of more experienced lawyers, they often find there is little profit in these kinds of cases and, unless they take a personal interest in the defendant and his position or see some broader purpose to the case, have a vested interest in getting the case over with rapidly. Of course, many attorneys appointed by the court do a conscientious job. Furthermore, in quite a few states the Legal Aid Society seeks to help indigents, but it is dependent almost entirely on private contributions.

In most states, it would probably be accurate to say that the poorer you are, the poorer are your chances for an adequate defense in court. In states where the public defender system works extremely well, however, this pattern is probably modified somewhat and the low-income person who does not quite qualify as an indigent is probably the least well represented.

The Press and Criminal Procedure   A major issue in the field of civil rights and liberties has been that of balancing the right of freedom of the press against the right of an individual to a fair trial. One of the few certainties in life is that if a newspaper editor is denied information he wants, he will scream, or at least print in 14-point type and boldface, that the historic freedom of the press is being invaded and this constitutes a dangerous threat to democracy. He apparently is likely to make the most noise or use the boldest type when he is denied information that he thinks will help sell newspapers. The responsibility of judges and legislators is, of course, not one of trying to keep newspapers solvent, but rather of trying to protect the basic elements of a fair trial. Many judges have emphasized that the American system of jurisprudence calls for trial by court and not by newspaper, but their arguments are frequently rejected by editors.

In 1959, the editor of the Eugene, Oregon, **Register Guard** said: "Whenever a boy is arrested on a major charge, we will print his name if we can get it, and of course we can get it. I don't think the public would want us to do otherwise." [21] This pious statement misses the point, of course. The question is not what the public would like. Much of the public would like to have as many of the enticing, dramatic details of a crime as a newspaper is willing to print. The fundamental question centers around the conditions under which an individual can be given a fair trial and those who are accused, but innocent, can be protected from a life-long stigma.

In 1965, the Columbia Broadcasting System announced "standards of self-restraint which we are adopting for ourselves; we will resist imposition by outsiders of rules concerning what we can and cannot report." CBS News specifically said that it would not make references to confessions or previous

[20] Murray T. Bloom, "Justice for the Poor," **National Civic Review**, 54:131–135, March, 1965.
[21] Quoted in **Publicity and Juvenile Courts,** Freedom of Information Center, University of Missouri, Columbia, Mo., Publication no. 140, 1965.

criminal records of accused persons until they had been admitted in evidence at a trial. CBS News, in other words, recognized that such detail may serve to prejudice a juror and that this might serve to prejudice the rights of either the state or the defendants to a fair trial.[22]

Although the press has sometimes abused its powers and privileges, it also performs a highly important function as a critic of those in power. Thomas Jefferson put it this way: [23] "No government ought to be without censors, and while the press is free none will." But criticism of the law and those who execute it and the reporting of events is not, according to our traditions, supposed to prejudice the rights of individuals.

Civil Liberties

Freedom of Expression   One specialist on civil liberties has noted that: [24]

In days when communications were slow, questions of freedom of expression were generally left to local courts which applied local values. With mass communications media, the old practice became less appropriate and local rulings were increasingly often challenged.

Prior to 1957, the Supreme Court had never squarely faced the issues of the censorship of obscene printed matter. In that year, the Court examined the validity of the Federal mail statute which declares obscene printed matter to be nonmailable.[25] The Court upheld the validity of the statute and declared that obscenity is not within the area of constitutionally protected speech and press. The Court noted that historically the constitutional protection for freedom of the press was not considered to cover every utterance. It reasoned that "all ideas having the slightest redeeming social importance—unorthodox ideas, controversial ideas, even ideas hateful to the prevailing climate of opinion—have the full protection of the guarantees. . . ." But the Court concluded that obscenity is utterly without redeeming social importance.

The importance of the *Roth* case is not the conclusion that obscenity has no constitutional protection; few people would seriously argue for such a position. The importance lies in its attempt to establish a standard for measuring what is and what is not obscene. The Court established the following obscenity standard: whether to the average person, applying contemporary community standards, the dominant theme of the material taken as a whole appeals to prurient interests, and to nothing else.

In the 1960s, only four states had motion picture censorship boards. The Kansas board, which was established in 1917, has altered somewhere between 10 and 20 percent of the films it has reviewed. The censorship boards have, however, had many critics. These have included liberals, who believe that any form of prior censorship is undemocratic, the press, often for the same reasons, and commercial interests, who see such boards as an economic threat.

Censorship boards have encountered increasing scrutiny by the courts.

[22] CBS News release, May 24, 1965.
[23] Letter, Thomas Jefferson to George Washington, 1792.
[24] Way, *op. cit.*, p. 40.
[25] *Roth v. United States*, 354 U.S. 476 (1957).

In 1951, the New York Censorship Board banned an Italian film, "The Miracle," on the ground that it was "sacrilegious." The Supreme Court, however, ruled that this term was too ambiguous to serve as a basis for censorship.[26] The Court also indicated that it was not the responsibility or even the right of government to protect any religion from views its leaders consider distasteful. In 1952, the Supreme Court reversed New York and Ohio cases and implied that the term "immoral" was also too ambiguous a basis for prior censorship.[27] Censorship boards or procedures are also to be found in a number of large cities, including Chicago and Detroit. In 1957, in reversing a Chicago censorship board, the Court held that obscenity is not protected by the First Amendment, but that matters related to sex were not in themselves to be interpreted as obscene.[28]

In an attempt to save for itself some powers of censorship, the Kansas board in 1959 adopted a narrow definition of obscenity by saying that:

A film or reel shall be deemed obscene when to the average person, applying contemporary community standards, the dominant theme of the material, taken as a whole, appeals to prurient interest, that is, a shameful or morbid interest in nudity, sex, or excretions and if it goes substantially beyond contemporary limitations of candor or representation of such matters.

This rule borrowed from the language of the Supreme Court decision in the *Roth* case.[29] The effect of this case, according to the literary critic and poet John Ciardi of the **Saturday Review,** is to allow the movie producer or book publisher to win in most obscenity cases if he is willing to spend the money necessary in order to appeal until he reaches a court level where the censorship decision must be reversed.[30] The reason for this is that it is virtually impossible to show that a particular film or book is without "any redeeming social importance," a condition imposed by the Supreme Court in the *Roth* case. The Supreme Court has also held that a state may not authorize mass seizures of material [31] unless it can be proved that the distributors knew that the material was regarded as obscene by law, and state officials must specifically describe the allegedly obscene items to be seized.[32]

Criminal Syndicalist Laws   World War I, and particularly the "Red scare" that followed it, provoked many state legislatures into enacting laws relative to subversion. Between 1917 and 1920, seventeen states enacted such laws. Because much of the concern about subversion prior to the Communist revolution in the Soviet Union in 1917 had centered around a radical movement that began in France in the 1890s, known as "syndicalism," these statutes were commonly called "criminal syndicalist laws." In general, they prohibited behavior advocating crime, sabotage, violence, or other unlawful forms of terror-

---

[26] K. A. Harris, "Censorship in Kansas: A Dilemma," **Your Government,** 19:1–3, Dec. 15, 1963.
[27] *Burstyn v. Wilson,* 343 U.S. 495 (1952). "The Miracle" case.
[28] *Times Film Corp. v. Chicago,* 244 F. 2d 423 (1957).
[29] *Roth v. United States,* 354 U.S. 476 (1957).
[30] John Ciardi, "Manner of Speaking," **Saturday Review,** Mar. 6, 1965, p. 14. Ciardi may have exaggerated, however. See, *Ginzburg v. United States,* 16 L. Ed. 2d 31 (1966), and *Mishkin v. New York,* 16 L. Ed. 2d 560 (1966).
[31] *Smith v. California,* 361 U.S. 147 (1959).
[32] *Marcus v. Search Warrants,* 367 U.S. 717 (1961).

ism as a means of securing political and economic reform. The law adopted in Michigan during this period (1919) resulted in a conviction only once (1923).[33] It is possible, however, that the threat of the use of the law has had an inhibiting influence which would not have existed in its absence.

Eighteen states have enacted statutes relative to sedition, which is defined in a number of ways. Between 1917 and 1951, thirty-two states passed laws prohibiting the display of red flags, the symbol of Marxism, "apparently on the theory that abolition of the symbol would prevent the reality of revolution." Twenty-six of these were enacted in 1919 at the height of the post-World War I "Red scare." [34]

Freedom of Education   Charges of discrimination against Negroes through segregation in schools are common in all parts of the country, not just in the South. The school board in the city of New York had a great deal of difficulty in the 1960s in trying to break up actual segregation by transporting students by bus to schools which were not always the closest to their own homes. This measure produced a great deal of controversy, just as the neglect of *de facto* segregation did earlier. In 1965, heavy pressure was placed upon the superintendent of schools in Chicago to break up *de facto* segregation and the mayor's office was picketed that summer in protest against existing policies. Even in Portland, Oregon, a city with relatively few Negroes, the Board of Education thought it necessary to appoint a large study committee to investigate charges of *de facto* segregation.

Public institutions of higher learning are sometimes subjected to severe criticism by legislators, particularly when members of their faculty make public statements that deviate seriously from the teachings of conventional wisdom. For example, in 1962, the recently established University of South Florida was subjected to criticism by a legislative committee which claimed that it had been "soft on Communism," that it harbored homosexuals, that some of its textbooks or required reading were vulgar, and that the University sponsored antireligious teachings. In the last case, the criticism apparently was directed at three chapters in a single book which occupied one day of discussion in a single course. This effort to apply small-town ideology as a basis for censorship of a university and a means by which to restrict academic freedom failed, although it did damage the university at a time when its leaders were attempting to secure appropriations needed for expansion in accord with the growing population and demands for public higher education in the state.[35]

Freedom to Vote   In the summer of 1962, a Georgia sheriff commented: [36]

We are a little fed up with this voter registration business. . . . We want our colored people to live like they've been living for the last hundred years—peaceful and happy. . . . There's nothing like fear to keep the niggers in line.

[33] Robert J. Mowitz, "State and Local Attacks on Subversion," in Walter Gellhorn (ed.), **The States and Subversion,** Cornell University Press, Ithaca, N.Y., 1952, pp. 185–189.
[34] Gellhorn, *op. cit.,* pp. 360–361.
[35] **Tampa Tribune** (Tampa, Fla.), Aug. 25–26, 1962.
[36] Quoted in Way, *op. cit.,* pp. 12–13.

The ability to vote is critical to the possession of political power—a fact that was known to the Georgia sheriff as well as to Negro leaders. Although nonvoting among Negroes is in part a result of an apolitical subculture (see Tables 15 and 16), it has also been in part a result of intimidation by some state and local official. The result was Negro demands for Federal action.

Table 15   Why Negroes Have Not Registered

	TOTAL,* %	NEGROES IN SOUTH, %
Just haven't got around to it	64	64
Not qualified (residency, education)	13	2
Election officials wouldn't allow	6	11
Can't be effective in voting, politics	6	7
Don't believe in voting	5	10
Can't pay poll tax	2	4
Illness	4	2

* Total: Members of a random nationwide sample of Negroes.
SOURCE: William Brink and Louis Harris, **The Negro Revolution in America,** Simon and Schuster, Inc., New York, 1964, p. 84.

Table 16   Why Negroes Who Tried to Register Were Not Able to

	NATIONWIDE, %
Turned back, threatened by authorities	33
Papers not in order	19
Lacked education requirements	15
Asked questions until finally couldn't answer	14
Couldn't pay poll tax	14
Whites kept getting in line ahead of me	5

SOURCE: William Brink and Louis Harris, **The Negro Revolution in America,** Simon and Schuster, Inc., New York, 1964, p. 85.

On August 9, 1965, the U.S. Department of Justice began to register Negroes who were eligible as voters under the Voting Rights Act of 1965. The registrars began work that day in Alabama, Georgia, Louisiana, Mississippi, and South Carolina. The Department of Justice announced that it would not send the registrars into areas except where persons eligible to vote under the act would not likely be voluntarily registered by state and local officials.

After President Johnson signed the Voting Rights Act, enforcement was applied in three phases. First, the use of literacy tests as a prerequisite for voting was suspended in Alabama, Alaska (where it had not been effectively enforced, anyway), Georgia, North Carolina (twenty-six counties), South Carolina, and Virginia. In addition, one county in Arizona was involved. Second, the Department of Justice filed suits in Alabama, Mississippi, Texas, and Virginia, asking that the poll tax be abolished as a requirement for voting. These were the only states still having a poll tax requirement in 1965. The third phase consisted of the assignment of registrars to the states indicated.[37]

Freedom of Religion   State and local governments have been involved in civil rights and liberties questions touching upon such matters as the dissemination of birth-control information and contraceptives and of aid to or opposition to the activities of religious groups. Such fundamentalist sects as the Jehovah's Witnesses and the Seventh-day Adventists have raised delicate questions concerning the balance between the police power of the state and freedom of religion. Some of these questions have involved problems of conditions under which a religious parade or religious solicitation may be made.[38]

A statement issued in 1940 by the General Conference Committee of the Seventh-day Adventist Church stated that: [39]

Seventh-Day Adventists believe they are, according to the Scriptures, called to proclaim the message of Christ's soon return to all men, of whatever class or race, respecting and helping all alike. This view precludes their taking sides with any organization that employs measures in any way contrary or prejudicial to the interests of the various classes of society, because by resorting to force, Seventh-Day Adventists would sacrifice their opportunity for unprejudiced and sincere efforts in behalf of both groups in a labor and capital controversy.

In other words, this church has argued that its members conscientiously object to being required to join a labor union on the grounds that such a union encourages a class struggle that is in violation of Christian teachings. On this basis, leaders of the Seventh-day Adventist Church have opposed repeal of right-to-work laws or repeal of section 14 (B) of the Taft-Hartley Act, which permits states to enact such laws even in cases where they affect interstate commerce.

Separation of Church and State   The states were faced with the question of separation of church and state before the national government was. More than a generation ago, the state of Louisiana decided that it had the right to provide free textbooks to children in schools, whether parochial or public, because the child would benefit from these books whether they were used in a public or other type of school. This decision was upheld by the United States Supreme Court.[40] At least two other states supply textbooks to school children irrespective of the school they attend, but the Oregon Supreme Court has held that the supplying of textbooks to parochial school children is a violation of the state constitution,[41] and the Wisconsin court has reached the same conclusion concerning the provision of bus transportation for children to parochial schools.[42]

[37] **New York Times,** Aug. 8, 1965.
[38] Way, *op. cit.,* pp. 81–89.
[39] W. Melvin Adams, "Compulsory Unionism and Individual Conscience," **Liberty,** July–August, 1965, pp. 12–13.
[40] Way, *op. cit.,* chap. 4.
[41] *Cochran v. Louisiana,* 281 U.S. 37 (1930); *Dickman v. School District 62-C,* 366 P. 2d 533 (1961).
[42] *Wisconsin v. Nusbaum,* 115 N.W. 2d 761 (1962).

Shortly after World War II, the United States Supreme Court ruled that local boards of education could not authorize pupils, on an optional basis, to attend religious instruction in the classroom or on public school property, even though no public funds were used for instruction and the religious teachers were provided by the various religious sects. The Court concluded that such instruction amounted to the use of tax-supported property for religious instruction.[43] The Court later retreated from this absolutist position and ruled it permissible for public school children to be dismissed during school hours to receive religious instruction at places other than the public school.[44] But in the state of Washington, this decision, which involved school children in New York, was ruled to violate the state constitution. The Washington Supreme Court held that a dismissed-time arrangement was little different from one which involved the use of public facilities.[45]

In 1962, the United States Supreme Court held unconstitutional the use of a simple, nondenominational prayer in the public schools of a state.[46] At the time, forty states, particularly those in the East and South, made use of Bible readings and prayers regularly in the public schools. In one-fourth of these states, their use was required; in others, it was a matter of local choice. The next year, the Court outlawed Bible readings and prayers whether or not they had official governmental sanction.[47] By this decision, the Court seemed to move back closer to its decision of fifteen years earlier in taking the position that on religious matters, the state must be neutral and not advance or inhibit religion in any way.[48]

The Civil Rights Movement

World War II marked the end of the acceptance of second-class citizenship by American Negroes. Earlier, other minority groups had rejected such status, and had been successful in claiming a right to treatment closer to that of equality. But the task of the Negro was much more difficult, as systematic discrimination against him was often supported by the sanctions of state and local governments.

During the civil rights movement of the 1960s, local officials in rural areas of the South generally resisted the efforts of civil rights leaders and so did most state legislatures and many Southern governors. The behavior of the legislators can probably be explained partly in terms of the malapportionment of legislatures in the South. And because most Southern states are relatively more rural than are states in the rest of the country, even governors for the most part found it politically expedient to resist the movement. There were some exceptions, such as Governor Leroy Collins in Florida, but for the most part, it was the officials of large cities, and particularly mayors, who sought to

---

[43] McCollum v. Champaign Board of Education, 333 U.S. 203 (1948).
[44] Zorach v. Clauson, 343 U.S. 306 (1952).
[45] Perry v. School District 81, 344 P. 2d 1026 (1959).
[46] Engel v. Vitale, 370 U.S. 421 (1962).
[47] School District of Abington Twp. v. Schempp, 374 U.S. 203 (1963).
[48] Way, op. cit., pp. 78–81.

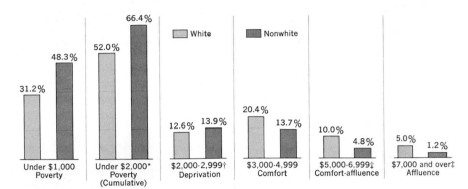

Comparative Income Status of
White and Nonwhite Individuals, 1960

Percent of white and nonwhite unrelated individuals
with annual money incomes of indicated amounts

☐ White   ■ Nonwhite

	66.4%
52.0%	
48.3%	
31.2%	

| Under $1,000 Poverty | Under $2,000* Poverty (Cumulative) | $2,000-2,999† Deprivation | $3,000-4,999 Comfort | $5,000-6,999‡ Comfort-affluence | $7,000 and over‡ Affluence |
| 31.2% / 48.3% | 52.0% / 66.4% | 12.6% / 13.9% | 20.4% / 13.7% | 10.0% / 4.8% | 5.0% / 1.2% |

Fig. 16-1   Racial Discrimination's Economic Effects⊅

* Comprising 4.9 million white unrelated individuals out of total of 9.4 million white unrelated individuals, and 1.0 million nonwhite unrelated individuals out of total of 1.5 million nonwhite unrelated individuals.
† Comprising 1.2 million white unrelated individuals and 0.2 million nonwhite.
‡ Data in income range from $5,000 to $7,499 used elsewhere in this study not available in data series from which this chart was prepared.
Data: U.S. Bureau of the Census.
SOURCE: **Poverty and Deprivation in the U.S.,** Conference on Economic Progress, Washington, D.C., 1962, p. 60.

rise to the occasion and to perform the traditional function of compromising among the conflicting interests and to meet partway the demands of the civil-rights leaders.

Characteristics of the Battleground   The politics of Negro advancement and of Negro-white relationships are characterized by a number of factors. These include the following: [49]

1. Lower-class members of the Negro social structure are relatively far more numerous than they are in the parallel white social structure.

2. Members of the Negro middle class are generally unable or unwilling to identify themselves with the lower class and to provide leadership for it. The Negro lower class is generally interested in the politics of welfare, while the middle class is concerned with the politics of status.

3. Persons under the age of about twenty-five constitute a particularly large percentage of the Negro social structures compared with the white and they have considerably more education than did their parents. Indeed, they have more education than can be absorbed in the current labor market, given the traditional restrictions upon Negro career opportunities.

4. Negro businessmen are relatively few, with the result that professional persons are even more important than they are in the white community. Most

[49] Edward C. Banfield and James V. Wilson, **City Politics,** Harvard University Press, Cambridge, Mass., 1964, pp. 297–300.

businesses in Negro areas of cities are owned by whites. This has long been a source of resentment to Negroes and has quite often resulted in resentful retaliation, as happened in the Los Angeles (Watts) riots of 1965.

5. Many Negroes have a vested interest in the existing social structure, which means that they benefit from discrimination and segregation and would stand to lose economically by its elimination, or at least its elimination would pose such a threat. The result of this is that some Negroes are cross pressured between a desire for economic advancement and a desire for status advancement. Segregation, of course, permits some Negroes to compete effectively with one another without having the additional burden of having to compete successfully with whites. In addition, many Negro ministers, politicians, educators, businessmen, and leaders of welfare organizations owe their positions to the system of segregation.

6. Negro civic organizations are small in membership and have few resources. As a result, in the past Negro leadership has been weak and ineffective.

The older, established Negro political-action organizations are the National Association for the Advancement of Colored People (NAACP), and the Urban League. The newer organizations are the Congress of Racial Equality (CORE), the Student Nonviolent Coordinating Committee (SNCC), the Southern Christian Leadership Conference (headed by the Reverend Martin Luther King, Jr.), and a fourth group of loosely organized Northern Negroes, led principally by Negro ministers, who have sought to get Negroes to boycott business firms which do not provide jobs or promotions for Negroes. None of these organizations has had much appeal to lower-class Negroes and all of them are financed principally by white citizens.

The heavy emphasis in the American culture upon present-day considerations and the assumption that "tomorrow will take care of itself" has contributed to the difficulties of intergroup relations. Many a community leader could make the comment that was made in the San Francisco Bay area that if: [50]

communities had done a more effective job of making room for Negro newcomers during the past two decades, one could be more hopeful about the two decades ahead, a period in which the Negro population will more than double. In looking at developments since 1940 one cannot avoid being struck by the fantastic growth of the Negro population and the rapid development of Negro-white tensions. Equally impressive is the fact that not a single city in the Bay area had, or tried to develop, plans for easing the movement of Negroes or for directing inescapable conflicts into affirmative civic channels.

Negro Opinion   In a sample survey of Negro opinion concerning civil rights in the Boston area, Negroes in the younger age groups, and especially women, had little knowledge about civil rights questions, but often had strong feelings on the subject. This corresponds with the general pattern in American politics in which younger people are relatively uninformed and relatively unlikely to

[50] Wilson Record, **Minority Groups and Intergroup Relations in the San Francisco Bay Area**, Institute of Governmental Studies, University of California, Berkeley, Calif., 1963, p. 48.

Table 17 Who Has Done Most for Negro Rights?

	TOTAL RANK AND FILE, %	NON-SOUTH, %	SOUTH, %	LEADERS, %
NAACP	45	46	44	57
Martin Luther King, Jr.	26	27	25	27
President Kennedy	9	7	11	1
U.S. Supreme Court	5	5	5	10
Medgar Evers	2	2	2	
CORE	1	1	2	2
Robert Kennedy	1		2	
The Kennedys	1	1	1	
Urban League	1	2	1	3
Roosevelt	1	1	1	2
Black Muslims	1	1	1	1
Thurgood Marshall	1	1		4
Democrats	1	1		
Adam Clayton Powell	1	2	1	1
SNCC				3
Not sure	4	3	5	

SOURCE: William Brink and Louis Harris, **The Negro Revolution in America**, Simon and Schuster, Inc., New York, 1964, p. 116.

Table 18 Negroes Assess Intentions of Most Whites

MOST WHITES WANT:	TOTAL RANK AND FILE, %	NON-SOUTH, %	SOUTH, %	LEADERS, %
Better break for Negroes	25	28	23	52
To keep Negroes down	42	35	47	9
Don't care one way or other	17	21	13	31
Not sure	16	16	17	8

SOURCE: William Brink and Louis Harris, **The Negro Revolution in America**, Simon and Schuster, Inc., New York, 1964, p. 126.

participate in the decision-making process. It was also found that low-income, unskilled men were generally apathetic concerning civil rights questions, but at the same time demonstrated strong feelings of hostility toward white men. They were generally cynical concerning the efficacy of political participation. In general, the more education a Negro had, the more aware and informed he was concerning civil rights matters. By comparing the responses of Negroes with those of whites, this study concluded a "widening chasm exists between the American Negro and the American white, with each firmly convinced that his position is soundly grounded in the basic values of our society." [51]

[51] George D. Blackwood, "Civil Rights and Direct Action in the Urban North," a paper read at the 1964 meetings of the American Political Science Association, Chicago. Also Thomas F. Pettigrew, **A Profile of the Negro American**, D. Van Nostrand Company, Inc., Princeton, N.J., 1964.

Table 19   White Attitudes Five Years from Now

	TOTAL RANK AND FILE, %	LEADERS, %
Better attitude	73	93
Worse attitude	2	
Stay same	11	4
Not sure	14	3

SOURCE: William Brink and Louis Harris, **The Negro Revolution in America,** Simon and Schuster, Inc., New York, 1964, p. 136.

Table 20   Negroes Assess the Government

	TOTAL RANK AND FILE, %	LEADERS, %
Congress:		
More helpful	54	31
More harmful	9	40
Not sure	37	29
State government:		
More helpful	35	34
More harmful	32	39
Not sure	33	27
Local authorities:		
More helpful	30	38
More harmful	35	45
Not sure	35	17

SOURCE: William Brink and Louis Harris, **The Negro Revolution in America,** Simon and Schuster, Inc., New York, 1964, p. 132.

In the nation as a whole, Negroes expect to make progress in the coming years. They expect most help to come from private direct-action groups, and they expect more help from the Federal government than from state or local governments.

Direct Action and Government   The first Negro sit-in appears to have taken place in Greensboro, North Carolina, in February, 1960. The technique spread rapidly through the South and then through the North. Since 1963, sit-ins and demonstrations to protest discrimination and segregation in education, employment, transportation, and housing have been commonplace.

Although religious leaders are not in accord as to the condition under which a citizen may, or should, violate the law, religious persons, not necessarily leaders, have quite often refused to obey the law and have used as a defense the argument that obedience would violate their personal religious

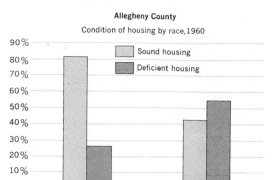

Fig. 16-2   Discrimination and Housing Patterns.
Housing in Pittsburgh and Allegheny County, Pa.
SOURCE: **Pittsburgh Press** (Pittsburgh, Pa.), June 26, 1963.

beliefs and hence should be a matter of choice. They argue that obedience to the law in violation of one's religious beliefs could be required only in defiance of the constitutional guarantee of freedom of religion. Using such arguments, persons have refused to pay that portion of their personal income tax that they believe would be used for national defense purposes. They have refused to take shelter during air-raid drills. During civil rights demonstrations and sit-ins, they have refused to obey instructions from police officers and have blocked streets and entrances to public buildings in violation of state laws and local ordinances. As part of the civil rights movement, Negroes have deliberately violated municipal ordinances which they view as improper. Their technique has been to sit at a lunch counter until the police arrive, and then to submit peaceably to arrest.[52]

In March, 1965, the Reverend Martin Luther King, Jr., led thousands of persons, Negro and white, from Selma, Alabama, to Montgomery. The leader of the march said that its purpose was "to make it clear that we are determined to make brotherhood a reality for all men." The march of approximately 50 miles took five days. At the end of it, King and his followers attempted unsuccessfully to file a formal protest with the governor of Alabama concerning the denial of Negro voting rights. Although the march was conducted through hostile territory, it took place virtually without incident, in part because of excellent planning by the leaders, but also significantly because of the presence in large numbers of nationalized units of the Alabama National Guard. The President had undertaken to provide the protection that the state of Alabama failed to provide.

The civil rights movement of Negroes in the 1960s has been punctuated from time to time by violence, including full-fledged riots which have raged out of control for hours and days at a time. They are most likely to occur in

[52] Murray S. Stedman, Jr., **Religion and Politics in America,** Harcourt, Brace & World, Inc., New York, 1964, chap. 2.

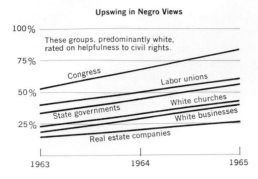

Fig. 16-3 . **The Negro Sees State Governments as of Limited Helpfulness.**
Although Negroes see many social institutions as increasingly helpful on civil rights, the states rate below the Federal government.
SOURCE: **Newsweek, Feb. 15, 1965.**

Northern slums, where frustrated lower-class Negroes are more willing to resort to violence than are national Negro leaders (see Table 21). Each such occasion is a basis for speculative editorial writing and frenetic activity by public officeholders. In the great riot in the Watts district of Los Angeles in 1965, for example, at least 36 persons were killed, at least 900 were injured, property damage ran to not less than $200 million, and more than 4,000 persons were arrested. After California National Guard units, operating under virtually full combat conditions, and the Los Angeles police finally restored order, the politicians began to play pin the tail on the donkey. The mayor of Los Angeles, the governor of California, and the director of the Federal anti-poverty program all attempted to explain the factors that caused the riot and to show that the policies they had advocated were policies that would alleviate tension in the area and that they were not themselves to blame. (Mayor Samuel Yorty did not seem to fare so well as the others in the propaganda battle. Among other things, he had made the serious mistake—one that was certain to hurt him in the eyes of persons on all sides of the issue—of leaving the city in the midst of the riot in order to make a political speech in San Francisco.) [53] Pundits of all kinds also immediately sought to explain the causes of the event. Left-wing leaders of the Negro movement for civil rights reaffirmed their view that occasional violence was necessary in the struggle. Persons committed to nonviolence, such as Martin Luther King, Jr., tried to talk to the people of the area in terms of what was being done and why some patience and certainly nonviolence was a necessary approach, but he made little impact with his highly sophisticated arguments upon the emotion-ridden people of the area, most of whom had little education, had had only brief urban life experiences, and had little prospects for economic advancement, whatever their color. Persons embracing the suburbanite ideology deplored the violence and law violation as well as the social and psychological condition in which the people

[53] **Newsweek, Aug. 30, 1965.**

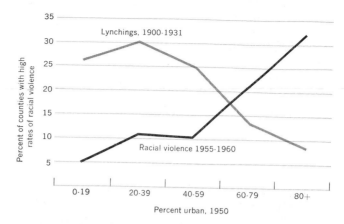

Fig. 16-4   Racial Conflict Differs by Type of Community.

Lynching of Negroes, now quite rare, was a behavior characteristically restricted to rural and small-town areas. Racial violence (such as riots) takes place in urban areas.

SOURCE: Donald R. Matthews and James W. Prothro, "Political Factors and Negro Voter Registration in the South," **American Political Science Review,** 57: fig. 2, June, 1963.

of the area lived. Others, still committed to the small-town ideology, insisted that the participants "must be prosecuted and punished," and that "a society that tolerates such self-indulgence oughn't to be surprised when the destructive flame suddenly lashes up." [54]

Table 21   Willingness to Resort to Violence

FUTURE ACTION SHOULD BE	NON-SOUTHERN LOW-INCOME NEGROES	TOTAL NEGRO SAMPLE	NEGRO LEADERS
Nonviolent	50	63	93
Violent	25	22	4
Not sure	25	15	3

SOURCE: William Brink and Louis Harris, **The Negro Revolution in America,** Simon and Schuster, Inc., New York, 1964, p. 73.

Violent action of this type can be explained only in terms of the facts that (1) it results from a cumulation of many factors and events, and (2) in any society that is not a complete police state, social order is fundamentally dependent upon the willingness of members of society to abide by the rules. As every policeman who has ever been involved in a riot situation knows, latent aggressive behavior erupts in many people as soon as they recognize that the normal rules, constraints, and sanctions are not being applied. Once a riot begins, the psychological factors governing the mob are evoked and the psychological factors contributing to social control are temporarily set aside.

[54] **National Review,** Aug. 31, 1965.

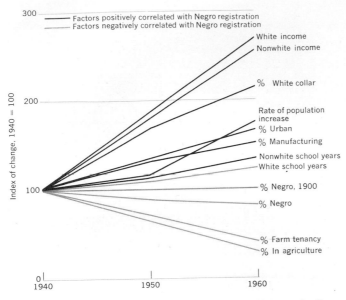

Fig. 16-5   Negro Voter Registration Related to Changes in the South.

Urbanization and rapid population growth in the South are favorable factors for Negro voting possibilities.

SOURCE: Donald R. Matthews and James W. Prothro, "Social and Economic Factors and Negro Voter Registration in the South," **American Political Science Review, 57:** fig. 8, Mar., 1963.

Under such circumstances, persons will do things, including murder, which they would not do under any other circumstances. To hundreds of people it is an opportunity to react aggressively against any persons or groups against whom they feel aggrieved.

A tendency also exists, as is always the case where conventional wisdom is involved, to find simple explanations for such riots, even though the causes are certainly multiple and the behavior pattern is complex. Mayor Yorty, for example, first blamed the state police for the riot, because of an arrest they had made. Yet, the arrest was a routine one for alleged drunken driving. The Communists and some non-Communist left-wing groups were his next target. He said they were responsible for the riot through their insistence that the police had behaved brutally toward the Negroes of the city. Later, he blamed Sargent Shriver, director of the Federal antipoverty program, for being slow in providing funds to the Los Angeles area. Still later, he engaged in a loud political controversy with Governor Edmund G. (Pat) Brown of California over the causes.[55]

The reporting to the public was by no means all ignorant, self-seeking, or simplistic. **Newsweek** reporters, for example, noted that: "Yet, for all the public finger-pointing, there were no short answers as to why the riots happened—or how to keep them from happening again."

[55] **Newsweek,** Aug. 30, 1965.

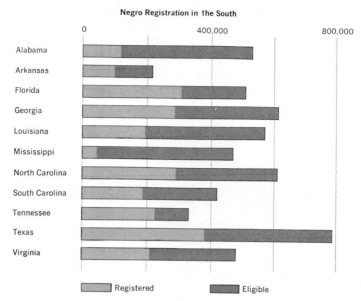

Negro Registration in the South

Fig. 16-6   **Most Southern Negroes Were Not Registered in 1965.**
SOURCE: **Newsweek,** June 7, 1965.

Opponents of Civil Liberties   State and local governments have been faced for a long time with groups that oppose the granting of equality to all people and who sometimes resort to violence or even to seeking to substitute their own administration of the law for that of public officials. Neighborhood "civic associations" sometimes seek to act in this fashion, especially to control access to local housing areas. White Citizens' Councils often are organized to oppose Negro civil rights groups. The most notorious antirights group is the Ku Klux Klan. A capsule description of the Ku Klux Klan in the 1920s has been provided by Frederick Lewis Allen: [56]

Not only could it [the Klan] be represented to potential members as the defender of the white against the black, of Gentile against Jew, and of Protestant against Catholic, and thus trade on all the newly inflamed fears of the credulous small-towner, but its white robe and hood, its flaming cross, its secrecy, and the preposterous vocabulary of its ritual could be made the vehicle for all that infantile love of hocus-pocus and mummery, that lust for secret adventure, which survives in the adult whose lot is cast in drab places.

For a time in the 1920s, the Ku Klux Klan dominated the state legislatures of Arkansas, California, Indiana, Ohio, Oklahoma, and Texas.

In Defense of Liberties   Some non-Negro groups and some Southern (as well as Northern) public officials have sought to protect civil rights and liberties. The American Civil Liberties Union (ACLU) was founded in 1920 by Roger

[56] Frederick Lewis Allen, **Only Yesterday,** Harper & Row, Publishers, Incorporated, New York, 1931, p. 54. Paperback by Perennial Library.

Baldwin. In general, the ACLU has attempted to defend the underdog in criminal proceedings. That is, it has attempted to help the person who is not likely to find the rules rigged in his favor or to find judge and jury sympathetic toward him. The concern of the ACLU has been to protect the elements of a fair trial as they have historically been understood in American jurisprudence. As such, it probably is more militantly in favor of civil rights than is the typical citizen and so is sometimes criticized as being "ultraliberal," and even pro-Communist. The ACLU is, of course, not the latter, since it seeks to preserve rather than to destroy American democracy. Although it is liberal in the sense of wanting to preserve the rights of defendants in criminal proceedings, it has defended a great variety of persons, most of them individuals who could not win a popularity contest, and many of these have been right-wing extremists.

It has defended Communists and Fascists. It defended Nicola Sacco and Bartolomeo Vanzetti in the 1920s. Later, it defended the rabble-rouser, Gerald L. K. Smith, and the segregationist, Governor Ross Barnett of Mississippi. In 1925, it provided the defense team for John T. Scopes in the so-called "monkey trial," which was concerned with the teaching of evolution in defiance of a Tennessee statute. It defended Henry Ford's right of free speech in 1937 before the National Labor Relations Board and during World War II attempted to defend the civil rights of Japanese-Americans who were forcibly relocated into camps in the West. As is likely to happen to any successful organization, the ACLU has achieved a high degree of respectability. It is now an organization which any middle-class do-gooder can support without embarrassment to himself.[57]

One of the endless problems in evaluating the work of government is in trying to determine what is trivial and what is fundamental, what is important for the moment, and what is important for democracy in the long run. The Long family of Louisiana, for example, has historically been opposed by leaders of the middle class, including newspaper editors. During the period when efficiency, economy, and honesty were regarded as among the most important characteristics of a political leader, the Long family was in eclipse. But when civil rights, the humane treatment of human beings (as defined by the dominant values in the culture), and a concern for the advancement of the underprivileged became important, members of the Long family, particularly Governor Earl Long, were given a second look.

Earl Long once said that "you got to recognize that niggers is human beings. . . . I plead with you in all candor. I'm a candidate for Governor. If it hurts me, it will just have to hurt." [58] Long always opposed candidates from the city of New Orleans and the New Orleans newspapers, but he also vigorously opposed the White Citizens' Council and extremists on segregation.

Direct-action Groups and Local Government   Until the late 1950s, local governments were generally viewed as purveyors of consumer services. They had always had some hand in the development of social policies, of course. The

57 Carter Van Lopik, "ACLU's Roger Baldwin," **Detroit Free Press**, May 3, 1964.
58 A. J. Liebling, **The Earl of Louisiana**, Ballantine Books, Inc., New York, 1960, pp. 144–145.

large city machines were important social welfare agencies through the 1930s. The policies of the mayor and the chief of police were of central importance in relation to the question of acceptance of unionization in the 1930s and early 1940s, and of such things as the racial integration of public facilities. But it has been only with the contemporary civil rights movement that cities have become deeply involved in social conflict. This also applies to school districts, counties, and other local governments. The fact that these agencies control police forces and the public schools is enough to make their leaders targets for civil rights reformers. The typical direct-action techniques of the civil rights activists are effective against local leaders. Demonstrations and sit-ins can be centered around city halls and board of education buildings, or around a particular school, park, or beach.

Providing leadership for the settlement of civil rights disputes might be extremely difficult for local officials. This is true for one reason because the extreme left, like the extreme right, is generally idealistic and hence unwilling to compromise. Indeed, proposals for compromise may only be infuriating to them. For another thing, civil rights activists include a great variety of persons. There are middle-class reformers, who are reluctant to support plans for passive resistance or in any other way to violate the law or to incur mild disapproval of friends and neighbors. There are also professional Negro leaders, for the most part highly trained, highly intelligent, and highly articulate; and there are a handful of Communist party-liners, who as always, exploit any type of social discontent and who glory in having the movement erroneously identified with and attributed to them. In addition, almost every civil rights action group includes a few "beatniks," and often persons desiring individual publicity, which the newspapermen are quite willing to provide. These last two groups, because of their disproportionate publicity, give the nonparticipating public a seriously distorted view of the kinds of persons involved in the civil rights movement. The left-wing extremists are typically just as intolerant as are right-wing extremists, but they have a major resource at their disposal: they are able to appeal to the individual's conscience, while the far right can appeal only to his romanticism. Because they appeal to what Freud would call the superego of the individual American, civil rights reformers must be taken seriously by state and local decision makers.

SELECTED READINGS

Anderson, J. W.: **Eisenhower, Brownell, and the Congress—The Tangled Origins of the Civil Rights Bill of 1956–1957,** The Bobbs-Merrill Company, Inc., Indianapolis, ICP no. 80, 1964.

Boles, Donald E.: **The Bible, Religion, and the Public Schools,** 3d ed., The Iowa State University Press, Ames, Iowa, 1965. (Court decisions and attitudes of various publics toward them.)

Brink, William, and Louis Harris: **The Negro Revolution in America,** Simon and Schuster, Inc., New York, 1964. (A report on an opinion survey conducted for **Newsweek** magazine.)

Brooks, Thomas R.: "Necessary Force—Or Police Brutality?" **New York Times Magazine,** Dec. 5, 1965, pp. 60ff.

Fellman, David: **The Defendant's Rights,** Holt, Rinehart and Winston, Inc., New York, 1958.

Gellhorn, Walter (ed.): **The States and Subversion,** Cornell University Press, Ithaca, N.Y., 1952.   (A report on state activities relative to subversion at the beginning of the McCarthy era.)

Karlen, Delmar: **The Citizen in Court,** Holt, Rinehart and Winston, Inc., New York, 1964.

Maloney, Joseph F.: **"The Lonesome Train" in Levittown,** The Bobbs-Merrill Company, Inc., Indianapolis, ICP no. 39, 1958.   (Questions of freedom of public schools from public opinion censorship.)

Mayers, Lewis: **The American Legal System,** Harper & Row, Publishers, Incorporated, New York, 1955.

Orfield, L. B.: **Criminal Procedure from Arrest to Appeal,** National Conference of Judicial Councils, Chicago, 1947.

Pierce, Neal R., J. G. Phillips, and Victoria Velsey (eds.): **Revolution in Civil Rights,** Congressional Quarterly Service, Washington, 1965.   (Detailed history and summary of legislation.)

Schroth, Thomas N., and others: **Congress and the Nation, 1945–1964,** Congressional Quarterly Service, Washington, 1965, chaps. 15–16.

Sherwood, Frank P., and Beatrice Markey: **The Mayor and the Fire Chief,** The Bobbs-Merrill Company, Inc., Indianapolis, ICP no. 43, 1959.   (Attempt by Mayor Norris Poulson to get fire department to desegregate. The chief feared desegregation would damage morale and efficiency.)

Silver, James W.: **Mississippi: The Closed Society,** Harcourt, Brace & World, Inc., New York, 1964.   (One view of the 1962 riot at the University of Mississippi when the first Negro was enrolled.)

Stokes, Anson P., and Leo Pfeffer: **Church and State in the United States,** Harper & Row, Publishers, Incorporated, New York, 1965.   (An abridgment of an original three-volume study by Stokes.)

Templin, Ralph T.: **Democracy and Nonviolence,** Porter Sargent, Publisher, Boston, 1965.   (A liberal's view of the civil rights and other movements.)

Westin, Alan F.: **The Miracle Case: The Supreme Court and the Movies,** The Bobbs-Merrill Company, Inc., Indianapolis, ICP no. 64, 1961.   (Are films a means of expression protected by the First Amendment? Is sacrilege a basis for censorship?)

Woodward, C. Vann: **The Strange Career of Jim Crow,** 2d ed., Oxford University Press, Fair Lawn, N.J., 1966. In paperback. Original publication, 1955.   (A classic study of racial segregation.)

See also bibliography for Chap. 15.

17

REVENUES AND EXPENDITURES

As we noted at the beginning of Chapter 3, state and local expenditures have expanded enormously in the last three generations. Public education was the largest item in the expenditure budget of governments at these levels in 1902 and still was in 1966.[1] Roads, which cost $175 million each year at the beginning of the century, had changed from rut-filled dirt lanes to hard-surfaced and often limited-access divided highways. Similar changes took place in almost every area of activity.

No doubt citizens in 1902, before hard-surfaced highways, consolidated schools, rehabilitative mental-health programs, and unemployment compensation, complained of taxes as we do today. But they paid only $11.08 per capita in state and local taxes. In 1957, we each paid $171.63.

An expansion of services and of their costs of this magnitude cannot be met without a considerable amount of effort. Part of the cost has been offset by a great increase in the standard of living and consequent ability to pay. But the problem has also helped to incite a desperate search for new revenue sources. The property tax remains the most important local tax, but state governments have turned to sales, excise, and income taxes as they have increasingly withdrawn from use of the property tax. Local governments have sought to broaden their tax bases, looking to sales, excise, and income taxes. But in the period since World War II, spending has exceeded collections and state and local debt has been rising.

[1] Figures in this section are from **Facts and Figures on Government Finance,** 13th ed., Tax Foundation, Inc., New York, 1965, and the **Book of the States,** Council of State Governments, Chicago, 1965. No correction is made here for the changing value of the dollar.

Why Taxes?   The typical citizen probably has little understanding of the relationships that exist between government revenues and expenditures. The traditional practice of politicians is one of promising to perform more services in
a better fashion and at lower cost than can or will the opposition. This has
probably helped preserve the citizen's habit of making no association between
service levels and costs. Each person, of course, has some knowledge about
taxes. Every home owner understands his property tax; at least he is able to
determine how much he must pay, and he is likely to know whether it is more
or less than the preceding year. The sales tax is known to most people because
of the general practice of adding it to the marked price of goods in making a
sale. The income tax cannot escape the attention of the employed person in
any state which levies it, especially since most states do not use the withholding system but require payment in one or two installments—each of which
produces anguish on the part of the citizen. Yet, the economic effects of particular taxes are unknown to the typical citizen. He knows little more about the
services that his taxes buy (except that he may associate the property tax with
schools), and he does not attempt to find his way through a wonderland of
double taxation,* grants-in-aid, shared taxes, dedicated funds, joint financing,
and service charges.

*** DEDICATED FUNDS are produced from taxes whose use is reserved for a particular
governmental function. DOUBLE TAXATION is the application of two taxes to the
same source of funds. GRANTS-IN-AID are gifts made by one government to another.
Usually conditions are attached. SHARED TAXES are collected by one government but
shared with other governments on the basis of some formula. JOINT FINANCING involves payment by more than one government for a single project. SERVICE CHARGES
differ from taxes in that they are based on benefits received rather than on income or
wealth. Public water-supply departments commonly levy service charges, for example.**

It is easy for the citizen to agree with the politician or commentator who
tells him that taxes are too high, since he has no criterion against which to
measure them. He balks from time to time when major tax increases are submitted to him on referendum, and his reluctance to pay taxes which he does
not associate with services has encouraged the extensive use in America of
dedicated funds. These help the citizen understand why it is being asked for
and help persuade him to accept it. Thus, an additional cent on the gasoline
tax is pledged for road building; extra millage on the property tax may be exclusively to build new schools; most of the state sales tax may be pledged for
grants to aid school operations; increases in hunting- and fishing-license fees
will go only for the stocking of more deer and trout. The use of dedicated funds
has long been denounced by specialists in financial administration because of
the rigidity it produces in the system. It leaves less room for the executive or
legislative branches to make adjustments for changing demands. But the practice undoubtedly makes the acceptance of new taxes or service charges more
palatable to the typical citizen.

The dedication of state taxes has been a declining practice. In the decade
following 1954, earmarked state taxes declined from 51 percent of total state

tax collections to 41 percent. In ten states, however, the percentage of ear-marked taxes increased. In general, the decline results principally from the disproportionate increase in the rate of nonearmarked taxes. Revenues com-mitted to specific purposes have been most often for education, but have also been used for a vast number of other purposes. Parts of the property tax have been the most commonly earmarked, but retail sales, tobacco, alcohol bever-age, and insurance company gross receipt taxes have also been earmarked. All of these have been tied to specific use in at least twenty states.[2]

Expenditure Patterns

Some of the tremendous increases in state and local expenditures during the twentieth century were noted at the beginning of this chapter. Service-level expectations, and hence costs, have increased especially since the end of World War II. New functions of government have been added, but none of them have replaced the traditional ones in financial importance. There have been some basic changes, however, in the pattern since the beginning of the cen-tury.[3] Among them are these:

1. New functions of government have appeared and have begun to chal-lenge the old functions in importance, including unemployment compensation urban redevelopment, public housing, smoke abatement, airports, and parking lots.

2. Old functions have been greatly expanded and changed in concept. This applies to recreation, conservation, mental health, highway, higher edu-cation, health, and welfare programs. For example, the old minimum-care, custodial approach to the care of psychotics has been largely replaced by expensive rehabilitative mental-health programs.

3. State governments have assumed an increasingly important role at the state-local levels. In 1902, state expenditures accounted for only 12 per-cent of total state-local expenditures. By the early 1960s, they accounted for over 35 percent of the total. The states have enormously expanded the number, and increased the quality, of their direct services to the public in the present century.

4. The states have gradually been becoming more and more collection agencies for local governments. In the early 1960s, about two-thirds of state government education expenditures were actually in the form of payments to local governments. The same disposition was made of about 20 percent of state highway fund expenditures and over 40 percent of state welfare ex-penditures. Shared taxes and grants-in-aid were also important parts of other state budget items. This pattern represents, in part, the result of legislative recognition of the need for additional revenues at the local level combined with an unwillingness to delegate adequate taxing powers to local governments, so the states collect the money and then disburse it to their local governments.

[2] **Earmarked State Taxes,** Tax Foundation, Inc., New York, 1965.
[3] See U.S. Bureau of the Census, **Historical Statistics on State and Local Government Finances,** 1955.

5. State and local expenditures have represented an increasingly large proportion of society's earnings, as measured by the gross national product (GNP). This increase has not been enormous, but it has been significant. In the 1920s, expenditures ran around 8 percent of the GNP; in the early 1960s, they had increased to 11 percent.

Postwar Fiscal Development   When World War II ended, state budgets were low. This was a result of many factors: materials controls prevented wartime capital-outlay programs and caused cutbacks in the operations of state programs; revenue rates were very high; debt had been reduced and most states had surpluses. By 1958, much of the backlog of capital-outlay needs resulting from World War II and later the Korean conflict had been eliminated, but so had surpluses and reserves. Long-term debt had increased dramatically, as had expenditure levels. Revenues had nearly kept pace with the increased spending patterns, but only through the levying of new taxes or the increasing of old ones. The future prospect for most states was for further increases.[4] Although their postwar debts had not increased at a rate equal to that of the states, in general, local governments had followed the same pattern.[5]

The reasons for these state and local expenditure and debt increases have already been discussed. They include the added costs resulting from population growth and its concentration into relatively small physical space, the relatively high prosperity and rising standard of living in the last generation, the rising price level and the fact that the cost of goods and services bought by state and local governments has risen more rapidly than have other goods and services, and the change in popular expectations concerning government.

Reasonable Expenditure Levels   What are reasonable expenditure levels for state and local governments? The citizen is bombarded with propaganda, much of it conflicting, which tells him of the unfinished business of government in providing highways, mental-health programs, recreation for increasing leisure time, and so forth, but also of increasing debt burdens, of the need for increased taxes if current service levels are to be maintained, and of "all-encroaching government." The citizen wonders whether a new or increased tax is fair or whether he is being taken advantage of.

The question the citizen raises cannot easily be answered. Essentially, expenditure levels are culturally determined. In the 1920s, Americans would not permit elaborate welfare or unemployment-compensation programs, to say nothing of public housing or limited-access highways. But since the Great Depression, Americans have come to expect government to provide a measure of security that is not otherwise available in an interdependent society, and they trust government further and are now willing to allow it to experiment with new programs where needs are believed to exist.

The relative ease with which money can be raised is also important in

[4] See Epilogue for future trends.
[5] See U.S. Bureau of the Census, **Historical Statistics on State and Local Government Finances** and **Summary of Governmental Finances in 1956,** 1957.

determining expenditure levels. Congress agrees more readily than does a state legislature to add a new grant-in-aid program because it is relatively easy for Congress to raise the additional billions. A city or state that cannot increase services without also raising taxes or adding new taxes will be slow to do so and will demand impressive proof before acting. But if a local unit of government is relatively prosperous, it is also likely to be relatively generous in expanding its budget. Services not now performed are often wanted; the problem comes in making the marginal sacrifice necessary in order to pay for them.

Item: Studies of municipal costs and tax rates indicate that local expenditures vary according to the income of local residents. In other words, as income of residents increases, the marginal sacrifice involved in meeting higher budgets is less and people do not resist as much as they do in lower-income communities.[6]

Item: Because citizens want more governmental services than they are willing to afford and because they do not clearly associate tax levels with specific services, governments tend to seize all available revenue possibilities and nearly always spend all funds available. Thus in West Virginia, county governments receive a fixed proportion of the local property tax. Increasing expenditures for schools in that state have therefore had the effect of increasing the property tax for the counties automatically. But county functions have not expanded at a rate comparable to that of the schools. Yet "with extremely rare exceptions" the counties have levied the maximum levies permitted and have spent these moneys "often on projects neither specified nor contemplated by the framers of the Constitution, or by the authors of the legislative act which allocates levies. . . ."[7]

Item: Conservatives *—individuals or groups who want government expenditures at a lower portion of gross national product than do most people— try to keep governments from making maximum use of their taxing and spending powers. They seek to restrict spending, not so much through counterpressures upon governing bodies, though that is an important technique for them, as through the adoption of restrictive constitutional and charter provisions. Once nestled in this protective armor, restrictions cannot usually be dislodged except by an extraordinary majority vote or a complicated procedure or both. The fact that most state constitutions have such restrictions built into them, commonly by an accumulation of amendments, makes the conservative an opponent of constitutional revision. Thus, the Citizens Public Expenditure Survey of New York opposed a 1957 proposal for a constitutional convention in that state, pointing out that "had the convention proposition been approved . . . there would have been many pressures upon the delegates to enlarge

[6] Walter Isard and Robert Coughlin, **Municipal Costs and Revenues Resulting from Community Growth,** Chandler-Davis Publishing Co., Wellesley, Mass., 1957. See also Stanley Scott and E. L. Feder, **Factors Associated with Variations in Municipal Expenditure Levels,** Institute of Public Administration, University of California, Berkeley, Calif., 1957, and Robert Wood, **1400 Governments,** Harvard University Press, Cambridge, Mass., 1961.
[7] **Report of the Trend in Costs of Maintaining Ordinary Functions of County Government in West Virginia,** West Virginia Chamber of Commerce, Charleston, W.Va., 1957.

government functions and open the door to increased spending on both state and local levels."[8]

* CONSERVATIVE. One who believes that change in social and economic systems should be cautious and relatively slow, and that the burden of proof should be carried by advocates of change.

The Budget

The budget document of a modern state or large city is an enormous thing. The 1958 New York State budget covered 1,794 pages in two volumes, including a ninety-four-page message from the governor explaining why he was asking for expenditures totalling more than $1,617 million. Even the budgets of relatively small states such as Connecticut or Alabama exceed in size the summer catalog of a large mail-order house. In small villages, cities, counties, or towns, the budget document is simpler and is often printed only in the local newspapers, where its columns of figures are found unintelligible by the typical citizen.

Trend toward Executive Budget   The trend toward centralized administration, the increasing number of functions of government, and the increasing complexity of those functions have contributed to the rapid rise in the use of the executive budget in the United States since the beginning of the century. The nature of this budget and the change it has brought about has been discussed earlier.[9]

Until recent years, every budget dealt with all of the minutiae that are needed to operate an office or function of government. Often the budget consisted of "line items" specifying the exact amount to be spent on a particular aspect of a function, and the funds were commonly not transferable from one line in the budget to another, even within the same department. The emphasis was upon the things to be acquired—paper clips, snow shovels, wheelbarrows—rather than upon the services to be rendered. This was necessary when public funds had to be guarded at all times against ingenious attempts at fraud. It encouraged, however, the citizen's habit of disassociating taxes from services provided. Many specialists in the field of fiscal administration have long urged that the budget should propose appropriations on a lump-sum basis. Under this plan, each agency or major subdivision would receive a single sum of money which the responsible administrator would then spend as he thought best—within generally established policies of the chief executive and the legislative body. Flexibility to meet unexpected emergencies and changes in service demands would result.

Since the original Hoover Commission reports in the late 1940s, a trend has been established toward a "performance" budget. This is a method of classifying expenditures so that each agency receives a lump sum for the operation of each of its different activities: so much for snow removal, so much for purchase of new park land, so much for public-welfare programs. Although

[8] **New York State Taxpayer,** 18:1, November, 1957.
[9] See Chap. 11.

the method has its faults, it is designed to help make clear to both legislators and the public what funds are being used for; it makes it easier to compare past performances with future requests; and it may encourage agencies to do a better job of thinking through their needs in making requests. The budget is designed to reduce the tendency under the older budget method (appropriation by objects) to stockpile materials and accelerate the purchase of services in order to exhaust appropriations. Legislators are sometimes cool toward the performance budget idea, believing that it has the effect of transferring still more fiscal power to the chief executive and the bureaucracy.[10] The most rapid adoption of the performance budget has come in council-manager cities. It is used in other cities as large as Los Angeles, and some state budgets are based on it in part.

The Budget as Policy   The budgeting function "is a specialized way of looking at problems in decision-making." [11] It is something of a negative view in the sense that after the agencies and interest groups have made known their positions, the budget examiners, and ultimately the chief executive, must balance off the various interests against one another and against a plausible estimate of income, often reducing requests. Budget making is also positive in the sense that a public budget is a basic statement of program and policy by the chief executive. He explains in it how he would balance off the various demands upon the public funds, gives reasons in his message for taking the stand that he does on the more controversial aspects of the program, and necessarily must stand willing to defend the explicit and implicit policies proposed in the budget. Many state and local governments require agencies to estimate capital-outlay needs for several years—perhaps five years—in advance, thus making this part of the budget a long-range planning instrument, since capital needs cannot be considered apart from program needs. If the mental-health department, for example, must estimate its building construction needs for the next five years, it will also have to consider population and mental illness trends as well as whether it will continue a custodial emphasis which implies slow patient turnover or will switch to a rehabilitation emphasis which might increase turnover rates. The latter would also increase operating costs (treatment is expensive), but might lower the rate of increase of patient population, thus requiring smaller capital outlays for fewer square feet of hospital space. The budget, in this way, becomes to each agency a means for promoting both fiscal and program planning.

Contemporary budget practices have given state and local chief executives: [12]

an opportunity to take the initiative in the most encompassing set of policy decisions that a legislative session makes. Budget decisions are in detail decisions to continue,

[10] On performance budgeting, see the textbooks in public administration or Jesse Burkhead, **Government Budgeting,** John Wiley & Sons, Inc., New York, 1956, chap. 6.
[11] Paul Appleby, "The Role of the Budget Division," **Public Administration Review,** 17:156–158, Summer, 1957.
[12] Karl A. Bosworth, "Lawmaking in State Governments," **The Forty-eight States: Their Tasks as Policy Makers and Administrators,** The American Assembly, Graduate School of Business, Columbia University, New York, 1955, p. 106.

discontinue, extend, or diminish existing programs and to initiate new programs and at a particular scale. They are also decisions about proposed buildings and other construction and capital outlay. Budget decisions are, on a more general level, decisions on tax rates and tax policy and on the general scale of [governmental] activity. How much money agencies "need" depends upon the premises entertained by the estimator, and the estimates can vary substantially.

The Parts of a Budget   A budget consists of many parts. It usually begins with a message from the chief executive which may say simply, in effect, Here is the budget for the next fiscal year, or it may explain proposed new expenditures, tell why tax changes are requested, and otherwise explain policy positions. A brief summary of the budget for the benefit of citizens and reporters usually follows. Next comes the detailed breakdown. It may start with a statement of anticipated revenues from all taxes and other sources. This will be followed by the expenditures section, often broken down by funds: the general fund plus a small or large number of others, such as a highway fund, a fish-and-game fund, sometimes even a municipal-band fund. A capital-outlay budget for new roads, buildings, and other structures will usually be presented separately from the operations budget, and the same may be true of utilities budgets, such as that of a municipal water-supply system. Provision must also often be made for governmental debt service. The budget may conclude with a statement concerning new taxes needed, or in local governments the property tax levy necessary, to bring the budget into balance.

Preparing the Budget   In state and local governments operating under the executive-budget plan, the document is prepared by a budget officer or controller under the chief executive. In a few state and local governments, the budget is prepared by an independent, elected controller. In some cases, an ex officio board prepares it. In Texas, one budget officer prepares a budget on behalf of the governor; another does so on behalf of the legislature. Local government legislative bodies often prepare the budgets themselves or do so through committees.

The preparation of the budget begins with the collection of estimates for the following year's needs prepared by the various agencies. These are gone over by budget analysts, who look for padding, inaccuracies, and inconsistencies. There may be conferences between the agencies and members of the budget division when differences arise. Such differences are likely to result from differing premises. The chief executive's own ideology, and his evaluation of his political strategy requirements, will affect his view of how "needs" should be interpreted in each agency. The agency will, however, probably use different criteria in arriving at "needs." It may base these upon professional concepts of standards, or upon the pet interests of the agency head, or upon demands of interest groups, or upon other considerations.

After detailed estimates of the needs of each department for the coming year are made available, they are set out in parallel columns with statements of the estimated expenditures for the same items in the current year and the actual expenditures for those items in the fiscal year just completed. The budget officer next examines the document in detail with the chief executive in order that proposed changes in policy may be incorporated in the estimates.

The completely assembled budget is then ready to be sent to the legislative body. Enclosed with it may also be the political future of the governor or mayor, the career prospects of the young city manager, the hopes of the chief executive's critics for new ammunition in their fight to displace him, and the welfare of all the publics that reside within the boundaries of the unit of government involved.

Enacting the Budget   The legislative body has responsibility for adopting the budget. It does so, nearly always with some, more commonly with many, modifications.[13] It will usually hold budget hearings, either before the full body, if it is small enough, or before the tax and appropriations committees, the chairmen of which are normally senior legislators of great power. These hearings do not often give legislators information they do not already have, but they serve to allow groups and individuals to vent their annoyances, bitterness, or frustrations. They are an important part of the democratic process. A budget hearing is more likely to be attended by representatives of interest groups, however, than by a representative cross section of the general public. Some department heads may lobby at this time to get a bigger share of the pie than was given to them by the budget office. If the chief executive is weak administratively, this may be done quite openly. If he is strong, however, it must be done more subtly, for a dissident department head may risk his job if he bypasses the executive. Pressure groups will at this time try to get favorable hearings, and those that find the legislative climate more receptive than was the executive may succeed in getting an increase in the department budgets in which they are interested. Other groups will have to fight to retain the level of funds recommended in the executive budget as legislators strive to reestablish a balance between income and outgo. Public employees may take the opportunity to try to improve their working conditions and pay, and newspaper editors may use the occasion to view with alarm the ever-increasing cost of government.

Usually the legislative branch is free to add, reduce, delete, or modify any part of the budget, although in some cases it may only reduce items or leave them unchanged. In two-house legislatures, the balance of forces and individual interests of legislators may be different in each house. Much struggling may take place before compromises are reached and budget and tax bills are finally passed. Often the chief executive has the final word if he has the power of the item veto.

Administering the Budget   In governmental units and states with the executive budget, the head of each department must submit a work program to the chief executive (or, often in practice, to the controller) before the beginning of each fiscal year. This program will show how much of the total appropriation for that department is desired in each month or quarter of the coming fiscal year. This

13 See above, pp. 333–335.

is known as the "allotment system." After approval, the allotments are turned over to the accounting division of the controller's office, which will then refuse to allow any money to be spent by that department unless it is both authorized by the appropriations ordinance or statute and falls within the time provided in the allotment schedule. In cases where budget administration is less well organized, no allotment system may exist, and the auditor may be the only one to check for the legality of expenditure. In small units, the governing body may itself exercise the control function by passing directly on individual bills presented for payment.

The Financial Officers   The public officials most concerned with finance are the chief executive, the treasurer, the controller, the assessor, and the auditor. These have already been discussed.[14] State fiscal administration is seldom integrated into a single department, as it frequently is in council-manager cities. It is often divided among many agencies, including perhaps an elected treasurer, an elected auditor who may exercise both control functions before agencies spend and audit functions afterwards, a controller appointed by the governor but sometimes elected, a state tax commission to handle property tax appeals and sometimes to administer other taxes, a secretary of state, usually elected, who handles some tax administration, especially of automobile and truck license fees, the head of the conservation department, who may have his own machinery for the purpose of collecting hunting and fishing license fees, and others. Cities and other local units may be organized along similar lines.

Revenues

As might be expected in a society growing increasingly dependent upon government for the performance of services, state and local revenue yields have grown enormously in the twentieth century. Sources of these revenues have become considerably diversified.

While state and local revenue totals increased about forty-five times between 1902 and 1957, some increases have been even more spectacular. Thus, state and local liquor store receipts were a mere $2 million in 1902 but were $1,284 million in 1963. There were no general state sales taxes at all in 1902, and this source produced only $499 million in 1940. But in 1963, it brought in $5,533 million in state revenues. The state personal income tax was also nonexistent at the beginning of the century. It produced only $206 million in 1940 but had reached $2,954 million by 1963 and was widely regarded as the tax most likely to expand in the future. Other tax sources untapped at the beginning of the century but now important bearers of revenue include the motor fuel, motor vehicle, cigarette, severance, and corporate income taxes and unemployment-compensation insurance charges. The general property tax, which produced over 50 percent of state tax revenues in 1902, had declined in im-

[14] See above, Chap. 11. City financial officers are discussed in Charles R. Adrian, **Governing Urban America,** 2d ed., McGraw-Hill Book Company, New York, 1961, pp. 331–335.

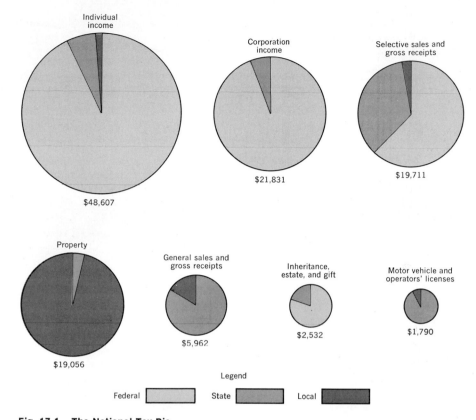

Fig. 17-1   The National Tax Pie.
1962 Tax Collections, in millions.
SOURCE: U.S. Advisory Commission on Intergovernmental Relations, **Tax Overlapping in the United States**, 1964, p. 14.

portance by 1963 to such an extent that it accounted for only 3.1 percent of revenue at that level.

Local governments received 73 percent of their tax revenues from the general property tax in 1902. This figure had declined to 55 percent in 1962, (see Figure 17-2). Yet, the dollar increase in property tax collections during this period amounted to more than a twentyfold rise. Personal income and especially sales tax receipts had become important for local governments, as had utility and liquor store profits.

As compared with the beginning of the twentieth century, the most impressive change in local receipts has been in the growth of state grants and shared taxes. Local governments received less than 6 percent of their total revenue from state intergovernmental payments in 1902; this had increased to 25 percent fifty-five years later, though some of this was Federal money distributed by the states. Federal direct grants have increased in importance, too, but at a far smaller rate than the attention paid to them would indicate. In 1902, 0.4 percent of local revenues came from Federal grants; in 1957, this

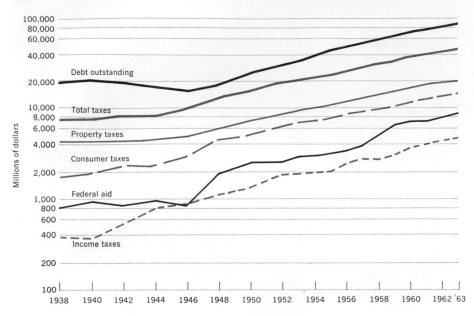

Fig. 17-2   Sources of State and Local Government Financing.
Fiscal years and current (uncorrected) dollars are used.
SOURCE: U.S. Advisory Commission on Intergovernmental Relations, **Tax Overlapping in the United States,** 1964, p. 1.

percentage had increased to 1.1. Major trends indicate a development of the local sales tax as the principal expanding source of income for governments at these levels.

Tax Sources   All taxes are ultimately derived from one of two sources: total wealth or annual income. Taxes are theoretically based upon some criterion of ability to pay, although the criteria used in various periods of history have not been the same, and a tax created in one period equitable at that time may be continued into a time of another life style when its justification becomes less apparent. In some instances, payments to the government are based upon a benefit theory rather than on ability to pay, but such payments are more in the nature of service charges than of taxes. The benefit theory is used, for example, in cases of special assessments for street, sidewalk, street lighting, and similar improvements. It is also applied to water and light charges, hunting and fishing licenses, gasoline taxes, and, to a degree, in determining motor-vehicle license fees. There is another strong tradition which holds that all persons have an equal obligation to pay taxes. This argument makes it right for the government to collect taxes as involuntary contributions. It is also used, especially by conservatives, as a basis for holding that every adult should participate in the payment of a major tax. The theory would thus reject a personal income tax which exempted low-income persons.[15]

[15] On the general subject of taxes, see one of the textbooks on public finance.

Limits on Taxing   Local governments have only those powers of taxation which are granted to them by the state. The only exceptions to this rule are to be found in a few home-rule states, notably California and Wisconsin, where court interpretations of the constitutional home-rule clause have given cities a general grant of powers to levy taxes. (Even in Wisconsin a general act limiting municipal taxing powers at the discretion of the legislature is valid.) Either through the constitution or state statutes the taxing powers of local governments are ordinarily limited. The law usually states a maximum tax rate relative to some limiting factor, the most common being to a certain percentage of the assessed value of taxable property within the local unit of government. The states also often impose conditions and regulations on the administration of local finances [16] and may deprive a local unit of a portion of its tax base by exempting state property, for example, or by providing for "homestead exemptions," which exclude part or all of the value of owner-occupied homes from the general property tax.

The effects of tax restrictions are many. They have encouraged the creation of special districts which have low public visibility but an independent basis for taxation and hence can serve as a means of avoiding the restriction. They have encouraged borrowing under circumstances where costs could have been met from current revenues and where bonds sometimes, through interest payments, greatly increased the cost of financing municipal services. They have required legislatures to work their way through great numbers of bills calling for special legislation and have crowded court dockets with taxpayer suits.[17]

States, too, are limited as to taxation. Many of their constitutions place limits of one kind or another on legislative taxing powers. The courts tend to hold to a narrow interpretation of authorizations to tax, and although state legislatures are less restricted than are local governing bodies, they are not free to decide taxing levels uninhibited.

Limitations on Subjects of Taxation   The subjects that may be taxed by local governments are normally controlled by the state. Nearly all of the states tell their local governments which taxes they may levy, for what period of time they may be levied, and under what conditions. A local government that finds its property tax consistently inadequate may not, for example, decide to levy a payroll or a sales tax. The state must first authorize such a levy on a new subject.

The state government is also frequently limited as to the subjects that may be taxed. The constitution may prohibit the state from levying certain kinds of taxes or may limit the amount of the tax. Some states are thus restricted on the use of property, income, and sales taxes.

[16] See, for example, T. E. McMillan, Jr., **State Supervision of Municipal Finance,** Institute of Public Affairs, University of Texas, Austin, Tex., 1953; W. M. Griffin, **State Supervision of Local Assessments,** Bureau of Governmental Research, Florida State University, Tallahassee, Fla., 1957.
[17] U.S. Advisory Commission on Intergovernmental Relations, **State Constitutional and Statutory Restrictions on Local Taxing Powers,** 1962.

Evasion of Limitations   Tax limitations result from economy pressures, and these pressures are felt especially in depression times. When property owners are faced with the prospect of losing their investments to the mortgage holder in such times, it is not difficult to convince them that they should vote to limit the property tax levy. Later, as revenue is badly needed, it becomes necessary to evade the limitation. Usually it is more difficult to find a way to levy a prohibited tax (e.g., the income tax) than it is to evade a limitation feature on an existing tax.

The Concept of Equity   Legislators, when they plan long-range tax policies, must consider both adequacy and equity. "Equity" is usually thought of as meaning ability to pay. In colonial America, ability to pay could best be measured in terms of property or total wealth. Today, when most people receive a regular pay check (unlike the situation in the predominantly agricultural colonies), income is considered by most economists to be a better criterion.

The income tax takes into consideration the fact that not all property is equally able to pay taxes. A home, most Americans would hold, is less suitable for taxation than is a factory. A factory that is losing money is less a subject for taxation than one that is making a profit (although it could be argued that it should pay some taxes nonetheless). The property tax makes them pay equally, the income tax does not. Saxophones, to an amateur musician, are as much a consumer good as are rutabagas; yet the former are (theoretically) taxable in many states as property. The income tax, in a complicated modern world, can be more equitably administered and is less subject to evasion than is the property tax.

The General Property Tax   Although the property tax has been bitterly attacked in recent years as unsuitable for a modern, and especially an urban, society, it remains by far the most important source of revenue for local government (see Figure 17-2). This is especially true of local units other than cities and school districts. The former are succeeding to some extent in diversifying their tax base, while the latter are becoming increasingly dependent upon state aid.

The general property tax was the principal source of income for state governments from colonial times until the Great Depression. In the 1930s defalcations on the tax reached great numbers, the states needed better sources of revenue, and the whole of the property tax, to the extent that it could be collected, was needed by local governments. The result was that the states shifted to the income, and especially to the sales, tax. By 1964, Nebraska was the only state which received more than 20 percent of its tax revenues from the property tax. Most states no longer make a general levy at all.

The great authority on the property tax, E. R. A. Seligman, once suggested that there is nothing the matter with the general property tax except that it is wrong in theory and does not work in practice. The objections to the tax are many. It has already been suggested that the property tax is no longer a good measurement of ability to pay and is hence inequitable. It is often poorly administered and is in any case difficult to administer.[18]

Property-tax Assessment   The pattern of local property-tax assessment differs from one state to another, but although the dates may not be the same, the pattern is generally along the following lines: [19]

The local government assessor must complete his work by December 31 of each year. By the first Monday in April, local boards of tax review must have heard any appeals made by citizens or corporations. Within the next month, county boards of equalization are expected to have "equalized," or balanced on an equitable basis, the tax burden of local units within the county. Within approximately a month thereafter, the state board of tax equalization must have decided on the equalization, or relative percentage of taxes, to be paid by each of the counties of the state. In May or June, village and city taxes are due and school and township taxes are due in December, by which time the local assessor has begun his work for the oncoming year.

The Politics of Equalization   Most assessors are probably honest in their efforts, but they have little training for their jobs. Local pressures make it difficult for them to place on the tax roll everything that legally belongs there or to relate tax valuation to market value. In some cases, wide discrepancies exist in judgment by assessors; in others, influential persons and businesses are given favorable valuations. As a device designed to overcome these problems, machinery for review and equalization of property taxes exists in every taxing jurisdiction. The board of review may be a special body, or it may be the governing board.

There is a tendency toward competitive underassessment whenever an assessor's figures are used as the basis for a tax by more than one unit of government. Thus, where the assessor is selected from a unit of government smaller than the county, each assessor will want to make his valuations as small as possible in order to minimize the amount of county property tax his constituents will have to pay. The same pressure exists if a school district covers more than one assessing unit and if the state levies a property tax millage. There are thus needs for equalization boards at the state, and often the county, levels. These bodies are supposed to achieve equity between assessing units. They differ as to powers, competence, and the amount of effort they put into their work. Usually, the equalization boards can merely make a percentage increase or decrease in the total valuation of an assessing unit as a whole, but in some cases they can reassess individual properties or order a complete reassessment of an assessing unit.

Boards of equalization generally have inadequate staffs to do the compli-

[18] Griffin, *op. cit.;* Adrian, *op. cit.,* pp. 310–313; U.S. Department of Agriculture, **Taxes Levied on Farm Property in the United States,** 1956; Robert H. Pealy, **A Comparative Study of Property Tax Administration in Illinois and Michigan,** Institute of Public Administration, University of Michigan, Ann Arbor, Mich., 1956.
[19] Charles Press, **A Michigan Local Property Tax Primer,** Institute for Community Development, Michigan State University, East Lansing, Mich., 1962.

cated work that is legally expected of them. Governing bodies will seldom give them the staff needed, since to do so would be politically unpopular—citizens generally do not want technically competent assessment; each taxpayer hopes to gain favor or advantage through his own assessor and fears that effective equalization will mean higher tax bills for him.

Equalization is further complicated by the variety of pressures involved in the process. Rural areas traditionally want few services and low assessments, but urban areas often need high assessments to overcome the debt limitations placed upon them by state laws or constitutions. Debts may usually not exceed a certain percentage of assessed valuation. The higher the valuation, therefore, the better the possibilities for issuing bonds for capital outlays. In many cases, state school-aid funds are distributed partly on the basis of the ability of each district to pay as determined by assessed valuation per pupil. Where this is the case, each superintendent seeks to make his own valuation as low as possible and to exert pressure for higher valuations in other districts so as to maximize his own state aid. In this atmosphere of numerous cross pressures, lack of public support, and inadequate staff, the equalization boards attempt to do a job which, under the best of conditions, would be extremely difficult.

Why Is the Property Tax Retained?   If there are so many problems connected with the property tax, why is it retained as the backbone of local government finance? There are a number of reasons, including inertia and the venerable argument holding that any old tax is a good tax and any new tax is a bad tax. This argument is at least partly valid, for taxpayers have accommodated to an old tax, but a new one causes much uncertainty.

The property tax is also one of the few taxes whose subjects will stay put. Most real property (if not personal property) is not easily moved out of the taxing jurisdiction on assessment day. Local sales taxes tend to drive buyers out of the taxing jurisdiction. Taxes upon income tend to cause political complications if levied upon nonresidents and if not, tend to drive homeowners, businesses, and industry outside the jurisdiction. The property tax is also retained because it produces a high yield, except in severe depressions. Local units of government are badly in need of money, and no one has suggested a substitute satisfactory enough to replace the tax. Cities in particular, among local units, have tried to ease the burden upon the property owner by diversifying the tax base through the addition of other taxes. These have served to supplement, rather than replace, the basic tax, however.

The Search for New Sources   As noted above, the states largely withdrew from the general property-tax field during the Great Depression. If there was ever a possibility of their reentering this field, it disappeared in the rear of rapidly advancing local government costs. In looking for a foundation for their tax systems, most states turned to a broad-base sales tax. This proved to be a fortunate choice so far as raising revenue in difficult times was concerned. Because it ordinarily applies to all retail transactions including necessities such as food and fuel, the tax yields relatively well in both depression and boom times. After watching the sales tax returns of their neighbors, one

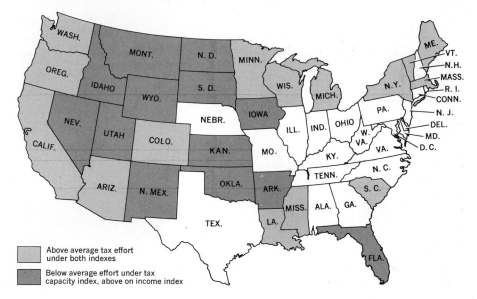

Fig. 17-3   State Tax Efforts Vary Widely.

About one-half the states seem to be making above-average tax efforts on the basis of income, but fall below average when collections are related to taxable capacity. States in light grey are making average efforts or less. Data for Alaska and Hawaii unavailable.

SOURCE: U.S. Advisory Commission on Intergovernmental Relations, **Measures of State and Local Fiscal Capacity and Tax Effort,** 1962, fig. 8.

state after another adopted the tax until, by 1964, thirty-eight states used it in one version or another.[20]

Some states, as the result of the balancing off of local political forces, adopted the personal or corporate income tax or both, rather than the sales tax. Generally, however, these taxes appeared as supplements to the sales tax. In 1965, thirty-seven states levied personal income taxes and thirty-eight states had corporation income taxes.

The increasing financial pressures felt by state governments after wartime surpluses had been absorbed precipitated a large number of state tax studies in the 1950s, just as expanded governmental functions had produced "Little Hoover" studies in the preceding decade. In 1955 alone, twenty-five states authorized such studies. The result was a trend both toward increasing existing taxes and imposing both sales and personal income taxes at the state —and sometimes also at the local—level of government. The picture was complicated by increasing urbanization and the need to finance metropolitanwide urban services.[21]

In 1963, thirty-five of the forty-seven state legislatures that met increased

[20] U. S. Bureau of the Census, **Historical Statistics on State and Local Government Finances,** 1955; **State Tax Rates and Collections,** Tax Foundation, Inc., New York, 1956; and see the most recent edition of **Facts and Figures on Government Finance,** published biennially by the Tax Foundation, Inc., New York.

[21] See Lyle C. Fitch, "Fiscal and Political Problems of Increasing Urbanization," **Political Science Quarterly,** 71:71–89, March, 1956; Harvey E. Brazer, "The Role of Major Metropolitan Centers in State and Local Finance," **American Economic Review,** 48:305–316, May, 1958.

Table 22 Increase in State Tax Rates and Sources, 1965

STATE	SALES TAX	INCOME TAX	TOBACCO TAX	ALCOHOLIC BEVERAGE TAX	MOTOR FUELS TAX	OTHER
Arizona	x	x	x		x	
Arkansas			x		x	x
California	x				x	
Colorado	x		x		x	
Connecticut		x	x		x	
Delaware			x		x	xn
Florida	x					x
Hawaii	x	x	x	x		x
Idaho	n					x
Illinois	x		x			x
Indiana	x		x			n
Iowa	x	x	x		x	x
Kansas	x	x	x	x		
Maine	x		x			
Massachusetts					x	
Minnesota		x				
Missouri	x					
Montana		x				x
Nebraska		n	x	x	x	x
New Hampshire			x	x		x
New York	n		x			x
North Dakota	x	x	x			
Oklahoma			x			
Rhode Island	x					
South Dakota	x		x			x
Texas			x			
Utah		x		x		
Vermont			x			
Washington	x		x	x		x
West Virginia	x					
Wisconsin		x	x			
Wyoming	x					

x Indicates increase in existing tax.
n Indicates adoption of new tax.
SOURCE: **State Tax Action in 1965,** Tax Foundation, Inc., New York, September, 1965, p. 38.

major tax rates, broadened bases, or enacted new taxes. The increase was approximately 5 percent over existing tax levels. In 1964, an off year, when most state legislatures did not meet in regular session, nine states increased major taxes. State tax collections in the 1950s and early 1960s increased by an average rate of 8 percent a year. Between 1950 and 1963, state debt increased from $5 billion to $23 billion.[22]

[22] "State Tax Action in 1964," **Tax Review,** 25:37–40, October, 1964.

Sales Taxes   Sales taxes, or excises, are levied in all the states. In thirty-eight states the tax applies to the sale of all or most items as a "retail sales," "gross receipts," or some similar type of tax. Other states levy specific sales taxes upon gasoline, alcoholic beverages, cigarettes, and other selected items. The objects selected for taxation are usually those for which the demand is highly inelastic, that is, things that people will tend to buy whether the price is relatively high or low. Thus a specific tax on alcohol yields well because people see no obvious substitute for the product; a specific tax on cauliflower would yield practically nothing, because people would buy cabbage or brussels sprouts instead. Taxing alcoholic beverages or cigarettes is commonly justified on the grounds that these products should not be used by people anyway and anything that can be done to discourage their use is desirable—a manifestation of America's strong Puritan tradition. The taxation of gasoline, which also has a highly inelastic demand, cannot be rationalized in the same way. The argument used instead is that those who can afford to own the automobiles and trucks that operate on the highways should pay the cost of construction and maintenance through a special tax and that the gasoline tax is a good means for determining relative use. All states levy gasoline, alcohol, and cigarette taxes.

The broad-base sales tax exists in several forms. The most common type is the retail sales tax. Some states also tax charges for services, such as for television repair or dental care. West Virginia has a gross income tax, which is a sales tax expanded to include taxes on rent, wages, salary, dividends, and other income. At this level, the tax becomes virtually a flat-rate personal and corporate income tax combined with a sales tax.

In 1963, Indiana substituted four different taxes for the gross income tax which it had used since the days of the Great Depression. These were a sales tax, a net income tax, a gross income tax on corporations, and a net

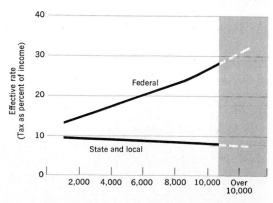

Fig. 17-4   State and Local Taxes Are Not Based on Ability to Pay.

SOURCE: Richard A. Musgrave and others, **Compendium of the Joint Committee on the Economic Report,** United States Congress, Washington, D.C., Nov. 9, 1957, p. 98.

income tax on corporations. Actually, the two taxes on corporations amount to a single one, for a given firm must pay only whichever one is greater.

The sales tax has also become increasingly popular as a secondary tax for city governments since it was first used by New York in 1934. It is authorized in several states and has been especially popular in California. The broad-base state sales tax has been popular with legislators because it yields well even under relatively depressed economic conditions, with tax administrators who find it quite easy to collect, and with the general public which prefers—if it must pay taxes at all—to pay a few pennies at a time rather than taxes that require budgeting and call loud attention to themselves at payment time, as does the income tax. The principal objections to the sales tax come, first, from merchants, who feel that it hurts their businesses and who dislike the paper work it imposes upon them (they become unpaid tax collectors for the government). Other objections come from persons—liberals, labor leaders, and some economists—who do not like the regressive * feature of the tax. The argument on regressivity, though economically sound, does not impress most people of either low or high income. They undoubtedly prefer the sales to the income tax.

* REGRESSIVE TAX. A tax, the burden of which is lessened as ability to pay increases. A sales tax which applies to food, fuel, and other necessities (as most of them do) is considered regressive, even though the rate does not vary, because persons with low incomes spend a larger percentage of their income on necessities than do those with high incomes.

Income Taxes   Probably the most unpopular tax in America is the personal income tax. It is unpopular because of the unending barrage of vilification directed against it over several decades by groups financed by high-income conservatives who prefer regressive taxes, because it requires infrequent large payments that are felt more than are sales taxes, and because the Federal income tax, since the early 1940s, has been at higher levels than the American culture will easily tolerate. The Federal government has been able to collect its tax despite a fairly high rate and steep progressivity, principally because (1) it has been justified as necessary for the defense of the nation and (2) it has a withholding system by which the taxpayer never sees the money he is paying under the tax and hence comes to think of his income exclusively in take-home terms—he usually objects only if he must pay more than was withheld. Until the financial crises of the late 1950s, few cities or states had used the withholding system. This was the case because conservatives had convinced legislators that withholding is an insidious device and because it complicates administration. None of the cities or states can use the national defense argument. Yet, the income tax is being used more and more on the state and local levels.

State income taxes generally are only slightly graduated. That is, the tax rate increases only slightly as income increases. None of the states levy taxes the rate of which increases at anywhere near the rate of the Federal income tax. The Colorado tax, for example, in 1964, ranged from 3 to 8 percent, the highest bracket applying on incomes above $10,000. Alaska had perhaps the most graduated income tax among states, ranging from 3 to 15 percent. In contrast, several states had taxes which ranged from 2 to 4 percent—in Mississippi the 4 percent did not apply except to incomes of over $25,000. Exemptions, deductions, and progressivity vary from one state to another, but in general economists view the tax as the most fair of state taxes. It yields well under most conditions but tends to collapse in times of depression when state revenue needs are high.

The income tax has been largely preempted by state and Federal governments. Philadelphia, however, adopted an income tax in 1939, and many other cities have since done so, particularly in Pennsylvania and Ohio. Most city income taxes might more accurately be called "payroll taxes," for typically they are not graduated and do not permit any deductions but are simply a certain percentage of the total amount of money earned by individuals, and sometimes corporations, within a city. The Philadelphia tax, for example, applies only to earned income and not to income from stocks, bonds, and rents. As such, it is regressive in character.[23]

It seems likely that in the future an increase will be made in the personal income tax at the local, and especially the state, level of government. States not using the tax were, in the 1960s, looking toward it, and states with it were considering the use of withholding and changes in the rules on deductions as a basis for increasing the rate and yield of the tax.[24]

In the five-year period preceding 1965, state tax collections increased by one-third, and the leading increases were in corporate and personal income taxes, which increased by almost 50 percent.

Corporation Income Taxes   Corporation income or profits taxes produce about two-thirds as much revenue for states as does the personal income tax, but the great bulk of the total collected is paid in only four states: California, New York, Pennsylvania, and Wisconsin.[25] In other states, the corporation income tax is often a mere token and in such highly industrialized states as Illinois, Michigan, Ohio, and Texas was not levied at all in 1965. Politicians are commonly subjected to pressure to adopt a corporation income tax, especially on three grounds: (1) that if individuals pay the tax, so should corporations (the argument is politically, if not economically or logically, sound); (2) that if small businessmen bear the burden of the sales tax with all of its nuisances and possible discouragement to business, the large manufacturing businesses which are incorporated should also be burdened with a tax; and (3) that the tax is based only on profits and so does not hurt anyone, certainly not the small taxpayer who is burdened with the various sales taxes.

But the tax is opposed by the most powerful and largest corporations in

[23] See L. J. Quinto, **Municipal Income Taxation in the United States,** Institute of Public Administration, New York, 1952; and Robert A. Sigafoos, **The Municipal Income Tax: Its History and Problems,** Public Administration Service, Chicago, 1954.
[24] See "Methods of State Income Tax Withholding Described," **Tax Administrators News,** 20: December, 1956; "Income Taxes Head State Revenue Gain," **Tax Administrators News,** 20: September, 1956; **Monthly Tax Features,** Tax Foundation, Inc., 1: entire issue, August, 1957.
[25] **Facts and Figures on Governmental Finance,** 1965, table 140.

each state. The managers of these companies view it as their duty to keep costs down, and to a corporation each tax is a cost item. Generally, they have been able to kill tax bills introduced in the legislatures. Indeed, except for the four states mentioned as having a relatively high-yielding tax, the corporate income tax is most likely to be found in the states with relatively few large corporations.

Economists sometimes oppose the corporation income tax on the ground that it does not measure ability to pay adequately. Their argument is that the profits of a corporation should more logically be passed along to the stockholders and the state's share should be reclaimed at that point as personal income tax. This would assure that there could be no truth to the old claim that the corporation income tax sometimes takes bread from widows and orphans, a brass gong that is sounded each time the tax is considered. Liberals often argue that corporate profits really belong to all of society and that, after stockholders are allowed a reasonable return on their investment, what is left (after the Federal government takes its considerable bite, around 50 percent in the postwar years) properly belongs to the people of the state. For liberal politicians, the tax has another attraction: most of their constituents are not stockholders and can be convinced that the tax will raise a lot of money without hurting anyone. Stockholders sometimes argue that the tax is unfair because it results in double taxation, once as corporate income, a second time as personal income. But double taxation is common in American government. For that matter, so is triple and quadruple taxation.

In addition to the tax on profits, all states levy taxes on corporations in the form of licenses and taxes on the privilege of doing business. These taxes are based on a variety of formulas, but profits are not the basic part of them. In these cases, it is a matter of allowing a corporation the right to be recognized as an artificial person and to enjoy the various special privileges which corporations have that individual proprietorships and partnerships do not have.

Other Taxes   In addition to those already mentioned, states collect a variety of other taxes. An important source of income is from motor-vehicle and operators' licenses. These are determined according to many formulas, and charges vary greatly. In states with important mining industries or with oil and gas wells, severance taxes may be important. These tax the removal from the ground of a resource that can never be replaced. In Louisiana, Minnesota, Oklahoma, and Texas, severance levies are major sources of state revenue. Because of the size and power of companies engaged in the extractive industries, power which is arrayed against popular opposition to exploitation and exhaustion of resources, histories of the adoption of severance taxes are likely to be dramatic.

States all have death and gift taxes, based on many formulas, and in several states are of some importance as a source of revenue. Other taxes are levied on the gross receipts of public utilities (usually in lieu of property taxes) and on parimutuel betting. Unemployment-compensation taxes are collected by all states, but they are really insurance premiums and not taxes. Local governments may use some or all of the above taxes and others as well. They are likely to have business taxes, often primarily levies to pay the cost of supervising businesses directly affecting the public health, but often set at a profitable level. Taxes on hotel-room occupancy are becoming popular, and so are admission taxes for theaters, motion pictures, and sports events, since theaters and stadiums are relatively immovable.

Nontax Revenues   State and local governments receive some money annually from fines and fees. The fines are paid for violating ordinances and laws. The fees are charges for certain services, such as issuing licenses or transferring real estate. They also make some profits from operating what are essentially business enterprises. These include the sale of water, fertilizer (from sewage-disposal plants), and liquor, and the operation of ferry boats, toll bridges, and roads. Some states have a monopoly over the wholesale distribution or retail sale of liquor. This is defended as aiding in the policing of the liquor business at all levels of operation; it is also enormously profitable. State and local governments operate retail liquor stores—usually package sales only, but sometimes also liquor by the drink.

Service Charges   Rather than pay for many services from general taxes, often local governments levy service charges. These have traditionally been used for water supply. In recent years, they have also been levied in the form of charges on sewerage, garbage collection, street lighting and cleaning, snow removal, weed cutting, and other services. Charges are often levied as a means of avoiding an increase in the general tax rate. It is a way of causing the tax level to appear to be lower than it actually is. Service charges can also be used to promote equity in local taxation by making it possible to charge tax-exempt property, of which there is a good deal in some cities, and by forcing industries which contribute disproportionate amounts of waste to the sewage system to pay appropriate costs. Service charges are also put to use when local governments have come close to their legal tax limits, since they are not usually counted as taxes for limitation purposes.

In addition to service charges, another important means of paying for services by use of the benefit theory is the special assessment.*

* SPECIAL ASSESSMENT. An extra levy upon specific pieces of property designed to defray the costs of services or conveniences of particular value to that property. Practices in their application vary widely, as do the rules by which the property owner pays for them.[26]

Intergovernmental Payments

In the United States, financial centralization has preceded administrative centralization to a much greater degree than has been the case in other urbanized and industrialized nations.[27] The two have a tendency to proceed together in

[26] See William O. Winter, **The Special Assessment Today**, Institute of Public Administration, University of Michigan, Ann Arbor, Mich., 1952.
[27] For a comparison of practices in the United States, Great Britain, and Scandinavia, see Kjeld Philip, **Intergovernmental Fiscal Relations**, Ejnar Munksgaard, Copenhagen, Denmark, 1954.

other countries, but American traditions militate against the transfer of powers to higher levels of government. We have, therefore, sought to solve financial problems at particular levels by the use of shared taxes and grants-in-aid, both of which are devices for bridging the gap between the appropriate spending unit and the most efficient tax-raising unit.[28] Shared taxes and grants are also made sometimes simply in response to sufficiently powerful pressures.

The size of intergovernmental payments has been increasing over the years.

In 1902, less than 1 percent of state and local general revenues came from Federal grants-in-aid. Sixty years later, this figure had increased to 13.5 percent. The amount was no longer entirely in the form of grants, however, although this was the principal form. State and local governments also shared some revenues and received contractual payments for scientific research and certain public services.

State and local expenditures, however, are not only increasing faster than are Federal domestic expenditures, but at a faster rate than all Federal expenditures. Indeed, by the early 1970s, state and local expenditures may pass total Federal expenditures, including those for defense and foreign aid.[29]

Local units of government have received increasing amounts of fiscal help in the form of grants from the Federal government (usually through the states) and grants and shared taxes from the state governments. Payments from state governments increased from $56 million in 1902 to $3,501 million in 1948 and $11,885 million in 1963. Yet, local spending increased at such a great rate in the decade following 1948 that state grants diminished slightly as a portion of total local expenditures.

Grants-in-aid   Grants-in-aid are payments made by voluntary appropriation from one level of government to a lower level of government. The amount of a grant is generally independent of the yield from any particular tax or other source of income.[30]

Specific grants are normally made with conditions attached. These conditions may require, for example, matching funds, the use of technically trained personnel in administering them, the maintenance of technical standards of equipment and material, or the use of the money only for certain specific purposes.

Three principal objections are usually levied against the use of grants-in-aid.[31] First, that they may stimulate extravagant expenditures because the locality is spending funds which are not an immediate and obvious burden upon local taxpayers. Thus, if local officials spend money that they need not

[28] Robert S. Ford, "State and Local Finance," **Annals,** 266:15–23, November, 1949. This entire issue deals with various aspects of governmental finance.

[29] John Anderson, "Can the States Live on Crumbs?" **Saturday Review,** Jan. 9, 1965, pp. 31ff.

[30] On grants, see J. R. McKinley, **Local Revenue Problems and Trends,** Bureau of Public Administration, University of California, Berkeley, Calif., 1949, and the various state and local revenue studies that have been made.

[31] Ford, *op. cit.* See also, Joseh P. Harris, "The Future of Grants-in-aid," **Annals,** 207:14–26, January, 1940; **Federal Grants-in-aid,** Council of State Governments, Chicago, 1949; E. J. Sady, **Research in Federal-State Relations,** The Brookings Institution, Washington, D.C., 1957; and the Commission on Intergovernmental Relations, **A Report to the President** (1955), chap. 5.

solicit from the voters, they may feel no need to spend it wisely or on necessities. Second, grants are considered a threat to local self-government and local responsibility. Since the state or national governments provide the funds only if certain conditions are met, they may come to supplant local government in the making of policies in these areas. Last, grants are held, potentially at least, to lead toward disproportionate expenditures in favor of those functions receiving grants. In other words, regardless of the merits or need of the various functions performed, some will always have a plentiful budgetary appropriation because of the grants, while others, perhaps more needy and deserving (by local value standards), may be skimped. Grants for venereal-disease and tuberculosis control may promote these services while other functions of the health department shrivel for lack of funds. Although these objections arise virtually every time grants-in-aid are discussed, there appears to be little empirical study to support their validity. They may well be proper objections, but further research is needed on the matter of the effects of grants-in-aid.

Shared Taxes   A shared tax is one imposed by one unit of government but shared with other governments according to a formula. The amount sent to each receiving unit is sometimes intended to be representative of the portion of the tax produced within the area of that unit, but shared taxes may be distributed on any basis the collector chooses. Unlike the grant-in-aid, a shared tax delivers no fixed amount; rather, receipts are dependent upon the yield of the tax.[32]

Shared taxes have become increasingly popular in recent decades, and they seem to be preferred by local officials to either grants-in-aid or an enlargement of the taxing powers of local governments. Part of the reason for this is that fewer strings are attached to shared taxes than to grants. Shared taxes also bring less criticism from local citizens than does the enactment of additional local taxes.

Taxes that are most often shared by the state with local units of government include those on motor fuel, motor vehicles, liquor sales, and income. Shared taxes are sometimes defended as being less in the nature of charity than the grant-in-aid, for although they are state-imposed and state-collected, they are levied upon local wealth and hence are not a largess. Since they are viewed as a local tax with the state acting as a collecting agent, local units are usually more free in using the revenue as they see fit than they are in the case of grants.

Many criticisms are made of shared taxes, however. New York state commissions, in 1936 and again in 1946, discouraged their use.[33] These study groups pointed out that shared taxes cannot be adjusted to local needs. Some areas with little need receive more from such taxes than they can spend, while others receive much less than their needs require. Grants-in-aid are better adjustable to need. Shared taxes, further, do not help to stabilize local rev-

---

[32] McKinley, *op. cit.*, pp. 22–27.
[33] See **Report of the New York Commission on State Aid to Municipal Subdivisions**, State of New York, Albany, N.Y., 1936; **Report of the New York State Commission on Municipal Revenues**, State of New York, Albany, N.Y., 1946.

enues. They yield well in prosperous times but tend to be withdrawn by the state during business depressions, when local need for funds is most critical. Last, the manner in which shared taxes are used is less subject to control than are grants. From an ideological viewpoint this may be argued as either an advantage or a disadvantage. But from the viewpoint of imposing standards, the state cannot be so effective through shared taxes as it can be through grants. Whatever the arguments, a long look into the future will no doubt reveal the shared tax still with us.

Postwar Trends   Intergovernmental financial payments exist between the Federal government and the states; to a much smaller extent, between the Federal government and local units; between the states and their political subdivisions; and even between units of local governments. The amounts spent for each of these has been increasing in recent years, and the principal way by which most local governments have diversified their revenue sources and relieved the pressure on the property tax has been through the receipt of grants and shared taxes.[34]

In 1948, the states received $1,643 million from the Federal government for various programs. This figure had increased to $7,566 million by 1963. But in the meanwhile, state expenditures, taken collectively, increased so rapidly that the Federal portion of total state revenues had changed hardly at all. The same situation was true of state revenue trends in relation to local government spending.

In 1964, the Heller Plan—named for Walter W. Heller, a professor of economics at the University of Minnesota and chairman of the Council of Economic Advisors under President John F. Kennedy—received a great deal of attention. His proposal was to offer to the states Federal "block" grants with no strings attached as a means for strengthening state finances. Although Heller was regarded by informed persons as a "liberal," other liberals were not enthusiastic about his plan and many strongly opposed it on the grounds that the states would not use the money efficiently for the advancement of programs needed (in their opinion) to meet the problems of an urban, industrial society.[35] Conservatives, who have for more than a generation opposed Federal grants-in-aid of all types, fearing that they would lead to greater Federal controls, were not enthusiastic. President Lyndon Johnson, in 1964 and later, ignored the Heller Plan in his recommendations to Congress, probably to the relief of both liberals and conservatives.

Patterns vary greatly from state to state on policies for intergovernmental payments. A very low percentage of total state expenditures are for local government aid in New England (except for Massachusetts), Montana, and South Dakota; a very high percentage in Wisconsin, California, and Colorado. The pattern of state payments to political subdivisions seems to be a function more of the balances among existing local pressures than of anything else. The

[34] See Rowland Egger, "Nature over Art: No More Local Finance," **American Political Science Review,** 47:461–477, June, 1955; U.S. Bureau of the Census, **Historical Statistics on State and Local Government Finances,** 1955.
[35] Christopher Jencks, "Why Bail Out the States?" **New Republic,** Dec. 12, 1964, pp. 8–10.

national pattern does not appear to show a high correlation with any factors whether one considers geography (except for the New England situation), rural-urban balances, or ranking by personal income as a measure of relative wealth. New York, an urban Eastern state, has an elaborate and generous program of state payments to local units. Pennsylvania, another urban Eastern state, ranks low in percentage of state budget devoted to payments to local units.

Federal payments to state and local governments were discussed in Chapter 3. Most state payments to local governments are in the areas of education, welfare, and highways. Collectively, they make up about 85 percent of the total, though practice varies by states. Payments are also made for public safety, health, hospitals, nonhighway transportation, housing, urban redevelopment, and natural resources, among others, and some are lump-sum, or block, grants for no prescribed purpose. Intergovernmental payments are important parts of the revenues of all units of government below the Federal level, and they seem destined to continue.

Debt Policies and Issues

A conflict that arises in every state or local unit of government from time to time centers on the alternatives of paying for capital improvements by issuing bonds or by increasing taxes and paying cash. The principles of borrowing on these levels are different from those on the national level. The national government itself is the principal institution for the establishment of credit-creating institutions, chiefly the banks. If the national government borrows from banks, it is borrowing credit made possible largely by its own rules. Furthermore, the internally held national debt is not passed on to other generations.

The credit of the United States is psychologically intertwined with that which is held worthwhile by most Americans. The borrowing power of the national government is limited only by the faith the American people have in their government, and that faith is enormous. The national government can, except in national defense emergencies, manage to borrow mostly in times of economic recession when interest rates are low, and the money pumped into the system thereby serves to prime the economic pump.

State and local governments enjoy none of the borrowing advantages of the national government. They cannot create credit. State and local governments usually have to borrow money in boom times to provide services a prosperous people want. But they must pay high interest rates to get the money. In contrast, in depressions when people need jobs, interest rates are low, and borrowing conditions are therefore favorable, state and local governments tend to decrease spending and avoid borrowing. The public faith in any given state or community is also immensely less than the faith in the United States. State and local government borrowing power is accordingly greatly limited. Except as they contain nontaxable income features, bonds of these units of government are treated with no more respect on the open market than are the bonds of private corporations.

When to Borrow   Almost all economists are agreed that a state or local unit of government should not borrow money to meet current operating expenses. In the past this has happened, either because a depression had dried up the revenue sources and the situation was one of desperation, or because public officials desired to keep taxes low as a vote-attracting technique for the next election. Borrowing to pay for permanent improvements is another matter, especially if the bonds are to be paid off before the improvement becomes obsolescent or dilapidated. Borrowing to cover a period greater than the life of the improvement is not economically sound, although it may be politically sound.

Sometimes the question of whether or not to borrow never actually confronts the governing body, since the conditions governing indebtedness are often prescribed by state constitution or city charter. Most of the states have restrictions upon the borrowing power of both state and local governments.[36] These vary in detail. Some of them may be waived by popular referendum.

Types of Bonds   Limitations upon the borrowing power of state and local governments apply particularly (though not exclusively) to the pledging of the full faith and credit of the government to "general-obligation bonds." In issuing these bonds, the community agrees to levy whatever tax is necessary in order to pay the interest and eventually to retire the bonds. If the issuing of these bonds is limited (sometimes it is completely prohibited) by statute or constitution, the governing body can turn to "mortgage bonds" or "revenue bonds." *

* MORTGAGE BONDS are normally used in connection with the purchase or construction of utilities, and they offer a mortgage on the utility as security. This type of bond has usually required a higher interest rate than bonds of general obligation (because the purchasers have less confidence in getting their money back) and as a result has been less popular with borrowing units. Sometimes mortgage bonds also involve a pledge of full faith and credit. REVENUE BONDS are retired from the income of the utility for which they were issued.

Revenue bonds have become increasingly popular since the 1930s. Generally, fewer constitutional and other legalities restrict their issue, and commonly no popular referendum is required, as is almost always the case with general obligation bonds. Their interest rate is usually higher, however, than if full faith and credit is pledged. These bonds are secured by a pledge of the revenue from some self-liquidating project. Toll roads or bridges, tunnels, electricity-generating plants, water-supply systems, and college dormitories may be financed in this way. Governments must agree to set rates high enough to pay the debt charges. Sometimes the bondholders are also given a mortgage on the utilities.

[36] See **Provisions in State Constitutions Controlling Debt,** Tax Foundation, Inc., New York, 1945; B. U. Ratchford, **American State Debts,** Duke University Press, Durham, N.C., 1941; C. H. Chatters and A. M. Hillhouse, **Local Government Debt Administration,** Prentice-Hall, Inc., Englewood Cliffs, N.J., 1939; A. M. Hillhouse, **Municipal Bonds: A Century of Experience,** Municipal Finance Officers' Association, Chicago, 1936; Alvin D. Sokolow, **State Review of Local Borrowing,** Institute for Community Development, Michigan State University, East Lansing, Mich., 1963.

Slightly over 53 percent of the outstanding state debt in 1963 was non-guaranteed, that is, was based upon revenue or mortgage bonds rather than general-obligation bonds. In 1948, only 14 percent of it had been of this type.

Repayment of Bonds   Traditionally, state and local government bonds have been retired by the establishment of a "sinking fund" which would, supposedly, provide sufficient funds to retire the bonds when they came due. Most bonds of this type would be issued so that all of them would fall due at the same time. The sinking-fund method has proved to be defective in several respects, however, particularly because (1) the governing body often failed to make adequate appropriations to the fund, which must be built up systematically, or the fund was otherwise tampered with; and (2) the sinking fund could come to disaster in economic depressions if its investments failed.

More recently, there has been a trend toward the use of "serial bonds." These bonds mature gradually, a certain percentage of them each year. The governing body then, instead of appropriating money into a sinking fund, appropriates the necessary amount for the direct retirement of part of the debt. This is the same plan that is so popular in bank loans to private individuals: part of the principal is paid back each month, thus simplifying the planning for retiring the debt.

Bond Prices and National Government Policies   Two national government policies have had an important effect upon the bond market for state and local government issues. The monetary policies of the national government are a major factor in determining the interest rates that must be paid on bonds. This is not the only factor, but it can be an important one. When the Federal government follows an easy-credit policy, state and local governments are encouraged to borrow; possibly they are encouraged beyond what they may later consider to have been prudent. When the Federal government follows a hard-credit policy, state and local governments find it more expensive to borrow money in order to make improvements they believe to be needed. In a time of expanding school-age populations, for example, it may be necessary to build schools regardless of the current cost of borrowing money. Federal policies are tied to political ideologies or to the business cycle; they do not consider current state and local needs and may work hardships on these units of government.

A second national government money policy of importance to state and local governments is that of exempting the income from their bonds from taxation by the national government. A series of nineteenth-century Supreme Court decisions established the principle of intergovernmental tax immunity, according to which one government cannot tax the instrumentalities of another. This principle was in effect set aside by the Supreme Court around 1940, but Congress has not taxed the yield of state and local bonds because of opposition from those units of governments, from bond houses, and from holders of the bonds. Tax-exempt bonds carry a lower interest rate than do those that are taxable. This encourages state and local governments to go into debt. The only persons who find them profitable to buy are high-income persons. The exemption feature thus, in effect, subsidizes those who least need it. The benefiting units of government nevertheless prefer to keep the present system, with its relatively low cost, even though it raises some questions of equity.[37]

Public Attitudes toward Debt   Since the end of World War II, there has been a great increase in state and local borrowing. Between 1950 and 1964, indebtedness at these levels increased by 258 percent. Highway construction has been the main reason for borrowing by state governments; education, by local governments. The need for local utilities (water-supply, electric, gas-supply, and transit systems) has also been responsible for much indebtedness.[38]

A few items should be noted about borrowing patterns:

1. Cultural values and the priorities they establish are important factors in determining the kinds of things the public will go into debt for. Thus, it is easier to gain approval for bonds for school construction than for sewage-disposal plants; for highway construction than for mental hospitals.

2. The public will sometimes refuse to permit a general-obligation bond issue at a referendum but will not seriously oppose a revenue bond issue intended for the same purpose. The latter usually does not require a referendum, and the complaints which follow its approval by the governing body are often mild, while they might be vigorous if a referendum campaign were conducted.

3. Economic conditions and interest rates affect public attitudes toward bond issues. In 1953, when interest rates were low, 90 percent of the referendums on general-obligation bond issues in Michigan passed; in 1956, when interest rates were the highest in decades, only 42 percent passed.

4. Per capita debt tends to increase with the population of local governmental units and is likely to be higher in growing than in stable communities.[39]

5. A direct relationship exists between the degree of urbanism of a state and its per capita debt. In addition, debt patterns tend to be grouped geographically, with the East and the Pacific Northwest states having relatively high debts. All of the Eastern states north of Virginia have higher per capita debts than the national average, except for Vermont. These figures indicate that debt patterns are related to cultural values. There are some startling differences between neighboring states, however. In 1963, Louisiana had a per capita debt of $146, Texas of only $45; New Mexico of $67, Arizona of a mere $15.[40]

Closing Note   Public finance is not a science. Although the economist can give technical advice concerning the possible approximate yield of a particular tax under certain conditions and although he has fairly well-developed ideas about the way in which the burden of a tax is distributed—that is, whether it

---

[37] For more on the subject, see Adrian, *op. cit.*, pp. 328–329.
[38] See U.S. Bureau of the Census, **State and Local Government Indebtedness**, 1957; **The Financial Challenge to the States**, Tax Foundation, Inc., New York, 1958, pp. 14–15; **Facts and Figures on Government Finance**, 1965, table 1.
[39] See Wylie Kilpatrick, **Revenue and Debt of Florida Municipalities**, Public Administration Clearing Service, University of Florida, Gainesville, Fla., 1953.
[40] **Facts and Figures of Government Finance**, 1965, table 166.

is regressive or progressive, is borne by the person or thing taxed, or is passed on to someone else—his information will be only one of the factors considered by legislators in passing tax laws. Two things are more important: the value patterns of the society which will have to pay any tax that is adopted and the balance of forces of the interest groups pressuring the legislative body. Out of these two considerations, balanced against the service demands of that same society and the same pressure groups, will come a tax system, or rather a group of not necessarily coordinated taxes. These will be combined with various other sources of government revenue in such a manner as to make possible the rough balancing of a budget.

SELECTED READINGS

Burkhead, Jesse: **Government Budgeting,** John Wiley & Sons, Inc., New York, 1956.

————: **Public School Finance: Economics and Politics,** Syracuse University Press, Syracuse, N.Y., 1964.

Chatters, Carl H., and A. M. Hillhouse: **Local Government Debt Administration,** Prentice-Hall, Inc., Englewood Cliffs, N.J., 1939.

Commission on Intergovernmental Relations: **A Report to the President,** 1955.

Earle, Valerie A., and Chester B. Earle: **Taxing the Southern Railway in Alabama,** rev. ed., The Bobbs-Merrill Company, Inc., Indianapolis, ICP no. 18, 1959.

Hillhouse, A. M.: **Municipal Bonds: A Century of Experience,** Municipal Finance Officers' Association, Chicago, 1936.

Isard, Walter, and Robert Coughlin: **Municipal Costs and Revenues Resulting from Community Growth,** Chandler-Davis Publishing Company, Wellesley, Massachusetts, 1957.

Martin, Roscoe C.: **The Cities and the Federal System,** Atherton Press, New York, 1965.

Peabody, Robert L.: **Seattle Seeks a Tax,** The Bobbs-Merrill Company, Inc., Indianapolis, ICP no. 49, 1959.

Penniman, Clara, and Walter Heller: **State Income Tax Administration,** Public Administration Service, Chicago, 1960.

Philip, Kjeld: **Intergovernmental Fiscal Relations,** Ejnar Munksgaard, Copenhagen, Denmark, 1954.

Provisions in State Constitutions Controlling Debt, Tax Foundation, Inc., New York, 1945.

Quinto, L. J.: **Municipal Income Taxation in the United States,** Institute of Public Administration, New York, 1952.

Sady, E. J.: **Research in Federal-State Relations,** The Brookings Institution, Washington, D.C., 1957.

Schroth, Thomas N., and others: **Congress and the Nation, 1945–1964,** Congressional Quarterly Service, Washington, 1965, chap. 10.

Scott, Stanley, and E. L. Feder: **Factors Associated with Variations in Municipal Expenditure Levels,** Institute of Public Administration, University of California, Berkeley, Calif., 1957.

Sigafoos, Robert A.: **The Municipal Income Tax: Its History and Problems,** Public Administration Service, Chicago, 1954.

U.S. Advisory Commission on Intergovernmental Relations: **Measures of State and Local Fiscal Capacity and Tax Effort,** 1962.

————: **The Role of Equalization in Federal Grants,** 1964.

————: **State Constitutional and Statutory Restrictions in Local Government Debt,** 1961.

————: **State Constitutional and Statutory Restrictions on Local Taxing Powers,** 1962.

————: **Tax Overlapping in the United States,** 1964.

Winter, William O.: **The Special Assessment Today,** Institute of Public Administration, University of Michigan, Ann Arbor, Mich., 1952.

18

EDUCATION

American parents have always wanted their children to be well educated; usually they have wanted them to have more education than they themselves had. In an open-class, socially mobile culture, education and status advancement have been closely linked. Frontier egalitarianism produced the public school system and gave it its character as a locally controlled and locally financed institution. Coupled with this desire for educational opportunity was, however, the strong belief that an educated person should not be a highbrow and that his learning should be pragmatic and put to use for the benefit of society. Out of frontier life came a powerful tradition in support of learning and in opposition to intellectualism. Within that general framework of values, American educational policy was developed.

History of Public Education

Two ideologies of education were brought to the shores of this land by the colonists. One was that of the class-ordered society to be found in all of Western Europe in the sixteenth and seventeenth centuries. It held that each family had an obligation to provide privately for the education of its children and that the community need offer only the barest rudiments of an educational system, and that only for the poor. Such a general concept was natural to the social structure of Europe and was accepted in America quite widely in colonial days, especially in the South.

This traditional view encountered opposition, however, from a competing philosophy. In those areas, notably in New England, where Calvinist religious beliefs were strong, the idea was advanced that education was a collective responsibility and a right equally for all. This concept, fitting neatly into the fluid class system of America and into the later training needs of an increasingly complex industrial society, spread westward. The aristocratic private-responsibility concept—which in practice meant education only for the economically privileged—maintained itself in the plantation economy of the South but did not advance with the frontier.[1]

The Coming of Free, Public Education   In 1647—six generations before the War of Independence—the Massachusetts colonial legislature required the towns to provide for the education of their youth. This requirement spread through New England and out along the fringe of civilization. After independence was won, but before the Constitution was adopted, Congress under the Articles of Confederation called for public education in the expanding West and provided land subsidies for that purpose. The rich prose of the Northwest Ordinance (1787) established a policy never abandoned on the frontier and provided words to be fashioned in stone, brass, or, more recently, stainless steel on the walls of schools from Ohio to California: "Religion, morality, and knowledge being necessary to good government and the happiness of mankind, schools and the means of education shall forever be encouraged."

But free public education was not easily afforded. Public instruction, in its earliest form, was sketchy and rudimentary, at best. In the early nineteenth century, many persons in all parts of the country still thought the idea of education for all a dangerous, radical concept. It was argued that the common man had never been educated and did not need instruction, that it would only make him discontented. Others thought it outrageous to propose that one person be taxed to help pay for educating another's children:[2] "It is probable that, with the exception of the slavery question, no other issue has ever faced the American people which was treated so emotionally or which aroused such bitter antagonisms."

It was not until the late 1840s that the principle of tax-supported common schools for all children became general in the North, and in many states it was more a principle than a practice. The use of taxes for school purposes was allowed in every state except Arkansas by 1850, but education was still very simple, and except in the older, wealthier states of the North, some tuition was usually charged. In 1860, the average American was getting only 434 days of schooling in his lifetime. As late as 1870, one-fifth of all Americans could neither read nor write—though many of these were immigrants. Only a few hundred high schools, or public "academies," existed prior to the Civil War. The high school, a unique American institution, appeared first when local school districts, acting alone or in concert, were permitted to offer "academic" courses, that is, courses that would help a student pass the qualifying examinations for entrance into college. These institutions developed rapidly after

---

[1] Lawrence A. Cremin, **The American Common School,** Teachers College, Columbia University, New York, 1951, outlines the values upon which public education was built.
[2] R. T. Gregg, "The Battle for Tax Supported Schools," **Nation's Schools,** 69:49–50, July, 1957. See also R. T. Gregg, "The Struggle for Free Schools," **Nation's Schools,** 85–86, June, 1957, and E. P. Cubberley, **Public Education in the United States,** Houghton Mifflin Company, Boston, 1919.

the Civil War. Yet, in 1900, only 8 percent of high school–age youngsters were in school. This figure compares with over 80 percent in 1957, and the percentage at that time was even higher in all areas outside the South. But by the beginning of the twentieth century, free public education for all was accepted everywhere, though in the East particularly some wealthy families still preferred that their children have private educations, and some religious groups did, too. Ironically, the Calvinists, leaders in the movement for public education, were, in the mid-twentieth century, maintaining many parochial schools: some of them had abandoned support of public education because it had become almost wholly secularized.

The Development of Public Education In the last half of the nineteenth century, the one-room school remained the predominant type. Schoolhouses were, in many parts of the nation, located two miles apart, within walking distance of all children. Teachers were mostly men, though by 1900, the pattern had changed so from the early days of the public school that women teachers exceeded men in number by over 5 to 1 in rural areas of Iowa.[3] Educational policy was locally controlled and financed. Educational administration was just emerging as a profession. Standards were low, both in terms of the training of teachers and the number of days spent in school each year by the typical pupil. In 1875, the school year in Hardin County, Iowa, was seven and one-half months; in Mississippi, four months. Forty percent of the white children and 36 percent of the Negro were in school in Mississippi. In Iowa, men teachers averaged $33.98 a month in salary, women $5 less. As late as 1900, the Mississippi state school superintendent reported that 90 percent of the teachers of the state had no professional training and that 75 percent had no education beyond the rural school. This was not an atypical situation of a poor Southern state; rural Iowa apparently was in little or no better condition.

By the beginning of the twentieth century, educators were becoming aware of the deficiencies of the rural school, and rural isolation was already declining. The National Education Association was studying the rural-school problem. These schools were unable to compete with the cities for personnel, and they had to depend upon young inexperienced teachers. Standards in cities were higher, and the schools were graded; but they were poorly equipped, had short school years, and many children did not attend. In the East, a monitorial system was common with older students teaching younger ones, acting as "monitors."

The Consolidation Movement The technical revolution both in the city and on the farm made traditional education inadequate. The movement of surplus farm populations into the cities, especially after the beginning of the twentieth century, helped emphasize the obsolete character of the one-room school. Con-

[3] George S. May, "Iowa's Consolidated Schools," **Palimpsest**, 37: January, 1956, entire issue. See also, H. G. Good, **A History of American Education**, The Macmillan Company, New York, 1956; E. W. Knight, **Fifty Years of American Education**, The Ronald Press Company, New York, 1952; Wilbur B. Brookover and David Gottlieb, **A Sociology of Education**, 2d ed., American Book Company, New York, 1964.

solidation of the traditional four-square-mile districts became necessary if education were to be carried beyond eight grades. The first such consolidation took place in Massachusetts in 1875; the first in the Midwest was in Indiana in 1889. Generally the combining of districts took place at a slow rate until the coming of the engine-driven school bus around the time of World War I. State financial aid became common as a device for encouraging consolidation, and further impetus was added by the Smith-Hughes Act of 1917, which provided Federal aid to districts offering high school training in agriculture and home economics.

There was considerable resistance to the abandonment of the local district, however. Pressure for change was opposed by (1) the traditional conservatism of those who work the land; (2) the once-common rural attitude that "luxuries" were for city people and beyond the reach of farmers and small-town dwellers; (3) the feeling that consolidated schools meant urban control of education and that this would make the curriculum unsuited for rural needs; (4) the fear that traveling into urban areas for education would mean "corruption of morals" and the "evil" influence of city ways; (5) the belief that the farmer, through the general property tax, would have to pay more than his share of educational costs under consolidation; (6) the reluctance of Catholics, Lutherans, Calvinists, and others who sent children to parochial schools to help pay for expensive educational facilities that they would not use; and (7) the loss of local control over education and with it the possibility of becoming a school-board member, which had been a ready means of social recognition in a rural community.[4]

In the period after World War II, consolidations took place at a great rate. The tendency was toward the reduction of the number of school districts to the point where every child would live in a twelve-grade district, thus reestablishing the practice of having the district offer the number of years of schooling that was generally expected of each child. Legislators were pressed to withdraw state aid to districts offering less than twelve grades of education. Townsmen competed with one another to secure annexations, since the hinterland areas tended to trade where their children went to school. By 1955, three-fourths of the one-room schools in existence in 1929 had disappeared.

Education Today

The Current Function of Public Education   The problems of school-board members and the issues confronting the public are complicated by the dual function performed by contemporary schools. They serve both as educational and custodial institutions, a fact that is often overlooked in controversies over school-curriculum policies.

The current function of education (Latin, *educare*, "to bring up a child") has resulted from a basic shift in the economic position of the child in the family. In an agricultural society, boys in particular, but girls as well, were economic assets. They were put to work at an early age doing general farm

4 May, *op. cit.*, pp. 36–45.

work. They were kept out of school for plowing and planting and at corn-picking time; they quit for good at an early age. In an urban society, children are an economic liability. There is no incentive to keep them out of school. In fact, the opposite is the case. On the farm, child labor was acceptable, indeed considered necessary for the development of firm character. In the city, it is regarded as dangerous, a threat to health and morals, and it is generally prohibited by law. But the small home in the suburb or apartment in the city is no fit place for an active, noisy, but unemployed teen-ager. The result is that parents exert pressure on school boards and on legislatures to require children to attend school at least until the age of sixteen. Large numbers of youngsters intellectually or emotionally unsuited for being educated are thus foisted upon teachers. Under such circumstances the threat of failing a student in a course or of "flunking out" of school is reduced almost to nonexistence. Furthermore, it becomes necessary for teachers to devise ways by which to keep youngsters adequately motivated in the face of very considerable obstacles. And to add to the complexity of the school as a social institution, it is simultaneously expected to transmit the culture to the next generation and to prepare highly intelligent, highly motivated youngsters for college and for later leadership roles in society. (Except in the East, few young people, even from among the most intelligent or the most wealthy, attend private preparatory schools before entering college.)

The school year, with a long summer vacation, was based on an agricultural society. The change to a year-round system with occasional breaks for short periods has not been made, perhaps partly because children can play outside the home in summer, because family vacations would be difficult to schedule if schools were on a twelve-month basis, and because educational costs, especially teachers' salaries, but also for screens and cooling equipment, would rise if a change were made.

Public and Private Education   Although private secular schools continued to have a place in American education and although parochial schools enjoyed a large growth in the prosperous years after World War II, the bulk of American children attend public schools, and this practice seems to be so basic a part of the culture that it is not likely to change in the foreseeable future. In 1954, over 87 percent of grade school children and 90 percent of those in high schools were in public institutions.

Education Becomes Universal   Almost all children under fourteen years of age, except submorons, attend school in contemporary America. In the high school years, some children continue to drop out, but the increase in attendance has been dramatic. In 1890, over 93 percent of high school–age youngsters were not in a school of any kind. Even in 1920, at the beginning of the period of the school bus and the consolidated school, only one high school–age person in three was in attendance. By the mid-1950s, this figure had reached four out of five and was still increasing.[5] About two-thirds of the children of

[5] See U.S. Office of Education, **Statistical Summary of Education,** 1957.

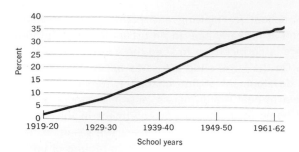

Fig. 18-1 School Buses Carry More than One-third of Public School Students.
SOURCE: **Motor Truck Facts,** Automobile Manufacturers' Association, Detroit, Mich., 1964.

high school age were, in the 1960s, being graduated from the twelfth grade. The average length of the school term, which had been 130 days in 1890, had increased to 179 in 1954. The average number of days attended by those actually enrolled had climbed from 86 to 159. Equipment and the amount of training given teachers were immensely greater in the 1960s than they had been a few generations earlier. Americans, taken as a total group, had more and better education than they had ever before had or than the people of any other land had.

American traditions relative to social advancement are powerful and influence persons even in the areas of the nation where the possibilities of advancement are poorest. Thus, in Kentucky: [6]

Many of the mountaineers value education even though most never went beyond the 8th grade themselves. They want lives for their children that are better than they had, but they do not know, and cannot know, what a good education is, or the kind of effort it requires. Although eastern Kentucky, with substantial amounts of state aid, has made great progress in education in the past five years, eliminating one-room schools, raising teacher salaries, and increasing the proportion of teachers who are certified with a degree from a college, the education its schools provide is still far behind most of the nation.

School Organization   Each state has a state department of education headed by a chief state school officer. The heads of state departments of education have been elective officials, particularly in the South, Midwest, and West. Under pressure from professional educators, however, the trend has been toward appointment of the chief state school officer either by boards of education or by the governor. The number of elected chief state school officers declined from thirty-three in 1942 to twenty in 1965. In addition, because most states operate their schools through numerous small school districts, many of which have limited resources, intermediate school units often exist. These units, operating between the state and local district levels, include counties, parts of counties, and various other groupings of districts. At both

[6] Peter Schrag, "The Schools of Appalachia," **Saturday Review,** May 15, 1965, pp. 68ff.

the state and intermediate levels, the principal responsibility has been not the operation of schools or control of school policy, but the furnishing of consultative, advisory, and statistical services. There has been, however, a trend toward the exercise of regulatory and inspection functions by these levels of administration.[7] The state department has also often been given a veto power over proposed school consolidations and in some states has control over the approval of textbooks and equipment.

The operation of schools remains, in nearly all states, the responsibility of local school districts under the control of locally selected board members. The school district is nearly always a special district of government, independent of the general unit of local government in the area. Even in New England, where the usual pattern is for the schools to be operated by a school committee under the town government, the practice has developed for these committees to act autonomously. Their budgets are often, in fact, not subject to review by the town government.

In the Midwest, the original school district was commonly based on the township, in accordance with advice given by Horace Greeley. But in practice, as in Michigan and Iowa, the subdistricts became virtually or completely independent of the township district. Local board members are ordinarily elected, although they are in some cases appointed by the mayor or a judge, or are elected by township or city governing boards.

The number of local school districts has been declining since the trend toward consolidation began. There were 127,422 districts in the United States in 1932; only 42,825 in 1954. The great bulk of the districts were in the Midwest, with over 60 percent of them in the nine states of Iowa, Kansas, Michigan, Minnesota, Missouri, Nebraska, North Dakota, South Dakota, and Wisconsin. These are the states where the four-square-mile-district tradition was the strongest. Some of the Southern states and Pennsylvania also had over 1,000 districts each, but in the sparsely settled West and in much of the East and South, districts were large in size. Delaware (with some districts excepted), Hawaii, and North Carolina operate virtually state systems of education.[8]

Organization and Politics   By tradition, school boards in the United States are independent of other units of government. They, in the ideal model, are responsible for fiscal and other noneducational aspects of school programs. Professional administrators and teachers are responsible for educational activities. In fact, however, school finances are closely tied in with city and county political decisions as well as those at the state and national levels. Futhermore, both the board of education and various interest groups have a voice in the curriculum of schools. Furthermore, all decisions about finances at

---

[7] See U.S. Office of Education, **Statistics of State Schools Systems,** 1956.

[8] See Paul Dolan, **The Government and Administration of Delaware,** Thomas Y. Crowell Company, New York, 1956, chap. 13; Robert S. Rankin, **The Government and Administration of North Carolina,** Thomas Y. Crowell Company, New York, 1955, chap. 13. For a case study by a political scientist, see Robert L. Morlan, **Intergovernmental Relations in Education,** The University of Minnesota Press, Minneapolis, 1950. There is a vast literature on the school district reorganization movement.

whatever level have some influence upon educational policy as it affects the children in public schools. Furthermore, despite the ideal model which is often treated as if it were a realistic description of actual educational processes, school superintendents are deeply involved in politics. Indeed: [9]

The public school superintendency, especially in the seething big cities, is hardly a position immune to pressure by special interest groups. [Some superintendents must spend] long hours in session with spokesmen of violently conflicting views on education and integration. Nobody challenges the superintendent's solemn duty to have sound educational practices uppermost in his mind and, in the course of such sessions, to be determined not to agree to anything that would jeopardize such practices. But it is absurd to suggest that these sessions are not political bargaining to evolve the most workable consensus, satisfying the greatest number without doing violence to anyone's educational rights.

Growth, Finance, and Politics   Persons who move to the suburbs often are aware only of the promises made by the real-estate salesman. Once they have purchased a home and entered their children in school, the complications resulting from the rapid growth of population in a given area come to their attention.

A school district about 50 miles north of New York City, for example, had 875 students in its public school system in 1951. By 1965, this number had increased to 5,664, an almost sevenfold increase. As a result of the enrollment pressure, it was necessary to begin asking for approval of bond issues to permit borrowing of money for the construction of new buildings. The first two proposals for funds to provide adequate space for school children were defeated and for four years grammar school children had to attend split sessions —that is, they could attend only one-half days. Eventually, a bond issue was approved for school construction, but by the time it was, competent estimates indicated that within another decade the total public school enrollment would nearly double.[10]

School Finance   Huge amounts of money are spent annually on education at the elementary and secondary levels. In the nation at large in the early 1960s, approximately $18 billion, or something like 2.5 percent of the gross national product, was being spent annually from public moneys for school buildings, equipment, and operations. Additional billions were spent for books, ballet slippers, gym shoes, PTA suppers, clarinets, and other purchases by parents on behalf of the education of their children. It is hardly surprising that a great deal of politics in any community centers around the schools—these institutions spend great amounts of money, and in many small towns, the consolidated school is the largest single purchaser of the goods and services provided by local merchants.

In the early days of public education, the cost was paid for in part by donations and endowments by the wealthy, but mostly through general prop-

[9] Fred M. Hechinger, "Who Runs Our Big City Schools?" **Saturday Review,** Apr. 17, 1965, pp. 70ff.
[10] Elaine Zimbel, "When a Community Votes 'No.'" **Saturday Review,** Jan. 16, 1965, pp. 54–55.

The institutions

Elementary† schools	88,600
Secondary† schools	30,500
Universities, colleges and junior colleges	2,170
Total	121,270

The learners

Elementary school pupils	
Public schools	26,379,000
Nonpublic (private and parochial)	5,400,000
Total	31,779,000
Secondary school students	
Public	15,321,000
Nonpublic	1,400,000
Total	16,721,000
College and university full- and part-time students enrolled for credit toward degrees	
Public	3,519,000
Private	1,916,000
Total	5,435,000
Grand total students enrolled	53,935,000

The teachers

Public school teachers	
Elementary	959,000
Secondary	716,000
Nonpublic school teachers	
Elementary	155,000
Secondary	80,000
College and university teachers	
Public institutions	235,000
Private institutions	190,000
Total	2,335,000

Administrators and supervisors

Superintendents of schools	14,130
Principals and supervisors	108,300
College and university presidents	2,170
Other college administrative and library staff	70,400
Total	195,000

Board members

Local school board members	137,100
State board members	470
College and university board members	40,000
Total	177,570

Fig. 18-2   The American Educational System Is of Enormous Size.*

* Figures are based on the latest available estimates from the U.S. Office of Education.
† Grades 7 and 8 are counted as elementary in systems under the 8-4 plan and as secondary when they are part of junior high schools.

SOURCE: **Saturday Review,** Sept. 11, 1965, p. 68.

erty tax levies. In recent years, school boards have been approving, albeit with compunction, budgets of enormous size. School costs are a heavy burden to citizens, especially in newer "bedroom" suburbs. But in our child-centered society, these large budgets are approved by most people, though certainly there are loud, and sometimes effective, dissenters. The reasons for the high budgets were discussed above in connection with historical developments in American education. The school remains today, even in larger cities, a community center, as it has always been. As such, it serves to symbolize the relative status of communities, just as the size and grandeur of the local church or cathedral did in medieval Europe. In the search for higher prestige, citizens approve expenditures for elaborate swimming pools, fancy band uniforms, and well-equipped football stadiums and basketball gymnasiums. The cost is high, but the psychological satisfaction felt by the people of Vertigo Heights when they know that they have a high school swimming pool while the people of Sequoia Grove do not is important to them. And, of course, so is the belief that one's children are being given as much in the way of a total education as can be afforded.

The high cost of the present pattern of education has strained the property tax, and other funds have been sought, especially since the end of World War II. The principal source of these has come through the expansion of state aid for school operation. The importance of the use of conditional state aid for putting pressure upon local areas to consolidate is reflected in the fact that state aid is highest in states which have reduced the number of districts most in the years since 1950, lowest in those with the least change.

All states, however, provide some direct grants for school operations. An important issue before state legislatures has concerned the details of the school-aid formula, particularly the degree to which state aid should depend upon local ability to pay as against the use of a simple head count. The poorer districts lobby for the former, the wealthier for the latter.

The increasing expense of providing educational facilities at the level expected by contemporary society has brought pressure for a diversification of the base of support for schools through the use of Federal grants-in-aid. The Federal aid question has been debated even more hotly than was the aid question on the state level. The fact that Federal aids to education are not new and have been made for many decades is often overlooked.[11] The future would seem to hold still more state and Federal financing of school programs; there is no other place to turn unless budgets and programs are cut back, and the public seems unwilling to do that.

School Politics and Issues

Because of the great amounts of money involved and the importance placed upon children and their welfare, local politics often centers around school elections and board of education meetings. Almost all local interest groups concerned with general local government also attempt to influence school

[11] See below, pp. 484–486.

policy. In addition, groups organized specifically around education are common. The issues are many.[12]

Educational Groups   Various educational interest groups are commonly active at the local level. In larger cities these may sometimes be divided along liberal and conservative lines, sometimes along religious lines. They may be organized as *ad hoc* groups to aid in a bond issue campaign. The best known local group is the parent-teacher association. Because its membership is made up jointly of parents, teachers, and administrators, it serves as a communications medium through which the professional educators' views are disseminated throughout the community and criticisms of educators' policies are countered.

At the state level, education groups are frequently among the most powerful to appear before the legislatures. Probably every state has an association of school-board members and of school administrators. On behalf of the teachers, there is the state (and local) branch of the National Education Association and of the American Federation of Teachers (AFL-CIO). The PTA is less active at the state level than elsewhere, and lay interests in education are less well represented than are those of the teachers, administrators, and school-board members.

Educational groups at the state level are interested in such things as state aid to school districts, curriculum and teacher certification requirements, minimum salaries for teachers, school district reorganization laws, and the rules concerning school-bus transportation (e.g., the conditions under which parochial students may be transported, if at all, or the distance a student must ride in order for the local district to get state financial aid for his transportation cost).

The administrators, faculties, and alumni of state-controlled colleges and universities are also important lobbies before state legislatures. It is necessary for state schools to compete for funds against the other possible uses for which they might be appropriated, and to convince legislators to provide educational services at the level the schools' administrators regard as desirable. In anticipation of the greatly increased numbers of college applicants expected after about 1960, state institutions have sought legislation to provide buildings and other capital outlays in time for the expected need and to develop long-range capital-outlay plans.

The Drive for More Funds   Educational interest groups in recent years have campaigned for more state school aid and for guaranteed payments under aid formulas to replace dependence upon the yield of a particular tax. They have, however, also sought to secure dedicated funds from high-yielding taxes. They oppose taxpayers' groups which want constitutional limitations upon spending or tax levies and which question the existence of a "school crisis."

In states where the legislature has voted funds for school operations only, leaving the financing of new plant and equipment to the local district,

[12] For a case study, see A. J. Vidich and Joseph Bensman, **Small Town in Mass Society**, Princeton University Press, Princeton, N.J., 1958, chap. 7.

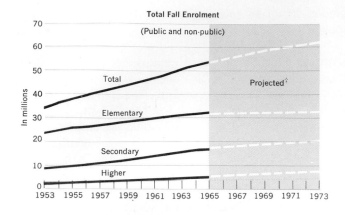

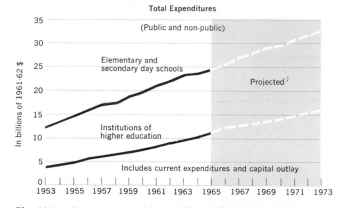

Fig. 18-3   Enrolments and Costs Will Continue to Increase.
* Grades 7 and 8 are counted as elementary in systems under the 8-4 plan and as secondary when they are a part of junior high schools.
† USOE projection of educational statistics to 1973–1974, OE-10030.
SOURCE: **Saturday Review,** Sept. 11, 1965, p. 69.

pressure has been exerted, with increasing success, for aid for school construction. The difficulty that the less prosperous districts have in marketing their small bond issues and the high costs of marketing them have led to demands in some states for some kind of plan whereby the state can buy local bonds or market them, using the superior borrowing power of the state government in order to reduce costs.

The opponents of expanding public school budgets are forced to disguise their opposition by phrasing their arguments in terms of socially accepted values. In general, those who have sought to serve as "depressants" have included business groups with a low-tax ideology, those who want to emphasize local control at the expense of state financial aid, politicians who are cautious in adopting new approaches in the face of conflicting public attitude, and the frequent naiveté of educators themselves. The Roman Catholic Church is powerful in New England because it has numerous and often highly dedicated members. Yet, "there is no evidence whatsoever to suggest that the Roman Catholic Church has been a depressant upon state aid to the public education. Neither is there any evidence to suggest that the Church hierarchy has taken leadership in the struggle for additional state aid, although there is substantial evidence that individual Catholic laymen have provided strong, if intermittent, leadership for the achievement of breakthroughs at the state level in granting additional financial assistance to local school districts." [13] The last part of this statement may be principally a result of the fact that a very large percentage of New England politicians are Roman Catholics.

One study found that persons who give least support to bond issues in suburban areas are those living in the least densely populated areas, those over fifty years of age, with twelve years or less of education, working in a blue-collar job, and with no children in the public schools.[14]

The Large-city Problem   In the largest cities, problems of maintaining standards of education have been especially difficult in recent years because of the eroding of the core-city tax base and the exodus of the education-emphasizing middle class to the suburbs. Large cities, for a variety of reasons, including the need to pay higher teacher salaries and demands for greater specialization, have high per pupil costs. During the 1955–56 school year, cities of over 100,000 population spent an average of $322 per pupil on education; middle-sized cities spent only $275.[15]

The Suburban School   As an area on the fringe of a city comes under the eye of land-development companies and gives up its bucolic existence, it is characteristically overrun by children, for those who move into new developments are predominantly young couples. The newcomers find the established governmental structure in the hands of farmers and small-town merchants who have a low-tax attitude. The newcomers demand expanded urban services— beginning with the schools. Generally the first battles between the newcomers and the old-timers center around the questions of issuing bonds to expand the school system and replacing the farm-oriented curriculum with one designed to prepare suburban children for college—for a degree is a cherished goal established by suburban parents for their children. These battles are often furious, but the newcomers practically always win through force of numbers and a common purpose.

Because suburbs usually are established with almost no school plant in existence and because the ratio of children to total population in them is high, the financial burden of providing schools of a type the migrants from the core city expect is often very heavy. School tax rates in Levittown, New York, increased by nearly 500 percent in the ten years following 1945.[16] To have them double in less than a decade is common. Because this is so, the puzzled and

[13] Stephen K. Bailey, Richard T. Frost, Paul E. Marsh, and Robert C. Wood, **Schoolmen and Politics,** Syracuse University Press, Syracuse, N.Y., 1962, chap. 3. Quotation from p. 46.
[14] Gary W. King, Walter E. Freeman, and Christopher Sower, **Conflict over Schools,** Institute for Community Development, Michigan State University, East Lansing, Mich., 1963.
[15] U.S. Office of Education, **Current Expenditures per Pupil in Public School Systems,** 1957.
[16] Benjamin Fine, "Educational Problems in the Suburbs," in William Dobriner (ed.), **The Suburban Community,** G. P. Putnam's Sons, New York, 1958.

Fig. 18-4   Educational and Income Levels Are Closely Linked.
* Excludes 0.5 million families not reporting education of family head.
Data: U.S. Bureau of the Census.
SOURCE: **Poverty and Deprivation in the U.S.,** Conference on Economic Progress, Washington, D.C., 1962, p. 63.

perhaps angered suburbanite, who had thought that fringe living was inexpensive, is likely to join in the call for state and Federal aid for his schools.

The Federal Aid Controversy   Great conflict has resulted from postwar efforts to secure Federal aid for public school operations or capital outlay or both.

The battle was fought as if Federal grants in this area would be invading virgin territory. Actually, however, Federal aid to education began with land grants in the Survey Ordinance of 1785. Congress has voted money grants each year for specific types of Federal school aid from the time of the Education of the Blind Act in 1879. Since then, Federal funds have also been made available for vocational education, school lunch and milk programs, foreign student exchange programs, research and surveys of school needs, and for school construction in areas especially affected by Federal activities. The opponents of Federal aid have felt, however, that providing general grants would be far more undesirable than providing these kinds of assistance.

Arguments against Federal aid center around the assertion that aid would eventually result in the national government's taking control over educational policies away from state and local governments and that policy would come to be made by an anonymous bureaucracy in Washington which would be answerable, if to anyone, to the professional educator interests. Some school administrators at both the state and local levels object to Federal aid as a threat to their discretionary powers or even to their survival. The politics of teacher certification is involved: a sharp increase in standards induced by Federal aid requirements, for example, would threaten the very existence of marginal teachers colleges, though it would further the goals of the good ones. But a great many educational groups, including the powerful National Education Association, support Federal aid as being necessary for the establishment of a national minimum standard and in order to finance the ever-rising costs of school operations.

Those who favor Federal aid point out that vast differences exist between states as to educational levels and that this is undesirable in a nation with a high degree of physical mobility. There are, indeed, great differences between states, and these seem to stem more from a variation in ability to pay than from differences in willingness to make an effort to provide education. In 1962, expenditures per pupil varied from $628 in New York to $229 in Mississippi. The average number of school years completed ranged from 12 in Utah to 7.6 in Louisiana and South Carolina.

In 1958, Congress passed a general aid act by tying it to the anti-poverty program, although part of the formula was based on state-local effort. The money was to be given to districts to spend as they saw fit, subject to state and Federal law.

Despite the impressive statistical case that is made for Federal aid and despite the strong support given it by study commissions, educational groups, and Presidents since Truman, Congress was reluctant to act. The reason for this hesitancy is probably to be found in the impressive line-up of opposition forces, which included:

1. Conservative taxpayer groups which fear that a small beginning of Federal aid will lead to great costs and a transfer of basic financial responsibility from the local property tax and other state and local taxes to the Federal income tax. They argued that the line should be held short of any general grant, for once this was made, it would be easy for proponents to have the act

expanded in scope. Low-tax interests, such as the Chamber of Commerce of the United States and the National Association of Manufacturers, are among the opposing groups.

2. Some members of the Catholic Church hierarchy who have argued that a Federal aid plan should include all schools, whether private or not. Their position is strongly opposed by congressmen from basically Protestant areas.

3. Desegregationists who want to use Federal aid as a weapon in a larger struggle. Thus, Harlem congressman Adam Clayton Powell has insisted that any Federal aid measure should make funds available only to desegregated schools, a policy that is unacceptable to Southern congressmen.

4. Citizens and officials of the wealthier states who object to subsidizing so expensive a function in other states. Many of them would accept a mildly equalizing formula but not one based principally on need. This kind of opposition leads either to a formula that will not produce the results that proponents desire or to one that would be fantastically expensive, giving generous amounts to states in little need of it.

Utilizing Physical Plant   The number of children enrolling in schools continues to place pressure upon communities for more money and tends to keep school plants overcrowded (see Figure 18-2). Various plans have been submitted to school boards and legislatures for consideration that would make more concentrated use of the already vast school plants. These generally included proposals for (1) summer attendance by high school students on an optional basis; (2) conducting regular school classes on a year-round basis, with students being required to attend three of the four quarters, with vacation periods staggered; and (3) conducting regular school classes on a year-round basis, with attendance of pupils for all four quarters, with intermittent brief vacations.

The first of these proposals would be helpful for retarded and gifted children and would give teachers year-round employment, but it would add to, rather than reduce, education costs. If the second plan were adopted in areas with severe winters, mothers would riot in every city and hamlet at the thought of having to live through a winter quarter with their children in the cramped space of a contemporary home. The third proposal might raise educational standards but would also increase costs. Only the second plan would offer a hope of reducing physical plant needs, and it would not likely be acceptable to most parents.[17]

The Issue of Consolidation   Although opposition to the consolidation of districts offering less than twelve grades of education appears now to be only a rear-guard and losing action, it is still vigorous, especially in the Midwest.[18] Opponents object to the loss of local control over school policy, to the power

---

[17] But see an article in **U.S. News & World Report,** Aug. 2, 1957, pp. 48–51.
[18] See John C. Bollens, **Special District Governments in the United States,** University of California Press, Berkeley, Calif., 1957, chap. 6.

state departments of education often have to make final decisions on consolidations, to the decline in the personal touch possible in the one-room school, and to the added costs. Rural districts, with their physical plants paid for, are not anxious to join in bond issues for new plants in consolidated districts. If the state pays part of the tuition for sending children to nearby districts for high schooling, they are especially reluctant.

Proponents of consolidation point out that the small districts of the nineteenth century were based on earlier means of transportation and upon an expectation that few children would go beyond eight grades. Today, with twelve grades the standard, they argue, districts should provide twelve grades of schooling. They also hold that consolidation provides better learning opportunities through specialization of faculty and superiority of equipment.[19] Partly because the proponents of consolidation and of expanded school expenditures are better organized and partly because their views seem to be generally supported by most of the public, they are winning out in the conflict.[20]

Issues in Transportation   By 1920, all states had authorized the transportation of children, although only 1.6 percent were hauled by bus. In 1962, 36 percent of the total number of public school children were transported.[21] The high cost of moving one school-age child in three by bus has produced demands for state aid to support this program, and most of the states have in the past, or still do, provide special grants for this purpose. Parents have always been somewhat apprehensive about the transporting of pupils: some children must spend long hours on buses that may be over- or under-heated. Road conditions are sometimes dangerous in winter months. Drivers may not be competent. Equipment may be faulty and poorly maintained. These and similar concerns have caused parents both to support large expenditures for transportation equipment and to encourage the establishment of state standards as a means of keeping the local board and its employees alert. Since the precise route a school bus takes may determine whether a particular child will stand on a lonely corner in cold weather waiting for a bus or will be picked up in front of his home, the laying out of the routes by the school board may involve a good deal of controversy.

Dropouts: Pupils and Teachers   Although the number of children remaining in school until completion of the twelfth grade is constantly growing, there are still many who drop out at an earlier time. Most of those who leave school prefer work to further education and do not expect to strive for jobs that would require much formal education. Since the economy needs many such persons, these dropouts may not be serious. Still, 15 percent of those leaving in one study indicated they did so for financial reasons (other than a desire for spending money), and some of these, at least, could be presumed to have been able

[19] Carl Eisemann, "In Reorganized Districts Children Do Learn More," The Nation's Schools, 59:61–63, June, 1957. On the amount of reorganization that has taken place, see U.S. Office of Education publications.
[20] For a case study, see R. F. Still, The Gilmer-Aiken Bills: A Study in the Legislative Process, Steck Co., Austin, Tex., 1950.
[21] Motor Truck Facts, Automobile Manufacturers Association, Detroit, 1964, p. 26.

to make a greater contribution to society by staying in school longer. Dropout rates tend to increase with the size of the city, for in the anonymity of larger cities, there is less social pressure to remain in school or for parents to seek to keep children in school. Rarely, however, do children leave school at their parents' suggestion, and there is a high correlation between pregraduation dropouts and juvenile delinquency. Keeping youngsters in school would, then, appear to be a matter of concern broader than that of the individual and his family.[22]

Teachers who give up teaching as a career have always been a threat to the standards of American public education. To have two or three teachers in a single year was not uncommon in the rural one-room school. The problem has remained serious throughout the history of public education. Of those who were graduated with teaching certificates in 1956, 30 percent did not enter the teaching profession at all. One-half of those who did were expected to drop out within five years, though some would return again later—especially women, after they have raised a family. Since more than two-thirds of all teachers are women, most of whom do not intend to have a full-time career, the turnover problem appears to be chronic. The result is a highly inefficient utilization of manpower. School boards have been generally unwilling, however, to pay salaries that would be necessary to attract more men and career women into the profession.

The Curriculum: Ideological Battleground   There has always been a tendency, under a system of public education with school boards responsible to the voting public, for the curriculum to reflect local cultural values and economic interests. In rural areas, the emphasis is upon agriculture and home economics; in middle-class suburbs, upon preparation for entering college; in working-class areas, upon preparation for a vocation. The colleges of education, influenced by the philosophy of John Dewey and other pragmatists, and by the interests of ordinary citizens, have emphasized the desirability of meeting mass needs. On the other hand, persons dedicated to the European tradition of an intellectual elite—they are concentrated in liberal arts colleges —have bemoaned the leveling effects of an ideology designed to make schools fit the average student rather than the excellent student. They especially object to the seeming unwillingness of public schools to give special encouragement to gifted children—the future Ph.D.s, M.D.s, and intellectual leaders. This type of concern became even more sharply verbalized after the Russians launched the first successful earth satellite ahead of the United States in 1957.

It is not uncommon to find comments to the effect that "if the tendency [to be found in contemporary public education] continues, it seems destined to create nothing less than a New Illiteracy." [23] The figures previously cited

[22] See two publications by the U.S. Office of Education: **Why Do Boys and Girls Drop Out of School?** 1953, and **Retention in High Schools in Large Cities,** 1957. There is a good case study in A. B. Hollingshead, **Elmtown's Youth,** John Wiley & Sons, Inc., New York, 1949.
[23] Ernest Stabler, "The Intellectual and America Today," **AAUP Bulletin,** 43:331, June, 1957. See also, W. H. Whyte, Jr., "The New Illiteracy," **Saturday Review,** Nov. 21, 1953, pp. 33–35.

give little reason to take this type of alarmist sentiment seriously, however. Despite outcries concerning present educational policies and their alleged tendency to weaken "the humane tradition of the liberal arts and sciences," coupled with complaints that television leads to indolent unwillingness to read or think, two dozen American companies publish quality books in paperbound editions. A great many of the paperbound books sold are of high scholarly or literary merit.

Public Education and the "Hard Courses"   In the area of the sciences, education has been much criticized. Yet the criticisms concerning an alleged failure to emphasize these subjects tend to make unfair comparisons of mathematics and science enrollments between pupils attending high school in an earlier time with those of today. A valid comparison would require percentages to be based upon all youths of high school age living in the United States at the times to be compared. Since only 8 percent of all those of high school age were in school in 1900, as against 64 percent in 1950, even a de-emphasis of science leaves a greater percentage of those of high school age taking these courses. In foreign languages, twice as many children, in percentage terms, were enrolled in 1950 as in 1900, and five times as many in mathematics and science courses.[24] This does not mean, of course, that we are producing enough scientists. It was estimated in 1958 that the United States had fewer scientists and was producing fewer scientists than the U.S.S.R. Estimates also indicated that the need for scientists in the future would grow disproportionately to the population or the training rate.

The American public has received a general impression that so-called progressive education has taken over the schools, although in fact about 60 percent of the courses are still in the category of academic and are required. Traditional methods, the progressive educator argues, still dominate our schools and continue to emphasize discipline, obedience, and learning by rote. Persons committed to the tradition of the intellectual elite feel, however, that schools today waste a great amount of time on trivia (courses in manual training, "life adjustment," the family, recreation) and too little on basic courses of language, mathematics, and the sciences. They tend to favor isolating the best students for academic high school work and sending the others to frankly vocational types of schools.[25] Such a plan would approach the standard policies of European countries.[26]

It is difficult to evaluate the criticisms that public education is subjected to. It would seem that our culture calls for a variety of educational programs, serving the interests of both the custodial and educational functions of the

[24] See H. C. Hand, "Black Horses Eat More Than White Horses," **AAUP Bulletin,** 43:266–279, June, 1957. This is a criticism of statistics used in "We Are Less Educated than 50 Years Ago," **U.S. News & World Report,** Nov. 30, 1956. Further discussion appears in the **AAUP Bulletin,** 44:476–494, June, 1958.

[25] See the publications, for example, of the Council for Basic Education or "What Went Wrong with U.S. Schools?" **U.S. News & World Report,** Jan. 24, 1958.

[26] In light of modern controversies, it may be interesting to read the comments of an aristocrat concerning the inadequacies of a classical education in an industrialized society. See Henry Adams, **The Education of Henry Adams,** Houghton Mifflin Company, Boston, 1907.

schools. There must be both vocational and academic training for teen-agers. Little room exists for the notion of an intellectual elite in America, but on the other hand the vast majority of college professors believe that their students are inadequately prepared for collegiate work by most high schools; and many of the ablest students complete high school with little or no challenge to their intellectual capacities.

To compare American public education with that of other lands would also be difficult. One observer has made the following observation: [27]

> The ordinary American of today, the ubiquitous high school product, knows far more about names . . . and what is what in general than the ordinary Englishman of the 19th century, or even the ordinary Englishman of today, who seldom gets past a basic elementary school education. He knows more particularly about psychology, but he does not necessarily think more. He is more sophisticated, but he is less sure of himself.

As a cultural institution meeting a mass social need, public education seems to have done, in general, the job expected of it; as an educational institution seeking to train the best of our young minds, it remains highly controversial.

Nonsegregation as a National Policy   In the period between the Civil War and World War II, the dominant view in the United States was that all persons, regardless of race, should be entitled to public education. But it was also generally believed that educational facilities need not be integrated and made available to all. The "separate but equal" doctrine regarding educational opportunities probably fitted the prevailing social attitudes when it was first announced by the Supreme Court in 1896.[28] Indeed, segregated schools existed throughout much of the nation and as far north as the top tier of states in the 1880s. Southern Indiana and Illinois did not desegregate until after World War II.

Yet, there were many who doubted whether the maintenance of social inferiority through the separation of facilities was in keeping with American values. The Supreme Court and the lower Federal courts continued to hold to the separation doctrine but occasionally held that segregated schools must be kept, in fact, equal to one another. At least as early as 1903, Frank A. Critz, a candidate for governor of Mississippi, expressed the fear that if Negro schools were to be closed (as his opponent advocated), the Federal government might require that Negroes be admitted to white schools.[29]

In the postwar years, a civil rights–conscious Supreme Court decided to

[27] Quoted from Geoffrey Moore, "American Novels Mislead Europeans," **Western World**, November, 1957, pp. 24–28. See also, Denis W. Brogan, **The American Character**, Alfred A. Knopf, Inc., New York, 1944.

[28] *Plessy v. Ferguson*, 163 U.S. 537 (1896), first applied the doctrine to public transportation. It was shortly applied to schools as well. See C. E. Williams, "Implementation of the Supreme Court's Decision on Racial Segregation in Public Education," **AAUP Bulletin**, 43:295–305, June, 1957.

[29] A. D. Kirwan, **Revolt of the Rednecks**, University of Kentucky Press, Lexington, Ky., 1951, p. 151.

impose a national policy of integrated public schools. The Court, setting aside precedents almost a century old, held that even if school facilities for both races were in fact equal—as they often were not—the psychological barrier to equality created by segregation was insurmountable and constituted a denial of equal protection of the laws.[30] A great battle had begun.

The Court said that school districts should proceed "with all deliberate speed," and there followed a series of decisions designed to overcome stalling tactics. The decisions threatened some of the principal values in the dominant culture of the states where slavery had once been the central institution of the economy. Educational segregation was there viewed not only as normal—it had always been practiced—but as a means for discouraging racial inter-marriage as well as for maintaining a semicaste system. There was, in the South, an enormous increase in the number of organizations dedicated to the maintenance of segregation. Labor unions which gave support to racial equality but which were at the same time seeking to recruit membership in the indus-trializing South found the two goals largely incompatible. But some integration took place fairly promptly, especially in the Border states. By 1957, 18 percent of the Southern school districts having both white and Negro children had begun or completed programs of integration.[31] Elsewhere, resistance was strong. Desegregation ranged, in 1965, from complete formal compliance in Kentucky to only token response in Alabama, Arkansas, Georgia, Louisiana, Mississippi, North Carolina, and South Carolina.[32] At issue was the question of whether the Federal courts could successfully impose upon the nation at large a single ethical concept of equality. The judges seemed to be as deter-mined as were their opponents.

School segregation, in actual practice, is common in both the North and the South. Chicago schools, in the mid-1960s, for example, were highly segre-gated, especially at the elementary level. Ninety percent of elementary stu-dents in Chicago in 1965 attended either all-white or all-Negro schools.[33] The situation was somewhat different at the high school level, probably only because high school attendance districts are much larger than those of elementary schools. In 1965 in Chicago, 82 percent of the high schools were completely segregated. The principal difference between the North and the South in the mid-1960s was that in the North Negroes had considerably more political power and their leaders were increasingly in a position to demand equal facilities. Segregation in both the North and South had obviously discriminated against the Negro pupil. In Chicago as well as in the most segregationist-minded areas in the South, Negro schools were more overcrowded than those of white chil-dren; they had the least experienced teachers, the highest rate of dropouts, and the highest truancy rates.

[30] *Brown v. Topeka Board of Education*, 347 U.S. 483 (1954).
[31] Southern Education Reporting Service, **With All Deliberate Speed**, Harper & Row, Publishers, Incorporated, New York, 1957. For the effect of inferior education for Negroes upon the social organization of Northern industrial cities, see "The Far-flowing Negro Tide," **Newsweek**, Dec. 23, 1957.
[32] **Southern School News**, June, 1965.
[33] Jack Star, "Chicago's Troubled Schools," **Look**, May 4, 1965, pp. 59–61.

Public Colleges and Universities

A public system of colleges and universities was a logical step beyond the provision of public grade and high schools. The early colonizers of what became the Eastern states established institutions for higher learning; but these were generally church-affiliated, and admission was rigidly restricted both intellectually and socially. Thomas Jefferson assisted in the founding of the first state university in his native Virginia. This particular institution spread throughout the South and along the frontier. Although many fine private liberal arts colleges were founded in these areas, few great private universities were developed outside the East. Eventually, the Morrill Act made possible colleges of agriculture in all states, and by the end of World War II, nearly all states had their own public universities.

Gradually a distinctly American pattern of public higher education developed both in the state universities and in the state agriculture and teachers colleges. It emphasized liberal admissions policies, departmentalization, the development of extensive vocational programs, many service functions, concentration on applied as well as basic research, specialization rather than broad training in the traditional liberal arts, and the collecting under the name of the university of a potpourri of professional and technical schools.[34]

Governing Organization   The governing body of state colleges and universities may be selected in a number of ways. The most common are by popular election, appointment by the governor, election by the legislature, membership ex officio, or by some combination of these. There may be one body for all state schools of higher learning, or each institution may have its own board. The legislature may legally have as much power over the public colleges and universities as it has over other state institutions, or it may be constitutionally limited to the voting of bloc grants, with the school established as an independent body politic under its own governing board. The board selects a president who often sits on the board and may preside over it. The governing body necessarily delegates a great deal of authority to the president, who is nearly always a professional administrator. In varying degrees, he will involve the faculty in decision making, but some degree of friction likely exists between him (and his professional staff) and the faculty proper. The latter, devoted to the tradition of independent scholarship, makes a psychological distinction between itself and the administration.

Struggles for actual control over the state university and colleges are quite common. These schools spend a great deal of money (over $4.2 billion among them all in 1963), and the educational policies they follow profoundly affect the attitudes of the next generation of social, economic, and political leaders in the state. Conflicts may exist between the public college or university president and the legislature, between the legislative leaders and the governor,

[34] W. C. DeVane, **The American University in the Twentieth Century,** Louisiana State University Press, Baton Rouge, La., 1957.

between the governing board and the legislative leaders, between the administration and the faculty, and between a large number of other possible combinations. There may also be struggles for power and appropriations among public universities and colleges in the same state.[35]

In the early 1960s, nearly 350 colleges and universities were under the general supervision of state boards of education or state superintendents of education. In 1965, around three-quarters of a million students were enrolled on a full-time basis in junior and community colleges, most of them under the control of the local board of education and school superintendents. The involvement of boards of education and school administrators whose principal responsibility is that of primary and secondary education has been a major matter of controversy. Administrators and faculty members in institutions of higher education have been generally critical of this type of involvement and have questioned the competence of public school administrators and teachers in educational matters beyond the twelfth grade.[36]

Finance   Public institutions of higher learning are founded on the assumption that it is in the interest of society generally to educate competent young people and to assess much of the cost upon society at large without regard to direct benefits received. In contrast to the pattern in the first twelve grades, however, the college student or his parents are usually expected to pay some part of the cost of a college education. Considerable conflict centers around the question of the part that students should pay directly. Whenever a legislature reaches a financial crisis, it is tempted to raise tuition and fees. This is generally opposed by liberals, many educators, and some of the general public. The question of the amount of the cost of higher education that should be paid by the student is a negotiable matter to be settled through the political process. Policy formulation is complicated because much of the budget of a public institution of higher learning is designated, not for instruction, but for research and service activities.

Although only 35 percent of all colleges and universities were under public control in 1965, these schools employed 55 percent of the faculty and enrolled 65 percent of the resident college students. Privately controlled institutions receive more than 40 percent of their income from tuition and fees, but public institutions received less than 11 percent from this source.

The Junior College Movement   The junior or community college is viewed by many as one possible solution to the demands for an adequate program of higher education in the face of expanding enrollments. Every year the number of junior colleges in the United States increases; the number doubled between 1930 and 1957.

The functions of the junior college are varied. Some students want to prepare for transfer to four-year colleges and universities; others for vocations;

[35] See O. C. Carmichael, Jr., **New York Establishes a State University: A Case Study in the Processes of Policy Formation,** Vanderbilt University Press, Nashville, Tenn., 1955.
[36] Editorial, **The School Administrator,** 20:2, Mar. 15, 1963.

still others for two-year terminal programs of various kinds, but chiefly those with a vocational bent; and others for a "fuller life" by enrolling in general liberal arts courses after regular working hours. The success of this particular institution, with its potential advantages of convenience and minimum cost for both the taxpayer and the student, may ultimately depend upon its ability to recruit faculty and to provide library and laboratory facilities of adequate caliber to maintain genuine college-level work.[37] The number of junior colleges is expected to increase sharply in the coming years. Pressures for state financial aid to these schools will increase, and a struggle may ensue for their control between persons dedicated to the traditions of the humanism of liberal arts colleges and of pragmatism as found in the colleges of education.

Issues in Higher Education Perhaps the major issue confronting public higher education in the 1960s concerned the means of financing an enormous increase in enrollment and the schedule to be followed in preparing for it. As the high birthrates of the years after 1941 have increasingly affected higher education, enrollment in colleges and universities expanded. This has created great problems of financing, of maintaining standards, and of recruiting a competent faculty.[38] Legislators will demand that expensive research and service programs be reexamined. Traditional teaching techniques requiring expensive personal attention and much classroom time will be questioned.

There is likely to be increasing pressure for higher tuition and fee rates. Much controversy will center around the question, who should attend? Not only do increasing numbers of parents want to send their children to college, but it has been estimated by the Office of Education that 30 percent of the best high school students still do not go on to attend college, largely owing to financial reasons. But the increasing need for college-trained personnel is a characteristic of a modern economy, and the shortage of engineers and scientists is still serious in the 1960s.

Public higher education in the United States is under constant pressure from legislators who do not want standards raised. The legislator, in turn, is under such pressure from his constituents. The typical citizen can distinguish between admission to a college or university and rejection, between graduation and flunking out, but he cannot distinguish between an excellent education and a mediocre one. His greatest concern is to have his children admitted to and to attend a college or university, both for status reasons and because of the demonstrated effect upon earning capacity by level of education.

Considerable interest is being shown in state scholarships as a means of maximizing opportunity for college education as well as in student loans to be repaid after graduation. The fact that the college graduate earns much more than the high school graduate helps to make this approach feasible and attractive to the student interested in his personal opportunities.

[37] See N. B. Henry (ed.), **The Public Junior College,** The University of Chicago Press, Chicago, 1956.
[38] President's Committee on Education Beyond the High School, **Second Report to the President,** 1957.

As the cost of education increases, there will be mounting pressure for state government officials and legislators to be given a voice in the budgeting, accounting, purchasing, and personnel practices of state schools. These views will be increasingly resisted by the professional administration of these institutions, for they, like all interests, prefer autonomy.[39]

Other major issues in higher education center around the methods of organization of various higher education bodies within a state and their relationship to one another—how to coordinate their activities, and the function to be performed by various public universities, colleges, and junior (or community) colleges. The demands for higher public education and the costs of it are so great that administrative and legislative leaders are demanding comprehensive planning, but this is not easy to provide in some states, particularly in those states in which educational institutions directly compete for scarce public funds.

Those in favor of expanding public education often attempt to increase their relative power by forming coalitions and establishing organizations that serve as mediums of communication. In New England: [40]

The coalition may express itself as a permanent organization; it may be a strategic device of a state department of education, as appears to be the case in Rhode Island and possibly New Hampshire, or it may be an *ad hoc* one-time affair as in Massachusetts. But the need is obvious and the trend toward cooperative action unmistakable.

In the state of New York, the Educational Conference Board has served as an alliance of the major educational interests, including the New York State Teachers' Association, the New York State School Boards' Association, the New York State Congress of Parents and Teachers, the Public Education Association of New York City, the New York State Citizens Committee for the Public Schools, the New York State Association of District Superintendents of Schools, the New York State Council of School Superintendents, the New York State Association of Secondary School Principals, and the New York State Association of Elementary School Principals. This board has served as "a sounding board for and a refiner of the deliberations of an inner core of seven school men. These seven leaders included two from the state Department of Education, two from the State Teachers' Association, two from the School Boards' Association, and one, the leader until his death in 1962, from Teachers College at Columbia University." [41]

The citizen in the 1970s will be called upon to help make basic decisions about the means of financing higher education, the students who are to be admitted, and the amount of research that such institutions are to engage in. In future generations of college students, the percentage enrolled in public institutions will be higher than ever. The costs will be great, and considerable effort will be required if they are to be met without lowering educational stand-

[39] See "The States and Higher Education," **State Government**, 29:253–257, December, 1956.
[40] Bailey and others, *op. cit.*, p. 36.
[41] *Ibid.*

ards. The principal issue at stake is not one of the amount of money to be spent, however. The real concern centers around the fact that in a highly complex technological society, and one which involves a great amount of international competition, "no aspect of our national life outweighs higher education in its bearing on our future security, our economic advance and our free institutions." [42]

SELECTED READINGS

Adams, Frank T., Jr.: **The Gainesville School Problem,** The Bobbs-Merrill Company, Inc., Indianapolis, ICP no. 15, 1953. (Problems of administrative change following long tenure by a superintendent.)

Bollens, John C.: **Special District Governments in the United States,** University of California Press, Berkeley, Calif., 1957.

Butts, R. Freeman, and Lawrence A. Cremin: **A History of Education,** Holt, Rinehart and Winston, Inc., New York, 1953.

Carmichael, O. C., Jr.: **New York Establishes a State University: A Case Study in the Processes of Policy Formation,** Vanderbilt University Press, Nashville, Tenn., 1955.

Cremin, Lawrence A.: **The American Common School,** Teachers College, Columbia University, New York, 1951.

Cubberley, E. P.: **Public Education in the United States,** Houghton Mifflin Company, Boston, 1919.

DeVane, W. C.: **The American University in the Twentieth Century,** Louisiana State University Press, Baton Rouge, La., 1957.

Dunbar, Ernest: "The Plot to Take Over the PTA," **Look,** Sept. 7, 1965, pp. 27ff. (The actions of the far right in seeking to take over the PTA and use it against school boards and administrations.)

Gregg, R. T.: "The Battle for Tax Supported Schools," **Nation's Schools,** 69:49–50, July, 1957.

————: "The Struggle for Free Schools," **Nation's Schools,** 69:85–86, June, 1957.

Henry, N. B. (ed.): **The Public Junior College,** The University of Chicago Press, Chicago, 1956.

Hollingshead, A. B.: **Elmtown's Youth,** John Wiley & Sons, Inc., New York, 1949. (A case study.)

Masters, Nicholas A., Robert H. Salisbury, and Thomas H. Eliot: **State Politics and the Public Schools,** Alfred A. Knopf, Inc., New York, 1964. (A comparative study of school politics in three Midwestern states.)

Mathiasen, Carolyn, Victor Block, and Victoria Velsey (eds.): **Federal Role in Education,** Congressional Quarterly Service, Washington, 1965. (Detailed history, and summary of legislation.)

Menand, Louis, III: **Hanover Builds a High School,** The Bobbs-Merrill Company, Inc., Indianapolis, ICP no. 51, 1959.

Miller, James L., Jr.: **State Budgeting for Higher Education,** Institute of Public Administration, University of Michigan, Ann Arbor, Mich., 1964.

Morlan, Robert L.: **Intergovernmental Relations in Education,** The University of Minnesota Press, Minneapolis, 1950.

Schroth, Thomas N., and others: **Congress and the Nation, 1945–1964,** Congressional Quarterly Service, Washington, 1965, chap. 8.

---

[42] *Ibid.,* p. 257.

Sigel, Roberta S.: **Detroit Experiment: Citizens Plan for a New High School,** The Bobbs-Merrill Company, Inc., Indianapolis, ICP no. 95, 1966.

Silverman, Corinne: **The Little Rock Story,** rev. ed., The Bobbs-Merrill Company, Inc., Indianapolis, ICP no. 41, 1959.   (Background leading to 1959 integration.)

Southern Education Reporting Service: **With All Deliberate Speed,** Harper & Row, Publishers, Incorporated, New York, 1957.

Still, R. F.: **The Gilmer-Aiken Bills: A Study in the Legislative Process,** Steck Company, Austin, Tex., 1950.   (A case study.)

U.S. Office of Education: **Contemporary Issues in American Education,** 1965.

————: **Progress of Public Education in the United States of America,** 1964.

————: **Projections of Educational Statistics,** 1964.

Ziblatt, David: **Public School Politics,** Institute for Community Development, Michigan State University, East Lansing, Mich., 1963.   (A bibliography.)

19

PUBLIC HEALTH AND WELFARE

Some functions of government are normally administered in such a way that most of their activity takes place below the level of attention of the typical citizen. These tend to be functions which rest on a foundation of stable cultural values, thus involving relatively little controversy. Since issues, under these circumstances, seldom reach the political arena, the functions tend to be taken over by a professional bureaucracy that administers them according to its own (culturally acceptable) standards.

Yet, even when consensus exists over a long period of time, changing environmental, social, technological, and philosophical conditions as well as fortuitous factors may disrupt the stability of a function. It may then gradually, or perhaps suddenly, be thrown into the arena of political conflict.

Matters of health and welfare fit generally into the above category. They have become highly professionalized, and typical citizens devote little time or thought to them under most conditions. But from time to time, throughout history, they have become the subject of intense political controversy. Thus, discovery of the germ theory of disease, coupled with cholera and typhoid epidemics, resulted in sharp public debate, which was followed by heavy public outlays and daring engineering projects designed to reach unpolluted water sources. Mary Jane Ward wrote a book—at the propitious moment—and coined a phrase, "the snake pit," to describe a type of mental institution that had existed for centuries, and in so doing contributed immensely to the destruction of public satisfaction with one approach for the handling of the mentally ill.[1] Public welfare based on the harsh seventeenth-century poor law fitted so well into the American belief system that it was not seriously challenged until the Great Depression, during which attitudes quickly changed.

[1] Mary Jane Ward, The Snake Pit, Random House, Inc., New York, 1946.

Public-welfare recipients and others who were potentially members of welfare clientele groups became politically conscious and active. Yet the long period of stable attitudes toward welfare could also block the development of concepts for a contemporary approach, thus delaying the maturation of a new public-welfare system.

In times of transition a governmental function may rise to the level of perception and concern of the average citizen. It is then that each of us may help to contribute to the construction of a new concept of the content of that function.

Public Health

Water Supply and Public Safety: A Case Study [2] On the evening of July 27, 1955, a freight train was wrecked within the city limits of Gastonia, North Carolina. The Southern Railway followed routine procedures for such circumstances, and within a few hours, the railroad and the community appeared to have returned to normal. But such was not the case. Early the next morning, the Gaston County Health Department received an urgent call from the operator of the water-filtration plant of a textile mill outside the city. He reported that he was confronted with a serious odor problem of an unidentified type. The public-health engineer made some technical suggestions, but they did not solve the problem. Use of the water was discontinued. The South Fork River, the source of the water, was inspected and found to be filled with dead fish. All communities using the river as a source of raw water were warned to stop using it. The engineer then suspected that the train wreck of the night before might be a factor, and a check with the railroad revealed that 8,000 gallons of an octyl alcohol had been spilled from a tank car. It was quickly determined how the spillage had found its way to the river.

How toxic to human beings were octyl alcohols? No one in the county health department knew. These industrial chemicals are not often a public-health problem. A telephone call was placed to the state board of health at Raleigh. A state sanitary engineer was dispatched to the scene, and shortly the state laboratory reported that the pollutant should be considered toxic. Emergency water supplies were arranged for from a neighboring town and an unaffected stream, and corrective flushing out of filter plants, storage tanks, and mains was undertaken. Three days after the first alarm was sounded, all water systems in the area were operating normally again.

This case demonstrates not only the effectiveness of public-health systems but also the importance of cooperative action, especially in emergencies. In this case, each person performed his function in such a way that not a single individual was poisoned. But to accomplish this, the cooperation of many persons and groups was required: the railroad removed many cubic yards of polluted soil from its right of way; the state worked closely with local governments; two textile firms lent a hand; a neighboring community allowed one

[2] Based on F. R. Blaisdell, "The Accidental Pollution of North Carolina Water Supply by Octyl Alcohol," **Journal of the American Water Works Association,** 48:1052–1054, August, 1956.

mill to connect temporarily to its system; and volunteers cleared the river of dead fish. An emergency had been successfully met.

The Concept of Public Health Whenever people come into contact with one another, they become targets for communicable diseases. Great cities, with their high concentration of people in confined areas, are especially vulnerable. Because of the obvious concern of society with this type of threat, local governments have long had responsibilities for the protection of health. The states, too, became active in this field beginning in the 1870s.

The fact that some diseases were in some manner contagious was discovered long ago. Resulting from this knowledge came the practice of having local governments require the isolation of afflicted persons. The pesthouse was an early form of isolation. Quarantining of persons in their houses also became a local responsibility. A flag or sign beside the doorway of the homes of those with contagious diseases was the responsibility of the public-health officer.

During the Great Plague (bubonic plague) that struck London in 1665–1666, for example, the houses of the afflicted were marked with red crosses on the door, "searchers" were sent out to certify the cause of deaths, and municipal authorities sent men to kill the dogs who were mistakenly blamed for spreading the disease. Local governments, aided by considerable progress in medical knowledge, still perform these functions. Their tasks have become ever greater and their successes in lowering the death rate ever more impressive.

Another development in local health activities, and a logical development out of the older practice of isolation, came with the discovery of the techniques of vaccination and inoculation against communicable diseases. A conflict has developed over the question of whether these practices are "treatments" that should be cared for by private physicians, or preventive medicine, and as such a public-health function. In the United States, the former view has generally prevailed, except for the vaccination of school children in some cases and the emergency treatment of populations in the event of epidemics.

A third factor in the development of public-health departments was the popularity of the filth theory of disease in the middle years of the nineteenth century. This notion led to heavy emphasis upon sanitation, especially in the construction of sewers, the collection of garbage, and the abatement of nuisances. During this period public-health departments became common and were expanded in size beyond that of a local physician acting on a part-time basis. Although the collection and disposal of sewage and garbage is still a function of the health department in some cities, it has generally been transferred to the public-works department. But the health department is still responsible for the health supervision of such activities, and it has been entrusted with an increasing number of other functions.

Public-health Administration The American Public Health Association believes that specialization is so important in a proper health program that its

Committee on Local Health Units has recommended the establishment of health units so organized as to contain not less than 50,000 people.[3] Smaller units not only cannot develop specialization, but are likely to be unable to finance successful programs. This means, of course, that the county or a special-purpose district would have to be used as the health unit, except for fair-sized cities. The professional organization also suggests standards that few communities now meet. Cities and villages are still the standard units established by state law, although countywide and city-county departments are increasingly taking over health functions and standards are rising. For example, Michigan law provides that any city failing to maintain a full-time health officer comes automatically under the county health department and that the city and county may, by mutual agreement, share the services of a single health officer to supervise both departments. In rural areas, the county is now, with few exceptions, the area for health administration, although in some states counties may join together in public-health districts.[4]

There is a trend toward municipal health departments under a single head who reports to the chief executive. Most local governments, however, still make use of the traditional board of health. (General local health departments first became popular in the heyday of the independent board and commission.) The board of health often consists partly of physicians and partly of laymen. In some cities or counties, at least one seat must be given to an engineer. The American Public Health Association and other medical groups favor a heavy representation of physicians on the board. This can perhaps be justified on the basis of the superior interest of these men, but undoubtedly they are also wanted there to "protect" the private medical profession against those who would expand the scope of public-health functions.

State health agencies are organized in a manner similar to that of large cities, with a health officer who frequently holds a Doctor of Public Health degree in addition to an M.D., an advisory board, and a number of bureaus.

Between 1945, the end of World War II, and 1960, the staff and service levels of public-health departments increased somewhat in the United States. Most of this increase took place in the mental health and chronic diseases areas, however. The number of physicians in state and local health departments actually declined during this period. The increase in personnel was, therefore, the result of increases in the number of nurses, sanitarians, and clerks.[5]

Public-health Functions A great many health activities are performed by state and local governments, sometimes in cooperation with the U.S. Public Health Service. The principal direct health services are performed by local

[3] American Public Health Association, **Local Health Units for the Nation,** The Commonwealth Fund, New York, 1946.
[4] On the growth of local health units, see National Health Assembly, **America's Health,** Harper & Row, Publishers, Incorporated, New York, 1949, p. 60.
[5] Herbert Domke, **Change in Local Health Department Administrative Patterns,** unpublished manuscript, 1962.

governments, with the higher agencies acting in educational, technical advisory, and sometimes supervisory capacities. Except in small communities, the health department is normally divided into several specialized divisions.

The earliest function of the health department centered around communicable-disease control, and this remains important despite the sharp drop in the incidence of these diseases in the decades since the beginning of the twentieth century. A special program now deals with tuberculosis, a disease that struck about as many people in the 1960s (120,000 new cases each year) as it did in 1930, but annual deaths had been reduced by over 80 percent during that time. Another special program seeks to carry on an educational campaign concerning the nature of venereal diseases and to treat victims. Despite the development of highly effective treatment medicines, venereal disease cases apparently continue to increase in number. Expanded programs are being urged for control purposes.[6]

Maternal- and child-care programs, chiefly of an educational nature, are commonly carried on. Other areas of activity include milk and restaurant inspections, the operation of municipal hospitals, public-health education (so that people may know of the dangers of food or water poisoning, for example), the keeping of vital statistics, assistance to crippled and afflicted children, hospital planning and financial assistance (a state-administered program financed in part through Federal grants-in-aid under the Hill-Burton Act), dental care for school children, environmental sanitation (control over sewage disposal, use of septic tanks, and water pollution), research into the causes of cancer, heart disease, diabetes, and other diseases, air-pollution control, cannery inspection, malaria and mosquito control, rodent control, chronic-illness care, water purification, and many other activities.

Public Awareness and Attitudes The public is not well informed concerning the services performed by public-health agencies. Many private organizations are active in the health field (such as the American Social Health Association, local tuberculosis organizations, the National Foundation), and these are often confused with public organizations. Furthermore, in one community, 84 percent of the working-class sample, 51 percent of the lower-middle-class, and 24 percent of the upper-middle-class, could not name one specific activity that was carried on by their local (county) public-health agency. This, despite the fact that the professional staff comes into daily contact with the public. This seeming paradox probably results from the high degree of professionalization in this field and the stable cultural attitudes that exist toward public-health functions and administrators.

Important controversies before local and state governing bodies center around several items, but perhaps especially in relation to the establishment of state hospitals for the chronically ill (a group of increasing size in our society, a by-product of lengthening life expectancy), the development of home-care programs by local health units at which patients not in need of hospital-

---

[6] **Today's VD Control Problem,** The Association of State and Territorial Health Officers, Chicago, 1957.

ization or other institutional care may be cared for and followed up in their own homes after hospital release, the public purchase of Salk polio vaccine for children, and the development of publicly financed medical-service centers in rural areas with too little population to support hospitals or even physicians. All of these and some other items being urged as proper areas for public-health activity are controversial, not only because they are potentially expensive, but also because they raise the long-standing question of the proper balance between public health and private medicine.

Mental Health

Mental-health programs are generally a part of public-health department operations, although in about one-third of the states these large and expensive programs are operated independently of the health department. The problem of mental health is particularly one of state government, with some assistance from local units. About 85 percent of all hospitalized patients are in state and local hospitals; all but 2 percent—persons in private institutions—of the remainder are cared for under the U.S. Veterans Administration program.

State and local mental-health programs require far more of the public's money each year than do all other public-health programs combined. Around 640,000 patients were cared for in state and local institutions in 1965, and the states alone spend about $1,000 million in capital outlay and operations budgets each year for care and treatment of the mentally ill and mentally deficient.[7] One person in ten in the United States suffers from some form of mental illness and these diseases are significant factors when related to crime, delinquency, suicide, alcoholism, narcotics addiction, and divorce rates.[8] Another 3 percent of the population is handicapped by mental deficiencies of sufficient degree to require special training or institutionalization. One out of every two hospital beds is occupied by a mental patient.[9] Each year, about 290,000 new patients are admitted to mental hospitals, and some 2.5 million persons of all ages are treated in hospitals, clinics, or by private psychiatrists.

A large proportion of persons in state mental hospitals are senile, or suffer from a combination of mental illness and senility. In 1963, for example, 34.4 percent of the patients in Texas state mental hospitals were sixty years of age or older.[10]

From Custody toward Treatment   Until very recent years, the mentally ill were treated much as if they were criminals. The nature of their difficulties was not recognized. They were "insane," perhaps as a punishment for wrongdoing, either of their own or of their families'. There was otherwise no understanding of their problems and no hope for cure, except by divine intervention. Persons

[7] Letter to the author from Sidney Spector, director of the Interstate Clearing House on Mental Health, Chicago, Mar. 14, 1957.
[8] **What Are the Facts about Mental Illness?** National Committee Against Mental Illness, New York, 1957.
[9] Mike Gorman, **Every Other Bed,** The World Publishing Company, Cleveland, 1956.
[10] C. J. Ruilmann, "The Aged in Texas State Mental Hospitals," **Public Affairs Comment,** 10:1–4, July, 1964.

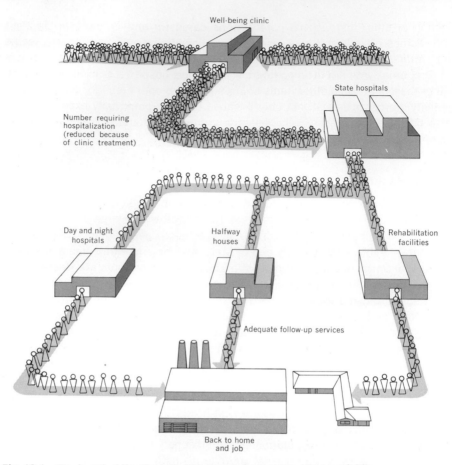

Fig. 19-1   Treatment of the Mentally Ill Is Increasingly a Local Responsibility.
SOURCE: **What Are the Facts about Mental Illness?** National Committee against Mental Illness, New York, 1957.

were cared for at home unless they became too great a burden to the family or too much of a threat to the community, in which case they were committed by a court to become inmates in so-called insane asylums—not for their own benefit, but to protect society. There they usually remained for the rest of their lives, often harshly treated by incompetent or sadistic custodians, poorly fed, subject to every communicable disease. But the typical citizen regarded them as being so far beyond reason that these facts were unimportant.

The beginnings of a movement away from strict custodial treatment of the mentally ill and an attitude toward these people which indicated that they were being punished by God for their presumed earlier misdeeds came in the 1840s. A social reformer, Dorothea Dix, conducted a lengthy and determined campaign to get the mentally ill out of jails, basements, and stables and into mental institutions operated by the states. These early institutions were primitive, and most of them remained so until after World War II, but they were better than the almost animallike treatment earlier given the mentally ill. Miss Dix began her campaign in 1841 when she first visited a Massachusetts prison and learned of the conditions of the mentally ill in those institutions.

Two books in particular served to publicize and popularize concern with mental illness. Both were written by former patients at state hospitals. One by Cliffords Beers, **A Mind That Found Itself** (1907), helped inspire both reform in state hospitals and the establishment of what is today the National Association of Mental Health. The book by Mary Jane Ward, **The Snake Pit** (1946), was influential in the post-World War II campaigns by reformers to secure modern treatment programs in state and local mental institutions.[11]

With the development of the theories of Sigmund Freud in the 1890s came a new concept of insanity. People learned that mental illness represented distortions of normal behavior, that it was indeed only an illness, and that it was potentially amenable to treatment. Others contributed, too, to the science and art of psychiatry. Medicines were discovered to help prevent certain kinds of mental illness (niacin to prevent pellagra, thyroid to treat cretinism, penicillin to prevent the psychosis of advanced syphilis), and after World War II, the great tranquilizing drugs were developed to give mental patients symptomatic—though not curative—relief.[12]

The states did not leap at the opportunity to rehabilitate their hospital residents. Little, in fact, was done to change from custodial to treatment approaches until after World War II. In the late 1940s, however, various groups began to push hard for legislative appropriations for treatment, research, and training. Some governors, such as Luther Youngdahl of Minnesota, made mental-hospital reform a central policy issue. In 1950, Allan Shivers of Texas, governor of one of our wealthiest states, complained: "I have found only one mental hospital where patients might achieve some peace of mind by attending church services. . . . I saw dilapidated, non-fireproof buildings without fire escapes, with hundreds of mentally ill persons locked in them . . . Texas, the proud Lone Star State—first in oil—48th in mental hospitals." [13] Shivers was unduly contrite. Much the same situation existed in many other states at the time.

But changes were taking place. Changes in attitude—as symbolized by the altering of the name of the New Mexico Insane Asylum in 1955 to the New Mexico State Hospital—were being followed by changes in appropriations. Some of the states lagged behind as usual—in 1966, a few of them still had no treatment programs—but rehabilitation was now hoped for, and to some extent expected by, the public.

The treatment of the mentally ill through clinical psychology and psychiatry is still far less exact than is the treatment of physical illnesses. The traditional caution of the medical profession, combined with this lack of certainty concerning both the diagnoses and treatment of mental illness "makes the psychiatrist very reluctant to have anything to do with criminal

[11] Clifford Beers, **A Mind That Found Itself,** Doubleday and Company, Inc., Garden City, N.Y., 1953. Originally published in 1907. Ward, *op. cit.*
[12] Gilbert Cant, **New Medicines for the Mind,** Public Affairs Press, Washington, D.C., 1955.
[13] Quoted in S. S. McKay, **Texas and the Fair Deal,** Naylor Co., San Antonio, Tex., 1954, p. 308.

patients, and they don't want to have anything to do with indigent patients. It is one profession that probably does less for the indigent than any other, because they are so tremendously in demand." [14] That is, the shortage of psychiatrists is great and charges for psychiatric treatment and salaries for state and local staff psychiatrists are high.

The greatly expanded cost led to demands for faster and better treatment and for outpatient treatment wherever possible. In 1956, the average per capita cost of a resident patient was $3.26 per day—and the average stay of a patient was eight years. But that year, for the first time in history, the number of persons in state hospitals declined, even in the face of a rapidly growing population. This was a result of more patients being treated on an outpatient basis, the development of local government child and adult mental-health clinics for early diagnosis, expanding therapeutic programs in hospitals, development of transitional devices between hospital and community such as family-care programs, "halfway houses," sheltered workshops, and other private and public agencies.[15]

The Federal government has, through the National Institute of Mental Health, established a grant-in-aid program designed to assist in the building of community health centers for the mentally ill in their own home towns or as close to them as possible, rather than in large and sometimes distant state mental hospitals. By the mid-1960s, all states were taking advantage of the program. The objective is to make it unnecessary for the mentally ill, except for the most difficult to manage and treat patients, to be cared for outside their own communities.

The program was faced with problems when it was established, of course. It was expected that many small towns would not view favorably the idea of local mental-health treatment centers or Federal aid to promote them. Some question exists as to whether enough trained personnel would be available if thousands of communities were to establish such centers. In 1965, only about 17,000 psychiatrists were active in the entire United States, the great bulk of them in private practice. For some years, the number of mentally ill has been increasing at a faster rate than the number of trained psychiatrists. In 1964, mental-health admissions were 70 percent above those of a decade earlier. In early 1965, the number of patients in mental hospitals totaled 491,000, but this represented a drop of 69,000 from a decade earlier. New techniques for meeting the needs of the mentally ill through halfway houses and tranquilizers, in particular, had made this possible. The estimate of the number of persons with clinically identifiable neuroses or psychoses remained at 10 percent of the total population, as it had been a decade earlier.

In order to qualify for Federal funds under the 1963 legislation, community mental-health centers have to provide both inpatient and outpatient

---

[14] Hugh J. McGee, quoted in, "To Protect the Constitutional Rights of the Mentally Ill," **Hearings,** Subcommittee on Constitutional Rights, Committee on the Judiciary, United States Senate, 1963, p. 221.
[15] This section uses data from a letter to the author from Sidney Spector, director of the Interstate Clearing House on Mental Health, Chicago, March 14, 1957, and **What Are the Facts about Mental Illness?** National Committee against Mental Illness, New York, 1957.

care, day care for those able to return to their homes on evenings and weekends, and a consultation and educational service.[16]

Local outpatient clinics are generally effective and relatively inexpensive: [17]

It usually costs much less to operate outpatient, multi-discipline mental health clinics than to provide psychiatric in-patient treatment in local hospitals or state mental institutions. Most community clinics are financed by a combination of tax resources, patient fees, and voluntary contributions. . . . Most states provide state grants covering up to 50 per cent of the expenses of their local clinics, but the public clinics in Kansas [some of the best in the nation] are almost completely locally financed.

The states still spend only about 1.5 percent of their mental-health budgets on research, and most state hospitals are far from comfortable homes; but great changes have taken place. The future, with the rate of mental illness not declining, offers problems for state and local governments. Grave shortages of hospital psychiatrists, clinical psychologists, nurses, and capable attendants still exist. Curative treatment is not only enormously expensive, but it must be applied early for best chances for recovery of the patient. It would appear that chemical symptomatic treatment offers the best immediate hope for returning patients to their own homes. Local governments will probably be expected to expand their outpatient treatment facilities for these persons. Hospitalized treatment will probably be far too expensive to be universally utilized, and the states will probably never be able to hire enough psychiatrists. The hospitals may eventually be reserved principally for the unmanageable and untreatable.

The Mentally Retarded   Care of the mentally retarded has followed a pattern similar to that of the mentally ill. In an earlier day, if the afflicted could not be cared for at home, they were sent to asylums for the "feebleminded." In more recent years, a less harsh term has been applied, something like "state home and training school." Although little progress has been made toward curing or preventing mental retardation, the conditions of hospitalization have improved, and local government programs are helping teach relatives to care at home for the retarded child or adult. Persons with an IQ above 50 and not otherwise afflicted are thought to be generally trainable for satisfactory life in the community. Others ordinarily enter state institutions as infants or young children and may be confined for a lifetime. Often, long waiting lists contribute to the anguish of parents who recognize that they must give up a hopelessly retarded child. Conditions are improving in state institutions, however, and better diagnoses and training programs have been introduced in the years since World War II.[18]

[16] **National Observer,** May 24, 1965.
[17] William H. Cape, "Mental Health Clinics," **Your Government,** 19:1–3, Feb. 15, 1964.
[18] **The Child Nobody Knows,** National Association for Retarded Children, New York, 1954.

Public Welfare

The ancient responsibility of the state to protect the welfare of the people is not limited to public-assistance programs. The problems of caring for the unemployed and those injured in industrial accidents and of providing housing for the aged, care of the chronically ill, and programs for veterans all are general state responsibilities. Many programs are handled on intergovernmental arrangements, with national, state, and local agencies taking part in varying combinations for different programs. These include the care of the poor, the care of children whose parents cannot or will not support them, and support for old people who can neither work nor support themselves from their savings. Delinquents, disabled persons, and the mentally handicapped are also cared for by welfare agencies in some cities and states.

Responsibility for Public Aid The responsibility for public-assistance aid rests with the state, but it has been delegated to local units of government ever since the Elizabethan Poor Law of 1601, the principles of which were adopted in colonial America. The basic approach taken in the days of the first Elizabeth in England remained unchanged in the American states until its archaism became obvious during the Great Depression. In the years since the Federal government established its grants-in-aid program with the Social Security Act of 1935, however, there has been a shift of emphasis from the city or township as the administrative unit to the county or the state itself.

Some activities by the states were designed to modify the ancient poor law even before the Great Depression. In the 1880s, for example, some Eastern private child-welfare agencies would gather up whole trainloads of large-city waifs and bring them to the Midwest to be delivered to farmers who waited at railroad stations. The theory apparently was that any Midwest farmer who offered a child a home would provide a better place than could be found in a large city. The potential abuses of this method of child placement were so great that in the mid-1880s, Midwestern states enacted legislation bringing child placement under state control.

The needs of the elderly, as distinguished from those of the employable, became obvious as the special problems of urban living made impossible the old system of being taken into the large farm homes of relatives. Even before the Great Depression, a number of states, including Montana, Kentucky, Wisconsin, and Nevada had adopted some form of old-age assistance. But generally programs for the aged were adopted after the passage of the Social Security Act in 1935.

The Federal government furnishes grants-in-aid to the states to help in caring for certain categories of persons: old-age assistance, aid to the blind, aid to dependent children, aid to the permanently and totally disabled (since 1950), aid for hospital care for anyone eligible under the four programs (since 1956), and medical care for the aged (since 1966). Some of the states administer these programs through field officers, but in most states they are administered by the counties or other local governments under state aid and supervision.

General direct relief other than the categorical aids is usually adminis-tered by the municipalities in incorporated areas or by the counties, and in a few states by the towns or townships. Local welfare agencies are often en-trusted, in addition, with the licensing of private child-caring agencies, the provision of foster care for children unable to live in their own homes, the supervision of adoption services, work with children's courts, provision for medical and dental care for the needy, and the supervision of private charities.

Persons Dependent upon Public Aid   The idea that some persons might not be capable of caring for their own basic economic needs was long essentially alien to the American tradition of self-sufficiency. Those who went on relief were often characterized as lazy and shiftless. Although this idea has by no

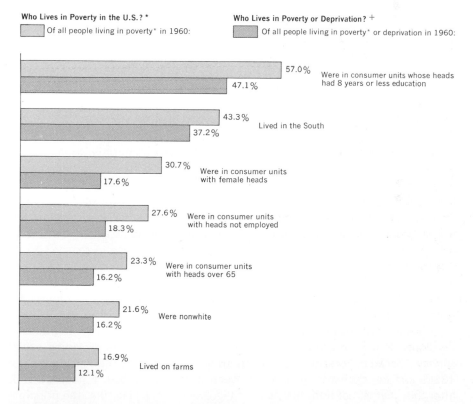

Who Lives in Poverty in the U.S.? *

Of all people living in poverty* in 1960:

Who Lives in Poverty or Deprivation? +

Of all people living in poverty* or deprivation in 1960:

57.0% / 47.1% — Were in consumer units whose heads had 8 years or less education

43.3% / 37.2% — Lived in the South

30.7% / 17.6% — Were in consumer units with female heads

27.6% / 18.3% — Were in consumer units with heads not employed

23.3% / 16.2% — Were in consumer units with heads over 65

21.6% / 16.2% — Were nonwhite

16.9% / 12.1% — Lived on farms

Fig. 19-2   Poverty Is Not Randomly Distributed.

* Total number of people in multiple person families with money incomes under $4,000 plus un-attached individuals with money incomes under $2,000.

† Total number of people in multiple person families with money incomes under $6,000 plus unattached individuals with money incomes under $3,000.

Data: Estimated by CEP on basis of census income and general family size data.

SOURCE: **Poverty and Deprivation in the U.S.,** Conference on Economic Progress, Washington, D.C., 1962, p. 74.

means been laid to rest in American folklore, the Great Depression made it clear that on some occasions, at least, the best efforts of a willing worker to find a job were unavailing. As a reaction to the earlier tendency to despise the destitute, some idealists came to describe the marginal members of the working force in glowing terms, ennobling them as martyrs, somewhat as the romantic Rousseau had considered the "noble savage."

In fact, welfare clients are a motley group made up of persons suffering from an extended period of bad luck; lazy persons, drunkards, and psychologically unstable personalities; mentally retarded persons not requiring institutionalization; persons who married young, have several children, but still have low seniority in their factory jobs and are thus often laid off; and many other types. The misfortunes that can bring a family onto public-welfare aid are many—exhaustion of unemployment-compensation benefits, successive years of crop failure on the farm, serious and prolonged illness on the part of the breadwinner, and dozens of others.

The attitude of social workers toward their clients is affected by both practical problems and social values. There are, in fact, two general ideologies toward people in need. One holds in essence that all men are rational beings who should be allowed to make decisions for themselves and that social service should provide emergency assistance only if it is wanted; the other is paternalistic in nature, with the caseworker often making decisions for the individual on behalf of society and with the welfare administrator deciding whether or not the client should receive a particular service.[19]

Welfare Administration   Public welfare is another function of government that has often been supervised by an administrative board with considerable autonomy from the rest of government. Professional social workers and the influential persons of the community who frequently interest themselves in social work as an avocation tend to favor autonomy. Social workers point out that the welfare budget is very large and that the temptation for elective officials to use these funds in order to help win votes is great. This type of reasoning was implicit in the requirement of the Social Security Act, written by professional social workers, that merit systems of personnel administration be established in each state that wished to qualify for Federal aid. Conflicts of interest between politicians and professionals sometimes result.[20]

Social work began as a form of upper-class charitable activity. It gradually developed into an organized profession and the institutions providing social services became bureaucratized. The trend began to be noticeable in the 1880s and the transition had largely been made by 1930.[21] It was not until after this, that is, not until the years of the Great Depression, that the principal

[19] See Alan Keith-Lucas, "The Political Theory Implicit in Social Casework Theory," **American Political Science Review,** 47:1076–1091, December, 1953, and by the same author, **Decisions about People in Need,** The University of North Carolina Press, Chapel Hill, N.C., 1957.
[20] For a case study, see Paul N. Ylvisaker, **The Battle of Blue Earth County,** rev. ed., University of Alabama Press, University, Ala., 1955.
[21] Roy Lubove, **The Professional Altruist: The Emergence of Social Work as a Career,** Harvard University Press, Cambridge, Mass., 1965.

center of social work transferred from private or voluntary institutions to those of government.

Late in the nineteenth century, persons interested in social welfare began to organize private charities on an increasing scale, and these institutions came to dominate the relief scene from that time until after World War I. It was through them that the casework system was developed, resulting in the basic administrative techniques still employed. These charities became so accepted that they were frequently subsidized by local governments, and they began to attract university-trained social workers. During the Great Depression, basic responsibility for welfare aid was shifted to government. Today, private social service agencies carry only a small part of the total load, but they remain important in a great many areas, particularly in activities for the young and old. Their professionally administered fund-raising campaigns are an annual feature of every community. The moneys collected are used to support the Boy Scouts, the YMCA, the Catholic Youth Organization; for the care of polio and muscular dystrophy victims; to maintain nursing homes for the aged; to assist persons in need who cannot qualify for a public-welfare program; to help in the rehabilitation of alcoholics; to care for unmarried mothers; and for dozens of other purposes.

Some Welfare Programs   Public-welfare agencies at both the state and local levels concern themselves with more than the various assistance programs. Their other activities include special clientele (migrants, veterans, the young, the old), housing, and insurance programs.

Workmen's Compensation   Through the early years of an industrialized America, employers could usually avoid paying for injuries resulting to employees in industrial accidents. The only remedy the worker had was to sue the employer, a process that was too slow and expensive to do him much good, as a rule. Furthermore, the ancient common law, based on pre-industrial conditions, provided many defenses for the employer, freeing him from obligation in most cases where suits were brought. This failure to assume responsibility for an expense that was economically a part of the cost of doing business and that could ill be afforded by the ordinary worker was a major source of dissatisfaction among industrial employees and a basis for much agitation. Early in the twentieth century New York, gradually followed by all states, abandoned the common law rules of legal responsibility and adopted a system of workmen's compensation. Practices vary widely from state to state. Sometimes the insurance system is administered entirely by the state government. In other cases, the employer may use the state fund or insure through a private company or even insure himself if he has sufficient resources. Often a referee decides cases of disagreement and a state appeal board may be resorted to if either side remains dissatisfied. The courts are generally excluded from the process (if they were used, the worker could not afford to carry through appeals) except to decide cases involving interpretation of the meaning of the law.

Unemployment Compensation   Some European nations had unemployment compensation long before the American states adopted it. This program is essentially an insurance device designed to provide a continuing income for persons who, through no fault of their own, are laid off from their jobs. Each state administers such an insurance plan, with employers paying into the fund under complicated formulas that vary from state to state. Unemployment compensation was slow in being adopted in the United States, partly because each state was afraid that to levy assessments for a compensation fund would tend to drive employers out of the state and into others where the costs of operation would be lower. Another reason was that many working people were opposed to the plan—even though under existing law they often had to depend upon public or private dole in the event of a layoff of extended duration. As late as 1931, the national convention of the American Federation of Labor adopted a resolution rejecting unemployment compensation as being a welfare handout. Today, however, labor organizations take every opportunity in seeking to increase benefits under the plan.

Wisconsin was the first state (in 1932) to adopt an unemployment-compensation plan. By 1935, eight states had done so. The Social Security Act of 1935 deliberately sought to force the issue in the others. It did not establish a Federal system of compensation but prodded the states by levying a payroll tax, nine-tenths of which would be retained by any state that adopted a plan. The other states then acted. Issues in the field of compensation center around the question of the differential that should exist between average compensation and average wage of the employee (the benefit rates); around the question of the duration of benefits, with organized labor arguing for extending the period of eligibility to at least twenty-six weeks; and around the various qualifying provisions in the laws which limit the conditions of eligibility.

The trend in unemployment-insurance benefits has been toward increasing the duration of benefits. Some states have also provided for temporary increases in unemployment-insurance benefits during periods of high unemployment. But, characteristically, "the states have waited to be prodded by Federal legislation to extend duration in periods of national recession. In 1958 and 1959, 17 states temporarily extended duration in cooperation with the Federal government under the Temporary Unemployment Compensation Act of 1958. . . ." [22]

Unemployment and Rehabilitation   The centuries-old concept of work as being good for everyone and necessary for good citizenship will probably clash with policies that will be developed to cope with work innovations of the last half of the twentieth century, especially with those related to automation. Most specialists believe that automation will produce high unemployment rates. If this is the result, there will be little economic logic in insisting that partially disabled persons find work. The problem will be one of maintaining their morale and their sense of social worth, given the typical citizen's view

[22] Harry Malisoff, **The Financing of Extended Unemployment Insurance Benefits in the United States,** Upjohn Institute for Employment Research, Kalamazoo, Mich., 1963, p. 1.

Sacramento, Cal.

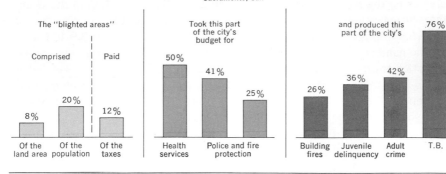

The "blighted areas"			Took this part of the city's budget for		and produced this part of the city's			
Comprised	Paid							76%
8%	20%	12%	50%	41%	25%	26%	36%	42%
Of the land area	Of the population	Of the taxes	Health services	Police and fire protection	Building fires	Juvenile delinquency	Adult crime	T.B.

Los Angeles, Cal.

Comparing "blighted areas" with a control "good area"
(On a per capita basis)

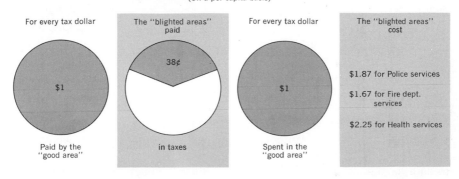

For every tax dollar

$1

Paid by the "good area"

The "blighted areas" paid

38¢

in taxes

For every tax dollar

$1

Spent in the "good area"

The "blighted areas" cost

$1.87 for Police services

$1.67 for Fire dept. services

$2.25 for Health services

Louisville, Ky.

Comparing a substandard area with a control "good area"
(With the same population)

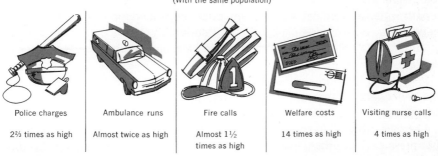

Police charges	Ambulance runs	Fire calls	Welfare costs	Visiting nurse calls
2⅔ times as high	Almost twice as high	Almost 1½ times as high	14 times as high	4 times as high

Fig. 19-3   The High Social Costs of Poverty.
SOURCE: **Poverty and Deprivation in the U.S.,** Conference on Economic Progress, Washington, D.C., 1962, p. 69.

that everyone should find a way of being gainfully employed, a view that even professional rehabilitation workers usually assume to be the goal of their activities.[23]

[23] Terrence E. Carroll, "The Ideology of Work," **Journal of Rehabilitation,** 31:26, July–August, 1965.

Services for the Aging   Between 1890 and 1960, the population in the United States sixty-five years of age and over increased from about 2.5 million to more than 16.5 million. In percentage terms, the increase was from 3.9 to 9.2, so that the number of persons sixty-five years of age and older more than doubled in relation to the rest of the population. Modern medical science has helped man to live longer. Contemporary industrial social organization gives man less independence and security for his old age than was enjoyed under an agricultural society. As the number of persons beyond retirement age increases, problems of insecurity increase and the politician becomes sharply aware of the political power of this group. The result has been a postwar development of a variety of state and local programs for the elderly. The Council of State Governments argues that the Federal government ought to stay out of this area and leave programs to the states. Many states have studied programs for expanded medical care and homelike institutional care facilities for older people, for recreational services, and for housing for the aged. A few states have adopted special housing programs. Increasingly, older people are demanding equal employment rights. In the coming decades, state and local welfare agencies will probably play an ever greater role in providing services to older people, and many of these will be expensive.

Services for Children   Dependent and neglected children have always formally been the responsibility of the state. In recent decades, special juvenile courts have been established both to supervise the care of such children and to take jurisdiction over youthful law violators who, if older, would come before the criminal courts. Juvenile judges must decide whether parents are fit to care for their children, and whether children without proper homes should be placed in private homes or in institutions. The judges turn over many responsibilities to other governmental agencies. The process of investigating complaints about alleged mistreatment of children is commonly left to police departments, and social workers are often depended upon to make recommendations to the judge concerning the suitability of foster homes or of the conditions in a home that is alleged not to have satisfactory conditions for the children of the family.

Children who violate the law or whose behavior places them in the juvenile delinquent category must also be treated by joint action of the police, the juvenile court, and public and private welfare agencies. Juvenile delinquency is a serious problem in contemporary society, resulting from various conditions that are a part of urban society, but it is not a recent phenomenon. In 1858, the **New York Herald** complained that the youth of the day was "brutal, cold-blooded, savage and cowardly," and that the "more heinous crimes of the calendar" were generally committed by "youth who are at the age when the heart is believed to be the most generous. . . ."[24] As urbanism expands in scope and the number of children in cities increases, the need for local government programs to assist in meeting the problems of delinquency will in-

[24] Quoted in an Associated Press dispatch, May 10, 1958.

crease. And the problems long known in cities have also become serious in smaller cities and rural areas.

The state government usually has responsibility for the custody of institutionalized delinquents. The social-welfare departments commonly administer the state reform schools—most of which are not supported by the public at a level that gives them opportunity to do much reforming, although their inmates are probably for the most part potentially able to adjust satisfactorily to the behavior requirements of society. The state also frequently has licensing and inspectorial powers over public and private child-caring institutions, child-placing agencies, boarding homes and schools for children, maternity homes for unmarried mothers, homes for handicapped children, children's summer camps, day care centers, and nursery schools.

Services for Migrant Laborers   Areas of the nation that use seasonal labor for truck farming or fruit harvests experience particular problems. These people come to the West or North from the South or from Mexico. The living quarters furnished them may be inadequate by contemporary minimum standards. Other problems arise, too, in relation to medical care, communicable diseases, the education of migrant children, recreation, acceptance in community business places, and the protection of the rights of migrants under workmen's compensation and civil liberties. States and especially local governments seek to develop programs to care for the health, education, and welfare of migrants. The work frequently involves propaganda campaigns aimed at employers and the communities whose economy is partially supported by the work done by these people.

Services for Veterans   Veterans are particularly effective when acting through interest groups because there is no balancing group to counter their demands. Politicians generally regard it as important to seek to gain support from veterans as veterans. Opposing arguments that veterans should be cared for in relation to service-connected disabilities but should otherwise be treated as other citizens are generally unavailing.

After World War I and again after World War II and the Korean conflict, many states provided cash bonuses for veterans, although in each case it was less than one-half of the states.[25] Other special benefits are commonly provided by the states and to some extent by local governments. These include rehabilitation loans, housing loans, grants for hospitalization, medical care in state university hospitals, care of dependents, financial assistance for education, property tax exemptions up to a certain amount, burial expenses for the veteran and his dependents, welfare aid under less restrictive conditions than for nonveterans, civil service employment preference, eligibility to spend retirement years in a soldiers' home, use of public facilities for meetings of veterans' groups, exemption from certain license fees, special employment, psychological or educational counseling services, and dozens of others.[26] All

[25] See "Korean War Bonus Developments," **Tax Review**, 17:1, September, 1956.
[26] For a complete list, see The President's Commission on Veterans' Pensions, **State Veterans' Laws**, 1956.

of these items cost a great deal of money—the states spent over $3,010 million in the first nine years after World War II—and many of the services are not available to nonveterans who, in some cases, stand in greater need of them.

Housing   Local governments have long had building codes providing minimum standards for building construction and human occupancy. The code (or series of codes, for they are not always unified or administered by a single agency) makes provisions for standards of lighting and ventilation, sanitation, and fire prevention and protection. Historically, these codes have often been subject to pressure demands of manufacturers, builders, real-estate people, tenement owners, and building-trades unions. As a result, in some communities minimum standards well below those that contemporary society would accept as an absolute minimum have been established. On the other hand, in some cases, building codes require materials of a quality far beyond what is reasonably necessary (for example, the use of metal conduits for basement wiring), thus raising the cost of housing. Codes have been revised in recent years: in the suburbs as persons investing in housing seek to protect neighborhood values, in the core cities as residents and businessmen become concerned with threatened declines in property values. Still many communities, especially on the outer fringe of cities, permit jerry-building. Some cities do not permit modern building techniques (for example, the use of dry-wall construction) or permit the construction of low-rent housing, thus depriving lower-income persons of adequate housing.[27]

In addition to controls over construction and occupancy by local governments, the states have sought to encourage housing construction by aiding in the financing of housing for veterans and the elderly. A large number of state and local governments have cooperated with the Federal government in the construction of public housing. Generally, housing authorities are established as special districts of local government, although some are partly integrated into the general government of the community.

Public housing has long been a controversial matter in America. Few precedents for it existed prior to the introduction of a program of Federal aid in the Housing Act of 1937. That act sought to help provide work for the unemployed during the Great Depression and to encourage better housing for low-income persons than was being provided for by the conversion of old homes and buildings into apartments. But public housing is low-status housing, and most families seek to avoid living in such projects. In the postwar years, housing projects came to be occupied increasingly by "problem" families, social nonconformists, and the chronically unemployed. To some extent, interest in public housing was revived by attempts to build projects less institutional in appearance and to concentrate upon using such housing for persons displaced from areas of cities to be torn down and redeveloped.

[27] See Edward C. Banfield and Morton Grodzins, **Government and Housing**, McGraw-Hill Book Company, New York, 1958.

Public housing accounted for just over 1 percent of the housing starts in 1965. Opposition by private realtors to public housing has been strong. Attempts have been made to require local referendums before public-housing projects can be begun, and some states have adopted such legislation. There will probably continue to be a role for public housing in the United States, but —except possibly housing for the elderly—it will continue to be a modest part of both the housing industry and the activities of welfare agencies.

Housing Factors in the 1960s 1. Between 1950 and 1960, despite the fact that housing, both urban and rural, fell into the substandard category more rapidly than renewal projects could eliminate such housing, some progress in the direction of culturally approved conditions was made. For example, in 1950, only 63 percent of housing units in the United States had plumbing. In 1960, this figure had increased to 73 percent. Owner occupancy had increased only slightly, from 55 to 56 percent. Nonwhite (mostly Negro) housing continued to be far behind that of the rest of the nation. The national average for per-centage of owner occupancy of housing units in 1960 was 56 percent, while that for nonwhites was only 38 percent. And while the average for homes with complete plumbing facilities was 73 percent, that for nonwhites was only 43 percent.[28]

Federal programs of the 1960s sought to provide incentives for adding to the new housing supply with policies that would be acceptable to the private business interests of realtors, developers, builders, and housing-management firms. The Federal Housing Administration (FHA) has insured private home-mortgage loans since 1934, the Veterans Administration (VA) since 1944. The Federal National Mortgage Association (FNMA, or "Fannie Mae") has pur-chased mortgages so as to release private funds for reinvestment. The Housing Act of 1965 permitted the leasing of privately owned units of low-income housing to be administered by local public housing authorities, and placed the interest rate below market levels for loans on privately built low- and medium-income housing.

2. One of the areas in which state governments have most commonly exercised their right to place stipulations upon the use of Federal aid by local units of government has been that of housing. In Iowa, which is one of the states in which the legislature has a definite small-town–oriented ideology, any municipality that wants to establish a public housing project must hold a special election on the proposition and it must secure the approval of 60 percent of the persons voting in the election. Before 1960, it was not even possible for Iowa communities to take part in the public housing program. Realtors, homebuilders, and savings and loan associations have been among the leaders in opposing the liberalization of the law in that and other states.

In 1965, forty-seven states had laws permitting local governments to par-ticipate in the public housing program. Nine of these states required an election before a municipality could participate. None required more than a

[28] U.S. Bureau of the Census, **1960 Census of Housing.**

simple majority, however, except for Iowa. Of the states requiring a referendum, four were in the Midwest, three in the West, one in New England, and one in the South.

3. The creation of a new Federal Cabinet post to deal with urban areas was accompanied by many structural changes relative to housing and urban renewal at the local level. In Pittsburgh, in 1965, for example, the offices of director of planning and urban renewal coordinator were combined into a single office. A few months earlier, San Francisco established the position of Coordinator of Planning, Housing, and Redevelopment. The objective was to coordinate the city's various development programs, but the mayor had difficulty in filling the new position. Professionals in the fields of planning, housing, and urban renewal have differing professional backgrounds and they must work with a variety of different Federal as well as state agencies. The task of coordination is difficult and the pressures and role expectations of such a coordinator are different in each of three areas of activity. Milwaukee, after five years' experience with a Department of City Development, still found that coordination was unsatisfactory, although there had been a definite move toward bringing the various city and school programs into harmony with one another.

In 1965, Mayor Robert F. Wagner of New York appointed the city's first Coordinator of Housing and Development, with responsibility for urban renewal, housing, building-code enforcement, and industrial park development. The coordinator was expected to serve not only to bring the parts of the program into line with one another, but also to be a major policy advisor to the mayor.[29]

4. Although city officials and judges have been timid in approaching slum clearance problems, some evidence indicates that local officials are becoming somewhat more determined. Chicago, in 1964, for example, secured 187 court orders to have slum tenements declared unfit for human habitation and vacated. The year before, the city had secured only 78 such orders. The Department of Buildings secured 223 mandatory injunctions requiring slum owners to bring buildings up to code standards or face contempt of court proceedings. In addition, 4,045 buildings were repaired as the result of administrative or judicial notices. Slum owners spent $21.5 million in complying with these code enforcement orders, an increase in expenditures of 14 percent over the previous year. The Building and Fire Department Compliance Board heard 23,396 cases in 1964, an increase of one-third over the previous year. During 1964, the Department of Law (city attorney's office) filed 441 suits asking for court decrees to order dilapidated and hazardous buildings demolished. The courts granted 393 of these requests. In addition, the city itself demolished 195 buildings when the owners failed to comply with decrees. In each case, liens for the cost of demolition were obtained against the owners. The City Department of Law also filed nearly 10,000 suits against slum owners for code violations. But these suits were more a matter of mild harassment than a

29 **Journal of Housing,** July, 1965, pp. 144–145.

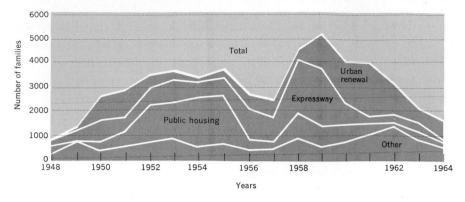

Fig. 19-4   Families Are Uprooted by Land-use Changes.
Shows number of families moved in Chicago, by program and year.
SOURCE: **Housing and Urban Renewal Progress Report,** City of Chicago, Chicago, 1964, p. 6.

threat of financial punishment, for fines during the year against those found guilty of code violations averaged less than $15 each.[30]

5. A major political problem in the future will be that of providing housing appropriate to middle-class status for middle-class Negroes. In the 1960s, the great majority of white citizens were still unable to distinguish between Negroes of the middle class and of the working class and tended to lump them together, a distinction that was painful to many members of the Negro middle class—a rapidly growing group—as well as to some of the leaders of the Negro working class. In the 1960s, "non-white families generally are housed in older, less expensive and lower quality housing than white families of similar incomes. Furthermore, the discrepancy is largely unchanged as the non-white family income rises." In other words, the pattern has been for discrimination to result in an equally large discrepancy between Negro and white housing, regardless of social class.[31]

Urban Redevelopment   A few efforts were made by state and local governments during the 1930s to encourage private endeavor to clear slums and build new homes. Tax exemptions were most commonly offered, but they were inadequate inducements. The state of New York worked out a plan for redevelopment corporations in 1941, but World War II interfered with putting it into effect. A few cities, notably Pittsburgh, have completed outstanding renewal programs with local finance. Most communities have not been able to do this.

The Federal Housing Act of 1949, among other things, offered aid to communities for slum clearance and urban redevelopment. Grants could be made to local units to acquire, clear, and prepare blighted areas for the construction of new dwellings. The cleared land could then either be used for public-housing projects or be resold to private builders for redevelopment.

Some slums were cleared away as a result of the 1949 act, but only ten projects were completed in the decade that followed its adoption. New slums

[30] Chicago Community Renewal Program, **Progress Report,** City of Chicago, Chicago, Dec. 31, 1964.
[31] U.S. Housing and Home Finance Agency, press release, Dec. 28, 1962.

developed at a faster rate than existing ones were cleared. The Housing Acts of 1954 and after, therefore, emphasized urban renewal. This orientation was reinforced by the concern felt by local businessmen and realtors over the downward trend in land values in the older parts of cities.

Under the urban-renewal provisions, communities, private business, and the Federal government were to cooperate to prevent the spread of urban blight to new areas, to rehabilitate and conserve areas that could still be restored at reasonable cost, and to clear and redevelop areas that could not be saved. The community was required to prepare an urban-renewal plan, to adopt adequate land-use controls, and to have a comprehensive physical plan for the whole community.

Table 23   Downtown Redevelopment Attitudes

	SUPPORT, %	UNDECIDED, %	OPPOSE, %
City dwellers:			
Low education	59	10	31
Medium and high education	66	11	23
Fringe dwellers:			
Low education	31	21	48
Medium and high education	65	16	18

SOURCE: Robert E. Agger and others, **The Rulers and the Ruled,** John Wiley & Sons, Inc., New York, 1964, table 12-1.

Federal aids are available to assist in the "main phases of project clearance, redevelopment or rehabilitation, rehousing of displaced families, and in community planning and other special operations." Grants and loans cannot be used for the construction or rehabilitation of structures, but the FHA mortgage-insurance program has been expanded to such activities.

The laws of the 1950s sought to overcome some of the earlier problems —of relocating displaced persons, of inducing private business to take part in renewal, of poor planning. But the amount of urban renewal that actually took place during the first few years after passage of the acts was relatively modest for several reasons: Persons in areas to be renewed objected to relocation, fearing that adequate housing would not be available to them, or would be too costly; slum owners feared loss of income and of valuable property if renewal plans went forward; some conservatives, even though they owned urban property, regarded government-assisted renewal as radicalism and thus undesirable. In 1957, only fifty-nine slum-clearance and urban-renewal projects were approved, and by the end of that year, the total of Federally assisted projects under way was only 491 in the entire nation.[32] A total of 299 communities were involved in these projects. According to past performances, some of these would take over ten years to complete. Some would not be completed at all.

[32] J. D. Lange, "Housing and Urban Renewal Developments in 1957," **Municipal Year Book, 1958,** International City Managers' Association, Chicago, 1958, pp. 306–313.

More than 1 million housing starts have been made in the United States in each year beginning in 1949. The great bulk of these have been one- and two-family units. Despite the slum-clearance and urban-renewal provisions of the Federal housing acts and supportive state laws, blight continues to spread and the problem of housing low-income people has not been solved.

Urban renewal and highway development in metropolitan areas has resulted in inconvenience to large numbers of persons and quite a few businesses. If more serious efforts at urban renewal are made in the future, these discommodations will increase in scope. In a study of 100 cities of over 100,000 population in 1964, more than 36,900 families and 5,800 business concerns were displaced. Most cities found a shortage of standard housing for low-income groups, and found that the relocating of Negroes was particularly a problem. Among the businesses that were displaced by urban renewal and highway programs, small businesses offered the greatest problem and most of these were persons near or beyond the age of sixty-five. Most of their businesses involved retail or personal service operations and were dependent upon neighborhood patronage. When the neighborhood was destroyed, so was their business opportunity.[33]

The popular impression is that urban renewal is essentially a big-city undertaking, but the bulk of urban-renewal projects are actually located in small cities and villages. Similarly, slums are associated in the minds of most citizens with large cities, but the percentage of rural families living in substandard housing is twice that of urban families. In 1960, almost 20 percent of the families living in rural areas and in small towns had substandard dwellings. More than 1 million rural homes were classified as "dilapidated" in 1960. One-third of rural homes did not have bath facilities; 20 percent did not have running water; 60 percent lacked central heating. At least one-half of the rural families whose income level was such as to include them among the poor were living in dilapidated housing.

Efforts to eliminate or at least to reduce the number of rural slums and substandard houses have not come from state or local governments. The principal effort has come from the Farmer's Home Administration of the Federal government, which makes direct loans to those who qualify, in contrast to the FHA procedure of guaranteeing the mortgage.

Smaller communities, when they enjoy general agreement among citizens and leaders concerning desirable public policies, can act more quickly than can large cities. Such communities either enjoy the benefits of direct support for particular activities, or their leaders quickly learn that support is not forthcoming, and probably will not be forthcoming. In 1965, for example, 70 percent of the communities participating in the Federal urban-renewal program had populations of 50,000 or less. Almost one-fourth of them had populations of less than 10,000.[34]

[33] U.S. Advisory Committee on Intergovernmental Relations, **Relocation: Unequal Treatment of People and Businesses Displaced by Governments,** 1965.
[34] **Journal of Home Building,** June, 1965.

Criticism of Urban Renewal   Liberal critics of urban renewal have generally concentrated upon the question of adequacy. They have complained that Federal and state programs offer "too little, too late." They also criticize the programs for lack of adequate involvement of local residents in the decision-making process. This is a general criticism made of the antipoverty program, which came along after urban-renewal policies were largely institutionalized. Conservative critics of the program have complained that it has cost more than is justified, has been destructive of personal liberty by causing the involuntary displacement of persons and businesses, has actually reduced the amount of low-rent housing available to low-income persons, and has thus created new slums rather than reduced the size of our slum population. They also say the program has been particularly a hardship upon Negro and Puerto Rican persons, applies widely differing and almost arbitrary definitions of standard housing if one compares one community with another, does not pay the displaced businessman for his loss of regular customers, "good will," and cost of relocation, has caused a decrease in urban tax revenues as a result of renewal, and has failed to generate the investment of private capital in renewed areas.[35]

Urban renewal is one of many professional fields of activity in which pressures exist both for political integration and for independence. Persons outside the housing and planning professions often argue that urban renewal should be a municipal activity, subject to the usual political processes, with leadership and control vested in the mayor and the council. Professionals in the area, emphasizing that urban renewal is a particularly important activity (at least as they view it), argue that this function of government should have a high degree of autonomy and should not be subject to the usual rules of political procedures of local government.[36]

SELECTED READINGS

Altshuler, Alan: **The Ancker Hospital Site Controversy,** The Bobbs-Merrill Company, Inc., Indianapolis, ICP no. 82, 1964.   (Problems involved in contradictory technical information reflecting different professional values—in this case medical administrators and urban planners.)

American Public Health Association: **Local Health Units for the Nation,** The Commonwealth Fund, New York, 1946.

Ascher, Charles S.: "Aren't We All?" **Public Administration Review,** 17:264–271, Autumn, 1957.   (A review of books on mental illness and its treatment.)

Banfield, Edward C., and Morton Grodzins: **Government and Housing,** McGraw-Hill Book Company, New York, 1958.

Barron, M. L.: **The Juvenile in Delinquent Society,** Alfred A. Knopf, Inc., New York, 1955.

Bosselman, B. C.: **The Troubled Mind,** The Ronald Press Company, New York, 1953.

[35] Martin Anderson, **The Federal Bulldozer,** The M.I.T. Press, Cambridge, Mass., 1964.
[36] George S. Duggar, "The Relation of Local Government Structure to Urban Renewal," **Law and Contemporary Problems,** 26:49–69, Winter, 1961.

Bruno, F. J., and L. Towley: **Trends in Social Work,** 2d ed., Columbia University Press, New York, 1957.

Cant, Gilbert: **New Medicines for the Mind,** Public Affairs Press, Washington, D.C., 1955.   (The effects of tranquilizers upon the management of mental illness.)

Colean, Miles L.: **Renewing Our Cities,** The Twentieth Century Fund, Inc., New York, 1953.

Daland, Robert T.: **Government and Health: The Alabama Experience,** Bureau of Public Administration, University of Alabama, University, Ala., 1955.

de Grazia, Alfred (ed.): **Grass Roots Private Welfare,** New York University Press, New York, 1958.

Drake, J. T.: **The Aged in American Society,** The Ronald Press Company, New York, 1958.

Duggar, George S. (ed.): **The New Renewal,** Bureau of Public Administration, University of California, Berkeley, Calif., 1961.   (Urban renewal issues of the 1960s, particularly the problem of meeting the normative goal of avoiding uniformity.)

————— and Patrick Ford: **Urban Renewal Administration,** Bureau of Public Administration, University of California, Berkeley, Calif., 1957.

Dworkis, M. B. (ed.): **The Impact of Puerto Rican Migration on Governmental Services in New York City,** New York University Press, New York, 1957.   (A case study.)

Epstein, Abraham: **Insecurity: A Challenge to America,** Random House, Inc., New York, 1938.

Greenblatt, Milton, and others: **From Custodial to Therapeutic Patient Care in Mental Hospitals,** Russell Sage Foundation, New York, 1955.

Greer, Scott: **Urban Renewal and American Cities,** The Bobbs-Merrill Company, Inc., Indianapolis, 1965.

Hanlon, J. J.: **Principles of Public Health Administration,** 4th ed., The C. V. Mosby Company, St. Louis, 1964.

Hogarty, Richard A.: **New Jersey Farmers and Migrant Housing Rules,** The Bobbs-Merrill Company, Inc., Indianapolis, ICP no. 94, 1966.   (Should the state require New Jersey farmers to provide hot water for migrant laborers? Involves ideologies and tactics of leaders on each side.)

Kaplan, Harold: **Urban Renewal Politics,** Columbia University Press, New York, 1963.   (Urban renewal policy making in Newark is dominated by the professionals.)

Keith-Lucas, Alan: **Decisions About People in Need,** The University of North Carolina Press, Chapel Hill, N.C., 1957.   (The unarticulated value assumptions of social casework.)

Koos, E. L.: **The Health of Regionville,** Columbia University Press, New York, 1954.

"The Legislative History of Public Housing Traced through 25 Years," **Journal of Housing,** 19:431–445, October, 1962.   (History of the Housing Act of 1937 and later amendments.)

Lubove, Roy: **The Professional Altruist: The Emergence of Social Work as a Career, 1880–1930,** Harvard University Press, Cambridge, Mass., 1965.

MacDonald, Dwight: "Our Invisible Poor," **New Yorker,** Jan. 19, 1963, pp. 82–132. (A review of books on poverty.)

McMillen, Wayne: **Community Organization for Social Welfare,** The University of Chicago Press, Chicago, 1945.

Meriam, Lewis, and others: **The Cost and Financing of Social Security,** The Brookings Institution, Washington, D.C., 1950.

Pasamanick, Benjamin, and others: "Mental Disease Prevalence in an Urban Population," **Public Health Reports,** 72:574–576, July, 1957.

Paul, B. J. (ed.): **Health, Culture, and Community,** Russell Sage Foundation, New York, 1955.

Perkings, Ellen J.: **State and Local Financing of Public Assistance,** U.S. Department of Health, Education and Welfare, Bureau of Public Assistance, 1956.

Poverty and Deprivation in the United States: The Plight of Two-fifths of a Nation, Conference on Economic Progress, Washington, D.C., 1962.

Robinson, Mariana: **The Coming of Age of the Langley Porter Clinic,** The Bobbs-Merrill Company, Inc., Indianapolis, ICP no. 74, 1962. (Organizational change in a mental-health clinic.)

———— and Corinne Silverman: **The Reorganization of Philadelphia General Hospital,** The Bobbs-Merrill Company, Inc., Indianapolis, ICP no. 47, 1959.

Rossi, Peter H., and Robert A. Dentler: **The Politics of Urban Renewal,** The Free Press of Glencoe, New York, 1961.

Schroth, Thomas N., and others: **Congress and the Nation, 1945–1964,** Congressional Quarterly Service, Washington, D.C., 1965, chaps. 4 and 8.

Stout, Ronald M.: **The New York Farm Labor Camps, 1940–1946,** The Bobbs-Merrill Company, Inc., Indianapolis, ICP no. 12, 1953. (The political agency head as innovator.)

Senate Committee on the Judiciary, **Juvenile Delinquency,** 1954.

Senate Committee on Labor and Public Welfare, **Studies of the Aged and Aging: Federal and State Activities,** 1956.

Spitz, Allan A.: **Organization and Administration of the Hawaiian Homes Program,** Legislative Reference Bureau, University of Hawaii, Honolulu, 1963. (A study of a housing program for the indigenous Hawaiian population. The paternalistic approach of the original act of 1920 has resulted in constant controversy.)

Stein, Clarence S.: **Toward New Towns for America,** rev. ed., Reinhold Publishing Corporation, New York, 1957.

Steiner, P. O., and Robert Dorfman: **The Economic Status of the Aged,** University of California Press, Berkeley, Calif., 1958.

Stevenson, G. S.: **Mental Health Planning for Social Action,** McGraw-Hill Book Company, New York, 1956.

Stout, R. M.: **The New York Farm Labor Camps,** University of Alabama Press, University, Ala., 1953. (A case study.)

Thorpe, L. P.: **The Psychology of Mental Health,** The Ronald Press Company, New York, 1950.

Urban Development Guidebook, Chamber of Commerce of the United States, Washington, D.C., 1955.

U.S. Children's Bureau: **Child Welfare Services,** 1957.

U.S. Housing and Home Finance Agency: **Housing Statistics,** 1965.

U.S. Public Health Service: **Patients in Mental Institutions,** 1963.

————: **Tuberculosis in the United States,** 1963.

Waggaman, John S.: **Health Regulations and the Indiana Food Industry,** Institute of Public Administration, Indiana University, Bloomington, Ind., 1965. (A description of one state's activities.)

Ward, Mary Jane: **The Snake Pit,** Random House, Inc., New York, 1946. (A report on conditions in a mental hospital. The book's publication resulted in increased interest in the condition of the mentally ill.)

Woodbury, Coleman: **The Future of Cities and Urban Redevelopment,** The University of Chicago Press, Chicago, 1953.

Ylvisaker, Paul N.: **The Battle of Blue Earth County,** rev. ed., University of Alabama Press, University, Ala., 1955. (A case study.)

20

LAND AND WATER POLICIES

The allocation of land uses and the distribution of water resources are basic policy matters involving the welfare of all people. Increasingly, issues of policy at both state and local levels center around these two broad considerations. In a day when the question whether a community will prosper or stagnate may depend upon decisions relative to land-use controls and water policies or when more than 10 percent of the land in a county may be allocated to arterial highways, it is obvious that these items are of the utmost importance to many citizens.

Land Use and Land-use Controls

Land-use changes over time, problems related to urban space requirements, shifting agricultural needs, and changing rural social organization have created problems in many lands in many periods of history. For example, the enclosure movement in fifteenth- and sixteenth-century England, which ended the feudal land system and concentrated control in a relatively few large landowners, was disapproved of by the Crown because it weakened the traditional arrangements for the defense of the realm, caused technological unemployment, and created social problems and unrest in cities to which went persons displaced from their small holdings to make way for wool-producing sheep. The peasantry opposed the movement because it threatened them with beggarhood and an enforced change in their way of life. Yet, the change took place anyway, and in spite of much individual hardship. Eventually, the wool trade helped England to prosper and become the most powerful nation in the world. And the movement of peasants to the cities provided a supply of labor that several generations later made possible the high standard of living of an industrial age.

A shift in land use of equal magnitude has occurred in the twentieth century. The use of steel machinery and technological advancements in general have made it possible to increase greatly the productivity and efficiency of agriculture. As the production of food and fiber, which was once part of a unique way of life, becomes increasingly a business, excess farm populations and farmland are being surrendered to an ever-growing urban economy and society. Great shifts in public policy result. These include changes in policies toward agriculture, water usage, highway development, and the use of land. In the case of the last of these, the problems arising during the transitional phases in usage have encouraged the development of physical planning techniques and of controls to enforce planning decisions.

The Meaning of Planning   Planning "involves the appraisal of all manner of resources in men and materials and the marshaling of them in the community interest." [1] While systematic planning in the United States might be said to date from William Penn's 1682 layout of the city of Philadelphia, most American cities had a chaotic growth until recent decades. In rural areas, planning was even less a community concern until the coming of the automobile and telephone which made possible the ribbon developments along arterial highways and fringe-area slums just beyond the reach of established land-use controls (see Figure 20-1).

Planning of some kind has always existed of course. In the nineteenth century, informal committees composed of people interested in realty development or simply in "civic improvement" would sometimes present plans to the city council for consideration. Later, committees of the same sort were sometimes appointed by the mayor or council to study and make recommendations on plans. Once they made a report, like most study groups, their task was finished.

In typical American fashion, land-use decisions were, until recently, made by private businessmen: realtors, land developers, and bankers in particular. Characteristically, nineteenth-century Americans did not believe that a greater community interest stood above that of the profit motives of these men. Planners were thus concerned with their profit-and-loss statements rather than with making Ackroyd City an attractive community with an imaginative physical design. It would be difficult to exaggerate the effect of their short-range concerns upon the face of urban America. Because bankers decide who gets loans and realtors decide, through their realty boards, who is to be allowed to buy where, their decisions determined, within the limits of cultural values, the face of American cities. They decided the areas in which Negroes would live and the quality of housing they would have. They determined when deteriorating areas were to be permitted to switch from single-family dwellings to multi-family apartments and rooming houses. They selected sites for parks (if any), business areas, and factories and established a basic policy of urban growth

[1] Thomas H. Reed, **Municipal Management**, McGraw-Hill Book Company, New York, 1941, p. 304.

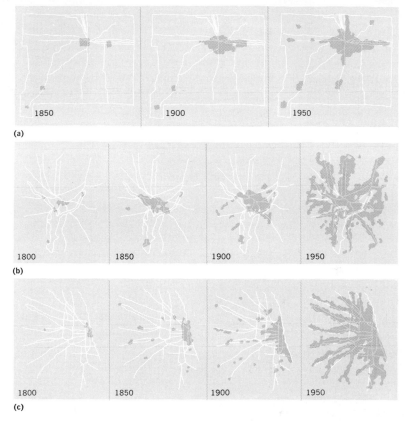

Fig. 20-1   Cities Usually Grow in a Spider Web Fashion.
(a) St. Joseph County, Indiana; (b) Washington, D.C.; (c) Chicago.
SOURCE: City Planning Commission, **Our Community,** City of Mishawaka, Ind., 1956.

through exodus and conversion, so that home construction took place for higher-income persons only (except for tenements), others taking the vacated property according to their status positions. It was a game of providing according to ability to pay with little concern for the decaying ugliness at the center.

But as American cities began to mature, this pattern changed. Some influential persons began to become concerned with growing blight. Property owners began to fear for the income value of the older sections. The retreating upper middle class began to run into rural- and fringe-area slums. Attitudes toward the uninhibited activities of private business began to change.

In 1907, a permanent planning commission as a municipal agency was established at Hartford, Connecticut. It set a pattern that has commonly been followed ever since. Once began, the movement spread rapidly, and in the 1960s 90 percent of the cities of 10,000 population or larger had official planning commissions. At first, realtors sought to dominate the planning commissions and were often successful in doing so. Gradually, however, a broader representation has been developed, with various community interests, including homeowners, represented, though realtors remain dominant in many communities.

Planning Today   The American political system is designed for incremental change. Policies are modified bit by bit and there are large numbers of veto loci, so that any proposed change must successfully overcome a whole series of hurdles and never merely one. The system furthermore tends to be highly parochial in character. Legislators and councilmen, especially those elected by boards or districts, tend to take a very narrow view of their interests and responsibilities. Public policy is expected to be a compromise among a host of parochial interests. Political figures may be more interested in maintaining a working political alliance than in the content of policy. Central development of policy (as distinguished from policy positions of the executive) and comprehensive planning to meet developing social situations are the exception.

This pattern of policy development and short-range, as distinguished from long-range, planning has frequently been criticized. It seems likely that reformers who denounce it and call for comprehensive planning "with muscle in it" do not understand fully the implications for change in the American system that this implies. It would sharply diminish the number of interests having access to the governmental decision-making process and would eliminate from the representational system many groups in society. Furthermore, the critics make the normative judgment that a comprehensive policy which includes careful consideration of future probabilities is better than that which does not. This may not necessarily be the case. Edward Banfield has pointed out that while a typical citizen may believe that "common sense" would say that a *personal decision,* which by its nature is made by some individual or group as a deliberate act, is better than a *social choice,* which by its nature is the accidental by-product of interested parties, the social-choice process is one in which any number of actors—individuals, groups, or institutions—seek to achieve their own ends, taking no more heed of other actors than the political situation requires. Such an approach to policy making produces only "outcomes," and not deliberate "solutions." Despite the fact that this system makes no "common sense," its results do seem to be accepted by most people most of the time.[2] We should note, however, a strong trend in the present century toward executive planning of all types, budgetary, physical plan, capital program, and policy planning. These plans are rarely accepted in their entirety and, by the logic of the system, are not intended to be. Instead, they serve as effective resources in the bargaining process on behalf of those who support them, including usually the chief executive.

Urban planning—one of the increasingly important forms of planning—is a relatively new profession and because it is oriented toward a particular process of decision making rather than toward the application of a body of knowledge to a particular function of government, planners sometimes come into conflict with other professionals and the chief executive or legislative

[2] Edward C. Banfield, **Political Influence,** The Free Press of Glencoe, New York, 1961, pp. 326–327.

body sometimes has to settle the resulting jurisdictional disputes. As one planner has put it: [3]

The city planners have carved out a field of special competence that overlaps the professional areas of other specialists. They are working toward legal definition of their profession because they fear the encroachment of others upon the professional territory which they regard as their exclusive domain. On the other hand, architects, engineers, and lawyers have sometimes accused planners of practicing aspects of *their* professions without license to do so.

Conflicts have arisen also between city planners and city managers. Planners claim they have more competence than city managers in certain aspects of community development and that they should therefore take their recommendations directly to the public and elected officials. City managers as executive officers believe, however, that the planners should report to them.

The Federal government's influence on planning has not yet been great: [4]

Although planning requirements are almost universally imposed in one form or another . . . the largest number of programs that do so actively promote functional planning only, and do not relate the added function with other functions in a comprehensive plan designed to achieve orderly development of the entire urban area. A majority of the programs that do recognize comprehensive planning, do so only passively. They do not require that such planning be done, but that only if it is done, it should not be disregarded.

The Planning Commission The central planning agency is almost always headed by a commission which coordinates the plans of the various municipal departments and carries on planning activities of a communitywide nature. The planning commission usually has five or seven memebers but may have as many as fifty. It may be entirely ex officio, consisting of designated public officials, or it may be made up of citizens serving without pay, or some combination of these two.

The problems facing planning commissioners are many. They are usually subjected to great pressures from land developers or realtors who may regard them more as obstacles in their particular business than as guardians of broader community interests. Commissioners may be urged to seek locations for industry in order to strengthen the local tax base, but almost any sites they select will be highly controversial—each citizen wants the industrial zone as far from his home as is physically possible. The commissioners are typically laymen, lacking in any technical knowledge of planning or sometimes even a knowledge as to what planning seeks to do. Yet professional staff is expensive and usually is ill provided for in commission budgets, since this agency lacks a clear-cut constituency to fight for it before the governing board at budget time. It lacks status, too, for although membership on the commission may

[3] Joseph M. Heikoff, "Planning Is the Responsibility of the Executive," **Public Management,** 47:156–161, July, 1965.
[4] Subcommittee on Intergovernmental Relations, Committee on Government Operations, United States Senate, **Impact of Federal Urban Development Programs on Local Government Organization and Planning,** 1964, p. 22.

be sought by "civic-minded" citizens, the typical resident is likely to view it as a haven for idle dreamers. The commission often lacks public, political, or administrative support, the last of these because various administrative agencies, like the realtors and bankers, have their own vested interests to which the planning commission is a potential threat. Planners in the agencies dealing with streets, housing, recreation, traffic control, industrial development, and others may fear that the commission will not give sufficient attention to the items they consider of top priority. Yet, lay concerns with the effects of possible land uses are becoming intensified, and with this trend, planning commissions are rising in status as well as in power in public policy making.

Planning is concerned not only with streets, utilities, and the regulation of private property, but also with parks, recreation, housing, slum clearance, airports, traffic, parking, public health, and a host of other things. It "is essentially a process of understanding human needs and of influencing and shaping future public policy to serve those needs most effectively." [5] Using prevailing cultural values and professional criteria, it seeks to correct or minimize the effects of past mistakes and to avoid them in future development.

The planning staff collects socioeconomic and population data; it offers community decision makers suggestions concerning alternative courses of action; it prepares brochures concerning the attractiveness of the community for industry, business, and residence; and it does the staff work in preparation for zoning and subdivision control decisions.[6]

The Plan   After a planning commission is established, a staff of professional planners may be hired (in other than large cities, a consulting firm may be retained instead, or a state agency may provide technical assistance). Surveys are made and basic data are gathered. It then becomes the job of the commission to interpret the data and to develop plans to fit it. Space must be allocated for various types of home building, for commerce, for light and heavy industry, for recreation, and for traffic flow. A master capital-improvements plan may be developed to supplement the land-use recommendations. The plan as it finally emerges will be a compromise between the professional recommendations of the staff and the demands of various interests which make their views known to the commission and the local governing body (see Figure 20-2).

Planning is a continuous operation, however. New data and new interpretations of the data must be constantly made by the commission in the light of unanticipated community developments. Master plans suffer from fairly rapid obsolescence. In 1791 Pierre L'Enfant drew up a master plan for the new city of Washington and his imagination was so wonderful and his foresight so great that the plan has never received serious alteration. Brigham Young demonstrated imagination in laying out Salt Lake City, but even his vision could not anticipate the crowded automobile traffic of today. The mag-

[5] D. H. Webster, **Urban Planning and Municipal Public Policy,** Harper & Row, Publishers, Incorporated, New York, 1958, p. 4.
[6] Charles E. Patterson, "The Politics of Planning in Small Cities," **Newsletter,** Bureau of Community Planning, University of Illinois, Urbana, Ill., November, 1963.

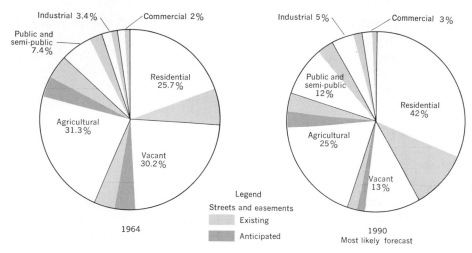

Industrial 3.4%   Commercial 2%

Public and
semi-public
7.4%

Residential
25.7%

Agricultural
31.3%

Vacant
30.2%

1964

Industrial 5%   Commercial 3%

Public and
semi-public
12%

Residential
42%

Agricultural
25%

Vacant
13%

1990
Most likely forecast

Legend
Streets and easements
☐ Existing
■ Anticipated

Fig. 20-2   Land Uses in Cities Are Expected to Change in the Next Generation.
SOURCE: City Planning Department, **Population,** City of Kansas City, Mo., 1964.

nificent boulevards of his city came about because he wanted to allow room for a Conestoga wagon to make a U-turn without backing up.

Most planners must start by accepting the existing situation, a heritage from the past that is not always fully welcome. They must make changes slowly and against the resistance of inertia and vested interests. Planners are rarely men of the vision of a L'Enfant. Even if they are, they encounter difficulties in long-range planning. A plan in the early nineteenth century founded upon a system of water transportation would have to be seriously altered with the coming of the railroad. Later, the automobile would require even greater changes. And the best plans laid out in 1850 or 1900 could not have made proper arrangements for an airport at a logical and convenient location.

Land-use Controls   The master plan drawn up by the commission is not usually enacted into law but serves as a basic guide for legislative and administrative officials. The governing body may instead formally adopt a map that becomes the official statement of policy. The policies implied in the map or in statements of principle that sometimes accompany it are put into effect through three types of land-use controls: subdivision regulations, zoning, and building construction codes.

Subdividing   Control over subdividing—the parceling of land into lots —is basic to the implementation of a plan. Subdividing is accomplished by requiring the land developer to present a "plat," that is, a map showing some or all of the following: lot sizes and shapes, utilities, topography, soil types, street sizes and patterns, and other relevant data. This plat must be in conformity with established policy and may be subject to review by the planning commission, as well as by health, highway, and other authorities before it is approved. No land can be built upon until a plat is approved, though platting may not be required in commercial, industrial, or rural nonfarm areas. With this control, planners can prevent the development of land without provision for necessary services.

Where subdivision regulations are vague or nonexistent, land developers have sometimes subdivided far beyond the foreseeable needs of a community and have pressured the governing body into furnishing utilities to otherwise vacant subdivisions. This, in effect, forces the taxpayers to subsidize speculation in real estate.[7]

Zoning   The control of the height, area, and the use of buildings or lots may be achieved either by zoning or by subdivision deed restrictions. The former is public policy enforceable at law, while the latter are private contractual relationships enforceable in civil action before the courts. Subdivision deed restrictions are often used to protect property values where inadequate or no zoning exists. They are not a substitute for zoning, however, for in order to enforce their provisions, a resident must bring a court action against the violator. This is expensive, time-consuming, perhaps embarrassing, and often not worth the bother.

Zoning has now become the standard method of ensuring the efficient use of land and of enforcing many of the provisions of the master plan. The community is normally divided up into residential, commercial, and industrial zones, and perhaps into further subcategories within these. Zones should not be taken too literally, however, as being belts or areas of the community. A zone may be very small: it may be a narrow strip along a street or railroad track—or it may be a single lot. The location of a single lot or of a few lots of one classification in the midst of a more preferred type—"spot zoning"—may be very profitable to an owner able to sell a lot in an area zoned for single-family homes to a filling-station or grocery-store operator. But it means a loss in the total value of the community. Because this loss is socialized among many persons who individually have less incentive to exert pressure than does the individual, such practices take place with frequency in some communities, sometimes reducing to an absurdity the concept of zoning.

Zoning decisions may, however, involve large sums of money. In Montgomery County, Maryland, the rezoning of 4,100 acres of land over a two-year period increased its value by $100 million. A 3-acre school site in the San Fernando Valley of Los Angeles, worth $35,000 in 1959, sold for $3 million in 1965, after it was rezoned for commercial use. An elderly lady in Washington, D.C., poor except for her ownership of 48 acres of nonproductive farmland near the city, sold her property for $1 million after it was rezoned for urban use. Her windfall was exceptional, however. Usually well-to-do speculators buy land that may be developed well before its potential value is recognized. Although they take the risk of losing a rezoning fight and must often tie up funds for many years before they receive a payoff, they are generally the major profit makers when land-use commitments are changed.[8]

---

[7] See Harold W. Lautner, **Subdivision Regulations,** Public Administration Service, Chicago, 1941; P. H. Cornick, **Premature Subdivision and Its Consequences,** Institute of Public Administration, Columbia University, New York, 1938.
[8] **Look,** Oct. 5, 1965.

Building Construction Codes   A community with land-use controls will have one or more building codes. These are usually known as building, plumbing, electrical, heating, and safe and sanitary housing codes. They seek to enforce the subdivision and zoning regulations and the housing standards desired in the community by requiring permits to build or install equipment. Inspections determine whether or not compliance has taken place or, in the case of safe and sanitary housing ordinances, is being maintained.

The building inspector, or zoning administrator, "can destroy the effectiveness of the [zoning ordinance or building code] by overlooking violations or permitting exceptions to the regulations." [9] He is subjected to great pressures and temptations. The physical appearance, not to say the reputation, of a community may depend upon his competence and incorruptibility. Because of inadequate codes and poor enforcement procedures, FHA regulations have, especially on the outer fringe, often given home buyers more protection than have those of the local government. [10]

Planning in the Suburbs   Urban areas have adopted procedures for planning and zoning, though long after they were first needed. Today, the principal growth in urban areas is on the periphery, and it is here, where planning and zoning are most needed today, that they are most often absent. Some efforts are being made to compensate for this pattern through county planning and zoning, and extraterritorial zoning jurisdiction for municipalities.

Suburbs, especially in their earliest years of development, are characterized by several factors that lead to blight. Premature subdividers are normally little supervised within the core city. In suburbs, and especially in unincorporated areas, they may encounter virtually no restrictions at all. They may be responsible for erratic, unplanned use of land. The outer fringe, which in a few years is to become an inner fringe, is characteristically the area where individuals try to build their own homes or purchase jerry-built shacks. With no building code or a very inadequate one, it may be possible for the person who cannot afford to build or buy a home in the city to construct one in the fringe area. He may be able to afford one that has too little floor space or is of too flimsy construction to meet the core-city building regulations.

In a few years, the outer fringe becomes truly suburban, with much subdividing and building. But the new homes are now interspersed with dilapidated shacks and nonconforming buildings according to the belatedly adopted zoning ordinances. In quite a number of metropolitan areas, a greater percentage of substandard and dilapidated homes exists in the suburbs than in the core city.

---

[9] Webster, *op. cit.*, p. 424.
[10] There is considerable material dealing with planning and zoning. See Webster, *op. cit.*, as well as his citations and those in Charles R. Adrian, **Governing Urban America**, 2d ed., McGraw-Hill Book Company, New York, 1961, chap. 20. A consideration of planning in light of population projections for the future is given in a series of articles in **Architectural Forum**, vol. 104, September, 1956. The realtors' point of view is stated in R. L. Nelson and F. T. Aschmen, **Real Estate and City Planning**, Urban Land Institute, Washington, D.C., 1957. A major concern of planners and businessmen is the threatened decay of the central business district. See John Rannels, **The Core of the City**, Columbia University Press, New York, 1956.

STATE AND LOCAL GOVERNMENTS

There are some exceptional situations around the nation, and certainly the new homeowners of suburbia quickly grasp the importance of planning and effective land-use controls in relation to their investment; but the major problem remains: chaotic land usage until the area becomes quite heavily populated and then a belated attempt to prevent the building of any more individual shacks. But by this time the opportunity for maximum efficiency of land use is probably gone forever.

Efforts at Metropolitan Planning Because our metropolitan areas are atomized politically while planning must by its nature extend continuously across the land, a hiatus exists between the need for planning and its political practicality. In order to fill this gap, somewhat of a trend has developed toward the development of metropolitan planning commissions or joint city-county commissions. Often these groups are private and unofficial, sometimes they are extralegal, or are provided for by state enabling acts, but almost always they are advisory only and have no coercive powers. Some of them have their own staffs, but quite a few share the staff of the core-city planning commission. Some have no staffs at all, but merely operate through occasional meetings.

Planning for utilities, parks and recreation, highways, the location of industry, and many other urban matters might logically be approached on an area or regional rather than a city basis. But it has been generally impossible to find a politically expedient method of representing the many communities of the area in a planning organization with effective powers over land use. Although metropolitan-area studies often recommend that planning should be a function of any areawide government that might be established, this function is undoubtedly one over which local landowners most want to keep control close to themselves.

The Federal government has urged metropolitan planning by requiring it as a condition of receiving certain grants-in-aid. Thus the Federal Aid Highway Act provides the beginning in 1965—highway projects in metropolitan areas will not be approved unless "such projects are based on a continuing comprehensive transportation plan in process, carried on cooperatively by states and local communities." When this requirement went into effect on July 1, 1965, only about one-third of the 216 metropolitan areas had existing planning programs that could qualify or could easily be made to qualify under the requirements of the Act.[11]

State Planning Organizations The idea of any kind of controls that would inhibit property owners from determining the use to which they should put their land was viewed with horror in the years before the Great Depression. Three decades later, it was still not fully accepted. But interest in controls has expanded, even at the state level.

The first semblance of state planning came in the 1930s, when grants-in-aid through the National Resources Planning Board encouraged states to

---

[11] Subcommittee on Intergovernmental Relations, Committee on Government Operations, United States Senate, **Metropolitan Planning**, 1963, p. 27.

establish planning boards. These agencies gathered a good deal of data and began to make moves toward statewide land-use plans, but when the Federal government withdrew its support in the conservative period of the late 1940s, many of them disappeared. The Housing Act of 1954, however, provided for the distribution of Federal redevelopment money through state planning agencies, and again gave impetus to demands for some kind of state organization.

In the 1960s, no more than one-fourth of the states had effective planning agencies at work. Most of the others designated agencies whose principal responsibilities were to attract tourists or new industries or were designated simply to qualify the state for redevelopment aid. In the 1960s and 1970s, states are expected, by some specialists, to become increasingly important institutions for the provision of regional (including metropolitan) planning.

Conservation and Recreation

Conservation has long been established as essentially a national or state government function. Parks and recreation activities, on the other hand, are engaged in by all governments, including special districts and school districts. Actually, conservation, parks, and recreation activities are three different functions supported by varying and sometimes conflicting interest groups. But they are often lumped together into a single state or local agency, which acts as a kind of holding company, administering each program on a more or less autonomous basis. These activities are, furthermore, not restricted to public-agency operations. Many recreation programs are operated by private agencies (such as the YMCA or CYO) financed by voluntary contributions, endowments, or bequests. And, in the field of conservation, a large lumbering firm has emphasized in its advertising that it plants a tree for each one it cuts down. The ubiquitous Federal government, of course, also operates in each of these areas.

Public policies relative to conservation and natural resources "have not been rooted in explicit, fully developed ideological concepts. Instead, they have grown out of the necessities and desires to deal with narrowly defined problems." This program area thus serves as a paradigm of the American politico-governmental process which stresses pragmatic problem solving. Among the persons with ideas concerning public policy in this area, the two areas of agreement among them concern, first, the social character of the interests in conservation and resource development, and second, a consensus on the notion that only government can ultimately achieve the desired goals.[12]

Natural Resources   The conservation movement began as a Federal activity, and most of the state programs have been pale imitations of the ideals expressed by Theodore Roosevelt and Gifford Pinchot at the beginning of the century. The states are not natural units for resources administration and their activities in the area have not only been generally haphazard if not inept, but

[12] Norman Wengert, "The Ideological Basis of Conservation and Natural-resources Policies and Programs," **Annals**, 344:65–75, November, 1962.

they have tended to be dominated frequently by the very interests which they were established to control. Thus, forestry programs have often been dominated by lumbering companies; Western water policies, by irrigators; Eastern water policies, by industrial users.

States have passed laws and appropriated moneys for the administration of programs dealing with protecting forest lands and with reforestation. They seek to control the water resources and grazing lands of the state. They try to develop fish and game resources, particularly if a tourist industry is supported by the state. Yet, one observer has concluded: [13]

In most states some resource agencies are doing an effective job on some phases of resources administration, such as the development of state parks, the management of state lands, forest fire prevention and the conservation of wild life; but no state is carrying on a well coordinated multiple-purpose program of resource administration.

Issues of Policy   Public-policy questions abound in connection with hunting, fishing, and the preservation of natural resources. Many interest groups are organized around these activities. In general, they claim to want better recreation areas, a maintenance of existing forests, and better conditions for hunting and fishing. These interests are frequently tied up, of course, with those of the tourist and resort industry, which is important in many states. Examples of these groups include state united conservation clubs (to represent collective conservation interests), state tourist bureaus, the Michigan Bear Hunters' Association, and the state federations of garden clubs.

Conflicts among groups in the field of conservation and between them and other groups are many. Hence, hunters want liberal open seasons, but resort owners and businessmen in hunting areas want seasons restrictive enough to keep the supply of game at or near capacity levels. Farmers and landowners want the state to assist in the draining of marshland (it would greatly increase the value of the land), but conservationists and sportsmen want to preserve marshland, which is vital for good duck hunting. In nearly all of the Western states, state agencies control water use in one way or another. Here conservationists and farmers disagree on the use of irrigation. In nonarid Eastern states, a potential conflict exists between agricultural interests which are increasingly seeking supplementary irrigation rights and fishermen who oppose stream pollution, for excessive use of water for irrigation results in stream levels that are too low to treat sewage and industrial wastes properly.

A conflict over land use exists in some parts of the nation between recreation and the production of petroleum. Oil wells, when successfully drilled, provide jobs and income for many persons. On the other hand, land which has been reserved for recreational uses can be destroyed by oil well drilling. Not only is the landscape made ugly, but a successful well attracts homes and trailers and, in the absence of careful and expensive controls, will result in polluted streams which are destroyed for fishing purposes.

[13] Vincent Ostrom, "State Administration of Natural Resources in the West," **American Political Science Review**, 47:478–493, June, 1953. Quotation from p. 493.

Governments at all three levels have been attempting in recent years to save the American ocean and lake shoreline. These areas have been disappearing rapidly and available sites are highly attractive to private developers, who hope to profit from the view from their shoreline apartments, a view which they have not purchased, but which is potentially extremely profitable to them. In the New York borough of Queens, for example, an attempt was made to establish a park on the ocean front at Breezy Point. Those favoring the park included an *ad hoc* group, the Committee for a Park at Breezy Point, the Regional Plan Association of New York, the Metropolitan Council on Housing, the Citizens' Committee for Children, the National Association for the Advancement of Colored People, and the Urban League. Opponents of the park included the Queens' Chamber of Commerce, the Rockaway Council of Civic Organizations, the Breezy Point Cooperative, and the Atlantic Improvement Corporation. The last of these was a firm proposing to build apartments on the site of the proposed park.[14]

Most persons interested in the field of conservation and natural resources agree that government plays a properly important role in their use and control. Within this general area of agreement, however, are many ideological differences. One of the conflicts involves a difference in emphasis between a concern for the use of natural resources to benefit people and a concern for preserving nature, as such. The constitution of New York, for example, requires that state forests are to be maintained "forever wild," emphasizing the preservation of natural phenomena rather than the use of these resources to benefit people under the control of professional foresters.[15]

Parks and Recreation   Parks and recreation programs are sometimes administered by the same agency; sometimes they are separated. Both state and local governments operate parks; recreation programs are often in the hands of city and school district governments.

Recreation programs are designed to provide activities for youngsters during the summer months, especially in the crowded sections of cities. But they are also planned by recreationists for all ages and for all seasons of the year. Programs for older persons are becoming increasingly important. A recreation program may include "rifle clubs, junior symphonies, dog obedience classes, toy workshops, baton twirling classes, charm schools, Hallowe'en window painting classes, show wagons, and drama clubs." [16]

Little planning for parks took place in early American cities. Either these areas of grass, shrubs, flowers, and birds were not provided for at all, or they were located wherever some local philanthropist happened to own land that he chose to leave to the city. Through special efforts, some cities—such as Minneapolis, Chicago, and Boston—have provided beautiful park systems, but many communities are forced to develop park sites miles beyond the corporate limits. Where this is the case, it causes inconvenience and traffic haz-

---

[14] **New York Times,** July 22, 1963.
[15] Wengert, *op. cit.*
[16] George D. Butler, "Parks and Recreation Developments in 1952," **Municipal Year Book, 1953,** International City Managers' Association, Chicago, 1953, p. 470.

ards on weekends. To those in the lowest-income group, who have no automobiles but who most need the facilities, these areas are often quite inaccessible.

After the automobile became the property of the average man, many counties and states began to develop park systems. Increasing urbanization has also made the public park more important. While city parks have traditionally been laid out in the style of an English country gentleman's estate, parks of the automobile age have tended to appeal to the "back to nature" interests. The result has been the development of parks not laid out in formal design, but that retain their natural topography and flora and fauna. Recreational facilities now often include those for camping sites which can be used for tents or house trailers. Swimming, picnicking, fishing, boating, hiking, and nature study are activities that citizens wish to engage in at state, regional, or county parks.

Issues and conflicts in parks administration are varied and complex. The tourist industry wants to encourage the development of parks as an added attraction for its clientele. But resort owners do not want state parks of such excellence that people who can afford to pay for private recreational facilities will not feel the desire to do so. Motel owners do not want overnight facilities to be so adequate that they will attract others than those who want to rough it. An important issue concerns admission fees for park use. Legislatures tend to adopt a benefit theory of taxation wherever they find that the public will accept this approach, and they therefore look hopefully toward the use of fees for park financing. Liberals tend to disapprove of this method, pointing out that higher-income persons use private resorts but that public parks are for the persons whose vacation budgets are modest. Yet, one study indicated that only 7 percent of actual state park users were opposed to any fee system.[17] Cities do not charge fees, and the urban park is ill suited for it, but many suburbs require a car sticker or property tax receipt for admission as a means of reserving their parks for use by their own residents.

Agriculture

State and county governments carry on programs designed to promote agricultural production and improve rural life. The best known program of agricultural assistance is the Cooperative Extension Service, which is staffed and financed jointly by the Federal, state, and county governments, with the program coordinated through each of the state agricultural colleges. Much of the research in the field of agriculture is performed by the state colleges, assisted by considerable Federal aid.

The state governments carry on regulatory activities designed to control plant and animal diseases and harmful insects. They inspect food, dairy herds, and meat. Other activities include the grading of agricultural products, control

[17] T. L. Dahle, **Michigan State Park Users Survey,** Michigan Department of Conservation, Lansing, Mich., 1956, table 6.

of farmers' and public markets, and a variety of policing activities loosely related to agriculture and often historically of concern to farmers, such as inspection of weights and measures. The Cooperative Extension Service is essentially an educational program, though it also acts as a technical consulting agency. Its services extend to the 4-H program for young people, home economics demonstrations, soil surveys, land-use studies, and many other activities. States also have programs in soil conservation.

The counties are also important units of government in agricultural work. They pay the travel and office-maintenance costs of the local county agricultural agent. Since the county governing board has the final decision in the selection of the agent, this person, though a staff member of the state agricultural college, is subjected to heavy local sanctions and tends to fit his program to prevailing local cultural values. Counties vary as to the services they provide for farmers, but the following are sometimes included: weed-eradication programs and the operation of limestone quarries and of agricultural marketing centers. They also administer some state regulatory programs.

Agricultural and Rural Interest Although rural life, once romanticized by farmer, politician, and rural sociologist, is becoming each year less distinguishable from urban life, interests of those who live on farms and in small towns still differ from those of persons in larger communities. Most state constitutions were written when farmers made up a majority of the population, and rural groups now oppose constitutional conventions that might reconsider legislative apportionment. They would almost certainly lose political strength by any reapportionment.

The values of rural dwellers still tend to emphasize the importance of self-sufficiency. This comes into conflict with the urbanite's interest in unemployment compensation, retirement benefits, programs for assistance to the aged, welfare legislation of many types, and other social service programs. Conflicts on a rural versus urban basis also center around the formula for allocating grants-in-aid to education and for the distribution of gasoline tax moneys. But a large and increasing number of "farmers" are actually employed in cities and farm on a part-time basis. They are often subjected to numerous cross pressures. Many of them, for example, belong to both farm and labor organizations simultaneously.

Because of the historical pattern of representation before state legislatures, agricultural groups have tended to be powerful beyond the size of their membership in society. Strangely enough, county governments where a medium- or large-sized city is part of the county have been less gerrymandered than are state governments as a general pattern. Under both the commissioner and supervisor form of county government, giving control to the rural minority is more difficult than is the same feat at the state level.

The principal farm groups include the Farm Bureau Federation, conservative, especially strong in the corn belt of the Midwest and the cotton belt of the central South, and generally representative of the interests of the more prosperous farmers; the Grange, older, at least as conservative, and especially strong in the East and New England; and the Farmers Union, liberal to radical, strong in the wheat belt extending from Texas to the Dakotas, and elsewhere generally representative of the low-income, marginal farmer.

It must not be assumed that farmers, any more than businessmen, labor leaders, or sportsmen, are always united. The kinds of conflicts that may exist may be demonstrated from the Minnesota scene of the depression-ridden 1930s when Governor Floyd B. Olson presented a plan for a Rural Credit Bureau which was to advance loans to farmers threatened with losing their farms. His plan failed because the less-hard-hit farmers of southern Minnesota (corn-hog and Farm Bureau country) felt that it was a scheme by which they would, through their tax payments, bail out the bankrupt farmers of the northern part of the state (wheat and Farmers Union country).

Corn-belt farmers are relatively prosperous and essentially conservative; the cotton belt is naturally a plantation economy, and the Bourbon families tend to control its politics; the wheat belt is politically volatile, and its degree of radicalism varies inversely with the price of wheat; dairying regions are generally prosperous and conservative. However, technological developments in agriculture are making more and more farmers marginal operators who are gradually being forced off the farm into urban living. These changes are putting ever greater amounts of pressure upon state legislatures to assist the large numbers of farmers who are chronically in difficulties. These farmers are less well represented by interest groups than are their more successful neighbors, but legislators are aware of their voting strength. Most of the pressures for subsidies and other forms of financial assistance have been aimed at Congress, but state legislatures feel them, too, particularly in the form of demands for tax relief and privileges and for restrictions in expenditures for strictly urban services.

The Issue of Farm Policy   Although the farmer has been urged since the 1870s to "raise less corn and more hell," the tendency has been for him to raise more of each. The result has been continuing political pressure of a type designed to be of the greatest help to the marginal farmer in the short run but of the least help in finding a long-range agricultural policy that fits the needs of American society generally. The problem is too complex to be considered here, but the long-range tendency is for a smaller percentage of the total population in each generation to produce the foods and fibers needed by all. And with the farmer's way of life becoming ever more potentially like that of the urbanite, "agribusiness" is gradually coming to replace the rural way of life. But the transition, and especially the transplantation of thousands of families who prefer to remain where they are into urban settings, will produce many painful problems. State and local governments will be called upon to assist in providing retraining programs, temporary public assistance, effective land-retirement plans, and in many other ways. The problem will by no means be exclusively one for the Federal government.

Water Policies

Probably no single governmental domestic policy is of more importance to the future pattern of development of the United States than is that of water. It has been said, without exaggeration, that "you could write the story of man's growth in terms of his epic concerns with water." [18] Man is utterly dependent upon it. It determined where he first settled as he moved into new lands. It dictates the location of most heavy industry. It controls the size to which a city, whether it be Denver, New York, or Los Angeles, may grow. It limits possible land uses. Its quality affects the state of the public health, the size of the municipal budget, and the taste of a highball. Its quantity determines whether bluegrass lawns may be watered in August, a rowboat must be kept in the garage as an escape vehicle from a flash flood, or the economy of a resort area will flourish or wither. In all aspects of water policy, government, national, state, and local, is involved.

The importance of water to social and economic development is dramatically shown in the state of Hawaii. The island of Oahu is the third largest in the island state, but it has 80 percent of the state's population. The other islands have all of the same attractions as does Oahu, with one difference: On no other island is a plentiful supply of fresh water available. The mountainous backbone of Oahu consists of porous rocks that catch and retain rain water. The other islands of the state will be restricted in the number of residents they can support until an inexpensive process of desalination of sea water is developed.

Changing Needs   Although the population of the United States only doubled between 1900 and 1955, per capita use of water quadrupled. This was a result not only of changing agricultural and industrial uses but also of the labor-saving devices that have been adopted in the contemporary home: the garbage grinder, the automatic washing machine, the dishwasher, and the air-conditioning unit.

Here are some relevant facts:

1. The average American family used at least 145 gallons of water a day for household needs in 1958. It used less than 95 gallons in 1890.

2. Homes with garbage grinders discharge 50 percent more organic matter into sewers than those without them. This adds greatly to the sewage-treatment problem and potentially to water pollution and to the existence of favorable conditions for the growth of fish in streams.

3. Commercial uses of water are enormous. Domestic uses of water account for only about 5 percent of the total. The rest is divided about equally between irrigation and industrial uses, the latter of which is growing much faster than the former. It requires about 110 gallons of water to manufacture

[18] Bernard Frank, "The Story of Water as the Story of Man," in Alfred Stefferud (ed.), **Water**, Government Printing Office, Washington, D.C., 1955.

a pound of rayon, 300 gallons for a gallon of beer, 65,000 gallons for a ton of steel, and 600,000 gallons for a ton of synthetic rubber.[19]

4. Both industrial and domestic effluent produce problems of water pollution that affect the welfare of downstream communities, of fish and game, and of recreation programs. Of approximately 16,000 American communities that have public water systems, only 9,000 have sewer systems, and of these no more than 6,000 are connected to sewage-treatment plants.

5. Increasing urban usage of lands adds to flood hazards and drainage problems, for land largely covered by roofs and concrete has much greater runoff than does other land.

6. The increasing concentration of the population in urban clusters involving a small percentage of the total land area has added greatly to the problem both of obtaining adequate water and of disposing of treated and untreated wastes.

Water Control and Supply Programs   The responsibility for getting the right amount of water of the right quality in the right place at the right time is shared by national, state, and local governments. The nature of the problems involved varies geographically and according to use. In the East, for example, the principal problems center around the distribution and quality of water; in the West, the major concern is with quantity. Some industries may be able to use raw water, whereas others need the highest quality; but much of the need is taken care of by industry itself, and governments need concern themselves only about regulation. Because water resources do not follow state or local boundaries, intergovernmental arrangements and potential problems and conflicts abound. Increasingly the states must arbitrate interlocal disputes and the Federal government those that are interstate.

Local Activities   Municipal and other local governments bear the primary responsibility for water supply for household use and much of it for industry. They are also basically responsible for sewage treatment, including septic-tank installation practices, and for the carrying off of rain water through storm drains and holding back floods through the construction (often with the aid of Federal funds) of levees and retaining walls. All of these activities cost a good deal of money. Sewerage and sewage-disposal plants are among the most expensive of municipal capital outlays, and great controversies center about the means of financing them and of holding costs to a minimum. Public forums in a city considering a new sewage-disposal plant give one the distinct impression that every taxpayer is also an expert in sanitary engineering. Storm drains, too, are matters of great concern to citizens—though usually only during wet springs. A complex cost-benefit problem is frequently involved. As a result, the citizen feels convinced in April that a new storm-drain system in his neighborhood is necessary at any cost. By August, he has forgotten his earlier view and is now certain that larger water mains or better supply sources are needed so as to make it possible for him to preserve the color of his precious bluegrass during dry spells.

[19] **State Administration of Water Resources,** Council of State Governments, Chicago, 1957, p. 5.

Water-supply problems of cities are as old as are cities themselves. In America, searches for more and better water used to follow disastrous fires and terrible epidemics, such as the cholera wave of 1832 that convinced New Yorkers to try the then daring engineering feat of going 30 miles to the Croton River for safe water.[20]

Waste Disposal   The frontier approach to garbage, sewage, and industrial waste disposal was to dump it in the nearest stream or body of water. America's waste production is so high now, however, that this simple and relatively inexpensive method will no longer satisfy health requirements. Lake Erie is already so badly polluted that it cannot cleanse itself and large areas of the lake contain "dead" or inert water, useless to both man and fish. Indeed: [21]

Americans now find themselves faced with the fact that the wastes exceed the ability of the surface waters to absorb them. Indeed, where septic tanks are close, even the earth is spongy with wastes that befoul the underground water. The situation is in crisis; the problem must be met, and no longer by half-hearted, meagerly, half-financed measures.

Despite the health hazards presented by inadequate sewage disposal facilities, even the more densely populated metropolitan areas do not have complete sewage-disposal facilities. The Philadelphia metropolitan area, for example, has nearly 900,000 of its people in homes not connected to sewers; this is 18 percent of the total population of the area.[22]

Politically, the popular thing for both builders and local office holders in the outer ring of suburbs had been to encourage the use of septic tanks. If their effort is successful, new home buyers can incorporate the cost of sewage disposal into the mortgage loan while the older resident of the area are not forced to help pay for expensive disposal facilities which they would not have needed if the area had remained sparsely settled. Thus, on the outer fringes of the Philadelphia area: [23]

In the early days of the post-war housing boom, there was little effort to control on-lot disposal, either by zoning or subdivision regulations of municipalities, or by the regulations of state or municipal health departments. The widespread and sometimes dramatic failures of on-lot facilities had only begun to make their appearance. The need for controls had not yet made itself felt.

Municipalities now receiving the brunt of suburban growth generally try to forestall the need for sewers and treatment plants by permitting on-lot disposal, but subjecting it to regulation under zoning, subdivision, or sanitation ordinances.

Generally speaking, large-lot zoning has been local government's answer to the rising cost of providing public services. If lots are large enough, the assumption is that sewer systems will not be required, and there will be fewer children for the community to educate. But large-lot zoning carries with it many hidden costs. . . .

[20] Nelson M. Blake, **Water for the Cities**, Syracuse University Press, Syracuse, New York, 1957.
[21] Robert Rienow and Leona T. Rienow, "Last Chance for the Nation's Waterways," **Saturday Review**, May 22, 1965, p. 35.
[22] John W. Bodine and others, **Sewage Disposal in the Penjerdel Region**, Penjerdel, Philadelphia, 1964.
[23] *Ibid.*

Suburban residents on large lots are willing, apparently, to pay these and other costs for the sake of their particular way of life.

Today, water supply is regarded as vital for the operation of a modern home and for the irrigation of suburban lawns and gardens. But it is also at times a matter of sheer survival, if we judge from the public reaction in New York, which had serious water-supply problems in 1949 and 1950 as a result of inadequate rainfall. At the time, there were [24]

daily front-page bulletins showing net gains and losses of precious water in city reservoirs; periodic prayers for rain offered at St. Patrick's Cathedral; fantastic solutions suggested by panicky citizens; bathless Fridays; official announcements that beards will be considered municipal "badges of honor"; official New York City rainmakers who drive around in the Catskill reservoir area, their trailers emitting the magical silver iodide smoke to squeeze water out of reluctant clouds; complaints from sufficiently water-supplied suburbs that the city is thus causing unnecessary snowstorms.

During the serious water shortage in New York City in 1965, a committee appointed to study possible solutions to the problem urged that the city order that water meters be installed in each building in the city. It was estimated that at least 150 million gallons of water could be saved each day if persons were required to pay according to amount used rather than on a flat-rate basis. The project would cost considerable money for the purchase of the meters and the plan was generally unpopular politically. As a result, the proposal was vetoed by Mayor Robert F. Wagner. Opposition came not only from owners of single-family detached homes, but also from apartment house owners, who would, in effect, be called upon to bear responsibility for the water wastefulness of their clients, since there would only be one meter for each apartment house. Mayor Wagner said that unlimited water is "part of the social philosophy of the people of the city," even though the city every few years is threatened with the exhaustion of its water supply and even though metering is a standard practice in almost all other American cities.[25] In early 1967, the New York water crisis remained unsolved.

State Activities   State governments increasingly are called upon to allocate as well as to preserve water resources. Pollution problems, especially in urbanized areas, are particularly keen. They are difficult to solve because, although the citizen will demand pure water from a health standpoint, he is concerned with sewage only to the extent that it is carried away from his home. Until recent years, it was common to dump it into the nearest lake or stream. The dangers created for the health of downstream residents and for fish and wildlife have made it necessary for the state to establish an agency to take a wider view than that of the local citizen, who is often concerned only with preventing pollution or offensive odors in his own community. State stream-control agen-

[24] Albert Lepawsky, "Water Resources and American Federalism," **American Political Science Review,** 44:639. Used by permission.
[25] **New York Times,** Aug. 20, 1965.

cies or environmental sanitation sections of health departments increasingly control the location and technical conditions of new sewage-treatment plants.[26] They may order suburbs that are polluting streams by overdependence upon septic tanks to install sewers and treatment plants. They may prevent a city from installing a plant that will be inadequate a few years after it is built or from dumping treatment-plant effluent too close to the water intake of a down-river community. In each of these cases, its orders will increase costs to the offending community, and this will result in anguished outcries followed by litigation; but the agency, through a competent and sufficient staff, has an obligation to protect the interests of other communities.

Water Quality Control The principal responsibility for the regulation of water quality is with the states. State agencies for water pollution control set standards, enforce laws and regulations, conduct surveys, and engage in research and planning activities. More than one-half of the states have water pollution control agencies. The others leave pollution control to state health departments or water resources agencies. All of the state health departments regulate to some degree water and sewage-disposal facilities in urban areas. In more than one-half of the states, the health agencies have some control over subdivision development relative to water- and sewage-disposal facilities proposed in new subdivisions. In most states the water pollution control agencies have power to establish quality standards and to determine the best social and economic use of waters. In seeking to enforce water quality standards, most state agencies rely on the cooperation of water users. This is a time-consuming procedure and efforts to abate certain types of pollution, especially industrial pollution that would be extremely costly to eliminate, may be dragged out for years. Regulations to conserve water have been politically unpopular and the same is true of efforts to abate pollution. Most of the states now can force municipalities as well as industries that are polluting streams and lakes to clean up the mess they are making, but enforcement efforts in most states have not been vigorous: [27]

The serious economic and political repercussion which can result from the enforcement of stringent provisions usually means that they are employed relatively rarely. . . . When the benefits of improved pollution abatement appear slight and the costs excessive, municipalities are likely to oppose the efforts of a State Pollution Control Agency with vigor. . . .

Perhaps the most potent constraint on State pollution control is competition for new industry and the fear of driving existing industries from the state. Industry, fearing the loss of competitive position if required to make up the tremendous backlog of industrial waste treatment, often has threatened to move. Differentials among the States in standards and levels of enforcement make these threats possible. Industrial groups generally favor pollution standards based on public health requirements, liberal dilution of untreated wastes, and strict controls only when the wastes have

[26] **State Administration of Water Resources,** Council of State Governments, Chicago, 1957.
[27] U.S. Advisory Commission on Intergovernmental Relations, **Intergovernmental Responsibilities for Water Supply and Sewage Disposal in Metropolitan Areas,** 1962, pp. 69–71.

been proved harmful. In many states industrial operators have shown relatively little concern for the recreational, wildlife, and esthetic values of water.

Although the political problems of ending industrial pollution are great, the technical problems are not. They are merely expensive. States with effective efforts to end industrial pollution generally require industry to submit plans and specifications for the treatment of wastes. If these meet state standards, the pollution control agency will issue a permit to install and operate the necessary equipment.

Waste Disposal Control   It has been commonplace for decision makers of industries which have large amounts of waste materials to insist upon state rather than Federal controls of standards in relation to water pollution. Thus, in 1965, the United States House of Representatives passed a bill leaving the question of quality of water to control by the states. Interest groups pressuring for state control in such cases seem to be more interested in avoiding any effective controls over their practices than in the principles of states' rights. Chemical and meat-packing firms, in particular, commonly emit large amounts of effluent. From their point of view, the most efficient disposal method is to dump the materials into a nearby body of water. Thus, as recently as 1966, the meat-packing plants of Omaha continued to dump their untreated refuse into the Missouri River.

Air Pollution Control   One of the major problems in contemporary metropolitan America is that of air pollution. The Federal government has restricted its activities to research and advice. Most states that have done anything at all have also restricted themselves to these functions. In 1961, however, only nine states were spending more than $25,000 annually on air pollution and the majority were spending nothing. Local governments and special districts are usually responsible for air pollution control, but they do not always have adequate legal authority from the state government to perform the task and eliminate the pollution. Furthermore, in metropolitan areas, local governments are generally not in a position to perform the task effectively. An areawide approach is necessary and in many industrial communities it is likely that the state is the most appropriate unit for air pollution, as it is for water pollution control. But the story is a familiar one: [28] "Although engineering methods are now available to combat most sources of air pollution, the states have generally failed to establish programs capable of solving the problem of air pollution control."

Noise Abatement   Another problem of metropolitan life is that of noise. Although the psychological costs cannot be calculated, they must be enormous. The problem is an old one, actually, and many communities enacted ordinances in the nineteenth century prohibiting dogs from barking or roosters from crowing between midnight and some hour of the morning. Many of these ordinances are still on the books, but they cannot usually be enforced. Industrial noises, which are among the most serious, have always been viewed as a

[28] Kenneth G. Bueche and Morris J. Schur, **Air Pollution Control**, Bureau of Governmental Research and Service, University of Colorado, Boulder, Colo., 1963, p. 28.

business cost to be socialized. State and local governments themselves are among the worst noise offenders, however, for the highway, street, and utilities jackhammer has become ubiquitous in American society. Although some efforts have been made at noise abatement, efforts by the mid-1960s were still timid on the part of both state and local governments.

Issues   Issues of policy are many in the water field. Northern California wants to keep its plentiful water supply as a hedge against the future. Southern California badly needs and wants the water now. Cities compete with irrigation farmers; they compete with other cities for the waters of the same stream or lake. One of the greatest struggles is over the question of the use of the appropriation doctrine or of the riparian doctrine of water rights. The latter is traditional and holds that persons who own or control rivers or lakes may freely use the water but must not materially decrease the flow or damage the quality. In water-scarce areas, this doctrine is inadequate. In the West, therefore, the appropriation doctrine was developed, which permits a person to file a claim, administered through a government agency, for a certain amount of water withdrawal. Water is distributed on a "first come, first served" basis. Interest in irrigation has spread toward the eastern part of the country and with it pressure to adopt the appropriation doctrine. Industry in some areas also favors it. But conservationists want to keep the riparian doctrine, since lowering of stream flow or lake levels is damaging to fish and game life. The issue will become intensified in the immediate future, as will issues related to water diversion for municipal use. As our population grows and concentrates in cities, water policies will be ever more sharply fought before city councils, in state legislatures, and in Congress. The fate of the nation is literally at stake in these decisions.

Highways

Nineteenth-century roads were nearly all rutted lanes, maintained by the most local of units of government and involving a very modest expenditure of public funds for maintenance. The predecessor of the modern gasoline tax was the road tax, but a man could, and often did, work on the road a certain number of days a year and supply a team of horses in lieu of payment. Toll roads, built by private companies, were constructed to connect some of the major cities, and the states appointed highway commissioners to provide some improved free roads. The Federal government entered the field in 1808 with Albert Gallatin's plan for a national turnpike through the Appalachian Mountains. This highway, the Cumberland Road, was built from Cumberland, Maryland, as far as Vandalia, Illinois, before Federal participation stopped. Road building, even in those days, was expensive. The mountainous portion of this first Federal-aid highway cost around $13,000 a mile (in early nineteenth-century dollars).

Early Highways   Basic transportation in frontier America was via waterways. Rivers were important highways, although they also were barriers to overland travel to the West (most American rivers flow in directions unsuited for the westward movement, the Ohio excepted). Canals were helpful though expensive. For much of the westward movement, land travel was necessary. Fords and ferryboats, which were cheaper than bridges, were used to cross streams. Travel on the Wilderness Road, the Natchez Trace, or the Boston Post Road was a memorable experience filled with hardships. After 1850, the ferryboat, stagecoach, and Conestoga wagon gave way to the railroads. Demands for first-rate highways were still decades away.

The automobile changed more than American travel and transportation practices. It created a new pattern of life, and this pattern has developed in a very short space of time. As late as 1906, Woodrow Wilson described the automobile as "a picture of the arrogance of wealth." Less than a decade later, Henry Ford had developed the assembly-line technique and was selling his Model T for $265. The motoring public soon became almost every adult in the country, and the campaign for adequate highways was under way.

In Europe, heavy taxes have continued to be imposed on the purchase, licensing, and fueling of motor vehicles, and this is regarded as equitable, since ownership is indicative of affluence. In the United States, however, taxes of these kinds are regarded as unfair levies on the common man if they are very heavy. The public has, however, generally accepted a benefit theory of taxation in connection with automobiles. Gasoline has come to have a highly inelastic demand, and the public pays taxes on it with perhaps less grumbling than results from taxes based on ability to pay. Motorists know that they can demand high-quality roads in return for payment of the gasoline tax.

Once the cost of the automobile dropped within range of the average wage earner, changes developed rapidly. The first mile of concrete highway was laid on Michigan's Saginaw Trail in 1909. In 1916, the first Federal-aid Highway Act was passed, and it prodded all states that had not already acted to establish highway departments. After World War I, powerful demands were heard for the construction of roads to connect the larger cities.[29] This was followed by demands to "get the farmer out of the mud." Roads could not be built fast enough to keep up with the number of vehicles using them. Congestion on city streets followed the construction of roads designed to bring people into the city. Road maintenance was transferred from the most local unit to the county and state. By the end of World War II, it was clear that highway-construction and road-design techniques had lagged behind demand and would have to be modernized.

Postwar Highway Planning   The Federal-aid Highway Act of 1921 had required state highway departments to plan interstate and intercounty routes in cooperation with the Federal Bureau of Public Roads and with neighboring states. This system was the only one that could receive Federal money. The Federal Aid Highway Act of 1944, anticipating postwar needs, built upon this pattern and made three major provisions for modernizing highways: (1) It recognized that a highway did not end at the city limits and that many of the worst trans-

[29] F. L. Paxson, "The Highway Movement, 1916–1935," **American Historical Review,** 51:236–253, January, 1946.

Fig. 20-3 The National Freeways System.

SOURCE: Businessmen's Guide to the Road Program, Chamber of Commerce of the United States, Washington, D.C., 1958.

portation problems were arising within, not between, cities and therefore permitted Federal funds to be spent in urban areas; (2) it provided for a secondary system of roads, the so-called "farm-to-market" roads; and (3) it established a framework for the designation of 40,000 (later increased to 41,000) miles of a national system of interstate highways. The 1954 act called for estimation of the cost of constructing such a system and for the projection of trends so as to build a system of highways that would be adequate for traffic loads twenty years hence.

The modern highway plan thus devised called for an interstate system of limited-access, multilane, divided highways to carry traffic around cities, or into the heart of them, at much less hazard and far greater average speed than was possible on roads built to prewar standards. This greatest of all road-building projects was estimated to cost over $27.4 billion, of which 90 percent was to be paid for by the Federal government. It would take at least fifteen years to complete construction. At the same time, other highways would continue to receive Federal aid on a fifty-fifty matching basis. The plan was originally intended to operate on a pay-as-you-go basis.

The legislation establishing the interstate system—which, incidentally, was responsible for the termination of a postwar revival of toll-road building— was expected to create a great many problems. It called for numerous, time-consuming local hearings as specific routes were planned, but basic and final decisions would be made in Washington. Interchanges for entrance and exit are natural targets for all types of eyesores if the areas around them are not subject to land-use controls. A great battle was begun as soon as the act was under consideration over whether billboards should be permitted or rigidly controlled. Many communities, dependent upon tourist trade, were threatened with the need to revamp their local economies after they were bypassed. Business, trade, and land-use patterns were subject to enormous changes. Land values for miles around the new roads and along the replaced routes changed greatly. The plan threatened to hasten even more the impending elimination of passenger trains. The economic and social patterns of every state in the union are being altered in the process of completing this vast new system.

Other Highways   The interstate system, when completed, will carry 20 percent of the total highway traffic on about 1 percent of the total highway mileage, and it will connect more than 90 percent of the cities of over 50,000 population. The remainder of the traffic will be handled by other Federally aided highways and by state, county, city, and other local roads.

Highways have become increasingly complex, both in design and in maintenance procedures. The result has been that in most of the states there has been a trend toward centralized control over highway policies. In some states, in fact, veritable state systems have been established over all roads. In others, county road administrators have had their duties increasingly detailed in state law, and they have been brought into close cooperation with state highway departments. Even where political patronage is important, the tendency is toward the professionalization of highway departments at all levels.

City Streets   Urban areas are generally plagued by congestion and parking problems. Neither of these is new. In 1837, Asa Greene complained that New York's Broadway "is now too narrow for the immense travel, business, and locomotion of various kinds, of which it is the constant scene." [30] Had he been alive six generations later, he would have had no need to change his words. Federal aid has helped to meet some of the problems of moving urban traffic, but elaborate expressway systems have tended to generate so much additional traffic that they become inadequate in the largest cities almost as soon as they are built. Expressways are enormously expensive. They damage property values along their routes but enhance the values of property at either end of them. One of their main purposes is to shore up sagging property values in the downtown area and to keep up the dollar volume of business in downtown stores. Yet, downtown property owners have not been anxious to help pay for them through special assessments.

Places to Park   The number of automobiles increased from just over 8 million in 1920 to 30 million at the beginning of World War II. They increased to nearly 72 million in 1965, and the number of trucks registered increased at an even greater rate. There were more than 14 million of them in 1965.[31] And while the number of automobiles increased, their importance as prestige symbols in our society was largely responsible for their increase in size. The two factors taken together produced a staggering parking problem. Parking lots can hold only 60 percent as many recent-year model autos as they could 1939 models. (St. Louis once banned Cadillacs from municipal lots because they took up too much room.)

The postwar intracity freeway made it easier to get downtown, but it aggravated the parking situation. Clearing of land is costly, and until the mid-1950s it was thought too expensive to buy land merely for parking purposes. Multistory parking garages are likewise expensive to build. Despite this, various efforts are being made to meet demands for parking space. In cities where rapid transit still exists, it is possible to convince drivers to park on the fringe of downtown and ride from there. After a rather slow postwar start, cities became increasingly committed to the development of municipal parking lots and structures. Pressure from central business district merchants was strong. More than two-thirds of all cities have some parking lots or structures, paid for largely through revenue bond issues. Merchants often pay parking charges for customers, and this policy has encouraged the building of more parking facilities. Building codes have been altered to permit special rules for constructing parking garages at lower cost than if they were treated as enclosed buildings.

Adequate parking space is, economically speaking, a cost of doing business and hence a responsibility of the firm for whom the driver works or the store to which the driver-shopper is headed. Because business districts were

---

[30] Quoted in Alexander Klein (ed.), **The Empire City,** Holt, Rinehart and Winston, Inc., New York, 1955.
[31] See **Automobile Facts and Figures,** Automobile Manufacturers Association, Detroit, Mich., 1965.

built before the automobile was developed, such provisions have not always been made. Most cities now attempt to require all new commercial places to furnish adequate parking spaces off the street. A part of the problem in many cities in procuring sufficient parking facilities from private sources is related to the fact that the business is monopolized in the hands of one or a few large lot owners possessing considerable political power.

Parking difficulties in the central business district have, of course, encouraged the movement of retail firms, business places, and factories to the suburbs. The heavy traffic, cost and scarcity of parking, and the necessity for rigid enforcement of parking-meter regulations have discouraged use of the downtown area. Yet, these factors alone do not account for the decline in downtown business and property values. The obsolescent character of the buildings and the greater proximity of the suburban shopping center and medical clinic to the suburban home are continuing to generate further declines in the importance of the central business district, even after parking ceases to be a serious problem.

Highway Safety   With around 48,000 persons being killed on American highways each year and with millions of accidents taking place which involve personal injury or property damage, Americans have become concerned about highway safety measures. State and local governments have joined private groups in encouraging safety publicity campaigns (see Figure 20-4). Coercive measures for taking incompetent drivers off the road have not had a great deal of public support, however. In popular attitude, a person has almost a constitutional right to drive a car, and, short of incarceration, it is virtually impossible to keep some persons with revoked licenses or those who have failed qualifying examinations from driving. Many persons, however, fear losing their licenses, and the threat of taking them away for repeated violations is in these cases effective.

About 90 percent of all licensed drivers consider themselves to be above average both in driving skills and in obeying traffic laws. In one study, *all* drivers with a record of traffic violations claimed to be above average in driving skills.[32] Obviously, then, one of the major problems in traffic safety relates to the inability of the incompetent driver to recognize his own weaknesses. This attitude of unwarranted self-confidence also leads to lack of citizen support for safety procedures and regulations. The typical citizen probably favors no maximum speed limit on highways and freeways. He opposes vehicle inspection programs that would help to disclose mechanical inadequacies in automobiles. In general, the typical citizen opposes programs for accident prevention if they cause him any personal inconvenience.

Vigorous court action against negligent drivers in the form of fines and jail sentences is often urged, but the typical citizen tends to identify with the defendant driver, and this weakens the willingness of a jury to deliver a guilty verdict and mitigates the penalties a judge may exact. Cities and states have found, however, that increasing the number of policemen and of patrol cars

[32] Associated Press dispatch, Apr. 22, 1961.

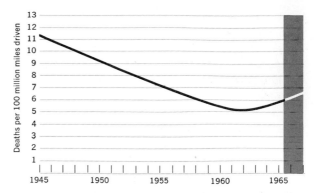

Fig. 20-4   In the 1960s, Automobile Accident Death Rates Have Increased.

Before 1961, improving quality of highways helped decrease highway traffic death rates. Since then, annual increases probably have resulted mostly from driver incompetence, excessive speed, lack of attention to safety features in designing autos, and increased numbers of young drivers with their own vehicles.

SOURCE: National Safety Council.

on the road is probably the best means of reducing traffic hazards. Improved highway-construction patterns are also helping. High speed is the greatest single cause of accidents and auto deaths, and rigid policing of speed limits and the use of reasonable posted limits seem to be especially important. Because of the importance of speed as a factor, motor-vehicle deaths tend to be lowest in urban states and highest in rural states, where the vast lonely distances encourage overspeeding.

Despite a common notion to the contrary, American highways are becoming safer, rather than more dangerous. In 1926, there were 18 deaths per 100 million vehicle miles driven. In 1961, the figure had dropped to 5.2 deaths. Between 1961 and 1964, the death rate climbed slightly, to 5.7, still far lower by almost any measure, than a generation earlier.[33] Because of the superior strength of construction and larger size of American cars and the better highways, traffic fatality rates in the United States are only one-fourth to one-third as high as they are in most Western European countries (on the basis of mileage).

After the highway death rate began to climb in 1961, increasing demands were made for greater safety standards in the construction of automobiles. The states generally failed to act but Congress actively considered national minimum standards, beginning with its 1965 session.[34]

Groups and Interests   Highways have become one of the costliest of state and local functions, and it is therefore to be expected that many interests will seek to influence highway decisions. To name a few of the interests: cities and

[33] National Safety Council figures.
[34] See Ralph Nader, **Unsafe at Any Speed**, Grossman Publishers, Inc., New York, 1965.

counties seek a greater share of the state gasoline taxes, their views are likely to run counter to those of the state highway department, and lobbyists for cities may in turn split with those of the counties over the percentage each is to get of the gasoline tax fund. The state highway department may have to fight off both these groups as well as those who would pay the cost of the state highway patrol or police from the highway fund. Motorists want limited-access, divided, high-speed highways which bypass cities. Cities may agree that state highways should be planned in this way in the interests of safety. This is not likely to be the view, however, in tourist and resort areas where each hamlet feels it has a right to seek to get the motorist to break his journey at that point and to make purchases from local merchants. Some businessmen try to get state or local governments to impose road construction requirements which will enable them to have a special advantage over competitors.[35] All those engaged in road building or repair find lobbying useful, if indeed not vital to their businesses. Most states have a "good roads" federation and various highway-users groups (e.g., a state motor bus association, heavy haulers association, movers and warehousemen's association) have their own construction and financing programs to recommend.

Many pressures are brought to bear upon the right-of-way divisions of highway departments as they select routes for new roads. The decisions made by highway planners may vitally affect the social and economic circumstances of every individual and community along a route.

PTA and neighborhood association groups often lead the fight for increasing the number of stop signs and traffic lights in their areas. The highway engineers who must make decisions about such things feel these pressures as well as counterpressures from travelers and commuters to put as few such hurdles in their paths as possible. Different policy recommendations concerning traffic rules on a state highway through a particular city frequently come from the state highway department and from local officials. The former are primarily concerned with moving vehicles through the community, and they tend to view the city as a traffic bottleneck. The latter are primarily concerned with the safety of pedestrians, noise suppression, and providing for parking places in front of local stores. They tend to view the transient motorist as a threat to the peace and well-being of the community. In most states, where a compromise cannot be reached, the views of the state agency usually prevail.

Many a traffic light or speed limit sign is erected on the basis of pressures upon elective officials, although engineers would prefer to locate them on the basis of traffic-flow studies.[36] Generally, the citizen wants his home and his children's school area to be surrounded by a forest of stop signs, traffic lights, and low-speed-limit controls; but once he is out of his own neighborhood, he demands a clear, unimpeded, safe, high-speed road to the door of his place of work and to the shopping center. It is within such an environment that traffic and highway planners must operate.

[35] For a case study, see Paul N. Ylvisaker, **The Natural Cement Issue,** Committee on Public Administration Cases, Washington, D.C., 1950.
[36] For case illustrations, see F. J. Herring, "Human Relationships Are the Key to Effective Traffic Engineering," **Traffic Quarterly,** 10:387–397, July, 1956.

SELECTED READINGS

Altshuler, Alan: **The City Planning Process: A Political Analysis,** Cornell University Press, Ithaca, N.Y., 1965.   (By a political scientist.)

————: **A Land-use Plan for St. Paul,** The Bobbs-Merrill Company, Inc., Indianapolis, ICP no. 90, 1965.   (Study of values, interests, and processes of preparing a plan.)

————: **Locating the Intercity Freeway,** The Bobbs-Merrill Company, Inc., Indianapolis, ICP no. 88, 1965.   (The conflicting values and interests of highway engineers, city planners, and businessmen.)

Anderson, Martin: **The Federal Bulldozer: A Critical Analysis of Urban Renewal,** The M.I.T. Press, Cambridge, Mass., 1964.   (A harsh, exaggerated criticism by a business school professor. Worthwhile as an application of the ideology of industrial individualism to a contemporary urban program.)

Bell, Daniel: "Crime as an American Way of Life," **Antioch Review,** 42:131–154, June, 1953.

Benedict, Murray R.: **Farm Policies of the United States, 1790–1950,** The Twentieth Century Fund, New York, 1953.

Blake, Nathan M.: **Water for the Cities,** Syracuse University Press, Syracuse, N.Y., 1957.

Butler, George D.: **Introduction to Community Recreation,** 3d ed., McGraw-Hill Book Company, New York, 1959.

Callison, C. H. (ed.): **America's Natural Resources,** The Ronald Press Company, New York, 1957.

Chapin, F. Stuart, Jr.: **Urban Land Use Planning,** 2d ed., University of Illinois Press, Urbana, Ill., 1964.

Cooley, Richard A.: **Politics and Conservation: The Decline of the Alaska Salmon,** Harper & Row, Publishers, Incorporated, New York, 1963.   (A thorough study of politics and the salmon industry. The author's personal normative values are undisguised.)

Cornick, Philip H.: **Premature Subdivision and Its Consequences,** Institute of Public Administration, Columbia University, New York, 1938.

"The Crisis in Water," **Saturday Review,** Oct. 23, 1965.   (Entire section devoted to source and pollution problems.)

Curtiss, C. D.: "The New Highway Program," **Traffic Quarterly,** 11:5–17, January, 1957.

Daland, Robert T.: **The County Buys Dunwoodie Golf Course,** The Bobbs-Merrill Company, Inc., Indianapolis, ICP no. 61, 1961.   (Interest groups and land-use conflicts.)

DeVoto, Bernard: "Roads of the Past," **The Lamp,** 38:10–15, Fall, 1956.

Duke, Richard D.: **Gaming-simulation in Urban Research,** Institute for Community Development, Michigan State University, East Lansing, Mich., 1964.

Durisch, L. L., and R. E. Lowry: "State Watershed Policy and Administration in Tennessee," **Public Administration Review,** 15:17–20, Winter, 1955.

"The Fouling of the American Environment," **Saturday Review,** May 22, 1965. (Entire section devoted to the subject. Articles by many specialists.)

Green, Arnold W.: **Recreation, Leisure, and Politics,** McGraw-Hill Book Company, New York, 1964.

Gross, Leonard: "Big Zoning Battle," **Look,** Oct. 5, 1965, pp. 93–98.   (The importance of zoning decisions in contemporary urban society.)

Hayes, Forbes B.: **Community Leadership,** Columbia University Press, New York, 1965.   (A history of the Regional Plan Association, a private organization in the New York metropolitan area.)

Horwitz, Robert H., and Norman Meller: **Land and Politics in Hawaii,** 2d ed., University of Hawaii Press, Honolulu, 1966.   (Land allocation patterns in a state where usable land is especially scarce.)

Hunter, N. D.: "Problems of the Colorado River as Reflected in Arizona Politics," **Western Political Quarterly,** 4:634–643, December, 1951.

Jacobs, Jane: **The Death and Life of Great American Cities,** Random House, Inc., New York, 1961.   (A vigorous criticism of the values, goals, and methods of the urban planning profession.)

Johnson, V. W., and Raleigh Barlowe: **Land Problems and Policies,** McGraw-Hill Book Company, New York, 1954.

Keeley, John B.: **Moses on the Green,** The Bobbs-Merrill Company, Inc., Indianapolis, ICP no. 45, 1959.   (Study of proposal to convert part of Central Park into a parking lot for a privately owned restaurant.)

Lautner, Harold W.: **Subdivision Regulations,** Public Administration Service, Chicago, 1941.

Lepawsky, Albert: "Water Resources and American Federalism," **American Political Science Review,** 44:631–649, Sept., 1950.

Mann, Dean E.: **The Politics of Water in Arizona,** University of Arizona Press, Tucson, Ariz., 1963.

Martin, W. T.: **The Rural-urban Fringe,** University of Oregon Press, Eugene, Ore., 1953.

————: "Ecological Change in Satellite Rural Areas," **American Sociological Review,** 22:173–183, Apr., 1957.

Miller, Howard: **Mr. Planning Commissioner,** Public Administration Service, Chicago, 1954.

Moore, E. H., and Raleigh Barlowe: **Effects of Suburbanization Upon Rural Land Use,** Agricultural Experiment Station, Michigan State University, East Lansing, Mich., 1955.

Nash, Peter H., and Dennis Durden: "A Task Force Approach to Replace the Planning Board," **Journal of the American Institute of Planners,** 30:10–26, February, 1964.

Nelson, R. L., and F. T. Aschmen: **Real Estate and City Planning,** Urban Land Institute, Washington, D.C., 1957.   (The realtor's position.)

Ostrom, Vincent: "State Administration of Natural Resources in the West," **American Political Science Review,** 47:478–493, June, 1953.

Owens, John R.: **A Wildlife Agency and Its Possessive Public,** The Bobbs-Merrill Company, Inc., Indianapolis, ICP no. 87, 1965.   (The California Department of Fish and Game.)

Parsons, Malcolm B.: "Party and Pressure Politics in Arizona: Opposition to Colorado River Development," **Pacific Historical Review,** 19:47–58, February, 1950.

Paxson, F. L.: "The Highway Movement 1916–1935," **American Historical Review,** 51:236–253, January, 1946.

Reps, John W.: **The Making of Urban America: A History of City Planning in the United States,** Princeton University Press, Princeton, N.J., 1964.

Schroth, Thomas N., and others: **Congress and the Nation, 1945–1964,** Congressional Quarterly Service, Washington, D.C., 1965, chaps. 4, 6, and 7.

Senate Subcommittee on Intergovernmental Relations, **National Survey of Metropolitan Planning,** 1963.

Srole, Leo, and others: **Mental Health in the Metropolis,** McGraw-Hill Book Company, New York, 1962.   (A survey covering eight years; 1660 residents of midtown Manhattan.)

State Administration of Water Resources, Council of State Governments, Chicago, 1957.

Tyler, Poyntz (ed.): **American Highways Today,** The H. W. Wilson Company, New York, 1957.

U.S. Advisory Commission on Intergovernmental Relations: **Intergovernmental Responsibilities for Water Supply and Sewage Disposal in Metropolitan Areas,** 1962.

Water Resource Activities in the United States: Future Water Requirements for Municipal Use, Senate Select Committee on National Water Resources, 86th Cong., 2d Sess., 1960.

Webster, Donald H.: **Urban Planning and Municipal Public Policy,** Harper & Row, Publishers, Incorporated, New York, 1958.

Wengert, Norman: **Natural Resources and the Political Struggle,** Doubleday & Company, Inc., Garden City, N.Y., 1955.

Wilson, James Q.: "Planning and Politics: Citizen Participation in Urban Renewal," **Journal of the American Institute of Planners,** 29:210–236, November, 1963.

Ylvisaker, Paul N.: **The Natural Cement Issue,** Committee on Public Administration Cases, Washington, D.C., 1950.   (A case study.)

Ziffren, Kenneth (ed.): "Land Planning and the Law," **UCLA Law Review,** 12:entire issue, March, 1965.

21

REGULATION AND PUBLIC SAFETY

Let us here recall the principal point made at the beginning of this book: government is one of the instrumentalities of social control. As its policy-making processes function in our democracy, the cultural values in society are applied to various aspects of human behavior so as to control them in a manner that the dominant groups consider to be desirable. Just as values change over time, so do the controlling popular concepts of the degree and type of controls over individuals or businesses that are preferred. In the nineteenth century, business was largely unrestrained, since it was then widely believed that society could prosper only as business found ways by which to profit. In the years since the Great Depression, this concept has been modified a good deal. Similarly, culturally defined crime and punishment changes over time. A few of the state and local activities and issues in the area of regulation of businesses and individuals will be examined in this chapter.

Public Utilities

Public utilities are not necessarily publicly owned. Many of them are, but the majority are actually owned and operated by private corporations; and some, by individual proprietors. A list of utilities includes railroads, commercial buses and trucks, and telephone, telegraph, electricity, water, and gas services. Other functions that are of the nature of utilities, although not always fully accepted as such, are auditoriums, port facilities, slaughterhouses, airports, and possibly toll bridges, toll roads, sewers, and public markets.

Public utilities, then, are businesses which, in terms of cultural values, are expected to be subjected to more than a normal amount of governmental control. They are often granted a monopoly within their areas of operation. This is because experience has shown that competition is wasteful of resources and results in inferior and more costly services to the consumers. A public utility normally has a right to use public property (over which to string electric wires or to operate buses) and to exercise the state's power of eminent domain. It usually charges for services rendered on a benefits-received basis, and it is subject to the control of some type of public-service commission whose legal responsibility is to protect both the provider and the purchaser of services.

Regulation In the nineteenth century, utilities were normally operated on the basis of a "franchise" which was granted to utilities by the state or city. A franchise is a license stipulating the conditions under which a utility may operate and the privileges it is to enjoy. A franchise usually stated the quality of service that was expected of the utility and the rates that could be charged. In practice, utilities firms were often little inhibited by their franchises. Sometimes they resorted to bribery of public officials, sometimes they won judicial interpretations of ambiguous provisions of the franchise by the use of superior legal talent, and in almost no cases was there a public body that had the legal authority to hold the utility to the terms of its agreement.

One of the major areas of activity of reform forces at the turn of the present century was that of public-utility regulation. The method of control that gradually evolved centered around a public-service commission (bearing various titles in various states) whose duty it was to determine rates after investigations and hearings and to supervise both the service and the management of the utilities. Most commissions today prescribe uniform accounting methods, they often must approve expansion plans and the issuance of new securities, and they may sometimes even be authorized to order such expansions. Commissions are constantly at work overseeing the activities of the utilities, but there is considerable variation in the degree to which they are effective.

Franchises are still granted, but they are no longer so detailed as they were in the days before public-service commissions. They are usually limited to a term of years (perhaps twenty-five) rather than made to exist in perpetuity, as was once common. A franchise usually provides for the privileges to be enjoyed by the utility, it may provide for a special tax structure for it, and for some conditions which must be met by the utility. It leaves most other controls to the public-service commission.

Issues in Regulation Many problems and issues center around regulatory activities. The major one, discussed below, is perhaps that of rate determination. Others include questions of state versus local control over utilities that operate essentially as local services and of whether or not utilities should be locally owned. The interests to be regulated work hard to influence the behavior of the public-service commission members and their staffs, while these people in turn usually seek to remain independent of such control. Another problem is one of keeping commissions politically responsive to the legislatures that create them. Legislatures often fail or refuse outright to provide adequate staff for effective enforcement activities. Pressures tor favoritism, reenforced by contributions to political party campaign coffers, remain high. Problems of this kind in the field of public utilities are chronic; yet the services are generally provided at a fairly high level and at prices that most of the public probably regards (except perhaps for bus transportation within cities) as not unreasonable.

The Determination of Rates The question of rate determination is one that can easily take up most of a semester in a college course in public-utility regulations without providing an answer satisfactory to all. The problem in practice has evolved around a question that is almost impossible to answer: What is the true value of a large and complex corporation? If rates are so low that the utility does not receive a fair rate of return on its investment, confiscation of private property results, and that is prohibited by the due-process clause of the Fifth Amendment. But what is the investment or worth of a utility? Should the value of a utility for rate purposes be based upon reproduction costs at current prices, less depreciation, or at actual, historic costs of construction, or upon some combination of these two methods? The formula used may make a great difference in the allowable rates. Should changes in the price index be considered? Should any value be placed on the franchise, "good will," or "going concern"?

In an attempt to answer these questions, public-service commissions have made valuation studies; but these often take years to complete and are inconclusive, and by the time they are completed their results are no longer applicable to existing conditions. Since due process of law is involved, utilities controversies are commonly adjudicated in the courts on appeal from the commissions. In seeking equity, the United States Supreme Court has for years struggled between the cost-of-reproduction and the actual-amount-of-prudent-investment theories.[1] While the most recent decision leans toward actual investment of capital without considering the problem of subsequent influences of inflation or deflation, the Court still has not settled on a definitive formula. Even with a formula, many questions and problems remain. Rate determination, despite able research staffs, is still in large part based upon folklore and subjective evaluations, and it is very costly.

Other Regulatory Activities

Banking and Insurance "The banking profession is not easy to regulate," an experienced state administrator has noted. "It prefers to go along in the *caveat emptor* theory. Little and big, all banks and bankers naturally hang together in opposition to public control. Strike one link and the whole chain shivers."[2]

The statement is probably correct, but it is doubtful whether bankers be-

[1] See *Smyth v. Ames*, 169 U.S. 466 (1898), the first landmark case; *Southwestern Bell Telephone Co. v. Missouri*, 262 U.S. 276 (1923); *F. P. C. v. Hope Natural Gas Co.*, 320 U.S. 591 (1944), the ruling case at present.
[2] Robert Moses, quoted in Frank Freidel, **Franklin D. Roosevelt: The Triumph**, Little, Brown and Company, Boston, 1956, p. 188.

have any differently in this respect from other businessmen who are subject to control. Banks, insurance companies, finance companies, building and loan associations, credit unions, and other financial institutions are generally subject to special state controls. In practice, each type of institution is likely to be governed by a different set of rules, and practices differ from one state to another.

The states nearly all have banking and insurance departments that have general supervisory control over these institutions. They audit their books, often control the issuance of their securities, and control the level of reserves or the conditions under which loans may be made. Insurance departments grant licenses to companies and agents and may revoke such licenses by following a certain procedure and for certain reasons. They also control, or administer state laws controlling, the conditions under which policies are issued and the provisions of policies, and the premiums that may be charged. Financial and insurance businesses are generally subject to Federal as well as state control, banks if they are members of the Federal Deposit Insurance Corporation, insurance companies if they do business in more than one state.

Banking and insurance departments, like public-service commissions, are subject to great political pressure, and those who are subject to control not infrequently succeed in gaining domination over the state agency that is to control them.[3] This is not surprising, for bankers have a great financial interest in the regulation of their profession. As with utility company officials, they find it worthwhile to pay legal and research talent to present their case in a convincing manner.

Bankers and allied financial leaders generally favor a certain amount of state regulation. They want their businesses to be favorably perceived by society. The marginal cheat who seeks to take advantage of the poor and ignorant damages popular acceptance of other members of the profession. Government is, therefore, a logical and popularly accepted institution for the establishment of rules of behavior that will encourage public tolerance of financial institutions.

Other Businesses   State laws control all businesses to some extent. They determine the conditions under which a partnership may operate or a charter may be issued for a corporation. They control the issuance of stock, the rules under which a corporation chartered in one state may operate in another. The general pattern of state government behavior in this field offers a good case example of the reasons why Federal activities and controls have been expanded over the years. Although many states had "blue sky" laws designed to prevent fraud and misrepresentation in the sale of stocks and bonds before the Great Depression, business pressures were generally sufficient to prevent the effective enforcement of these laws. Partly as a result of this, especially of activities in the securities-mad 1920s, the Federal government entered this field with a comprehensive program beginning with the Securities Exchange Act of 1934.

[3] See Bray Hammond, **Banks and Politics in America from the Revolution to the Civil War**, Princeton University Press, Princeton, N.J., 1957; Freidel, *op. cit.*, pp. 184–187.

States also control the sale of adulterated foods and drugs, the use of weights and measures, the production of oil and gas, mining and quarrying practices, and other business activities. Local governments control many businesses in the interests of health and safety. They thus establish and maintain health standards in restaurants, fire exit regulations from theaters, and smoke control practices of industries. In all of these cases, the local governments find their basic authority in state law.

Licensing of Trades and Professions   Many trades and professions require high degrees of skill, and society, not unreasonably, expects that some kind of standards of education and practice must be met before persons should be permitted to begin practice of such activities. It is difficult for the ordinary citizen to know whether the man who proposes to defend him in court, remove his gall bladder, or survey his property is actually qualified to do the job. Members of the various trades and professions, in turn, do not want to be subjected to competition that might come from persons who have invested less time and money in training or who seek to take advantage of public ignorance and gullibility. Trades and professions that require licensing or registration include the various branches of medicine, nursing, law, engineering, plumbing, teaching, pharmacy, embalming, and others.

Many issues of policy arise in connection with licensing practices. Efforts to protect the public against the incompetent or the shyster involve laws and rules which may also be diverted to the purpose of restricting the number of persons authorized to perform some professional function and, hence, to raise the cost of having that function performed, to the profit of those authorized to practice the profession.[4]

Each trade or profession seeks to control its own licensing board and to keep it independent of the remainder of state government. If it succeeds at this, it may become tempted to raise standards of qualification as a means for cutting down competition. Standards are necessary, nearly all citizens would agree, but when are they unnecessarily high? It is difficult to judge—and practically everyone qualified to offer a professional opinion belongs to the group that is seeking to raise standards. Is it really necessary for a barber to be a high school graduate? Are physicians trained in Europe really likely to have so inferior an education that special licensing procedures should apply to them? Is it really necessary for an attorney or an engineer to be a citizen? These are not easy questions to answer.

In addition to the pressure to raise standards of qualification, a continuing demand exists for state legislatures to bring additional trades or professions under licensing or registration regulations. Urban planners are interested in registration requirements. Mental-hospital attendants claim that they have a specialized occupation that is as deserving as is that of the practical nurse for licensing. Television repairmen, who frequently lose work to untrained competitors and suffer a loss of reputation in the process, demand that their

4 See Gary P. Brazier, "The Ohio Architect's Guild," in Richard T. Frost (ed.), **Cases in State and Local Government,** Prentice-Hall, Inc., Englewood Cliffs, N.J., 1961, pp. 41–49.

trade be licensed. Many citizens, especially in larger cities, agree with them. As labor becomes increasingly specialized in the future, we can expect that the trend toward increased requirements for licensing or registration will continue.[5]

Labor Law   Labor law has expanded in scope as America has changed from a belief that, if in doubt, the employer was right to one that holds that labor-management conflicts are properly a matter of government concern. As control over the existence of more and more jobs has become dependent upon the decisions of anonymous bureaucrats buried in the structure of large corporations, persons who seek those jobs or who hold them one day and lose them the next have become increasingly interested in government assistance in achieving some measure of economic security.

Labor legislation is another field where responsibility is divided between Federal and state governments. The Federal law applies only to industry that affects interstate commerce, but this concept has been gradually broadened over time.

State labor law began with legislation concerning the regulation of working conditions, particularly relative to health and safety. Other early laws dealt with requirements that workers be paid within stated intervals of time and sometimes prescribed the method of payment. States conceded the need to regulate the hours and conditions of labor for children and women earlier than for men.

Throughout the twentieth century, labor law has gradually accumulated. Many states have regulations of maximum hours of work; some have minimum-wage laws. The conditions under which court injunctions can be used in labor disturbances are controlled in some states; some have rules relating to the internal affairs of unions. Every state has legislation relative to strikes, boycotts, and picketing, and many seek to mediate labor disputes. Every state also has legislation concerning the right to bargain collectively and to join a union. Some states outlaw labor-management agreements establishing the "closed shop." * In the 1950s, there was a widespread movement to outlaw agreements for the "union shop" by legislation which advocates so-called right-to-work laws. A number of states have adopted such legislation, but the more industrialized states have usually rejected it after bitter struggles.

* **CLOSED SHOP. A firm that will hire persons only if they are already members of a particular union. A UNION SHOP requires a new employee to join a particular union within a certain length of time after being hired. An OPEN SHOP hires union or non-union labor and recognizes no union as exclusive bargaining agent for employees.**

Every aspect of labor legislation is highly controversial, and both labor and management groups are constantly working to modify it in their favor or to create a favorable public opinion for seeking changes at some future time. Both trade unions and management have much at stake in this struggle.

[5] See J. A. C. Grant, "The Guild Returns to America," **Journal of Politics,** 4:303–336, 458–477, August and November, 1942.

Intergroup Relations An increasingly important activity of both state and local governments deals with the problems of potential and actual conflict between racial or ethnic groups. Urbanism has resulted in bringing these groups together in close physical proximity and in situations where social relationships cannot be kept isolated, as they often were when different ethnic groups lived in the same general area in nineteenth-century rural America. A variety of other factors have also contributed to a rising demand for social equality on the part of minority groups. Discontent with inferior social status and economic opportunity has brought about the use of voting power to seek governmental assistance in overcoming discrimination.

In the mid-1960s, about one-third of the states had organizations of some kind to deal with intergroup problems. Some of them were concerned only with fair-employment practices; others conceived of their jobs more broadly. Most state agencies have some enforcement powers through the courts, but several are advisory only. The emphasis in seeking to get groups to work together is necessarily upon education and conciliation. States with legislation on inter-group relations are to be found especially in the East but to some extent in all areas outside the South. They are generally the most populous and urbanized states. The acts usually apply to employers, labor unions, and local units of government as well as to state government.

City governments also have adopted charter amendments or ordinances providing for intergroup organizations, including all of the five largest cities in the nation. Because intergroup conflicts are most likely to occur in large urban areas and because minority groups are most likely to be politically powerful in such places, most municipal agencies are to be found in cities of over 100,000 and especially in those of over one-half million.

Most municipal agencies have only advisory and noncoercive powers, although some of them have power to bring court actions against offenders which may result in both restraining orders and criminal punishments. The municipality may not be an adequate unit to handle intergroup relations. The problem is widespread, and the state appears to be in a better position to finance, support, and enforce programs in this area. Civil rights advocates generally want both state and local agencies.

Fire Protection

Cost versus Results American communities have the finest fire equipment in the world, but they also have the greatest annual fire losses. Such losses, in 1958, set an all-time record of over $1,000 million—most of it in cities. Americans are not very economy-conscious. Europeans, endowed with fewer of nature's gifts, must be conservationists. Americans, for example, are seldom prosecuted for contributory negligence in cases of fires. Losses, it is felt, are somehow "paid by the insurance company." Insurance rates are not associated with fire rates. In nearly all American states, as a reflection of this attitude fire-insurance rates are determined by the quality of fire-defense equipment in each community, with no consideration given to actual fire-loss experience.

The core cities of urban areas typically have modern, professional fire departments. The larger the city, the more specialized and costly the equipment is likely to be. Suburbs, small cities, and rural areas, on the other hand, often depend upon amateur departments. Some small residential communities make it a practice to hire a few full-time members who man the station and equipment, with volunteer amateurs on call to follow along at each fire alarm. There is a trend toward the training and use of men as both policemen and firemen, especially in suburban areas. Fire departments generally have important responsibilities in the area of fire prevention, both in seeking to prevent common hazards and in carrying on educational campaigns among school children and the general public.

Fire protection has traditionally been a responsibility of local government, usually municipalities, townships, towns, and special fire districts. The states have not been active in the area except in relation to the prevention and fighting of forest fires and in certain kinds of fire-prevention activities and the investigation of suspected arson cases through state fire marshal's offices.

Police Protection

The Police Function   The police function of government is one that has the responsibility of translating the public's concept of antisocial behavior into a program for controlling individuals and, where necessary, apprehending violators of established codes.

Two of the major problems in connection with police work in recent years have been the continuing increase in the crime rate in America and the increasing cost of police protection. Why the high cost of crime?

Sociological Factors   Part of our difficulty in suppressing crime stems from an ambivalent attitude. We have inherited certain puritanical values which condemn gambling and purely pleasurable activity. On the other hand, we live in a culture that is dynamic, complex, impersonal, and materialistic. Our whole economic and cultural pattern is based upon competition and getting ahead. Gambling and crimes against property are, therefore, partly a result of a hope for gain, a desperate need to succeed. Establishments for performing abortions—another illegal occupation—exist because women have a great fear of loss of status through the bearing of an illegitimate child. Loss of status comes easily in our culture and symbolizes failure.

In our competitive society, it is often difficult to distinguish the criminal from the noncriminal. Many business activities verge on the classification of racketeering, certainly they often violate the moral values of many individuals. "Anything's fair in business that you can get away with." If so, how does one distinguish legitimate from illegitimate businesses? Many Americans believe that you cannot do so. Americans have never strongly believed that all laws should be obeyed. If "everyone has his racket," why should we condemn the gamblers, prostitutes, abortionists, or bootleggers?

Sometimes social mores and criminal law agree nicely—as in the case of murder; sometimes they do not. Laws in serious conflict with the mores of society become unenforceable. The public or at least a large segment of it does not want the laws on gambling rigidly enforced. An even larger segment is indifferent to the question of how they are enforced.

Legal Factors   Americans, especially of the middle classes, have a rather naive faith in law and punishment as solutions for social problems.[6] As a result, the superficial action of making an occupation illegal is mistaken for a move toward the abolition of the occupation. Psychological and sociological phenomena cannot be legislated away, for their causes are complex and deep-seated. Since demand is not eliminated by making the occupation illegal, such action merely has the effect of creating racketeering, gangsterism, and an increased disrespect for the law.

Organized crime is common in a society torn between the values of puritanism and hedonism, where nearly all of our symbols of status and achievement are measured in material terms. Juvenile delinquency results when the teen-ager has no socially important function, is subjected to the impressions of the mass communications devices, and stands in revolt against neglect and misunderstanding.

Citizens tend to blame the police for the high crime rate, the vandalism of delinquents, and organized crime. Most police departments, in fact, enforce the law to the extent that they are permitted by public opinion as reflected in the political process. It is not the fault of the police that Americans want certain kinds of behavior carried in the statutes as crimes but do not want those statutes enforced or do not care whether or not they are enforced.

The Crime Rate   The crime rate increased at about four times the rate of the population in the period of one generation following World War II. Significant increases have taken place in all types of crimes, except murder and man-slaughter. One reason for this, perhaps, is that the odds are in favor of the robber, auto thief, or burglar each time he commits a crime (unless he resorts to violence). The police catch relatively few thieves—in only about three cases in ten is anyone even charged with the offense. The public does not tolerate a similar lack of success where a person loses life, and solutions of such crimes are usually easier than in the case of crimes against property.

The American crime rate is several times as high as that of any European nation; yet as in the case of the fire department, the police are the best equipped in the world. A well-known police chief once said: "Despite the technology that has been acquired through no small effort and expense, the police service today fulfills its task with no greater success than it did a quarter- or half-century ago."[7]

Americans tend to be careless of property losses resulting from robbery just as they tend to be careless of fire losses. The poor record of American police is, therefore, in large part a result of public apathy. Furthermore, "the

[6] D. R. Taft, **Criminology**, 3d ed., The Macmillan Company, New York, 1956, p. 235.
[7] William H. Parker, "The Police Challenge in Our Great Cities," **Annals**, 291:5–13, January, 1954.

individual police officer operates with a remarkable lack of public support, cooperation or trust." [8] The police are sometimes hampered partly by efforts on the part of public officials or the citizenry at large to "save" tax money. American police forces are small by comparison with European forces.

Crime rates vary through time, reflecting changes in social and economic conditions and in attitudes toward those changing conditions. For example, between 1935 and 1965, the urban murder rate in the United States declined by about 40 percent. On the other hand, the more serious types of physical assaults increased by 50 percent.[9] Whatever the social and economic (and perhaps psychological) reasons for these changes, they were certainly not the result of stiffer penalties. In the 1930s, the death penalty was commonly applied for murder in most American states. By the mid-1960s, executions of the death penalty had become rare. The penalty for both murder and assault changed in the same direction, the rates in opposite directions.

In conventional wisdom, punishment is discouraging to criminal behavior. Hence, it follows that if crime is increasing the effective solution is to increase the severity and probability of punishment. Although the evidence of historians, anthropologists, and sociologists indicates that this belief is false, it is so logical (superficially) and so widely accepted in the culture that judges are under constant pressure to accept the belief. Some of them probably believe it themselves. In 1964 and 1965, the judges of New York City, under heavy pressure from various groups and from newspaper editors to "do something" about a sharply rising crime rate, decided to increase the length of prison terms, to refuse leniency in doubtful cases, and to refuse probation. But none of these decisions had any measurable effect upon the rate of increase of crimes reported, arrests made, or cases scheduled for trial. The judges cleared more cases from the docket than in any other period in New York history, but at the end of the 1965 fiscal year, twice as many cases were pending as had been the case at the beginning of it.

Crime rates are unrelated to punishment practices, but they are related to a large number of other factors. These include unfavorable social conditions, poverty in the midst of general prosperity, and ignorance in a highly educated society. Attitudes toward the legitimacy of the law and the honesty and impartiality of justice are also relevant. If we believe, as large numbers of Americans seem to, that the law applies only to those who get caught, that judges and juries discriminate against the poor and those without political connections, there is less reason to obey the law. If many people, at least secretly, admire a clever "operator" rather than condemn him as someone who does not honor the rules of the game, operators are encouraged and because some of them will be caught, the crime rate increases. Given the American emphasis upon "getting ahead," it is easy for the armed robber to picture himself as a Robin Hood. If he does not rob only from the rich, he does rob from the affluent and he gives to the poor—himself and his family.

The sharp increase in crimes against property has been accompanied by

[8] *Ibid.*, p. 5.
[9] United Press-International dispatch, May 9, 1965.

a similar increase in crimes against the person. These are interrelated. Frequently, a citizen is injured in the course of being robbed, for example. The increase in sex crimes is probably related to the increase in crimes against property. That is, some beliefs, such as that anything you can get away with is all right, also apply here. Sex is, among other things, a commodity. In conventional wisdom, the increase in sex crimes is usually accorded to the decline in the importance of the family as an institution and to the decline in discipline and instruction at home. These may be factors, but they must be weighed along with other considerations already mentioned, as well as the effect of a switch from a rural to a metropolitan society in which large numbers of people are stacked, almost literally, on top of one another in apartments and tenements. Furthermore, sex behavior disapproved of in rural areas can be disguised, and in some cases, behavior that is not considered criminal in a rural society of primary relationships may be treated as criminal in an impersonal, urban environment. Primary-group controls in rural areas, such as gossip and social ostracism, are often not effective in the city. The law must be relied upon, instead, as is the case in many other social and economic relationships.

Finally, a large portion of the alleged increase in crime rates can be attributed to improved reporting techniques. The actual crime rates in the United States a century ago are not known and cannot be known, for adequate records were not kept. Today our conscious attention to the gathering of data may lead us to exaggerate rates of change, such as those in the case of crime.

Police Organization   Police and fire departments, by tradition, are organized along quasi-military lines. The head of the police department is commonly a professional policeman called the chief. In some cities, especially the largest cities, the highest ranking uniformed officer may be subordinate to a lay department head, called the commissioner, director, or in a few cities, the chief. The lay department head does not usually perform details of departmental administration. His job is to serve as liaison officer between the force and the chief executive. At one time a council committee or an autonomous board administered the police department. A few such cases still exist, but they are giving way to control by the chief executive.

Under the chief and depending largely upon the size of the city are numerous supervisory officers arranged in a hierarchy. They are traditionally given military titles. The force is organized with patrol, detective, traffic, vice, juvenile, and women's divisions.

As a result of charges made in many cities alleging selective law enforcement, particularly discrimination against Negroes by police departments, leaders of the civil rights movement have pressed for the establishment of civilian review boards attached to police departments and having the right to review alleged cases of discriminatory treatment and police brutality. Policemen and command officers alike have resisted these pressures. They argue that review boards would destroy the morale of police departments and would make law enforcement more difficult and perhaps impossible because persons accused of serious crimes would have little to lose by appealing to these boards, claiming that they were brutally treated. A few decisions against police officers would, it is argued, discourage policemen from attempting to enforce the law against veteran criminals. Political leaders have been reluctant to side with either position. In 1965, the mayor of Newark, New Jersey, decided not to establish such a review board, but instead proposed a procedure by which the Federal Bureau of Investigation would be called upon to investigate cases of alleged brutality. His proposal had the considerable political advantage of calling in a professional police organization that, until the mid-1960s, had been almost immune to public criticism. But many civil rights leaders were likely to be dissatisfied with a proposal that would have professional police officers investigating the behavior of other professional police officers.[10]

Recruiting Police American policemen, although improving in ability, are generally considered by authorities to be of inferior quality when compared with European policemen. A part of the cause may be traced to lower prestige but also to both the fact that entrance salaries and maximum salaries (short of promotion) are low in comparison with the qualifications required of competent police officers. Furthermore, policemen cannot easily make comparisons between their and similar jobs in private industry, as can the government accountant or highway engineer.

The earliest salaried policemen in America were political appointees. Gradually applicants came to be subjected to physical, mental, and moral examinations or scrutiny. In many cities of all sizes, the recruitment and disciplining of police are under the control of the municipal personnel agency. Training academies have been established in the largest cities.

Americans have not been willing to pay very much for police protection. This is demonstrated by the fact that per capita expenditures in cities of from 10,000 to 25,000 population were only $8.36 in 1957. As is the case with many urban functions, costs increase with the size of community. Cities of over 500,000 spend about twice as much per capita, $16.65 in 1957, as do the small cities just mentioned.[11] The need to pay higher salaries, the impersonality of the large city, and the greater complexity of the work requiring greater specialization all contribute to this higher cost.

The Image of the Police The police in America are not so highly regarded as they are in most European countries and there are far fewer of them in ratio to population. Partly because of low status, police departments do not find it easy to recruit and are usually undermanned, even by the standards of the numbers permitted them by law or appropriations. In addition to the suspicions a freedom-loving people have of police—many Americans are descended from people who came from countries where the police were extremely oppressive—Americans commonly believe that "everyone has his racket" and that the police

[10] **New York Times**, Sept. 16, 1965.
[11] See the most recent **Municipal Year Book**, International City Managers' Association, Chicago, 1958.

are, hence, probably often corrupt. Many citizens are quick to blame them in the event of any serious public disturbances.

The police themselves contribute to the low esteem in which they are held. Every year some serious police scandal occurs in a major city. Similar scandals also occur in small towns and small cities. Although the vast bulk of our police forces are undoubtedly men of honor who want to do good jobs, the ones who get the headlines establish the public image. High-ranking police officers sometimes make serious tactical blunders, too. In 1960, for example, the police commissioner of Detroit, responding to the perennial public demand for a "crackdown" after a widely publicized violent crime, arrested hundreds of persons who appeared on the streets at night and who were deemed "suspicious," almost all of them Negroes. For a while, a virtual curfew was imposed upon the major Negro slum area of Detroit. The result was extremely bad publicity for the police force and retaliatory voting against the mayor in the next election.

The police often try to build up a favorable image of themselves among grammar school children, hoping thus to develop an attitude that will carry over into their adult life. Unfortunately for the police, much of this image is undone when the children become adolescents and begin to drive automobiles. Every college student knows that the police watch younger drivers especially carefully and that they are less likely to be given the benefit of the doubt in marginal cases. It is also likely that the police, on the average, are less courteous to young drivers than they are to older ones. The police have a reason for their suspicion of young drivers, of course. These represent, by all odds, the least competent drivers on the road, as a group, and the ones most likely to cause accidents and to have serious injuries in the event of accidents. But whatever the cause of the attitude, it is damaging to the image of the police officer and probably has its effect upon the citizen in later life.

The police have difficulties in developing an image of a trustworthy, reliable organization among other portions of the population, too. To many members of minority groups, a policeman is a mercenary hired to enforce the customs and protect the interests of the dominant social class. These persons believe that the law is designed to work against their interests, rather than being neutral or a protection for them. The policeman becomes a symbol for a system that denies them equal rights.[12] The heavy emphasis the John Birch Society has given to the desirability of accepting police methods and its slogan, "Support Your Local Police," have also damaged the image of the police force in some parts of the nation, for any organization that is strongly supported by groups at the extremes of the political continuum is certain to be viewed with some suspicion by political moderates, not to mention extremists at the opposite end of the continuum.

The County Sheriff   The traditional law officer in America is the county sheriff. Although the job is one generally requiring professional competence, sheriffs

[12] Herbert Carter of the Los Angeles County Commission on Human Relations, cited in **The Los Angeles Herald-Examiner,** Apr. 30, 1965.

are still nearly all elected to office. They have responsibility for apprehending criminals outside of municipalities, they maintain the county jail, and they usually serve as the bailiffs of the local courts of record. It is not uncommon for them to be assigned sundry other duties by state law. In some urban areas, sheriffs' departments have come to resemble large-city police departments, complete with traffic control and detective divisions, but the typical rural sheriff continues to operate a small office with a few friends appointed as deputies and another as the jail turnkey. If he needs assistance with a difficult case, he is likely to call upon the state police or state detective bureau. Much of the responsibility for policing the main highways of his county has been assumed by state police or state highway patrols. But the sheriff nonetheless remains an important executive officer of the law.

Except in the most urbanized areas, sheriffs' offices are still operated in accord with the caretaker traditions of small town ideology. In 1964, for example, the Michigan State Police budget was approximately twice the size of the budget of all eighty-three sheriffs' departments in the state. The largest expenditure for public safety is made, however, by municipalities. In that same year, they spent more than three times as much as did the state government in providing police protection. In the enforcement of the criminal statutes, more than 70 percent of the cost, in Michigan, is devoted to police protection. The second largest expenditure is for the operation of prisons, for probation and parole. These activities account for about 21 percent of total expenditures. The remainder is devoted to the operation of the courts and the prosecution of alleged criminal offenders.[13]

In 1965, Multnomah County, Oregon (the Portland area), became the first local government in the United States to require that all uniformed and detective personnel in the county police force hold college degrees.

State Police   The first state police system was that of the Texas Rangers, which was organized early in the twentieth century. As means of transportation and communication have grown more rapid and crime detection more technical, there have been increasing demands for police officers of jurisdiction wider than that of the county. Gradually, state police forces came into being. Around the time of World War I, they fell into temporary unpopularity because they were often used for strikebreaking, but the reputation gained at that time has now been lived down in most states.

Some states have general police forces, while others have only detective agencies and highway patrols; but it is common for the latter to have full police powers. Usually, state police do not work within municipalities except upon request. Often they follow a rule of not entering a local labor, race, or other mass disturbance unless the local sheriff or chief states that he cannot handle the situation. Generally, state police are directly responsible, through a superintendent or commissioner, to the governor, and most state departments have able recruits, wide public acceptance, and high prestige.

[13] Raymond T. Galvin and Paul R. Falzone, "The Administration of Criminal Justice in Michigan," **Michigan Economic Record,** 7:3–6, January, 1965.

The increasing responsibilities of state police are considerable. They have largely taken over from the National Guard responsibility for restoring order in case of mass disturbances, assumed responsibility from county sheriffs for policing traffic on major highways, replaced the local sheriff or small-town policemen in the solving of crimes requiring the use of technical equipment, and absorbed the duties of the state fire marshal's office.

It may be expected that state police forces will expand in size and importance in the future. They will provide professional-quality police protection in areas where sheriffs or local police departments fail to do so.

Civil Defense   With Federal aid, both state and local governments have established civil defense units and programs. The American public, even in metropolitan areas that would appear to be prime H-bomb targets in the event of war, has been almost completely apathetic toward the development of a system of defense. The public regards the problem either as futile or as a technical one not involving popular participation at this time. Even industry has resisted Federal government policies of deconcentration.

Many states and cities have done little to further planning. They have experienced difficulties in getting volunteers to fill posts in local organizations. Some cities and states have effectively combined the program with a disaster plan, so that they are prepared for such emergencies as floods and tornadoes.

Punishment and Rehabilitation

Prisons and related institutions date primarily from the late eighteenth century, and innovations concerning them have taken place chiefly in the United States. In an earlier day, extended imprisonment took place usually only for debt. The usual punishment for crime was death, fine, flogging, mutilation, branding, the stocks, pillory, or ducking stool. The alternative to these, and perhaps the closest equivalent to imprisonment, was transportation—the sending of the convicted person to a remote place to work in a labor camp of some kind. This plan was economical, convenient, and provided a labor supply for the tapping of natural resources. With the almost total settlement of the world, the plan became impractical and is little used today, though some cases remain. The Soviet Union has labor camps in Siberia, for example.

The Development of the Prison System   The Society of Friends, or Quakers, introduced the prison system in Pennsylvania, starting with the Walnut Street Jail of Philadelphia in 1790, although there were antecedents in the commonwealth. The objective of the Quakers was to avoid physical punishment and to encourage the prisoner to meditate on his alleged wrongs, thus encouraging him to conform to society's will. The prison system, however, may perhaps best be viewed as the most obvious way, short of death, of removing from the community persons regarded by society as being a threat to its values and safety. It did not necessarily prove to be a more humane way of handling persons convicted of crimes.

After the idea of imprisonment spread, with modifications, to the state of New York (where the "Auburn system" became a model still followed in handling maximum security prisoners), other punishment methods died out, except for the use of the fine and the death penalty.

New York, in addition to the tight-security prison, also developed the "house of refuge" for juvenile delinquents and the "reformatory" concept (the first was at Elmira) for young prisoners regarded as having a good chance for rehabilitation.

No relationship exists between the length of prison terms and crime deterrence, but imprisonment does perform at least two functions useful to society. First, it provides a means by which persons who, in terms of personality and psychological motivation, are a threat to other members of society can be isolated and controlled. Second, imprisonment offers a means by which persons rebellious against or a threat to society can be given rehabilitative treatment which will, in some cases at least, convert the person from a threat to a useful member of society.

Although the idea of rehabilitation through the contemplation of moral and religious problems was a part of the Quaker philosophy from the beginning, the nineteenth-century prison did little to encourage this type of program and it became essentially a device for isolating from society those who had violated its rules of behavior. The idea of retribution and of catharsis through deprivation was also important, as was the belief that imprisonment of offenders would serve as a deterrent to others.

Gradually, prison reformers came back to the original argument that the job of departments of correction was essentially one of rehabilitation, to make the prisoner a useful member of society and to encourage him to want to live by society's rules. This involved the development of policies involving probation and supervised parole. The use of the indeterminate sentence became important. It was designed to fit the stay in prison to the individual's rehabilitation needs, in contrast to the older revenge concept of a prescribed number of years for manslaughter and a different number for stealing a watch. The sentence was to be applied to the individual criminal, not to the criminal act. (In practice, the indeterminate sentence has not been used for its original purpose as much as it has for the purpose of compelling conformity to prison rules. By its nature, it is a powerful club in the hands of prison administrators.) Within the prison, constructive use of time, especially in learning a trade, was to be encouraged, and psychological counseling was regarded as a cornerstone of the prison program.

The introduction and operation of rehabilitative programs involve many problems. A rehabilitation-oriented prison is far more difficult and expensive to administer than is one concerned only with security. There is a great lack of trained people available for work in prisons. In 1957, there were somewhat over 160,000 inmates in state prisons—and only twenty-three full-time psychiatrists. Although there were psychologists and psychiatric social workers on the job, in most state prisons rehabilitation remained, according to a former Minnesota warden, "largely the consequence of a prisoner's do-it-yourself project." [14] Many persons in prisons are so totally in revolt against society and its values that they probably must be held in prison for the rest of their lives in order to protect others, but the great majority of inmates are potentially capable of making a positive contribution to society. Yet the pressures upon inmates from their existence in the prison society with its special subculture are such as to make rehabilitation difficult and unlikely without substantial help from skilled persons.

Time Spent in Prison   The tendency toward the use of indeterminate sentences and of considerable variation in sentences permitted by the use of time off for good behavior has tended to make the stay of the average prisoner a short one. Inmates serving ten-year sentences are, on the average, released in four and one-half years; those with life sentences are released after ten years, on the average. In 1946, only 3.4 percent of the prisoners in state institutions had been there for more than ten years, and only 0.4 percent over twenty years.

A large majority of persons paroled from prisons return there, however, either for violation of parole or for committing another crime. About 60 percent of all released persons are returned to prison within five years. Many citizens conclude that this shows that "criminal types" cannot be rehabilitated. But the truth is that most of the prisons in the United States do relatively little to prepare the inmate for successful return to society. An intelligent, thirty-year-old inmate with a skilled trade was released on parole from a state prison in 1965. In commenting on his chances, he pointed out the typical dilemma in which the ex-convict finds himself. He said: [15]

Sure, I'm ready to get a job, to settle down. But who's going to hire me? There are two things I can do when I go to look for a job. I can tell them I'm an ex-convict, and let them say no on the spot. Or I can lie to them and have to worry about being found out later. What do I really think will happen when I get out? The truth is I think I'll wind up right back here in this prison.

Types of Prisons   About one-third of the male prisoners in state institutions are serving sentences of not over five years. Few of these need more than minimum security measures of the reformatory or work-camp type. Because most can expect to be released in about a year and one-half, they are not usually serious escape risks. Other inmates require medium, or ordinary, security prisons. Not over one-third are incorrigibles or psychopaths who require maximum security.

State prison physical plants require some facilities in each of the categories from work camp to supersecurity cells, although the various types are often combined within the area of a single prison. It is also necessary to have some kind of arrangement for women prisoners and for juvenile delinquents, but the latter are usually cared for by the social welfare, rather than the corrections, agency of state government.

[14] A. C. Schnur, quoted in the **State Journal,** Lansing, Mich., Dec. 27, 1957.
[15] James F. Fixx, "Must They Return?" **Saturday Review,** May 8, 1965, p. 24.

Issues in Prison Administration   Some of the important issues in connection
with prisons are the following:

1. Rational rehabilitation and physical-plant policies are often modified
as a result of the public's attitude toward prison inmates. The typical citizen
fears inmates. His greatest concern is that they escape. Even after they are
released, he probably expects that they will remain antisocial, a threat to his
person and property. As a result, in the event of a prison riot the citizen is
primarily concerned that it does not result in a mass break. He wants order
restored for his own safety, and he is not likely to inquire far into the aspects
of prison administration or finance that may have brought on the riot; to him
a riot is merely another example of antisocial people behaving badly. This
attitude has also had its effects upon prison architecture. The public wants
prisons that will hold the toughest inmate likely to be sent there. This results
in overly expensive prisons, fortresslike structures with expensive walls, bars
twice as strong as those used in zoos to hold lions or Kodiak bears,[16] and a
gloomy atmosphere well calculated to chill the prospects for any rehabilitation
program. Thus, the enormous Western Penitentiary of Pennsylvania, begun in
1872 and as imposing as a great castle, was outmoded by the standards of
progressive penologists even before the plans left the drawing table. By professional standards state prisons generally are much inferior to those of the
Federal government.

2. The public has not supported rehabilitation programs to any great
extent. The result is that these programs have been understaffed. Much of the
public does not have confidence in rehabilitation programs, believing that the
duty of the state is to keep antisocial persons behind bars. Because prisons
as built are often very expensive, legislatures seek to save money by cutting
down on "nonessential" (i.e., noncustodial) personnel, by overcrowding the
prisons, and by building them for large inmate populations. Many major state
prisons are larger than the size recommended by the Federal Bureau of
Prisons: a maximum of 1,200 inmates. The largest of them all, the State Prison
of Southern Michigan, at Jackson, is designed to house 5,735. In large prisons,
impersonal relationships become necessary, and individual rehabilitation programs are likely to suffer.

3. Competent personnel, both for treatment and custodial care, are not
often available. This is perhaps in part because prison jobs have frequently
been assigned on a patronage basis but more likely because public indifference
has made it impossible for the state to pay salaries that would attract an able
work force.

4. Labor unions and manufacturers oppose the public sale or distribution
of prison-made goods. They view cheap prison labor as unfair competition. Yet,
a central part of a rehabilitation program calls for the teaching of trades to
inmates. The state uses prison goods and foods raised on prison farms within
the corrections department and distributes them to other state agencies (many

---

[16] According to Alfred Hopkins, noted prison architect, cited in U.S. Bureau of Prisons, **Handbook of Correctional Institution Design and Construction**, 1949, p. 32. This book gives a fine
description of the history of punishment and of contemporary practices.

a governor's office is partly furnished from this source), but state laws often seriously limit the manufacturing program at prisons and frequently prohibit public sale of products.

5. Some trend exists toward the use of work camps operating on an "honor system" with virtually no custodial force. Many prison administrators believe this inexpensive type of operation provides the best possible chance of rehabilitation for young, short-term prisoners who are not psychopaths. Yet, there is opposition to the movement, principally from two sources. Some informed persons believe that the plan encourages judges to sentence to the work camps young men who would otherwise be good probation risks, and many citizens oppose the plan because of their fear and distrust of prisoners of all types.

6. The use of the death penalty and the means of executing it are hardy topics of debate in state legislatures.[17] There has been a slow trend toward abolition of the death penalty, even for murder. It is seldom invoked for any other crime today. Even in states which authorize the penalty, it is being used in a diminishing percentage of cases. Most citizens who support the penalty probably do so out of a primitive revenge motive, and there is no evidence at all that it serves as a deterrent to crime—murder is usually committed under conditions of great emotional stress when the murderer is not likely to stop and reflect upon the punishment that may await him. State legislatures are constantly being urged to increase or decrease the use of the penalty or to change the means of executing it. Debates on the issue are frequently of a highly emotional nature.

Jails   Cities and counties have traditionally maintained jails as a responsibility of their police or sheriff's departments. These local prisons are primarily of a congregate type of design, while most state prisons are organized on a cellular principle. A large "bull pen" is likely to house most prisoners, with perhaps a few cells to house notoriously tough prisoners and the violently insane. Jails are seldom constructed to meet the multifunctional demands placed upon them. They house an even greater variety of persons than do most state prisons: major offenders awaiting trial; habitual misdemeanants, many of them psychopaths; elderly degenerates; youthful minor offenders; traffic violators; drunks locked up for a single night; vagrants; material witnesses; and others.[18] At least 1 million persons spend some time in jail each year. It is doubtful if many profit from the experience.

Few sheriffs or police chiefs know much about penology or are interested in it. The jail caretakers are often unskilled friends of the local sheriff. The jails themselves are often badly designed, and the holding of prisoners in them is sometimes financed on a per diem allowance basis to the sheriff or turnkey who can profit by skimping on food allowances to the prisoners. The Federal government will house its prisoners in local jails only after it has inspected and approved them. Since it is profitable to the local unit of government to

[17] See "Murder and the Penalty of Death," **Annals,** 284: November, 1952, entire issue.
[18] U.S. Bureau of Prisons, *op. cit.,* p. 168.

house Federal prisoners who are being held for trial or have been given short sentences, there has been some incentive to improve local jail administration, but this does not apply in many rural counties. The general public has never regarded jails as being of much importance and does not approve of the expenditure of large amounts of money "to make things comfortable for crooks and drunks."

With only a few exceptions, state and local prisons have failed both as educational and disciplinary institutions. The rehabilitation of those who have failed to accept the behavior patterns imposed by the dominant groups in our society is a function of government that has been poorly met throughout American history. Public apathy, despite rapidly rising crime rates, is likely to forestall major changes in the near future.

SELECTED READINGS

Barnes, I. R.: **The Economics of Public Utility Regulation,** Appleton-Century-Crofts, Inc., New York, 1942.

Bauer, John: **The Public Utility Franchise: Its Functions and Terms under State Regulation,** Public Administration Service, Chicago, 1946.

Bernstein, Marver H.: **Regulating Business by Independent Commission,** Princeton University Press, Princeton, N.J., 1955.

Clemmer, Donald: **The Prison Community,** Christopher Publishing House, Boston, 1940.

Colebrook, Joan: "Prison Chronicle," **New Yorker,** June 12, 1965, pp. 47ff.   (A description of life in the Massachusetts Correctional Institution for Women, at Framingham.)

Fesler, James W.: **The Independence of State Regulatory Agencies,** Public Administration Service, Chicago, 1942.

Fox, Vernon: **Violence Behind Bars,** Vantage Press, Inc., New York, 1956.   (The story of a major prison riot as told by a member of the rehabilitation staff.)

Glaser, Daniel: **The Effectiveness of a Prison and Parole System,** The Bobbs-Merrill Company, Inc., Indianapolis, 1964.   (A report on a major study conducted at the University of Illinois.)

Grant, J. A. C.: "The Guild Returns to America," **Journal of Politics,** 4:303–336, 458–477, August and November, 1942.

Hammond, Bray: **Banks and Politics in America from the Revolution to the Civil War,** Princeton University Press, Princeton, N.J., 1957.

Lewis, W. David: **From Newgate to Dannemora: The Rise of the Penitentiary in New York,** Cornell University Press, Ithaca, N.Y., 1964.   (A study of the politics of penal reform in New York, 1796–1848, and the ideology of punishment in early New York.)

Logue, John, and Edwin A. Bock: **The Demotion of Deputy Chief Inspector Goldberg,** The Bobbs-Merrill Company, Inc., Indianapolis, ICP no. 78, 1963.   (Study in the politics of law enforcement [New York City].)

McCleery, Richard H.: **Policy Change in Prison Management,** Bureau of Social and Political Research, Michigan State University, East Lansing, Mich., 1957.

"Murder and the Penalty of Death," **Annals,** 284, November, 1952.

Occupational Licensing Legislation in the States, Council of State Governments, Chicago, 1952.

Parker, William H.: "The Police Challenge in Our Great Cities," **Annals,** 291:5–13, January, 1954.

Powelson, Harvey, and Reinhard Bendix, "Psychiatry in Prison," **Psychiatry,** 14: 73–86, February, 1951.

Schroth, Thomas N., and others: **Congress and the Nation, 1945–1964,** Congressional Quarterly Service, Washington, 1965, chap. 5.

Stefferud, Alfred (ed.): **Water,** Government Printing Office, Washington, D.C., 1955.

U.S. Bureau of Prisons: **Handbook of Correctional Institution Design and Construction,** 1949.

Wilson, O. W.: **Police Administration,** 2d ed., McGraw-Hill Book Company, New York, 1963.

EPILOGUE

American state and local governments have been romanticized, spoken of in awe and nostalgia, viewed with alarm, and seen as institutions passing into final eclipse. It is probably safe to discard the extreme points of view. There is likely to be a continued important function for state and local governments in the provision of services to people and in the making of policy decisions about those services.

The tasks of the states and communities, in the future as in the past, will be to perform those functions that are demanded by influential groups—within the limits of revenues that can be raised through the political process. In determining types and levels of services and how to pay for them, government will, as always, have to strike a balance.

The American culture is a product created by people interacting upon one another. It is an independent variable which must be accepted as a basis for understanding present and future American government. Projections seem to show that the future holds "more of the same," with increasing pressures, but of the same sort that have existed for many years. Citizens in the future will be called upon to meet the problems of living together in vast numbers, problems that seemingly will become more complicated rather than simpler as time passes. If the political process as well as trends in state and local government services are understood, these future challenges will become more understandable, and workable policies perhaps somewhat easier to discover.[1]

SELECTED READINGS

America's Needs and Resources, J. Frederic Dewhurst and Associates, New York, 1955.

Brown, Harrison: The Next Hundred Years: Man's Natural and Technological Resources, The Viking Press, Inc., New York, 1957.

"The Challenge of Automation," Newsweek, Jan. 25, 1965, pp. 73–80.

Drucker, Peter F.: America's Next Twenty Years, Harper & Row, Publishers, Incorporated, New York, 1957.

Karsh, Bernard: "Automation's Brave, New World," The Nation, 185:208–210, Oct. 5, 1957.

[1] On trends, see Charles R. Adrian and Charles Press, The American Political Process, McGraw-Hill Book Company, New York, 1965, chap. 22.

Raskin, A. H.: "Automation: Road to Lifetime Jobs?" **Saturday Review,** Nov. 28, 1964, pp. 14ff.

Stieber, Jack (ed.): **United States Industrial Relations: The Next Twenty Years,** Labor and Industrial Relations Center, Michigan State University, East Lansing, Mich., 1958.

Wernette, J. P.: **The Future of American Prosperity,** The Macmillan Company, New York, 1955.

FOR FURTHER READING

For general bibliography, see James Herndon, Charles Press, and Oliver P. Williams, **A Selected Bibliography of Materials on State Government and Politics,** Bureau of Government Research, University of Kentucky, Lexington, Ky., 1963; and Charles Press and Oliver P. Williams, **State Manuals, Blue Books, and Election Results,** Institute of Governmental Studies, University of California, Berkeley, Calif., 1962. V. O. Key, Jr., **State Politics: An Introduction,** Alfred A. Knopf, Inc., New York, 1956, has many bibliographical references, and discusses politics in some individual states. See also Roy V. Peel, **State Government Today,** University of New Mexico Press, Albuquerque, N.Mex., 1948; and W. Brooke Graves and others, **American State Government and Administration: A State by State Bibliography,** Council of State Governments, Chicago, 1949. A basic bibliography for city government is to be found in Charles R. Adrian, **Governing Urban America,** 2d ed., McGraw-Hill Book Company, New York, 1961.

Some of the more important books, monographs, and articles on individual states, also useful as bibliographical sources, include the following:

ALABAMA:

Key, V. O., Jr., and Alexander Heard: **Southern Politics,** Alfred A. Knopf, Inc., New York, 1949.

ALASKA:

Bebout, John: **Local Government Under the Alaska Constitution,** Public Administration Service, Chicago, 1959.

Slotnick, Herman: "Alaska: Empire of the North," in Frank H. Jonas (ed.), **Western Politics,** University of Utah Press, Salt Lake City, Utah, 1961.

ARIZONA:

Mason, Bruce B.: **Arizona General Election Results, 1911–1960,** Arizona State University Press, Tempe, Ariz., 1961.

Rice, Ross R.: "Amazing Arizona: Politics in Transition," in Frank H. Jonas (ed.), **Western Politics,** University of Utah Press, Salt Lake City, Utah, 1961.

————: "Bibliography of Arizona Politics," **Western Political Quarterly,** 11:13–22, Supplement, December, 1958.

ARKANSAS:

Alexander, Henry M.: **Government in Arkansas: Organization and Function at State, County, and Municipal Levels,** rev. ed., University of Arkansas Press, Little Rock, Ark., 1959.

Key, V. O., Jr., and Alexander Heard: **Southern Politics,** Alfred A. Knopf, Inc., New York, 1949.

CALIFORNIA:

Anderson, T. J.: "Bibliography of California Politics," **Western Political Quarterly,** 11:23–50, Supplement, December, 1958.

————: "California: Enigma of National Politics," in Frank H. Jonas (ed.), **Western Politics,** University of Utah Press, Salt Lake City, Utah, 1961.

Broder, David S.: "California's Political Free-for-all," **Look,** July 13, 1965.

Cresap, D. R.: **Party Politics in the Golden State,** The Haynes Foundation, Los Angeles, Calif., 1954.

Crouch, Winston W., John C. Bollens, Stanley Scott, and Dean McHenry: **California Government and Politics,** 4th ed., Prentice-Hall, Inc., Englewood Cliffs, N.J., 1967.

Harris, Joseph P.: **California Politics,** 3d ed., Stanford University Press, Stanford, Calif., 1961.

Jacobs, Clyde E., and John F. Gallagher: **California Government,** The Macmillan Company, New York, 1966, paperback.

Leuthold, David A.: **California Politics and Problems, 1900–1963: A Selective Bibliography,** Institute of Governmental Studies, University of California, Berkeley, Calif., 1965.

Schlessinger, Philip J., and Richard Wright: **Elements of Government in California,** Holt, Rinehart and Winston, Inc., New York, 1962.

Turner, Henry A., and John A. Vieg: **The Government and Politics of California,** 2d ed., McGraw-Hill Book Company, New York, 1964.

COLORADO:

Martin, Curtis: "Bibliography of Colorado Politics," **Western Political Quarterly,** 11:51–53, Supplement, December, 1958.

CONNECTICUT:

Lockard, Duane: **New England State Politics,** Princeton University Press, Princeton, N.J., 1959.

White, Max R., and Shirley Raissi: **Forms of Town Government in Connecticut,** Institute of Public Service, University of Connecticut, Storrs, Conn., 1952.

DELAWARE:

Dolan, Paul: **The Government and Administration of Delaware,** Thomas Y. Crowell Company, New York, 1956.

FLORIDA:

Bibliography of Florida Government, Florida Legislative Council, Committee on Governmental Organization, Tallahassee, Fla., 1960.

Doyle, W. K.: **The Government and Administration of Florida,** Thomas Y. Crowell Company, New York, 1954.

Havard, William C., and Loren P. Beth: **The Politics of Mis-representation: Rural-urban Conflict in the Florida Legislature,** Louisiana State University Press, Baton Rouge, La., 1962.

Key, V. O., Jr., and Alexander Heard: **Southern Politics,** Alfred A. Knopf, Inc., New York, 1949.

Morris, Allen, and Ann Waldron: **Your Florida Government,** University of Florida Press, Gainesville, Fla., 1964.

Price, H. Douglas, and Bruce B. Mason: **Florida Voters' Guide,** rev. ed., University of Florida Press, Gainesville, Fla., 1960.

GEORGIA:

Gosnell, Cullen B., and D. C. Anderson: **The Government and Administration of Georgia,** Thomas Y. Crowell Company, New York, 1956.

Key, V. O., Jr., and Alexander Heard: **Southern Politics,** Alfred A. Knopf, Inc., New York, 1949.

HAWAII:

Fuchs, Lawrence H.: **Hawaii Pono,** Harcourt, Brace & World, Inc., New York, 1961.

Meller, Norman, and Daniel W. Tuttle, Jr.: "Hawaii: The Aloha State," in Frank H. Jonas (ed.), **Western Politics,** University of Utah Press, Salt Lake City, Utah, 1961.

IDAHO:

Martin, Boyd A.: "Idaho: The Sectional State," in Frank H. Jonas (ed.), **Western Politics,** University of Utah Press, Salt Lake City, Utah, 1961.

Martin, Boyd, and R. D. Humphrey: "Bibliography of Idaho Politics," **Western Political Quarterly,** 11:54–64, Supplement, December, 1958.

ILLINOIS:

Fenton, John H.: **Midwest Politics,** Holt, Rinehart, and Winston, Inc., New York, 1966.

Garvey, Neal F.: **The Government and Administration of Illinois,** Thomas Y. Crowell Company, New York, 1958.

Gove, Samuel K. (ed.): **Illinois Votes,** Institute of Government and Public Affairs, University of Illinois, Urbana, Ill., 1960. Supplemented by Gove, "Illinois Votes, 1960–1962," **Illinois Government,** March, 1964.

———— (ed.): **State and Local Government in Illinois: A Bibliography,** Institute of Public Affairs, University of Illinois, Urbana, Ill., 1953, with 1958 Supplement.

Ranney, Austin: **Illinois Politics,** New York University Press, New York, 1960.

Steiner, Gilbert Y., and Samuel K. Gove: **Legislative Politics in Illinois,** The University of Illinois Press, Urbana, Ill., 1960.

INDIANA:

Fenton, John H.: **Midwest Politics,** Holt, Rinehart, and Winston, Inc., New York, 1966.

Francis, Wayne L., and Sharron E. Doerner (eds.): **Indiana Votes,** Indiana University Press, Bloomington, Ind., 1962.

Pitchell, Robert J. (ed.): **Indiana Votes,** Indiana University Press, Bloomington, Ind., 1960.

Sikes, P. S.: **Indiana State and Local Government,** rev. ed., Principia Press, Bloomington, Ind., 1946.

IOWA:

Mather, George B.: **Voting in Iowa,** Bureau of Public Affairs, University of Iowa, Iowa City, Iowa, 1960.

Ross, Russell M.: **The Government and Administration of Iowa,** Thomas Y. Crowell Company, New York, 1957.

KANSAS:

Drury, James W., and Associates: **The Government of Kansas,** Governmental Research Bureau, University of Kansas, Lawrence, Kans., 1961.

KENTUCKY:

Fenton, John H.: **Politics in the Border States,** The Hauser Press, New Orleans, La., 1957.

Jewell, Malcolm E.: **Kentucky Votes,** 2 vols., University of Kentucky Press, Lexington, Ky., 1963.

Reeves, John E.: **Kentucky Government,** 4th ed., University of Kentucky Press, Lexington, Ky., 1960.

LOUISIANA:

Howard, P. H.: **Political Tendencies in Louisiana, 1812–1952,** Louisiana State University Press, Baton Rouge, La., 1956.

Key, V. O., Jr., and Alexander Heard: **Southern Politics,** Alfred A. Knopf, Inc., New York, 1949.

Sindler, Allen P.: **Huey Long's Louisiana,** The Johns Hopkins Press, Baltimore, 1956.

MAINE:

Lockard, Duane: **New England State Politics,** Princeton University Press, Princeton, N.J., 1959.

Walker, David B.: **Politics and Ethnocentrism: The Case of the Franco-Americans,** Government Research Series, no. 23, Bowdoin College, Brunswick, Maine, 1961.

Wilson, James, and Robert W. Crowe: **Managers in Maine,** Government Research Series, no. 24, Bowdoin College, Brunswick, Maine, 1962.

MARYLAND:

Fenton, John H.: **Politics in the Border States,** The Hauser Press, New Orleans, La., 1957.

Friedman, Robert S.: **A Selected Bibliography of Maryland State and Local Government,** Bureau of Government Research, University of Maryland, College Park, Md., 1956.

MASSACHUSETTS:

Latham, Earl, and George Goodwin, Jr.: **Massachusetts Politics,** rev. ed., Massachusetts Center for Education in Politics, Medford, Mass., 1960.

Lockard, Duane: **New England State Politics,** Princeton University Press, Princeton, N.J., 1959.

Mallen, John P., and George Blackwood: "The Tax That Beat a Governor: The Ordeal of Massachusetts," in Alan F. Westin (ed.), **The Uses of Power,** Harcourt, Brace & World, Inc., New York, 1962.

MICHIGAN:

Fenton, John H.: **Midwest Politics,** Holt, Rinehart, and Winston, Inc., New York, 1966.

LaPalombara, Joseph: **Guide to Michigan Politics,** rev. ed., Bureau of Social and Political Research, Michigan State University, East Lansing, Mich., 1960.

Press, Charles (comp.): **Selected Bibliography, Michigan Government and Politics,** Institute for Community Government, Michigan State University, East Lansing, Mich., 1963.

Sarasohn, Stephen B., and Vera H. Sarasohn: **Political Party Patterns in Michigan,** Wayne State University Press, Detroit, Mich., 1957.

Turano, Peter J.: **Michigan State and Local Government and Politics: A Bibliography,** Institute of Public Administration, University of Michigan, Ann Arbor, Mich., 1955.

White, John P.: **Michigan Votes: Election Statistics, 1928–1956,** Supplements for 1960 and 1962 Elections, Institute of Public Administration, University of Michigan, Ann Arbor, Mich., 1958.

MINNESOTA:

Fenton, John H.: **Midwest Politics,** Holt, Rinehart, and Winston, Inc., New York, 1966.

Mitau, G. Theodore: **Politics in Minnesota,** The University of Minnesota Press, Minneapolis, 1960.

MISSISSIPPI:

Highsaw, Robert B., and C. N. Fortenberry: **The Government and Administration in Mississippi,** Thomas Y. Crowell Company, New York, 1954.

Key, V. O., Jr., and Alexander Heard: **Southern Politics,** Alfred A. Knopf, Inc., New York, 1949.

MISSOURI:

Fenton, John H.: **Politics in the Border States,** The Hauser Press, New Orleans, La., 1957.

Karsh, Robert F.: **The Government of Missouri,** 7th ed., Lucas Brothers, Columbia, Mo., 1961.

Montana:

Payne, Thomas: "Bibliography of Montana Politics," **Western Political Quarterly,** 11:65–72, Supplement, December, 1958.

————: "Under the Copper Dome: Politics in Montana," in Frank H. Jonas (ed.), **Western Politics,** University of Utah Press, Salt Lake City, Utah, 1961.

Renne, R. R.: **The Government and Administration of Montana,** Thomas Y. Crowell Company, New York, 1958.

Nebraska:

Breckenridge, Adam C.: **One House for Two,** University of Nebraska Press, Lincoln, Nebr., 1958.

Nebraska State Government, The League of Women Voters in Nebraska, Lincoln, Nebr., 1961.

Report of the Committee on Reorganization of County Government, Nebraska Legislative Council, State of Nebraska, Lincoln, Nebr., 1950.

Nevada:

Driggs, D. W.: "Bibliography of Nevada Politics," **Western Political Quarterly,** 11:73–76, Supplement, December, 1958.

————: "Nevada: The Silver Dollar State," in Frank H. Jonas (ed.), **Western Politics,** University of Utah Press, Salt Lake City, Utah, 1961.

New Hampshire:

Lockard, Duane: **New England State Politics,** Princeton University Press, Princeton, N.J., 1959.

New Jersey:

Rich, Bennett M.: **The Government and Administration of New Jersey,** Thomas Y. Crowell Company, New York, 1957.

New Mexico:

Donnelly, Thomas C.: **The Government of New Mexico,** rev. ed., The University of New Mexico Press, Albuquerque, N.Mex., 1953.

Irion, Frederick C.: "Bibliography of New Mexico Politics," **Western Political Quarterly,** 11:77–109, Supplement, December, 1958.

————: "New Mexico: The Political State," in Frank H. Jonas (ed.), **Western Politics,** University of Utah Press, Salt Lake City, Utah, 1961.

New York:

Caldwell, Lynton K.: **The Government and Administration of New York,** Thomas Y. Crowell Company, New York, 1954.

Garrett, Charles: **The La Guardia Years: Machine and Reform Politics in New York City,** Rutgers University Press, New Brunswick, N.J., 1961.

Moscow, Warren: **Politics in the Empire State,** Alfred A. Knopf, Inc., New York, 1948.

Munger, Frank, and Ralph Straetz: **New York Politics,** New York University Press, New York, 1960.

Sayre, Wallace S., and Herbert Kaufman: **Governing New York City,** Russell Sage Foundation, New York, 1960.

Shaw, Frederick: **The History of the New York City Legislature,** Columbia University Press, New York, 1954.

Thomas, Samuel F.: **Nassau County: Its Governments and Their Expenditure Patterns,** New York City College Press, New York, 1960.

North Carolina:

Hodges, Luther H.: **Businessman in the Statehouse: Six Years as Governor of North Carolina,** The University of North Carolina Press, Chapel Hill, N.C., 1962.

Key, V. O., Jr., and Alexander Heard: **Southern Politics,** Alfred A. Knopf, Inc., New York, 1949.

Matthews, Donald R. (comp.): **North Carolina Votes,** The University of North Carolina Press, Chapel Hill, N.C., 1962.

Rankin, Robert S.: **The Government and Administration of North Carolina,** Thomas Y. Crowell Company, New York, 1955.

NORTH DAKOTA:

Legislative Handbook on State Governmental Agencies and Their Principal Duties, North Dakota Legislative Research Committee, State of North Dakota, Bismarck, N.D., 1960.

Morlan, Robert L.: **Political Prairie Fire: The Nonpartisan League,** The University of Minnesota Press, Minneapolis, 1955.

OHIO:

Aumann, Francis R., and Harvey Walker: **The Government and Administration of Ohio,** Thomas Y. Crowell Company, New York, 1956.

Fenton, John H.: **Midwest Politics,** Holt, Rinehart, and Winston, Inc., New York, 1966.

Flinn, Thomas A.: "The Outline of Ohio Politics," **Western Political Quarterly,** September, 1960.

OKLAHOMA:

McReynolds, E. C.: **Oklahoma: A History of the Sooner State,** University of Oklahoma Press, Norman, Okla., 1954.

Thornton, H. V.: **An Outline of Oklahoma Government,** Rickner's Book Store, Norman, Okla., 1956.

OREGON:

Seligman, Lester G., and Martha Swanson: "Bibliography of Oregon Politics," **Western Political Quarterly,** 11:110–131, Supplement, December, 1958.

Swarthout, John M.: "Oregon: Political Experiment Station," in Frank H. Jonas (ed.), **Western Politics,** University of Utah Press, Salt Lake City, Utah, 1961.

PENNSYLVANIA:

Cooke, Edward F., and Edward G. Janosik: **Pennsylvania Politics,** rev. ed., Holt, Rinehart and Winston, Inc., New York, 1965.

Tanger, Jacob, and others: **Pennsylvania's Government: State and Local,** 3d ed., Penns Valley Publishers, University Park, Pa., 1950.

RHODE ISLAND:

Lockard, Duane: **New England State Politics,** Princeton University Press, Princeton, N.J., 1959.

Stitely, John O.: **An Outline of Rhode Island State Government,** University of Rhode Island, Kingston, R.I., 1961.

SOUTH CAROLINA:

Key, V. O., Jr., and Alexander Heard: **Southern Politics,** Alfred A. Knopf, Inc., New York, 1949.

SOUTH DAKOTA

Farber, William O., T. C. Geary, and W. H. Cape: **Government of South Dakota,** Bureau of Governmental Research, University of South Dakota, Sioux Falls, S.Dak., 1962.

Parmelee, Gertrude (comp.): **A South Dakota Bibliography,** University of South Dakota, Vermillion, S.Dak., 1960.

TENNESSEE:

Goodman, William: **Inherited Domain: Political Parties in Tennessee,** Bureau of Public Administration, University of Tennessee, Knoxville, Tenn., 1954.

Greene, Lee S., and Robert S. Avery: **Government in Tennessee,** University of Tennessee Press, Knoxville, Tenn., 1962.

Key, V. O., Jr., and Alexander Heard: **Southern Politics,** Alfred A. Knopf, Inc., New York, 1949.

TEXAS:

Key, V. O., Jr., and Alexander Heard: **Southern Politics,** Alfred A. Knopf, Inc., New York, 1949.

MacCorkle, Stuart A., and Dick Smith: **Texas Government,** 5th ed., McGraw-Hill Book Company, New York, 1964.

McKay, S. S.: **Texas Politics,** Texas Tech Press, Lubbock, Tex., 1952.

————: **Texas and the Fair Deal,** The Naylor Company, San Antonio, Tex., 1954.

UTAH:

Jonas, Frank H.: "Bibliography of Utah Politics," **Western Political Quarterly,** 11:132–150, Supplement, December, 1958.

————: "Utah: Crossroads of the West," in Frank H. Jonas (ed.), **Western Politics,** University of Utah Press, Salt Lake City, Utah, 1961.

Local Government in Utah, Local Government Survey Commission, State of Utah, Salt Lake City, Utah, 1956.

VERMONT:

Lockard, Duane: **New England State Politics,** Princeton University Press, Princeton, N.J., 1959.

VIRGINIA:

Key, V. O., Jr., and Alexander Heard: **Southern Politics,** Alfred A. Knopf, Inc., New York, 1949.

Kraus, Joe W.: **Notes on Virginia State Bibliography,** 2d ed., State of Virginia, Richmond, 1960.

WASHINGTON:

Bone, Hugh A.: "Washington State: Free Style Politics," in Frank H. Jonas (ed.), **Western Politics,** University of Utah Press, Salt Lake City, Utah, 1961.

————, and W. H. Leavel: "Bibliography of Washington Politics," **Western Political Quarterly,** 11:151–163, Supplement, December, 1958.

Ogden, Daniel M., Jr., and Hugh A. Bone: **Washington Politics,** New York University Press, New York, 1960.

Webster, Donald H., and others: **Washington State Government,** 2d ed., University of Washington Press, Seattle, Wash., 1962.

WEST VIRGINIA:

Fenton, John H.: **Politics in the Border States,** The Hauser Press, New Orleans, La., 1957.

Lambert, O. D.: **West Virginia and Its Government,** D. C. Heath and Company, Boston, 1951.

Ross, William R.: **An Introduction to the Electoral Process in West Virginia,** Bureau of Government Research, West Virginia University, Morgantown, W.Va., 1962.

WISCONSIN:

Donoghue, James R.: **How Wisconsin Voted, 1848–1960,** Governmental Research Bureau, University of Wisconsin, Madison, Wis., 1962.

Epstein, Leon: **Politics in Wisconsin,** The University of Wisconsin Press, Madison, Wis., 1958.

Fenton, John H.: **Midwest Politics,** Holt, Rinehart, and Winston, Inc., New York, 1966.

Wyoming:

Beall, Charles P.: "Wyoming: The Equality State," in Frank H. Jonas (ed.), **Western Politics,** University of Utah Press, Salt Lake City, Utah, 1961.

Trachsel, H. H.: "Bibliography of Wyoming Politics," **Western Political Quarterly,** 11:164–167, Supplement, December, 1958.

————, and R. M. Wade: **The Government and Administration of Wyoming,** Thomas Y. Crowell Company, New York, 1956.

In addition to the above, the usual periodical indexes in libraries will provide information on articles from professional and popular sources. The volumes of the state historical societies often have articles on state and local politics and politicians, as do state histories. The reader wanting information on a particular state or community might also be rewarded by writing to the librarian of the appropriate state university, for many libraries possess copies of mimeographed bibliographies related to state and local government.

NAME INDEX

NAME INDEX

SUBJECT INDEX

SUBJECT INDEX